Welfare Economics and Antitrust Policy—Vol. II

Richard S. Markovits

Welfare Economics and Antitrust Policy—Vol. II

Mergers, Vertical Practices, Joint Ventures, Internal Growth, and U.S. and E.U. Law

Springer

Richard S. Markovits
School of Law
The University of Texas at Austin
Austin, TX, USA

ISBN 978-3-030-96481-8 ISBN 978-3-030-96482-5 (eBook)
https://doi.org/10.1007/978-3-030-96482-5

This Springer imprint is published by the registered company Springer Nature Switzerland AG
The registered company address is: Gewerbestrasse 11, 6330 Cham, Switzerland

Preface

This book is Volume II of a two-volume study of antitrust policy. The study has three parts. Part I (Chaps. 1–8) delineates the basic welfare-economics, competition-theory, moral, and legal concepts and analytic protocols the study uses to analyze (1) the impacts of antitrust-policy-coverable business conduct on economic efficiency, liberal moral rights, and the instantiation of various utilitarian and other egalitarian conceptions of the moral good and (2) the ability of a liberal-moral-rights-constrained government to increase economic efficiency, secure liberal moral rights, and instantiate the various egalitarian conceptions of the moral good by responding appropriately to antitrust-policy-coverable conduct. Part II (Chaps. 9–16) applies these concepts and analytic protocols to investigate the above impacts of eight categories of antitrust-policy-coverable business conduct and the ability of a government of a liberal-moral-rights-based society to increase economic efficiency, secure liberal moral rights, and promote the egalitarian moral good by responding appropriately to exemplars of each such category of conduct. Part III (Chaps. 17 and 18) describes the tests of illegality and conduct and actor coverages of U.S. antitrust law and E.U. competition law correctly interpreted as matters of law and analyzes the implications of the differences in these two bodies of law for their respective potentials to increase economic efficiency, secure liberal moral rights, and instantiate various egalitarian conceptions of the moral good.

Volume I of this study contains Part I and the first two chapters of Part II (which focus respectively on oligopolistic and predatory conduct). This book (Volume II of this study) contains the last six chapters of Part II (Chaps. 11–16, which focus respectively on horizontal mergers and acquisitions [M&A]s, conglomerate [M&A]s, surrogates for vertical integration, vertical [M&A]s, joint ventures, and internal growth) and Part III (Chaps. 17 and 18).

Before proceeding, I want to point out two differences between the economic-efficiency analyses of Chaps. 11–16 and the economic-efficiency analyses of Chaps. 9 and 10 . Chapters 11–16's analyses of the impact on economic efficiency of the categories of business conduct on which they respectively focus will ignore two ways in which all such conduct may decrease economic efficiency that Chaps. 9 and 10 consider: (1) by causing production-optimum misallocation by inducing the resulting firm or the perpetrator to operate more sloppily by increasing its potential supernormal profits and (2) by causing UO-to-UO misallocation by increasing the potential supernormal profits of the perpetrators or perpetrator, derivatively the compensation the perpetrators or perpetrator pay their or its managers and employees, hence the tax-rate applied to the managers' and employees' marginal taxable income, hence the misallocation that the combination of tax-rates that increase with taxable income and tax policies of applying a lower or a zero tax-rate to more-attractive working conditions and certain fringe benefits than to monetary compensation causes managers and employees to generate by substituting lower-taxed attractive working-conditions and fringe benefits for the goods they would otherwise have purchased with the higher-taxed monetary compensation they sacrificed in exchange for the superior working-conditions and fringe benefits in question. Chapters 11–16 ignore these possibilities because I think their empirical importance is sufficiently reduced by the operation of the takeover market to make it sensible to save the space.

Austin, USA Richard S. Markovits

Contents

Part II The Morally-Relevant Effects of Specific Categories of Antitrust-Policy-Coverable Conduct and the Ability of Government to Secure Better Outcomes (Continued)

11 Horizontal Mergers and Acquisitions 3
11.1 The 16 Ways in Which Horizontal (M&A)s Can Increase Their Participants' Profits 4
11.1.1 The 8 "Sherman-Act-Licit" Ways in Which Horizontal (M&A)s Can Increase Their Participants' Profits—That Is, Can Do So Without Increasing Those Profits by Reducing the Absolute Attractiveness of the Most-Attractive Offers Against Which They Will Have to Compete in a Way That Would Render the (M or A) Profitable Even If It Would Have Been Economically Inefficient in an oPp Economy 4
11.1.2 The 8 Sherman-Act-Illicit Ways in Which a Horizontal (M or A) Can Increase Its Participants' Profits 6

11.2 The Determinants of the Amount of Profits a Horizontal (M or A) Will Yield Its Participants in Each of the 16 Ways in Which It Can Yield Them Profits, the Relationship Between Each of These 16 Profit-Yields and the (M or A)'s Associated Impact on Economic Efficiency, the Relevance of the Fact That a Horizontal (M or A) Yields Its Participants Profits in Each of the 16 Ways in Which It Can Do So to the (M or A)'s Liberal-Moral-Rights-Violativeness, and the Relevance of the Fact That a Horizontal (M or A) Yields Its Participants Profits in Each of the 16 Ways in Which It Can Do So for the (M or A)'s Serving or Disserving the Instantiation of the Various Pure (Utilitarian, Equal-Utility, Equal-Resource, and Other-Equal-Opportunity) and Mixed Egalitarian Conceptions of the Moral Good 8
11.2.1 Analyses That Relate to Any Static Marginal-Cost Efficiencies a Horizontal (M or A) Generates 8
11.2.2 Analyses That Relate to Any Static Fixed-Cost Efficiencies a Horizontal (M or A) Generates 21
11.2.3 Analyses That Relate to Any Dynamic Efficiencies That a Horizontal (M or A) Generates 38
11.2.4 Analyses That Relate to a Horizontal (M or A)'s Increasing Its Participants' Profits by Substituting for a Situation in Which No Participant Could Profit by Making a QV or PPR Investment Even Though at Least Two of Them Would Have Found Such an Investment Profitable If It Would Not Have Induced Another Participant to Make an Investment a Situation in Which the Resulting Firm Can Make One Such Investment Without Inducing Anyone to Make Another 41
11.2.5 Analyses That Relate to a Horizontal (M or A)'s Increasing Its Participants' Profits by Creating a Resulting Firm Whose Selection of the Investments It Will Make Is Influenced by the Alternative Investments' Impacts on the Profits Yielded by the Other Projects of All Participants 45

11.2.6 Analyses That Relate to a Horizontal (M or A)'s Increasing Its Participants' Profits or Equivalent-Dollar Gains by Enabling the Owner or Owner/Manager of One Participant to Liquidate His or Her Assets and Retire from Management 47

11.2.7 Analyses That Relate to the Equivalent-Dollar Gains a Horizontal (M or A) Yields Its Participants by Creating a Resulting Firm That Can Take Advantage of a Tax-Loss Incurred by a Participant That Could Not Use It as a Separate Entity 48

11.2.8 Analyses That Relate to Any Horizontal (M or A)'s Yielding Its Participants Profits by Enabling Them (and Their Rivals) to Make Additional (Jointly-Profitable) Expenditures on Political Campaigns/Parties/Candidates and Government-Decision-Making-Process Participation 51

11.2.9 Analyses That Relate to Any Profits a Horizontal (M or A) Yields Its Participants by Increasing Their HNOPs by Freeing Them From Each Other's Price-Competition 53

11.2.10 Analyses That Relate to Any Profits a Horizontal (M or A) Yields Its Participants by Freeing Them From Each Other's Investment-Competition 59

11.2.11 Analyses That Relate to Any Profits a Horizontal (M or A) Yields Its Participants by Creating a Resulting Firm That Realizes More Profits by Driving Out Extant Rival Investors by Engaging in Predatory Pricing, Predatory Advertizing, or Making Other Predatory Moves Than the Participants Would Have Done as Separate Entities 64

11.2.12 Analyses That Relate to Any Profits a Horizontal (M or A) Yields Its Participants by (Predatorily) Critically Increasing the Retaliation Barrier to Entry Faced by an Otherwise-Effective Potential Competitor or the Retaliation Barrier to Expansion Faced by an Otherwise-Effective Established-Firm Potential Investment-Expander 69

11.2.13 Analyses That Relate to Any Horizontal (M or A)'s Increasing Its Participants' Profits by Predatorily Inducing an Established Rival to Change the Product-Space Location of an Existing Investment or by Predatorily Inducing an Established Rival or Potential Entrant to Change the Product-Space Location of a New Investment (When the Location-Change Does Not Increase Economic Efficiency) ... 72
11.2.14 Analyses That Relate to Any Horizontal (M or A)'s Increasing Its Participants' Profits by Creating a Resulting Firm That Is Better Able Than the Participants Would Have Been to Increase Their and Their Mutual Rivals' Across-the Board HNOPs by Altering the Sequence in Which They and Their Mutual Rivals Announce and "Lock Themselves Into" Their Prices ... 74
11.3 The Economic Efficiency of Particular Horizontal (M or A)s and the Ability of a Liberal-Moral-Rights-Constrained Government to Increase Economic Efficiency by Responding Appropriately to Proposed/Consummated Horizontal (M&A)s ... 76
11.3.1 The Economic Efficiency of Particular Horizontal (M&A)s ... 76
11.3.2 The Ability of a Liberal-Moral-Rights-Constrained Government to Increase Economic Efficiency by Responding in Appropriate Ways to Proposed/Consummated Horizontal (M&A)s ... 78
11.4 The Liberal-Moral-Rights-Violativeness of Horizontal (M&A)s and the Ability of a Government to Instantiate Its Liberal Justice-Commitments by Responding Appropriately to Horizontal (M&A)s ... 87
11.4.1 The Liberal-Moral-Rights-Violativeness of Horizontal (M&A)s ... 87
11.4.2 The Ability of a Liberal-Moral-Rights-Constrained Government to Reduce the Liberal-Moral-Rights-Violations Firms Commit When Consummating Horizontal (M&A)s and Operating the Resulting Firms ... 87

11.5 The Impact of Horizontal (M&A)s on the Instantiation of the Utilitarian and Non-Utilitarian-Egalitarian Conceptions of the Moral Good and the Ability of Liberal-Moral-Rights-Constrained Governments to Instantiate These Various Egalitarian Conceptions of the Moral Good by Responding Appropriately to Proposed and Consummated Horizontal (M&A)s 89
11.5.1 The Impact of Horizontal (M&A)s on the Instantiation of the Utilitarian and Non-Utilitarian-Egalitarian Conceptions of the Moral Good 89
11.5.2 The Ability of a Liberal-Moral-Rights-Constrained Government to Serve the Instantiation of the Utilitarian and Non-Utilitarian-Egalitarian Conceptions of the Moral Good by Responding Appropriately to Proposed and Consummated Horizontal (M&A)s 89
11.6 Conclusion 90
References 96

12 Conglomerate Mergers and Acquisitions 97
12.1 The Differences in the Ways in Which Conglomerate and Horizontal (M&A)s Can Yield Their Participants Profits and the Relationship Between the Determinants of the Magnitudes of the Impacts That Conglomerate and Horizontal (M&A)s Will Have on Their Participants' Profits 98
12.1.1 The Relevant Differences Between Conglomerate and Horizontal (M&A)s When Neither Participant Is an Effective Potential Competitor of the Other 98
12.1.2 The Relevance of One or Both Participants' Being an Effective Potential Competitor of the Other to the Profits That a Conglomerate (M or A) Yields Its Participants and the Determinants of the Impacts That a Conglomerate (M or A) Will Have on Its Participants' Profits by Virtue of One or More Participants' Being an Effective Potential Competitor of the Other in Various Situations 102

12.2 The Economic Efficiency of Particular Conglomerate (M or A)s and the Ability of a Liberal-Moral-Rights-Constrained Government to Increase Economic Efficiency by Responding Appropriately to Proposed/Consummated Conglomerate (M&A)s ... 111
12.2.1 The Economic Efficiency of Particular Conglomerate (M or A)s ... 111
12.2.2 The Ability of a Liberal-Moral-Rights-Constrained Government to Increase Economic Efficiency by Responding Appropriately to Proposed/Consummated Conglomerate (M&A)s ... 115
12.3 The Liberal-Moral-Rights-Violativeness of Conglomerate (M or A)s and the Ability of a Government to Instantiate the Liberal Conception of Justice by Responding Appropriately to Proposed/Consummated Conglomerate (M&A)s ... 116
12.4 The Impact of Conglomerate (M&A)s on the Instantiation of the Utilitarian and Non-Utilitarian-Egalitarian Conceptions of the Moral Good and the Ability of a Liberal-Moral-Rights-Constrained Government to Instantiate These Egalitarian Conceptions of the Moral Good by Responding Appropriately to Conglomerate (M&A)s ... 116
References ... 119

13 Surrogates for Vertical Integration ... 121
13.1 "Fancy" Pricing-Techniques ... 125
13.1.1 The Functions of Fancy Horizontal Pricing-Techniques ... 125
13.1.2 The Economic Efficiency of Those Sellers' That Find It Profitable to Do So Substituting Each Fancy Pricing-Technique I Have Identified for Single Pricing and the Economic Efficiency of the Government's Deterring the Use of Each Such Type of Fancy Pricing-Technique ... 133
13.1.3 The Liberal-Moral-Rights-Violativeness of Substitutions of Fancy Pricing-Techniques for Single Pricing ... 147

13.1.4 The Impact of Shifts From Single Pricing to Each of the Various Fancy Pricing-Techniques on the Instantiation of the Utilitarian and Different Non-Utilitarian-Egalitarian Conceptions of the Moral Good 148
13.2 Tie-Ins and Reciprocity Agreements That Should Not Be Described as Pricing-Techniques 150
13.2.1 The Functions of "Non-Pricing-Techniques" Tie-Ins and Reciprocity 151
13.2.2 The Economic Efficiency of Non-Pricing-Technique Tie-Ins and Reciprocity Agreements and the Ability of the Government of a Liberal-Moral-Rights-Based Society to Increase Economic Efficiency by Deterring Economically-Inefficient Tie-Ins and Reciprocity Agreements 158
13.2.3 The Liberal-Moral-Rights-Violativeness of Non-Pricing-Technique Tie-Ins and Reciprocity Agreements and the Ability of the Government of a Liberal-Moral-Rights-Based Society to Secure Liberal-Moral-Rights-Related Interests by Responding Appropriately to Such Tie-Ins and Reciprocity Agreements 164
13.2.4 The Impact of Non-Pricing-Technique Tying and Reciprocity Agreements on the Instantiation of the Utilitarian and Various Non-Utilitarian-Egalitarian Conceptions of the Moral Good and the Ability of the Government of a Liberal-Moral-Rights-Based Society to Instantiate These Conceptions of the Moral Good by Deterring and Allowing Such Tying and Reciprocity Agreements 166
13.3 Minimum-Price-Setting-Resale-Price-Maintenance (RPM) Clauses and Vertical-Customer-Allocation (VCA) Clauses That Are Surrogates for Vertical Integration 174
13.3.1 The Functions of Minimum-Price-Setting-RPM Clauses and VCA Clauses That Are Surrogates for Vertical Integration 174

13.3.2 The Economic Efficiency of Minimum-Price-Setting-RPM Clauses and VCA Clauses That Are Surrogates for Vertical Integration and the Ability of the Government of a Liberal-Moral-Rights-Based Society to Increase Economic Efficiency by Responding Appropriately to a Producer's Use of Such Vertical-Integration Surrogates 177
13.3.3 The Liberal-Moral-Rights-Violativeness of Minimum-Price-Setting-RPM Clauses and VCA Clauses and the Ability of the Antitrust-Policy-Implementation Authorities of a Liberal-Moral-Rights-Based Society to Secure Liberal Moral Rights by Responding Appropriately to the Use of Such Clauses 202
13.3.4 The Impact of Minimum-Price-Setting-RPM Clauses and VCA Clauses on the Instantiation of the Utilitarian and Various Non-Utilitarian-Egalitarian Conceptions of the Moral Good and the Ability of a Government of a Liberal-Moral-Rights-Based Society to Secure the Moral Good by Responding Appropriately to Such Clauses 204
13.4 Maximum-Price-Setting-RPM Clauses 205
13.4.1 The Functions That Maximum-Price-Setting-RPM Clauses Can Perform 205
13.4.2 The Economic Efficiency of Maximum-Price-Setting-RPM Clauses and the Ability of the Government of a Liberal-Moral-Rights-Based Society to Increase Economic Efficiency by Responding Appropriately to a Producer's Using Such Clauses 207
13.4.3 The Liberal-Moral-Rights-Violativeness of Maximum-Price-Setting-RPM Clauses and the Ability of the Government of a Liberal-Moral-Rights-Based Society to Secure Liberal Moral Rights by Responding Appropriately to a Producers' Using Such Clauses 219

13.4.4 The Impact of a Producer's Using Maximum-Price-Setting-RPM Clauses on Total Utility and the Instantiation of Various Non-Utilitarian-Egalitarian Conceptions of the Moral Good and the Ability of the Government of a Liberal-Moral-Rights-Based Society to Instantiate Any Such Conception of the Moral Good by Responding Appropriately to a Producer's Use of Maximum-Price-Setting-RPM Clauses 220
13.5 Single-Brand Exclusive Dealerships 220
13.5.1 The Functions of Single-Brand Exclusive Dealerships 220
13.5.2 The Economic Efficiency of Single-Brand Exclusive Dealerships and the Economic Efficiency of the Government of a Liberal-Moral-Rights-Based Society's Responding to Single-Brand Exclusive Dealerships in Various Ways 221
13.5.3 The Liberal-Moral-Rights-Violativeness of Single-Brand Exclusive Dealerships and the Ability of the Government of a Liberal-Moral-Rights-Based Society to Secure Liberal Moral Rights by Responding Appropriately to the Creation of Such Dealerships 229
13.5.4 The Impact of Single-Brand Exclusive Dealerships on the Instantiation of the Utilitarian and Various Non-Utilitarian-Egalitarian Conceptions of the Moral Good and the Ability of the Government of a Liberal-Moral-Rights-Based Society to Instantiate These Conceptions of the Moral Good by Responding Appropriately to Uses of Single-Brand Exclusive Dealerships 229
13.6 Long-Term Full-Requirements Contracts and Long-Term Total-Output-Supply Contracts 230
13.6.1 The Functions of Long-Term Full-Requirements Contracts and Long-Term Total-Output-Supply Contracts 230

13.6.2 The Economic Efficiency of Long-Term Full-Requirements Contracts and Long-Term Total-Output-Supply Contracts and the Ability of the Government of a Liberal-Moral-Rights-Based Society to Increase Economic Efficiency by Responding Appropriately to Them 231
13.6.3 The Liberal-Moral-Rights-Violativeness of Long-Term Provisions in Full-Requirements Contracts or Total-Output-Supply Contracts and the Ability of the Government of a Liberal-Moral-Rights-Based Society to Secure Liberal Moral Rights by Responding Appropriately to Such Long-Term Provisions 237
13.6.4 The Impact of the Inclusion of Long-Term Provisions in Full-Requirements and Total-Output-Supply Contracts on Total Utility and the Instantiation of Various Non-Utilitarian-Egalitarian Conceptions of the Moral Good and the Ability of the Government of a Liberal-Moral-Rights-Based Society to Instantiate Various Egalitarian Conceptions of the Moral Good by Responding Appropriately to the Inclusion of Such Provisions in Such Contracts 238
References 241

14 Vertical Mergers and Acquisitions 243
14.1 The Differences Between the Ways in Which Vertical (M&A)s and Horizontal (M&A)s Can Yield Their Participants Profits 244
14.2 The Economic Efficiency of (Profitable) Vertical (M&A)s and the Ability of the Liberal-Moral-Rights-Constrained Government of a Liberal-Moral-Rights-Based Society to Increase Economic Efficiency by Responding Appropriately to Vertical (M&A)s 246
14.3 The Liberal-Moral-Rights-Violativeness of Vertical (M&A)s and the Ability of the Government of a Liberal-Moral-Rights-Based Society to Secure Liberal Moral Rights by Responding Appropriately to Vertical (M&A)s 251

14.4 The Impact of Profitable Vertical (M&A)s on the Instantiation of the Utilitarian and Other Pure or Mixed Egalitarian Conceptions of the Moral Good and the Ability of a Liberal-Moral-Rights-Constrained Government to Instantiate These Conceptions of the Moral Good by Responding Appropriately to Profitable Vertical (M&A)s ... 252
Reference ... 253

15 Joint Ventures (and Functionally-Analogous Collaborative Arrangements) ... 255
15.1 The Functions of Joint Ventures ... 257
15.2 The Economic Efficiency of Joint Ventures and the Ability of a Liberal-Moral-Rights-Constrained Government to Increase Economic Efficiency by Responding Appropriately to Joint Ventures ... 265
15.3 The Liberal-Moral-Rights-Violativeness of Joint Ventures, Functionally-Analogous Collaborations, and Any Restrictive Provisions Joint-Venture Agreements Contain and the Ability of a Government to Secure Liberal Moral Rights by Responding Appropriately to Such Arrangements and Provisions ... 275
15.4 The Impact of Joint Ventures, Functionally-Analogous Collaborative Arrangements, and Any Restrictive Provisions in Joint-Venture Agreements on the Instantiation of Various Egalitarian Conceptions of the Moral Good and the Ability of the Government of a Liberal-Moral-Rights-Based Society to Instantiate Various Egalitarian Conceptions of the Moral Good by Responding Appropriately to Such Arrangements and Provisions ... 276
References ... 281

16 Internal Growth ... 283
16.1 The Functions of Internal Growth ... 284
16.2 The Impact of Internal Growth on Economic Efficiency and the Ability of a Liberal-Moral-Rights-Constrained Government to Increase Economic Efficiency by Responding Appropriately to Internal Growth ... 287
16.3 The Liberal-Moral-Rights-Violativeness of Internal Growth and the Ability of the Government of a Liberal-Moral-Rights-Based Society to Secure Liberal Moral Rights by Responding Appropriately to Internal Growth ... 289

16.4 The Impact of Internal-Growth Investments on the Instantiation of Various Egalitarian Conceptions of the Moral Good and the Ability of the Government of a Liberal-Moral-Rights-Based Society to Secure the Instantiation of These Conceptions of the Moral Good by Responding Appropriately to Internal-Growth Investments 290
References 291

Part III The Economic Efficiency, Liberal Justness, and Non-Liberal-Egalitarian Moral Desirability of U.S. Antitrust Law and E.U. Competition Law, Correctly Interpreted and Applied as a Matter of Law

17 U.S. Antitrust Law and E.U. Competition Law, Correctly Interpreted and Applied as Matters of Law: The Tests of Illegality They Respectively Promulgate and the Business Entities and Conduct to Which Those Tests Respectively Apply 297
17.1 The Business Entities Covered by, the Tests of Illegality Respectively Promulgated by, and the Conduct Respectively Covered by the Sherman Act, the Clayton Act, and the Federal Trade Commission Act—The 3 Major Sources of U.S. Federal Antitrust Law 298
17.1.1 The Test of Illegality Promulgated by and the Conduct-Coverage of the Sherman Act 298
17.1.2 The Conduct-Coverage of and Test of Illegality Promulgated by the Clayton Act 301
17.1.3 The Test of Illegality and Conduct-Coverage of the Federal Trade Commission Act 306
17.2 The Business Entities Respectively Covered by, the Tests of Illegality Respectively Promulgated by, and the Conduct Respectively Covered by What Is Now Article 101 of the 2009 Treaty of Lisbon, What Is Now Article 102 of the 2009 Treaty of Lisbon, and the EMCR 307
17.2.1 Article 101 of What Is Now the 2009 Treaty of Lisbon 307
17.2.2 Article 102 of What Is Now the 2009 Treaty of Lisbon 311
17.2.3 The European Merger Control Regulation (EMCR) 313

17.3 The Relationship Between the Business-Entity Coverages of, the Conduct-Coverage of, and the Tests of Illegality Promulgated Respectively by U.S. Antitrust Law, Correctly Interpreted and Applied, and E.U. Competition Law, Correctly Interpreted and Applied 316
17.3.1 Contrived-Oligopolistic and Natural-Oligopolistic Conduct 317
17.3.2 Predatory Conduct 319
17.3.3 Horizontal Mergers and Acquisitions 320
17.3.4 Conglomerate Mergers and Acquisitions 321
17.3.5 Surrogates for Vertical Integration 321
17.3.6 Vertical Mergers and Acquisitions 327
17.3.7 Joint Ventures and Functionally-Analogous Collaborative Arrangements of Other Sorts (Such as Patent Pools) 329
17.3.8 Internal Growth 332
References 335

18 The Differences in the Potentials of U.S. Antitrust Law and E.U. Competition Law as Written to Increase Economic Efficiency, Secure Liberal Moral Rights, and Instantiate Various Utilitarian and Other Egalitarian Conceptions of the Moral Good 337
18.1 Oligopolistic Conduct: The Differences Between Written U.S. Antitrust Law's and Written E.U. Competition Law's Respective Potentials to Increase Economic Efficiency, Secure Liberal Moral Rights, and Instantiate Any Egalitarian Conception of the Moral Good That Are Attributable to Their Disparate Treatments of Oligopolistic Conduct 338
18.1.1 Natural Oligopolistic Pricing and Contrived-Oligopolistic Pricing 338
18.1.2 Natural-Oligopolistic Investment-Restrictions and Contrived-Oligopolistic Investment-Restrictions 341
18.1.3 Contrived-Oligopolistic Conduct That Is Designed to Enable Its Participants to Make a Different Set of Investments That Are Collectively More Economically Efficient as Well as More Profitable Because They Are Less-Economic-Inefficiently-Duplicative 346
18.1.4 Contrived-Oligopolistic Purchasing 348

18.2 Predatory Conduct: The Differences (If Any) Between Written U.S. Antitrust Law's and Written E.U. Competition Law's Respective Potentials to Increase Economic Efficiency, Secure Liberal Moral Rights, and Serve the Instantiation of any Egalitarian Conception of the Moral Good That Can Be Attributed to Their Disparate Treatments of Predatory Conduct 349
18.2.1 Predatory Pricing 350
18.2.2 Predatory Investing 352
18.2.3 Predatory Advertizing That Is Not Unfairly Competitive 356
18.2.4 Predatory Unfair Competition 358
18.2.5 Predatory Refusals to Deal 361
18.2.6 Allegedly-Predatory Systems Rivalry 366
18.3 Horizontal Mergers and Acquisitions 371
18.4 Conglomerate Mergers and Acquisitions 374
18.5 Surrogates for Vertical Integration 374
18.5.1 Pricing-Techniques 376
18.5.2 Non-Pricing-Technique Tying and Reciprocity Agreements 378
18.5.3 Minimum-Price-Setting-RPM, Maximum-Price-Setting-RPM, and Vertical-Customer-Allocation (VCA) Clauses in Distributorship Agreements 379
18.5.4 Contractual Clauses Obligating Distributors to Place Specific Quantities and/or Qualities of Media Advertizing, to Provide Specified Quantities and/or Qualities of Promotional Displays, to Supply Specified Quantities and Qualities of Salesmanship, to Provide Specified Quantities and Qualities of Shelf-Space, to Provide Specified Repair-and-Maintenance Services (Perhaps Related to Warrantees), and to Use Specified Architectural Layouts and Contractual Clauses in Which a Producer Agrees to Subsidize/(Pay for) Distributor (Expenditures of These Kinds)/(Shelf-Space Allocations) 382
18.5.5 Sales-Policies: A Producer's Communicating to Its Distributors Its Intention Not to Renew Their Distributorships If They Do Not Follow Its "Recommendations" and a Producer's Not Renewing the Distributorships of Distributors That Do Not Follow Its "Recommendations" 382

18.5.6 Clauses in Distributorship Agreements That Impose Single-Brand Restrictions on the Distributor 384
18.6 Vertical Mergers and Acquisitions 385
18.7 Joint Ventures, Functionally-Related Collaborative Arrangements, and Any Restrictive Clauses the Contract That Creates Them Contain 387
18.8 Internal Growth 389

Conclusion 393

Part II

The Morally-Relevant Effects of Specific Categories of Antitrust-Policy-Coverable Conduct and the Ability of Government to Secure Better Outcomes (Continued)

Horizontal Mergers and Acquisitions 11

A horizontal merger or acquisition (M or A) is an (M or A) consummated by two or more firms at least one of whose use of one or more of its pre-(M or A) investments reduced the profits yielded by at least one investment of at least one of the other participants because, for example, at least two of the participants were uniquely-privately-equal-best-placed to secure the patronage of one or more given buyers or because two of the participants were respectively uniquely-privately-best-placed and uniquely-privately-second-placed to secure the patronage of one or more buyers. This chapter's analysis of horizontal-(M&A) policy is presented in five sections. Section 11.1 delineates 16 ways in which a horizontal [M or A] can increase its participants' profits (eight of which do not or may not involve the [M or A]'s reducing the absolute attractiveness of the best offers against which the participants will have to compete in one or more ways that would render the [M or A] profitable though economically inefficient in an otherwise-Pareto-perfect economy and eight of which do involve the [M or A]'s having such an effect). Section 11.2 analyzes for each of the 16 ways in which a horizontal (M or A) can increase its participants' profits the determinants of the magnitude of the profit-yield in question, the determinants of the (M or A)'s associated effect on economic efficiency, the relevance of the fact that an (M or A) yields its participants profits in the way in question to the (M or A)'s liberal-moral-rights-violativeness, and the relevance of the fact that an (M or A) yields its participants profits in the relevant way to its serving or disserving the instantiation of various conceptions of the moral good. Section 11.3 examines the implications of Sects. 11.1 and 11.2 and Chaps. 1 and 8 for the economic efficiency of horizontal (M&A)s and the ability of a government to increase economic efficiency without violating liberal moral rights (1) by prohibiting horizontal (M or A)s that it concludes were/would be economically inefficient, (2) by allowing firms that want to engage in a horizontal (M or A) to do so only if they alter the horizontal (M or A) they proposed (say, by divesting one or more of their investments) so as to render it (more?) economically efficient, (3) by conditioning its consent to the (M or A) on the participants' agreeing to their prices being regulated post-(M or A), (4) by selling to firms

R. S. Markovits, *Welfare Economics and Antitrust Policy—Vol. II*,
https://doi.org/10.1007/978-3-030-96482-5_11

that propose a horizontal (M or A) the right to consummate it for a price the government concludes the participants would be willing to pay only if the combination of the (M or A), its participants' paying the price in question for the right to consummate it, and the government's responses to its receipt of the required payment would increase economic efficiency, and/or (5) by prohibiting horizontal (M&A)s not only that it concludes would decrease economic efficiency but also that it concludes would increase economic efficiency by less than economic efficiency would be increased by the conduct its participants would substitute for the (M or A) in question (for example, the horizontal [M or A][s] they would substitute for the [M or A] in question) if that (M or A) were prohibited. Section 11.4 examines the implications of Sects. 11.1 and 11.2 and Chap. 2 for the more-specific conditions under which a horizontal (M or A) was or would be liberal-moral-rights-violative as well as for the ability of government to secure liberal-moral-rights-related interests by responding in various ways to proposed or consummated horizontal (M&A)s. Section 11.5 examines the implications of Sect. 11.2 for the conditions under which horizontal (M&A)s will disserve and serve the instantiation of various pure (utilitarian, equal-utility, equal-resource, and various other equal-opportunity) and mixed egalitarian conceptions of the moral good and for the ability of government to secure the instantiation of these various conceptions of the moral good without violating any liberal moral rights by responding in various appropriate ways to proposed/consummated horizontal (M&A)s.

This chapter is exhaustive and exhausting. It will identify and analyze a huge number of possibilities, some of which will frequently or possibly even usually not be third-best allocatively efficient, liberal-moral-rights-securing, or morally good for the government to consider. But one cannot decide whether it would be "worthwhile" for the government to consider a possibility in a given case or in various defined sets of cases unless one recognizes its existence and possible salience. I am striving to put analysts in a position to make "desirable" investigative choices. To quote Isaiah: "If not now, when?" And, if I may be self-indulgent: "If not I, who?."

11.1 The 16 Ways in Which Horizontal (M&A)s Can Increase Their Participants' Profits

11.1.1 The 8 "Sherman-Act-Licit" Ways in Which Horizontal (M&A)s Can Increase Their Participants' Profits—That Is, Can Do So Without Increasing Those Profits by Reducing the Absolute Attractiveness of the Most-Attractive Offers Against Which They Will Have to Compete in a Way That Would Render the (M or A) Profitable Even If It Would Have Been Economically Inefficient in an oPp Economy

A horizontal (M or A) can increase its participants' profits in eight Sherman-Act-licit ways:

(1) directly by generating "static marginal-cost efficiencies"—that is, by creating a firm that is more proficient at using one or more participant-investments than

the participant would have been (for example, that faces a lower marginal-cost curve than the participant would have faced),

(2) directly, by generating "static" fixed-cost efficiencies"—that is, by creating a firm that is able to renew or replace a participant's production plant or distributive outlet more cheaply than the participant could have done),

(3) by generating "dynamic efficiencies"—that is, by creating a firm that faces lower ($\Pi_D + R$) barriers to making a QV or PPR investment than any participant would have faced,

(4) by enabling the resulting firm to profit by making an individual investment when no participant could have done so by converting a situation in which the participants caused each other to face natural-oligopolistic investment-disincentives into one in which the resulting firm faced no such disincentives (had the option of making an investment whose creation/execution would not induce a rival [namely, another participant] to make an investment when that rival would not otherwise have made an investment),

(5) by creating a resulting firm that can make one or more investments that are more profitable for it than the investment or investments the participants would have made as separate entities would have been for them jointly because the resulting firm would take account of the impact that any investment it made would have on the profits yielded by all participants' other investments, whereas each individual participant would take account of the impact that its investment(s) would have on the profits yielded only by its own other investments,

(6) by enabling an owner or owner/manager of a (usually small) firm that is participating in the (M or A) who wants to liquidate his or her assets and escape the burden of management to do so,

(7) by enabling a participant that has a tax-loss that it cannot use itself (because the relevant society's tax laws limit the number of years that such tax-losses can be carried forward and used to offset subsequent-year taxable income and the participant has not realized and would not realize sufficient taxable income in the years following the loss to enable it to take advantage of the operative carry-forward provision)—in essence, to sell the tax-loss it cannot itself use to another (M or A) participant that has taxable income that can be offset by the tax-loss in question, and

(8) by enabling the participants (and their remaining rivals) to overcome to at least some extent the "public-good type" problem that militates against their spending as much money on political-party-contributions, specific political campaigns, specific political candidates, and participation in government legislative, administrative, and adjudicative decision-making processes as would be in the participants' joint interest when the profits the relevant expenditures yield are not Sherman-Act-illicit. (Section 11.1.2 recognizes that the profits that some expenditures of these kinds yield are Sherman-Act-illicit—are motivated by predatory intent or a desire to have government make decisions

that place rivals at a competitive disadvantage that is not warranted by the allocative efficiency of the rivals' making sales. The analysis of the "moral desirability" of prohibiting firms from making expenditures of these kinds that are so motivated is complicated by their—that is, their shareholders'—possible liberal-moral-rights-based interest in influencing their government's decisions. In U.S. law, the compromise decision-rule is to permit firms to participate in governmental decision-making processes to secure their parochial interests so long as they play fair—do not tell lies, intentionally make misleading statements, or pay individuals perceived to be neutral experts to take policy-positions that the firms favor without revealing that they are being paid to do so by the firms.)

11.1.2 The 8 Sherman-Act-Illicit Ways in Which a Horizontal (M or A) Can Increase Its Participants' Profits

A horizontal (M or A) can increase its participants' profits in the following eight Sherman-Act-illicit ways:

(1) by increasing the resulting firm's HNOPs above those of the participants by freeing the participants from each other's price-competition,
(2) by increasing the NOMs the resulting firm can obtain above those the participants could have obtained by increasing the resulting firm's OCAs above those of the participants, in across-the-board-pricing contexts by creating a resulting firm whose prominence enables it to orchestrate its and its rivals' announcing a series of "premature" price-announcements that facilitates their obtaining OMs naturally, and by creating a resulting firm that is more able to obtain OMs naturally because it is better able to take advantage of organizational economies of scale in changing its initial prices (the conclusion that these profits are "illicit" is consistent with the fact that they cannot be morally justified and with the fact that the choices that yield them are economically inefficient, may be liberal-moral-rights-violative, and disserve all egalitarian conceptions of the moral good: however, I admit that their characterization as "Sherman-Act-illicit" is called into question by the fact that the Sherman Act does not cover natural –oligopolistic conduct),

(3) by creating a resulting firm that obtains more COMs than the participants would have obtained,
(4) by freeing the participants from each other's investment-competition when each participant would have found it unprofitable to make an investment if it did not believe that its failure to invest would result in the other participant's making an investment when no-one else would do so that would reduce the former participant's profits by more than the former participant's investment would reduce those profits relative to the *status quo ante*,
(5) by creating a resulting firm that profits more by reducing the absolute attractiveness of the best offers against which it must compete by driving out existing-rival investments—by engaging in predatory pricing, placing predatory advertizements, and/or making other predatory moves,
(6) by creating a resulting firm that faces less competition from its participants' rivals than its participants would have faced because the resulting firm will find it more profitable than any participant would have done to reduce the absolute attractiveness of the best offers against which it must compete by predatorily raising the retaliation barriers to investment facing an otherwise-effective potential competitor or an otherwise-effective established-rival potential investment-expander,
(7) by creating a resulting firm that is better able than the participants would have been to orchestrate the relevant ARDEPPS' sellers' raising their HNOPs by announcing their prices and making choices that render it costly for them to change their initially-announced prices in a sequence that increases the HNOPs of the participants and their mutual rivals (an analog to the parenthetical that concludes Item (2) in this list could be inserted here), and
(8) by enabling the participants (that is, the resulting firm) and the participants' mutual rivals to overcome to at least some extent the "public-good-type" problem that militates against their spending as much money on political parties/campaigns/candidates and government-decision-making-process participation as would be in their collective and the participants' joint interest when the profits yielded would reflect the government's making decisions that increase the participants' profits by reducing the absolute attractiveness of the best offers against which they must compete in one or more ways that would render the expenditures profitable though economically inefficient in an oPp economy.

11.2 The Determinants of the Amount of Profits a Horizontal (M or A) Will Yield Its Participants in Each of the 16 Ways in Which It Can Yield Them Profits, the Relationship Between Each of These 16 Profit-Yields and the (M or A)'s Associated Impact on Economic Efficiency, the Relevance of the Fact That a Horizontal (M or A) Yields Its Participants Profits in Each of the 16 Ways in Which It Can Do So to the (M or A)'s Liberal-Moral-Rights-Violativeness, and the Relevance of the Fact That a Horizontal (M or A) Yields Its Participants Profits in Each of the 16 Ways in Which It Can Do So for the (M or A)'s Serving or Disserving the Instantiation of the Various Pure (Utilitarian, Equal-Utility, Equal-Resource, and Other-Equal-Opportunity) and Mixed Egalitarian Conceptions of the Moral Good

11.2.1 Analyses That Relate to Any Static Marginal-Cost Efficiencies a Horizontal (M or A) Generates

For convenience, I will assume that any static marginal-cost efficiencies a horizontal (M or A) generates will be manifest in the (M or A)'s reducing by a constant amount the per-unit marginal cost the resulting firm must incur to produce each unit of each product of each of its participants. I will also assume that the static (private) marginal-cost efficiencies on which this section focuses are associated with allocative-cost savings—do not reflect the resulting firm's having more bargaining-power than the participants would have had that enables it to buy inputs more cheaply than they could have done for reasons that have nothing to do with the resulting firm's being a more-allocatively-efficient buyer than the participants would have been.

11.2.1.1 The Determinants of the Profits That a Horizontal (M or A) Will Yield Its Participants by Generating Static Marginal-Cost Efficiencies

The relevant analyses will vary somewhat with whether single pricing or across-the-board pricing is practiced in the ARDEPPS in which the relevant horizontal (M or A) is consummated. I will focus first on situations in which single pricing is practiced by the participants and their mutual rivals.

When the (M or A) is consummated in a single-pricing ARDEPPS, any static marginal-cost efficiencies it generates

(1) will increase the profits the participants realize on unit sales they would have made absent the (M or A) by the sum of the following mathematical products for each product the participants would have sold on their own—(the number

of units the participant[s] would have sold of the product in question absent the [M or A]) *times* (the marginal-cost reduction the [M or A] effectuated),

(2) will yield the participants profits by making the resulting firm privately-best-placed to make sales that no participant would have been privately-best-placed to make equal to the sum of the following mathematical products for each product a participant produced—(the number of unit-sales of the product in question that the marginal-cost efficiencies the horizontal [M or A] in question generate rendered the resulting firm privately-best-placed to make) *times* (the average difference between the marginal-cost reduction in question and the number of dollars by which the participant[s] that was [were] privately-better-placed than any other participant to make any of the sales in question would have been privately-worse-than-best-placed to make the sales in question),

(3) will increase the profits the participants realize by driving out an existing rival by critically worsening its array of competitive positions—in particular, if one ignores any effects the marginal-cost efficiencies have on this account by enabling the resulting firm to obtain higher NOMs and COMs than the participants could have obtained and assumes that the efficiencies will not on this account alter the buyer surplus the participants' customers secure, will on this account increase the participants' profits by the sum of the OCAs the resulting firm enjoys in its relations with buyers it is privately-best-placed to supply (via its current or future investments) but an exiting rival would have been privately-best-placed to supply *plus* the sum of the extra OCAs the resulting firm enjoys because the exiting rivals would have been uniquely-privately-second-placed to supply buyers the resulting firm was privately-best-placed to supply (the sum of the OCAs the exiting rival would have enjoyed over those buyers' privately-third-placed suppliers),

(4) will increase the profits the participants realize by critically raising the barriers to investment faced by an otherwise-effective potential investor (be it a potential entrant or rival established firm) in the ARDEPPS in question by worsening its array of prospective competitive positions—in particular, if one ignores any associated effects on the amounts of NOMs and COMs the resulting firm will obtain relative to those the participants would have obtained and assumes that the marginal-cost efficiencies will not on this account alter the amount of buyer surplus the resulting firm's customers obtain, will increase the participants' profits by either (A) if the rival investment in question would otherwise have been made, the sum of the OCAs the resulting firm enjoyed in its relations with buyers it was privately-best-placed to supply (via its current or future investments) but the owner of the deterred investment would have been privately-best-placed to supply had it made the deterred investment *plus* the additional OCAs the resulting firm enjoyed in its relations with buyers it was privately-best-placed to supply and the deterred investor would have been uniquely-privately-second-placed to supply had it made the deterred investment or (B) the "cost" to the participants of any move one of them or another rival would otherwise have made to deter the rival investment the marginal-cost efficiencies deterred (for example, the loss a participant would have incurred

relative to the *status quo ante* to make an investment that would deter the rival investment the marginal-cost efficiencies deterred),

(5) will increase the amount of profits the participants realize by the amount by which the static marginal-cost efficiencies the horizontal (M or A) generates cause the NOMs the resulting firm secures when using the participants' investments to exceed the NOMs the participants would have secured when using them, and

(6) will increase/decrease the amount of profits the participants realize by the amount by which the static marginal-cost efficiencies the (M or A) generates cause the COMs the resulting firm obtains when using the participants' investments (to exceed)/(to be lower than) the COMs the participants would have secured when using them.

I need to explain points (5) and (6) in this list and to acknowledge that point (6) may be inappropriate. I will start with point (5).

At least if the relevant society's government had not succeeded in preventing all natural-oligopolistic pricing, any static marginal-cost efficiencies a horizontal (M or A) generates will tend to increase the NOMs the resulting firm obtains when using the participants' investments above the NOMs the participants would have obtained when using them by increasing (1) the resulting firm's OCAs in its relations with buyers a participant would have been privately-best-placed to supply above the OCAs the participant would have enjoyed in it relations with those buyers, hence (2) the difference between the price that the resulting firm would have to include in a revised offer to any relevant buyer if the resulting firm's initial offer was beaten by a rival to beat the rival's superior offer and the marginal cost the resulting firm would have to incur to supply that buyer above the counterpart difference for the relevant participant, hence (3) the frequency with which the above (reduced-price *minus* marginal-cost) difference for the resulting firm would exceed the extra cost it would have to incur to change its initial offer above its counterpart for the relevant participant.

I move now to point (6). Even if the relevant society's government has not succeeded in preventing its firms from engaging in contrived-oligopolistic pricing, I do not think that the static marginal-cost efficiencies a horizontal (M or A) operates will tend to increase the profits its participants realize by engaging in contrived-oligopolistic pricing when they are charging individualized prices. I believe that 7 points are most salient.

First, the static marginal-cost efficiencies a horizontal (M or A) generates will tend to make it less profitable for the resulting firm to charge contrived-oligopolistic prices to buyers a participant would have been privately-best-placed to supply than it would have been for the participant to do so by increasing the safe profits the resulting firm must put at risk to do so (its [OCA + NOM] total) above the safe profits the participant would have had to put at risk to do so. Second, it is unclear whether the static marginal-cost efficiencies a horizontal (M or A) generates will render contrivance more/less profitable for the resulting firm relative to the participant when the participant would have been privately-best-placed to supply the buyer in question by causing the resulting firm to be (more able to)/(less able to) reciprocate to rival cooperation than the participant would have been—whether such efficiencies (1) will cause the resulting firm to be uniquely-privately-second-placed to obtain its relevant rivals' customers more or less often than the relevant participant would have been and (2) will cause the average amount by which the resulting firm is better-placed than the privately-third-placed supplier of the customers of the relevant rivals when the resulting firm is those buyers' privately-second-placed supplier to exceed or be exceeded by the average amount by which the relevant participant would have been privately-better-placed than the privately-third-placed supplier of customers of the relevant rivals when the participant would have been its privately-second-placed supplier. Third, it is unclear whether the static marginal-cost efficiencies a horizontal (M or A) generates will cause the resulting firm to be privately-better-placed than the relevant participant would have been to retaliate against non-cooperators: the efficiencies will worsen the harm-inflicted to loss-incurred ratio by reducing the number of buyers the non-cooperators are privately-best-placed to supply and the average amount by which they are privately-best-placed to supply the buyers to which the resulting firm and participants could make retaliatory offers and will have an uncertain effect on the relative frequencies with which the resulting firm and the relevant participant would be a non-cooperating rival's closest competitor for the patronage of buyers a non-cooperator was privately-best-placed to supply and the resulting firm and the relevant participant were different amounts worse-than-privately-second-placed to supply. Fourth, the static marginal-cost-efficiencies a horizontal (M or A) generates may cause the resulting firm to engage in more contrived-oligopolistic pricing than the relevant participant would have done by making the resulting firm privately-best-placed by a relatively-small amount to supply buyers no participant was privately-best-placed to supply. Fifth, if the static marginal-cost efficiencies a horizontal (M or A) generates cause one or more mutual rivals to exit, deter a potential entrant from entering the ARDEPPS of consummation, or perhaps deter a mutual established rival of the participants from executing an investment-expansion in that ARDEPPS, they may on that account cause the resulting firm to engage in more contrived-oligopolistic pricing than the participants would have done by reducing the number of rivals to which the resulting firm would have to communicate its contrived oligopolistic intentions and the number of potential non-cooperators it would have to check out when trying to identify its non-cooperators below the number with which the individual participants would have had to be concerned. Sixth, regardless of whether the static marginal-cost efficiencies a horizontal (M or A) generated would reduce the quantity of investment in the ARDEPPS of consummation owned by firms other than the participants but particularly if it did reduce that quantity, those efficiencies would tend to make contrived-oligopolistic pricing more profitable for the resulting firm than for the participants by increasing their unit sales and hence their ability to infer non-cooperation by comparing sales in the most recent period with historic sales. Seventh, if the static marginal-cost efficiencies a horizontal (M or

A) generates cause an existing investment to be withdrawn or deters a potential entrant or small established firm from making an investment in the ARDEPPS of consummation, they may on that account make contrived-oligopolistic pricing more profitable for the resulting firm than it would have been for the participants by rendering the resulting firm more able than the participants would have been to coordinate reciprocation to cooperators and retaliation against non-cooperators with other ARDEPPS contrivers.

I recognize that the following conclusion is contestable. However, in my judgment, everything considered, the static marginal-cost efficiencies a horizontal (M or A) generates will almost always cause the resulting firm to engage in less contrived-oligopolistic pricing than the participants would have practiced.

I turn now to the impact that any static marginal-cost efficiencies a horizontal (M or A) generates will have on its participants' profits when the resulting firm and its rivals set across-the-board prices. The analysis that follows will be less precise than the just-completed counterpart analysis for horizontal (M or A)s that take place in ARDEPPSes in which individualized prices are charged. Even if I assume that all relevant sellers face marginal-cost curves that are horizontal over their relevant ranges and that any static marginal-cost efficiencies a horizontal (M or A) generates will not affect the NOMs or COMs the participants obtain, a full analysis would have to take into account (in addition to the magnitudes of the static marginal-cost efficiencies that were generated for each participant-product) the pre-(M or A) marginal costs of the participants for each of their products, the marginal costs that the participants' rivals faced on each of their products, the product-by-product BPA/BPD arrays of the participants and each of the resulting firm's rivals, the sequence in which the participants and their mutual rivals announced their prices pre-(M or A), and the sequence in which the resulting firm and its rivals announce their prices post-(M or A) (that is, any effect that the static marginal-cost efficiencies the [M or A] generated would have on this sequence), and I do not think it would be "cost-effective" for me to work through examples that take full account of all these parameters. Instead, I will assume here and throughout this chapter that the static marginal-cost efficiencies that are generated by any horizontal (M or A) that takes place in an ARDEPPS in which across-the-board pricing is practiced will (1) reduce the prices the resulting firm charges below those the participants would have charged, (2) increase the (P–MC) gaps for the participants' products, (3) reduce the prices the resulting firm's rivals charge for their products, and (4) increase the resulting firm's unit sales of the participants' products above the unit sales they would have made of their products after the date of the (M or A). These assumptions are favored by the fact that—effects on NOMs and COMs aside—the static marginal-cost efficiencies (1) will tend to reduce the prices that will be profit-maximizing for the resulting firm to charge for the participants' products below the prices the participants would have found most profitable to charge for their products both by reducing the resulting firm's marginal-cost curves below the marginal-cost curves the participants would have faced and by causing the resulting firm's rivals to lower their prices and (2) as I have just asserted, will tend to cause the resulting firm's rivals to reduce their prices. These assumption are disfavored by the fact that—to the extent that the static marginal-cost efficiencies a horizontal (M or A) generates induce a resulting-firm not to renew a QV investment it would have renewed absent the (M or A) and/or deters a potential competitor or a resulting-firm established rival from making a QV investment that would increase the ARDEPPS' equilibrium-QV-investment quantity–they will tend on this account to increase the prices the resulting firm charges for the participants' products above the prices they would have charged for them and to increase the prices the resulting firm's rivals charges for their products. These assumptions also ignore the very real possibility that the static marginal-cost efficiencies generated by a horizontal (M or A) that is consummated in an ARDEPPS in which across-the-board prices are set may induce a resulting firm's rival to increase its prices when, pre-(M or A), that rival charged a price that was lower than the price some of its customers would have been willing to pay to enable itself to make sales at supra-marginal-cost prices to buyers that one or more participants were almost as well-placed (in BCA terms) to supply (an objective that would no longer be as attainable or attractive after the [M or A] reduced the prices the resulting firm charged below the prices its participants would have charged).

In any event, any static marginal-cost efficiencies generated by a horizontal (M or A) that was consummated in an ARDEPPS in which across-the-board prices are charged

(1) will increase the profits the participants realize on the unit sales they would have made absent the (M or A) by the sum of the following mathematical products—(the number of units the participants would have sold of each product on which they would have made sales absent the [M or A]) *times* (the amount by which the efficiencies would have increased the [P–MC] gap for that product had they not induced a rival-exit or deterred a rival investment),
(2) will yield the participants additional profits directly (that is, even if they do not induce established-rival exits or deter any rival investment) by increasing the resulting firm's unit sales above the unit sales the participants would have made by the sum of the following mathematical products for each product produced by a participant—(the additional unit sales the resulting firm would have made of each participant-product on this account had the efficiencies not driven a rival out or deterred a rival investment) *times* (the difference between the price the resulting firm would have charged for the product in question had the efficiencies not driven a rival out or deterred a rival investment and the resulting firm's marginal cost for the product in question),
(3) will yield the participants profits indirectly by driving out an extant rival by worsening its competitive-position array or deterring one or more potential investors from adding to the ARDEPPS' equilibrium-investment total by worsening its or their prospective competitive-position array(s) by (A) the sum of the following mathematical products—(the number of units of each participant-product that the resulting firm was privately-best-placed to supply

that the exiting rival or deterred rival-investor would have been privately-best-placed to supply) *times* (the post-[M or A] [P–MC] gap for the product in question) *plus* (B) the sum of the following mathematical products–(the number of units of each participant-product that the resulting firm would have sold had the static marginal-cost efficiencies not driven a rival out or deterred a rival investment) *times* (the amount by which static marginal-cost-efficiency-induced rival-exits or rival-investment-deterrence increased the resulting firm's profit-maximizing price), and

(4) will increase the profits the resulting firm will realize on its future investments by driving a rival out or deterring a rival investment by an amount equal to the sum of the following mathematical products for each product the resulting-firm's future investment would create—([the number of units by which the exiting rival or deterred rival-investor would have reduced the unit sales the resulting firm would have made of each such future product] *times* [the average profits per-unit the resulting firm would have made on those lost unit sales]) *plus* ([the number of units of the new products that the resulting firm would have sold of each new product even if the existing firm had not exited or the deterred investment not been deterred] *times* [the amount by which the withdrawn product or deterred investment would have reduced the average per-unit profits the sale of the new product would yield the resulting firm]), and

(5) will increase the NOMs the resulting firm obtains above those the participating firms would have obtained by increasing the resulting firm's (HNOP–MC) gaps for product-units a participant would have sold above the relevant participating firms' corresponding (HNOP–MC) gaps on those units by increasing the (HNOP–MC) gaps for the resulting firm above their counterparts for the participants.

This list does not reference the possibility that any static marginal-cost efficiencies a horizontal (M or A) generates might increase the COMs the resulting firm secures above those the participants would have secured when across-the-board pricing is practiced in the ARDEPPS of consummation because I do not know whether across all "cases" such efficiencies will tend to increase or decrease the COMs the resulting firm secures relative to those the participants would have secured. The relevant efficiencies will tend to lower the participants' COMs by increasing their (HNOP–MC) gaps and NOMs for buyers in relation to which a participant enjoyed a BCA pre-(M or A)—that is, by increasing the safe profits the resulting firm must put at risk to attempt to obtain a COM from such buyers. However, the relevant efficiencies will tend to increase the participants' COMs (1) by giving the resulting firm low BCAs in its relations with buyers in relation to which no participant enjoyed a BCA and (2) by making it more likely that the resulting firm will be able to participate in joint retaliation with its rivals than the participants could with their mutual rivals, by driving a mutual rival of a participant out, by deterring a potential competitor from entering, or by deterring a resulting-firm established rival with a small share of ARDEPPS-investment from investing (that is, by concentrating the seller-side of the relevant ARDEPPS). Everything considered, I think the most-accurate guess is that any static marginal-cost efficiencies a horizontal (M or A) generates would have no effect on the participants' COMs even if the relevant society's laws did not completely deter its firms from practicing contrived-oligopolistic pricing when it would have been profitable for them to do so if such conduct were not illegal.

11.2.1.2 The Determinants of the Impact That Any Static Marginal-Cost Efficiencies a Horizontal (M or A) Generates Will Have on Economic Efficiency

I will continue to assume that the relevant static marginal-cost efficiencies cause the marginal-cost curves the resulting firm faces to be lower than but parallel to the respective marginal-cost curves the participants would have faced and that the (M or A)-generated reduction in marginal cost may differ from participant-product to participant product. I will analyze the impact that the static marginal-cost efficiencies a horizontal (M or A) generates will have on economic efficiency first in situations in which individualized pricing is practiced in the ARDEPPS of consummation and then when that ARDEPPS' sellers set across-the-board prices. In both situations, I will initially ignore any impact the static marginal-cost efficiencies the horizontal (M or A) generates has on the participants' practice of natural and contrived oligopolistic-pricing.

When individualized single pricing is practiced in the ARDEPPS of consummation, the increase in economic efficiency that will result from any static marginal-cost efficiencies a horizontal (M or A) generates will equal the sum of the following five totals, the first two of which are totals of a set of mathematical products whose members relate to an individual product produced by an individual participant:

(1) the total across all participant-products of the following mathematical products for each participant product—(the number of units of the relevant product the participant in question would have sold after the date of the [M or A] had the [M or A] not been consummated) *times* (the per-unit reduction in the marginal cost of producing each unit of that product the [M or A] in question generated) *times* (the ratio of [the (M or A)-generated reduction in the per-unit marginal allocative cost of producing successive units of the product in question] to [the (M or A)-generated reduction in the per-unit marginal (private) cost of producing successive units of the product in question]) *plus*
(2) the total across all participant-products of the following mathematical products for each participant-product—([the positive difference between the unit sales the resulting firm made of the product in question and the unit sales that the participating firm would have made of the product in question after the date of the relevant (M or A)] *times* [the average BPA the resulting firm enjoyed when selling the extra units in question (which might be negative)]) *plus* ([the positive difference between the unit sales the resulting firm made of the product in question and the unit sales the participating firm would have made of the

product in question after the date of the relevant (M or A)] *times* [the average MCA the resulting firm enjoyed over its respective closest competitors for the unit sales in question, which may be negative] *times* [the ratio of (the per-unit reduction in the marginal *allocative* cost of producing successive units of the product in question) to (the per-unit reduction in the marginal [private] cost of producing successive units of the product in question)] *plus*

(3) if the investments in the ARDEPPS of consummation are QV investments and the relevant society's government has not adopted policies that prevent the society from continuing to devote too many resources from the perspective of economic efficiency to QV-investment creation, the increase in economic efficiency the static marginal-cost efficiencies the (M or A) yields will generate by reducing equilibrium QV investment in the ARDEPPS of consummation by reducing the prices charged for the participants' products, thereby reducing the profits their mutual rivals realize on their QV investments, thereby inducing one or more of the participants' mutual rivals to not renew one or more of their QV investments in the ARDEPPS of consummation[1] *plus*

(4) the amount by which the relevant static marginal-cost efficiencies will increase economic efficiency by reducing poverty and inequality (primarily by yielding equivalent-dollar gains to the relevant ARDEPPS' buyers[2]) *minus*

(5) the amount by which the relevant static marginal-cost efficiencies will decrease economic efficiency by concentrating the seller-side of the ARDEPPS of consummation (by creating a resulting firm that renews a participant QV investment that the participant would not have renewed, by deterring one or more established firms from renewing a QV investment by worsening the array of competitive positions it or they would occupy when using the QV investment[s] in question, and/or by deterring a potential entrant or a smaller established firm from making one or more deconcentrating new QV investments in the ARDEPPS in question by worsening the array of competitive positions these deterred investors would anticipate facing on the deterred investments) and thereby increasing the amount of economic inefficiency government generates when making decisions that affect the ARDEPPS' sellers' profits by increasing the expenditures the ARDEPPS' sellers make on political parties/campaigns/candidates and on government-decision-making-process participation.

As already indicated, the preceding list ignores the possibility that the static marginal-cost efficiencies a horizontal (M or A) generates may affect economic efficiency by increasing or decreasing the incidences of natural-oligopolistic conduct, contrived-oligopolistic conduct, or predatory conduct in which the ARDEPPS' sellers engage. Chapters 9 and 10 argued that, with the possible exception of some exemplars of predatory conduct that reduce equilibrium QV investment in the ARDEPPS in which it is practiced, all such conduct generates economic inefficiency. I have ignored the possibility that the marginal-cost efficiencies that a horizontal (M or A) generates may affect economic efficiency by altering the incidences of these types of conduct not only for the dubious reason that these possibilities might muddle my claim that the profits a horizontal

(M or A) yields its participants by generating static marginal-cost efficiencies are Sherman-Act-licit but also for the excusable reason that I do not know whether the static marginal-cost efficiencies a horizontal (M or A) generates will increase or decrease the incidence of these three types of conduct taken together. Thus, although the static marginal-cost efficiencies a horizontal (M or A) generates will tend to cause the NOMs the resulting firm obtains to exceed the NOMs the participants would have obtained as separate entities by increasing the resulting firm's OCAs in its relations with buyers a participant would have been privately-best-placed to supply above those the participant would have enjoyed, those efficiencies will tend to reduce the NOMs the participants' mutual rivals secure by reducing their OCAs in their relations with buyers they are still privately-best-placed to supply post-(M or A) and will have an uncertain effect on the OCA of the seller that is privately-best-placed to supply buyers that the resulting firm is privately-best-placed to supply but a resulting-firm rival would have been privately-best-placed to supply absent the (M or A), and I do not know whether all tolled the static marginal-cost efficiencies a horizontal (M or A) generates will (so to speak) increase the participants' NOMs by more or less than they decrease the NOMs of the participants' mutual rivals. Similarly, although I suspect that the static marginal-cost efficiencies a horizontal (M or A) generates will cause the resulting firm to engage in less contrived-oligopolistic pricing than the participants would have done (by increasing the safe profits the resulting firm must put at risk to try to obtain COMs—I recognize that a complete analysis is far more complicated), I suspect that the static marginal-cost efficiencies a horizontal (M or A) generates will increase the amount of contrived-oligopolistic pricing that the resulting firm's rivals practice (both by reducing the safe profits they must put at risk to do so and by causing retaliation against the resulting firm to be more "cost-effective" than retaliation against the participants would have been [by creating a resulting firm with higher OCAs and enabling a rival to retaliate against the resulting firm by charging retaliatory prices to customers of both participants]). I also find it difficult to predict whether the static marginal-cost efficiencies a horizontal (M or A) generates will tend to increase or decrease the profitability of predation either for the resulting firm relative to the separate participants or for the participants' mutual rivals. Because I cannot predict whether, all tolled, the static marginal-cost efficiencies a horizontal (M or A) generates will tend to increase or decrease the incidence of natural-oligopolistic, contrived-oligopolistic, and predatory conduct and doubt that it will be TBLE to try to resolve this issue in individual cases or sets of cases, I feel justified in ignoring the possibility that the static marginal-cost efficiencies a horizontal (M or A) generates might affect economic efficiency by altering the incidence of such conduct (even if one makes realistic assumptions about the extent to which actual antitrust policies will deter such conduct).

I will now consider the impact that any static marginal-cost efficiencies a horizontal (M or A) generates will have on economic efficiency when the sellers in the ARDEPPS in which the (M or A) was consummated set across-the-board prices. In my judgment, the only differences that the type of pricing practiced in the (M or A)-ARDEPPS makes to the economic-efficiency impact of the static marginal-cost efficiencies the (M or A) generates relate to the following possibility: If those efficiencies make the resulting firm more prominent by increasing its share of ARDEPPS sales both directly by increasing the number of buyers it is best-placed to supply without inducing a rival to exit or deterring a rival investment and/or by making it profitable for the resulting firm to renew a QV investment a participant would not have renewed and indirectly by inducing one or more resulting-firm rivals to exit and/or deterring one or more investments by actual or potential competitors of the resulting firm, they may on that account (1) increase the prices in the (M or A)-ARDEPPS HNOP-array by enabling the resulting firm to influence the order in which it and its rivals announce their prices, (2) increase the NOMs secured by the sellers in the (M or A)-ARDEPPS by enhancing the ability of the resulting firm to orchestrate a series of natural-oligopolistic-pricing-enabling "premature" price-announcements and perhaps by increasing the ARDEPPS' sellers' (HNOP–MC) gaps ("perhaps" because the static marginal-cost efficiencies the [M or A] generates will probably decrease the [HNOP–MC] gaps of the resulting firm's rivals by improving the resulting firm's competitive-position array at the same time that it increases the resulting firm's [HNOP–MC] gaps by improving its competitive-position array and will increase all ARDEPPS-sellers' [HNOP–MC] gaps by enabling the resulting firm to alter the sequence in which those sellers announce their prices), and (3) increase the COMs secured by the (M or A)-ARDEPPS' sellers by concentrating the subset of the ARDEPPS' sellers that are prospective contrivers (as opposed to being prospective non-cooperators), by increasing the resulting firm's sales, and perhaps by driving one or more resulting-firm rivals out and/or deterring one or more actual or potential competitors of the resulting firm from making a new investment in the ARDEPPS in question (and thereby reducing the public-good-type obstacle and the coordination obstacle to the prospective contrivers' engaging in as much retaliation against non-cooperators as would be in the contrivers' collective interest).

I should admit that I doubt the importance of these possibilities and *a fortiori* the third-best allocative efficiency of an antitrust-law-enforcement authority's taking them into consideration. Nevertheless, for the sake of completeness, I will point out (1) that any increase that the static marginal-cost efficiencies a horizontal (M or A) generates yields in these ways in the HNOPs, NOMs, and COMs of the (M or A)-ARDEPPS' sellers will (A) decrease economic efficiency by increasing the ARDEPPS' equilibrium-QV-investment quantity when its investments are QV investments (on the assumption that the relevant society's government has not prevented its continuing to devote too many resources to QV-investment creation from the perspective of economic efficiency) and (B) will decrease economic efficiency by increasing poverty and material inequality and (2) that any increase that the static marginal-cost efficiencies a horizontal (M or A) generates yields in the incidence of contrived-oligopolistic pricing in the ARDEPPS in which the (M or A) was consummated will decrease economic efficiency (A) because contrived-oligopolistic pricing would be allocative-transaction-costly even if it did not lead to offensive and defensive retaliation and (B) because contrived-oligopolistic pricing does tend to lead to offensive and defensive retaliation, which generate allocative transaction costs and intra-ARDEPPS UO-to-UO misallocation, and (3) any tendency the static marginal-cost efficiencies a horizontal (M or A) generates has to concentrate the seller-side of the ARDEPPS of consummation by deterring the renewal of a QV investment by a mutual rival of the participants or by deterring the creation of a new QV investment by a potential entrant or by an established firm that owned a relatively-low percentage of the relevant ARDEPPS' investment (by worsening the competitive-position array the deterred investors would face when using the renewed/new QV investments in question) will decrease economic efficiency by reducing the public-good-type obstacle to the ARDEPPS' sellers' spending as much on political parties/campaigns/candidates and government-decision-making-process participation as would be in their collective interest.

11.2.1.3 The Relevance of Any Static Marginal-Cost Efficiencies a Horizontal (M or A) Generates to Its Violating Liberal Moral Rights

In my judgment, a horizontal (M or A) will be liberal-moral-rights-violative in two sets of circumstances: (1) when one or more participants' *ex ante* belief that it would be at least normally profitable was critically affected by its (their) perception that it would increase its (their) profits by reducing the absolute attractiveness of the best offers against which it (they) would have to compete in one or more ways that would render the (M or A) profitable even though it would be economically inefficient in an oPp economy or (2) when one or more participants (A) believe *ex ante* that it would increase the profits the participant could realize by engaging in post-(M or A) oligopolistic or predatory conduct, which would itself be liberal-moral-rights-violative and (B) intended *ex ante* to take advantage of the opportunity the (M or A) would give it/them to make profits by engaging in such liberal-moral-rights-violative conduct. The fact that the static marginal-cost efficiencies a horizontal (M or A) generates will yield its participants Sherman-Act-licit profits disfavors the conclusion that the (M or A) is liberal-moral-rights-violative for the first of the above two reasons, though it does not eliminate the possibility that the (M or A) is liberal-moral-rights-violative for that reason since it is compatible with the (M or A)'s not generating or not being perceived by its participants *ex ante* to generate sufficient Sherman-Act-licit profits to be *ex ante* at least normally profitable on their account. The fact that the static marginal-cost efficiencies a horizontal (M or A) generates will tend to increase the frequency with which the participants could obtain OMs naturally, and the reality that the static marginal-cost efficiencies that some horizontal (M or A)s generate will increase the profitability of contrived-oligopolistic pricing and predation to their participants (even if such efficiencies do not *tend* to do so) warrants the conclusion that in some cases the static marginal-cost efficiencies that some horizontal (M or A)s generate will result in their being liberal-moral-rights-violative for either or both of the reasons articulated in the first sentence of this paragraph. However, I should point out that, standing alone, proof that the resulting firm did engage in oligopolistic or predatory conduct will not establish that either of these sets of conditions is fulfilled.

11.2.1.4 The Relevance of Any Static Marginal-Cost Efficiencies a Horizontal (M or A) Generates to Its Serving or Disserving the Utilitarian and Various Non-Utilitarian-Egalitarian Conceptions of the Moral Good

I will start by examining the impact of the static marginal-cost efficiencies a horizontal (M or A) generates will have on its instantiation of the total-utility variant of the utilitarian conception of the moral good. For the following two reasons, I believe that the fact that a horizontal (M or A) generates static marginal-cost efficiencies favors its increasing total utility. First, as Sect. 11.2.1's analyses reveal, the static marginal-cost efficiencies a horizontal (M or A) generates will virtually always increase economic efficiency. Second, the static marginal-cost efficiencies a horizontal (M or A) generates will virtually always have a distributive impact that is desirable from the utilitarian perspective—that is, the average-marginal-utility gain generated by the equivalent-dollar gains a horizontal (M or A)'s static marginal-cost efficiencies yield will virtually always exceed the average-marginal-utility loss generated by the equivalent-dollar losses a horizontal (M or A)'s static marginal-cost efficiencies yield. With one qualification, this second conclusion would follow from the following five claims if they were correct: (1) the static marginal-cost efficiencies a horizontal (M or A) generates will confer equivalent-dollar gains on buyers of the products produced in the ARDEPPS of consummation, will confer equivalent-dollar gains on the shareholders/creditors/managers/employees of the participants, will impose equivalent-dollar losses on the shareholders/creditors/managers/employees of the mutual rivals of the participants, will inflict equivalent-dollar losses on the suppliers of the inputs the static marginal-cost efficiencies enable the resulting firm to save when producing the outputs the participants would have produced after the date of the (M or A) had they not participated in the (M or A), and will confer equivalent-dollar gains on the consumers of the products whose producers were input-rivals of the participants; (2) taken as classes, the buyers of the relevant ARDEPPS' products will usually be less-well-off than the shareholders/creditors/managers/employees of either the participants or their mutual rivals; (3) taken as classes, the shareholders/creditors/managers/employees of the participants and of the participants' mutual rivals are equally-well-off; (4) taken as classes, the suppliers of the inputs the static marginal-cost efficiencies save are equally-well-off as the buyers of the products whose producers are the alternative users of the saved inputs; and (5) the marginal utility of money for an individual decreases as his or her (wealth/income)-position improves.

With the same qualification, whose salience I acknowledge when discussing the distributive desirability from a utilitarian perspective of the distributive impact of any static marginal-cost efficiencies a horizontal (M or A) generates, if the above five claims are correct, (1) they would justify the conclusion that any static marginal-cost efficiencies a horizontal (M or A) generates favors the (M or A)'s serving the instantiation of the equal-utility conception of the moral good, (2) the first four of the preceding five claims would justify the conclusion that any static marginal-cost efficiencies a horizontal (M or A) generates favors the (M or

A)'s serving the instantiation of the equal-resource conception of the moral good, and (3) the combination of the first four of the preceding five claims and a variant of the fifth that asserts that the relevant (non-utility-experiencing)-opportunity value of marginal dollar-gains decreases as the relevant individual's income/wealth positions improves would justify the conclusion that any static marginal-cost efficiencies a horizontal (M or A) generates favors the (M or A)'s serving the instantiation of egalitarian non-utility-experiencing-opportunities conceptions of the moral good.

I need to explain the qualification referenced at the beginning of the preceding two sentences. It relates to the fact that—although the static marginal-cost efficiencies a horizontal (M or A) generates will tend to decrease the extent to which the buyers of the relevant ARDEPPS' products are poorer than the shareholders/creditors/managers/employees of the mutual rivals of the participants—they may increase the extent to which the participants' shareholders/creditors/managers/employees are better-off both than the relevant ARDEPPS' buyers and than the shareholders/creditors/managers/employees of the participants' mutual rivals. The qualification is that, in some cases, the static marginal-cost efficiencies a horizontal (M or A) generates (1) may tend to disserve the instantiation of the utilitarian conception of the moral good by increasing the difference between the income/wealth positions of the shareholders/creditors/managers/employees of the participants on the one hand and the income/wealth positions of the participants' mutual rivals on the other and (2) may tend to disserve the instantiation of the various non-utilitarian-egalitarian conceptions of the moral good I have distinguished not only in the above way but also by increasing the difference between the income/wealth positions of the shareholders/creditors/managers/employees of the participants on the one hand and the income/wealth positions of the relevant buyers on the other (by giving the former group larger equivalent-dollar gains than it gives the latter). I recognize that, to assess the importance of this possibility in a given case, one would have to know not only the relevant equivalent-dollar-gain-and-loss facts but also the appropriate metric for inequality. Since I do not know the distributions of the relevant fact-patterns and do not have anything useful to say about the apposite inequality-metric, I will restrict myself to asserting that the qualification on which I am now focusing will rarely if ever critically affect the correctness of my original qualitative conclusion that the static marginal-cost efficiencies a horizontal (M or A) generates will favor the conclusion that they will serve the instantiation of all these egalitarian conceptions of the moral good.

11.2.2 Analyses That Relate to Any Static Fixed-Cost Efficiencies a Horizontal (M or A) Generates

When the static fixed-cost efficiencies a horizontal (M or A) generates relate to the use of one or more QV investments the participants owned, they will be manifest in the resulting firm's having to incur lower fixed costs than the relevant participant(s) would have had to incur to renew or rebuild the production plant used to produce the product(s) the relevant QV investment(s) created, to renew or rebuild the distributive outlet(s) the relevant QV investment(s) created, or to renew or rebuild the production-capacity the relevant QV investment(s) created. When the static fixed-cost efficiencies a horizontal (M or A) generates relate to the use of one or more PPR investments (discovered production processes), they will be manifest in the resulting firm's having to incur lower fixed costs than the relevant participant(s) would have had to incur to renew or rebuild the production plant(s) built for using the discovered production process(es).

This section assumes that any static fixed-cost efficiencies a horizontal (M or A) generates will not affect the marginal-cost curves or average-variable-cost curves that the resulting firm faces and will not affect the product or distributive service that is being supplied. Like Sect. 11.2.1, this section assumes as well that the fixed-cost efficiencies it analyzes are allocative as well as private—that is, do not manifest the fact that the resulting firm has more buyer power than the participants would have had that enables the resulting firm to purchase inputs more cheaply than the participants could have done independent of whether the resulting firm is a more-allocatively-efficient buyer than the participants would have been.

11.2.2.1 The Determinants of the Profits That a Horizontal (M or A) Will Yield Its Participants by Generating Static Fixed-Cost Efficiencies

The static fixed-cost efficiencies a horizontal (M or A) generates could relate either (1) to the fixed costs of renewing or rebuilding a participant production-or-distributive facility that the participant constructed when making a QV investment or (2) to the fixed costs of renewing or rebuilding a production plant that enabled a participant to use a production-process discovery it had made. The distinction between these two possibilities is salient because (1) the decision of a resulting firm to renew or rebuild a participant's QV-investment-related production or distributive facility that the relevant participant would not have renewed or rebuilt will sometimes deter a resulting-firm rival from making a QV investment in the ARDEPPS of consummation but (2) a resulting firm's decision to renew or rebuild a production plant that enabled its participant-owner to use a production process it discovered that the relevant participant would not have renewed or rebuilt will not deter a resulting-firm rival from executing a PPR project.

It should not be surprising that the profits that any fixed-cost efficiencies a horizontal (M or A) generates confer on the resulting firm will depend in part on (1) how those efficiencies affect the renewing/rebuilding-investment decisions of the resulting firm relative to their counterparts for the relevant participant and (2) how those efficiencies affect the QV-investment decisions of the resulting firm's rivals. It may be somewhat less obvious that four different scenarios need to be distinguished:

(1) in the first, the relevant resulting firm would have renewed or rebuilt the production plant or distributive outlet in question if it had remained a separate entity, and the static fixed-cost efficiencies the horizontal (M or A) generated

will simply reduce the private cost to the resulting firm of the relevant investment below the private cost the participant would have incurred to renew or rebuild its production/distributive facility,

(2) in the second, the private fixed-cost efficiencies the horizontal (M or A) generates (A) will cause the resulting firm to renew or rebuild a participant's production plant or distributive outlet that the participant would not have renewed or rebuilt and (B) in so doing will not deter a resulting-firm rival from making an investment in the ARDEPPS of consummation,

(3) in the third, the private fixed-cost efficiencies a horizontal (M or A) generates (A) will cause the resulting firm to renew or rebuild a participant's QV-investment-related production or distributive facility and (B) in so doing, will deter a resulting-firm rival from making (say) an equally-large investment in the ARDEPPS of consummation, and

(4) in the fourth, the private fixed-cost efficiencies a horizontal (M or A) generates will actually reduce equilibrium investment in the ARDEPPS of consummation by substituting for a situation in which a mutual rival of the participants would have added a QV investment to the ARDEPPS a situation in which neither that mutual rival of the participants nor the resulting firm will make a QV investment in the ARDEPPS of consummation because the relevant mutual rival and the resulting firm will confront each other with critical natural-oligopolistic investment-disincentives—an outcome that will obtain when (A) the static fixed-cost efficiencies the horizontal (M or A) generates would make it profitable for the resulting firm to renew or rebuild a participant production/distributive facility if its decision to do so would not induce a rival to make an investment when it would not have been profitable for the relevant participant to do so in the circumstances in question, (B) would make it profitable for the resulting firm to renew or rebuild the QV-investment-related production/distributive facility of a participant once a rival had added a QV investment to the relevant ARDEPPS when it would not otherwise have been profitable for the relevant participant to do so, and (C) would—given "(B)"—make it unprofitable for a mutual rival of the participants that would have found it profitable to add a QV investment to the ARDEPPS of consummation absent the (M or A) to do so post-(M or A) because the static fixed-cost efficiencies the (M or A) generated would make it profitable for the resulting firm to respond to the rival's QV investment by renewing or rebuilding a participant's production/distributive facility when the relevant participant would not as an independent entity have responded to the rival's QV investment by renewing or rebuilding its production/distributive facility.

If the horizontal-(M or A) participant would in any event have renewed or rebuilt the production facility or distribute outlet whose renewal's or rebuilding's profitability was increased by the static fixed-cost efficiencies the relevant horizontal (M or A) generated, the profits that the static fixed-cost efficiencies a horizontal (M or A) generates yield the resulting firm will equal the reduction in the (private) fixed cost of renewing or rebuilding the production facility or distributive outlet in question. If the relevant horizontal-(M or A) participant would not otherwise have renewed or rebuilt the production facility or distributive outlet whose renewal or replacement cost was reduced by the horizontal (M or A) in question and the participant's decision not to renew or rebuild that facility would not have induced any rival to make a QV investment in the ARDEPPS of consummation—that is, if the resulting firm's decision to renew the participant's production/distributive facility would not deter a rival QV investment, the profits that the relevant static fixed-cost efficiencies will confer on the participants will equal (1) the supernormal profits the renewed investment would be calculated to yield the resulting firm if one ignored its use's impact on the profits yielded by the resulting firm's other investments *minus* (2) any amount by which the renewed investment reduced the profits yielded by the resulting firm's other investments by competing against them and/or by inducing the resulting firm's rivals to respond to the investment's renewal by making non-investment moves that would reduce the profit-yields of the resulting firm's other projects *plus* (3) when the renewed or rebuilt investment was a QV-investment component, the number of dollars by which the continued use of the participant's investment increases the profits the resulting firm obtains by selling other products in the same product-line (since each product in a product-line increases the dollar-value to buyers of other products in that product-line in that buyers prefer to have multiple products in a product-line for aesthetic reasons and/or because the uses and methods of use of the products in a given line of products are similar whereas they differ among product-lines) *plus* (4) when the renewed or rebuilt investment is a component of a QV investment, the profits the continued use of the investment in question enables the resulting firm to earn when selling complements of the product it uses the renewed or rebuilt product to produce *plus* (5) the profits the renewal/rebuilding of the production/distributive facility in question enables the resulting firm to realize because (A) the quality of the product/service the renewed/rebuilt production/distributive facility enables the resulting firm to produce or the production process the renewed/rebuilt production facility enables the resulting firm to continue to use is high and (B) the relevant product or service's continued supply or the relevant production process' continued use causes potential buyers of the resulting firm's other products (who buy units of the product or service the investment's renewal enables to be produced, observe the performance of the newly-produced units of that product for their consumers, or are told by those units' consumers of their high quality or observe the functioning of the production process whose continued employment the renewed investment enables) to revise upward their dollar-valuations of those products *plus* (6) any additional COMs the static fixed-cost-efficiency-induced renewal/rebuilding of a participant's (production facility)/(distributive outlet) enables the resulting firm to realize when using its other investments by enabling it to reciprocate to cooperators or retaliate against non-cooperators via the renewed investment, by increasing the resulting firm's sales and hence its ability to infer non-cooperation from its sales-records, and (particularly if the resulting firm makes a high percentage of the relevant ARDEPPS' sales) by improving its ability to induce the ARDEPPS' potential contrivers to cooperate in their contrivance activities *plus* (7) any additional profits the static fixed-cost efficiencies the horizontal (M or A) generates will enable its participants to realize by engaging in predatory behavior (by using the renewed investment predatorily) *plus* (8) any additional profits the static fixed-cost efficiencies the horizontal (M or A) enables the participants to obtain by increasing the expenditures that the resulting firm and its rivals make on political parties/campaigns/candidates and government-decision-making-process participation by increasing the concentration of the seller-side of the ARDEPPS of consummation by increasing the resulting firm's sales when it already made a relative-large percentage of the ARDEPPS' sales).[3]

If the horizontal-(M or A) participant to whose production/distributive facility's renewal or rebuilding the (M or A)-generated static private-fixed-cost efficiencies relate would not otherwise have continued to use the investment in question and its decision not to use that investment would have resulted in a mutual rival of the participants' making an equally-large investment in the ARDEPPS of consummation, the static private-fixed-cost efficiencies the relevant (M or A) generated would yield the participants profits equal to the total delineated in the preceding sentence *plus* any monopolistic investment-incentive the resulting firm had to continue to use the participant's investment or *minus* the monopolistic investment-disincentive the resulting firm had to continue to use the participant's investment where any such investment-incentive/disincentive would reflect *inter alia* the impact that the substitution of the renewed investment for the deterred investment would have on the resulting firm's NOMs and COMs and on the profits the resulting firm realized by engaging in predation (by using the renewed investment predatorily).

If the static fixed-cost efficiencies a horizontal (M or A) generates (1) substitutes (A) a situation in which the resulting firm does not renew the participant's production/distributive facility and no resulting-firm rival adds a QV investment to the ARDEPPS of consummation for (B) a situation in which a mutual rival of the participants would otherwise have added a QV investment to that ARDEPPS (2) by substituting a situation in which the resulting firm and that rival confronted each other with critical natural-oligopolistic QV-investment disincentives for a situation in which that rival would otherwise have invested, the static fixed-cost efficiencies the horizontal (M or A) generated will increase the participants' profits by the amount by which the deterred rival investment would have decreased their profits.

11.2.2.2 The Determinants of the Impact That Any Static Fixed-Cost Efficiencies a Horizontal (M or A) Generates Will Have on Economic Efficiency

The analysis of the economic-efficiency impact of any static fixed-cost efficiencies a horizontal (M or A) generates will focus separately on the four possible scenarios Sect. 11.2.2.1 distinguished. However, before proceeding, I will address two issues whose resolution will affect the economic-efficiency impact of any static fixed-cost efficiencies a horizontal (M or A) generates the first of which will also affect the impact of such efficiencies on the instantiation of the utilitarian and the various non-utilitarian-egalitarian conceptions of the moral good in each of the 4 situations

I have distinguished. The first of these issues is: What are the determinants of the impact of any static fixed-cost efficiencies a horizontal (M or A) generates on poverty and material inequality? The second of these issues is: What are the determinants of the impact of such efficiencies on the concentration of the seller-side of the ARDEPPS of consummation and hence on the expenditures its sellers make on political parties/campaigns/candidates and government-decision-making-process participation and (possibly) on the amount of contrived-oligopolistic and predatory conduct in which its sellers engage? I should admit at the outset that the distributive-impact analyses that follow will be far from complete—will consider only the most obvious (and I hope the most significant) distributive effects the static fixed-cost efficiencies in question will generate.

In the situation in which the static fixed-cost efficiencies a horizontal (M or A) generates simply enable the resulting firm to renew or rebuild at lower cost a production or distributive facility that a relevant participant would have renewed or rebuilt, the static fixed-cost efficiencies will confer equivalent-dollar gains on the shareholders/creditors/managers/employees of the participants, impose equivalent-dollar losses on the suppliers of the inputs that the resulting firm used less of (to renew or rebuild the participant's facility) than the relevant participant would have employed for this purpose, and confer equivalent-dollar gains on the suppliers of any inputs that the resulting firm used more of than the relevant participant would have employed for the relevant purpose. I will assume that the latter group of benefited input-suppliers is smaller than the former group of harmed input-suppliers: indeed, in some cases, no input-suppliers may be benefited. I will also assume that, taken as a group, the shareholders/creditors/managers/employees of the participants are better-off than are their counterparts for either set of input-suppliers just referenced and that, taken as groups, the shareholders/creditors/managers/employees of the two sets of input-suppliers are equally-well-off. On these last two assumptions, in the situation on which I am now focusing, the static fixed-cost-efficiencies at issue will tend to increase poverty and material inequality. In the situation on which I am now focusing, any static fixed-cost efficiencies a horizontal (M or A) generates will have no impact on the concentration of the seller-side of the ARDEPPS of consummation and hence will have no effect on its sellers' political activities or government-decision-making-process participation. (The combination of these last conclusions and my assumption that any static fixed-cost efficiencies a horizontal [M or A] generates will not affect the marginal-cost curve or average-variable-cost curve for using the production/distributive facility in question accounts for my implicit assumption that in this situation any static fixed-cost efficiencies a horizontal [M or A] generates will not have any impact on the buyers of the participants or their mutual rivals.)

In the situation in which the static fixed-cost efficiencies a horizontal (M or A) generates increase equilibrium QV investment in the ARDEPPS of consummation by causing the resulting firm to renew or rebuild a production/distributive facility of a participant that would not have done so when the participant's failure to do so would not have led anyone else to make an (equally-large) QV investment in the ARDEPPS of consummation, the static fixed-cost efficiencies the horizontal (M or A) generates will confer equivalent-dollar gains on the shareholders/creditors/managers/employees of the participants, will impose equivalent-dollar losses on the shareholders/creditors/managers/employees of the resulting firm's rivals in the ARDEPPS of consummation, will confer equivalent-dollar gains on buyers of the product(s)/service(s) the renewed/rebuilt facilities produce and on buyers of the other products/services supplied in the ARDEPPS of consummation, will confer equivalent-dollar gains on the suppliers of the inputs used to renew or rebuild the facility the efficiencies cause to be renewed or rebuilt, will confer equivalent-dollar losses on the shareholders/creditors/managers/employees of the firms that are the alternative purchasers of the inputs that the resulting firm used to renew or rebuild the relevant participant's facility, and will impose equivalent-dollar losses on the prospective buyers of the "goods and services" the resources used to renew or rebuild the participant's facility would otherwise have been used to produce as well as on the buyers of those goods' and services' product-rivals. The assumptions that (1) the shareholders/creditors/managers/employees of the resulting firm are equally-well-off as their counterparts for the resulting firm's product and input rivals, (2) the buyers of the products produced in the ARDEPPS of consummation are equally-well-off as the buyers of the goods that would have been produced with the resources used either to renew or rebuild the relevant participant's production/distributive facility or to produce the extra units of the goods supplied by sellers in the ARDEPPS of consummation because the continued operation of the participant's facility caused prices in the ARDEPPS of consummation to drop, (3) the suppliers of the inputs used to renew or repair the participant's facility and of the inputs used to produce the additional units of the relevant ARDEPPS' products that the continued operation of a participant's facility causes to be produced are equally-well-off as the buyers of the products produced by the ARDEPPS of consummation and the buyers of the products whose prices are increased by the induced increase in inputs-demand by the resulting firm and its product-demand by the resulting firm and its product-rivals, and (4) taken as groups, the shareholders/creditors/managers/employees of the suppliers and buyers referenced in Item (3) of this list are less-well-off than the shareholders/creditors/managers/employees of the firm referenced in Item (1) of this list do not seem to me to favor any qualitative conclusion about the impact that the static fixed-cost efficiencies a horizontal (M or A) yields will have on poverty or material inequality. I am also unable to generate any conclusion about whether, in the situation now under consideration, any static fixed-cost efficiencies a horizontal (M or A) generates will tend to increase or decrease the concentration of the seller-side of the ARDEPPS of consummation (and hence the sellers' political and government-decision-making-process expenditures and/or practice of contrived-oligopolistic and predatory conduct). In individual cases, the above effects will be determined by whether the resulting firm had a relatively-low percentage of ARDEPPS-sales or ARDEPPS-investment (in which case the continued operation of the participant's facility would tend to decrease seller-concentration) or a relatively-high percentage of ARDEPPS-sales or ARDEPPS-investment (in which case the continued operation of the participant's facility would tend to decrease seller-concentration). (I acknowledge that the preceding generalizations are crude.)

In the situation in which the static fixed-cost efficiencies a horizontal (M or A) generates cause a resulting-firm renewal or rebuilding of a participant's facility to be substituted for a rival QV investment (which the resulting-firm investment deters), the static fixed-cost efficiencies will confer equivalent-dollar gains on the stockholders/creditors/managers/employees of the participants, will impose equivalent-dollar losses on their counterparts for the deterred resulting-firm rival, will impose equivalent-dollar losses on the buyers in the ARDEPPS of consummation if the deterred QV investor is a potential competitor or possibly if the deterred QV investor owns a lower percentage of the ARDEPPS' QV investment than the resulting firm would own if it did not renew or rebuild the relevant facility (to the extent that in this situation the substitution of the resulting firm's investment for the deterred rival QV investment would increase the amount of contrived-oligopolistic pricing practiced in the ARDEPPS of consummation), and possibly could confer equivalent-dollar gains on the relevant ARDEPPS' buyers if the deterred QV investor was an established rival of the resulting firm whose ARDEPPS-QV-investment quantity was higher than the quantity of QV investment the resulting firm would own if it did not renew or rebuild the participant's facility (for the reason just referenced). On the assumptions I have been making, the preceding conclusions imply that, in situations in which the static fixed-cost efficiencies a horizontal (M or A) generates cause a resulting-firm renewing/rebuilding investment to be substituted for a rival QV investment, those static fixed-cost efficiencies will tend to increase poverty and material inequality if the deterred investor is a potential entrant or perhaps if it is an established firm that owned less QV investment in the relevant ARDEPPS than the resulting firm would own if it did not renew or rebuild the relevant participant's facility and will tend to decrease poverty and material inequality if the deterred investor is an established firm that owns more QV investment in the ARDEPPS of consummation than the resulting firm would own if it did not renew or rebuild the relevant participant's facility. In the situation now under consideration, the static fixed-cost efficiencies a horizontal (M or A) generates will increase the concentration of the seller-side of the ARDEPPS of consummation when the deterred QV investor was a potential competitor or an established firm whose QV investment in the ARDEPPS was lower than the QV investment the resulting firm would own if it did renew or rebuild the participant's facility and would decrease the concentration of the seller-side of the ARDEPPS of consummation if the deterred QV investor was an established firm in that ARDEPPS whose QV investment in it was lower than the QV investment the resulting firm would own if it did not renew or rebuild the participant's facility.

In the situation in which the static fixed-cost efficiencies a horizontal (M or A) generated would reduce equilibrium QV investment in the ARDEPPS of consummation by substituting for a situation in which a resulting-firm rival would have made a QV investment in that ARDEPPS a situation in which neither it nor the resulting firm do so because they confront each other with critical natural-oligopolistic QV-investment disincentives, those efficiencies will impose an equivalent-dollar loss on the shareholders/creditors/managers/employees of the deterred rival of the resulting firm, will confer an equivalent-dollar gain on the shareholders/creditors/managers/employees of the participants by deterring a mutual-rival QV investment that would have reduced the participants' profits, will impose an equivalent-dollar loss on the buyers in the ARDEPPS of consummation by depriving them of the buyer surplus the use of the deterred QV investment would have generated and the equivalent-dollar gains its use would have conferred on buyers of other products produced in the ARDEPPS of consummation by causing their prices to be reduced, will impose equivalent-dollar losses on the shareholders/creditors/managers/employees of the suppliers of the inputs that would have been used to create and operate the deterred QV investment, and will confer equivalent-dollar gains on the shareholders/creditors/managers/employees of the firms that were the alternative buyers of those inputs and on the buyers of the products those alternative input-buyers would have produced with them and on the buyers of the products with which those products competed. On the assumptions I have been making, I see no reason to believe that, in this type of situation, the static fixed-cost efficiencies a horizontal (M or A) generates will tend either to increase or to decrease poverty or material inequality across all cases. In this type of situation, the static fixed-cost efficiencies a horizontal (M or A) generates will increase the concentration of the seller-side of the ARDEPPS of consummation when the deterred QV investor is a potential competitor or an established firm that owned a relatively-low percentage of the ARDEPPS' QV investment and will decease seller-concentration when the deterred QV investor owned a relatively-high percentage of the ARDEPPS' QV investment.

I will now proceed to analyze the impact that any static fixed-cost efficiencies a horizontal (M or A) generates will have on economic efficiency in the four types of situations I distinguished. If the static fixed-cost efficiencies a horizontal (M or A) generates do not cause the resulting firm to renew a QV investment that the relevant participant would not have renewed—i.e., if they simply reduce the private fixed cost the resulting firm had to incur to renew or rebuild a production plant or distributive outlet that the relevant participant would have renewed or rebuilt at a higher private fixed cost, the static fixed-cost efficiencies a horizontal (M or A) generates will increase economic efficiency by (the reduction in private fixed costs) *times* (the ratio of the fixed-allocative-cost savings to the fixed-private-cost savings, which I believe will always exceed one and will depend on the proportions of the saved resources that would have been withdrawn from [would be devoted to] the various other categories of use [from which they would be withdrawn]/[to which they would be devoted] and all the factors that determine the percentage-distortions in the private benefits the resources in question [would have generated]/[would generate] in their alternative uses).

If the static fixed-cost efficiencies a horizontal (M or A) generates do cause the resulting firm to renew a QV investment (renew or rebuild a production plant or distributive outlet) that the relevant participant would not have renewed or rebuilt and the withdrawal of the QV investment in question would not have caused anyone else (neither a mutual rival of the participants nor another participant) to introduce any QV investment into the ARDEPPS of consummation, the static private-fixed-cost efficiencies the (M or A) generated would increase economic efficiency by (1) the profits the renewal and use of the investment would yield the resulting firm if it did not affect the profits it made on its other investments *plus* (2) the buyer surplus that the continued use of the renewed QV investment would be deemed to have yielded if one defines buyer surplus to equal the difference between the price a buyer believed he or she could pay for a unit of a product and remain equally-well-off and the cost to the buyer of purchasing that unit of the product in question *minus* (3) what I assume will be the negative distortion in the private cost of renewing and using the relevant QV investment *plus/minus* (4) any negative/positive difference between the net allocative gain generated by the consumption of the units of the good or service supplied by using the renewed/rebuilt production/distribution facility that were sold and their buyers' perceptions of their dollar-value to them (generated by buyer errors and externalities of consumption) *plus* (5) any sales/excise/VAT/consumption taxes collected on the sales of the product produced with the renewed/rebuilt production/distributive facility *plus* (6) any increase in the allocative value of the units of other products in the product-line of the product produced through the use of renewed/rebuilt production/distributive facility that resulted from the relevant product's sale *plus/minus* (7) any increase/decrease in economic efficiency that was generated by the sale of complements of the product/service produced with the renewed/rebuilt production/distributive facility *plus* (8) any increase in economy efficiency that resulted from buyers being better-informed about the quality of the resulting firm's other products as a result of the sale and consummation of the goods/services produced with the renewed/rebuilt production/distributive facility *minus* or *plus* (9) any decrease in economic inefficiency the static fixed-cost efficiencies the horizontal (M or A) generated would cause by increasing/decreasing the extent to which the resulting firm engaged in contrived-oligopolistic pricing and predation (where both practices reduce economic efficiency by generating allocative transaction costs and intra-ARDEPPS UO-to-UO misallocation, contrived-oligopolistic pricing tends to generate economic inefficiency by increasing equilibrium QV investment in the ARDEPPS in which it is practiced, and predation could increase/decrease/have no impact on economic efficiency by affecting equilibrium QV investment in the ARDEPPS in which it is practiced because it can increase/decrease/have no impact on equilibrium QV investment in that ARDEPPS) *plus* (10) the increase in economic efficiency the static private-fixed-cost efficiencies would generate by reducing poverty and probably material inequality primarily as a result of their conferring equivalent-dollar gains on the relevant ARDEPPS' buyers at least in what I take to be the vast majority of cases in which the static fixed-cost efficiencies do not inflict a net equivalent-dollar loss on such buyers all tolled because they lead to additional contrivance and/or predation that reduce the relevant ARDEPPS' equilibrium-QV-investment quantity *plus/minus* (11) any increase/decrease in economic efficiency the efficiencies in question would generate by deconcentrating/concentrating the seller-side of the ARDEPPS in question (depending on whether the resulting firm had a relatively-low or relatively-high share of the ARDEPPS' QV investment and on whether the static fixed-cost efficiencies lead to predation that increases/decreases the concentration of the seller-side of the ARDEPPS of consummation) and thereby decreasing/increasing the expenditures the ARDEPPS' sellers make on political parties/campaigns/candidates and government-decision-making-process participation.

If the static fixed-cost efficiencies a horizontal (M or A) generates do cause the resulting firm to renew or rebuild a participant's production/distributive facility that the relevant participant would not have renewed or rebuilt in circumstances in which, absent the (M or A), neither a mutual rival of the participants nor another participant would have "replaced" the facility the relevant participant would have stopped using absent the (M or A) with an equally-large QV investment of its own, the static private-fixed-cost efficiencies the (M or A) generates would increase economic efficiency by (1) the amount by which the renewing/rebuilding investment was more economically efficient than the QV investment it deterred (see below: the deterred QV investment might be intrinsically more economically efficient or intrinsically less economically efficient than the renewing/rebuilding investments) *plus/minus* (2) the amount by which the substitution of the renewing/rebuilding investment for the deterred QV investment increased/decreased economic efficiency because it decreased/increased poverty and material inequality (see below) *plus/minus* (3) the amount by which the substitution of the renewing/rebuilding investment for the deterred QV investment decreased/increased economic efficiency by increasing/decreasing the (P–MC) gaps in the ARDEPPS of consummation at the quantity of QV investment the ARDEPPS would contain after the participant's facility was renewed (see below) and thereby increasing/decreasing the ARDEPPS' equilibrium-QV-investment quantity *plus/minus* (4) the amount by which the substitution of the renewing/rebuilding investment for the deterred QV investment decreased/increased economic efficiency because it increased/decreased the concentration of the seller-side of the ARDEPPS of consummation (see below) and thereby increased/decreased the ARDEPPS' sellers' expenditures on political parties/campaigns/candidates and government-decision-making-process participation *plus* (5) the amount by which the substitution of the renewing/rebuilding investment for the deterred QV investment decreased/increased economic efficiency by decreasing/increasing the amount of natural-oligopolistic pricing, contrived-oligopolistic pricing, and predatory conduct practiced in the ARDEPPS of consummation.

I will now comment on each of the four pairs of possibilities I indicated would be considered below. The first issue that needs to be addressed is: Will the renewing/rebuilding investment tend to be intrinsically-more or intrinsically-less economically efficient than the QV investment it deters? Throughout this study, I have been making what I take to be the plausible assumptions that (1) investments that are made tend to be more profitable than the investments they deter (or, more generally, that the investments that are made in any ARDEPPS tend to be made in the order of their profitability) and (2) unless one has good reason to doubt this conclusion in a particular context, (put crudely) the relative profitability of two investments in a given ARDEPPS will be strongly positively correlated with their relative economic efficiency. If correct, those assumptions would favor the conclusion that the private-fixed-cost efficiencies a horizontal (M or A) generates will tend to increase economic efficiency to the extent that they cause the resulting firm to renew or rebuild a participant facility whose renewal deters the creation of an equally-large QV investment. In fact, another argument can be made for the conclusion that the renewing/rebuilding investment will tend to be more economically efficient than any QV investment it deters: the renewing/rebuilding investment will take (so to speak) a free ride on the investment the participant made in designing and promoting the product or distributive service produced by the production/distributive facility the relevant resulting-firm investment renews or rebuilds. However, I acknowledge that two counterarguments can be made against the claim that any static fixed-cost-efficiency-induced renewing/rebuilding investment will be more economically efficient than any QV investment it deters. First, (1) when the deterred QV investment would have been made by a new entrant, an investment-renewal might be executed even when it was less profitable and therefore (presumptively) less-economically-efficient than the deterred investment because established firms learn of investment-opportunities before outsiders do and can make less-profitable investments that deter more-profitable entries, and (2) when the deterred QV investment would have been made by a new entrant to the ARDEPPS of consummation (that would have no monopolistic QV-investment incentive to make it) or by an established firm in the ARDEPPS of consummation whose total QV investment in the ARDEPPS of consummation was lower than the resulting firm's total QV investment in that ARDEPPS (that would tend to have had a smaller QV-investment incentive to make its deterred investment than the resulting firm had to renew the participant's QV investment), there is some reason to believe that the substitution of the deterred QV investment for the renewed QV investment would increase economic efficiency (if one ignored any differences in their respective impacts on poverty, material inequality, and ARDEPPS-seller expenditures on political parties/campaigns/candidates and government-decision-making-process participation) because such expenditures yield those that make them private benefits that are substantially inflated (indeed, are inflated by more than 100% in that their generation is associated, if anything, with decreases in economic efficiency).

The second issue that needs to be addressed is: Will the substitution of a renewing/rebuilding investment for a deterred QV investment increase or decrease poverty and material inequality? Once more, the answer to this question depends on the attributes of the deterred investor. Put crudely, if the deterred investor is a potential competitor or an established firm that owns less QV investment in the ARDEPPS of consummation than the resulting firm would own if it did not renew or rebuild the participant's facility, the substitution will tend to increase poverty and material inequality because, in these circumstances, the use of the renewed QV investment will tend to cause prices to drop less than the use of the deterred QV investment would have done; if the deterred investor owns more QV investment in the ARDEPPS of consummation than the resulting firm would own if it did not renew or rebuild the participant's facility, the substitution will decrease poverty and material inequality because the use of the renewed participant-QV-investment will tend to cause prices to drop more than the use of the deterred QV investment would have done.

The analysis of the third issue that needs to be addressed—Will the substitution of the renewing/rebuilding investment for the deterred QV investment increase the amount by which the static private-fixed-cost efficiencies a horizontal (M or A) generates affect economic efficiency by affecting equilibrium QV investment in the ARDEPPS of consummation?—is identical to the analysis of the second since the impact on equilibrium QV investment depends on the impact on the (P–MC)s for the ARDEPPS' products at the immediate-post-renewal ARDEPPS-QV-investment quantity.

The analysis of the fourth issue that needs to be addressed—Will the substitution of the renewing/rebuilding investment for the deterred QV investment increase or decrease the concentration of the seller-side of the ARDEPPS of consummation?—is identical to its two predecessors since the answer to this question depends on the same attributes of the resulting firm and deterred investor that determine the effect of the substitution on the relevant (P–MC) figures.

All generalizations are false (unless one takes account of the fact that they are generalizations). The combination of the preceding analyses and my estimates or guesstimates of the magnitudes of the parameters whose salience they establish leads me to the following three conclusions:

(1) horizontal-(M or A)-generated static fixed-cost efficiencies that reduce the private fixed costs a resulting firm must incur to renew or rebuild a production facility or distributive outlet a relevant participant would have renewed or rebuilt as an independent entity will always or virtually always increase economic efficiency by considerably more than they reduce the static fixed costs the resulting firm had to incur to renew or rebuild the participant's relevant facility below the private fixed costs the relevant participant would have had to incur to do so;

(2) in cases in which (A) the static fixed-cost efficiencies a horizontal (M or A) generates induce the resulting firm to renew or rebuild a participant's production plant or distributive outlet, (B) the participant would not have renewed or rebuilt the facility in question as an independent entity, and (C) the resulting firm's induced investment does not deter any rival QV investment, I do not know whether the static fixed-cost efficiencies the horizontal (M or A) generates will tend to increase or decrease economic efficiency when the government of the society in question has not adopted policies to prevent its continuing to devote too many resources to QV-investment creation from the perspective of economic efficiency (the outcome will depend on whether the profits the induced investment yields the investor are higher than the positive distortion in those profits), though I suspect that such static fixed-cost efficiencies will tend to increase economic efficiency if the relevant society's government has adopted policies that eliminate the positive distortion in the profits yielded by QV-investment creation and use;

(3) I do not know whether horizontal-(M or A)-generated static fixed-cost efficiencies will tend to increase or decrease economic efficiency in situations in which the efficiencies (A) induce the resulting firm to renew or rebuild a participant production plant or distributive outlet that the participant would not have renewed or rebuilt and (B) the resulting firm's induced investment deters a rival from making an equally-large investment; and
(4) in situations in which the static fixed-cost efficiencies a horizontal (M or A) generates reduce the equilibrium quantity of QV investment in the ARDEPPS of consummation by substituting for a situation in which a resulting-firm rival or a participant would have made a QV investment a situation in which the resulting firm and its relevant rival are deterred from making a QV investment by the natural-oligopolistic QV-investment disincentives with which they confront each other, the static fixed-cost efficiencies the horizontal (M or A) generates will tend to increase economic efficiency if (as I suspect will be the case) the government of the society in question has not adopted policies to prevent its continuing to devote too many resources to QV-investment creation-and-use from the perspective of economic efficiency (at least if as I suspect the profits the deterred investment would have yielded the investor absent the [M or A] would have been lower than the positive distortion in those profits).

11.2.2.3 The Relevance of Any Static Fixed-Cost Efficiencies a Horizontal (M or A) Generates to Its Violating Liberal Moral Rights

A horizontal (M or A) is liberal-moral-rights-violative if (1) at least one participant's *ex ante* perception that it was at least normally profitable was critically affected by a belief that it would or might increase the profits the resulting firm would realize by engaging in liberal-moral-rights-violative conduct above the profits the participants would have earned by doing so and/or (2) at least one participant believed that the (M or A) would create a resulting firm that could realize more profits by engaging in liberal-moral-rights-violative conduct than the participants could have done and intended the resulting firm to take advantage of this opportunity.[4] Section 11.2.2.1 discussion of the various ways in which the static fixed-cost efficiencies a horizontal (M or A) generates will or may increase its participants' profits warrants the following two conclusions:

(1) the fact that the static fixed-cost efficiencies a horizontal (M or A) generates will yield its participants profits in ways that are not liberal-moral-rights-violative implies that any such efficiencies a horizontal (M or A) generates will favor the conclusion that the (M or A) is not liberal-moral-rights-violative though it does not guarantee that the relevant (M or A) is not liberal-moral-rights-violative (A) because the liberal-moral-rights-non-violative profits the (M or A) should have been predicted to generate *ex ante* might not have rendered it *ex ante* at least normally profitable on their account, (B) because even if the participants should have realized *ex ante* that their horizontal (M or A)

was rendered at least normally profitable by the profits it should have been predicted to yield in liberal-moral-rights-non-violative ways, they might not have done so—that is, their decision to consummate the (M or A) might have been critically affected by their belief that it would yield them profits in some liberal-moral-rights-violative ways, and (C) because, even if a horizontal (M or A)'s participants believed *ex ante* that it was rendered *ex ante* at least normally profitable by profits it would yield them in liberal-moral-rights-non-violative ways, the (M or A) would be liberal-moral-rights-violative if one or more participants believed that it would increase the profits it or they could realize by engaging in liberal-moral-rights-violative conduct and intended the resulting firm to "take advantage" of the enhanced opportunity with which the (M or A) would provide them to profit from engaging in liberal-moral-rights-violative conduct, and

(2) the fact that the static fixed-cost efficiencies a horizontal (M or A) generates can yield its participants profits by creating a resulting firm that can profit more by engaging in liberal-moral-rights-violative conduct than the participants could have done creates the possibility that individual horizontal (M&A)s may be liberal-moral-rights-violative but does not imply that horizontal (M or A)s that create one or more such possibilities are liberal-moral-rights-violative (A)(i) because the relevant (M or A)s may have been rendered *ex ante* at least normally profitable by the profits they should have been predicted to generate in ways that do not involve the resulting firm's engaging in liberal-moral-rights-violative conduct and (ii) because, even if the condition articulated after "(A)(i)" was not satisfied, all the participants may have believed *ex ante* that it was satisfied and (B) because no participant in the (M or A) in question may have intended *ex ante* the resulting firm to take advantage of any tendency that the static fixed-cost efficiencies the relevant (M or A) would generate might have to increase the profits it could realize by engaging in liberal-moral-rights-violative conduct regardless of whether any participant realized that such efficiencies would have this effect. (The preceding analysis ignores the possibility that conduct that is motivated by specific anticompetitive intent may not be liberal-moral-rights-violative if its perpetrator believes *ex ante* that the economy's extant Pareto imperfections render the conduct *ex ante* economically efficient. Such conduct may not be liberal-moral-rights-violative because in the situation in question the perpetrator's decision to engage in the conduct in question will not manifest the perpetrator's placing a lower value on the average equivalent-dollar it causes others to lose than on the average equivalent-dollar it causes the perpetrator to gain. Indeed, in some instances, economically-efficient choices that are motivated by specific anticompetitive intent may not impose a net equivalent-dollar loss on nonchoosers. I have ignored and continue to ignore this possibility not because I doubt that choices that are motivated by specific anticompetitive intent will ever be economically efficient (think of exemplars of such choices that are critically motivated by the perpetrators' desire to free themselves from each other's QV-investment competition and that, relatedly, will increase economic

efficiency by reducing equilibrium QV investment in the economy in which they are made) but because I suspect that few if any perpetrators of choices that are motivated by specific anticompetitive intent will be aware *ex ante* of their economic efficiency and because I believe that what might be called unsuccessful attempts to make liberal-moral-rights-violative choices (decisions that the chooser [incorrectly] believes will impose net equivalent-dollar losses on others that exceed the equivalent-dollar gains they will confer on the chooser) are liberal-moral-rights-violative.

11.2.2.4 The Relevance of Any Static Fixed-Cost Efficiencies a Horizontal (M or A) Generates to Its Serving or Disserving the Instantiation of the Utilitarian and Various Non-Utilitarian-Egalitarian Conceptions of the Moral Good

The impacts that any static fixed-cost efficiencies a horizontal (M or A) generates have on economic efficiency and material inequality vary with whether the efficiencies (1) simply reduce the private cost the resulting firm must incur to renew or rebuild a production or distributive facility a relevant participant would have renewed or rebuilt as a separate entity without deterring a rival from making a QV investment in the ARDEPPS of consummation, (2) cause the resulting firm to renew or rebuild a facility the relevant participant would not have renewed or rebuilt when the resulting firm's doing so does not deter a rival from making a QV investment in the ARDEPPS of consummation, (3) cause the resulting firm to renew or rebuild a participant's facility when the participant would not have done so when the resulting firm's action does deter a rival from making an (equally-large) QV investment in the ARDEPPS of consummation, or (4) reduce equilibrium QV investment in the ARDEPPS of consummation by substituting a situation in which the resulting firm and a rival confront each other with critical, natural-oligopolistic QV-investment disincentives for a situation in which a rival would otherwise have made a QV investment in the ARDEPPS of consummation. For this reason, this section's analyses focus separately on each of these 4 situations.

Section 11.2.2 concluded that, when the static fixed-cost efficiencies a horizontal (M or A) generates simply reduce the private (and allocative) cost the resulting firm must incur (generate) to renew a production or distributive facility a participant would have renewed/rebuilt had it remained an independent entity, the efficiencies in question will increase economic efficiency and tend to increase material inequality. I suspect that the increase in economic efficiency that the efficiencies in question will generate in this class of cases will be sufficiently large relative to the increase in material inequality they will generate in such situations for the efficiencies to increase total utility in virtually all cases in this category. However, if I am right that in this class of cases any static fixed-cost efficiencies a horizontal (M or A) generates will tend to increase material inequality (by imposing equivalent-dollar losses on the prospective suppliers of the inputs whose use the static fixed-cost efficiencies obviates), those efficiencies will tend to cause the horizontal (M&A)s that generate them to disserve the instantiation of all non-utilitarian-egalitarian conceptions of the moral good.

Section 11.2.2 concluded that, when the static fixed-cost efficiencies a horizontal (M or A) generates cause the resulting firm to renew or rebuild a participant's production or distributive facility that the participant would not have renewed or rebuilt in circumstances in which the resulting firm's conduct does not deter a rival from making a QV investment in the ARDEPPS of consummation, the efficiencies (1) will sometimes increase and sometimes decrease economic efficiency in societies (unfortunately, in virtually all actual societies) whose governments have not prevented them from continuing to devote too many resources to QV-investment creation from the perspective of economic efficiency, (2) will tend neither to increase nor decrease economic efficiency across all such cases, and (3) will have no tendency to either increase or decrease material inequality. If these conclusions are correct, across all cases in this category, the static fixed-cost efficiencies that horizontal (M&A)s generate will neither serve nor disserve the instantiation of either the utilitarian or any non-utilitarian-egalitarian conception of the moral good. Of course, this conclusion is compatible with (1) such efficiencies' either serving or disserving the instantiation of these various conceptions of the moral good in individual cases in this category and (2) one or more of these conceptions of the moral good's being served by government efforts to investigate these issues on a case-to-case basis within this category of cases (although I doubt that any such government efforts will prove to be morally good from any utilitarian, non-utilitarian-egalitarian, or mixed egalitarian normative perspective).

Section 11.2.2 concluded that, when the static fixed-cost efficiencies a horizontal (M or A) generates cause the resulting firm to renew or rebuild a participant's production or distributive facility that the participant would not have renewed or rebuilt and in so doing deterred an equally-large QV investment of a rival, those efficiencies (1) will tend to decrease economic efficiency if the deterred rival is a potential entrant or an established firm whose QV investment in the ARDEPPS of consummation is lower than the QV investment the resulting firm would own in that ARDEPPS if it did not renew or rebuild the participant's relevant facility, (2) will tend to increase economic efficiency if the deterred rival is an established firm whose QV investment in the ARDEPPS of consummation is higher than the QV investment the resulting firm would own in the ARDEPPS of consummation if it did not renew the participant's relevant facility, (3) seem unlikely to either increase or decrease economic efficiency across all cases in this category, (4) will tend to increase material inequality when the deterred investor is a potential entrant or an established firm that owns less QV investment in the ARDEPPS of consummation than the resulting firm would own if it did not renew or rebuild the participant's relevant facility, (5) will tend to decrease material inequality when the deterred investor is an established firm that owns more QV investment in the ARDEPPS of consummation than the resulting firm would own if it did not renew or rebuild the participant's relevant facility, and (6) seem unlikely to either increase or decrease material inequality across all cases in this category. If these conclusions are correct, (1) across all cases in this category, the static fixed-cost efficiencies a horizontal

(M or A) generates will tend neither to serve nor to disserve the instantiation of either the utilitarian or the non-utilitarian-egalitarian conceptions of the moral good, (2) will tend to disserve the instantiation of both the utilitarian conception of the moral good and all non-utilitarian-egalitarian conceptions of the moral good when the deterred QV investor is a potential entrant or owns less QV investment in the ARDEPPS of consummation than the resulting firm would own if it did not renew or rebuild the participant's relevant facility, and (3) will tend to serve the instantiations of both the utilitarian and the various non-utilitarian-egalitarian conceptions of the moral good when the deterred QV investor is an established firm that owns more QV investment in the ARDEPPS of consummation than the resulting firm would own if it did not renew or rebuild the participant's relevant facility.

Section 11.2.2 concluded that, in those cases in which the static marginal-cost efficiencies a horizontal (M or A) generates would reduce equilibrium QV investment in the ARDEPPS of consummation (an effect I agree will be evanescent), (1) those efficiencies will increase economic efficiency if one makes the realistic assumption that the government of the society in question has not prevented it from continuing to devote too many resources to QV-investment creation from the perspective of economic efficiency and (2) will have no effect on material inequality. If these conclusions are correct, in this category of situation, the static fixed-cost efficiencies that horizontal (M&A)s generate will serve the instantiation of the utilitarian conception of the moral good and will have no impact on the instantiation of non-utilitarian-egalitarian conceptions of the moral good.

I have not ventured any opinion about whether, across all cases, the static fixed-cost efficiencies that horizontal (M&A)s generate will serve or disserve the instantiation of the utilitarian and/or the several non-utilitarian-egalitarian conceptions of the moral good. I have not done so because I am not prepared even to guesstimate (1) the percentages of cases that fall into the four categories I have distinguished, (2) the percentages of cases that fall into the various subcategories I have identified of the four categories of cases in question, or (3) the relative magnitudes of the economic-efficiency and material-inequality impacts whose signs I have predicted. I am not averse to basing conclusions on crude estimates or guesstimates. But I hope I know when the best course of action is to keep silent.

11.2.3 Analyses That Relate to Any Dynamic Efficiencies That a Horizontal (M or A) Generates

In my terminology, a horizontal (M or A) is said to generate dynamic efficiencies if and to the extent that the resulting firm faces lower ($\Pi_D + R$) barriers to making a new QV investment or executing a PPR project in the ARDEPPS of consummation than the participants would have faced. The impacts that any dynamic efficiencies a horizontal (M or A) generates has on the participants' profits, on economic efficiency, on the relevant (M or A)'s liberal-moral-rights-violativeness, and on the instantiation of the utilitarian conceptions of the moral good depend *inter alia* on whether those efficiencies (1) result in the resulting firm's substituting a more *ex ante* supernormally profitable QV investment or PPR project for the *ex ante* normally profitable or *ex ante* less supernormally profitable QV investment or PPR project a participant would have executed, (2) result in the resulting firm's creating a QV investment or executing a PPR project in the ARDEPPS of consummation when no participant and no mutual rival of the participants would have done so, (3) result in the resulting firm's creating a QV investment or executing a PPR project in the ARDEPPS of consummation that deters a rival from making an equally-large investment of the relevant type in that ARDEPPS, or (4) substitute for a situation in which a mutual rival of the participants would have created a QV investment or executed a PPR project in the ARDEPPS of consummation a situation in which neither that rival of the participants not the resulting firm makes an investment in that ARDEPPS because the efficiencies create a situation in which the relevant mutual rival of the participants and the resulting firm confront each other with critical natural-oligopolistic investment-disincentives when the participants and their relevant mutual rival would not have confronted each other with such disincentives. In this important respect, Sect. 11.3 analyses of the impacts of any dynamic efficiencies a horizontal (M or A) generates on the participants' profits, on economic efficiency, on liberal moral rights, and on the instantiation of various conceptions of the moral good will resemble Sect. 11.2 analyses of these impacts of any static fixed-cost efficiencies a horizontal (M or A) generates.

However, the analyses of Sect. 11.3 will differ from those of Sect. 11.2 for two reasons (one of which I will ignore). The first difference relates to the fact (manifest in the text of the preceding paragraph) that the dynamic efficiencies that a horizontal (M or A) generates can relate to the investments in PPR that the participants may want to make as well as to the QV investments the firms may want to make. This difference is salient not only because it affects the frequency with which horizontal (M&A)s generate dynamic efficiencies but also because—if one makes the realistic assumption that the government of any relevant society will not have prevented it from continuing to devote too many resources to QV-investment creation and not enough to PPR execution from the perspective of economic efficiency—the fact that the dynamic efficiencies a horizontal (M or A) generates will increase/decrease equilibrium PPR in the ARDEPPS of consummation will make the (M or A) more/less economically efficient whereas (as Sect. 11.2 indicated) the fact that the dynamic efficiencies a horizontal (M or A) generates will increase equilibrium QV investment in the ARDEPPS of consummation could either make it more or less economically efficient and the fact that the dynamic efficiencies a horizontal (M or A) generates will decrease equilibrium QV investment in the ARDEPPS of consummation will make it more economically efficient.

The second reason why it might be appropriate for this section's analyses to differ from their Sect. 11.2 counterparts is that, in generating dynamic efficiencies, a horizontal (M or A) might alter the QV investment that is created or the PPR project that is executed in a way that causes the demand curve for the "created" product or discovered production processes to diverge from the demand curve for the product or production process whose creation was deterred and/or the marginal-cost curve for producing the created product or for using the discovered production process to diverge from its counterpart for producing the product whose creation was deterred or for using the production process whose discovery was deterred. This possibility is relevant to the economic-efficiency impact of the dynamic efficiencies a horizontal (M or A) generates not only because such demand and marginal-cost curve alterations may result in the use of the created QV investment's or production-process discovery's generating a different amount of profit-deflating buyer surplus than would have been generated by the use of the deterred QV investment or prevented production-process discovery but also because the variable cost of producing a created product or using a discovered production process is (in my judgment) virtually always deflated so that the profits that the dynamic efficiencies a horizontal (M or A) generates for its participants when they cause one QV investment to be substituted for another or one PPR project to be substituted for another will tend to be inflated to the extent that the total variable cost of using the made investment is higher than the total variable cost of using the deterred investment and will tend to be deflated to the extent that the variable cost of using the made investment is lower than the total variable cost of using the deterred investment. This possibility is also relevant to the analysis of the impact that the dynamic efficiencies a horizontal (M or A) generates will have on poverty and material inequality (and on that account on economic efficiency and the instantiation of the utilitarian and non-utilitarian-egalitarian conceptions of the moral good) in cases in which those dynamic efficiencies alter the QV investment that is created or the PPR project that is executed and in so doing the demand and marginal-cost curves for the (changing) product that is produced or for the use of the (changing) production-process discovery that is made. The text that follows ignores this second possible difference between dynamic efficiencies and static fixed-cost efficiencies not only to save space and avoid testing reader patience but also because I doubt that it will ever be TBLE, *ex ante* liberal-moral-rights-securing, or *ex ante* moral-good securing for a government to try to identify situations in which the dynamic efficiencies a horizontal (M or A) will generate increases or decreases in the total variable cost of using the (changing) QV investment or production-process discovery that is made or increases or decreases in the buyer surplus that is yielded by the use of the changing QV investment that is made or the changing production process that is discovered.

If it is appropriate to ignore the possibility that in individual instances the dynamic efficiencies a horizontal (M or A) generates will not only change the QV investment that is created or the PPR project that is executed but in so doing will also substitute for one QV investment or production-process discovery whose use is associated with a given pair of demand and marginal-cost curves another QV investment or production-process discovery whose use is associated with a different pair of demand and/or marginal-cost curves, the only differences between Sect. 11.3 dynamic-efficiency-impact analyses and Sect. 11.2 static fixed-cost-efficiency-impact analyses are that (1) dynamic efficiencies may relate to the resulting firm's PPR investments as well as to its QV investments and (2) in the actual economies that continue to devote too may resources to QV-investment creation and not enough to PPR execution from the perspective of economic efficiency, the fact that the dynamic efficiencies a horizontal (M or A) generates will increase/decrease equilibrium PPR in the ARDEPPS of consummation will render the (M or A) in question more/less economically efficient whereas the fact that the dynamic efficiencies a horizontal (M or A) generates will increase equilibrium QV investment in the ARDEPPS of consummation can be associated with the (M or A)'s being either more or less economically efficient than it otherwise would have been whereas the fact that the dynamic efficiencies a horizontal (M or A) generates will decrease equilibrium QV investment in the ARDEPPS of consummation will render the (M or A) more economically efficient than it otherwise would have been.

11.2.4 Analyses That Relate to a Horizontal (M or A)'s Increasing Its Participants' Profits by Substituting for a Situation in Which No Participant Could Profit by Making a QV or PPR Investment Even Though at Least Two of Them Would Have Found Such an Investment Profitable If It Would Not Have Induced Another Participant to Make an Investment a Situation in Which the Resulting Firm Can Make One Such Investment Without Inducing Anyone to Make Another

11.2.4.1 The Determinants of the Profits That a Horizontal (M or A) Can Yield Its Participants by "Substituting" a Resulting Firm That Does Not Face (Critical) Natural-Oligopolistic Investment-Disincentives for Participants That Did Confront Each Other With Critical Natural-Oligopolistic Investment-Disincentives

The determinants of the profits that a horizontal (M or A) will yield its participants in this way are (1) the determinants of the supernormal profits that the investment the resulting firm will make that no participant would have made would be calculated to yield if one ignored the impact that the investment in question would have on the profits yielded by the resulting firm's other projects and (2) the determinants of the impact that the relevant resulting-firm investment would have on the profit-yields of the resulting firm's other investments (of both the negative impacts the investment in question would have on the resulting firm's other projects by competing against them directly and inducing the resulting firm's rivals to respond [say, by lowering their prices] in ways that reduced the resulting firm's other projects' profit-yields] and the positive impacts the investment in question would have on the resulting firm's other projects by filling out its product-line, by improving those other investments' potential patrons' perceptions of the resulting firm's other products, by generating joint-cost efficiencies, and by increasing the amount of profits the resulting firm realizes relative to the total amount the participants would have realized by engaging in contrived-oligopolistic and predatory conduct).

11.2.4.2 The Determinants of the Impact That Any Horizontal (M or A) That Yields Its Participants Profits in This Way Will Have on Economic Efficiency on This Account

Here is a partial list of the determinants of the impact on which this section is focusing:

(1) the determinants of the profits the resulting firm will realize on the investment the (M or A) results in its making for this reason,
(2) if the investment in question is a QV investment and the government of the relevant society has not eliminated the positive distortion in the profits yielded by creating and using a new QV investment, the determinants of that positive distortion—(A) the percentages of the resources devoted to creating and using the QV investment in question that are withdrawn from UO-producing-and-consuming, QV-investment-creating-and-using, and PPR-executing-and-using uses and (B) the magnitudes of the Pareto imperfections that would in an oPp world individually distort the private benefits that the resources in question would yield the UO producers, QV investors, and production-process researchers from which the resources would be withdrawn,
(3) if the investment in question is an investment in PPR and the government of the relevant society has not eliminated the negative distortion in the profits yielded by the execution of PPR projects and the use of the discoveries they yield, the PPR counterparts of the determinants referenced in Items (2)(A) and (2)(B) in this list,
(4) (A) the determinants of whether and the extent to which the induced investment causes the resulting firm to engage in more contrived-oligopolistic and predatory conduct than it otherwise would have practiced and (B) the determinants of the impact on economic efficiency of any additional contrived-oligopolistic and/or predatory conduct in which the induced investment causes the resulting firm to engage,
(5) (A) the determinants of the impact of the induced investment on the concentration of the seller-side of the ARDEPPS of consummation (e.g., the share

of the ARDEPPS' investment the resulting firm would have owned had it not made the investment in question), (B) the determinants of the impact that any related change in seller-concentration would have on the expenditures that all sellers in the ARDEPPS of consummation make on political parties/campaigns/candidates and government-decision-making-process participation, and (C) the determinants of the impact that any related change in seller-expenditures of these kinds would have on the economic efficiency of government decisions, and

(6) (A) the determinants of the impact that the induced investment would have on poverty and material inequality and (B) the determinants of the impacts that any related changes in poverty and/or material inequality would have on the various categories of economic inefficiency whose magnitudes poverty and material inequality can affect.

11.2.4.3 The Relevance of a Horizontal (M or A)'s Yielding Its Participants Profits in This Way to the (M or A)'s Liberal-Moral-Rights-Violativeness

If, contrary to my view, natural-oligopolistic-disincentive-induced decisions not to make particular choices that would benefit others violate the prospective beneficiaries' liberal moral rights, the fact that a horizontal (M or A) creates a resulting firm that makes an investment that no participant would have made because the participants would have caused each other to face natural-oligopolistic investment-disincentives, (that is, the fact that an [M or A] yields its participants profits in this way) would tend to make it liberal-moral-rights-securing. More generally, the fact that a horizontal (M or A) yields its participants profits in this way will make it liberal-moral-rights-violative only if (1) at least one participant's *ex ante* perception that the (M or A) would be at least normally profitable was critically affected by its perception that the resulting firm it would create would or might realize more profits by engaging in liberal-moral-rights-violative conduct than the participants would have realized in this way because the investment the (M or A) would cause the resulting firm to make for the reason on which I am now focusing would increase its ability to profit from such conduct and/or (2) at least one participant (A) believed that the (M or A) would or might for the reason on which I am now focusing create a resulting firm that could realize more profits than the participants would have been able to realize by engaging in liberal-moral-rights-violative conduct and (B) intended the resulting firm to take advantage of this opportunity.

11.2.4.4 The Relevance of an (M or A)'s Yielding Its Participants Profits in This Way to the (M or A)'s Serving or Disserving the Instantiation of the Utilitarian and Various Other Egalitarian Conceptions of the Moral Good

This section will proceed on the following two assumptions:

(1) when a horizontal (M or A) induces the resulting firm to make an investment that increases equilibrium investment in the ARDEPPS of consummation by creating a resulting firm that does not face critical natural-oligopolistic investment-disincentives in a situation in which the participants would have faced such disincentives, the (M or A) will on this account tend to increase economic efficiency when the induced investment is an investment in PPR but will on this account tend to decrease economic efficiency when the induced investment is a QV investment, and
(2) because any such induced investment will confer equivalent-dollar gains on the customers of the resulting firm and the customers of the resulting firm's rivals and because, taken as a class, such buyers will tend to be less-well-off than the shareholders/creditors/managers/employees of the resulting firm and its product rivals, the distributive impact that a horizontal (M or A) will generate when it results in the resulting firm's increasing equilibrium investment in the ARDEPPS of consummation for the reason on which this section is concentrating (or for any other reason) will be desirable both from the utilitarian perspective and from the perspective of all non-utilitarian-egalitarian conceptions of the moral good.

If correct, these assumptions would warrant the following three conclusions:

(1) it is unclear whether the fact that a horizontal (M or A) yields its participants profits for the natural-oligopolistic-investment-disincentive-related reason on which this section is focusing tends to favor or disfavor the conclusion that the (M or A) in question will increase total utility when the induced investment is a QV investment;
(2) the fact that a horizontal (M or A) yields its participants profits for the natural-oligopolistic-investment-disincentive-related reason on which this section is focusing will clearly favor the conclusion that it will increase total utility when the induced investment is an investment in PPR; and
(3) the fact that a horizontal (M or A) yields its participants profits for the natural-oligopolistic-investment-disincentive-related reason on which this section is focusing will clearly favor the conclusion that the (M or A) in question will serve the instantiation of all non-utilitarian-egalitarian conceptions of the moral good, regardless of whether the induced investment is a QV investment or an investment in PPR.

11.2.5 Analyses That Relate to a Horizontal (M or A)'s Increasing Its Participants' Profits by Creating a Resulting Firm Whose Selection of the Investments It Will Make Is Influenced by the Alternative Investments' Impacts on the Profits Yielded by the Other Projects of All Participants

11.2.5.1 The Determinants of the Profits a Horizontal (M or A) Would Yield Its Participants Even If It Did Not Generate Any Static Fixed-Cost Efficiencies or Dynamic Efficiencies Because the Resulting Firm's Investment-Selections Will Reflect the Impact Each Alternative Would Have on the Profits Yielded by the Other Investments of All Participants

The amount of profits a horizontal (M or A) yields its participants in this way depends on (1) the number of investments the resulting firm finds profitable to make and (2) the average equivalent-dollar gain the resulting firm secures by substituting for an investment that a participant would have found most profitable an alternative investment that is more profitable for the resulting firm because its use lowers the profit-yields of other participants' investments by a smaller number of dollars than the number of dollars by which the investment of the former participant would have lowered the profits yielded by the investments of the other participant(s).

11.2.5.2 The Determinants of the Impact That a Horizontal (M or A) Will Have on Economic Efficiency by Virtue of Its Yielding Its Participants Profits in This Way

Across all cases, I do not think that the fact that a horizontal (M or A) yields its participants profits in this way will tend either to increase or to decrease its economic efficiency. The investments that, for this reason, the resulting firm substitutes for the investments the participants would have made will be less competitive with the participants' other investments than the prospective-participants-investments the resulting firm "rejects" would have been, but the investments the resulting firm makes for this reason will be more competitive with the investments of its rivals than the rejected prospective investments of its participants would have been with the investments of their mutual rivals (the resulting firm's rivals). I see no reason to believe that the specific-investment "swap" a horizontal (M or A) effectuates on this account will either increase or decrease economic efficiency.

11.2.5.3 The Relevance of a Horizontal (M or A)'s Yielding Its Participants Profits in This Way for Its Liberal-Moral-Rights-Violativeness

Because economic efficiency will not tend to be increased by decisions made by firms created by a horizontal (M or A) to increase its participants' profits by "substituting" a new investment that was less competitive with the resulting firm's other investments for an investment by one of the participants that would have been more competitive with the other participant's and its own other investments, the profits that a horizontal (M or A) yields in this way are Sherman-Act-illicit–would render the (M or A) profitable even though it would be economically inefficient in an oPp economy. If the participants' in a horizontal (M or A) *ex ante* perception that the (M or A) was at least normally profitable was critically positively affected by their belief that it would yield them profits in this way and they knew or should have realized that these profits were inflated, those facts would render the (M or A) liberal-moral-rights-violative. Because liberalism disfavors the imposition of positive duties on individuals to benefit others (in that the imposition of such duties undermines the obligor's perception that he is the author of his own life and thereby his disposition to take his life morally seriously), the preceding conclusion does not imply that existing firms have a liberal moral obligation to make an investment that confers a higher equivalent-dollar gain on others but is less profitable because it is more competitive with the investor's other investments rather than an investment that confers lower equivalent-dollar gains on others but is more profitable because it is less competitive with the investor's other investments.

11.2.5.4 The Relevance of a Horizontal (M or A)'s Yielding Its Participants Profits in This Way to Its Serving or Disserving the Instantiation of the Utilitarian and Various Other Egalitarian Conceptions of the Moral Good

A horizontal (M or A)'s yielding its participants profits in this way will be associated with its conferring equivalent-dollar gains on its participants' shareholders/creditors/managers/employees, imposing equivalent-dollar losses on actual and some possible buyers of its participants' products, imposing equivalent-dollar losses on the shareholders/creditors/managers/employees of the participants' product-rivals, and conferring equivalent-dollar gains on the buyers of the products of the participants' product-rivals. I see no reason to believe that a horizontal (M or A)'s yielding its participants profits in this way will tend to either increase or decrease poverty or material inequality. This conclusion implies that a horizontal (M or A)'s yielding its participants profits in this way will have no tendency either to favor or to disfavor its serving (disserving) the instantiation of any non-pure-utilitarian-egalitarian conception of the moral good. If I am correct in concluding that, across all exemplars, a horizontal (M or A)'s yielding its participants profits in this way will tend neither to favor nor to disfavor (1) its increasing (or decreasing) economic efficiency or (2) its increasing (or decreasing) material inequality, the fact that a horizontal (M or A) yields its participants profits in this way will have no bearing on whether it increases or decreases total utility.

11.2.6 Analyses That Relate to a Horizontal (M or A)'s Increasing Its Participants' Profits or Equivalent-Dollar Gains by Enabling the Owner or Owner/Manager of One Participant to Liquidate His or Her Assets and Retire from Management

Of course, horizontal (M&A)s that enable one of their participants to realize profits or equivalent-dollar gains in the above way can also yield their participants profits in other ways. Like all its counterparts, this section will ignore all the other ways in which horizontal (M&A)s that yield these types of gain benefit their participants. Because it will not take much space to consider in the current context the four issues on which Sect. 11.2 is focusing, I will not subdivide Sect. 11.2.6.

The equivalent-dollar gain a horizontal (M or A) would yield a participants by enabling him or her to liquidate his or her assets and to retire from management depends only on the equivalent-dollar value the relevant participant places on liquidating his or her assets and retiring from management. Any profits that a horizontal (M or A) that performs the functions on which this section is focusing generates because a competitor of the erstwhile seller/retiree can make more profits by using his or her company than a non-competitor could for either Sherman-Act-licit reasons (e.g., because a competitor could operate the retiree's company more-allocative-efficiently than any non-competitor could) or (for that matter) for one or more Sherman-Act-illicit reasons will be considered separately in sections that focus on the profits the relevant horizontal (M or A) yields its participants in those ways. Because the private equivalent-dollar gains a horizontal (M or A) yields a participant by enabling the participant to liquidate his or her assets and retire from management will be allocative as well as private, the determinants of the associated private gain will also be the determinants of the associated economic-efficiency gain. Because a horizontal (M or A)'s yielding its participants profits for this reason violates no liberal moral right, the fact that a horizontal (M or A) yields a participant equivalent-dollar gains for this reason favors the conclusion that the (M or A) is not liberal-moral-rights-violative. Indeed, horizontal (M or A)s that perform this function might well be said to secure the liberal-moral-rights-related interest of the seller in liquidating his or her property interests and escaping the burdens of management. Because the fact that a horizontal (M or A) yields its participants equivalent-dollar gains for this reason and does not cause the (M or A) to affect anyone else (if one ignores possible external-preference-generated effects), horizontal (M&A)s that yield their participants profits in this way will tend on this account to make them increase total utility. However, if as I suspect the seller/retiree in question and the shareholders/creditors/managers/employees of the "acquiring" firm are on the weighted average better-off than the average member of the society in question, the fact that a horizontal (M or A) yields its participants profits for this reason favors the conclusion that (in the absence of any other source of material inequality) the (M or A) would disserve the instantiation of all non-pure-utilitarian egalitarian conceptions of the moral good.

11.2.7 Analyses That Relate to the Equivalent-Dollar Gains a Horizontal (M or A) Yields Its Participants by Creating a Resulting Firm That Can Take Advantage of a Tax-Loss Incurred by a Participant That Could Not Use It as a Separate Entity

For the same reason that I did not subdivide Sect. 11.2.5, I will not subdivide this section. The tax-related profits that a horizontal (M or A) yields its participants increase with the tax-losses that a participant cannot use itself (because it will not realize taxable profits in the years in which it is allowed to carry forward the tax-losses it incurred in previous years that are as large as the tax-losses it incurred in the relevant previous years), the extent to which the taxable income the other participant has earned or the resulting firm will earn covers the relevant tax-losses the participant in question incurred, and the effective tax-rate that would have been applied to the resulting firm's offsetable taxable income. The fact that a horizontal (M or A) enables its participants to realize profits for this tax-related reason (1) will decrease economic efficiency by the allocative transaction costs the resulting firm generates when taking advantage of a participant's tax-losses and the allocative transaction costs the government generates when assessing the resulting firm's associated tax-claim, (2) will decrease/increase economic efficiency by the amount by which the government's responses to the loss of the tax-revenue in question decrease/increase economic efficiency, (3) will decrease/increase economic inefficiency to the extent that the resulting firm's taking advantage of a participant's tax-loss increases/decreases poverty and material inequality and derivatively the amount of inefficiency that is generated in the society in question because some of its members are poor and its income/wealth distribution is unequal, (4) could either increase or decrease economic efficiency by eliminating the negative step-wise-tax distortion our tax laws generate in small firms' making investments that might yield them losses (see below), and (5) will probably tend to increase economic efficiency by encouraging the creation of start-up companies whose investments could yield losses (by eliminating the step-wise-tax distortion in the profitability of their creation [see below]).

As indicated, the last two points in the preceding list require both explication and elaboration. I will begin by making three economic-efficiency-related points. To start, the fact that our tax laws impose positive taxes on the profits generated by firm-investments that turn out to be profitable but do not require the government to transfer money to firm-investors whose investments turn out to yield losses that the firm investors cannot set off against the profits their other investments yielded because the firm in question does not own investments that yield (sufficient) profits for this purpose (that our tax laws do not promulgate negative tax-rates to be applied to such investors' losses) can affect economic efficiency in two ways. First, it will reduce economic efficiency by increasing the risk costs borne by investors that (1) make investments that could yield either profits or losses, (2) do not realize sufficient profits on other investments to be able to make full use of any losses the investment in question might yield, and (3) do not have a portfolio of investments whose riskiness is not increased by any associated riskiness of the investment in question.

Next, this feature of our tax laws can affect economic efficiency by rendering subnormal for the category of investors just defined the after-tax certainty-equivalent rate-of-return of some investments that could yield either profits or losses whose pre-tax certainty-equivalent profit-rate is at least normal. Regrettably though predictably, the direct economic-efficiency implications of this last conclusion are complicated to analyze. If the tax law's imposing positive taxes on the profits yielded by firm-investments but not allowing firm-investors whose investments yield losses to secure a transfer from the government leads an investor in the relevant category to substitute an investment associated with a "less-unattractive" distribution of possible-loss outcomes but a lower certainty-equivalent-pre-tax supernormal profit-rate for an investment associated with a "more-unattractive" distribution of possible-loss outcomes but a higher certainty-equivalent pre-tax supernormal profit-rate, I would conclude that the tax-law reality in question would tend to cause economic inefficiency on that account. If the tax law's applying a positive tax-rate on firm investment-profits but not applying a negative tax-rate on firm investment-losses deters firms in the relevant category from making an investment that would increase the relevant ARDEPPS' equilibrium-investment quantity, I would suspect that, across all relevant instances, it would decrease economic efficiency when the deterred investment would have been an investment in PPR and would increase economic efficiency when the deterred investment would have been a QV investment, assuming that the government of the society in question has not adopted policies to prevent its continuing to devote too many resources to QV-investment creation and not enough to PPR execution from the perspective of economic efficiency (though I acknowledge that, if the deterred investment would have been substantially supernormally profitable, its deterrence might be economically inefficient). If the tax law's applying a positive tax-rate to firm-investment profits but not applying a negative tax-rate to firm-investment losses deters a firm in the category on which I am now focusing from making a QV or PPR investment that would have deterred another firm from making an equally-large QV or PPR investment in the ARDEPPS in question, I would be inclined to conclude that these features of the tax law would tend to decrease economic efficiency on this account because I am disposed to think that (1) the fact that the small firm whose investment was deterred by the tax law would otherwise have made the investment favors the conclusion that its investment was more *ex ante* pre-tax supernormally profitable than the investment the tax law would have deterred and (2) the fact that the small firm's deterred investment would have been more *ex ante* pre-tax supernormally profitable than the investment the tax law would have deterred favors the conclusion that the small-firm deterred investment would have been more economically efficient than the investment that "replaced" it.

Finally, the fact that the tax law applies a positive tax-rate to firm-investment profits but does not apply a negative tax-rate to firm-investment losses (that the firm cannot set off against profits it realizes on other investments because it does not have enough such profits for this purpose) will affect economic efficiency by deterring the formation of small firms that would make investments that could yield either losses or profits that could not in practice make tax-use of some or all of the losses it sustains: I have already explained in Sect. 11.2.6 why I think that the formation of such start-ups will tend to increase economic efficiency.

I will now explain the relevance of the preceding three points to the correct resolution of the issue on which I am now focusing. The fact that a horizontal (M or A) yields its participants profits by creating a resulting firm that can take advantage of a tax-loss a participant could not itself have used will be associated with the (M or A)'s increasing economic efficiency because the ability of small firms to participate in (M or A)s that yield them this type of advantage will increase economic efficiency by reducing the extent to which the tax law's failure to apply a negative tax-rate to losses that firms could not in practice use to offset other taxable profits they realized if they remained separate entities will reduce the amount of economic inefficiency this tax-law "omission" generates (1) by increasing the risk costs that the owners of relevant small firms bear, (2) across all cases, by deterring small firms from making investments that might yield them losses and by substituting less-loss-prone investments with lower certainty-equivalent rates-of-return for more-loss-prone investments with higher certainty-equivalent rates-of-return, and (3) by deterring the formation of start-ups.

Is there a relevant economic-efficiency-impact bottom line? Somewhat to my surprise, I am disposed to conclude that if the tax laws of the society in question do not apply a negative income tax to the tax-losses that individual investments yield firms that cannot in practice use them to offset taxable profits their other investments generate, the profits a horizontal (M or A) generates by creating a resulting firm that can take advantage of tax-losses one or more participants could not use will be associated with an increase in economic efficiency. If the relevant society's tax laws do contain such a negative-income-tax provision, any such profits a horizontal (M or A) yields its participants will be associated with a decrease in economic efficiency.

Because an investor's decision to consummate a horizontal (M or A) to enable it to take advantage of tax-losses it could not otherwise have used is not liberal-moral-rights-violative, the fact that a horizontal (M or A) yields its participants profits in this way, if anything, favors the conclusion that it is not liberal-moral-rights-violative.

Although (1) the resolution of any positive or normative distributive-impact-related issue depends on the way in which the government of the society in question will respond to any loss in government tax-revenue that a horizontal (M or A) generates by enabling the resulting firm to take advantage of a participant's tax-losses it could not have used as a separate entity (a tax-revenue impact that will also be affected by the horizontal [M or A]'s related effects on start-up decisions and investment-decisions) and (2) I have not analyzed the distributive impact of either this net-revenue effect or the relevant government's probable response to it, I will proceed on the assumption that the distributive impact of a horizontal (M or A)'s yielding its participants profits for this tax reason is undesirable from the utilitarian perspective and from all non-utilitarian-egalitarian perspectives. On this assumption, in a world in which the relevant conceptions of the moral good would otherwise be perfectly instantiated, (1) the impact that a horizontal (M or A) will have on total utility by virtue of its enabling its participants to profit by taking advantage of tax-losses will depend on whether its doing so will increase economic efficiency sufficiently to outweigh its having a distributive impact on this account that is undesirable from a utilitarian perspective, and (2) the fact that a horizontal (M or A) yields its participants this type of benefit will cause it to disserve the instantiation of all non-utilitarian-egalitarian conceptions of the moral good.

11.2.8 Analyses That Relate to Any Horizontal (M or A)'s Yielding Its Participants Profits by Enabling Them (and Their Rivals) to Make Additional (Jointly-Profitable) Expenditures on Political Campaigns/Parties/Candidates and Government-Decision-Making-Process Participation

I will not subdivide this section either. As I have previously argued, to the extent that a horizontal (M or A) increases the concentration of the seller-side of the ARDEPPS of consummation (1) by combining the participants, (2) by causing the resulting firm to renew or rebuild a production facility or distributive outlet of a participant that the participant would not have renewed or rebuilt when the resulting firm owned a relativey-large percentage of the ARDEPPS' investments or at least a larger percentage of those investments than the percentage owned by the actual or potential rival of the resulting firm whose investment its investment deterred, (3) by causing the resulting firm to make one or more investments in the ARDEPPS of consummation that the participants would not have made when the resulting firm owned a relatively-high percentage of the ARDEPPS' investments or a larger share of those investments than was owned by the potential or actual rival(s) of the resulting firm whose investment(s) was (were) deterred by the resulting firm's horizontal-(M or A)-induced expansions, and (4) by causing the resulting firm to engage in more predation than the participants would otherwise have practiced, it will tend to increase the profits that its participants realize (indeed, that its participants and its rivals in the ARDEPPS of consummation realize) by making expenditures on political parties/campaigns/candidates and on participation in government-decision-making processes by helping the participants and their mutual rivals overcome the public-good-type obstacles to their spending as much money in these ways as would be in their collective interest. To save space, I will not analyze the determinants of the extent to which any individual horizontal (M or A) will increase the expenditures of these kinds that its participants and their mutual rivals make or the determinants of the profits that any resulting increase in these actors' relevant expenditures will yield the participants (or the participants and their rivals).

As I have admitted, I am simply asserting that any increase in such expenditures a horizontal (M or A) generates will decrease economic efficiency not only because such expenditures are allocatively costly but also because I believe that the decisions they cause the government to make will not only be in the parochial interest of the participants but also will tend to be economically inefficient. I recognize that some of these expenditures may provide the government with empirical information and theoretical arguments that will enable it to make more-economically-efficient decisions, that any analysis of the economic-efficiency and moral-desirability impacts of any related increase in the political power of an individual horizontal (M or A)'s participants will depend on the political influence of its policy-allies and policy-opponents, and that the economic-efficiency and moral-desirability impacts of any tendency of all horizontal (M&A)s to increase the political power of their participants will have to take account both of the fact that different horizontal (M&A)s may individually increase the political power of political opponents and allies and the fact that political power would be distributed economic-inefficiently even if all horizontal (M&A)s were prohibited. Still, if (perish the thought) I were the economic-efficiency-analysis czar, I would assume that the profit-increases that individual (M&A)s yield their participants by reducing the public-good-type obstacles to their exercising political influence will tend to be associated with decreases in economic efficiency.

My assessment of the implications of a horizontal (M or A)'s yielding its participants profits in the way for its liberal-moral-rights-violativeness is based on the combination of (1) the moral assumption that it is not liberal-moral-rights-violative for a firm or an individual to pursue its parochial interest by trying to influence government decisions in this way so long as the expenditures in question do not involve its lying, making substantively-misleading statements, paying a supposed or actual expert to make statements that favor the firm's/individual's interest without revealing that he or she is on the relevant party's payroll, or playing unfair in some other way and (2) an empirical assumption that the relevant participants' extra expenditures are not on conduct that is unfair in the above or some similar way. I am making the just-stated normative assumption despite my conclusion that the government of a liberal-moral-rights-based society is morally obligated to put all its members in a position to exercise equal political influence because I am reluctant to conclude that society-members have a liberal moral duty to determine whether they have unfair excessive political influence and to restrain themselves from exercising their political power when they conclude that they have too much of it. My reluctance is not traceable to what I take to be an implicit claim that the individual members of society have a liberal political right to exercise all the political power they possess. Instead, my reluctance is traceable (1) to the difficulty of a firm's or an individual's identifying the conception of the moral good that would give equal weight to each society-member's set of moral-good positions, (2) to the difficulty of a firm's or individual's determining the extent to which the full set of government decisions has secured its shareholders' or his or her parochial interests or instantiated its shareholders' or his or her moral-good position relative to the extent to which those decisions have secured the parochial interests or instantiated the moral-good positions of others, and (3) to the possibility that it may be morally defensible for each firm to be legally obligated to serve the parochial interests or instantiate the moral-good positions of its shareholders. In any event, if it is liberal-moral-rights-licit for a horizontal (M or A) to benefit its participants by increasing their influence on government decisions (so long as they "play fair"), an individual (M or A)'s benefiting its participants in this way will favor the conclusion that it is not liberal-moral-rights-violative by making it more likely that none of its participants' *ex ante* perception that the (M or A) was at least *ex ante* normally profitable was critically affected by a belief that it would or might increase his or her profits in a liberal-moral-rights-violative way. I acknowledge that this argument is far from conclusive, particularly since many of the expenditures that firms make would not have been perceived by them *ex ante* to be at least normally profitable if they did not believe that the expenditures would or might elicit government decisions that would yield them profits by reducing the absolute attractiveness of the best offers against which they would have to compete in one or more ways that would render the expenditures economically inefficient in an oPp economy.

I believe that a horizontal (M or A)'s yielding its participants profits by increasing their political influence will be associated not only with its decreasing economic efficiency on this account but also with its increasing poverty and material inequality. If these beliefs are correct, the fact that a horizontal (M or A) increased its participants' profits in this way would favor the conclusion that it would tend on this account both to decrease total utility and to disserve the instantiation of all non-utilitarian-egalitarian conceptions of the moral good.

11.2.9 Analyses That Relate to Any Profits a Horizontal (M or A) Yields Its Participants by Increasing Their HNOPs by Freeing Them From Each Other's Price-Competition

If individualized pricing is practiced in the ARDEPPS of consummation, the equivalent-dollar gain a horizontal (M or A) will yield its participants in this way equals (1) (the number of "product"-units the participants were respectively uniquely-privately-best-placed and uniquely-privately-second-placed to sell) *times* (the average number of dollars by which in the relevant instances the privately-second-placed participant was privately-better-placed to sell that unit than was its privately-third-placed prospective seller) *plus* (2) (the number of "product"-units the participants were uniquely-privately-equal-best-placed to sell) *times* (the average number of dollars by which in these instances the participants were privately-better-placed to sell the units in question than was the privately-third-placed prospective seller of those "product"-units) where "product" is enquoted both because the product in question might be a service and because the relevant "products" of the relevant sellers may (usually will) differ.

A horizontal (M or A)'s yielding its participants profits in this way will be associated with its having the following impacts on economic efficiency (if I ignore for the moment any effects it has by altering the NOMs and COMs of the participants and their mutual rivals or by affecting the amount of predation the participants [post-merger as the resulting firm] and their mutual rivals practice):

(1) its decreasing economic efficiency by increasing poverty and material inequality (in the vast majority of cases, in which the buyers of the relevant ARDEPPS' products are less-well-off than are the shareholders/creditors/managers/employees of the participants and of their mutual rivals),
(2) its decreasing economic efficiency by increasing equilibrium investment in the ARDEPPS of consummation if that ARDEPPS' investments are QV investments and the government of their society in question has not prevented its continuing to devote too many resources from the perspective of economic efficiency to QV-investment creation, and
(3) its increasing economic efficiency by increasing equilibrium investment in the ARDEPPS of consummation if that ARDEPPS' investments are investments in PPR and the government of the society in question has not prevented its continuing to devote too few resources from the perspective of economic efficiency to the execution and use of PPR.

Since the profits a horizontal (M or A) yields its participants in the way on which this section is focusing are Sherman-Act-illicit (though it is not liberal-moral-rights-violative for the resulting firm to take advantage of this effect of the [M or A]—not to compete against itself), the fact that a horizontal (M or A) yields its participants profits in this way if anything makes it more likely that the (M or A) in question is liberal-moral-rights-violative, though (I suspect) many horizontal (M&A)s that yield their participants profits in this way are not liberal-moral-rights-violative in that they should have been predicted and would have been predicted by their participants to generate at least normal profits even if they would not yield their participants profits in this way.

If, as I believe, a horizontal (M or A)'s yielding its participants profits in this way would be associated with its increasing poverty and material inequality, that "reality" would imply that a horizontal (M or A)'s yielding its participants profits in this way would cause it (on the above assumption) to disserve the instantiation of all non-utilitarian-egalitarian conceptions of the moral good and would cause it to disserve the instantiation of the utilitarian conception of the moral good as well except in those instances in which it increases economic efficiency sufficiently by increasing equilibrium PPR in the ARDEPPS of consummation for it to increase total utility everything considered.

11.2.9.1 Analyses That Relate to Any Profits a Horizontal (M or A) Yields Its Participants by Increasing Their NOMs

A horizontal (M or A) can increase its participants' NOMs in at least three ways: (1) by creating a resulting firm whose OCAs are higher than the OCAs the participants would have enjoyed by generating static marginal-cost efficiencies, freeing the participants from each other's price-competition, creating a resulting firm that can substitute new investments that are less competitive with its old investments than the investments the participants would have made would have been with the other investments of all participants, etc., (2) by creating a resulting firm that can determine whether it has lost a sale to a competitive inferior and change its initial offers more-cost-effectively than the participants could have done, and (3) particularly when the participants and their mutual rivals are setting across-the-board prices, by creating a resulting firm that is more able than the participants would have been to induce its rivals to join it in making and implementing "premature" price-announcements that enable all to obtain OMs naturally.

With one addition, the economic-efficiency impacts that are associated with a horizontal (M or A)'s increasing its participants' NOMs are identical to their counterparts for a horizontal (M or A)'s increasing its participants' OCAs or HNOPs. The addition is that, to the extent that a horizontal (M or A)'s increasing its participants' NOMs is associated with the resulting firm's and its rivals' devoting more resources to arranging for their making and implementing "premature" price-announcements, a horizontal (M or A)'s yielding its participants profits in this way will tend to decrease economic inefficiency on this account.

My conclusions about the relevance of a horizontal (M or A)'s increasing its participants' profits by increasing their NOMs for its liberal-moral-rights-violativeness derive from the following three premises: (1) it is liberal-moral-rights-violative for a firm to take advantage of its ability to secure an OM naturally; (2) even if it would not be liberal-moral-rights-violative for a firm to charge an NOM when it can do so without doing anything it would not otherwise find profitable to do to put itself in such a position, it would be liberal-moral-rights-violative for a firm to expend resources to make and implement "premature" price-announcements and to induce its rivals to make and implement "premature" price-announcements to enable it and them to obtain OMs naturally; and (3) a horizontal (M or A) will be rendered liberal-moral-rights-violative by its increasing its participants' NOMs (as contrasted with "by its increasing its participants' abilities to obtain OMs naturally if they do not take advantage of the opportunity in question) not only if the participants' *ex ante* perception that the (M or A) would be at least normally profitable was critically affected by their belief that it would or might yield them profits in this way but also—even if that is not the case—by its participants' *ex ante* perception that it would give them an opportunity to increase their profits by securing NOMs and *ex ante* intent that the resulting firm would take advantage of this opportunity.

I will assume that a horizontal (M or A)'s increasing the NOMs that its participants (and their mutual rivals) secure would cause it to generate a distributive impact that was undesirable from both a utilitarian perspective and the perspectives of all non-utilitarian-egalitarian conceptions of the moral good. This conclusion implies that a horizontal (M or A)'s increasing its participants' NOMs would cause it to disserve the instantiation of all non-utilitarian-egalitarian conceptions of the moral good. In combination with the conclusions I have reached about the impact that a horizontal (M or A) will have on economic efficiency by virtue of its increasing its participants' NOMs, the conclusion that a horizontal (M or A) would generate a distributive impact that was undesirable from a utilitarian perspective by virtue of its increasing its participants' NOMs implies that a horizontal (M or A)'s increasing its participants' NOMs will cause it to decrease total utility unless it increased economic efficiency sufficiently by increasing the equilibrium-investment quantity in an ARDEPPS of consummation whose investments were investments in PPR for the opposite conclusion to be warranted.

11.2.9.2 Analyses That Relate to Any Profits That a Horizontal (M or A) Yields Its Participants by Increasing the COMs They Obtain

I begin by outlining why I believe that horizontal (M&A)s will not tend to increase the COMs their participants secure as well as why I believe that horizontal (M&A)s will tend to increase the COMs the resulting firm's rivals secure. The basic reason for my belief that horizontal (M&A)s will not tend to increase their participants' COMs (or the profits their participants realize by engaging in contrived-oligopolistic pricing) is that horizontal (M&A)s will tend to increase their participants OCAs[5] and NOMs[6] and in so doing will reduce the *ex ante* profitability of their participants' trying to secure COMs by increasing the amount of safe profits their participants must put at risk to try to secure COMs. I recognize that individual horizontal (M&A)s will tend to make contrived-oligopolistic pricing more profitable for the resulting firm than for the participants in one or more of large number of ways,[7] but I think that on balance horizontal (M&A)s will tend to decrease the amount of contrived-oligopolistic pricing in which their participants engage.

Although horizontal (M&A)s will tend to reduce the total COMs their participants' mutual rivals obtain by reducing the number of buyers their rivals are privately-best-placed to supply (by generating static efficiencies and creating a resulting firm that makes more investments in the ARDEPPS of consummation than its participants would have made), I suspect that horizontal (M&A)s will tend to increase the amount of COMs their participants' mutual rivals secure, everything considered, because the preceding effects will be outweighed (1) by the horizontal (M&A)s' reducing the OCAs the participants' mutual rivals enjoy and derivatively the NOMs their participants' mutual rivals obtain—that is, by reducing the amount of safe profits their participants' mutual rivals must put at risk to try to obtain a COM—and (2) by the horizontal (M&A)s' increasing the participants' mutual rivals' abilities to secure "the participants'" cooperation by promising to reciprocate to "the participants"—i.e., the resulting firm—(A) by increasing the frequency with which the rivals are privately-second-placed to secure the patronage of a buyer "the participants" are privately-best-placed to supply by increasing the number of buyers the resulting firm is privately-best-placed to supply above the total number of buyers the participants would have been privately-best-placed to supply, (B) by causing a mutual rival of the participants to be privately-second-placed to supply a customer of the resulting firm that the participants would have been either uniquely-privately-equal-best-placed to supply or respectively privately-best-placed and privately-second-placed to supply, and (C) by increasing the amount by which "the participants'" mutual rivals are privately-better-placed than the privately-third-placed supplier of buyers the resulting firm is privately-best-placed to supply and a relevant rival is privately-second-placed to supply in situations in which, absent the (M or A), one participant would have been privately-best-placed, the other participant would have been either uniquely-privately-equal-best-placed or uniquely-privately-second-placed to supply, and a mutual rival of the participants would otherwise have been either uniquely-privately-equal-second-placed or uniquely-privately-third-placed to supply, and (3) by the horizontal (M&A)s' increasing the harm-inflicted to loss-incurred ratio for the participants' mutual rivals' inflicting a given relevant amount of harm on the resulting firm above its counterpart for the participants as a separate entity (A) by increasing the number of buyers that the resulting firm is privately-best-placed to supply and the participants are privately-second-placed or close-to-privately-second-placed to supply above the number of buyers that the participants would as separate entities have been privately-best-placed to supply and their mutual rivals would have been privately-second-placed or privately-close-to-second-placed to supply, (B) by increasing the (OCA + NOM) totals of the resulting firm above their counterparts for the participants when as separate entities they would have been privately-best-placed to supply buyers, and (C) by enabling individual mutual rivals of the participants to retaliate against the resulting firm by charging retaliatory prices to customers of all participants and to buyers the resulting firm was privately-best-placed to supply that no participant would have been privately-best-placed to supply (that is, by spreading the resulting firm's defenses).

11.2.9.3 The Determinants of the Profits a Horizontal (M or A) Will Yield Its Participants by Increasing the Amount of Profits They Can Realize by Engaging in Contrived-Oligopolistic Pricing

The determinants of any profits a horizontal (M or A) will yield its participants by increasing the profits they realize by engaging in contrived-oligopolistic pricing include (1) those that have been discussed in footnotes 5–7 of this chapter and (2) the attributes of the law on contrived-oligopolistic pricing—(A) whether such pricing is prohibited, (B) whether the law makes such pricing a criminal offense, (C) whether the law entitles buyers that have been charged COMs to obtain judgments against the contrivers, (D) the standards of proof that apply in criminal and civil contrived-oligopolistic-pricing cases, (E) the severity of the criminal sentences (prison sentences, criminal fines) prescribed for convicted individual contrived-oligopolistic pricers, (F) the magnitude of the criminal fines and other sanctions that can be imposed on firms that are convicted of engaging in contrived-oligopolistic pricing, (G) if victims of contrived-oligopolistic pricing are given the legal right to obtain legal redress, the damage-awards to which they are legally entitled (compensatory damages, treble damages, etc.) (H) the help that the State provides private plaintiffs who or that bring contrived-oligopolistic-pricing suits, (I) the availability of the empirical data that bears on whether a defendant has engaged in contrived-oligopolistic pricing, (J) the resources that have been allocated to antitrust-law-enforcement authorities, and (K) the extent to which the relevant society's antitrust-law-enforcement authorities accept settlements in contrived-oligopolistic-pricing civil cases or accept plea-bargains in contrived-oligopolistic-pricing criminal cases that are more favorable to the defendants than are the evidence and the operative (damage award)/(criminal-sentencing) provisions.

11.2.9.4 The Determinants of the Economic-Efficiency Loss (Gain) a Horizontal (M or A) Will Generate by Virtue of Any Increase (Decrease) in Contrived-Oligopolistic Pricing It Generates

Section 9.1.1.1.2 analyzed the economic-efficiency impact of contrived-oligopolistic pricing. The determinants of the economic-efficiency effect of a horizontal (M or A)'s increasing or decreasing the amount of contrived-oligopolistic pricing in which its participants and their mutual rivals engage can be inferred from that subsection's analyses.

11.2.9.5 The Relevance of a Horizontal (M or A)'s Increasing the Profits Its Participants Realize by Practicing Contrived-Oligopolistic Pricing to Its Liberal-Moral-Rights-Violativeness

As Section 9.1.3 explained, contrived-oligopolistic pricing is liberal-moral-rights-violative. This conclusion implies that (1) if any horizontal-(M or A) participant's *ex ante* perception that the (M or A) would be at least normally profitable was critically affected by its belief that the (M or A) would or might increase the profits the resulting firm would realize by practicing contrived-oligopolistic pricing above the profits the participants would have realized by doing so, the (M or A) would be liberal-moral-rights-violative on that account and (2) even if no participant in a horizontal (M or A)'s perception that the (M or A) was *ex ante* at least normally profitable was critically affected by its belief that the (M or A) would or might increase the profits the resulting firm would or might realize by practicing contrived-oligopolistic pricing above the profits the participants could have realized by doing so, the (M or A) would be liberal-moral-rights-violative if a participant believed *ex ante* that it would or might increase the profits the resulting firm would or might realize by practicing contrived-oligopolistic pricing and expected *ex ante* the resulting firm to take advantage of any such profit-opportunity the (M or A) created.

11.2.9.6 The Relevance of a Horizontal (M or A)'s Increasing/Decreasing the Extent to Which Contrived-Oligopolistic Pricing Is Practiced to Its Serving or Disserving the Instantiation of the Utilitarian and the Various Non-Utilitarian-Egalitarian Conceptions of the Moral Good

Contrived-oligopolistic pricing (1) will virtually always decrease economic efficiency and (2) will virtually always generate a distributive impact that is undesirable from the perspective of utilitarianism and from the perspective of all non-utilitarian-egalitarian conceptions of the moral good (primarily because it will impose equivalent-dollar losses on the buyers in the ARDEPPS of consummation, who are almost always less-well-off than the average member of the society in question). For the above two reasons, a horizontal (M or A)'s increasing/decreasing the incidence of contrived-oligopolistic pricing will favor the conclusion that it will disserve/serve the instantiation of the utilitarian conception of the moral good, and, for the second of the above two reasons, a horizontal (M or A)'s increasing/decreasing the incidence of contrived-oligopolistic pricing will favor the conclusion that it will disserve/serve the instantiation of all non-utilitarian-egalitarian conceptions of the moral good.

11.2.10 Analyses That Relate to Any Profits a Horizontal (M or A) Yields Its Participants by Freeing Them From Each Other's Investment-Competition

11.2.10.1 The Determinants of the Profits a Horizontal (M or A) Will Yield Its Participants by Freeing Them From Each Other's Investment-Competition

A horizontal (M or A) can yield its participants profits by freeing them from each other's investment-competition by enabling the resulting firm not to make an investment that would have reduced its profits given its impact on the profits yielded by its other investments that a participant would have made because each participant realized that if it did not make an investment the other participant would do so—a possibility that will be likely to be salient only if the resulting firm's (or the participants') not making an investment would not induce a mutual rival of the participants (a rival of the resulting firm) to make an investment in the ARDEPPS of consummation. I suspect that, less often and more evanescently, a horizontal (M or A) can also yield its participants profits by freeing them from each other's investment-competition by creating a resulting firm that can make an investment that is profitable everything considered when no participant would find the same investment profitable even if it could design and execute the relevant investment as proficiently as the resulting firm could because each participant realized that if it made such an investment the other participant would make one too when the other participant would not otherwise make an investment given that it would recognize that its making an investment would induce the first participant to make an investment it would not otherwise make. (This possibility will also be salient only if the participants' failure to make an investment would not induce a mutual rival to make an investment in the relevant ARDEPPS.)

When a horizontal (M or A) yields its participants profits by enabling the resulting firm not to make an investment that it found unprofitable that a participant would have made despite the fact that it would have been unprofitable for all the (M or A)'s participants taken together, the determinants of the profits the (M or A) will yield the participants on this account are (1) the determinants of the profits the (M or A)-deterred investment would have yielded the participant that would have made it as an independent entity and (2) the determinants of the impact that the deterred investment would have had on the profit-yields of the investments of the other participants in the (M or A) in question. When a horizontal (M or A) yields its participants profits by enabling the resulting firm to make one investment that was profitable for it to make all things considered when no participant would have made the investment because the separate participants would have confronted each other with critical natural-oligopolistic investment-disincentives (because each participant would recognize that if it made an investment the other participant would make one too that the other would otherwise not have made), the determinants of the profits the (M or A) will yield the participants on this account will be (1) the determinants of the profits the (M or A)-induced investment would yield the resulting firm if it did not affect the profits yielded by its other investments and (2) the determinants of the impact that the induced investment would have on the profit-yields of the resulting firm's other investments.

11.2.10.2 The Determinants of the Impact That a Horizontal (M or A) Will Have on Economic Efficiency by Virtue of Its Freeing the Participants From Each Other's Investment-Competition

The impact that a horizontal (M or A) will have on economic efficiency by virtue of its freeing its participants from each other's investment-competition will depend on whether on this account the (M or A) creates a resulting firm that does not make an investment a participant but no other firm would have made or creates a resulting firm that makes an investment when neither a participant nor anyone else would otherwise have made an investment in the ARDEPPS of consummation. The first set of determinants that are relevant to the current enquiry are those that determine which of these two outcomes eventuates. The next set of relevant determinants can be inferred from the following accounts of the impact that a horizontal (M or A) will have on economic efficiency by virtue of its decreasing or increasing equilibrium investment in the ARDEPPS of consummation as a result of its freeing the participants from each other's investment-competition. When on this account the (M or A) creates a resulting firm that does not make an investment that a participant but no other firm would have made, the horizontal (M or A)'s freeing the participants from each other's investment-competition will affect economic efficiency in the following ways:

(1) when the deterred investment is a QV investment, will increase economic efficiency by an amount that is determined by the profits the deterred QV investment would have yielded the participant that would have made it and by all determinants of the positive distortion in the profits that would have been yielded by the deterred investment if the government of the relevant society has not prevented its continuing to allocate too many resources to QV-investment creation from the perspective of economic efficiency,
(2) when the deterred investment is an investment in PPR, will decrease economic efficiency by an amount that is determined by the profits that the deterred investment would have yielded the participant that would have made it and by all the determinants of the negative distortion in those profits that would have been yielded by the execution and use of the deterred PPR investment if the government of the society in question has not prevented its continuing to devote too few resources to PPR execution from the perspective of economic efficiency,
(3) will tend to decrease economic efficiency by increasing poverty and material inequality (by an amount that is determined primarily by the factors that influence the equivalent-dollar gain the deterred investment would have conferred on the buyers in the ARDEPPS of consummation, the amount by which the buyers of the relevant ARDEPPS' products are poorer than the average member of the society in question, and all the factors that determine the amount of economic inefficiency various amounts of poverty and material inequality generate), and
(4) will decrease/increase economic efficiency if the deterred investment would have increased/decreased the concentration of the seller-side of the ARDEPPS of consummation (depending [put crudely] on whether the resulting firm owned a relativey-low/relatively-high percentage of the investment in the ARDEPPS of consummation) by increasing/decreasing the expenditures the ARDEPPS' sellers make on political parties/campaigns/candidates and government-decision-making-process participation.

When the (M or A) in question creates a resulting firm that makes an investment when neither a participant nor anyone else would have made one in the ARDEPPS of consummation by eliminating a situation in which two (or more) participants confronted each other with critical natural-oligopolistic investment-disincentives, the horizontal (M or A) will on this account affect economic efficiency in the following ways:

(1) when the induced investment is a QV investment, will decrease economic efficiency by the profits the induced investment yields the resulting firm *minus* the positive distortion in those profits that will exist if the government of the society in question has not prevented its continuing to devote too many resources to QV-investment creation from the perspective of economic efficiency,
(2) when the induced investment is an investment in PPR, will increase economic efficiency by the profits the induced investment yields the resulting firm *plus*

the negative distortion in those profits that will exist if the government of the society in question has not prevented its continuing to devote too few resources to PPR execution from the perspective of economic efficiency,

(3) will tend to increase economic efficiency by reducing poverty and material inequality, and

(4) will decrease/increase economic efficiency if the induced investment increased/decreased the concentration of the seller-side of the ARDEPPS of consummation (depending [put crudely] on whether the resulting firm owned a relativey-high/relatively-low percentage of the investment in the ARDEPPS of consummation) by increasing/decreasing the relevant sellers' expenditures on political parties/campaigns/candidates and on government-decision-making-process participation).

11.2.10.3 The Relevance of a Horizontal (M or A)'s Yielding Its Participants Profits by Freeing Them From Each Other's Investment-Competition for Its Liberal-Moral-Rights-Violativeness

The conclusions on this issue that I think are warranted reflect my views that, when antitrust-policy-coverable conduct is at issue, (1) it is not liberal-moral-rights-violative for (a firm)/(an individual) to decide not to make choices that would confer a net equivalent-dollar gain on others and (2) it is liberal-moral-rights-violative for a firm/individual to make a choice it would not otherwise have found profitable to put itself in a position in which it could profit by deciding not to make a choice that would confer a net equivalent-dollar gain on others. These conclusions imply that the fact that a horizontal (M or A) yields its participants profits by freeing them from each other's investment-competition will make it more likely that the (M or A) is liberal-moral-rights-violative to the extent that it increases the probability that a participant's *ex ante* perception that the (M or A) was at least normally profitable was critically affected by the participant's *ex ante* belief that it would or might increase its profits in this way, but it certainly does not warrant the conclusion that any horizontal (M or A) that yields its participants profits in this way is liberal-moral-rights-violative on this account.

11.2.10.4 The Relevance of a Horizontal (M or A)'s Yielding Its Participants Profits by Freeing Them From Each Other's Investment-Competition to Its Serving or Disserving the Instantiation of the Utilitarian and Non-Utilitarian-Egalitarian Conceptions of the Moral Good

I will distinguish four sets of cases, each of which will be analyzed on the assumption that the government of the society in question has not prevented the relevant society's continuing to allocate from the perspective of economic efficiency too many resources to QV-investment creation and not enough to PPR execution. In the first, (1) the horizontal (M or A) in question's freeing its participants from each other's investment-competition will have resulted in the resulting firm's not making an investment that a participant would have made in circumstances in which the participant's investment would not have deterred a rival from investing and (2) the eliminated investment would have been a QV investment. In this case, the horizontal (M or A)'s freeing its participants from each other's competition could either tend to cause it to increase or to decrease economic efficiency and would usually cause it to increase poverty and material inequality if the affected buyers would not otherwise have been better-off than the other affected parties. In this case, then, the (M or A)'s yielding its participants profits by freeing them from each other's investment-competition would have an uncertain effect on its impact on total utility and would usually disserve the instantiation of all non-utilitarian-egalitarian conceptions of the moral good.

In the second set of cases, (1) the horizontal (M or A) in question's freeing its participants from each other's investment-competition will have resulted in the resulting firm's not making an investment that a participant would have made in circumstances in which the participant's investment would not have deterred a rival from investing and (2) the eliminated investment would have been an investment in PPR. In this case, the horizontal (M or A)'s freeing the participants from the investment-competition they would have waged against each other will almost always decrease economic efficiency and increase poverty and material inequality on the assumption that the affected buyers would otherwise have been worse-off than the other parties affected by the decision not to invest. In this case, the horizontal (M or A)'s freeing its participants from each other's investment-competition will almost certainly reduce total utility and disserve the instantiation of all non-utilitarian-egalitarian conceptions of the moral good.

In the third set of cases, (1) the horizontal (M or A)'s freeing its participants from each other's investment-competition will have resulted in the resulting firm's making an investment when neither participant nor anyone else would have done so and (2) the induced investment will be a QV investment. In this set of cases, (1) the horizontal (M or A)'s freeing its participants from each other's investment-competition will have an uncertain impact on economic efficiency (though, if I had to guess, I would guess that it would decrease economic efficiency more by increasing equilibrium QV investment in the economy than it would increase economic efficiency by reducing poverty and material inequality [the effect that the (M or A) would have on economic efficiency in this way by changing the quantity of the relevant ARDEPPS' sellers' expenditures on political parties/campaigns/candidates and government-decision-making participation is uncertain since on this account the [M or A] could either concentrate or deconcentrate the seller-side of the ARDEPPS of consummation) and (2) the distributive impact of the (M or A)'s freeing its participants from each other's investment-competition will be desirable from both the utilitarian and all other egalitarian perspectives if (as I assume will usually be the case) the affected buyers would otherwise be worse-off than the other affected parties. In this set of cases, then, a horizontal (M or A)'s freeing its participants from each other's investment-competition will have an uncertain effect on total utility but will usually serve the instantiation of all non-utilitarian-egalitarian conceptions of the moral good.

In the fourth set of cases, (1) the horizontal (M or A)'s freeing its participants from each other's investment-competition will have resulted in the resulting firm's making an investment when no participant and no other firm would otherwise have invested in the ARDEPPS of consummation and (2) the induced investment will be an investment in PPR. In this set of cases, the horizontal (M or A)'s freeing the participants from each other's investment-competition will almost always increase economic efficiency and reduce poverty and material inequality if, as I assume, the government of the relevant society has not eliminated the negative distortion in the profits yielded by investments in PPR and the affected buyers are almost always worse-off than the other parties that would be affected by the (M or A)'s freeing its participants from each other's investment-competition. Hence, in this set of cases, the horizontal (M or A)'s freeing its participants from each other's investment-competition will almost always tend to favor its instantiating the utilitarian and all non-utilitarian-egalitarian conceptions of the moral good.

11.2.11 Analyses That Relate to Any Profits a Horizontal (M or A) Yields Its Participants by Creating a Resulting Firm That Realizes More Profits by Driving Out Extant Rival Investors by Engaging in Predatory Pricing, Predatory Advertizing, or Making Other Predatory Moves Than the Participants Would Have Done as Separate Entities

11.2.11.1 The Determinants of the Profits That a Horizontal (M or A) Will Yield Its Participants by Creating a Resulting Firm That Realizes More Profits by Predatorily Driving Out Extant Rival Investments Than the Participants Would Have Realized in This Way as Separate Entities

Firms can predatorily drive out one or more rival investments in a wide variety of ways: *inter alia* (1) by predatorily denigrating a rival's product, (2) by predatorily obstructing a rival's place of business, (3) by placing predatory (inherently-unprofitable) advertizements promoting the predator's product, (4) by predatorily deterring suppliers of labor, finance, and other inputs from supplying them to the targeted rival by bribing them not to supply the target or misrepresenting the target's credit-worthiness or probable longevity, (5) by predatorily hiring workers or managers who would otherwise have supplied their labor to the target (by hiring them when it was inherently-unprofitable to do so]), (6) by making inherently-unprofitable, predatory purchases of IP rights or other non-labor inputs the target wished to purchase and refusing predatorily to sell them to the target on inherently-profitable terms, (7) by making inherently-unprofitable legal claims against the target in order to drive them out, (8) by participating in legislative and/or administrative processes in ways that were critically motivated by the parochial interest the predator had in driving a target out, (9) by setting predatorily-low prices to a target's customers, etc. The determinants of the impact that a horizontal (M or A) will have on the profits its participants will realize by engaging in predation that drives an existing rival out fall into four categories: (1) the determinants of the profitability of such predation for the participants acting as separate entities (which are relevant because even if an [M or A] makes such predation more profitable for the resulting firm than it would have been for any participant and even if the resulting firm would take advantage of any opportunity it had to earn profits by engaging in predation, the horizontal [M or A] would not increase the profits its participants obtained by engaging in predation if predation was still unprofitable post-[M or A] because the [M or A]-generated increase in the profitability of predation was lower than the amount by which the predation was unprofitable pre-[M or A]),[8] (2) the determinants of the amount by which a horizontal (M or A) would increase the profitability of such predation for its participants if the (M or A) would not affect the certainty-equivalent law-related cost of engaging in predation, (3) the determinants of the amount by which a horizontal (M or A) would cause the law-related cost of the resulting firm's practicing any variant of predation to exceed the law-related cost that a participant should have reckoned with incurring if it practiced that variant of predation to the same extent (by making antitrust-law-enforcement authorities and prospective private plaintiffs more watchful and triers-of-fact more inclined to find against the resulting firm, though this effect will be at least somewhat offset to the extent that the resulting firm can make more-cost-effective defense-counsel-hiring decisions than the individual participants could), and (4) the determinants of the intensity of the dispreferences of the relevant firms' directors, CEOs, high-level managers, and lower-level employees for violating the law pre-(M or A) and of the impact of the (M or A) on those dispreferences.

I will focus primarily on the determinants of the amount by which a horizontal (M or A) will make it more profitable for a resulting firm to drive an extant rival QV investment out than it would have been for the participants to do so acting separately. The first set of such determinants relates to the fact that the horizontal (M or A) will make any variant of predation more profitable for the resulting firm than it would have been for a participant to the extent that the exit of the targeted extant rival investment will benefit all participants in the (M or A), not just the individual participant that was contemplating engaging in such predation on its own. This fact implies that the determinants of the positive difference a horizontal (M or A) makes between the profits that the resulting firm can realize by predatorily driving an existing rival out and the profits that the participant that would have found it most profitable or least unprofitable to drive that existing rival out predatorily include all the determinants of the contribution that the exit of the extant-rival target would make to the profits that would be realized by the (M or A) participant(s) other than the (M or A) participant that was privately-best-placed to drive the relevant target out predatorily—(the unit-sales the target would have been privately-best-placed to make that one of the participants that was not privately-best-placed to engage in the predation would have been uniquely-privately-second-placed to make *times* the average amount by which that participant was privately-better-placed to supply the buyer in question than was its privately-third-placed supplier) *plus* (the unit-sales the target would have been privately-uniquely-second-placed to make that a participant that was not the privately-best-placed predator was privately-best-placed to supply *times* the average amount by which in those instances the target was better-placed to supply the buyers in question than were their privately-third-placed suppliers). The second set of such determinants is related to the facts that (1) the profitability of predation for a firm increases with its reputation for engaging in strategic conduct since the credibility of its threats increase with its reputation for carrying them out, (2) firms that result from horizontal (M&A)s often inherit the reputations of the participant that has the stronger or strongest reputation for engaging in strategic conduct, and (3) horizontal (M&A)s may create a resulting firm that has a stronger reputation for engaging in strategic conduct than any participant had because part of a firm's reputation for engaging in such conduct depends on the target's perception that such conduct would be profitable for the firm in question and there are organizational economies of scale in building and maintaining a reputation for engaging in strategic conduct and because the horizontal (M or A) may increase the profits the resulting firm can realize by engaging in predatory behavior by increasing the harm-inflicted to loss-incurred ratio for inflicting given requisite amounts of harm by practicing predatory pricing or predatory advertizing by enabling the resulting firm to charge predatory prices on all participants' products and to place predatory advertizements on all participants' products. The third set of such determinants contains the factors that determine the extent to which the horizontal (M or A) will reduce the cost the resulting firm will have to incur to inflict a given relevant amount of harm on the target by enabling the resulting firm to inflict harm on the target by charging predatory prices for two or more participants' products or placing predatory advertizements on two or more participants' products (which determinants can in part be inferred from Sect. 10.1.1's discussion at the beginning of the factors that determine the harm-inflicted to loss-incurred ratio for given acts of predatory pricing on a particular product). The fourth set of such determinants contains (1) the magnitudes of the static marginal-cost efficiencies the horizontal (M or A) generates and/or the magnitudes of the static fixed-cost efficiencies or dynamic efficiencies the horizontal (M or A) generates that cause the resulting firm to make one or more investments that no participant would have made all of which are relevant to the extent that they increase the harm-inflicted to loss-incurred ratio for a relevant amount of harm inflicted by predatory pricing for the resulting firm relative to that ratio's counterpart for any participant and (2) the other factors that determine whether or the extent to which the associated increase in the harm-inflicted to loss-incurred ratio for the resulting firm's predatory pricing is consequential.

Because the following reality is relevant to the overall economic efficiency of horizontal (M or A)s, it is also worth pointing out that horizontal (M&A)s may also affect the amount of predation that the participants' rivals practice against "the participants"—that is, against the resulting firm relative to the total amount they would have practiced against the separate participants. In the one direction, the horizontal (M or A) may reduce such resulting-firm-rival predation by substituting for smaller, more-vulnerable individual participants a larger, more-resistant resulting firm. In the other direction, a horizontal (M or A) may increase such resulting-firm-rival predation by creating a resulting firm whose defenses are more spread-out than are the defenses of the individual participants and by causing individual resulting-firm rivals to be the privately-second-placed supplier of more customers of the resulting firm than they were of customers of the participants both by causing the resulting firm to be privately-best-placed to supply more buyers than the participants would have been taken together and by making a mutual rival of the participants privately-second-placed to supply a customer of the resulting firm that the participants were respectively privately-best-placed and privately-second-placed to supply or privately-equal-best-placed to supply and the rival in question was privately-third-placed to supply pre-(M or A).

11.2.11.2 The Determinants of the Impact That a Horizontal (M or A) Will Have on Economic Efficiency by Virtue of Its Increasing the Amount of Profits the Resulting Firm Realizes by Driving Extant Rival-QV-Investments Out Relative to the Amount of Profits the Participants Would Have Realized by Doing So (and by Increasing the Amount of Predation Directed at the Resulting Firm Relative to the Amount That Would Have Been Directed at the Participants)

With one possible exception, any additional efforts a horizontal (M or A) causes to be made to drive out existing investments will be misallocative. Predatory pricing is misallocative in itself not only because it is allocative-transaction-costly but also because both it and any defensive retaliation it elicits cause intra-ARDEPPS UO-to-UO misallocation. The fact that all the other predatory moves that the introduction to Sect. 11.2.13 lists are allocative-transaction-costly would favor the conclusion that they were economically inefficient even if they did not reduce economic inefficiency by misinforming consumers, obstructing access to target businesses, preventing otherwise-profitable transactions between their targets and their targets' prospective suppliers, etc. I also suspect that the withdrawal of extant investments whose continued use would have been profitable had predation not been practiced will decease economic efficiency (though a complete analysis of this issue would have to take account of the facts that the profits that the exiting investments would have yielded will be inflated by the deflation in the cost to the investor of the resources it combines with its investment to produce its unit output of the product the existing investment created and will be deflated by any buyer surplus the target's continued use of its investment would have generated). I should note that the preceding conclusion does not apply to horizontal-(M or A)-generated predation in this category that is directed at preventing the renewal of an extant QV investment. Perhaps I should "handle" this exception by saying that predation that is directed at preventing the renewal or rebuilding of a production or distributive facility that is a component of an extant QV investment should really be classified together with predation that is directed at preventing the creation of a QV investment (a type of predation on which Sect. 11.2.14 focuses).

11.2.11.3 The Relevance of the Fact That a Horizontal (M or A)'s Increases the Profits the Resulting Firm Realizes by Engaging in Predatory Conduct to Drive an Extant Rival Investment Out Above the Profits Its Participants Would Have Realized by Engaging in Such Conduct to the (M or A)'s Liberal-Moral-Rights-Violativeness

If a participant in a horizontal (M or A)'s *ex ante* perception that the (M or A) was *ex ante* at least normally profitable was critically affected by its belief that the (M or A) would or might increase the profits the participant would realize by engaging in predation to drive an extant-rival investment out, the (M or A) would be liberal-moral-rights-violative on this account. Even if the perception of no participant in a horizontal (M or A) that it was *ex ante* at last normally profitable was critically affected by a belief that the (M or A) would or might increase the amount of profits the resulting firm would realize by practicing such predation above the profits the participants would have realized by engaging in such conduct, the (M or A) would be liberal-moral-rights-violative if a participant (1) believed *ex ante* that the (M or A) would or might create a resulting firm that could profit more from such conduct than the participants could and (2) intended *ex ante* that the resulting firm would take advantage of any such opportunity the (M or A) created.

11.2.11.4 The Relevance of a Horizontal (M or A)'s Creating a Resulting Firm That Will Realize More Profits by Engaging in Predatory Conduct That Drives an Extant Rival Investment Out Than the Participants Would Have Realized by Engaging in Such Conduct to the (M or A)'s Serving or Disserving the Instantiation of the Utilitarian and the Various Non-Utilitarian-Egalitarian Conceptions of the Moral Good

Section 11.2.13.2 argued that all or virtually all predation of the type under consideration that a horizontal (M or A) elicits will decrease economic efficiency. Moreover, all or virtually all such predation will also have a distributive impact that is undesirable from a utilitarian and all non-utilitarian-egalitarian normative perspectives because all or virtually all such predation will increase material inequality primarily because it will impose equivalent-dollar losses on the buyers of the products produced in the ARDEPPS of consummation. The second of the preceding claims favors the conclusion that a horizontal (M or A)'s creating a resulting firm that would realize more profits in this way than the participants would have done will tend to make it disserve the instantiation of all non-utilitarian-egalitarian conceptions of the moral good. And the two claims made in the first two sentences of this paragraph favor the conclusion that a horizontal (M or A)'s creating a resulting firm that will realize more profits in this way than the participants would have done favors the conclusion that the (M or A) will reduce total utility.

11.2.12 Analyses That Relate to Any Profits a Horizontal (M or A) Yields Its Participants by (Predatorily) Critically Increasing the Retaliation Barrier to Entry Faced by an Otherwise-Effective Potential Competitor or the Retaliation Barrier to Expansion Faced by an Otherwise-Effective Established-Firm Potential Investment-Expander

11.2.12.1 The Determinants of the Amount by Which a Horizontal (M or A) Will Increase Its Participants' Profits by Increasing the Profits the Resulting Firm Realizes by Erecting Retaliation Barriers to Investment Above the Profits the Participants Would Have Realized by Doing So

Obviously, any established firm will profit from an actual or potential rival's deciding not to make an investment that would raise the equilibrium-investment quantity in its ARDEPPS to the extent that the deterred investment (1) would have reduced the relevant beneficiary's OCAs by rendering the deterred investor (A) privately-best-placed to supply buyers the relevant beneficiary would be privately-best-placed to supply in its absence and/or (B) by rendering the deterred investor privately-uniquely-second-placed to supply buyers that the beneficiary was privately-best-placed to supply or by reducing the OCD of an investor that would in any event have been privately-second-placed to supply buyers the beneficiary was privately-best-placed to supply, (2) would have reduced the relevant beneficiary's NOMs by reducing the number of buyers the beneficiary was privately-best-placed to supply and the OCAs it enjoyed in its relations with buyers it would have been privately-best-placed to supply in any case, (3) would have reduced the profits the firm realized by practicing contrived-oligopolistic pricing by increasing the number of products that might be priced non-cooperatively and reducing the sales-data available to the beneficiary, and (4) would have reduced the profits the beneficiary realized as a result of its and its rivals' making expenditures on political parties/campaigns/candidates and government-decision-making-process participation by decreasing the concentration of the seller-side of the ARDEPPS in which the deterred investment would have been located (though, admittedly, in some instances, a deterred investment will benefit the relevant beneficiary in this way by concentrating the seller-side of that ARDEPPS). Indeed, a firm's deterring a potential or established rival from making an investment in its ARDEPPS can also yield the firm profits when doing so enables the firm to make a profitable investment in that ARDEPPS. It follows that it will sometimes be profitable for a firm to incur costs to deter one or more potential entrants or established-firm potential investment-expanders from making one or more investments in its ARDEPPS. One way in which a firm can deter a potential or established competitor from making an investment in its ARDEPPS is to inform the potential investor that—if it does invest in the firm's ARDEPPS—the firm will retaliate (will make inherently-unprofitable moves—for example, price-cuts, advertizing decisions) to stop the investor in question from using its investment and/or (more likely) to deter future potential investors in any of the ARDEPPSes in which the firm operates from making investments in it. Any conduct of this kind in which a firm engages deserves to be characterized as predatory.

A horizontal (M or A) can increase the profits its participants realize by engaging in this variant of predation by creating a resulting firm (1) that has more investments than either participant and can therefore take advantage of organizational economies of scale in establishing and maintaining a reputation for engaging in such strategic conduct (a reputation that will make its threats more credible, more effective, and therefore more profitable), (2) that has more profits to protect than either participant has, (3) that faces a higher harm-inflicted to less-incurred ratio for the necessary acts of retaliation than any participant faces both (A) because the (M or A) yields static marginal-cost efficiencies, static fixed-cost efficiencies, and/or dynamic efficiencies that, either directly or indirectly by inducing the resulting firm to renew or make one or more investments, cause the resulting firm to be privately-second-placed or privately-close-to-second-placed to secure the patronage of a target's customers more often than either participant would have been and (B) because the resulting firm can sometimes use retaliatory price-cutting more cost-effectively than the participants could have done as separate entities by cutting one participant's product's or products' prices to the target's customers more often and the other participant's products or products' prices to the target's customers less often than the participants would have found most cost-effective to do as separate entities, and (4) that can use retaliatory advertizing more-cost-effectively than the participants could have by placing more retaliatory advertizements of one participant's product or products and fewer of the other participant's product or products than the participants would have done as separate entities.

The determinants of the profits that a horizontal (M or A) will yield its participants by making it more profitable for the resulting firm to erect retaliation barriers to investment than it would have been for the participants to do so include (1) the determinants of the pre-(M or A) unprofitability of such predatory conduct for the participants, (2) the determinants of the amount by which the (M or A) would cause the profitability of such conduct for the resulting firm to exceed the profitability of such conduct for the participants if law-related costs were ignored (which can be inferred from the preceding paragraph), (3) the determinants of the impact that the (M or A) would have on the law-related cost of practicing this type of predation (which were discussed in Sect. 11.2.13.1), and (4) the determinants of the negative dollar-value that the firm's relevant personnel place on breaking laws that prohibit this type of predation (independent of the risk of their being fined or penalized for violating this prohibition).

11.2.12.2 The Determinants of the Economic-Efficiency Impact of a Horizontal (M or A)'s Yielding Its Participants Profits by Creating a Resulting Firm That Realizes More Profits by Raising the Retaliation Barriers to Investment Its Rivals Face Than the Participants Would Have Earned by Engaging in Such Conduct

If I continue my assumption that the government of the relevant society has not prevented its continuing to devote from the perspective of economic efficiency too many resources to QV-investment creation and too few to PPR execution, a horizontal (M or A)'s increasing the amount of this type of predation that the resulting firm will practice above the amount the participants would have practiced

(1) will tend to cause the (M or A) to increase economic efficiency if the extra predation decreases equilibrium investment in the ARDEPPS of consummation when that ARDEPPS' investments are QV investments,
(2) will tend to cause it to decrease economic efficiency if the extra predation decreases equilibrium investment in the ARDEPPS of consummation when that ARDEPPS' investments are investments in PPR,
(3) will (I suspect) tend to cause it to decrease economic efficiency if the extra predation "substitutes" a less-profitable resulting-firm investment for a more-profitable deterred investment,
(4) will tend to cause it to decrease economic efficiency by the allocative transaction cost of communicating the additional threats of retaliation,
(5) will tend to cause it to decrease economic efficiency if the threats have to be carried out because any associated retaliatory pricing and any associated retaliatory advertizing will be misallocative,
(6) will tend to cause it to decrease economic efficiency by increasing poverty and material inequality (primarily because it will be associated with the relevant ARDEPPS' buyers suffering equivalent-dollar loses), and
(7) will tend to cause it to decrease/increase economic efficiency if it increases/decreases the concentration of the seller-side of the ARDEPPS of consummation because in so doing it will tend to increase/decrease the amount of contrived-oligopolistic pricing practiced in the ARDEPPS and the expenditures the ARDEPPS' sellers make on political parties/campaigns/candidates and government-decision-making-process participation.

I leave it to readers to work out the determinants of the magnitudes of each of these possible economic-efficiency effects.

11.2.12.3 The Relevance of a Horizontal (M or A)'s Creating a Resulting Firm That Will Realize More Profits by Raising the Retaliation Barrier to Investment Its Rivals Face Than Its Participants Would Have Realized by Raising the Retaliation Barrier to Investment Their Mutual Rivals Would Have Faced to the (M or A)'s Liberal-Moral-Rights-Violativeness

A horizontal (M or A)'s having this effect will render it liberal-moral-rights-violative if (1) a participant's *ex ante* perception that the (M or A) was at least normally profitable was critically affected by its belief that it would or might yield it profits in this way or (2) if a participant (A) believed *ex ante* that the (M or A) would or might enable it to earn more profits in this way and (B) intended *ex ante* the resulting firm to take advantage of any such opportunity the (M or A) created.

11.2.12.4 The Relevance of a Horizontal (M or A)'s Creating a Resulting Firm That Will Realize More Profits by Raising the Retaliation Barriers to Investment Its Rivals Face Than Its Participants Would Have Realized by Engaging in Such Conduct to the (M or A)'s Serving or Disserving the Instantiation of the Utilitarian and Various Non-Utilitarian-Egalitarian Conceptions of the Moral Good

I will proceed on the assumptions that a horizontal (M or A)'s yielding its participants profits in this way will tend to make it less-economically-efficient and more prone to generate material inequality. These two assumptions imply that a horizontal (M or A)'s yielding its participants profits in this way will tend to decrease total utility, and the second of the above two assumptions imply that a horizontal (M or A)'s yielding its participants profits in this way will tend to make it disserve the instantiation of all non-utilitarian-egalitarian conceptions of the moral good.

11.2.13 Analyses That Relate to Any Horizontal (M or A)'s Increasing Its Participants' Profits by Predatorily Inducing an Established Rival to Change the Product-Space Location of an Existing Investment or by Predatorily Inducing an Established Rival or Potential Entrant to Change the Product-Space Location of a New Investment (When the Location-Change Does Not Increase Economic Efficiency)

The parenthetical at the end of this subsection's heading is redundant in that firm-efforts to induce rivals to make economically-efficient changes in the product-space location of one or more of their investments are not "predatory" in the sense in which I have defined this term (regardless of whether the economic efficiency of the induced rival-investment product-space-location change depends on the inducer's changing the product-space location of one or more of its own investments). Obviously, if it were costless to do so, firms would find it profitable to induce rivals to relocate current investments or change the location of future investments to product-space locations that result in the relocated investment's being less competitive with the inducing firm's investments. Firms that are attempting to induce a rival to relocate an existing or planned investment to a location that makes it less competitive with the inducing firm's projects will do so by threatening to charge inherently-unprofitably-low prices to the buyers its target would be privately-best-placed to supply if the target did not change the location of its extant or planned investment and/or by threatening to place inherently-unprofitable advertizements that are aimed at the target's customers. Horizontal (M&A)s can increase the profits their participants can earn by engaging in this types of predation in all the ways in which such (M&A)s can increase the profits their participants can realize by deterring rivals from making any new investment.

To save space, I will not write separate subsections on the relevance of a horizontal (M or A)'s increasing its participants' profits in this way to the (M or A)'s economic efficiency, liberal-moral-rights-violativeness, or impact on the moral good. Although I see no reason to believe that the investment-locations that horizontal (M&A)s that increase the amount of this type of predation their participants practice cause to be selected will tend to be either more or less economically efficient than the investment-locations that such horizontal ((M&A)s cause to be "rejected" to the extent that they lead to the practice of additional predation of this kind, the fact that a horizontal (M or A) increases the amount of such predation its participants practice disfavors the (M or A)'s economic efficiency (1) because the communication of the associated threats is allocative-transaction-costly, (2) because the carrying out of any such threats is economically inefficient (in that predatory price-cuts are allocative-transaction-costly to execute, lead directly to intra-ARDEPPS UO-to-UO misallocation, and may lead [the target]/[the perpetrator] to engage in defensive /further-offensive retaliation that is misallocative and in that inherently-unprofitable advertizing will tend to be misallocative even if it does not convey inaccurate or misleading information), and (3) because moving the product-space location of an existing investment and perhaps of a planned investment is allocative-transaction-costly.

I do think that the practice of this type of predation violates the liberal moral rights of its target and of the buyers on whom it imposes equivalent-dollar losses. For this reason, I believe that the fact that a horizontal (M or A) increases the extent to which its participants engage in this type of predation will render the (M or A) liberal-moral-rights-violative if (1) one or more participants would not have perceived the (M or A) to be at least normally profitable *ex ante* had the participant not believed it would or might increase its profits in this way or (2) one or more participants believed *ex ante* that the (M or A) would or might increase the amount of profits it could realize by practicing this type of predation and intended to take advantage of any such opportunity the (M or A) created. My assessment of the relevance of a horizontal (M or A)'s increasing the amount of this type of predation its participants practice to the (M or A)'s impact on total utility or on the various non-utilitarian-egalitarian conceptions of the moral good reflects in part my inability to predict whether such predation will tend to increase or decrease material inequality: such predation will confer equivalent-dollar gains on the shareholders/creditors/managers/employees of the predators, will impose equivalent-dollar losses on their counterparts for the targets of predation, and will have an uncertain net impact on the relevant ARDEPPS' buyers (will impose equivalent-dollar losses on the buyers that would have benefited from the rejected location-choice and confer equivalent-dollar gains on the buyers that benefited from the induced location-choice), and since there is no reason to believe that the predators' shareholders/creditors/managers/employees will be materially-better-off or materially-worse-off than their counterparts for the targets or that the benefited buyers will be materially-better-off or materially-worse-off than the harmed buyers, my best guess is that across all instances the distributive impact of such predation will be neither desirable nor undesirable from the perspective of any non-utilitarian-egalitarian conception of the moral good. However, the combination of the same distributive-desirability conclusion and my previous conclusion that this type of predation is economically inefficient implies that a horizontal (M or A)'s increasing the amount of this type of predation its participants practice favors the conclusion that the (M or A) in question will tend to decrease total utility and therefore disserve the instantiation of both the utilitarian conception of the moral good and any mixed-egalitarian conception of the moral good that places a positive value on total utility.

11.2.14 Analyses That Relate to Any Horizontal (M or A)'s Increasing Its Participants' Profits by Creating a Resulting Firm That Is Better Able Than the Participants Would Have Been to Increase Their and Their Mutual Rivals' Across-the Board HNOPs by Altering the Sequence in Which They and Their Mutual Rivals Announce and "Lock Themselves Into" Their Prices

Some horizontal (M or A)s create resulting firms whose size and prominence enables them to increase the extent to which their ARDEPPS' sellers announce their prices and lock themselves into their announced prices in an order that maximizes or at least increases the height of their HNOP arrays. To the extent that a horizontal (M or A) has this effect, it will on this account yield its participants (and their mutual rivals) profits. When the relevant ARDEPPS' investments are QV investments, a horizontal (M or A)'s increasing its participants' profits in this way will clearly tend to make it less economically efficient than it would otherwise have been because the associated increase in the prices charged by the ARDEPPS' sellers will cause economic inefficiency not only by increasing poverty and material inequality but also by increasing the ARDEPPS' and the economy's equilibrium-QV-investment quantity (if as seems likely it is correct to assume that the relevant society's government has not adopted policies to prevent its continuing to devote too many resources to QV-investment creation from the perspective of economic efficiency). (I acknowledge that these economic-efficiency losses will be offset to the extent that the increase in the relevant sellers' HNOPs deters them from practicing contrived-oligopolistic pricing, but I believe that the associated economic-efficiency gains will rarely if ever be larger than the previously-referenced economic-efficiency losses in part because the decrease in COMs will rarely be larger than the increases in HNOPs or [HNOPs + NOMs].) Admittedly, the associated increases in the prices charged by the ARDEPPS' sellers may increase economic efficiency when the investments in the relevant ARDEPPS are investments in PPR by increasing its equilibrium-PPR quantity if the relevant economy devotes too few resources to PPR from the perspective of economic efficiency—indeed, may increase economic efficiency everything considered in such a situation. However, I suspect that the vast majority of horizontal (M&A)s are consummated in ARDEPPSes whose investments are QV investments.

Because I believe that efforts by sellers to increase the prices in their HNOP arrays by controlling the sequence in which they announce their prices are liberal-moral-rights-violative, a horizontal (M or A)'s yielding its participants profits in the way on which this section is focusing will render the (M or A) liberal-moral-rights-violative if the participants know *ex ante* that the (M or A) would enable them to profit in the way in question, regardless of whether the participants' *ex ante* perception that the (M or A) would or might increase their profits in this way critically affected their belief that it would be at least normally profitable.

A horizontal (M or A)'s yielding its participants profits by creating a resulting firm that is able to orchestrate the timing of the relevant ARDEPPS' sellers' announcement of their prices and implementation of those price-announcements so as to increase their HNOP array will cause it to generate a distributive impact that is undesirable from the perspective of all non-utilitarian-egalitarian conceptions of the moral good and from the perspective of utilitarianism except in what I take to be the highly-unusual case in which, taken as classes, the relevant ARDEPPS' buyers are materially-better-off than are its sellers' shareholders/creditors/managers/employees. This conclusion implies that a horizontal (M&A)'s yielding its participants profits in this way will almost always tend to cause it to disserve the instantiation of all non-utilitarian-egalitarian conceptions of the moral good and will also tend to make it disserve the instantiation of the utilitarian conception of the moral good except when (1) the investments of the ARDEPPS of consummation are investments in PPR, (2) the government of the society in question has not prevented its continuing to devote too few resources to PPR-execution from the perspective of economic efficiency, and (3) the increase in economic efficiency the (M or A) generates on this account by increasing the relevant ARDEPPS' and derivatively the economy's equilibrium-PPR-investment quantity is sufficiently large to outweigh from a utilitarian perspective the economic-efficiency losses and utilitarian-distributive-desirability losses it will generate on this account by increasing poverty and material inequality.

11.3 The Economic Efficiency of Particular Horizontal (M or A)s and the Ability of a Liberal-Moral-Rights-Constrained Government to Increase Economic Efficiency by Responding Appropriately to Proposed/Consummated Horizontal (M&A)s

11.3.1 The Economic Efficiency of Particular Horizontal (M&A)s

Section 11.2 argues that individual horizontal (M or A)s can increase economic efficiency in various ways and can decrease economic efficiency in various ways. Thus, Sect. 11.2 argues that individual horizontal (M or A)s can increase economic efficiency *inter alia* in the following specific ways: (1) by generating static marginal-cost efficiencies that are allocative as well as private that increase the economic efficiency of using QV investments that would have been continued to be used in any event, (2) by generating static fixed-cost efficiencies that are allocative as well as private whose generation increases economic efficiency by reducing the allocative cost of renewing or rebuilding a production plant or distributive outlet that would have been renewed or rebuilt in any event or (in some instances) by causing the resulting firm to renew or rebuild a production facility or distributive outlet that the relevant participant would not have renewed or rebuilt, (3) by generating dynamic efficiencies that are allocative as well as private whose generation increase economic efficiency (A) by causing the resulting firm to substitute a more-allocatively-efficient QV investment or PPR project for the less-economically-efficient (QV investment)/(PPR project) that a participant would have created/executed, (B) by causing the resulting firm to (create a more-economically-efficient investment)/(execute a more-economically-efficient PPR project) that deters a less-economically-efficient (QV investment)/(PPR project) that a resulting-firm rival would otherwise have (created/executed), (C) by causing the resulting firm to execute an economically-efficient PPR project whose execution does not deter any resulting-firm rival from executing a PPR project in the ARDEPPS of consummation, or (D) by causing the resulting firm to create a QV investment whose creation does not deter any resulting-firm rival from making a QV investment in the ARDEPPS of consummation when the resulting firm's QV investment was not only profitable but economically efficient ("despite" the fact that its profitability was inflated by the interaction of the relevant economy's relevant Pareto imperfections and other salient parameters), (4) by generating static marginal-cost efficiencies, static fixed-cost efficiencies, and/or dynamic efficiencies that in the instant cases deconcentrate the seller-side of the ARDEPPS of consummation and in so doing reduce the amount of (economically-inefficient) contrived-oligopolistic and predatory conduct in which its sellers engage and the expenditures they made on political parties/campaigns/candidates and government-decision-making-process participation, (5) in some cases, by increasing economic efficiency by reducing poverty and material inequality primarily by conferring equivalent-dollar gains on the buyers in the ARDEPPS of consummation because the equivalent-dollar gains that the various static and dynamic efficiencies the (M or A) generates confer on them by decreasing prices "directly" and (sometimes) by increasing the relevant ARDEPPS' equilibrium-investment quantity exceed the equivalent-dollar losses the (M or A) in question imposes on the ARDEPPS' buyers by freeing the participants from each other's price-competition and investment-competition, creating a resulting firm that engages in more contrived-oligopolistic and predatory conduct than the participants would have done, and increasing the amount of such conduct in which the resulting firm's rivals engage, (6) in some cases, by decreasing equilibrium investment in the ARDEPPS of consummation when that ARDEPPS' investments are QV investments by freeing the participants from each other's investment-competition or creating a situation in which the resulting firm and a rival that would otherwise have invested confront each other with critical natural-oligopolistic investment-disincentives, (7) by increasing equilibrium PPR investment in the ARDEPPS of consummation and the economy by increasing that quantity in the ARDEPPS of consummation more by increasing the prices that would be charged for the ARDEPPS' production-process discoveries at various relevant ARDEPPS-PPR quantities than it decreases that quantity by reducing the intensity of the relevant ARDEPPS' PPR competition (primarily by freeing its participants from each other's investment-competition but also in some instances by creating a resulting firm that confronts its rivals with higher retaliation barriers to investment than the participants would have erected or creating a resulting firm that faces critical natural-oligopolistic investment-disincentives because it confronts a rival that would otherwise have invested with critical natural-oligopolistic investment-disincentives), and (9) when one of the participants is a small firm (especially when its owner/manager has left a managerial position in a well-established firm to start up a new company), by increasing economic efficiency in various ways by increasing the number of start-ups that are created by increasing the incentives individuals have to create start-ups by improving the terms on which they can sell up when they want to liquidate their assets and retire from management.

Section 11.2 also argues that individual (M or A)'s can decrease economic efficiency *inter alia* in the following specific ways: (1) by increasing the amount of contrived-oligopolistic pricing in which the resulting firm's rivals engage (which pricing would be allocatively inefficient if one ignored its impact on the relevant ARDEPPS' equilibrium-investment quantity because it is allocative-transaction-costly and because the non-cooperative responses, offensive retaliation, and defensive retaliation it generates reduce economic efficiency not only because they are allocative-transaction-costly but also because they yield intra-ARDEPPS UO-to-UO misallocation), (2) by increasing equilibrium QV investment in the ARDEPPS of consummation and derivatively in the economy (by increasing the prices that are charged for the ARDEPPS of consummation's products at relevant ARDEPPS-QV-investment quantities by raising the participants' OCAs by freeing them from each other's price-competition and relatedly by increasing the participants' NOMs) when its investments are QV investments and the relevant society's government has not prevented its continuing to devote too many resources from the perspective of economic efficiency to QV-investment creation, (3) by creating a resulting firm that finds it profitable to make a QV investment whose profitability has been critically inflated by the interaction of the economy's relevant Pareto imperfections, (4) by increasing the amount of economically-inefficient predation that is practiced in the ARDEPPS of consummation (I acknowledge that predation may be economically efficient if it deters the creation of a QV investment that would have increased the relevant ARDEPPS' equilibrium-QV-investment quantity), (5) by increasing poverty and material inequality (primarily as a result of its imposing equivalent-dollar losses on the relevant ARDEPPS' buyers and hence the amount of [poverty/material-inequality]-generated economic inefficiency the relevant economy contains), (6) by increasing the concentration of the seller-side of the ARDEPPS of consummation and hence the amount of (economic-inefficiency generating) expenditures its sellers make on political parties/campaigns/candidates and government-decision-making-process participation, (7) in some instances, by enabling their participants to secure tax benefits whose generation reduces economic efficiency by causing the government to make economically-inefficient decisions to make up the tax-revenue loss or to offset the loss in its revenues by canceling expenditures that would be economically efficient if their financing would not decrease economic efficiency, and (8) by generating the allocative transaction costs of negotiating the (M or A)s and finalizing the (M or A)-agreement.

Sections 11.2 also analyzes in some detail the factors that determine the amount by which an individual (M or A) will increase or decrease economic efficiency in each of the ways in which such an (M or A) can do so. I will not attempt to provide even a summary account of these analyses here. Instead, I will simply assert that a full account would reveal that some horizontal (M or A)s increase economic efficiency and that some decrease economic efficiency.

11.3.2 The Ability of a Liberal-Moral-Rights-Constrained Government to Increase Economic Efficiency by Responding in Appropriate Ways to Proposed/Consummated Horizontal (M&A)s

I will proceed on the assumptions (1) that the governments whose "abilities" to increase economic efficiency are under consideration govern liberal-moral-rights-based societies and that their choices are therefore constrained by the liberal moral rights of the members of their respective societies and (2) that liberalism implies the moral-rights-violativeness of any government's (A) coercing confessions, (B) obtaining evidence through "unreasonable" searches and seizures, (C) relying on evidence provided by non-government actors who secured it in some liberal-moral-rights-violative way, (D) using evidence in negotiations or adjudicative proceedings that has been obtained in a way that is liberal-moral-rights-violative, (E) failing to secure adequate legal representation for defendants in civil/criminal cases both in pre-trial interactions and in actual trials if the defendant cannot pay for such legal counsel, (F) reducing the standard of proof that must be satisfied to establish civil liability below proof by a preponderance of the evidence, (G) reducing the standard of proof that must be satisfied to establish criminal guilt below proof beyond a reasonable doubt (a concept that admittedly requires some operationalization), (H) possibly, depriving a defendant in a civil/criminal case of the right to have (civil liability)/guilt determined by a set of decision-makers that contains at least a minimum number of members and/or a minimum number or percentage of non-government officials (jurors), (I) creating a regime in which a defendant in a civil/criminal case can be found liable/guilty if the percentage of the decision-makers that vote for liability/guilt falls below some admittedly-difficult-to-specify number, (J) allowing defendants who have been found not liable/guilty to be retried, (K) imposing "costs" on defendants in civil/criminal cases who (that) have been found liable/guilty (civil fines, criminal fines, custodial sentences, and/or non-custodial restrictions or obligations) whose burdensomeness exceeds the seriousness of the wrongdoing for which the defendant has been convicted, (L) relatedly, negotiating civil settlements and criminal plea-deals whose burdensomeness exceeds the (seriousness of the alleged wrongdoing) *times* (the probability of guilt)—I recognize I am entering deep waters, etc.

What would be the most-allocatively-efficient way for a government subject to liberal-moral-rights constraints to respond to horizontal (M&A)s? I will make three sets of points related to this issue.

The first set contains nine broad, preliminary points. First, the most-allocatively-efficient response for such a government to make to horizontal (M or A)s will depend not only on the economic efficiency of the horizontal (M or A)s it allows and prohibits but also on the economic efficiency of the horizontal (M or A)s whose consummations the government's choices deter, the impact of the government's decisions on allocative risk costs, and the allocative cost of devising and implementing the government's approach to horizontal (M&A)s—the allocative cost of the resources devoted to these tasks and the allocative cost of financing the creation and implementation of the government's response. Second, I am certain that it will be TBLE for such a government to respond to horizontal (M&A)s selectively—that is, it will not be TBLE for the government of such a society to prohibit or allow all such (M&A)s, but (with three qualifications to be delineated below) it will be TBLE for the government of such a society to allow all such (M&A)s its antitrust-policy-implementation authority deems to be economically efficient and to prohibit all such (M&A)s its antitrust-policy-implementation authority deems to be economically inefficient. Third, a point that is a clarification of the second point. The clarification relates to whether the economic efficiency of a proposed horizontal (M or A) is to be determined by comparing the state of the world its consummation would produce with (1) the state of the world that would prevail if the prohibition of the proposed (M or A) would induce the participants to do nothing instead in the relevant ARDEPPS or (2) the state of the world that would prevail if the participants would respond to the prohibition of the proposed (M or A) by doing something else in the relevant ARDEPPS—for example, by consummating an alternative horizontal (M or A) in that ARDEPPS or making one or more additional investments on their own in that ARDEPPS. In my judgment, for three reasons, it will be TBLE for the government of such a society to assess the economic efficiency of a proposed horizontal (M or A) on the assumption that its prohibition would induce its proposers to do nothing in response in the relevant prohibition: (1) identifying merger/acquisition partners and negotiating merger/acquisition deals is allocative-costly so that, even if the proposers of a horizontal (M or A) would respond to its prohibition by making a more-economically-efficient move, the prohibition might on this account reduce economic efficiency; (2) the rejection of the "proponents-do-nothing-instead" baseline for economic-efficiency prediction in favor of the "move-the-participants-would-make-instead" baseline would deter some potential participants in economically-efficient horizontal (M or A)s from trying to consummate such (M or A)s; and (3) it is doubtful that the antitrust-policy-enforcement authorities of a liberal-moral-rights-based society will be able to identify the move (if any) that the proposers of a prohibited horizontal (M or A) would substitute for it and assess the economic efficiency of that alternative move sufficiently accurately or allocative-cheaply for the use of this alternative baseline to be TBLE. Fourth, the first qualification to the second introductory point: in some cases, the government of a liberal-moral-rights-based society may also be able to increase the *ex ante* allocative efficiency of its response to horizontal (M&A)s by conditioning its approval of proposed/consummated horizontal (M or A)s on the participants' agreeing to reduce the extent to which the (M or A) would reduce price-competition by divesting some of the participants'/(resulting firm's) investments (for example, to put into independent ownership one of any pair of investments the participants/[resulting firm] owned that were highly competitive with each other), though this response has some allocative-efficiency costs—the allocative transaction cost of the divestiture and any economic-efficiency loss that is generated because the buyer of the divested investment will operate it less proficiently than the resulting firm would have done. Fifth, the second qualification to the second introductory point: a liberal-moral-rights-constrained government may also be able to increase economic efficiency by responding to proposed or consummated horizontal (M&A)s by prohibiting resulting firms from raising the prices of the participants' products or services for a specified period of time (or by limiting the resulting firm to price-increases on these products equal to increases in their marginal costs that the resulting firm should not have prevented and/or to increases in the value of the "participants' products" that resulted from the resulting firm's increasing their quality [including their reliability]). (I acknowledge that at least three allocative-efficiency objections can be made to government's including such price-regulations in its response to horizontal [M&A]s: [1] the price-regulations will be allocative-transaction-costly to implement; [2] the price-regulations may decrease economic efficiency by deterring the resulting firm from making economically-efficient improvements in participant-products, given the difficulty of proving the product-improvement and its value to buyers; and [3] prospective horizontal-[M&A] proposers may defeat such price-regulations by increasing their prices to higher-than-otherwise-profit-maximizing levels before they propose the relevant [M or A] to government authorities or consummate it and in so doing generate various types of economic inefficiency.) (Although a liberal-moral-rights-constrained government might also be able to increase economic efficiency by including in its response to proposed or consummated horizontal [M&A]s regulations of the resulting firm's investment-decisions—for example, prohibitions of the resulting firm's or any of its rivals' making QV investments in the ARDEPPS of consummation for some period of time, constraints that limit the resulting firm to making only those QV investments that a specified regulatory authority operating in a specified way concludes are *ex ante* economically efficient, or requirements that the resulting firm execute at least some specified amount of PPR projects, I doubt that it will in practice be *ex ante* economically efficient for a government to include such prohibitions and positive requirements in its response to horizontal [M&A]s in part because of the inevitable arbitrariness of the definition of the relevant ARDEPPS and in part because of the difficulty of determining whether any proposed QV investment would be sufficiently more economically efficient than the relevant ARDEPPS' existing QV investments to be economically efficient despite the fact that ARDEPPS-investment was too high from the perspective of economic efficiency.) Sixth, the third qualification to the second introductory point: although I have substantial doubts about whether this implementation-technique will ever be TBLE, it may sometimes be TBLE for an antitrust-policy-implementation authority to allow horizontal-(M or A) proposers to consummate their proposed (M or A) only if they agree to pay a specified fee for the right to do so that is calculated to assure that the weighted-average-expected economic-efficiency impact of the paid-for (M or A) is positive or at least not negative—that the economic-efficiency gain the government's receipt of the payment is expected to yield on the weighted average will exceed any economic-efficiency loss the (M or A) would be expected on the weighted average to yield on its own. This proposal might be TBLE to implement if (1) horizontal (M&A)s that generate no static marginal cost, static fixed cost, or dynamic efficiencies will decrease economic efficiency, (2) the relevant antitrust-policy-enforcement authority will be able to predict with acceptable accuracy at non-prohibitive allocative cost the amount of profits and the amount of economic inefficiency a specific horizontal (M or A) would generate if it yielded no such efficiencies, (3) the static-marginal-cost, static-fixed-cost, and dynamic efficiencies a horizontal (M or A) generates will increase both the economic efficiency of the (M or A) in question and the profits it yields its participants, (4) the antitrust-policy-enforcement authorities will be able to determine with acceptable accuracy at non-prohibitive allocative cost the contributions that any static-marginal-cost, static-fixed-cost, and dynamic efficiencies of given magnitudes will make to the (M or A)'s economic efficiency and profit-yield, but (5) the antitrust-policy-enforcement authorities cannot determine with acceptable accuracy or at non-prohibitive cost the magnitudes of the static-marginal-cost, static-fixed-cost, or dynamic efficiencies that a proposed horizontal (M or A) would generate or perhaps that a consummated horizontal (M or A) did generate. Although I suspect that such an approach will be rendered third-best-allocatively-inefficient by the complexities associated with the fact that the relationship between the magnitudes of each of the three types of efficiencies I distinguished on the one hand and their respective impacts on the (M or A)'s economic efficiency and its participants' profits on the other differ from category of efficiency to category of efficiency, it is conceivable that it would be TBLE for an antitrust-policy-enforcement authority to condition its permission for a horizontal (M or A)'s consummation on the participants' paying a fee that they would be willing to pay (given the profits the [M or A] would yield them if it yielded no such efficiencies and the profits it would yield them by generating the efficiencies in question) only if those efficiencies were sufficiently large to render the (M or A) economically efficient or cause the (M or A) to reduce economic efficiency by less than the payment would increase economic efficiency by enabling the government to make economically-efficient expenditures or obviating the government's making economically-inefficient tax, price-of-government-supplied-goods-and-services, or money-printing decisions to finance its operations. If this government response was TBLE, its third-best allocative efficiency would be attributable to its obviating the enforcement authority's estimating the magnitudes of the efficiencies the (M or A) would generate. A variant of this policy-response that might be more likely to be TBLE would be one in which the antitrust-enforcement authority would condition its permission for any horizontal-(M or A)'s consummation on the resulting firm's paying a fine if post-consummation evidence revealed that the (M or A) did not yield sufficient efficiencies to be economically efficient, which fine would be set to render *ex ante* unprofitable any horizontal (M or A) that would be economically inefficient. This variant is more likely to be TBLE because the enforcement authorities will be more able to ascertain the efficiencies a horizontal (M or A) generate after it was consummated than to predict the efficiencies a proposed horizontal (M or A) will generate. Seventh, it will never or virtually never be TBLE for an antitrust-policy-implementation authority to determine as accurately as it can whether a particular determinant of the economic efficiency of a relevant horizontal (M or A) is or is not present (whether, for example, a proposed horizontal [M or A] will generate efficiencies of various kinds, whether the participants in a proposed horizontal [M or A] confronted each other with natural-oligopolistic investment-disincentives when operating as separate entities, whether a resulting firm's decision not to make an investment a participant would have made will result in a mutual rival of the participants' making an investment) or to estimate as accurately as it can the magnitudes of any parameter whose size is relevant to the economic efficiency of a horizontal (M or A). Eighth, if the government of the relevant society is operating as economic-efficiently as it can, given the liberal-moral-rights constraints on its decision-making, its antitrust-policy-implementation authorities will have at their disposal a great deal of information that bears on the economic efficiency of any horizontal (M or A)—for example, information about the formulas for the aggregate distortion in the profits yielded by exemplars of many categories of resource allocations whose magnitudes will be affected by any horizontal (M or A) and information about the pre-(M or A) magnitudes of the parameters in those formulas (primarily Pareto imperfections but also other factors). Ninth, in some cases, it will be TBLE for antitrust-policy-implementation authorities to base their prediction/post-diction of the economic efficiency of particular proposed/consummated horizontal (M or A)s on their assessments/estimates of only some of the possibilities/parameters that are relevant to the horizontal (M or A)'s economic efficiency: thus, if the antitrust-policy-implementation authority is confident that the proposers of a horizontal (M or A) are rarely privately-uniquely-equal-best-placed to supply given buyers, are better-placed than those suppliers' privately-third-placed suppliers by only small amounts when the participants are privately-uniquely-equal-best-placed, are rarely respectively privately-best-placed and privately-second-placed to supply given buyers and in those cases in which they are respectively privately-best-placed and privately-second-placed the privately-second-placed proposer is only slightly privately-better-placed than the relevant buyers' privately-third-placed supplier and that the (M or A) will generate substantial static and dynamic efficiencies, it may well be TBLE for the authorities not to consider the other possibilities and parameters that will affect the economic efficiency of the proposed (M or A), though I acknowledge that when a partial analysis will enable the authorities to determine that a consummated (M or A) was economically inefficient, the authorities might have to collect additional information to determine the sanctions whose imposition would be TBLE as well as to determine the sanctions that would deter liberal-moral-rights-violative horizontal (M&A)s, the damages that the victims of liberal-moral-rights-violating horizontal M&A)s are entitled to recover, and the sanctions that would best instantiate a relevant conception of the moral good.

The second set of points I will make at this juncture is more directly connected to the preceding analyses of the various ways in which horizontal (M&A)s can increase and decrease economic efficiency and the determinants of the extent to which particular horizontal (M or A)s will increase or decrease economic efficiency in each of these ways. More specifically, this set of points is actually a list of the facts that it would be economically efficient for an economic-efficiency analyst to ascertain for the purpose of predicting the economic efficiency of a proposed horizontal (M or A) if the analyst could ascertain these facts perfectly accurately at no allocative cost. This list would include (1) the factors that would determine the impact of the (M or A) on its participants' OCAs if the (M or A) would generate no relevant efficiencies (primarily by freeing the participants from each other's price-competition), (2) the factors that would determine the impact of the (M or A) on the participants' mutual rivals' OCAs if the horizontal (M or A) generated no relevant efficiencies, (3) the factors that would determine the horizontal (M or A)'s impact on the participants' NOMs if the (M or A) generated no relevant efficiencies, (4) the factors that would determine the horizontal (M or A)'s impact on the participants' mutual rivals' NOMs if the (M or A) generates no relevant efficiencies, (5) the factors that determine the amount of economic inefficiency that any horizontal (M or A) that yields no relevant efficiencies, does not affect the amount of contrived-oligopolistic pricing that is practiced, and does not affect equilibrium investment in the ARDEPPS of consummation would generate by increasing prices and derivatively poverty and material inequality, (6) the factors that would determine any horizontal (M or A)'s impact on the participants' COMs if the (M or A) generated no relevant efficiencies, (7) the factors that would determine a horizontal (M or A)'s impact on the COMs of the participants' mutual rivals if the (M or A) would generate no relevant efficiencies, (8) the factors that would determine the economic-inefficiency impact that any (M or A) would have if it did not generate any relevant efficiencies by altering the amount of contrived-oligopolistic pricing that is practiced, which relate to the allocative-transaction-costliness of such contrivance, the possibility that it might lead to retaliation that causes intra-ARDEPPS UO-to-UO misallocation, and the possibility that it may increase poverty and material inequality (which cause economic inefficiency), (9) the factors that determine the impact that a horizontal (M or A) that generates no relevant efficiencies would have on the amount of predatory pricing the participants and their mutual rivals practice and the factors that determine the amount of economic inefficiency predatory pricing would generate if it did not affect the relevant ARDEPPS' equilibrium-investment quantity, (10) the magnitudes of the static-marginal-cost, static-fixed-cost, and dynamic efficiencies a horizontal (M or A) under scrutiny would generate, (11) the factors that determine the relationship between the profit-yields and the economic-efficiency gains that are generated respectively by the static-marginal-cost and static-fixed-cost efficiencies a horizontal (M or A) generates, (12) the factors that would determine the relationship between the profit-yield and economic-efficiency gain the dynamic efficiencies a horizontal (M or A) would generate if those efficiencies simply caused the resulting firm to substitute more-economically-efficient for less-economically-efficient investment-renewals or new investments, (13) the factors that determine whether any dynamic efficiencies a horizontal (M or A) generates will cause the resulting firm or one of its rivals to increase the equilibrium-investment quantity of the ARDEPPS of consummation by affecting the intensity of its price-competition and investment-competition or will generate a reduction in the equilibrium-investment quantity of the ARDEPPS of consummation (in the same ways), (14) the factors that determine the impact that a horizontal (M or A) has on equilibrium investment in the ARDEPPS of consummation—*inter alia*, the factors that influence the (M or A)'s impact on prices at the pre-(M or A) equilibrium-investment quantity, the factors that influence the (M or A)'s impact on the incidence of predation in the ARDEPPS of consummation, the factors that influence the impact of predation in the relevant ARDEPPS on its equilibrium-investment quantity, the magnitudes of the various kinds of efficiencies the (M or A) generates, the factors that influence the impact of such efficiencies on the equilibrium-investment quantity of the ARDEPPS of consummation, (15) the factors that influence the loss that would have been generated post-(M or A) by the successive investments the (M or A) would deter or cause to be withdrawn and the factors that determine the profits that would be yielded by the successive investments the (M or A) would elicit, (16) the factors that determine the aggregate distortion in the profits (losses) that would have been yielded by the successive investments the (M or A) would deter and the profits that would be yielded by the successive investments the (M or A) would elicit—whether the investments in question are QV investments or investments in PPR, the alternative uses to which the resources that would have been devoted to a deterred investment would be allocated or the alternative uses from which the resources that were devoted to an elicited investment were withdrawn, and the post-(M or A) magnitudes of the parameters in the formula for the aggregate distortion in the profits (losses) that would have been yielded by the deterred investment(s) or would be yielded by the elicited investment(s), (17) the tax-losses the (M or A) would enable the resulting firm to use that a participant could not have used and the factors that determine the amount of economic inefficiency the associated loss of revenue to the government generates (by causing the government to forego economically-efficient expenditures or inducing the government to make up the loss of tax revenues by levying [additional] misallocative taxes, instituting economically-inefficient price-increases on goods or services it sells to the public, and/or causing [allocative-costly] inflation by printing money), and (18) the factors that determine the extent to which the horizontal (M or A) in question would increase the concentration of the seller-side of the ARDEPPS of consummation, the factors that determine the amount that any such increase in seller-concentration will raise the ARDEPPS' sellers' expenditures on political parties/campaigns/candidates and government-decision-making-process participation, and the factors that determine the amount by which the relevant increases in such seller-expenditures will increase the economic inefficiency of government decisions. I could lengthen this list both by making it address additional possibilities and by delineating the specific members of various sets of factors it references. But enough is enough. *Dayeinu.*

The third set of points relates to the methods that will be TBLE for the government of a liberal-moral-rights-based society to use to collect the various pieces of information that bear on the economic efficiency of a proposed or consummated horizontal (M or A). I will make two sets of three points.

The first three points relate to information that is relevant to the economic efficiency of a proposed or consummated horizontal (M or A) that it will almost certainly not be TBLE to obtain from the proponents of any horizontal (M or A). The first point is that this category of information includes information on the Pareto imperfections and other parameters that determine the distortion in the profits yielded by the various resource allocations to the ARDEPPS of consummation that a relevant horizontal (M or A) could elicit or deter. The second point is that—with two exceptions—this category of information also includes information about the alternative uses from which any resources the (M or A) causes to be used in some way in the ARDEPPS of consummation would be withdrawn and information about the alternative uses to which any resources the (M or A) causes not to be used in the ARDEPPS of consummation will be devoted: the exceptions are that it may well be TBLE for an antitrust-policy-implementation authority to obtain information from horizontal-merger proponents of the uses from which resources the resulting firm would devote to creating an investment would be withdrawn when the participants wanted to consummate the (M or A) at least in part to substitute a resulting-firm investment either for a different investment a participant would have made or for an investment a mutual rival of the participants would have made. The second point is that—with the just-referenced exceptions—the antitrust-policy-enforcement authority will have to obtain information on these factors by doing new research itself, by hiring outside experts to do the research, by using the results of research already done by academic economists by think-tanks (non-university research-organizations), or by the government. The third point in this set is that it will almost certainly be TBLE for the government of a liberal-moral-rights-based society to collect information on the Pareto imperfections the economy contains and on other parameters whose magnitudes affect the economic efficiency of various government decisions on a continuous, systematic basis: there are economies of scale in collecting such information, and most exemplars of such information are relevant to the economic efficiency of a wide variety of government and non-government decisions (as well as to those decisions' liberal-moral-rights-violativeness and impacts on the instantiation of various egalitarian conceptions of the moral good).

The second set of three points relates to information that could be supplied by the horizontal-(M or A) proposers/participants or by their managers employees, customers, and/or rivals. First, it may well be TBLE for the government of a liberal-moral-rights-based society to secure relevant information from relevant employees or managers by offering them immunity or positive rewards and from relevant buyers or rivals by offering them monetary rewards, by giving them a right to obtain legal redress for any losses that consummated illegal horizontal (M or A)s imposed on them, and by providing them with assistance in any such litigation or non-litigative claiming-efforts (even though the provisions of some such incentives may taint the evidence such individuals provide). Second, in more cases than many suppose, the antitrust-policy-enforcement authority will be able to obtain such information by subpoenaing or searching for e-mails, company-meeting minutes, company reports, and notes that company employees or managers kept of communications or meetings. Third, finally, and probably most importantly, it will almost certainly be TBLE for the antitrust-policy-implementation authority of a liberal-moral-rights-based society to secure such information from horizontal-(M or A) proposers by creating a "regulatory" regime in which significant horizontal (M or A)s will be allowed only if approved by the authority or a reviewing court through a process that requires horizontal-(M or A) proposers to supply the authority with the information at their disposal that bears on their proposed horizontal (M or A)'s economic efficiency.[9]

11.4 The Liberal-Moral-Rights-Violativeness of Horizontal (M&A)s and the Ability of a Government to Instantiate Its Liberal Justice-Commitments by Responding Appropriately to Horizontal (M&A)s

11.4.1 The Liberal-Moral-Rights-Violativeness of Horizontal (M&A)s

A horizontal (M or A) will be liberal-moral-rights-violative when either or both of two sets of conditions are fulfilled: (1) when a participant's *ex ante* perception that the (M or A) was at least normally profitable was critically affected by its belief that the (M or A) would or might increase its profits (A) by increasing the participant's OCAs by freeing it and its fellow-participant(s) from the price-competition each would otherwise wage against the other(s), (B) by increasing the NOMs that it and its fellow-participant(s) obtain, (C) by increasing the COMs it and its fellow-participant(s) obtain, (D) by increasing the profits it and its fellow-participant(s) obtain by engaging in other types of contrived-oligopolistic conduct, (E) by increasing the profits it and its fellow-participant(s) obtain by engaging in predatory conduct of all types, and (F) by increasing its and its fellow-participant's (or its fellow-participants') profits by freeing them from each other's investment-competition and thereby increasing the resulting firm's profits above those the participants would have realized by creating a resulting firm that can make no investment when the participants would have made one or more investments or that can make one or more investments when the participants would have made more investments and/or (2) when one or more participants believed *ex ante* that the horizontal (M or A) would create a resulting firm that could profit more by engaging in natural-oligopolistic pricing, contrived-oligopolistic conduct of one or more types, or predatory conduct of one or more types and intended *ex ante* that the resulting firm would take advantage of the opportunities the (M or A) would create for it to profit by engaging in such liberal-moral-rights-violative conduct. I am not able to make a useful estimate of the percentage of horizontal (M&A)s that would be proposed and consummated if they were never prohibited that would be liberal-moral-rights-violative, but I am confident that in the absence of such a prohibition a significant number of proposed and consummated horizontal (M&A)s would be liberal-moral-rights-violative.

11.4.2 The Ability of a Liberal-Moral-Rights-Constrained Government to Reduce the Liberal-Moral-Rights-Violations Firms Commit When Consummating Horizontal (M&A)s and Operating the Resulting Firms

Liberal-moral-rights-constrained governments clearly would not be able to prevent all liberal-moral-rights-violating horizontal (M&A)s even if their efforts to deter such (M&A)s would not preclude them from securing weightier liberal-moral-rights-related interests by using up resources. It will often not be possible for a liberal-moral-rights-constrained government (or, for that matter, for any government) to prove that a horizontal (M or A)'s participant's *ex ante* perception that it would be at least normally profitable was critically affected by its belief that it would or might yield it profits in one or more of the illicit ways listed in Sect. 11.4.1 and/or that one or more of its participants believed *ex ante* that the (M or A) would increase the profits the resulting firm could realize by engaging in liberal-moral-rights-violative conduct and intended *ex ante* the resulting firm to take advantage of some of the profit-opportunities of these kinds it thought the (M or A) would create. However, governments will sometimes be able to secure sufficient evidence on these issues to win civil or criminal cases against horizontal-(M or A) participants without violating liberal moral rights to deter liberal-moral-rights-violative horizontal (M&A)s by conditioning the right of firms to participate in such (M or A)s on their gaining the approval of an antitrust-policy-implementation authority or reviewing court through a process in which they are required to provide information from which the authority or court could infer that the proposed horizontal (M or A) would be liberal-moral-rights-violative, by securing the testimony of witnesses to whom the government may or may not have offered monetary rewards, immunity from prosecution, or lessened sentences, by obtaining through such individuals or by itself pertinent e-mails, notes of conversations recorded by proposer-employees or proposer-managers, copies of the minutes of proposer-meetings, and proposer-studies, or by collecting relevant information entirely independently. In fact, any government of a liberal-moral-rights-based society has a moral duty to deter liberal-moral-rights-violative horizontal (M&A)s to the maximum extent possible within the constraints liberalism imposes (1) by prohibiting liberal-moral-rights-violative (M&A)s, (2) by authorizing the imposition of civil fines, criminal fines, and custodial and non-custodial non-monetary sentences on convicted wrongdoers, (3) by investigating the liberal-moral-rights-violative character of proposed and consummated horizontal (M&A)s, (4) by negotiating appropriate civil settlements and/or plea-deals, (5) by trying relevant cases appropriately assiduously and making appropriate sentencing recommendations, (6) by providing victims of liberal-moral-rights-violative horizontal (M&A)s the right to obtain legal redress, and (7) when needed, by providing assistance to victims who are entitled to obtain legal redress.

11.5 The Impact of Horizontal (M&A)s on the Instantiation of the Utilitarian and Non-Utilitarian-Egalitarian Conceptions of the Moral Good and the Ability of Liberal-Moral-Rights-Constrained Governments to Instantiate These Various Egalitarian Conceptions of the Moral Good by Responding Appropriately to Proposed and Consummated Horizontal (M&A)s

11.5.1 The Impact of Horizontal (M&A)s on the Instantiation of the Utilitarian and Non-Utilitarian-Egalitarian Conceptions of the Moral Good

Some horizontal (M&A)s will increase total utility (1) by increasing economic efficiency and increasing material equality, (2) by increasing economic efficiency and having no impact on material inequality, (3) by increasing economic efficiency sufficiently for this effect to outweigh from the perspective of utilitarianism their decreasing material equality, (4) by increasing material equality and having no impact on economic efficiency, or (5) by increasing material equality sufficiently to outweigh from the perspective of utilitarianism their decreasing economic efficiency. Some horizontal (M&A)s will decrease total utility (1) by decreasing economic efficiency and decreasing material equality, (2) by decreasing economic efficiency and having no effect on material equality, (3) by decreasing economic efficiency and increasing material equality insufficiently for the latter impact to outweigh from the perspective of utilitarianism their decreasing economic efficiency, (4) by decreasing material equality and having no impact on economic efficiency, or (5) by decreasing material equality sufficiently for this impact to outweigh from the perspective of utilitarianism their increasing economic efficiency. Some horizontal (M or A)s will instantiate the various non-utilitarian-egalitarian conceptions of the moral good by increasing material equality, and some will disserve the instantiation of the various non-utilitarian-egalitarian conceptions of the moral good by decreasing material equality.

11.5.2 The Ability of a Liberal-Moral-Rights-Constrained Government to Serve the Instantiation of the Utilitarian and Non-Utilitarian-Egalitarian Conceptions of the Moral Good by Responding Appropriately to Proposed and Consummated Horizontal (M&A)s

I have explained the complexity and by implication the high allocative cost of predicting/post-dicting the impact of a proposed/consummated horizontal (M or A) on economic efficiency and material equality. Nevertheless, I am convinced that even a liberal-moral-rights-constrained government will be able to respond to proposed and consummated horizontal (M&A)s in ways that will increase total utility and/or instantiate the various non-utilitarian-egalitarian conceptions of the morel good. At the most abstract level, the responses that would achieve these goals would prohibit those horizontal (M&A)s whose prohibition would disserve the referenced conceptions of the moral good and implement those prohibitions in a way that would instantiate the relevant conception of the moral good, taking into account the allocative cost and/or distributive impact of the public financing and execution of the relevant implementation-techniques, The more concrete moral-good-promoting responses would include (1) conditioning firms' right to consummate a horizontal (M or A) on their gaining the approval of an antitrust-policy-implementing authority or reviewing court through a process that requires the (M or A)-proposers to supply information that bears on their proposed (M or A)'s impacts on economic efficiency and material equality, (2) eliciting relevant information in various ways from the proposers' employees, managers, rivals, suppliers, (3) systematically collecting information on the facts that affect the impacts of particular horizontal (M&A)s on economic efficiency and material inequality, (4) analyzing the impacts of particular proposed/consummated horizontal (M&A)s on economic efficiency and material equality, (5) devoting resources to analyzing the implications of the preceding predictions for the impact of the horizontal (M or A) in question on total utility or material equality, (6) prohibiting the consummation or continuation of horizontal (M&A)s that the government concludes will reduce total utility or disserve the instantiation of non-utilitarian-egalitarian conceptions of the moral good, perhaps, (7) conditioning the permission to participate in or continue a horizontal (M or A) on the participants' agreeing not to raise their products' prices for a period of time after the consummation of the (M or A) except to the extent that any price-increase was warranted by an increase in the marginal cost of producing the good in question that the resulting firm should not have prevented and/or by an increase in the dollar-value of the relevant "participant-product" to its prospective buyers attributable to changes the resulting firm made in it, and perhaps (8) conditioning the permission to participate in or continue a horizontal (M or A) on the participants' paying a price whose payment would justify the conclusion that the (M or A)-*plus*-payment package would instantiate the relevant conception of the moral good because the payment would enable the State to make choices that would increase total utility or material equality and the willingness of the participants to make the payment would evidence the (M or A) itself's having an acceptable effect on total utility or material equality.

11.6 Conclusion

I recognize that Chapter 11's policy-analysis of horizontal (M&A)s has been exhausting as well as exhaustive. Fortunately, it will enable me to shorten Chapter 12's and Chapter 14's respective policy-analyses of conglomerate and vertical (M&A)s: These chapters will focus exclusively on the policy-relevant differences between conglomerate and vertical (M&A)s on the one hand and horizontal (M&A)s on the other.

Notes

1. The text makes no reference to the possibility that the static marginal-cost efficiencies a horizontal (M or A) yields may affect economic efficiency by altering equilibrium investment when the investments in the ARDEPPS of consummation are investments in PPR because I do not believe that horizontal (M or A)s will ever reduce the marginal cost of using a PPR investment (of using the production process it discovers).
2. Some explanation is necessary. The static marginal-cost efficiencies a horizontal (M or A) generates will tend to confer equivalent-dollar gains both on the buyers of the participants' products and on the buyers of the products produced by the participants' mutual rivals by reducing the prices charged both for the participants' products and for their mutual rivals' products if the efficiencies did not deter a mutual rival from renewing an investment, deter a potential competitor or extant participant-rival from making an investment in the ARDEPPS of consummation, or increase the NOMs and COMs the relevant buyers paid. As the text also indicates, there are situations in which the static marginal-cost efficiencies a horizontal (M or A) generates will increase the HNOPs of one or more resulting-firm rivals. For reasons the preceding text explains, if the relevant society has not deterred all contrived-oligopolistic pricing, I think that the static marginal-cost efficiencies a horizontal (M or A) generates will tend to reduce the COMs its participants would have obtained. I acknowledge that, if the relevant society has not deterred all contrived-oligopolistic pricing, the static marginal-cost efficiencies a horizontal (M or A) generates will tend to increase the COMs the participants' mutual rivals obtain (1) by reducing their OCAs and NOMs, (2) by increasing the frequency with which they are privately-second-placed to supply buyers the resulting firm is privately-best-placed to supply above the frequency with which they would have been privately-second-placed to supply buyers a participant would have been privately-best-placed to supply (by increasing the number of buyers the resulting firm is privately-best-paced to supply above the number the participants would have been privately-best-placed to supply), and (3) by increasing their harm-inflicted to loss-incurred ratio for a given amount of harm inflicted on the resulting firm through retaliation for the counterpart ratio for the participants by increasing the resulting firm's OCAs above those of the participants (though these effects will be counteracted by the efficiencies' reducing the number of buyers in relation to which the resulting firm's rivals enjoy OCAs). I also acknowledge that the static marginal-cost efficiencies a horizontal (M or A) generates will tend to inflict equivalent-dollar losses on customers of the participants' mutual rivals to the extent that the efficiencies reduce equilibrium investment in the ARDEPPS of consummation by deterring an extant mutual rival of the participants from renewing a QV investment and/or deterring a potential entrant into or potential investment-expander in the ARDEPPS of consummation respectively from making an investment in that ARDEPPS. Finally, the static marginal-cost efficiencies a horizontal (M or A) generates will tend to reduce the NOMs customers of the resulting firm's rivals pay by reducing those rivals'

OCAs in relation to those buyers in relation to which they continue to enjoy OCAs post-(M or A). Everything considered, I do think that any static marginal-cost efficiencies that horizontal (M or A)s generate will tend to confer equivalent-dollar gains on buyers in the ARDEPPS of consummation.

3. I am not considering at this juncture the profits that the static (private) fixed-cost efficiencies a horizontal (M or A) generates would yield its participants if it made it profitable for the resulting firm to substitute for a QV investment a participant would have renewed a QV investment that would create a product or distributive outlet that was different from the QV investment a participant would have renewed: I am classifying such efficiencies as dynamic efficiencies. I am also ignoring at this juncture the possibility that the decision of one horizontal–(M or A) participant not to continue to use an investment that the resulting firm would continue to use might cause another participant in the horizontal (M or A) in question to make a QV investment in the ARDEPPS of consummation.
4. The relevant variants of liberal-moral-rights-violative conduct clearly include all variants of contrived-oligopolistic and predatory conduct. I also believe that decisions by a firm to make false claims about the value of its product(s) to buyers and possibly not to reveal to buyers negative attributes of its product(s) respectively are and may be liberal-moral-rights-violative and that a horizontal (M or A) may create a resulting firm that can profit more by making such false statements and failing to reveal relevant information to buyers by eliminating as a separate entity a participant that might point out another participant's relevant errors of commission and omission, particularly in situations in which the sellers in the ARDEPPPS of consummation would find it jointly profitable to conceal from the public information about their products' safety and desirability. Although I consider this conclusion to be contestable, I also believe that natural-oligopolstic pricing is liberal-moral-rights-violative. I am reluctant to conclude that a decision by a firm not to make an investment because the natural-oligopolistic investment-disincentives it faces critically reduce the profitability of the investment is liberal-moral-rights-violative. My reluctance to find such choices liberal-moral-rights-violative is connected to the reasons for liberalism's being disposed not to impose positive duties on moral-rights bearers to benefit others. My doubts about this conclusion are connected to the fact that a firm is not usually a moral-rights bearer (though, of course, the individuals that make a firm's decisions are moral-rights bearers). I choose not to take refuge in what I take to be the reality that it will rarely be possible to attribute a firm's decision not to invest to its facing natural-oligopolistic investment-disincentives. I am also uncertain about the liberal-moral-rights-violative status of decisions by a firm to make political expenditures or expenditures on government-decision-making-process participation that are motivated by specific anticompetitive intent (expenditures that the firm would not have found *ex ante* at least normally profitable if it did not believe that the expenditure would or might induce government to make economically-inefficient decisions that will yield the firm profits by reducing the absolute attractiveness of the best offers against which it will have

to compete in one or more ways that would render the expenditure *ex ante* profitable though *ex ante* economically inefficient in an oPp economy—for example, expenditures to induce the government to make economically-inefficient decisions to refuse a license to a prospective competitor, to find a competitor guilty of a patent infringement, to impose a tariff on a foreign competitor's product, to declare a competitor's product unsafe, etc.) The simple but perhaps simplistic "justification" for concluding that such expenditures are not liberal-moral-rights-violative is that all members of a liberal-moral-rights-based society have a moral right to have an equal influence on government decisions and that denying them the right to make political contributions and expenditures and to participate in government-decision-making processes violates that right in addition to depriving government-decision-makers of information and arguments that bear on the decision that would be "best" for them to make. This justification is simplistic because in all contemporary societies different individuals have widely different financial and other abilities to influence government decisions, and it is (in my admittedly-unexplained judgment) likely (despite the countervailing-power argument) that, by increasing the political influence of the firms in their ARDEPPSes of consummation, horizontal (M&A)s disserve the instantiation of the liberal conception of justice by increasing the inequality of political influence of the members of the society in which they take place.

5. As we have seen, horizontal (M&A)s will tend to increase their participants' OCAs *inter alia* (1) by freeing them from each other's price-competition, (2) by generating static marginal-cost efficiencies, (3) by generating dynamic efficiencies that enable the resulting firm to substitute for the investments the participant could have made investments that would give them a superior array of OCAs, (4) by generating dynamic efficiencies that cause the resulting firm to make one or more investments that deter rival investments, (5) by generating dynamic efficiencies that substitute for a situation in which a participant would have made an investment a situation in which it and a relevant rival face critical natural-oligopolistic investment-disincentives, (6) by creating a resulting firm that does not make an investment that a participant would have made that would have reduced the profits of all participants "combined" in part because it would not have deterred a mutual-rival investment, (7) by creating a resulting firm that substitutes for the investments the participants would have made investments that were less competitive with the participants' other investments than the investments the participants would have made would have been, (8) when the participants and their mutual rivals set across-the-board prices, by creating a resulting firm that is better able than the participants would have been acting separately to induce the relevant ARDEPPS' sellers to announce their prices and lock themselves into their announced prices in the sequence that most raises their array of HNOPS, and possibly (9) by creating a resulting firm that engages in more predatory conduct than the participants would have practiced.
6. Horizontal (M&A)s will tend to increase the NOMs their participants secure by creating a resulting firm that (1) possesses higher OCAs than the participants would have possessed, (2) can scrutize its customers' claims to have received

superior offers more-cost-effectively than the participants could have done, (3) can change its initially-announced or offered prices more cheaply than the participants could, and (4) in across-the-board-pricing situations, is better able than the participants would have been to induce the relevant ARDEPPS' sellers to make and implement "premature" price-announcements that facilitate their securing OMs naturally.

7. Horizontal (M&A)s will tend to increase the profitability of contrived-oligopolistic pricing to its participants (1) by reducing by one the number of possible non-cooperators and hence the number of rivals to which a contriver must communicate its anticompetitive, contrived-oligopolistic-pricing intentions and the number of rivals it must "check out" when trying to identify the rival that has failed to cooperate with it in individualized-pricing contexts, possibly (2) by causing the resulting firm to be privately-second-placed to secure its potential non-cooperators' customers more often and by a larger amount (relative to those buyers' privately-third-placed suppliers) than the participants would have been (by yielding static marginal-cost efficiencies, by creating a resulting firm that makes a relevant investment when neither participant would have done so, and by combining into the resulting firm participants that would otherwise have been privately-second-placed and privately-third-placed or privately-uniquely-equal-second-placed to supply a cooperator's customers and concomitantly by creating a resulting firm that is better-placed to reciprocate to cooperation than the participants would have been as separate entities), (3) by creating a resulting firm that is better able to secure cooperation by promising to reciprocate to it than the participants would have been acting separately by enabling the resulting firm to take advantage of any excess reciprocatory power a participant possessed, possibly (4) by causing the resulting firm to be privately-second-placed or privately-worse-than-second -placed by small amounts more often than the participants would have been and concomitantly to increase the harm-inflicted to loss-incurred ratio for a relevant amount of harm inflicted by price-retaliation against a non-cooperator for the resulting firm relative to its counterpart for the participants acting separately (though a full analysis would also have to take account of the [M or A]'s effect on the non-cooperator's OCA by altering the resulting firm's competitive positions in relation to the prospective non-cooperator's customers ([relative to the participants' competitive positions]) by generating static marginal-cost efficiencies, by causing the resulting firm to make different investment-decisions from those the participants would have made, and by increasing the resulting firm's CMCs above those the participants would have faced when considering charging a rival's customers particular prices by increasing the prices the resulting firm charged its own customers above those the participants would have charged those of the resulting firm's customers they would have been privately-best-placed to supply), (5) by creating a resulting firm that can retaliate more-cost-effectively against a non-cooperator than the participants could have done acting separately by increasing the amount of price-retaliation it carries out via one participant's product(s) and decreasing the amount it carries out via the other participant's product(s) when the harm-inflicted to loss-incurred ratio for the last act of retaliation that the former

participant would have carried out as a separate entity would have been higher than its counterpart for the other participant (I am assuming for simplicity and counterfactually that the [M or A] would not cause the amount of harm the resulting firm would have to inflict through price [and/or, for that matter, advertizing] retaliation would not be different from the amount the participants would have to inflict in this way), (6) by creating a resulting firm whose promises of reciprocation and/or threats of retaliation are more credible than their counterparts for the participants would have been (A) because the resulting firm enjoys the reputation for engaging in strategic conduct that the participant with the stronger reputation for engaging in such behavior enjoyed and/or (B) because there are economies of organizational scale in building and maintaining a reputation for engaging in strategic conduct, (7) in individualized-pricing contexts, by creating a resulting firm that has more data than any participant would have on the percentage of old customers it retained, the percentage of other sellers' customers it secured, and the percentage of new buyers in the ARDEPPS it obtained through time as well as on the identity and magnitudes through time of the parameters other than non-cooperation by a rival that determine those percentages—that is, that is more able than the individual participants would have been to infer from such circumstantial evidence that its contrived-oligopolistic offers have been beaten by a non-cooperating competitive inferior, (8) in individualized-pricing contexts, by creating a resulting firm that has access to information that all participants possess that will inform the identification of the actual non-cooperator, (9) in individualized-pricing contexts, by creating a resulting firm that can take better advantage of institutional economies of scale in determining whether one had lost sales to a non-cooperator and in identifying the non-cooperator, and (10) by creating a resulting firm that is better able to organize joint data-dissemination, joint reciprocation, and joint retaliation with its rivals than the participants would have been able to do with their mutual rivals.

8. The determinants of the pre-(M or A) unprofitability of predation include *inter alia* (1) the supernormal profits the target rival investment(s) would have yielded the target(s) if no predation were practiced, (2) the ability of the target(s) to withstand short-term losses—their retained earnings and abilities to secure credit from financial institutions or additional capital by issuing new stock shares, (3) the long-run interest of the target(s) in avoiding a reputation for succumbing to predatory and/or retaliatory efforts, (4) the amount by which the continued use of individual target-investments reduced the potential predator's profits—(A) the frequency with which the target-investment was privately-second-placed to supply the possible predator's customers and the average amount by which when the target-investment was privately-second-placed to secure such buyers' patronage it was better-paced than their privately-third-placed suppliers, (B) the frequency with which the target-investment was privately-best-placed to supply buyers the potential predator was privately-second-paled to supply and the average amount by which in those cases the potential predator was privately-better-placed to supply those buyers than were their privately-third-placed suppliers, (C) the amount by which the target was reducing the potential predator's profits by failing to

cooperate with its contrived-oligopolistic pricing, by failing to make "premature" price-announcements and implement such prematurely-announced prices that would enable the potential predator to obtain OMs naturally, and by refusing to announce and lock itself into across-the-board prices at a time that would increase the potential predator's (and their mutual rivals') across-the-board HNOPs, (5) the probability that the targeted investment would be replaced by a rival investment that would be as competitive (or different degrees less competitive) with the potential predator's investment(s) as (than) the target investment was, (6) the extent to which the potential predator can reduce the losses that the ability of other rivals to replace a withdrawn targeted investment impose on it by investing itself or threatening to retaliate and/or actually retaliating against any rival that considers replacing or does replace a withdrawn investment, (7) the extent to which—if the target investment is not withdrawn—its owner would lower the prospective predator's profits by making and using additional investments in the ARDEPPS of consummation.

9. For exemplars of such protocols, see the United States' Hart-Scott-Rodino Act, Public Law 94-435 (1976) and the E.U.'s Council Regulation 139/2004 on the Control of Concentrations Between Undertakings, OJ L241 (May 1, 2004). Of course, a full account of the version of this proposal that would be TBLE (consistent with the liberal conception of justice, most promotive of a relevant conception of the moral good) would have to specify *inter alia* (1) the attributes of a proposed horizontal (M or A) that would render it subject to this regime, (2) the information the horizontal-(M or A) proposers would have to provide the authority, (3) the right of any other actors to provide information of various sorts to the authority, (4) the number of days the authority would have to make its decision or request further information, (5) the number of days the authority would have to make a decision after receiving the requested additional information, (6) any obligation the authority would have to justify its decision, (7) the legal rights the proposers would have that information they supplied not be made public, (8) any provision for judicial review of decisions by the authority to approve or reject the horizontal-(M or A) proposal, etc.

References

E.U. Council Regulation 139/2004 on the Control of Concentrations Between Undertakings, OJ L24/1 (May 1, 2004).

Hart-Scott-Rodino Act, Public Law 94–435 (1976).

Conglomerate Mergers and Acquisitions

12

Conglomerate mergers and acquisitions (M&A)s are (M&A)s consummated by (typically two) participants that are neither both privately-well placed (paradigmatically, privately-uniquely-equal-best placed or, respectively, privately-best placed and privately-second placed) to secure the patronage of any given buyer nor in a supplier-supplied relationship to each other. The effects that an individual conglomerate (M&A) has on its participants' profits and on economic efficiency depend primarily on the efficiencies the (M or A) generates, on the impacts the (M or A) has on the amount of contrived-oligopolistic and predatory conduct in which the participants and their mutual rivals engage, and on whether one or more of their participants is/are an effective potential competitor of one or more other participants.

This chapter is structured similarly to Chap. 11. The only difference is that this chapter combines into one section—Sect. 12.1—its comments on the various ways in which conglomerate (M&A)s can yield their participants profits and its comments on the determinants of the magnitudes of the profit-yields that individual conglomerate (M or A)s would/did yield their participants in each of the ways in which conglomerate (M&A)s can yield its participants profits. Section 12.2 comments on the implications of Sect. 12.1 and Chaps. 1 and 8 for the impact that particular conglomerate (M&A)s would/did have on economic efficiency and for the ability of a liberal-moral-rights-constrained government to increase economic efficiency by responding appropriately to proposed or consummated conglomerate (M&A)s. Section 12.3 comments on the implications of Sect. 12.1 and Chap. 2 for the liberal-moral-rights-violativeness of particular conglomerate (M or A)s and for the ability of government to instantiate the liberal conception of justice by responding appropriately to proposed and consummated conglomerate (M&A)s. And Sect. 12.4 comments on the implications of Sects. 12.1 and 12.2 and Chaps. 1, 2, and 8 for the impact that particular conglomerate (M or A)s would/did have on the instantiation of the utilitarian and various non-utilitarian-egalitarian conceptions of the moral good and for the ability of a liberal-moral-rights-constrained

R. S. Markovits, *Welfare Economics and Antitrust Policy—Vol. II*,
https://doi.org/10.1007/978-3-030-96482-5_12

government to secure the instantiation of the utilitarian and other egalitarian conceptions of the moral good by responding appropriately to proposed or consummated conglomerate (M&A)s. The preceding outline of this chapter uses the expression "comments on" because, to save space, this chapter focuses primarily on the relevant differences between conglomerate and horizontal (M&A)s.

12.1 The Differences in the Ways in Which Conglomerate and Horizontal (M&A)s Can Yield Their Participants Profits and the Relationship Between the Determinants of the Magnitudes of the Impacts That Conglomerate and Horizontal (M&A)s Will Have on Their Participants' Profits

For simplicity, not only will Sect. 12.1 but all sections of this chapter will assume that conglomerate (M&A)s always involve only two participants. This assumption does not significantly affect any conclusion this chapter reaches.

12.1.1 The Relevant Differences Between Conglomerate and Horizontal (M&A)s When Neither Participant Is an Effective Potential Competitor of the Other

Nine differences are salient. First, unlike horizontal (M&A)s, conglomerate (M&A)s in which neither participant is an effective potential competitor of the other cannot yield their participants profits by creating a resulting firm whose investments are more profitable for it than the investments the participants would have made as separate entities would have been for the two of them because the resulting firm's investment-decisions will take account of the impact of its investments on the profits yielded by the investments of both participants whereas each participant's investment-decisions will take account of the impact that its investments have on the profits yielded by the other participant only to the extent that this impact influences the investing participant's profits by causing the other participant to respond to the investing participant's investment. Second, unlike horizontal (M&A)s, conglomerate (M&A)s in this category cannot yield their participants profits by concentrating the seller-side of any ARDEPPS by combining sellers that are competitive and thereby enabling them better to overcome the collective-action problem that may prevent them and their mutual rivals from spending as much on political parties/campaigns/candidates and government-decision-making-process participation as would be in their mutual interest: However, I should acknowledge that conglomerate (M&A)s can yield their participants (and their participants' mutual rivals) profits by reducing the collective-action problem that prevents them from spending as much money on political parties/campaigns/candidates and government-decision-making-process participation as would be in their collective interest by concentrating the seller-side of a relevant individual ARDEPPS by yielding static and/or dynamic efficiencies that have this concentrating effect, by creating a resulting firm that engages in more (seller-sale-concentrating) predation than the participants would have practiced, and/or by combining firms that operate in different ARDEPPSes that share a common interest in securing one or more government decisions. Third, unlike horizontal (M&A)s, conglomerate (M&A)s between participants neither of which is an effective potential competitor of the other will not yield its participants profits by increasing their OCAs by freeing them from each other's price competition when as separate entities they would have been either uniquely-privately-equal-best placed or, respectively, uniquely-privately-best placed and uniquely-privately-second placed to supply a given buyer. Fourth, and relatedly, unlike horizontal (M&A)s, conglomerate (M&A)s between participants neither of which is an effective potential competitor of the other will not increase the participants' profits by increasing the OMs they can obtain naturally by increasing their OCAs in the way delineated in the third item in this list, though it may enable the resulting firm to obtain more NOMs by yielding static-marginal-cost efficiencies that raise the resulting firm's OCAs above the OCAs a participant would have enjoyed, by generating dynamic efficiencies that enable the resulting firm to make investments that create "products" on which it can obtain NOMs, by creating a resulting firm that is more prominent than the participants would have been and on that account is more able to organize a series of premature across-the-board-price announcements whose implementation will increase all relevant sellers' abilities to secure NOMs, and/or by creating a resulting firm that is better placed than the participants to take advantage of organizational economies of scale in changing initially-announced prices. Fifth, conglomerate mergers in this category will not increase their participants' profits by creating a resulting firm that will choose not to make one or more investments that are rendered unprofitable by their reducing the profit-yields of the resulting firm's other investments when the decision of the resulting firm not to invest would not induce any rival to invest whereas one or more participants would have made an investment that would have reduced the "collective profits" of the participants because each participant knew that if it did not make a first additional investment the other participant(s) would and no participant would be deterred from investing by natural-oligopolistic investment-disincentives. Sixth, unlike horizontal (M&A)s, conglomerate (M&A)s neither of whose participants is an effective potential competitor of the other cannot yield their participants profits by creating a resulting firm that can profit by making an investment that is identical to the investment a participant could have made equally proficiently that the participant would not have found profitable to make because its making that investment as an independent entity would have induced the other participant to make an investment the other participant would not otherwise have made because each of the participants would have realized that any investment it would have made would have induced the other to invest when they were separate entities and both participants would have suffered a loss if two or more investments were made—that is, by creating a resulting firm whose creation eliminates the natural-oligopolistic investment-disincentive situation that would have rendered it unprofitable for any participant to make a single investment that would have been "collectively profitable" for both participants. Seventh, although, for reasons that Chap. 11 explained at the text that includes footnote 7 and in footnote 7 itself, I do not think that horizontal (M&A)s *tend to* increase the COMs their participants obtain, I suspect that conglomerate (M&A)s that do not end the independent status of any effective potential entrant will increase the COMs the resulting firm obtains above those the participants would have obtained even less often than do horizontal (M&A)s: However, it is important to note that conglomerate (M&A)s in this category can increase their participants' COMs (A) by creating a resulting firm that is larger than the participants and on that account is better able to take advantage of organizational economies of scale in building and maintaining a reputation for engaging in strategic conduct and (B) when the resulting firm faces one or more rivals that operate in both participants' ARDEPPSes, by creating a resulting firm that can secure the cooperation of such rivals more cost effectively than the individual participants could (i) because even if the conglomerate (M or A) does not generate any relevant static-marginal-cost efficiencies or dynamic efficiencies it will be able to retaliate more cost effectively than the participants could against a resulting-firm rival's non-cooperation because the harm-inflicted to loss-incurred ratio for the last act of price or advertizing retaliation that one participant would direct at the rival in question was higher than its counterpart for the last act of such retaliation the other participant would direct at that rival, (ii) because even if the conglomerate (M or A) does not generate any relevant static-marginal-cost efficiencies or dynamic efficiencies, the resulting firm will be more able to secure a rival's cooperation by promising to reciprocate to its cooperation by not beating that rival's contrived oligopolistic offers to its customers than the two participants could when one participant could provide the relevant rival with more benefits in this way than it needed to provide to secure that rival's cooperation or when the resulting firm could provide more benefits to a relevant rival by reciprocating to its cooperation than the participants could as independent entities in that the participants were, respectively, privately-second placed and privately-third placed to supply one or more buyers the rival was privately-best placed to supply, or (iii) because the conglomerate (M or A) would generate static-marginal-cost efficiencies or dynamic efficiencies that would lead the resulting firm to make investments that would increase the harm-inflicted to loss-incurred ratio for a requisite amount of retaliation by the resulting firm above its counterpart for the participants and/or increase the amount of benefits the resulting firm could confer on the rival by reciprocating to its cooperation above the benefits the participants could confer on the rival in this way. Eighth, although I suspect that conglomerate (M&A)s that do not end the independent status of an effective potential entrant will tend to raise the profits the resulting firm realizes by practicing predation above the profits the participants would have realized by doing so by less than horizontal (M&A)s do (because such conglomerate [M&A]s are less likely to increase the ability of the resulting firm to reciprocate to cooperators above the ability of the participants to do so and will tend to increase the cost effectiveness of the resulting firm's retaliation against non-cooperators above the cost effectiveness of the separate participants' retaliation against non-cooperators to a lesser extent than horizontal [M&A]s do), the differences in question will be less substantial when the relevant cooperators/non-cooperators are conglomerates that operate in more than one participant-ARDEPPS, and, like horizontal (M&A)s, conglomerate (M&A)s will be as likely as horizontal (M&A)s to enable their participants to take advantage of organizational economies of scale in building and maintaining a reputation for engaging in strategic conduct. (Because the following points are relevant to the economic efficiency of conglomerate [M&A]s, it may also be useful to state that conglomerate [M&A]s that create a resulting firm that operates in more ARDEPPSes in which one or more rivals of the resulting firm operate will also tend [1] to increase the amount of contrived-oligopolistic pricing that those rivals practice by enabling them to charge retaliatory prices to and direct retaliatory advertizements at the customers of both participants in the conglomerate [M or A] and to reciprocate to the resulting firm's cooperation by not beating its contrived-oligopolistic offers to both participants' customers and [2] to increase the amount of predation the resulting firm's rivals direct at it relative to the amount they would have directed at the participants by enabling the resulting firm's rivals to make predatory price-cuts to and to direct predatory advertizing at both participants' customers).

The preceding analysis implies or explicitly states that conglomerate (M&A)s neither of whose participants is an effective potential competitor of the other will yield their participants profits in many of the ways that horizontal (M&A)s can do so—for example, (1) by generating static-marginal-cost efficiencies, static-fixed-cost efficiencies, and dynamic efficiencies, (2) by increasing the participant's COMs (though they have no general tendency to do so) and NOMs (though not by increasing the resulting firm's OCAs by eliminating the price competition the participants waged against each other), (3) by increasing the profits the resulting firm can realize by engaging in predation above the "collective profits" the participants would have realized by doing so (though such conglomerate [M&A]s are likely to yield less profits in this way than are horizontal [M&A]s), (4) by increasing the expenditures the resulting firm and its rivals make on political parties/campaigns/candidates and government-decision-making-process participation by increasing the concentration of the seller-side of one or both participants' ARDEPPSes (though, once again, conglomerate [M&A]s in this category are less likely to concentrate the seller-side[s] of the participant's/participants' ARDEPPS[es] than are horizontal [M&A]s since conglomerate [M&A]s in this category do not combine sellers in the same ARDEPPS or prevent a [deconcentrating] entry, etc.). With the differences just referenced aside and admittedly some other differences the preceding sentence did not identify, Sect. 11.2's analyses of the determinants of the magnitudes of the contribution that horizontal (M&A)s can make to their participants' profits in the ways that not only they but also conglomerate (M&A)s that do not involve an effective potential competitor can do so apply fully to such conglomerate (M&A)s.

12.1.2 The Relevance of One or Both Participants' Being an Effective Potential Competitor of the Other to the Profits That a Conglomerate (M or A) Yields Its Participants and the Determinants of the Impacts That a Conglomerate (M or A) Will Have on Its Participants' Profits by Virtue of One or More Participants' Being an Effective Potential Competitor of the Other in Various Situations

In my terminology, a firm is "an effective potential competitor" of the firms established in an ARDEPPS or an effective potential entrant in relation to a particular ARDEPPS if it would enter the ARDEPPS in question if one or more of the ARDEPPS' established firms did not do something it or they would not otherwise have found unprofitable to do to deter the potential competitor/entrant from investing in the ARDEPPS in question. Chapter 5 explained (1) that the firm that is privately-best-placed to enter a particular ARDEPPS at a given point in time is the potential competitor that faces lower ($\Pi_D + R + S + L$) barriers to entry than does any other firm not already established in the ARDEPPS in question and (2) that the firm that is privately-best-placed to enter an ARDEPPS at a particular point in time will be an effective potential competitor of the established firms in that ARDEPPS if the sum of the (Π_D, R, S, and L) barriers to entry it faces are lower than (the sum of the Π_D, R, S, and L barriers to investment expansion) *plus* (the monopolistic or natural-oligopolistic investment-disincentives that would confront) or *minus* (the monopolistic investment-incentives that would be present for) the established firm that would be privately-best placed to make an additional investment in the ARDEPPS in question at the entry-barred expansion-preventing investment quantity in the ARDEPPS in question—the lowest quantity of investment the ARDEPPS in question would have to contain if (usually counterfactually) entry was barred for no established firm to find it profitable to add to the ARDEPPS' investment total. Chapter 5's analysis also implies that a potential competitor that is not the privately-best-placed potential competitor of an ARDEPPS' established firms will be an effective potential competitor of those firms if (1) the entry-barred expansion-preventing investment quantity in the relevant ARDEPPS is lower than the entry-preventing investment quantity in that ARDEPPS and (2) the worse-than-privately-best-placed potential entrant in question would find it profitable to enter after all privately-better-placed potential entrants had entered (because the entry-barred expansion-preventing investment quantity was lower than the entry-preventing investment quantity and the established firms [acting either separately or conceivably collaboratively] did not find it profitable to make sufficient [limit] investments (or in any event did not make sufficient limit investments] to deter the privately-better-placed potential entrants from entering).[1]

In my view, in almost all situations (see below), effective potential competition affects ARDEPPS outcomes either by becoming kinetic (i.e., by resulting in the effective potential competitor's entering) or by inducing one or more of the relevant ARDEPPS' established firms to make one or more investments it or they would otherwise not have made (to make one or more what I denominate "limit investments") to deter the effective potential competitor's entry. I hasten to add that—at least until recently and perhaps still now—most industrial organization economists (and U.S. judges and antitrust-law-enforcement officials[2]) did/do not subscribe to this position. They claimed or continue to claim that either in all situations or in many situations (namely when "barriers to entry"—a concept they never clearly define—are moderate to substantial[3]) established firms respond to effective potential competition not by investing to deter entry but by charging so-called limit prices—prices below their conventional profit-maximizing counterparts—to deter entry.

Before preceding to analyze the relevance of the fact that one participant in a conglomerate (M or A) is an effective potential competitor of the other participant in that (M or A) for the impact that the (M or A) will have on its participants' profits, I want to explain why with two possible exceptions whose empirical importance I doubt I do not think that established firms respond to the presence of one or more effective potential competitors by practicing limit pricing.[4]

For three categories of reasons, with the two possible qualifications to be discussed below, I reject the claim that firms respond to effective potential competition by charging lower prices than they would otherwise charge (by engaging in limit pricing). First, I reject the limit-pricing hypothesis because I think that the limit-pricing theorists have vastly exaggerated the efficacy of limit pricing. None of the four reasons that limit-pricing theorists have offered for limit pricing's alleged efficacy is as convincing to me as it seems to be to them: (1) both because effective potential competitors tend to be existing firms that are already operating in related ARDEPPSes and know a lot about the demand for the relevant ARDEPPS' products and because employees of limit pricers would have an incentive to sell to potential competitors (or exchange for better jobs) the employees' knowledge that their limit-pricing employers are charging prices that are lower than the higher, most-conventionally-profitable prices they could have charged, I doubt that limit pricing will be as successful at inducing potential competitors to underestimate the heights of the $H\Pi_E$ and $H\Pi_N$ curves as many limit-pricing theorists claim; (2) I also doubt that limit pricing will be as likely as some limit-pricing theorists allege to discourage entry by communicating to potential competitors the established firms' intention to retaliate against new entrants (I should also point out that some limit-pricing theorists do not realize that in individual cases limit pricing cannot deter entry both in this way and by deceiving potential entrants since this threat claim assumes that the potential competitors recognize that the established firms are charging prices that are lower than the prices that would be conventionally-profit-maximizing for them to charge); (3) my reasons for doubting the claim that limit pricing will deter entry by inducing potential competitors to underestimate the established firms' conventional-profit-maximizing prices also lead me to doubt the claim that some limit-pricing theorists make that limit pricing will deter entry by inducing potential competitors to underestimate the established firms' marginal costs; and (4) I am also unconvinced by the limit-pricing theorist argument that limit pricing will deter entry by depriving potential competitors of the opportunity to undermine the "goodwill" of the established firms by setting prices that are lower than the pre-entry prices the established firms charged: (A) I am never sure what is meant by "goodwill"—whether the referent is to buyers' placing a positive value on enabling the relevant supplier to earn profits by supplying them or to buyers' believing in the high quality/reliability of the firm's products/services, (B) I suspect that few established firms have "goodwill" in the first "sense" just delineated (the argument that they do seem to me to assume that the established firms are small shopkeepers in an English village), (C) to the extent that established firms have goodwill in the first of the just-referenced senses, I doubt that it would be diminished by a new entrant's beating the established firm's pre-entry prices (buyers would be likely to attribute such new-entrant conduct to the new entrant's engaging in promotional pricing rather than to the established supplier's having engaged in "price-gouging"), and (D) logically, there is no connection between an established seller's charging lower prices and its customers believing in its product's/services' high quality/reliability. Moreover, although I can think of two additional arguments for the efficacy of limit pricing that the limit-pricing theorists did not make—namely (5) even if limit pricing does not induce potential competitors to underestimate the heights of the $H\Pi_E$ and $H\Pi_N$ curves, it leaves them less certain of these curves' heights (i.e., of the established sellers' conventional profit-maximizing prices and marginal costs)—and concomitantly increases the R barrier to entry they face, and (6) limit pricing increases the L barrier to entry that potential competitors face by making the established firms' independently-delivered threats of retaliation more credible by lowering the law-related cost of retaliation to the established firms by putting them in a position to retaliate simply by not raising their prices post-entry (i.e., by enabling the established firms to retaliate in a way that is less detectable, less "objectively provable," and more difficult to convince juries of), I do not think that limit pricing will often be significantly efficacious on these accounts either.

Second, I reject the claim that established firms often or always respond to effective potential competition by engaging in limit pricing because, even if limit pricing was more efficacious than I believe and even if limit pricing was the only way established firms could deter effective potential competitors from entering, limit pricing would rarely be more profitable than charging conventional-profit-maximizing prices and allowing entry to occur. In the general case, effective limit pricing would be more profitable than conventional-profit-maximizing pricing only if limit pricing that would reduce the limit pricer's supernormal rate-of-return by (say) X percent in absolute terms would reduce the effective potential competitor's *ex ante* perception of its certainty-equivalent post-entry rate-of-return by more than X percent in absolute terms, and that condition seems extremely unlikely to be satisfied.

Third, I reject the claim that established firms often or always respond to effective potential competition by engaging in limit pricing because, even if limit pricing was always efficacious and more profitable than doing nothing to prevent entry, it would virtually never be more profitable than other choices established firms could make to deter entry—communicating threats of retaliation more conventionally, creating goodwill by providing reliable, high-quality goods, and services, inducing government authorities to impose tariffs or constrain entry, and (most importantly) making limit investments.

I should add that my skepticism about the empirical importance of limit pricing is reinforced by the fact that, to my knowledge, no one has ever provided an example of real-world limit pricing. The stories that economists tell that they claim to be stories of limit pricing always (in my experience) turn out to be stories of limit investing.

Admittedly, as previously suggested, I can imagine two situations in which limit pricing might be profitable and therefore practiced. In the first, a probably-small established seller in a "market niche" that (1) believed that its operation would be much less privately-proficient than the operation of the new entrant that would enter if the profit potential of the established firm's subarea of product-space became known and (2) could not make money by selling information about the profit potential of entering its subarea of product-space to a firm that could make use of it might engage in limit pricing to keep the profit potential of its subarea of product-space secret. In the second, one or more established firms might find it profitable to limit price if they thought that, if the profit potential of its or their area of product-space became known, more investment would flow into that area of product-space than could be sustained—that is, ARDEPPS investment would come to exceed equilibrium ARDEPPS investment. The fact that I do not know of any real-world examples of these possibilities makes me comfortable in ignoring them.

I will now analyze the impact that a two-firm conglomerate (M or A) one or both of whose participants are effective potential competitors of the other will have on the profits of its participants by virtue of this fact on the assumption that established firms will not respond to effective competition by charging limit prices. I will assume initially that such conglomerate (M&A)s do not generate any static or dynamic efficiencies and then investigate the relevance to their impact on participant profits of any tendency of conglomerate (M&A)s to be more-static-and-dynamic-efficiency-generative when one or both participants are an effective potential competitor of the other.

Even if one assumes that the relevant conglomerate (M&A)s yield no static or dynamic efficiencies, the impact of at least one conglomerate (M or A) participant's being an effective potential competitor of the other on the profits the (M or A) yields its participants will depend on which of ten possible scenarios transpires. To ease the exposition, I will assume that only one participant is an effective potential competitor of the other participant.

In the first scenario, the consequences of the conglomerate (M or A)'s converting an effective potential competitor of one participant into a component of the resulting firm are to reduce the relevant ARDEPPS' equilibrium investment quantity by substituting for (1) a situation in which the effective-potential-competitor participant would have introduced a new investment to the ARDEPPS because the participants and/or their mutual rivals would not have found it profitable to make sufficient investments to deter it from doing so (2) a situation in which no one introduces a new investment into the ARDEPPS because no other potential entrant finds it profitable to do so (because the barriers to entry facing all other potential entrants are critically higher than the barriers to entry facing the effective potential competitor in question) and the resulting firm and its established rivals will not find it profitable to invest because they did not find it profitable to invest pre-(M or A), the (M or A) eliminated their entry-deterring incentive to invest, and (on current assumptions) the (M or A) did not generate any dynamic efficiencies. In this situation, the fact that one of the participants in the conglomerate (M or A) in question was an effective potential competitor of the other would increase the (M or A) participants' profits by (the number of dollars by which the deterred investment of the effective-potential-competitor participant would have reduced the profit-yields of the other participant's investment[s]) *minus* (the supernormal profits the effective-potential-competitor participant would have realized on the deterred investment). To state what I hope is by now obvious, the deterred investment would have reduced the profits of the non-investing participant by (1) (the number of sales the investment of the effective-potential-competitor participant would have caused it to be privately-best placed to make that the other participant would otherwise have been privately-best placed to make) *times* (the average [P – MC] gap the non-investing participant would have secured on the sales in question [which depends on the associated OCAs, NOMs, and COMs]) *plus* (2) (the number of sales that the non-effective-potential-competitor participant on which the former firm would have obtained NOMs but for the entry that the entry would have prevented it from securing by reducing its OCAs [because the entered firm would have been the other participant's uniquely-privately-second-placed rival for those sales]) *times* (the average NOM the non-effective-potential-competitor participant would have obtained on those sales) *plus* (3) the amount by which the entry would have reduced the COMs the non-effective-potential-competitor participant obtained on the sales it would have made post-entry.

In the second scenario, the consequence of the conglomerate (M or A)'s converting an effective potential competitor into a component of the resulting firm is to substitute for (1) an investment by the effective privately-best-placed potential competitor (2) an investment by a potential competitor that was privately-second-placed to enter pre-(M or A). In this scenario, which I acknowledge is much less likely than the others I will discuss, the fact that the conglomerate (M or A) involved an effective potential competitor will (when it increases the participants' profits at all) increase the participants' profits by (1) the difference between the number of dollars by which the entry of the privately-second placed potential competitor reduced the profits yielded by the established-firm participant's investments and the number of dollars by which the investment that the effective-potential-competitor participant would have reduced the profit-yields of the established-firm participant's investments (a difference that may be positive both because the privately-second-placed potential entrant had a worse array of competitive positions than the privately-best-placed potential competitor would have had and because the investment of the privately-second-placed potential competitor was less competitive with the established-firm participant's investments relative to other investments in the ARDEPPS in question than the privately-best-placed potential competitor's investments would have been) *minus* (2) the supernormal profits the effective-potential-competitor participant would have realized on the investment it would have made as a separate entity.

In the third scenario, the consequence of the conglomerate (M or A)'s converting an effective potential competitor of one participant into a component of the resulting firm would be to substitute for (1) a situation in which a rival of the established-firm participant would have made a limit investment to deter the entry of the effective-potential-competitor participant because the established-firm participant would not have made a new investment to deter the effective-potential-competitor-participant or established-firm-participant-rival investment (2) a situation in which no new investment would be introduced into the ARDEPPS in question. In this situation, the fact that one of the participants in the conglomerate (M or A) in question was an effective potential competitor of the other would increase the participants' profits by the number of dollars by which the deterred established-firm-participant's rival's investment would have reduced the profit-yield(s) of the established-firm participant's investment(s).

In the fourth scenario, the consequence of the conglomerate (M or A)'s converting an effective potential competitor of one participant into a component of the resulting firm would be to substitute for (1) a situation in which the non-effective-potential-competitor participant would have introduced a new investment into its ARDEPPS to deter the entry of the effective-potential-competitor participant or the investment of a rival of the non-effective-potential-competitor participant that would otherwise have made a limit investment to deter the entry of the effective-potential-competitor participant (2) a situation in which no new investment would be introduced into the ARDEPPS in question. In this situation, the (M or A)s converting an effective potential competitor into a component of the resulting firm would increase the participants' profits by (1) the number of dollars by which the deterred limit investment of the non-effective-potential-competitor participant would have reduced its other investment's profit-yield or its other investments' profit-yields if it would not have deterred the effective-potential-competitor participant's entry or an established rival's limit investment *minus* (2) the supernormal profits the deterred investment would be calculated to yield if one ignored the impact it would be calculated to have had on the investor's profits by deterring a rival investment.

In the fifth scenario, the consequence of the conglomerate (M or A)s converting an effective potential competitor into a component of the resulting firm are to substitute for (1) an effective-potential-competitor entry that is more competitive with the non-effective-potential-competitor participant's investments (2) a resulting-firm investment that is less competitive with its other investments. In this situation, the conglomerate (M or A)s bringing the effective potential competitor "in house" will increase the participants' profits by (1) the positive difference between the number of dollars by which the resulting firm's new investment reduces the profits yielded by its old investment(s) and the number of dollars by which the entry of the independent effective potential competitor would have reduced the profits yielded by the non-effective-potential-competitor's investment(s) *minus* (2) the positive difference between the supernormal profits the effective potential competitor's entry would have yielded it and the supernormal profits the resulting firm's investment would be calculated to yield it if the investment's effects on the profits yielded by the resulting firm's other investment(s) were ignored.

In the sixth scenario, the fact that one of the participants in a conglomerate (M or A) is an effective potential competitor of the other does not change the relevant investment-outcome—that is, the resulting firm makes precisely the same investment the effective potential competitor would have made equally-privately-proficiently as the effective potential competitor would have made that investment. In this "case," the conglomerate (M or A)s substituting (1) a resulting firm investment for (2) an identical investment that would otherwise have been made by an independent effective potential competitor will increase the participant's profits by eliminating the price competition the participants would otherwise have waged against each other (thereby increasing their OCAs and NOMs), by creating a resulting firm that may be better able than the participants would have been to obtain NOMs for non-OCA-related reasons, (at least in some cases) by enabling the resulting firm to earn more profits than the participants could have earned by engaging in contrivance and predation, and by enabling the resulting firm to realize more profits through its own and its rivals' political activity and government-decision-making-process participation than the participants could have done by concentrating the seller-side of the relevant ARDEPPS.

In the seventh scenario or set of related scenarios, a conglomerate (M or A)'s converting an effective potential competitor into a component of the resulting firm deters the non-effective-potential-competitor participant and/or an established rival of that firm from continuing the life or lives of one or more of its/their extant QV investment(s) by renewing or rebuilding the production or distributive facility that is a part of the investment(s) in question by removing the incentive that the prospect of the effective-potential-competitor participant's entry would otherwise have given the firm(s) in question to make a limit investment. In the variant of this scenario in which the conglomerate (M or A)'s in question deters its non-effective-potential-competitor participant from making one or more limit renewing/rebuilding investments, the (M or A)s converting the effective-potential-competitor participant into a component of the resulting firm will increase the participants' profits by the loss the deterred non-effective-potential-competitor participant's limit investment(s) would have imposed on the non-effective-potential-competitor participant if the investment(s) would not have deterred the effective-potential-competitor participant's entry. In the variant of this scenario in which the conglomerate (M or A) in question deters an established rival of the non-effective-potential-competitor participant from making one or more limit renewing/rebuilding investments to prevent the entry of the effective-potential-competitor entry, the (M or A)'s converting the effective-potential-competitor participant into a component of the resulting firm will increase the participants' profits by the loss the established rival's deterred limit renewing/rebuilding investments would have imposed on the non-effective-potential-competitor participant. And, obviously, in the variant of this scenario in which the relevant (M or A) would deter both the non-effective-potential-competitor participant and one or more of its established rivals from making one or more limit renewing/rebuilding investments, the profits the (M or A) will confer on its participants by incorporating one participant's effective potential competitor into the resulting firm will equal the loss the deterred investments would have imposed on the non-effective potential-competitor participant.

It is arguable that the final three scenarios I will consider should not be included in this list since they are based on (contestable) empirical assumptions that the fact that one of the participants in a conglomerate (M or A) is an effective potential competitor of the other favors the (M or A)'s generating static-marginal-cost efficiencies static-fixed-cost efficiencies, and/or dynamic efficiencies. If one attributes the static-marginal-cost efficiencies, a relevant conglomerate (M or A) generates to its participants' being, respectively, an established firm in a particular ARDEPPS and an effective potential entrant into that ARDEPPS (as the eighth scenario does) and assumes that any such efficiencies will relate only to the use of the non-effective-potential-competitor's investments in the ARDEPPS into which the effective potential competitor might enter and the use of the investment the effective potential competitor might make in that ARDEPPS, the effect that the (M or A) will have on its participants' profits on this static-marginal-cost-efficiency-generation account will depend (1) on whether the generated static-marginal-cost efficiencies relate to the use of one or more of the non-effective-potential-competitor participant's QV investments (which strikes me as less likely) or to the use of any QV investment the effective-potential-competitor participant might make as an independent entity or the resulting firm would make by virtue of its ownership of the effective-potential-competitor's ideas and other assets and (2) in the latter case, on whether the prospective reduction in the (Π_D + R) barriers to making what was pre-(M or A) the effective potential competitor's investment would result in (A) the resulting firm's making a more-profitable investment than the effective potential competitor would have made as an independent entity or (B) a rival of the resulting firm's making an investment to deter the resulting firm from making an investment when it would not have made a limit investment to deter the effective-potential-competitor participant in the (M or A) from making the "less-proficient" investment it would have made as an independent entity. Section 12.2's analysis of the determinants of the magnitude of the profits a horizontal (M or A) will yield its participants by generating static-marginal-cost efficiencies applies fully to situations (1) and (2)(A) referenced in the preceding sentence. In the situation (2)(B) referenced in the sentence before last, the prospect of the relevant conglomerate (M or A)'s generating the relevant static-marginal-cost efficiencies will reduce its participant's profits by (1) the supernormal profits the effective-potential-competitor participant would have realized by making the investment it would have made as a separate entity *minus/plus* (2) the positive/negative difference between the number of dollars by which the effective potential competitor's investment would have reduced the other participant's profits and the number of dollars by which the other participant's established rival's limit investment reduced the other participant's profits.

The ninth scenario attributes to a relevant conglomerate (M or A)'s bringing "in-house" an effective potential competitor the (M or A)'s generating static-fixed-cost efficiencies that relate either (more likely) to the fixed cost the effective potential competitor would have to incur to enter (I recognize that this category of efficiency might be classified as a dynamic efficiency) or (less likely) to the fixed cost the non-effective-potential-competitor participant must incur to renew or rebuild the (production/distributive)-facility component of an existing QV investment. If the static-fixed-cost efficiencies relate to the non-effective-potential-competitor participant's renewing or rebuilding the (production–distributive)-facility component of one of its extant QV investments, Sect. 12.2's analysis of the determinants of the contribution that horizontal-(M or A)-generated efficiencies of this kind will make to the profits the horizontal (M or A) yields its participants applies fully. If the static-fixed-cost efficiencies relate to the effectuation of the investment that the effective-potential-competitor participant would have made as a new entrant, (1) the prospect of their generation will have no impact on whether a rival of the non-effective-potential-competitor participant would have made a limit investment to deter the effective-potential-competitor participant from entering or would make an investment to deter the resulting firm from investing post-(M or A), (2) if a rival (would have made)/(would make) such an investment, the relevant static-fixed-cost efficiency will not affect the (M or A)'s participants' profits because neither the effective-potential-competitor participant as an independent potential entrant nor the resulting firm would take advantage of the prospective static-fixed-cost efficiencies, and (3) if the effective-potential-competitor participant would have invested as an independent entity and the resulting firm does invest post-(M or A), the fact that the conglomerate (M or A) in question would generate the static-fixed-cost efficiencies will increase its participants' profits by the associated private-fixed-cost saving.

The tenth and final scenario attributes to a conglomerate (M or A)'s participants' being, respectively, a firm established in a particular ARDEPPS and a potential entrant into that ARDEPPS the (M or A)'s generating dynamic efficiencies that I assume are related to the resulting firm's making investments in the ARDEPPS in question other than the investment(s) the effective-potential-competitor participant would have made in that ARDEPPS as an independent entity. Section 12.2's analysis of the determinants of the effect that any such dynamic efficiencies a horizontal (M or A) generates on its participants' profits applies fully to the determinants of the effect that any dynamic efficiencies a conglomerate (M or A) generates has on its participants' profits by virtue of its participants' being, respectively, an established firm in an ARDEPPS and an effective potential competitor of that established firm.

12.2 The Economic Efficiency of Particular Conglomerate (M or A)s and the Ability of a Liberal-Moral-Rights-Constrained Government to Increase Economic Efficiency by Responding Appropriately to Proposed/Consummated Conglomerate (M&A)s

12.2.1 The Economic Efficiency of Particular Conglomerate (M or A)s

Section 11.3.1 articulates and justifies a number of conclusions about the economic-efficiency correlates of the various possible microeconomic effects of horizontal (M&A)s that are equally applicable when the relevant microeconomic effects are generated by conglomerate (M&A)s, though conglomerate (M&A)s will not be equally prone to generate some of those microeconomic effects as horizontal (M&A)s are. For example, for reasons that Sect. 11.3 explains, (1) any conglomerate (M or A) that generates static-marginal-cost efficiencies will generate allocative-cost savings on that account that exceed the private-variable-cost savings it generates, (2) any conglomerate (M or A) that generates static-fixed-cost savings on a (production/distributive)-facility renewal/rebuilding investment that the relevant participant would have executed anyway will generate allocative-cost savings that exceed the private-fixed-cost savings it generates, (3) any conglomerate (M or A) between a firm that is established in an ARDEPPS and a potential entrant to that ARDEPPS that creates a resulting firm that makes an investment that is less competitive with its other investments than the investment that the effective-potential-competitor participant would have made as a separate entity would have been with the other participant's investments will not tend to increase or decrease economic efficiency on that account, (4) any conglomerate (M or A) that increases/decreases the incidence of contrived-oligopolistic and predatory conduct will tend on that account to decrease/increase economic efficiency with four possible exceptions—any conglomerate (M or A) that increases contrived-oligopolistic conduct and hence equilibrium investment in an ARDEPPS of consummation whose investments are investments in PPR may increase economic efficiency all tolled, any conglomerate (M or A) that decreases contrived-oligopolistic conduct and hence equilibrium investment in an ARDEPPS of consummation whose investments are investments in PPR may decrease economic efficiency all tolled, any conglomerate (M or A)s that decreases the incidence of predation and as a result increases equilibrium investment in an ARDEPPS of consummation whose investments are QV investments may decrease economic efficiency all tolled, and any conglomerate (M or A) that increases the incidence of predation and as a result decreases equilibrium QV investment in an ARDEPPS of consummation may increase economic efficiency all tolled, (5) any conglomerate (M or A) that generates dynamic efficiencies by reducing the cost of creating and using a QV investment that would have been made and used anyway or the cost of executing a PPR project that would have been executed anyway will increase economic efficiency on this account by more than it increases its participants' profits on this account, (6) any conglomerate (M or A) that generates dynamic efficiencies that cause the resulting firm to make an investment in the ARDEPPS of consummation that increases the relevant ARDEPPS' equilibrium investment quantity will increase economic efficiency on this account by less than it increases the participants' profits on this account when the investment in question is a QV investment (indeed, may decrease economic efficiency on this account when the investment in question is a QV investment) and will increase economic efficiency on this account by more than it increases the participants' profits on this account when the investment in question is an investment in PPR, (7) any conglomerate (M or A) that would generate dynamic efficiencies that are never realized by the resulting firm because the (M or A) causes an established rival of the resulting firm to make an investment in the ARDEPPS of consummation when neither it nor any participant acting as a separate entity would otherwise have done so by creating a resulting firm that would invest if a rival did not deter it from doing so will decrease economic efficiency on this account when the relevant ARDEPPS' investments are QV investments and will increase economic efficiency on this account when the relevant ARDEPPS' investments are investments in PPR (though in both situations, the prospect of the [M or A]'s yielding realized dynamic efficiencies would decrease its profitability to its participants by the loss the induced rival investment imposed on the resulting firm), (8) conglomerate (M&A)s that increase the concentration of the seller-side of an affected ARDEPPS (say, by converting a situation in which an effective potential competitor would have entered into one in which it becomes a component of a resulting firm) will tend to decrease economic efficiency on that account by reducing the extent to which the ARDEPPS' sellers are deterred by collective-action problems from making "collectively profitable" expenditures on political parties/campaigns/candidates and government-decision-making-process participation, (9) to the extent that a conglomerate (M or A) decreases/increases poverty/(material inequality), it will tend to increase/decrease economic efficiency on that account, (10) conglomerate (M&A)s that create resulting firms that can take advantage of tax losses that one participant (or conceivably both participants if the [M or A] increases its participants' profits sufficiently in other ways) could not make use of will tend to decrease economic efficiency on that account by depriving the relevant society's government of tax revenues, though I acknowledge that a conglomerate (M&A)'s yielding its participants profits in this way may also increase economic efficiency by eliminating the negative distortion the tax laws would otherwise create in the certainty-equivalent profits that firms that could not otherwise use their tax losses would expect to realize on investments that could yield either losses or profits *ex post* and, when the firm that had the relevant tax loss was a start-up (particularly if it was a start-up founded by one or more individuals who were and would otherwise have remained employees/managers of well-established firms in the start-up's ARDEPPS) may also increase economic efficiency by inducing the creation of such start-ups, (11) conglomerate (M&A)s

one of whose participants is owned by one or more individuals who want to liquidate their holdings and retire from management will tend to increase economic efficiency not only by enabling these individuals to secure these objectives but also, when they had left a position in a well-established firm to create a start-up, by encouraging the managers and employees of well-established firms to leave their positions and form new companies, (12) conglomerate (M&A)s will always generate allocative transaction costs because it is allocative transaction costly for their participants to identify each other, negotiate their deal, and consolidate their operations—indeed, for reasons that Sect. 12.3 explained, the allocative costs conglomerate (M&A)s generate on this account will almost always be higher than the associated private transaction costs the (M or A)'s participants incurred. I could write much more but will stop here: although I acknowledge that this study provides much evidence to the contrary, I do sometimes restrain myself in deference to reader patience and production costs.

I want to close this section by addressing the economic efficiency of one response that a liberal-moral-rights-constrained government might make to a particular subcategory of conglomerate (M&A)s—geographical-diversification conglomerate (M&A)s. That response would be to allow a firm that wants to execute a geographic-diversification conglomerate (M or A)—say, a Colorado beer producer that wants to enter the New England beer "market" by acquiring or merging with a New England brewer—if and only if it proves that (1) it would not have entered the (say) New England "market" on its own and either (2) (A) the New England participant was a small producer in New England or (B) the New England participant was a medium-sized or large-sized producer in New England but the Colorado brewer had expended an acceptably-large amount of money to identify a smaller (M or A)-co-participant with which it could consummate an (M or A) that would be more profitable than not entering the New England market at all and had failed to identify such a possible co-participant.[5] This decision-rule would increase economic efficiency only if (1) it were not *ex ante* economically efficient for a liberal-moral-rights-constrained government to make more-refined determinations, (2) geographic-diversification (M&A)s that involve smaller firms in the diversified-into "market" tend as a class to be more economically efficient than geographic-diversification (M&A)s that involve larger firms in the diversified-into market, and (3) any economic-efficiency gain the decision-rule in question generated because "claim (2)" in this list was true would be larger than any economic-efficiency loss the rule would generate by deterring would-be diversifiers from engaging in diversification that would increase economic efficiency relative to the do-nothing option by raising the search cost of diversifying and reducing the profitability of the (M or A) that is consummated (search costs aside).

I disagree with all three claims articulated in the preceding sentence. Although I recognize that this is little more than an assertion: even if claims (2) and (3) were correct, in my judgment, the decision-rule I am now considering would be less *ex ante* allocative efficient than a more-refined approach. I also see no reason to believe that, all things considered, the economic efficiency of a geographic-diversification (M or A) will be inversely related to the size of the "acquired" firm.

Thus, I do not find particularly convincing the argument that the static-marginal-cost, static-fixed-cost, and dynamic efficiencies a geographic-diversification (M or A) enables the "acquired firm" to achieve will tend to be inversely related to the acquired firm's size because they are connected to the acquired-firm component of the resulting firm's taking advantage of organizational economies of scale. Moreover, as we have seen, the static-fixed-cost efficiencies and dynamic efficiencies an (M or A) generates may or may not increase its economic efficiency—depending on (1) whether the investments in the ARDEPPS of consummation are QV investments or investments in PPR and (2) on whether the efficiencies (A) cause the resulting firm to renew/rebuild an investment or make a new investment that is privately and allocatively superior to an investment a participant would have renewed/rebuilt or made anyway, (B) cause the resulting firm to renew/rebuild a QV investment or make a new QV or PPR investment that would otherwise not have been renewed/rebuilt or made anyway, or (C) cause a resulting-firm rival to renew or rebuild a QV investment or make a new QV or PPR investment that adds to the equilibrium-investment quantity in the ARDEPPS of consummation. In addition, even if the probability that an "acquired firm' has a tax loss it cannot use or is owned by individuals who want to liquidate their holdings and retire from management is inversely related to the size of the "acquired firm," I suspect that these considerations would not strongly favor the greater economic efficiency of geographic-diversification (M&A)s with smaller rather than larger "acquired firms" (even if one granted *ad arguendo* and contrary to my suspicions that allowing small firms to sell their tax losses increases economic efficiency). (I should add that it would almost certainly be more economically efficient to take these possibilities into account directly in more-fine-grained analyses than to do so indirectly by applying the "toe-hold-merger" doctrine I am now considering.) Moreover, to the extent that any static-marginal-cost efficiencies a geographic-diversification (M or A) yields are not connected to its enabling the "acquired-firm" component of the resulting firm to take advantage of organizational economies of scale, the associated economic-efficiency gains will be directly, not inversely, related to the "acquired firm's" sales. I could say more about this second claim but will stop here. Third, even if the first two claims made in the preceding paragraph were true, I suspect that the toe-hold-merger decision-rule might be economically inefficient because it would deter the diversification of firms that are interested in engaging in geographic-diversification (M&A)s that are more economically efficient than their not diversifying by critically increasing the cost of consummating a geographic-diversification (M or A) by increasing the search costs it will have to incur to do so and/or by requiring the would-be diversifier to execute an (M or A) that would be less profitable (search costs aside) rather than the more profitable (M or A) it would have consummated if its choices were not constrained by the toe-hold-merger doctrine.

12.2.2 The Ability of a Liberal-Moral-Rights-Constrained Government to Increase Economic Efficiency by Responding Appropriately to Proposed/Consummated Conglomerate (M&A)s

Section 11.3.2 argues that a liberal-moral-rights-constrained government will be able to increase economic efficiency by tailoring its responses to particular horizontal (M or A)s or different classes of horizontal (M&A)s to their specific characteristics. More specifically, Sect. 11.3.2 argues (1) that some proposed/consummated horizontal (M&A)s will increase economic efficiency, (2) that some will decrease economic efficiency, (3) that it will often be *ex ante* economically efficient for a liberal-moral-rights-constrained government to ascertain the facts that determine the economic efficiency of proposed/consummated horizontal (M&A)s and perhaps their alternatives (perhaps by charging their participants a price for the right to consummate or continue such an [M or A] that they would be willing to pay only if it were economically efficient for them to do so), and (4) that a liberal-moral-rights-constrained government will be able to increase economic efficiency by basing on estimates of the relevant facts (A) decisions to prohibit certain horizontal (M or A)s, (B) decisions to allow horizontal (M or A) proposers to consummate an (M or A) only if they agree to divest some of their investments, (C) decisions to condition approval of the horizontal (M or A) in question on the resulting firm's agreeing not to raise its prices for a specified period of time or to raise its prices during the relevant time-period only if it can establish that the price-increase is a response to an increase in its variable costs for which it was not a culpable cause or to an increase in "the product's" quality for which it deserves credit, (D) decisions to permit the participants to consummate/continue the horizontal (M or A) in question only if they pay a stated price for the right to do so, or (F) decisions to allow the proposed/consummated horizontal (M or A).

I see no reason to believe that Sect. 11.3.2's horizontal-(M&A)-related conclusions are not full applicable to conglomerate (M&A)s. In my judgment, (1) both conglomerate (M&A)s between participants neither of which is an effective potential competitor of the other and conglomerate (M&A)s between participants at least one of which is an effective potential competitor of the other can either increase or decrease economic efficiency relative either to the situation that would prevail if the participants would do nothing relevant if they were prohibited from consummating/continuing the (M or A) in question and to the situation that would prevail if the participants responded in some "positive" way to the prohibition of the (M or A) in question, and (2) a liberal-moral-rights constrained government will be able to increase economic efficiency by responding selectively to proposed/consummated conglomerate (M&A)s.

I will not try to prove the following assertion here. However, I do want to state that, in my judgment, both government officials and academic economists have (1) underestimated the frequency with which and the extent to which conglomerate

(M&A)s whose participants are not potential competitors will decrease economic efficiency and (2) misanalysed the microeconomic and economic-efficiency relevance of conglomerate (M&A)'s participants' being potential competitors.

12.3 The Liberal-Moral-Rights-Violativeness of Conglomerate (M or A)s and the Ability of a Government to Instantiate the Liberal Conception of Justice by Responding Appropriately to Proposed/Consummated Conglomerate (M&A)s

Section 11.4's analyses of the counterpart issues for horizontal (M&A)s apply *mutatis mutandis* when the business conduct at issue is conglomerate (M or A)s. The only additional conglomerate-(M or A)-related "wrinkle" is that conglomerate (M&A)s will be liberal-moral-rights-violative not only if their participants' *ex ante* perception that the relevant (M or A) would be at least normally profitable was critically affected by their belief that it would or might increase not only the profits they would realize by engaging in contrived-oligopolistic, natural-oligopolistic, and predatory conduct but also by the profits the conglomerate (M or A) would confer on them by converting one or more participants that were effective potential competitors of one or more other participants into components of the resulting firm. I should add that, like horizontal (M&A)s, conglomerate (M&A)s will also be liberal-moral-rights-violative if one or more participants intended *ex ante* the resulting firm to take advantage of the fact that the (M or A) would create a resulting firm that could earn more profits by engaging in natural-oligopolistic, contrived-oligopolistic, and predatory conduct than the participants could have done as separate entities even if no participant's *ex ante* perception that the (M or A) would be at least normally profitable was critically affected by a belief that the (M or A) would or might increase its profits by creating a resulting firm that realized more profits in these ways than the participants would have done as separate entities and/or by converting one or more participants that were effective potential competitors of one or more other participants into components of the resulting firm.

12.4 The Impact of Conglomerate (M&A)s on the Instantiation of the Utilitarian and Non-Utilitarian-Egalitarian Conceptions of the Moral Good and the Ability of a Liberal-Moral-Rights-Constrained Government to Instantiate These Egalitarian Conceptions of the Moral Good by Responding Appropriately to Conglomerate (M&A)s

Section 11.5's analyses of the counterpart issues for horizontal (M&A)s apply *mutatis mutandis* when the business conduct at issue is conglomerate (M&A)s. Of course, the relevant facts are different. Horizontal (M&A)s may be more likely to generate static-marginal-cost, static-fixed-cost, and dynamic efficiencies than are conglomerate (M&A)s. Horizontal (M&A)s will be more likely to affect economic efficiency and (usually) increase poverty and material inequality than are conglomerate (M&A)s because horizontal (M&A)s will always increase the HNOPs and NOMs in their ARDEPPSes of consummation by freeing the participants from each other's price competition, whereas conglomerate (M&A)s will do so only in some cases in which one or more participants are effective potential competitors of one or more other participants. But the relevant considerations and the structure of the relevant analyses are the same.

******

This chapter relies to a considerable extent on the related analyses of Chap. 11. Swings and roundabouts. This expositional choice makes this chapter shorter than Chap. 11. However, it prevents those who have not read Chap. 11 from fully understanding or at least assessing some of this chapter's analyses and conclusions.

Notes

1. The United States Department of Justice Conglomerate Merger Guidelines (1984) assumes that the three privately-best-placed potential entrants into any "market" will be effective potential competitors and that, in the absence of evidence to the contrary that is "particularly strong," potential entrants that are worse-than-privately-third placed to enter a "market" will not be effective potential competitors. I do not agree with either of these conclusions. Thus, in my judgment, in many situations, even the privately-best-placed potential entrant will not be an effective potential competitor because the entry-barred investment-expansion-preventing investment quantity equals or exceeds the entry-preventing investment quantity—that is because, $(\Pi_D + R + S + L) + (M \text{ or } O)$ for the established firm that would be privately-best placed to increase the relevant ARDEPPS' investment quantity at its entry-preventing investment quantity equals or is lower than $(\Pi_D + R + S + L)$ for the ARDEPPS' privately-best-placed potential entrant at that investment quantity. And, in my judgment, in many situations—most likely, when the demand for the ARDEPPS' product is rapidly increasing through time and/or the marginal-cost curves for producing the ARDEPPS' various products are rapidly decreasing through time—potential entrants that are worse-than-privately-third placed to enter the ARDEPPS in question will be effective potential competitors because the entry-preventing-investment quantity will be increasing at a rate that would cause the Π_D and R barriers the established firms would face on the last several investments they would have to make to prevent entry to be prohibitively high (given the rate at which they would have to expand their ARDEPPS investments to prevent entry)—that is, because in such situations the entry-barred expansion-preventing investment quantity will be far below the entry-preventing investment quantity.
2. See, *e.g.*, United States v. Penn-Olin Chemical Co., 378 U.S. 158 (1964), United States v. Faltaff Brewing Co., 410 U.S. 526 (1973), Yamaha Motor Co. v. FTC,

657 F.2d 971 (1981), and (United States) Department of Justice 1984 Conglomerate Merger Guidelines. I should indicate, however, (1) that since 1973, U.S. courts have been disinclined to conclude that particular potential competitors were effective—see *e.g.* United States v. Marine Bancorporation, 410 U.S. 602 (1974) and Tenneco Inc. v. FTC 689 F.2d 346 (2d Cir. 1982)—and (2) that the 1992 and 2010 (U.S.) Department of Justice and Federal Trade Commission Horizontal Merger Guidelines seem implicitly to reject limit-pricing theory.

3. The more limited position referenced in the parenthetical is the position of Joe Bain, one of the pioneers of the "limit-pricing hypothesis" the text that follows explains and criticizes. According to Bain ((1949 and 1956), limit pricing will not be practiced in "markets" in which barriers to entry are high because in such markets sellers can charge their profit-maximizing prices without making entry profitable for any potential competitor (because in such markets the conventional profit-maximizing price will be lower than the limit price), and limit pricing will not be practiced in "markets" in which barriers to entry are low because in such markets the price that the established firms would have to charge to deter entry (the limit price) would be so low (would yield them such a low rate-of-return) that they will find it more profitable to charge the conventional profit-maximizing price (to realize a higher supernormal profit rate before entry) and accept the lower supernormal profit-rate that entry will cause them to realize post-entry. On the other hand, Bain argues, when barriers to entry are moderate to substantial, firms will find it profitable to engage in limit pricing because they will have to do so to deter entry and the fact that the limit price will be relatively high (will yield them a relatively-high supernormal rate-of-return in such circumstances) will make limit pricing more profitable than conventional profit-maximizing pricing in such cases. These claims ignore the "facts" that (1) if, as most limit-pricing "theorists" claim, limit pricing will always deter entry if it is practiced, the critical issue is whether the limit-pricing supernormal profit rate (which will be constant) is higher or lower than the weighted average of the higher pre-entry conventional-profit-maximizing supernormal rate-of-return and the (on their view) lower post-entry conventional-profit-maximizing supernormal rate-of-return and (2) the limit price and limit-pricing supernormal rate-of-return will be strongly positively correlated with the pre-entry and the post-entry conventional-profit-maximizing rates-of-return. Thus, because the conventional profit-maximizing price will be high when barriers to entry are high, the fact that the limit price will be high when barriers to entry are high does not guarantee or perhaps even increase the probability that the limit price will be higher than the conventional profit-maximizing price when barriers to entry are high. And because both the pre-entry and the post-entry conventional profit-maximizing price and conventional-profit-maximizing supernormal rate-of-return will be higher when barriers to entry are moderate to substantial than their counterparts will be when barriers to entry are low, the fact that the limit price will be higher when barriers to entry are moderate to substantial than when they are low does not favor the conclusions that limit pricing will be more profitable than conventional-profit-maximizing pricing when barriers to

entry are moderate to substantial and less profitable than conventional profit-maximizing pricing when barriers to entry are low.

4. For a more-detailed critique of limit-pricing "theory," see Markovits, R. (2016) at pp. 221–234.
5. I address this possibility because some U.S. courts have promulgated and used an analogous approach—the so-called toe-hold merger doctrine—when applying the U.S. Clayton Act. Some U.S. courts have adopted this doctrine in the belief that its application will increase competition by inducing firms that want to engage in geographic diversification to substitute conglomerate (M&A)s with small firms ([M&A]s, which the doctrine's supporters incorrectly claim will tend to be more pro-competitive) for the conglomerate (M&A)s with larger firms the diversifier would otherwise consummate (which the doctrine's supporters claim will be less pro-competitive). For an explanation of why this doctrine is incorrect as a matter of economics and would be incorrect as a matter of U.S. law even if it were correct as a matter of economics, see Markovits, R. (2016) at pp. 201–218 and Sect. 12.2.1 *infra*. This so-called toe-hold merger doctrine was first promulgated and used by the U.S. Federal Trade Commission in 1970 in Bendix Corp., 77 F.T.C. 731 (1970). The FTC subsequently used the doctrine in other cases such as SKF Indus., 1979 Trade Reg. Rep. ¶2/595 at 21,724 (FTC) and Budd Co., 86 F.T.C. 518, 582–583 (1975). The United States Department of Justice implicitly accepted the doctrine in United States Department of Justice Conglomerate Merger Guidelines, 2 Trade Reg. Rep. 9/9 14,490–14,495 (1984). A number of U.S. Courts of Appeal have expressed sympathy with the doctrine—see, *e.g.*, Bendix Corp., 450 F.2d 534, 541–542 (6th Cir. 1971) and Kennecott Copper Corp. v. FTC, 467 F.2d 67, 79 (10th Cir. 1972), cert. denied, 416 U.S. 909 (1974)—and a number of District Court opinions have implicitly relied on it—see, *e.g.*, Washington Mt. Sav. Bank v. Federal Dep. Ins. Corp., 347 F. Supp. 790, 798–800 (W.D. Wash 1972), aff'd, 482 F.2d 459 (9th Cir. 1973) and United States v. Phillips Petro. Co., 367 F.Supp. 1226, 1258 (C.D. Cal. 1973), aff'd mem. 418 U.S. 906 (1974). The U.S. Supreme Court has never ruled on the doctrine—indeed, in one case expressly reserved the question of its correctness. See United States v. Falstaff Brewing Corp., 410 U.S. 526, 537 (1973).

References

Bain, J. S. (1949). A note on pricing in monopoly and oligopoly. *American Economic Review*, 39, 448–464.

Bain, J. S. (1956). *Barriers to new competition*. Cambridge, MA: Harvard University Press.

Bendix Corp., 77 F.T.C. 1291 (1976). vacated on procedural grounds, 450 F.2d 534 (6th Cir. 1971), consent order, 84 F.T.C. 1291 (1974).

Budd Co., 86 F.T.C. 518 (1975).

Kennecott Copper Corp. v FTC, 467 F.2d 67 (10th Cir. 1972), cert. denied, 416 U.S. 909 (1974).

Markovits, R. (2016). *Economics and the interpretation and application of U.S. and E.U. antitrust law*. Vol. II *Economics-based legal analyses of mergers, vertical practices, and joint ventures*. Heidelberg, New York, Dordrecht, London: Springer.
SKF Inclus., 1979 Trade Reg. Rep. ¶21,595 at 21,724 (FTC).
Tenneco, Inc. v. FTC, 689 F.2d 346 (2d Cir. 1982).
United States Department of Justice Conglomerate Merger Guidelines, 2 Trade Reg. Rep. 9¶1 14,490–14,495 (1984).
United States Department of Justice and Federal Trade Commission Horizontal Merger Guidelines (1992).
United States Department of Justice and Federal Trade Commission Horizontal Merger Guidelines (2010).
United States v. Falstaff Brewing Co., 410 U.S. 526 (1973).
United States v. Phillips Petro Co., 367 F. Supp. 1226, aff'd mem. 418 U.S. 906 (1974).
United States v. Marine Bancorporation, 410 U.S. 602 (1974).
United States v. Penn-Olin Chemical Co., 378 U.S. 158 (1964).
Washington Mt. Sav. Bank v. Federal Dep. Ins. Corp., 347 F. Supp. 1226 (W.D. Wash 1972), aff'd 482 F.2d 459 (9th Cir. 1973).
Yamaha Motor Co. v. FTC, 657 F.2d 971 (9th Cir. 1981).

Surrogates for Vertical Integration 13

A firm that is perfectly vertically integrated from input production through final-good production, distribution, and consumption will make a host of decisions to maximize its profits or equivalent-dollar gains. *Inter alia*, such a Robinson Crusoe will use the "most-organizationally-profitable" set of inputs to produce the output it produces, will produce the quantity of each of its products that is most-organizationally-profitable, and will consume all the units of its product that it produces. A final-good producer that is not perfectly vertically integrated may do worse than this Robinson Crusoe counterpart for a variety of reasons: it may produce its output with a different set of inputs than would be most profitable for Robinson Crusoe to use, it may price its product in one or more ways that allow buyer surplus to escape, relatedly it may produce fewer units of its product than the Robinson Crusoe firm would produce because—unlike Crusoe—it would be concerned with the way in which the transaction surplus its sales (the consumption of its output) generated was divided between its output's consumers and itself, it may lose profits because its independent distributors engaged in intra-brand price-competition that enabled its product's buyers to pay lower prices than they would have been willing to pay, it may lose profits because its independent distributors make more or less demand-increasing expenditures on or allocate more or less shelf-space to its product than is in the "organization's" (that is, all components of what could be a completely-vertically-integrated entity's) interest, it may suffer losses because its independent distributors do not inform it of product-uses or effective sales-pitches when the "organization" would profit from their doing so, it may lose profits because its independent distributors do not supply the warranteed repair and maintenance sources that would be organizationally profitable for them to supply, it may lose profits because its independent distributors do not take account of the impact that their prices have on the producer's profits by affecting potential buyers' perception of the producer's product's quality, the actual value of its product to buyers for whom the price of a product is one of its attributes, or the profits that the producer makes when selling other products (for various other

R. S. Markovits, *Welfare Economics and Antitrust Policy—Vol. II*,
https://doi.org/10.1007/978-3-030-96482-5_13

reasons), and it may lose profits because its independent distributors or customers combine its product with a complement whose use by these parties reduces the producer's profits by worsening what others perceive to be the performance of the producer's product.

I use the expression "surrogate for vertical integration" to cover the various pricing-techniques, minimum-resale-price-fixing and maximum-resale-price-fixing (resale-price-maintenance or RPM) clauses, vertical-customer-allocation (VCA) clauses, distributor-(demand-increasing-expenditure)/(shelf-space-allocation)-subsidization policies, sales/franchise-renewal policies, and single-brand exclusive dealerships that firms that are not perfectly vertically integrated use to reduce the losses their non-integration cause them to sustain on one or more of the above accounts.

Each of this chapters 6 sections focuses on one subset of surrogates for vertical integration—respectively, on (1) fancy pricing-techniques, (2) "non-pricing" tying and reciprocity agreements, (3) minimum-price-setting-RPM clauses and VCA clauses and the (demand-increasing-expenditure)/(shelf-space-allocation)-subsidization policies and sales/franchise-renewal policies that can be substituted for such clauses, (4) maximum-price-setting-RPM clauses, (5) single-brand exclusive dealerships, and (6) long-term full-requirement contracts and long-term total-output-supply contracts. Each of these sections is divided into four subsections: the first subsection explains the functions that the relevant surrogates for vertical integration can perform for the producer that uses them; the second analyzes the economic efficiency of the relevant subset of surrogates for vertical integration and the ability of the government of a liberal-moral-rights-based society to increase economic efficiency by responding appropriately to their actual and proposed use; the third analyzes the liberal-moral-rights-violativeness of the relevant subset of surrogates for vertical integration and the ability of the government of a liberal-moral-rights-based society to secure liberal-moral-rights-related interests by responding appropriately to their actual and proposed use; and the fourth analyzes the impact of the relevant surrogates for vertical integration on the instantiation of the utilitarian, various pure non-utilitarian-egalitarian, and various mixed egalitarian conceptions of the moral good and the ability of the government of a liberal-moral-rights-based society to increase the instantiation of any of these conceptions of the moral good by responding appropriately to exemplars of the relevant category of surrogates for vertical integration.

As Sect. "3" argues, sellers can also use RPM clauses to effectuate horizontal price-fixes and can use VCA clauses to effectuate horizontal "market"-divisions. This chapter largely ignores these possibilities because RPM and VCA clauses that are being used for these purposes are not functioning as surrogates for vertical integration: This chapter considers these possibilities only to the extent that they increase the difficulty of determining the functions that particular RPM and VCA clauses are performing.

As just indicated, this chapter analyzes (1) the functions of the various surrogates for vertical integration, (2) the effects these surrogates have on economic efficiency, the securing of liberal-moral-rights-related interests, and the instantiation of various morally-desirable conceptions of the moral good, and (3) the ability of the government of a liberal-moral-rights-based society to increase economic efficiency, secure liberal moral rights, and instantiate various conceptions of the moral good by responding appropriately to exemplars of the various surrogates for vertical integration. However, before proceeding with these analyses, I need to discuss two important, preliminary issues.

The first is "the relevant unit for analysis"—the analysand—issue: When analyzing the impact that a surrogate for vertical integration or its prohibition or "something related to a surrogate for vertical integration" has on economic efficiency, the instantiation of the liberal conception of justice, and/or the instantiation of a morally-defensible conception of the moral good, should one focus on (1) an individual firm's using the relevant surrogate for vertical integration or the prohibition of an individual firm's doing so or (2) all members of a set of product-rivals' that find it profitable to use the surrogate for vertical integration doing so or a rule prohibiting all members of a set of product-rivals' using that surrogate for vertical integration? In Markovits, (2014b) at pp. 377–378 and 499–501, I argued that, when the illegality respectively of any surrogate for vertical integration or any vertical (M or A) depends on whether it lessens competition, the analysand on which it is correct as a matter of law to focus is not an individual firm's use of the relevant surrogate or the consummation of a relevant vertical (M or A) but a rule allowing all members of a set of product-rivals to engage in the conduct in question. I justified this admittedly-non-standard legal conclusion by arguing that (1) a decision to focus on the competitive impact of an individual firm's vertical conduct would often lead to the conclusions that (A) a well-established firm's engaging in vertical conduct would be illegal because it would lessen competition (i) by causing one or more marginal established competitors to exit by worsening its (their) competitive-position array(s) by improving the perpetrator's competitive-position array and/or (ii) by preventing one or more new entries or established firm investment-expansions by worsening the relevant deterred investors' prospective competitive-position arrays by improving the perpetrator's competitive-position array whereas (B) a marginal established firm's or any non-well-established firm owner of a new investment's engaging in the same vertical conduct for the same reason would be lawful because, if anything, it would increase competition by (preventing the exit of the marginal firm)/(inducing a non-well-established firm to invest in the relevant ARDEPPS) by improving its actual/prospective array of competitive positions by performing the same functions for it that the relevant vertical conduct would perform for a well-established perpetrator and (2) this pattern of government decision-making is inconsistent with the level-playing-field norm of both U.S. antitrust law and E.U. competition law and these two legal regimes' related commitment to permitting firms to compete on the competitive merits (a commitment that contributes to these legal regimes' economic efficiency, liberal justness, and instantiation of the utilitarian conception of the moral good). The "fact" that making the vertical-conduct competitive-impact analysand a rule allowing all members of a set of product-rivals to engage in the conduct in question rather than an individual firm's engaging in that conduct would promote economic efficiency, secure liberal moral rights, and instantiate utilitarianism implies the appropriateness of making the above rule the vertical-conduct analysand in this policy-study. (I hasten to add that, when the relevant issue is whether a firm's using a surrogate for vertical integration [or vertically integrating] violates liberal moral rights directly because the firm's choice is motivated by specific anticompetitive intent, the relevant analysand is the individual firm's decision to use a surrogate for vertical integration [or to vertically integrate], but such conduct is not a surrogate for vertical integration).

The second preliminary issue I need to discuss is the impact-analysis-baseline issue: When calculating the impact of any exemplar of any category of vertical-integration surrogate, what behavior should one assume the firms that might be permitted by a relevant rule to use a particular surrogate for vertical integration will substitute for the conduct in question if they are prohibited from engaging in it? For example, since a producer that is prohibited from forbidding its independent distributors to resell its product for less than a specified minimum price will virtually always find it profitable to respond to this prohibition by increasing the per-unit price and reducing the lump-sum (franchise) fee it charges those distributors for its product, should not one analyze the effect of a rule permitting all members of a set of product-rivals to engage in such RPM on economic efficiency, liberal moral rights, total utility, and various other egalitarian conceptions of the moral good on the assumption that the prohibition of these firms' engaging in such RPM will lead them to increase their per-unit prices and reduce their lump-sum fees, at least if such a response would be lawful. Or, whenever a producer's decision to divide up the potential buyers to which each of its independent distributors may attempt to make sales so that only one such distributor is entitled to compete for the patronage of each potential buyer of the producer's product derives from its desire to make it profitable for each of its distributors to make expenditures on media advertizing, in-store promotions, and person-to-person sales-efforts that the producer finds profitable for the distributor to make, should not one analyze the relevant impacts of a rule allowing all members of a set of product-rivals to include such VCA clauses in their distributorship agreements on the assumption that their prohibition will lead the producers in question to subsidize their independent distributors' demand-increasing expenditures or to substitute their own media advertizing or in-store promotional displays for their distributors' (at least if analysis implies that this response would be [1] profitable for the producers and [2] lawful)? Even more universally, when analyzing the various impacts of a rule allowing all members of a set of product-rivals to use any surrogate for vertical integration, should one not compare the state of the world that would result from that surrogate's use by these firms with the state of the world that would result from the relevant firm's vertically integrating whenever (1) the prohibition of the surrogate in question would make it profitable for the firms in question to engage in vertical integration through merger, acquisition, joint venture, or internal growth if it would be lawful for them to do so and (2) such vertical integration would be lawful? Although an affirmative answer to these and various other analogous questions I could pose makes the necessary analysis more complicated, the correct answer to all such questions is clearly "Yes."

13.1 "Fancy" Pricing-Techniques

13.1.1 The Functions of Fancy Horizontal Pricing-Techniques

The "non-fancy" horizontal pricing-technique to which all the fancy pricing-techniques this section analyzes will be compared is the technique that all elementary micro-economic textbooks assume sellers usually employ—what I call "single pricing," the pricing-technique in which the seller charges each potential buyer the same per-unit price for all units of the seller's product the buyer chooses to purchase and no lump-sum fee for the right to purchase the seller's product at that per-unit price. When the seller in question is not a perfect competitor, with one empirically-unimportant exception,[1] the profits it will earn by charging the most profitable single price it can charge (the per-unit price at which its single-pricing marginal-revenue curve cuts its marginal-cost curve from above) will be lower than the gains a Robinson Crusoe would secure by producing and consuming the seller's product on two accounts: (1) the profit-maximizing single price will destroy some transaction surplus because it is higher than the seller's marginal cost at the output at which its demand curve cuts its marginal-cost curve from above (because it will reduce the seller's output below transaction-surplus-maximizing {TSM] output) and (2) the profit-maximizing single price will allow all its customers (none of whom is the seller) to obtain buyer surplus on all but the last unit it sells.[2]

The fancier pricing-techniques this section considers are designed to increase the seller's profits by reducing the "losses" that non-Robinson-Crusoe firms sustain on these combined accounts (in addition, sometimes, to performing other [profitable] functions for the sellers that employ them, which will be discussed below).

I will now address four fancy "pricing-techniques" that a seller may find profitable to employ when selling its product to an individual buyer. The first is perfect price discrimination, which a seller can execute in three ways that I will describe on the simplifying assumption that none of these arrangements will impose any risk costs on the buyer or seller and that the buyer does not possess any bargaining power (cannot secure buyer surplus by exercising bargaining power): (1) by offering to supply the buyer with successive units of its product each of which it prices at the highest price the buyer would be able to pay for the unit in question and just break even on the transaction, (2) by offering to supply the buyer with the transaction-surplus-maximizing quantity of its product (its TSM output) for a lump-sum fee equal to the area under the buyer's demand curve for the seller's product between output zero and the product's TSM output, or (3) by offering to supply the buyer with the TSM output of the seller's product if the buyer agrees to pay the seller a combination of the per-unit price for each unit equal to the height of the seller's demand curve for the product at its TSM output and a lump-sum fee equal to the area between the buyer's demand curve for the product and a horizontal line whose height equals the per-unit price charged. The seller's use of any variant of this pricing-technique will (ideally) remedy both deficiencies of single pricing—that is, will prevent truncation surplus from being destroyed by per-unit prices that exceed the seller's marginal cost at the output at which the demand curve the seller faces cuts its marginal-cost curve from above (at its transaction-surplus-maximizing [TSM] output) and will prevent the buyer from securing any buyer surplus. In addition, when the buyer is a wholesaler or *a fortiori* a retailer, the substitution of perfect price discrimination for single pricing will also tend to yield the seller profits by inducing the buyer to make demand-increasing expenditures and shelf-space allocations that are in the seller's interest by making those buyers' expenditures and allocations that are in the seller's interest profitable for the buyer by equating the cost of the good sold to the buyer with the marginal cost to the seller of supplying the good to the buyer (whereas single pricing by sellers that are not perfect competitors makes the cost of the good sold to the buyer [the single price] exceed the marginal cost to the seller of supplying relevant units to the buyers).

Unfortunately, any variant of this pricing-technique will also have various disadvantages from the perspective of the seller: (1) will require the seller to incur additional private transaction costs to estimate the buyer's demand curve for its product and its own marginal-cost curve over a larger range of outputs than it would have to make such estimates to practice single pricing, (2) if the arrangement covers a significant period of time, requires the seller to incur the transaction cost of drafting a contract, (3) if the seller has more than one buyer to which it wants to make sales, might require the seller to incur costs to prevent arbitrage[3] or to suffer losses from arbitrage by giving the buyer in question an incentive to engage in arbitrage by selling some units of the seller's product to other potential customers of the seller that value the units more than the seller's actual customer valued them (which would be the case for many units even if all seller's customers had the same demand curve for its product), (4) if the contract covers a significant period of time (to reduce the per-unit transaction cost of contracting) and the buyer and/or seller are uncertain about the buyer's demand curve for the seller's product, may increase the sum of the related risk costs the seller and buyer incur (assume, for example, that the seller uses the variant of perfect price discrimination that combines a per-unit price with a lump-sum fee and that the buyer and seller are uncertain about the buyer's quantity-demand for the seller's product over the period covered by the contract; in comparison with single pricing, this variant of perfect price discrimination will shift the risk of the buyer's demand for the seller's product's being higher or lower than both expected on the weighted average from the seller to the buyer by making part of the buyer's payment a lump-sum fee that does not vary with the buyer's actual quantity-demand; if the buyer is more risk-averse than the seller or faces more risk as a result of the transaction than the seller faces [because the buyer is a distributor that is concerned not only with the total resales of the seller's product by all resellers but also with its share of those sales while the seller is a producer that is concerned solely with the total resale of its product (I am simplifying)], the shift from single pricing to this variant of perfect price discrimination will increase the sum of the buyer's and seller's risk costs—an effect with which the seller will be concerned because the risk costs the buyer incurs by participating in the transaction will reduce dollar for dollar [at least when the buyer has no bargaining power] the lump-sum fee the buyer will be willing to pay the seller for the right to purchase the predicted TSM output of the seller's product at a per-unit price equal to the seller's marginal cost at that output),[4] and (5)(A) if the buyer underestimates the weighted-average-expected quantity of the seller's product it will purchase if it is charged a price equal to the seller's marginal cost at the TSM output, a variant of perfect price discrimination that entitles the buyer to purchase as much of the relevant product as it wishes to purchase at the seller's TSM per-unit price will on this account yield the seller lower profits than single pricing would yield it by reducing the lump-sum fee the buyer will be willing to agree to pay in advance below the lump-sum fee it could pay and break even on the transaction in question,[5] and (B) if the seller underestimates the quantity of its product the buyer should be expected to purchase on the weighted average if the seller charges the buyer a per-unit price equal to the seller's TSM-output-marginal cost, the variant of perfect price discrimination under which the buyer is charged a lump-sum fee for the right to purchase as much of the seller's product as it wishes to purchase for use in its own business at a per-unit price equal to the marginal cost the seller expects it will face at its TSM output will cost the seller money by precluding it from profiting on the buyer's purchases of its product that the seller does not anticipate (by causing the seller to charge the buyer a lump-sum fee that is lower than the lump-sum fee the buyer would have been willing to pay). Still, in some cases, prefect price discrimination (perhaps in combination with seller efforts to prevent arbitrage) will be more profitable than single pricing.

The second fancy horizontal pricing-technique a seller may employ in its relations with an individual buyer is to charge that buyer a lower lump-sum fee than it would be charged under the third variant of perfect price discrimination for the right to purchase as much of the seller's product as it wants to buy for its own use at a per-unit price that is higher than the seller's marginal cost at the seller's TSM output. A seller will find it profitable to shift from perfect price discrimination to this mixed lump-sum-fee *plus* supra-TSM-marginal-cost per-unit-price technique if (1) the losses this technique imposes on the seller by destroying transaction surplus by reducing unit sales (given the buyer's demand-increasing expenditures and shelf-space allocations) and by making it unprofitable for a wholesaler/retailer buyer to make demand-increasing expenditures or shelf-space allocations that would increase the producer's profits even if it had to compensate the distributor-buyer for making them (say, by reducing the distributor's franchise fee)[6] are lower than (2) the gains the shift to this technique will yield the seller by reducing the buyer's incentive to engage in arbitrage, the loss the seller incurs because of buyer pessimism about its quantity-demand for the seller's product at different prices, and the loss the seller incurs because of its own pessimism about the buyer's quantity-demand for the seller's product (at different prices) the sum of the risk costs the seller and buyer incur (by shifting risk from the buyer to the seller by lowering the lump-sum fee).

The third fancy horizontal pricing-technique a seller may employ when selling its product to an individual buyer is full-requirements tie-ins. Such tie-ins involve the seller's agreeing to supply the buyer with as many units as the buyer wishes to purchase of one product the seller produces itself (the so-called "tying product") for a lower per-unit price (plus usually a lump-sum fee) than the seller would charge the buyer for this product in a one-product transaction in exchange for the buyer's agreeing to purchase from the seller its full requirements of a second so-called tied product (which the seller may or may not produce itself) for a per-unit price that exceeds the per-unit price the buyer would otherwise have to pay for this tied product.[7]

Two variants of such full-requirements tie-ins should be distinguished. The first involves tying and tied products that are final products (typically complements) and a buyer that is typically a retailer (though it could be a wholesaler). Any seller that finds it profitable to use such a tie-in finds it profitable to do so because, by shifting the locus of some or all of the seller's supra-TSM-output-marginal-cost per-unit pricing from the tying product to the tied product, the tie-in (1) reduces the amount of transaction surplus it must destroy "directly"—i.e., without affecting the buyer's demand-increasing expenditures and shelf-space allocations—to remove a given amount of buyer surplus by charging supra-TSM-output-marginal-cost per-unit prices and (2) reduces the "loss" that supra-TSM-output-marginal-cost pricing that removes a given amount of buyer surplus imposes on the seller by causing the retailer/wholesaler buyer to make lower demand-increasing expenditures and less/less-attractive shelf-space allocations than would be in the seller's interest (even when one takes account of the fact that the seller will have to "compensate" the buyer for making such expenditures and shelf-space allocations, usually by reducing the franchise [lump-sum] fee the buyer must pay).

Both of these last two claims require some explanation. The first reflects one fact and one possibility. The relevant fact is that the ratio of (the seller surplus a seller can obtain by removing any given amount of buyer surplus by raising the per-unit price it charges the buyer above its TSM-output-marginal cost) to (the amount of buyer surplus the price-increase in question removes)—the (SS+)/(BS−) ratio for any such (BS−)—is positively related to the absolute slope of the buyer's demand curve for the seller's product between the two prices in question, is positively related to the TSM output of the product in question, and is negatively related to the absolute (positive) slope of the seller's marginal-cost curve between the outputs associated with the two prices in question.[8] To explore the relevant possibility, I will assume that the tying product is "A," the tied product is "B," the seller is "X," the buyer is "Y," "DD_{XAY}" stands for the demand curve X faces when selling A to Y, "DD^{RC}_{XBY}" stands for the demand curve X would face when selling B to Y if Y committed itself to purchasing from X all the B it bought ("RC" stands for [full] requirements contract), MC_{XAY} stands for the marginal-cost curve X faces when supplying A to Y, and MC_{XBY} stands for the marginal-cost curve X faces when selling B to Y. In this notation, the relevant possibility is that in some (I suspect, many) situations, the relevant facts—the difference between the absolute slopes of the DD_{XAY} and DD^{RC}_{XBY} curves over the relevant output ranges, the difference between the TSM outputs of A and B, and the difference between the slopes of MC_{XAY} and MC_{XBY} over the relevant range of outputs—will enable X to reduce the amount of transaction surplus it must destroy to remove—to increase the (SS+) it can secure by removing—a given amount of buyer surplus by charging Y supra-TSM-output-marginal-cost prices (demand-increasing-expenditure and shelf-space-decision consequences aside). For example, this outcome might obtain when X is a producer of A that has several competitors for Y's patronage (say, when A is designer suits or complicated farm machinery), Y is a retailer that faces no close competitor when selling A (is the only haberdasher or seller of complex farm machinery in the area) but operates in a tight oligopoly situation when selling A's complements B1…n (underclothes, socks, ties, and dress shirts all of which can also be bought in the one department store or dry-goods shop in the area or rakes, shovels, hoses that can also be bought in the one general store in Y's area).[9]

The preceding story also reveals why in some situations the second claim previously made will be justified—why the type of full-requirements tie-in on which I am now focusing may reduce the "loss" a producer will incur because its removing a given amount of buyer surplus by charging supra-TSM-output-marginal-cost per-unit prices for its product to its wholesalers or retailers deters them from making demand-increasing expenditures or shelf-space allocations that are in the producer's interest. *Ceteris paribus*, the importance of such expenditures and allocations and concomitantly the "loss" a seller's supra-TSM-output-marginal-cost pricing will impose on it by reducing its dealer's relevant expenditures/allocations increase with the extent to which the product in question is or can be differentiated, and, as in the above examples, it will sometimes (indeed, I suspect, typically) be the case that A is a differentiated product and B is a standardized good.

Of course, the preceding account ignores the costs that sellers must incur to employ the type of tie-in on which I am now focusing. X could have avoided the "losses" that this type of tie-in can reduce by setting A's price at X's TSM-output-marginal cost. Absent the tie-in, X would have found it unprofitable to charge such a TSM-output-marginal-cost price for A because doing so would impose costs on X by increasing Y's incentive to engage in arbitrage on A, by preventing X from reducing the consequences of its and/or Y's underestimating Y's demand for A, and by increasing the sum of the risk costs X's and Y's transaction on A imposed on them. For the type of tie-in on which I am now focusing to increase X's profits, it (1) must do better in these regards from X's perspective than charging a TSM-output-marginal-cost per-unit price for A or (2) put another way, must not perform these functions for X sufficiently worse than the sacrificed supra-TSM-output-marginal-cost pricing of A to be unprofitable all tolled. I will start with the bad news: not only does the tie-in not give X any protection against Y's engaging in arbitrage on A, it creates an additional problem for X by giving Y an incentive to violate its full-requirements obligation on B. The good news is that, if B is a complement of A, the tie-in may give X almost as much protection against its and Y's pessimism about Y's demand for the products it is purchasing from X as the supra-TSM-output-marginal-cost pricing of A would do since X and Y are likely to be pessimistic about Y's quantity-demand for B to the same extent as they are pessimistic about Y's quantity-demand for A (so that, for example, Y will underestimate the cost to itself of agreeing to the full-requirements constraint on B when it underestimates the value to it of the right to purchase A at a stipulated price [be willing to accept terms on B that are more costly to it than it believes when it underestimates its quantity-demand for A). Similarly, if B is a complement of A so that Y's actual quantity-demand for B deviates in pretty much the same way from Y's weighted-average-expected quantity-demand for B as Y's actual quantity-demand for A deviates from Y's weighted-average-expected quantity-demand for A, the tie-in will do pretty much as good a job of reducing the sum of X's and Y's risk costs as does the sacrificed supra-TSM-output-marginal-cost pricing of A. In many situations, this type of tie-in will be profitable for sellers—will be a profitable fancy pricing-technique.

In the second variant of this type of tie-in, the seller X is a manufacturer of an input A against which substitution is possible, the buyer Y is a manufacturer of a final good D, and Y can produce any (relevant) quantity of D by using different combinations of input A and another input B (perhaps together with another input C against which substitution is not possible). (X may or may not produce inputs B and/or C itself.) An input producer in X's position can find it advantageous to charge a supra-TSM-output-marginal-cost per-unit price for its product for the same reasons that a final-product producer X can find it advantageous to charge such a per-unit price for its product—namely, to discourage its customer from engaging in arbitrage on A, to reduce the loss is sustains because it and/or its customer is pessimistic about the customer's quantity-demand for A, and to reduce the sum of the risk costs it and its customer bear by shifting risk from its customer to itself. However, when the product a seller X produces is an input against which substitution is possible, X's charging a supra-TSM-output-marginal-cost price for its input A will lower its unit sales of A and the transaction surplus and seller surplus it respectively generates and realizes by producing and selling A in two ways: not only by reducing its customer Y's output of D by raising the marginal cost of D to Y but also by inducing Y to produce the output of D Y produces with less A and more B than is in the joint interest of X and Y and hence in X's interest (by inducing Y to make jointly-unprofitable substitutions of B for A). Any input producer in X's position may be able to use two variants of full-requirements tie-ins to prevent its supra-marginal-cost pricing from destroying transaction surplus by inducing Y to substitute B for A. In the first variant, X agrees to give Y an $\$\alpha$ gain by supplying Y with A for a lower per-unit price than X would charge Y for A in an independent transaction on A on condition that Y agree to incur an $\$\alpha$ loss by purchasing from X its full requirements of B from X as well for a price that exceeds B's normal market price by the same percentage as the percentage by which A's price in this tie-in exceeds the marginal cost to X of producing A and supplying it to Y. In the second variant, X agrees to give Y an $\$\alpha$ gain by supplying Y with A for a lower per-unit price than X would charge Y for A in an independent transaction on A on condition that Y agree to incur an $\$\alpha$ loss by purchasing from X its full requirements of input C against which substitution is not possible for a price that exceeds C's normal market price. Both these tie-in variants will yield X gains by preventing X's removing a given amount of buyer surplus by charging supra-TSM-output-marginal-cost prices from inducing Y to making jointly-unprofitable input-substitutions against A. This type of tie-in will give X the same protection against its and/or Y's pessimism about Y's quantity-demand for A and against Y's and its own risk-averseness as would the sacrificed supra-TSM-output-marginal-cost pricing of A. Although such tie-ins will impose some costs on X—the cost of drafting and negotiating the relevant agreement and the cost of enforcing Y's obligation to purchase its full requirements of B or C for more than its normal market price, there will be many situations in which the benefits it will yield X by deterring substitutions against A will exceed the latter costs—that is, in which this variant of full-requirements tie-ins will be profitable.[10] Admittedly, a producer of an input A against which substitution is possible may also be able to increase its profits by preventing jointly-unprofitable substitutions against its input by agreeing to lower its per-unit price for its input A in exchange for the buyer's agreeing to pay X an endproduct royalty on its sales of D or—as we shall see—to sell X its full output of D for less than the price it would otherwise charge for its product. However, in some circumstances, the tie-ins I have described will be more profitable (will involve lower enforcement-costs) than any such endproduct-royalty scheme or reciprocity agreement.

The fourth type of fancy pricing-technique a seller can use to increase the profits it can realize when supplying an individual buyer is a total-output-supply reciprocity agreement. This type of reciprocity agreement is most likely to be profitable when one participant—say, X—produces an input against which substitution is possible and the other participant—say, Y—uses or can use that input to produce a final product D. In some situations, X may find that the most profitable technique for it to use to prevent its non-marginal-cost "pricing" from reducing its profits by inducing Y to produce the quantity of D it produces with fewer units of A and more units of another unput B than would be in X's interest and indeed in X's and Y's joint interest for Y to use would be not to use one of the two subtypes of tie-ins just described or an endproduct-royalty scheme but to condition its sale of A to Y at a per-unit price equal to A's marginal cost to X at A's TSM output (*plus* perhaps a lump-sum fee) on Y's agreeing to sell to X its total output of D for a per-unit price that is sufficiently lower than the price Y would otherwise find profitable to charge for B to cancel out the gains Y obtained from the lower price of A. Such a reciprocity agreement would tend to be most profitable when it would be more cost-effective to enforce the total-output-supply obligation on D than to enforce the full-requirements-purchasing obligation on the substitutable input B and/or any input C against which substitution was not possible or the endproduct-royalty obligation. Although full-requirements-supply reciprocity agreements involving final products may also be profitable for the same reasons that their tie-in counterparts may be profitable, I doubt that the conditions that would have to be fulfilled for this to be the case are often satisfied.[11]

The fifth fancy pricing-technique a seller may find profitable to employ is inter-buyer price discrimination. Sellers can practice inter-buyer price discrimination both by charging different buyers different per-unit prices and no lump-sum fees (when doing so cannot be cost-justified) and by charging different buyers different (average-lump-sum-fee *plus* per-unit) prices (when doing so is not cost-justified). For simplicity, I will focus on the pure-per-unit-pricing variant of price discrimination (the variant that is the universal focus of price-discrimination scholarship).

I will analyze the profitability of conventional (pure per-unit-price) price discrimination by comparing the profits it yields with those yielded by non-discriminatory pure per-unit pricing—that is, with single pricing. A switch from single pricing to conventional price discrimination, which involves the seller's charging some buyers a higher per-unit price and some a lower per-unit price than the conventional non-discriminatory profit-maximizing per-unit price, confers benefits on the seller (1) by enabling it to secure a higher price for the units it continues to sell at the discriminatorily-high price that it would also have sold at its non-discriminatory price (benefits equal to the number of units sold at the discriminatorily-high price *times* the amount by which the discriminatorily-high price exceeds the non-discriminatory price) and (2) by enabling it to make profits on the extra units it sells at the discriminatorily-low price that it would not have sold at the non-discriminatory price (benefits equal to [the number of additional units the price discrimination enables the seller to sell] *times* [the difference between the discriminatorily-low per-unit-price and the average variable cost the price discriminator had to incur to supply the additional units in question]).[12] Sellers will also have to incur additional costs to shift from single pricing to conventional price discrimination: (1) the extra research costs they must incur to identify the buyers to whom/which they will find it profitable to charge respectively discriminatorily-high and discriminatorily-low prices, (2) the extra checkout-counter costs they will have to incur to charge different buyers different prices, (3) any costs they have to incur because conventional price discriminators gives those charged the discriminatory-low price an incentive to resell the seller's product to buyers from whom/which the seller is trying to obtain a discriminatorily-high price (the cost to the discriminator of preventing or allowing such arbitrage), (4) any goodwill-related loss the seller incurs because buyers charged discriminatorily-high prices resent that fact, and (5) in jurisdictions in which the seller's conventional price discrimination is legally prohibited or might be misperceived to be illegal, any law-related costs the seller must incur to engage in the practice. In some situations, the benefits a seller can obtain by substituting conventional price discrimination for single pricing will exceed the costs it must incur to do so.

13.1.2 The Economic Efficiency of Those Sellers' That Find It Profitable to Do So Substituting Each Fancy Pricing-Technique I Have Identified for Single Pricing and the Economic Efficiency of the Government's Deterring the Use of Each Such Type of Fancy Pricing-Technique

13.1.2.1 The Economic Efficiency of Sellers' That Find It Profitable to Do so Substituting Any of the 4 Fancy Pricing-Techniques Previously Described for Single Pricing

I will assume initially that the relevant firms will not vertically integrate forward if constrained to engage in single pricing and then comment on the significance of relaxing that assumption.

The Economic Efficiency of Sellers' Practicing Perfect Price Discrimination Rather that Single Pricing When Dealing with Individual Buyers

On the assumption that the relevant sellers will not vertically integrate forward if prohibited from using any fancy pricing-technique, the choice of those sellers that find it profitable to do so to practice perfect price discrimination rather than single pricing will or may affect economic efficiency in at least eight ways.

First, the switch to perfect price discrimination will tend to decrease economic efficiency by increasing "mechanical" allocative transaction costs (in my judgment by more than they increase "mechanical" private transaction costs). More specifically, this pricing-technique switch will decrease economic efficiency (1) by increasing the research costs the sellers must incur to estimate the buyers' demand curves, (2) by necessitating the sellers' drafting/negotiating/signing written sales-contracts, and often (3) by causing the sellers to incur costs to prevent the buyers from engaging in arbitrage.

Second, this pricing-technique switch will tend to decrease economic efficiency by increasing incentives the original buyer has to engage in arbitrage. More specifically, to the extent that this switch in pricing-technique increases the amount of arbitrage in which the original buyer engages, it will increase (1) the private and *a fortiori* the allocative cost that the parties involved in the transfer of the good from the producer to the ultimate buyer incur/generate to identify each other as profitable trading-partners, (2) the private and *a fortiori* the allocative contracting costs that are generated by substituting two contracts (the contract between the producer and the initial buyer and the contract between the initial buyer and the arbitrage buyer) for the one contract that would otherwise be formed between the producer and the arbitrage buyer, and (3) the private and *a fortiori* the allocative cost of delivering the arbitraged units to their ultimate buyer (by substituting a two-stage delivery from the producer to the initial buyer and from the initial buyer to the ultimate [arbitrage] buyer for a one-stage delivery from the producer to the ultimate buyer) and by delaying delivery. Relatedly, this pricing-technique switch will also tend to decrease economic efficiency by causing the original seller to include allocative-costly arbitrage-prohibiting clauses in its contracts of sale (which are allocatively costly to draft, negotiate, and enforce: the allocative enforcement-costs include not only those the original seller directly generates but also those the original buyer generates when defending itself and those the government generates when handling the related legal disputes).

Third, at least to the extent that the seller that switches from single pricing to perfect price discrimination uses a variant of perfect price discrimination that involves its charging the buyer a lump-sum fee either for the right to purchase the seller's product for a per-unit price equal to the seller's marginal cost at its expected TSM output or for the expected TSM output of the product in question, the switch will usually decrease economic efficiency by increasing the sum of the buyer's and seller's transaction-related risk costs, which are allocative as well as private (though I acknowledge that in some unusual cases the switch will increase economic efficiency by decreasing the sum of the seller's and buyer's risk costs).

Fourth, I suspect that, even in a realistically-Pareto-imperfect economy when the relevant buyer is a retailer (or perhaps a wholesaler) and the relevant seller is the producer of a good the relevant buyer resells, the switch to perfect price discrimination will tend to increase economic efficiency by making it profitable for the relevant buyer to make demand-increasing expenditures on media advertizing, in-store promotional installations, and in-person sales-efforts and to make shelf-space allocations that are in its and the relevant seller's joint interest by reducing the gaps between the cost to the buyer of various marginal and intra-marginal units of the seller's product and the cost to the seller of supplying the relevant buyer with those units.

Fifth, the switch from single pricing to perfect price discrimination will tend to decrease economic efficiency by increasing poverty (by reducing buyer surplus and increasing seller surplus and thereby conferring equivalent-dollar gains on the sellers' shareholders/creditors/managers/employees, at least if the number of relevant buyers who are poor or near-poor are higher than the number percentages of the sellers' shareholders/creditors/employees/manager who are poor or near-poor).

Sixth, the switch from single pricing to perfect price discrimination will tend to decrease economic efficiency by increasing material inequality on the distributive-impact assumptions made in the preceding paragraph.

Seventh, firms' substituting perfect price discrimination for single pricing may either increase or decrease the amount of economic efficiency they generate by spending money on political parties/campaigns/candidates and government-decision-making-process participation, depending on whether the shift to perfect price discrimination respectively increases or decrease the amount of money sellers devote to these activities. I am unable to provide any guesstimate worth consideration about the sign of the impact that perfect price discrimination will have on economic efficiency in this way because that impact will depend on whether perfect price discrimination tends to increase or decrease the concentration of the seller-side of the ARDEPPSes in which it is practiced and I have nothing worthwhile to say on this issue—that is, to say on (1) whether perfect price discrimination will increase or decrease equilibrium investment in the economy in which it is practiced (see below), (2) on the relevant extents to which any additional QV investments or investments in PPR that are induced by the practice of perfect price discrimination will be made by firms with atypically-large "ARDEPPS-shares," by firms with atypically-small ARDEPPS-shares, or by new entrants, or (3) on the relative extents to which any reduction in QV investment or investment in PPR that results from the practice of perfect price discrimination will be caused by decisions by firms with atypically-high ARDEPPS-shares, atypically-low ARDEPPS-shares, or potential entrants not to renew extant investments in the ARDEPPSes in question or not to make new investments in those ARDEPPSes.

Eighth, for somewhat-related reasons, I am unable to predict whether the specified shifts from single pricing to perfect price discrimination will increase or decrease the amount of economic inefficiency the relevant economy generates because, from the perspective of economic efficiency, it devotes too many resources to QV-investment creation and too few to the production of units of output of extant products and to the execution of production-process research. I am unable to predict whether all shifts from single pricing to perfect price discrimination that would be profitable would increase or decrease economic efficiency by altering the proportions of the relevant society's resources that are devoted respectively to UO production, QV creation, and PPR execution (1) because although the direct effect of any such shift will be to increase the unit output of the extant goods on which the perfect price discrimination is practiced (to increase the amount of resources the relevant economy devotes to producing extant products and to decrease the amounts it devotes to QV creation and PPR), the indirect effect of any such shift will be to increase equilibrium QV investment or equilibrium PPR in the ARDEPPS in which the perfect price discrimination is practiced by increasing the profit-rates that will be yielded by the investments it contains at any ARDEPPS-investment quantity (to increase the amounts of resources the relevant economy devotes to QV creation and PPR and to reduce concomitantly the amount it devotes to producing extant products), (2) because—given Item (1) in this list—I do not know whether the relevant shifts from single pricing to perfect price discrimination will increase or decrease the amounts of resources devoted respectively to producing extant products, QV creation, and PPR, and (3) because—given that from the perspective of economic efficiency too many resources are devoted to QV creation and too few to PPR—even if it were certain that profitable shifts from single pricing to perfect price discrimination would increase the amount of resources devoted to producing extant products—it might not be clear whether this resource allocation would increase or decrease economic efficiency. Admittedly, if I am right in thinking that the percentage-inflation in the profits yielded by QV investments is much higher than the percentage-deflation in the profits yielded by investments in PPR, that the percentage of resources devoted to QV-investment creation is much higher than the percentage devoted to PPR, and that about the same percentages of the resources devoted respectively to QV-investment creation and PPR execution can be cost-effectively used to produce units of extant products, profitable shifts from single pricing to perfect price discrimination would increase/decrease economic efficiency if they increased/decreased the amount of resources the relevant economy devotes to producing units of extant products.

The preceding analyses clearly do not constitute an a priori argument for the conclusion that the decisions of all sellers in an economy to shift from single pricing to perfect price discrimination whenever they find it individually profitable to do so will decrease economic efficiency. However, I am confident that such shifts to perfect price discrimination would decrease economic efficiency all tolled if the sellers that made them would not respond to their prohibition (or, more generally, to their using any pricing-technique other than single pricing) by vertically integrating forward. Admittedly, to the extent that the relevant sellers would respond to such a prohibition by engaging in otherwise-unprofitable vertical integration, that reality would have to be taken into account when assessing the economic efficiency of profitable perfect price discrimination since in the relevant cases the actual options between which relevant firms will choose will be not (1)(A) perfect price discrimination that was more profitable than single pricing or (B) single pricing (as I have implicitly assumed) but (2)(A) single pricing or (B) vertical integration that was more profitable than single pricing but less profitable than perfect price discrimination that was more profitable than single pricing. I assume that forward vertical integration will never be an option when the relevant buyer is a final consumer but will be a profitable option in some cases in which (1) the seller is an input-manufacturer or a distributor of an input and the buyer is a final-good producer or (2) the seller is a final-good producer and the buyer is a retailor or perhaps a wholesaler of the seller's output or (3) the seller is a wholesaler of a final product and the buyer is a retailor of that product. For the purposes of this analysis, I also assume that the relevant seller's vertical integration would not be legally prohibited, regardless of whether it was achieved by an (M or A), joint venture, or internal growth.

Three additional questions or pairs of related questions are therefore salient. First, in cases in which prohibiting a seller from substituting perfect price discrimination for single pricing would cause the seller to vertically integrate forward, what is the relationship between the misallocativeness of the shift from single pricing to perfect price discrimination and the misallocativeness of the shift from single pricing to vertical integration if a perpetrator-makes-no-relevant-change baseline is used to calculate the economic efficiency of each of the shifts in question? Second, in what percentage of the cases would a seller that would find it profitable to substitute perfect price discrimination for single pricing find it profitable to vertically integrate forward if it were prohibited from substituting perfect price discrimination (or any other fancy pricing-technique) for single pricing? If across all instances profitable shifts from single pricing to perfect price discrimination would generate economic inefficiency if they did not deter vertical integration and any vertical integration they deterred would have been less economically inefficient than the shift from single pricing to perfect price discrimination would be if it did not deter vertical integration, the practice of perfect price discrimination would be economically inefficient. However, if as I believe profitable shifts from single pricing to perfect price discrimination would generate economic inefficiency if they did not deter vertical integration, some such shifts would deter vertical integration, and any vertical integration such shifts deterred would have generated more economic inefficiency than the shift from single pricing to perfect price discrimination would be deemed to generate if the economic efficiency of both shifts was calculated using the perpetrator-makes-no-relevant-change baseline, whether profitable shifts from single pricing to perfect price discrimination as a class will increase or decrease economic efficiency will depend on (1) the percentage by which the economic inefficiency that would be generated by the deterred vertical integrations exceeds the economic inefficiency that would have been generated by the shifts from single pricing to perfect price discrimination if those shifts did not deter vertical integration and (2) the relative magnitudes of the shifts from single pricing to perfect price discrimination that would and would not deter vertical integration (where the magnitude of any such pricing-technique shift is measured by the economic inefficiency it would be calculated to generate if one uses a seller-does-nothing-relevant baseline). Third, assuming that some instances of shifts from single pricing to perfect price discrimination increase and some decrease economic inefficiency in part because some deter and some do not deter vertical integration, will it be TBLE to identify categories of shifts from single pricing to perfect price discrimination whose members seem appropriately likely to be respectively economically efficient and economically inefficient?

I will now comment on the answers to these three questions in the order in which they were posed. I will answer the first on two assumptions: (1) that the sellers in question have sufficient retained earnings, sufficient ability to raise capital from the debt or equity markets, sufficient managerial and labor capacity, or sufficient ability to expand their stock of managers and workers not to have to forego alternative investments that would otherwise yield significant supernormal profits to engage in vertical integration and (2) that the hierarchical-control devices that would be available to the sellers if they were vertically integrated would enable them to respond to the deficiencies of single pricing (when evaluated from a "Robinson Crusoe-baseline perspective) more cost-effectively than perfect price discrimination would do. On these assumptions, the fact that the relevant sellers found perfect price discrimination more profitable than vertical integration would imply that the vertically-integrated firm would perform the other functions of the downstream operation sufficiently-less-cost-effectively than independent contractors would preform them for the upstream firm for the associated profit-loss to exceed the previously-referenced profit-gain that the vertical integration would generate. This difference in cost-effectiveness will reflect some combination of independent contractors' being more skilled and assiduous than in-house staff and (possibly) the fact that independent contractors of given "productivity" need to be paid less than in-house staff of that productivity because at least some relevant individuals place a positive value on running their own business even as an independent contractor of another firm as opposed to being an employee of another firm. I suspect that some of the Robinson-Crusoe-related benefits of substituting vertical integration for perfect price discrimination (those related to buyer and seller pessimism) are "inflated" in the sense in which I use this term—are private benefits that exceed their allocative counterparts—while none of the private costs of substituting vertical integration for perfect price discrimination are "inflated" in the above sense. Indeed, I suspect that to the extent that independent contractors are more cost-effective than employees because independent contractors use fewer resources to execute given tasks than employees would use to do so, the private cost of substituting vertical integration for perfect price discrimination will be deflated. I am therefore inclined to conclude that (1) the profitability of substituting vertical integration for perfect price discrimination is inflated, (2) that the substitution of perfect price discrimination for vertical integration that was less profitable than the perfect price discrimination for which it would be substituted would decrease economic efficiency by more than it would decrease the relevant seller's profits, and (3) that the replacement of single pricing with perfect price discrimination that deters its practitioner from vertically integrating forward will be economically efficient (even if as I believe the substitution of perfect price discrimination for single pricing would be economically inefficient if it did not deter vertical integration).

If all the economic-efficiency conclusions I have argued for (should I say "asserted"?) were correct, what would follow? The answer depends on whether it would be TBLE to investigate whether a particular seller's (category of sellers') switch(es) from single pricing to perfect price discrimination would deter it (them) from vertically integrating forward. If it would be TBLE to investigate this issue and my other proffered economic-efficiency conclusions were correct, it would be TBLE to investigate whether particular individual sellers' (categories of sellers') substitution(s) of perfect price discrimination for single pricing would deter it (them) from vertically integrating forward and to conclude that any switch or category of switches to perfect price discrimination from single pricing would decrease economic efficiency if it did not deter vertical integration and would increase economic efficiency if it did deter vertical integration. I can think of two categories of potential perfect price discriminators whose use of this technique will clearly not deter them from engaging in forward vertical integration (for which it will be TBLE to make that determination): sellers that are supplying final consumers and sellers whose forward vertical integration is prohibited by law. Because vertical integration forward into final-good consumption will not be an option, the decision of sellers whose customers are final consumers to switch from single pricing to perfect price discrimination will on my other assumptions always be economically inefficient because such decisions will never deter the sellers that make them from vertically integrating forward into consumption. However, I do not think that this conclusion is empirically important because I suspect that suppliers of final consumers rarely if ever practice perfect price discrimination. Sellers' practice of perfect price discrimination will also be economically inefficient when the law prohibits them from vertically integrating forward. However, the real-world significance of this possibility is probably limited to situations in which the relevant sellers find vertical (M&A)s and vertical joint ventures critically more profitable than vertical internal growth: although the courts and antitrust-enforcement agencies of many countries (mistakenly) believe that vertical (M&A)s and vertical joint ventures often violate one or more of their tests of antitrust illegality, I know of no country whose antitrust law—either as written or as applied—prohibits vertical internal growth. As one of my previous observations implies, in those situations in which it is not TBLE to investigate whether any seller's (category of sellers') switch(es) from single pricing to perfect price discrimination would deter it (them) from vertically integrating forward, the relevant conclusion that would be TBLE to reach in the current context (1) would be a conclusion about the economic efficiency of all decisions combined of all sellers in this category to switch from single pricing to perfect price discrimination and would depend on estimates or guesstimates of (A) the percentage of the relevant switches that would and would not deter the relevant seller's forward vertical integration and (B) the relative average amounts by which the switches by sellers that might vertically integrate forward that would deter such vertical integration would increase economic efficiency and the switches by such sellers that would not deter such vertical integration would decrease economic efficiency. I wish I had more information or better-grounded intuitions that bear on these issues, but I do not. For what it's worth, I suspect that the practice of perfect price discrimination will rarely deter the practitioners from vertically integrating forward in situations in which the relevant buyer is not a final consumer and the vertical integration was not prohibited by law. If that is the case, the substitution of perfect price discrimination for single pricing in such situations will almost certainly decrease economic efficiency across all instances. I will proceed on the admittedly-contestable assumption that this is so.

The Economic Efficiency of a Seller's Switching From Single Pricing to a Pricing-Technique That Combines a Lump-Sum Fee and a Supra-TSM-Output-Marginal-Cost Per-Unit Price When Dealing With Individual Buyers

To simplify, I will assume that this switch does not deter the seller that makes it from vertically integrating forward and focus on the difference between the economic efficiency of this switch and the switch from single pricing to perfect price discrimination. The economic efficiency of this switch differs from the economic efficiency of the switch to perfect price discrimination for at least three reasons:

(1) because this switch is to a pricing-technique in which a higher per-unit price is charged than is charged for relevant units of the product in question under any variant of perfect price discrimination, this switch generates less misallocation than the switch to perfect price discrimination generates by causing the buyer involved to engage in arbitrage and/or the seller involved to take allocative-transaction-costly steps to prevent the buyer from engaging in arbitrage and to collect damages from buyers that violated their contractual obligations not to engage in arbitrage;
(2) because, in comparison to the switch to perfect price discrimination, this switch involves the charging of a lower lump-sum fee, it shifts less risk from

the seller to the buyer than does the shift to perfect price discrimination and hence causes less misallocation by raising (is more allocative costly in that it raises) the sum of the seller's and buyer's risk costs in the typical case in which the seller is less-risk-averse than the buyer and does not face the risk a reseller-buyer faces that its share of the resale market may be lower or higher than is expected; and

(3) because, in comparison to the switch to perfect price discrimination, this switch involves a smaller reduction in the difference between the per-unit price the seller is charging the buyer and the seller's TSM-output marginal cost, this switch will increase economic efficiency by less than the shift to perfect price discrimination will increase economic efficiency (A) by reducing the extent to which the buyer (if it is a retailer or perhaps a wholesaler) fails to make expenditures on media advertizing, in-store promotional displays, and salesperson training and sales-efforts and fails to make shelf-space allocations that on conventional assumptions about buyers' abilities to process information correctly and properly assess the value to them of product-images would be economically efficient (I recognize I am entering deep waters) and/or (B) by reducing the "allocative costs" that the seller generates to prevent its supra-marginal-cost per-unit pricing from producing this outcome (to subsidize the relevant reseller's expenditures, to train the reseller's sales-staffs, to place advertizements or set up promotional displays itself that are less allocatively efficient than those the independent-retailer buyer would have placed).

In short, there are two reasons for believing that the pricing-technique shift now under consideration will be more economically efficient than the shift to perfect price discrimination and one reason for believing that the shift now under consideration will be less economically efficient than the shift to perfect price discrimination. Unfortunately, I have no basis for generalizing about the relevant magnitudes of these differences. I recognize that my failures are adding up. But if I had to make the best guess I could muster, I would guess that, taken together, all shifts that sellers would find profitable to make from single pricing to the pricing-technique now under consideration would reduce economic efficiency—that any difference between the economic efficiency of these shifts and the economic efficiency of shifts to perfect price discrimination would not be critical.

The Economic Efficiency of a Seller's Shifting From Single Pricing One Product to a Particular Buyer to a Tie-In That Shifts to Another Product Part or All of Its Supra-TSM-Marginal-Cost Per-Unit Pricing to That Individual Buyer

Once more, to simplify, I will assume that the use of such tie-ins will not deter the sellers that employ them from vertically integrating forward. I will also adopt the last subsection's conclusion that the shift from single pricing to a one-product-oriented pricing-technique in which the seller charges the buyer a lump-sum fee and a per-unit price that exceeds the seller's TSM-output marginal cost will decrease economic efficiency. I will then analyze the economic efficiency of shifting from single pricing to the type of tie-in with which this subsection is concerned by analyzing the economic efficiency of shifting from the complicated one-product pricing-technique just described to this type of tie-in referenced in this section's heading and asking whether this latter shift could increase economic efficiency by more than the pricing-technique shift studied in the previous subsection decreased it. I will analyze separately the economic efficiency of the two variants of this type of tie-in that I distinguished in Sect. 13.1.1.

When the tying and tied products are final goods, the switch from the one-product-oriented complicated (mixed lump = sum fee plus supra-marginal-cost per-unit price) pricing-technique analyzed in the preceding subsection to the type of tie-in on which this subsection is focusing will affect economic efficiency for at least four reasons:

(1) I suspect that the switch will tend to decrease economic efficiency because the type of tie-in in question will be more allocative-transaction-costly to design, draft, and negotiate than the contract that would implement the complicated one-product pricing-technique on which the preceding subsection focused would be;
(2) the pricing-technique shift whose economic efficiency this paragraph is analyzing will tend to decrease economic efficiency by increasing the buyer's incentive to engage in arbitrage on the tying product A and by giving the buyer an incentive to violate its contractual obligation to purchase from the tying seller its full requirements of the tying product B for more than the tying product's normal market price—that is, will tend to cause economic inefficiency (A) by leading the tying seller to take allocative-costly steps to counteract the tie-in's tendency to increase the buyer's incentive to engage in arbitrage on the tying product A and to enforce the buyer's obligation to purchase its full requirements of B from the tying seller and (B) by leading to arbitrage, which increases the allocative distributive cost of supplying A to the arbitrage buyer and reduces the dollar value of the A to the arbitrage buyers both when the A is perishable and when the dollar value of the A to the arbitrage-buyer increases with the speed with which the A is delivered;
(3) at least on the conventional assumptions that retailer demand-increasing expenditures that are in the joint interest of the retailer and the producer are economically efficient, the pricing-technique shift from the complicated one-product-oriented-technique just analyzed to the type of tie-in now under consideration will tend to increase economic efficiency on balance by increasing the incentives of the buyer (usually a retailer) to make demand-increasing expenditures on the tying product A (by lowering the per-unit price of A closer to its marginal cost to the tying seller X) and decreasing the buyer's incentive to make demand-increasing expenditures on the tied product B (by increasing the per-unit price of B to the buyer Y above the marginal cost the seller X must incur to supply it to Y), at least if I am correct in assuming that, for other reasons related to the profitability of this type of tie-in, the tied product A will usually be a differentiated good (on which demand-increasing expenditures may well be in the joint interest of the retailer [buyer] and the producer

[seller]) while the tied product B will usually be a standardized good (on which demand-increasing expenditures are unlikely to be in the joint interest of the retailer and the producer); and

(4) when the tying and tied products are complements (which they will tend to be) that can be combined in varying proportions to each other (which, admittedly, is less likely to be the case), the shift from the complicated one-product-oriented pricing-technique considered in the last subsection to this type of tie-in will probably tend to increase economic efficiency by increasing the economic efficiency of the proportions in which the tying and tied products are combined (at least if I am correct in assuming [1] that the tie-in will bring the [P_A/MC_A] and [P_B/MC_B] ratios closer to each other [because B will usually be an undifferentiated good whose P/MC ratio in an independent transaction will be lower while A will usually be a differentiated product whose P/MC ratio in an independent transaction will tend to be higher even when in an independent transaction in which X would sell A for a lump-sum fee and a per-unit price that is significantly below its "profit-maximizing" single price] and [2] that it is TBLE to ignore the other Pareto imperfections that would individually in an otherwise-Pareto-perfect economy cause the above price [P] figures to diverge from the associated marginal-allocative-value [MLV] figures and the above marginal-cost [MC] figures to diverge from the associated marginal-allocative-cost [MLC] figures).

Once more, I must admit that my assessment of the net economic efficiency of the switch now directly under consideration is based on empirical guesstimates that—though not completely uninformed—could certainly be improved on. But I will not be deterred. In part because I have doubts about the economic efficiency of demand-increasing expenditures that increase the joint profits of the retailers that make them and their respective suppliers and in part because I suspect that the complements that are involved in final-good tie-ins of this type (for example, suits and [dress shirts and ties] or substantial agricultural machinery and [hoses, spades, etc.]) are usually not combined in proportions that are significantly affected by the relative prices of the individual goods involved in the tie-in, I believe that shifts from a one-product pricing-technique in which an individual buyer is charged a lump-sum fee and a supra-TSM-output-marginal-cost per-unit price to a tie-in in which the per-unit price of the "one product" and perhaps the lump-sum fee are reduced on condition that the buyer agrees to purchasing its full requirements of a second product for more than its normal market price decrease economic efficiency. If both this conclusion and my earlier conclusion that shifts from single pricing to the complicated one-product-oriented pricing-technique referenced in the preceding sentence are economically inefficient are correct, shifts from single pricing to this type of final-good tie-in will be economically inefficient across all exemplars. Although I admit that some individual shifts from the complicated one-product pricing-technique just referenced to this type of final-good tie-in and a smaller number of shifts from single pricing to this type of final-good tie-in might be economically efficient if the change in demand-increasing expenditures they effectuated generated a substantial increase in economic efficiency and they generate significant increases in economic efficiency by changing the proportions in which the tying and tied products are combined, I doubt both that such outcomes obtain in a significant percentage of the relevant cases and, relatedly, that it would be TBLE to consider this possibility.

When the tying and tied products are inputs (are an input A that the tying seller produces and either another input B that can be substituted against the tying seller's input A or another input C against which substitution is not possible that the relevant buyer Y uses to produce its final product D), the switch from the complicated one-product pricing-technique on which the preceding section focuses (in which the buyer is charged a lump-sum fee and a supra-TSM-output-marginal-cost per-unit price for A) to a tie-in in which the seller (perhaps in addition to lowering its lump-sum fee) lowers its per-unit price for A in exchange for the buyer's agreement to purchase its full requirements of either B (for a price that exceeds this second input's normal market price by the same percentage by which A's price under the tie-in exceeds the marginal cost of A to its producer X) or input C against which substitution in not possible (if such an input exists) for a price that exceeds its normal market price sufficiently for the related loss the tie-in imposes on Y to equal the gain it confers on Y by lowering the price of A (if I assume that Y does not benefit from the arrangement all tolled) will affect economic efficiency in 3 ways:

(1) will tend to decrease economic efficiency to the extent that it is more allocative-transaction-costly to formulate, draft, and negotiate the tie-in than the complicated-pricing-technique-incorporating contract on A,
(2) will tend to decrease economic efficiency by causing X to generate allocative transaction costs to combat the tie-in's increasing Y's incentive to engage in arbitrage on A and giving Y an incentive to violate its full-requirements obligation on B or C and by causing Y in essence to substitute less-allocatively-efficient sales to an arbitrage-buyer Z for more-allocatively-efficient sales by X to Z, but
(3) will tend to increase economic efficiency (A) by preventing economically-inefficient substitutions of B for A in what I take to be the normal situation in which (i) the ratio of B's normal market price to its marginal cost is lower than the ratio of the price that X would charge for A in an independent transaction to the related marginal cost of A to X and (ii) the other Pareto imperfections the relevant economy contains do not render the input-substitution the tie-in prevents economically efficient or (B) by obviating X's using endproduct royalties to prevent Y from substituting B for A (an alternative that I assume will be less-allocatively-efficient when it is less-profitable because it will be more private-transaction-costly and *a fortiori* more allocative-transaction-costly when it is less profitable).

I acknowledge once more the contestability of the conclusions I am about to assert. However, in my judgment, (1) all tolled, across all instances, the substitutions of this type of input tie-in for the complicated independent pricing of the input A against which substitution is possible will increase economic efficiency (in part because X will often be able to reduce the private and allocative cost of preventing Y from violating its obligation to purchase its full requirements of B or C from X by altering the B or C it produces or arranges to have someone else to produce for it in a way that makes "its" B readily identifiable), (2) across all instances, all tolled, the substitutions of this type of input tie-in for single pricing is also likely to increase economic efficiency (both the allocative costs and the allocative benefits of these substitutions will be higher than their counterparts for the substitution Item (1) in this list analyzed), and (3) it will probably not be TBLE to attempt to identify and treat separately those exemplars of this type of tie-in whose use is economically inefficient from those exemplars whose use is economically efficient.

The final type of individual-buyer-oriented pricing-technique to be discussed is reciprocity agreements. As indicated previously, the type of reciprocity agreement that deserves to be characterized as a pricing-technique is a functional counterpart to the input variant of the tie-ins just discussed. Thus, a seller X that produces an input A against which substitution is possible that would set a supra-marginal-cost price (as well as a lump-sum fee) for A in an independent transaction on that input will sometimes find it profitable to prevent the substitutions against A to which such pricing would lead by agreeing to supply A to final-good D producer Y that is the potential buyer of A at a price equal to A's TSM-output marginal cost on condition that Y agree to sell to X its total output of D for a price sufficiently below the price Y would otherwise charge for D for Y to suffer a loss on that account that just equals the gain Y secured from the associated reduction in A's per-unit price (if I assume for simplicity that Y breaks even on the pricing-technique switch in question). The switch from the "lump-sum-fee *plus* supra-TSM-marginal-cost per-unit price of A" pricing-technique to this type of reciprocity agreement will affect economic efficiency in 3 ways:

(1) will tend to decrease economic efficiency by increasing the allocative transaction cost of formulating, drafting, and negotiating the associated contract of sale,
(2) will tend to decrease economic efficiency by increasing Y's incentive to engage in arbitrage on A and giving Y an incentive to violate its total-output-supply obligation on D, and
(3) if the assumptions made previously are correct, will tend to increase economic efficiency by preventing substitutions of B for A or obviating X's entering into and enforcing an endproduct-royalty scheme on D.

I do not know whether the shifts to this type of reciprocity agreement now being considered will be more or less economically efficient than shifts to functionally analogous input tie-ins. I suspect that the shifts to the reciprocity agreements will tend to be more economically efficient because it will be less-allocative-transaction-costly for X to enforce Y's total-output-supply obligation than to enforce Y's full-requirements-input-purchase obligation. However, I suspect that the shifts to the reciprocity agreements will tend to be less economically effect to the extent that X is a less-economically-efficient distributor of D than Y would be. Still, I believe that when input producers in X's position choose to use this type of reciprocity agreement rather than full-requirements tie-ins to deter substitutions against their inputs, the choice of the reciprocity agreement over the tie-in will tend to be economically efficient. I therefore believe that, across all exemplars, shifts to this type of reciprocity agreement from both single pricing and the one-product pricing-technique that combines a lump-sum fee and a supra-TSM-output-marginal-cost per-unit price will increase economic efficiency and that it will not be TBLE to try to identify and prohibit those shifts in this category that decrease economic efficiency.

The last pricing-technique to be discussed—conventional inter-buyer price discrimination—relates to the prices that a seller offers more than one buyer. Usually, the expression "price discrimination" references a seller's charging different buyers different per-unit prices for the same good despite the fact that the seller had or would have to incur the same marginal cost to supply the buyers in question or, more generally, to a seller's charging different (price *minus* marginal cost) margins to different buyers (e.g., to a seller X's charging buyers Y1 and Y2 the same price despite the fact that the marginal cost X had to incur to supply "the good" to Y1 was different from the marginal cost X had to incur to supply the good to Y2, perhaps because the good was a delivered good and the cost of delivering it to Y1 was different from the cost of delivering it to Y2). In fact, it would also be appropriate to say that a seller practiced price discrimination if it charged different average lump-sum fees *plus* per-unit prices to buyers that it had to incur the same average incremental cost to supply. To save space and avoid taxing reader patience, I will limit this discussion of the economic efficiency of shifting from non-discriminatory single pricing to (inter-buyer) price discrimination (and subsequent analyses of this shift's liberal-moral-rights-violativeness and impact on the instantiation of the utilitarian and various non-utilitarian-egalitarian conceptions of the moral good) to the variant of price discrimination in which the seller charges no lump-sum fee to any buyer but different per-unit prices to different buyers when the per-unit-price differences cannot be (marginal-or-incremental)-cost- "justified."

This shift will tend to affect economic efficiency in five or six ways:

(1) will tend to decrease economic efficiency because the allocative cost of determining the two or more separate prices that are profitable to charge different subsets of potential buyers exceeds the allocative cost of identifying the most profitable uniform single price,
(2) will tend to decrease economic efficiency by substituting for a situation in which no buyer has an incentive to engage in arbitrage a situation in which buyers that are charged discriminatorily-low prices have an incentive to engage in arbitrage (by causing sellers to take allocative-costly steps to prevent arbitrage and by leading to the substitution for direct sales from the seller X to the arbitrage-buyer Y_{AB} two sales, one from seller X to the arbitrage-seller Y_{AS} and one from Y_{AS} to Y_{AB} (thereby increasing delivery costs, increasing

contracting transaction costs, and reducing value when the good is perishable or speed of delivery is valued),
(3) will tend to decrease economic efficiency when the good in question was created by a QV investment by increasing the amount of resources the economy devotes to QV-investment creation in both the ARDEPPS of practice and overall (by increasing the $I\Pi_E$ curve and its "counterpart" curve for the relevant ARDEPPS' successively-worse-placed potential entrants [for QV investments] without having any clear short-run effect on the discriminator's unit-sales),
(4) will tend to increase economic efficiency when the good in question is a production process by increasing the amount of resources the economy devotes to PPR in both the ARDEPPS of practice and overall for the same reasons that profitable price discrimination will increase equilibrium QV investment in the ARDEPPS of practice and overall when the good involved was created by a QV investment,
(5) will tend to increase economic efficiency by reducing poverty and material inequality (to the extent that the buyers that receive discriminatorily-low prices tend to be worse-off than the buyers that are charged discriminatorily-high prices), and
(6) will have an uncertain effect on economic efficiency by virtue of its impact on material inequality because its effect on material inequality is uncertain: (A) on the one hand, as I have just "asserted," it will tend to reduce material inequality among the buyers who are charged discriminatory prices but (B) on the other hand, it will tend to increase material inequality by benefiting the shareholders/creditors/managers/employees of the discriminators (though this conclusion depends on the relative size of the equivalent-dollar gains to the individual shareholders/creditors/managers/shareholders and to the favored buyers as well as on the relative positions that the shareholders/creditors/managers/employers, favored buyers, and disfavored buyers would respectively have occupied absent the discrimination).

In my contestable judgment, shifts from single pricing to per-unit-price price discrimination will decrease economic efficiency across all exemplars. I also doubt that it will be TBLE to try to identify instances or categories of exemplars of such price discrimination that will increase economic efficiency and to permit such acts of price discrimination while prohibiting acts of price discrimination deemed to be economically inefficient.

13.1.2.2 The Economic Efficiency of the Government's Attempting to Deter the Use of the Fancy Pricing-Techniques Whose Substitution for Single Pricing is Economically Inefficient

I will assume *ad arguendo* that the prohibition of any of these pricing-techniques will not induce their prospective employers to vertically integrate forward. On this assumption, I think it will usually be economically efficient for government to attempt to deter economically-inefficient substitutions of fancy pricing-techniques for single pricing. I reach this conclusion because it will be allocatively cheap for government to identify and prove the use of fancy pricing-techniques. Of course, it will not be economically efficient for government to deter substitutions for single pricing of categories of fancy pricing-techniques that are economically efficient—full-requirements tie-ins and total-output-supply reciprocity agreements that prevent substitutions against inputs (and conceivably full-requirements tie-ins that prevent complementary tying and tied products from being purchased in economically-inefficient proportions).

13.1.3 The Liberal-Moral-Rights-Violativeness of Substitutions of Fancy Pricing-Techniques for Single Pricing

Of course, the use of any pricing-technique including non-discriminatory single pricing will be liberal-moral-rights-violative if the seller is practicing contrived-oligopolistic or predatory pricing. Moreover, the percentage of exemplars of inter-buyer price discrimination that is associated with contrived-oligopolistic or predatory pricing is undoubtedly higher than the percentage of exemplars of non-discriminatory single pricing that involves contrived-oligopolistic or predatory pricing (though the connection between price discrimination and either contrived-oligopolistic pricing or predatory pricing is clearly too weak for evidence of price discrimination to be probative of either contrived-oligopolistic or predatory pricing). Still, I am confident that only a small percentage of the de facto switches from non-discriminatory single pricing to any of the fancy pricing-techniques I have discussed is rendered liberal-moral-rights-violative by the contrived-oligopolistic or predatory character of the exemplar of the fancy pricing-technique to which the seller is switching because (I suspect) only a small percentage of fancy-pricing-technique uses are contrived-oligopolistic or predatory. Moreover, those (few) switches from single pricing to fancy pricing-techniques whose relevant exemplars are not contrived-oligopolistic or predatory that impose losses on some buyers that deprive them of a morally-acceptable opportunity to take their lives morally seriously are not rendered liberal-moral-rights-violative on that account because on my understanding liberalism does not impose a duty on individuals when acting in non-political capacities to provide others with whom they are not intimately connected by birth or chosen non-commercial affiliation with the resources they need to have a meaningful opportunity to take their lives morally seriously.

13.1.3.1 The Fancy-Pricing-Technique-Related Duties of the Government of Liberal-Moral-Rights-Based Society

With two exceptions, the government of a liberal-moral-rights-based society has no liberal moral duty to prohibit shifts from single pricing to fancy pricing-techniques. First, the government of such a society has the same moral duty to prevent contrived-oligopolistic and predatory pricing when they are effectuated through the use of a fancy pricing-technique as when they are effectuated by (non-discriminatory) single pricing. Second, if particular efforts to prevent (or elicit) any such shift would effectuate the instantiation of a specific conception of the moral good or a specific mixed conception of the moral good that the liberal-moral-rights-based society's members' moral-good positions morally obligate its government to instantiate (in the service of its moral obligation to give the same weight to the morally-defensible moral-good positions of all of its members who have a liberal moral right to have their moral-good positions be given equal weight), the government of a liberal-moral-rights-based society would have a moral obligation to make the relevant fancy-pricing-technique-deterring/eliciting decision if it could do so without sacrificing weightier liberal-moral-rights-related interests or violating liberal moral rights that may not be violated come what may.

13.1.4 The Impact of Shifts From Single Pricing to Each of the Various Fancy Pricing-Techniques on the Instantiation of the Utilitarian and Different Non-Utilitarian-Egalitarian Conceptions of the Moral Good

Once again, I will assume that none of the shifts in question will deter the relevant seller from vertically integrating forward. On that assumption, I will first analyze the impact of each of the shifts on the instantiation of the utilitarian conception of the moral good and then analyze each such shift's impact on the instantiation of the various non-utilitarian-egalitarian conceptions of the moral good I have distinguished.

The impact of any of the pricing-technique shifts now under considerations on the total utility of all creatures whose utility counts depends on its impact on (1) economic efficiency and (2) material equality. I will start by reviewing my conclusions about the impacts of the relevant pricing-technique shifts on economic efficiency.

Section 13.1.2.1 argues that, with two or possibly three exceptions, all the pricing-technique shifts under consideration decrease economic efficiency. The clear exceptions are shifts from single pricing to (tied-product) full-requirements tie-ins that involve inputs and (final-good) total-output-supply reciprocity agreements that involve an input and a final product the input is used to produce that prevent substitutions against an input producer's input. The possible exception is shifts from single pricing to (tied-product) full-requirements contracts when the tied products are final-good complements that are combined in proportions that vary significantly with their respective P/MC ratios.

The next issue is the impact of the pricing-technique shifts now under consideration on material equality. I focus initially on pricing-technique shifts that involve the pricing of goods and/or services to an individual buyer. Shifts from single-buyer-focused single pricing to single-buyer-oriented fancier pricing-techniques virtually always increase material inequality. This conclusion is warranted by the following three "facts" (or should I say: plausible assumptions): (1) the weighted-average shareholder/creditor/manager/employee of the sellers that effectuate the pricing-technique shifts in question (where the weight assigned to each category of individuals depends on the number of individuals in the category and the average equivalent-dollar gain conferred on the individual members of the category) is better-off than the weighted-average affected potential/actual customer of the sellers changing their pricing-technique; (2) the pricing-technique shifts in question confer profits on their seller-effectuators and hence on those firms' shareholders/creditors/managers/employees; and (3) although individual pricing-technique shifts in these categories will confer equivalent-dollar gains on the buyers they directly affect if those buyers have substantial bargaining power (which enables them to share in the joint gain the shift yields them and the sellers by paying lower lump-sum fees than I have been assuming they are paying), such outcomes probably occur only when the executed pricing-technique is a tie-in or reciprocity agreement that involves a buyer that is a final-good producer or retailer and in those instances the "buyer's" shareholders/creditors/managers/employees are probably as well-off as the seller's and even in the rare instances in which the shift benefits the relevant buyers, I suspect the average equivalent-dollar gain to the buyer involved is lower than the average equivalent-dollar gain to the seller's shareholders/creditors/managers/employees. I focus second on pricing-technique shifts from non-discriminatory single pricing to the charging of discriminatory per-unit prices and no lump-sum fees to different buyers. I suspect that such pricing-technique shifts also increase material inequality primarily because they benefit the shareholders/creditors/managers/employees of the firms that make them, though they may tend to decrease material inequality by benefitting favored buyers (who tend to be materially-worse-off than the disfavored buyers) and imposing losses on disfavored buyers (who tend to be better-off than the favored buyers).

Taken together, the conclusions I have offered about the impacts of the pricing-technique shifts in question on economic efficiency and material inequality imply that, with two or three exceptions, all categories and subcategories of such shifts reduce total utility. The exceptions are shifts from single pricing to full-requirements tie-ins and total-output-supply reciprocity agreements that deter substitutions against an input the shifter produces and shifts from single pricing to what I take to be the small percentage of full-requirements tie-ins that involve complementary final goods that are combined in proportions that vary significantly with the difference between the P/MC ratios of tying and tied good.

I turn now to the impact that pricing-technique shifts from non-discriminatory single pricing to the various fancy pricing-techniques I have considered have on the instantiation of the various non-utilitarian-egalitarian conceptions of the moral good I have identified. This impact depends entirely on the relevant shifts' effect on material inequality. If correct, my conclusion that all these pricing-technique shifts increase material inequality implies that all disserve the instantiation of these non-utilitarian-egalitarian conceptions of the moral good.

I should also address the impact of the pricing-technique shifts under consideration on the instantiation of the mixed conceptions of the moral good in which two or more utilitarian and non-utilitarian-egalitarian conceptions of the moral goo play a positive role. My previous economic-efficiency and material-inequality conclusions imply that (1) shifts from non-discriminatory single pricing to all fancy pricing-techniques other than full-requirements tie-ins and total-output-supply reciprocity agreements that deter substitutions against an input and full-requirements tie-ins that prevent substantial substitutions of a final-good tied-product complement for a final-good tying product disserve the instantiation of all the mixed conceptions of the moral good just referenced, (2) the exceptions just referenced will be less desirable from the perspective of these mixed conceptions of the moral good than from the perspective of utilitarianism, and relatedly (3) it is not clear that any of the shifts that will increase total utility will instantiate any of these mixed conceptions of the moral good, but some may well do so.

13.1.4.1 The Ability of the Government of a Liberal-Moral-Rights-Based Society to Instantiate Utilitarianism or a Non-Utilitarian-Egalitarian Conception of the Moral Good Without Violating Any Liberal Moral Right by Deterring or Allowing Shifts From Non-Discriminatory Single Pricing to a Fancy Pricing-Technique

If the pricing-technique shifts on which this subsection is focusing would never deter vertical integration, my only doubts about the ability of the government of a liberal-moral-rights-based society to promote the moral good by prohibiting and allowing various shifts from non-discriminatory single pricing to a fancy pricing-technique would relate to the TBLE of determining the economic efficiency of the input-substitution-preventing tie-ins I have discussed. With those exceptions, I think it will be sufficiently allocatively cheap for such a government to identify and prove to the morally-obligatory degree of certainty that a seller has made a pricing-technique shift that disserves the moral good for government efforts to deter such pricing-technique shifts to serve the moral good.

I recognize that the preceding moral-good conclusions may be morally-irrelevant in a liberal-moral-rights-based society because the shareholders, at-risk creditors, and possibly the managers and employees of a company have a liberal property right that the company be permitted to charge any price it wants to charge when its doing so is not motivated by specific anticompetitive intent. Although I agree that liberalism favors the protection of property interest, I doubt that liberalism implies the existence of the just-referenced right.

13.2 Tie-Ins and Reciprocity Agreements That Should Not Be Described as Pricing-Techniques

This section distinguishes six functions or related sets of functions that "non-pricing-technique" tying and reciprocity agreements can perform and analyzes the economic efficiency, liberal-moral-rights-violativeness, and moral-good impacts of each such functional category of tying and reciprocity agreements. It ignores the fact that individual tying and reciprocity agreement may perform two or more of these "functions"—for example, that tie-ins can increase the cost-effectiveness of their employer's efforts both to control the quality of the complements its customers combine with its "tying product" and to practice meter pricing. Obviously, one cannot analyze the impact of a multi-function tying or reciprocity agreement without taking account of the relevant impacts it has by virtue of its performing each of the functions it performs. I do not think that any conclusion this section reaches is critically affected by my ignoring the reality that tying and reciprocity agreements can be multifunctional. But readers should be aware of my failure to take account of this complicating fact.

13.2.1 The Functions of "Non-Pricing-Techniques" Tie-Ins and Reciprocity[13]

I will first analyze the functions that non-pricing tie-ins can perform and then analyze the functions that non-pricing reciprocity agreements can reform. Non-pricing-technique tie-ins can perform five functions.

First, full-requirements tie-ins can increase the cost-effectiveness of the efforts of a producer of a tying product A to control the quality of a complementary tied product B its customers combine with its tying product A. For several reasons, a seller may have an interest in controlling the quality of the complement B its customers combine with its product A. Even if it is profitable for the customer to use an inferior or less-compatible complement (in that the related cost-saving exceeds the reduction in the dollar-value to it of the combination's performance), the customer's use of B will impose a loss on the producer of A (X) if the dollar-loss the use of the inferior complement imposes on X by damaging A's and perhaps the tying producer's general reputation when third parties (possibly observers of the performance of the A-B combination) attribute the combination's worsened performance to A exceeds the dollar-gain Y's use of the inferior complement B enables X to obtain by taking advantage of the inferior-complement-employing buyer's profiting from using the inferior complement. And if the tying-product producer's customer's decision to use an inferior (or less-compatible) complement is against that buyer's interest, that buyer's complement-choice will or may impose losses on the producer of the tying product both by deterring Y from being a repeat purchaser (if Y attributes the combination's disappointing performance to the tying product) and by damaging the reputation of the tying product A and perhaps its producer X more generally if the disappointed buyer bad-mouths the tying product to others (or, again, others observe the combination's compromised performance and attributes that performance to the tying product). Full-requirements tie-ins in which the producer of the tying product A obligates its customer(s) Y to purchase its (their) full requirements of a complement B from it will increase X's profits by increasing the cost-effectiveness of X's efforts to control the quality of the complement that Y combines with A when it is difficult for X to articulate the attributes that a complement must have to be suitable from X's perspective, costly to X to assess whether the complements that Y would use absent the tie-in are suitable from X's perspective, and cheap for X to enforce the full-requirements tied-product obligation because X can alter or mark the B it supplies Y to make the B it produces or orders other producers to produce for it easily identifiable.

Second, a seller X can use tie-ins to increase the cost-effectiveness of its efforts to prevent cross-selling of its product A. As we saw, a buyer may find it profitable to engage in arbitrage on A if the per-unit price that X is charging it for A is lower than the average-lump-sum fee *plus* per-unit price X is trying to obtain from other potential buyers of A. If (1) Y uses another product B each time it uses X's product A, (2) X knows the quantity of that product B that Y would combine with the quantity of A it purchased if it used all the A it purchased in its own business, and (3) it will be costly to Y to take delivery of some of the A it purchases from X and resell it, X will be able to reduce Y's incentive to engage in arbitrage on A at the low cost of drafting and negotiating the tie-in and arranging for the delivery of the requisite quantity of B by conditioning its sale of a particular or various quantities of A to Y on Y's agreeing to purchase from X at its normal price the quantity of B Y would use in its own operations if it used in its own operations all the A it purchased from X.

Third, in some circumstances, a seller X of two or more goods can use a package-pricing tie-in (in which it sells a package of goods for, in essence, a given total price) to reduce the market-research, personnel-training, and checkout-counter-sale-processing costs of practicing inter-buyer discrimination. Thus, if (ideally) the seller realizes that different buyers place different supra-marginal-cost dollar values on each member of a set of products it could sell them, does not know the dollar value that individual buyers place on each of the products in the potential package, but does know that all buyers place the same dollar-value on the package of products in question, the seller will be able to obtain the same total revenue it could obtain by charging the buyers in question the different prices for each product in the package that equal the dollar value of that product to the respective buyers in question without determining the dollar value of each product to each buyer, without training its checkout-counter personnel to identify the different buyers in question, and without incurring the time-costs of charging separate prices to each buyer for each product by charging all buyers the same price for the relevant packages of products—by tying the sales of the products in question together. In fact, even when these ideal conditions are not satisfied, sellers that believe that buyers that place a higher-than-average dollar value on some members of a set of products place a lower-than-average value on other members of the relevant product-set (ideally, a lower dollar value that exceeds the marginal cost the seller would have to incur to supply these buyers with these products) may be able to increase their profits for the above reasons by setting a uniform price for a package of products (that allows some buyer surplus to escape and/or costs it some profitable sales) or by price discriminating on the relevant package of products. Thus, a seller of a differentiated dishwashing powder or clothes-washing detergent (product A) may for the above reasons tie together the sale of that product with a coupon (product B) that entitles its owner to buy cheap dishes at a cheap price if the seller believes that (1) the dollar value of its differentiated product A to different buyers is primarily determined by and increases with the buyer's income while (2) the dollar value of the coupon to buyers is primarily determined by and is inversely related to the buyer's income.

Fourth, a seller may also use package-pricing tie-ins to reduce the apparent extent of and/or change the apparent locus of its inter-buyer price discrimination, predatory or illegally-retaliatory pricing, maximum-price-regulation or minimum-price-regulation violations, or tax or contract frauds. Thus, when, absent legal constraints, a seller X would find it most profitable to charge a buyer Y in separate transactions a price for A that is $\$\alpha$ below X's normal price for A or $\$\alpha$ below the minimum price a price regulation permits to be charged for A and a price for B that is $\$\alpha$ above X's normal price for B or the maximum price a price regulation permits to be charged for B, X may be able to increase the profits of engaging in such discriminatory and/or price-regulation-violating pricing by using a tie-in in which it charges Y the normal or permitted prices for A and B or a combined price for A and B that equals the sum of its normal or price-regulation-permitted prices for those two products—a tie-in that conceals what X is doing. Indeed, even when the relevant "numbers" do not allow X totally to conceal what it is doing, it may be able to use such tie-ins to conceal the extent of its price discrimination and/or price-regulation violations or the locus of its violations (when enforcement authorities or potential private plaintiffs pay more attention to what is going on in some areas of product-space than in others).

Sellers may also be able to use tie-ins to conceal contract and tax fraud. For example, if the percentage of sales to exhibitors that the director, writers, and actors who worked on film A are contractually entitled to receive (as royalties) exceed the percentage of such sales that their counterparts for film B are entitled to receive, the owner of films A and B may commit contract fraud by using tie-ins under which exhibitors are charged a lower price for the right to exhibit film A than they would otherwise have been charged for that right in an independent transaction on condition that they agree to pay more for the right to exhibit film B than they would have been willing to pay for that right in an independent transaction. Individuals or business firms can also use tie-ins to perpetrate tax fraud by changing the apparent source of the profits they earn. Thus, if the profits yielded by the sale of land are taxed as ordinary income while the profits yielded by the sale of timber is taxed at a lower, capital-gains tax-rate, a seller X of land and timber on that land can perpetrate tax fraud by agreeing to sell Y the land for a price that is lower than the price that Y would be willing to pay for the land in an independent transaction on condition that Y agree to purchase the timber on the land for a higher price than Y would have been willing to pay for the timber in an independent transaction. Before proceeding, I should point out the fact that tie-ins and reciprocity agreements that appear to or actually do perform the concealing functions on which I am now focusing can also perform economic-efficiency-enhancing functions and discuss the implications of this fact for the ability of antitrust-policy-enforcement authorities to increase economic efficiency by allowing and permitting exemplars of such agreements. Tie-ins that appear to or actually do perform concealing functions may also or instead enable their employer to control the quality of the complements B that the buyer-participants combine with the tying seller's product A and may also reduce the private transaction costs the tying seller must incur to supply the buyer with A and B by substituting a single tie-in transaction (package-deal) on A and B together for two separate transactions on A and B and (although this is less relevant from a policy perspective) may also reduce the market-research, checkout-counter-personnel training-costs, and checkout-counter-sales-processing costs the tying seller must incur to practice inter-buyer price discrimination. Reciprocity agreements that appear to or actually do perform concealing functions may also or instead enable a buyer of a final good to control the quality of the ingredients or other sorts of inputs its suppler incorporates into or uses to produce the product the supplier is supplying the buyer and/or may enable the two participants in the reciprocity agreement to reduce the transaction cost of dealing with each other by substituting one two-product transaction for two one-product transactions. These possibilities are relevant to the ability of government to increase economic efficiency, protect liberal-moral-rights-related interests, and instantiate various conceptions of the moral good because their existence complicates the task of determining whether particular tie-ins or reciprocity agreements (1) are performing concealing functions whose performance reduces economic efficiency, sacrifices liberal-moral-rights-related interests, and/or disserves one or more morally-defensible conceptions of the moral good and (2) are economically inefficient, liberal-moral-rights-violative, or moral-good disserving all tolled even when *inter alia* they do perform concealing functions. I should add that the difficulties that some of these possibilities pose is reduced by the fact that, to achieve the quality-control or one-deal for two-deal transaction-cost saving in question, the relevant tying and reciprocity agreements need not alter the prices of the goods in the package (though they must do so to perform their concealing functions or to increase the profitability of the seller's inter-buyer price discrimination in other ways). I should add that all these function-related and enforcement-related observations also apply to package-pricing tie-ins that reduce the market-research, personnel-training, and checkout-counter-sales-processing costs of inter-buyer price discrimination.

The fifth "non-pricing-technique" function that tie-ins can perform is increasing the cost-effectiveness of implementing a pricing-technique that substitutes for the outright sale of a durable machine, the right to operate a franchise, or the right to use a production process (which is a form of perfect price discrimination if the "product" is described as an individual use of the machine, franchise, or production process) the mixed pricing-technique in which the buyer is charged a lower lump-sum fee but a supra-marginal-cost (to the seller) per-unit (meter) price for each use of the machine, franchise, or production process. Section 13.1.1 explained why a producer X of durable machines, franchises, or production processes might find this pricing-technique shift profitable. The point here is that in many circumstances producers of durable machines, franchises, or production processes (tying product A) may find it most profitable to use tie-ins to implement this complicated pricing-technique. Thus, rather than (1) requiring the buyer Y to pay a meter rate for using a durable machine (attaching a meter to a button-fashioning machine or [less practicably] to a riveter and reading the meter) or (2) obligating the buyer Y to pay an endproduct royalty on its sales of the product it uses X's durable machine or production process to produce or the sales its franchised part of X's branded distributive chain makes (which requires X *inter alia* to monitor Y's books), X may find it more cost-effective to make Y pay a supra-marginal-cost price for each use it makes of X's durable machine, production process, or franchise idea by placing Y under a contractual obligation to purchase from X its full requirements of a second, tied product B for more than B's market price that Y either uses each time it uses X's product A or whose sales by Y are highly positively correlated with the frequency with which Y uses A—for example, for a producer X of a button-fastening machine/riveter to contractually obligate Y to purchase its full requirements of buttons/rivets for more than their normal market price, for a production-process discoverer X to require the licensee or purchaser Y of its discovered production process to purchase from X for more than its normal market price its full requirements of an input B that Y uses each time it uses X's production process, or for a fast-food-franchise designer/advertizer X to contractually obligate its franchisee Y to purchase from X for more than its market price its full requirements of hamburger meat, potatoes, and/or hamburger rolls.[14] Particularly when X is able at little or no cost to modify the B it produces or hires someone else to produce for Y's use (or the wrapping of the B it supplies Y to make the B it supplies readily identifiable), such tie-ins may be more cost-effective than any other method of implementing this pricing-technique—for example, than buying, installing, and reading meters or implementing endproduct-royalty schemes.

The sixth and final "non-pricing" function that sellers can use tie-ins to perform is deterring one or more tied-product-ARDEPPS entries. Although many economists believe that a significant number of tie-ins perform this function,[15] I am skeptical. The tie-ins that are alleged to perform this function are tie-ins in which producer X of a tying product A requires its customers to purchase from it their full requirements of a tied product B—a complement of A—to prevent possible independent producers of B from lowering the barriers to entering the A ARDEPPS they face by producing B and supplying it to A's buyers. (The use of this type of tie-in is sometimes denominated "systems rivalry)."[16] The argument is that an independent producer of B's producing B would lower the barriers it faced to entering the A ARDEPPS (1) by yielding it profits (even normal profits) it could use to finance its entry into the A ARDEPPS, (2) by enabling it to learn things about product A and/or its production that would reduce the Π_D and/or R barriers to entering the A ARDEPPS it faced, and (3) by enabling the independent producer of B to reduce the Π_D and R barriers to entering the A ARDEPPS it faced by enabling it to learn the names and addresses of A's buyers, to learn their respective relevant specific preferences and the sales-pitches to which they respond positively, and to impress buyers of A with its reliability. The economists who claim that a significant number of tie-ins function in this way appear to believe that those tie-ins that perform this function are in my terms motivated by specific anticompetitive intent: at least, this conclusion is favored by their claiming that the use of such tie-ins is "strategic," that such tie-ins "foreclose" competition and "exclude" competitors, that these tie-ins involve the exercise of "leverage" and the practice of "predation," and that the conduct in question is "anticompetitive."[17] My belief that the profitability of few tie-ins that make it more difficult for potential suppliers of the tied product to enter the tying-product market is critically affected by their having this effect is (1) partly attributable to my belief that the *ex ante* tying-seller-perceived profitability of most of the tie-ins that others claim were motivated by specific anticompetitive intent is attributable to the tying seller's belief that they would increase the cost-effectiveness of the seller's efforts to control the quality of the complements B that buyers combine with the seller's product A and/or the seller's practice of meter pricing on A and (2) partly attributable to my belief that potential suppliers of B are often effective potential entrants into ARDEPPS A. My belief that few of the tie-ins that deter entry deserve to be characterized as "*anti*competitive" or "predatory" reflects my belief that producers have a legal (and possibly a moral) right (1) to keep to themselves information about their products and the best way to produce them even when the producer does not have a patent right to the information (a legal right that is recognized by the law of many jurisdictions) and (2) to keep to themselves their customer-lists (a right that is also recognized in the law of many jurisdictions)—rights whose legal recognition may be liberal-moral and may in any event promote the moral good by preserving the incentive of individual firms to develop products and production-techniques and to identify potential customers and to convince them of the value to them of its product[s]).

I turn now to the "non-pricing" functions that reciprocity agreements can perform, which are analogous to or identical to the 5 "non-pricing" functions I argued tie-ins can perform. First, a firm X that seeks to control the quality of the ingredients or inputs A that a firm Y from which X wants to buy a final product D uses to produce D may employ a reciprocity agreement to increase the cost-effectiveness of its efforts to control the quality of the A that Y uses to produce D. Under such a reciprocity agreement, X would condition its agreeing to purchase D from Y on specified terms on Y's agreeing to purchase from X its full requirements of A (or perhaps its full requirements of the A Y uses to produce D for X) usually at A's normal market price. Such a reciprocity agreement will be particularly likely to be cost-effective if (1) X can at little or no cost render readily identifiable the A or the packaging of the A it wants Y to use when producing D for X and/or (2) it is difficult or costly to articulate the attributes an ingredient or input Y must incorporate into A or use to produce A for the A it produces to be acceptable to X and/or to test the of A Y produces to determine whether it satisfies X's requirements.

Second, a seller X of an input A to a buyer/final-good-D-producer Y that prices A to Y in a way that gives Y an incentive to engage in arbitrage on A may employ a reciprocity agreement to increase the cost-effectiveness of its efforts to deter Y from engaging in arbitrage on A. To achieve this result, X would condition its agreement to supply A to Y on specified terms on Y's agreeing to supply X with the amount of D it would produce if it used all the A it bought from X in its own operations at the price Y would otherwise charge for D. This type of reciprocity agreement will be more cost-effective the lower the cost-effectiveness of the other methods X could use to deter Y from cross-selling A and the smaller the loss X would have to incur to distribute itself or through a third firm the D with which Y would be supplying it under the reciprocity agreement.

Third, in some circumstances, firms may be able to use reciprocity agreements to increase their profits by concealing part or all of their (price discrimination)/(predatory or illegally-retaliatory pricing)/maximum-or-minimum-price-regulation violations) or to change the apparent locus of such pricing and to practice tax or contract fraud. Thus, if firm X wants to discriminate against firm Y when selling product A but wants to obtain a discriminatorily-low price on product B it purchase from Y, it can conceal part or all of its price discrimination by substituting for independent transactions on A and B a reciprocity agreement in which the prices of A and B are non-discriminatory (or less discriminatory) or only one monetary payment is specified. Obviously, reciprocity can perform the same function when X wants to violate a maximum-price regulation when selling A to Y or charge Y a discriminatorily-high price for A and to be charged by Y a price for B below the minimum allowed price for that product or a discriminatorily-low price. Equally obviously, in appropriate circumstances, reciprocity agreement can also enable a firm to commit contract fraud or tax fraud (as happens when a solo-practitioner lawyer provides free legal services to a doctor in exchange for the doctor's supplying the lawyer's family with free medical services).

Fourth, reciprocity agreements can also increase the cost-effectiveness of a seller X's substituting for the outright sale of a durable machine or the right to use a production process for a lump-sum fee (the functional equivalent of perfect price discrimination if the tying product [A] is defined to be a single use of the machine or production process [to produce a unit of the good the production process can be used to produce]) a mixed (meter-pricing) pricing-technique in which the lump-sum fee is reduced but the buyer is charged a per-unit price each time it "uses" the machine or production process (a per-unit price that exceeds X's marginal cost at A's TSM output—zero). In the relevant reciprocity agreement, X conditions its sales to Y of the right to use the machine or production process on stated terms on Y's agreeing to sell to X its total output of the product the machine or production process is used to produce for a price that is lower than the price Y would otherwise charge for its product.

Fifth, it is conceivable that a firm X that sells a final product D to another firm Y that produces an input A that is used to produce D could enter into a reciprocity agreement under which X conditions its sale of D to Y on specified terms on Y's agreeing to supply its total output of A to X (say) at the price Y would otherwise charge for A to deter potential entrants from investing in ARDEPPS D by preventing them from obtaining input A or worsening the terms on which they can purchase input A. It is even conceivable that X could get a series of firms Y1...n in the position I originally indicated Y was in to participant in such reciprocity agreements even though it was against their collective interest to do so (since they would profit from the entry of additional suppliers of D) because Y1...n were tyrannized by their small decisions. But I doubt that any significant number of reciprocity agreements perform this function for final-good producers. Indeed, the reasons that led me to doubt the empirical importance of predatory refusals to deal in Chapter 10 make me doubt that any real-world reciprocity agreements perform this function.[18]

13.2.2 The Economic Efficiency of Non-Pricing-Technique Tie-Ins and Reciprocity Agreements and the Ability of the Government of a Liberal-Moral-Rights-Based Society to Increase Economic Efficiency by Deterring Economically-Inefficient Tie-Ins and Reciprocity Agreements

Like Sect. 13.2.1, Sect. 13.2.2 proceeds on the assumption that the pricing-techniques whose cost-effectiveness may be increased by tie-ins and reciprocity agreements have not been deterred. Section 13.2.2 takes account of the possibility that the tie-ins and reciprocity agreements that can increase the profitability of particular pricing-techniques may sometimes critically affect those techniques' profitability—more relevantly, may cause their employers to use those techniques when they otherwise would not have done so. Section 13.2.2 analyzes together the economic efficiency of tie-ins and reciprocity agreements that perform the same function.

13.2.2.1 The Economic Efficiency of Each Functional Type of Non-Pricing-Technique Tie-In or Reciprocity Agreement

First, tie-ins that increase the cost-effectiveness of seller efforts to control the quality of the complements B that their customers combine with the seller's product A and reciprocity agreements that increase the cost-effectiveness of a buyer's efforts to control the quality of the inputs a supplier incorporates into the product it supplies the buyer in question will always or virtually always increase economic efficiency. If anything, the private control-cost savings the agreements generate will be lower than the associated allocative control-cost savings. And, I suspect, any increase in the control that is exercised will be associated with an increase in economic efficiency as well. (I wrote "suspect" because the tie-in-related conclusion assumes that the losses that the added control prevents the tying seller from sustaining by preventing its product's or its organization's reputation from being damaged by incorrect assessments of its product's quality will be associated with altered consumer purchase-choices that are misallocative).

Second, if tie-ins and reciprocity agreements that increase the cost-effectiveness of their employer's efforts to prevent its customers from engaging in arbitrage do not cause their employer to substitute for non-discriminatory single pricing a fancy pricing-technique whose use gives the buyers involved an incentive to engage in arbitrage, the tie-ins and reciprocity agreements in question will almost certainly increase economic efficiency: (1) to the extent that they reduce the private cost of preventing a given amount of arbitrage, the associated allocative cost-savings will if anything be higher than the private cost-savings and (2) to the extent that they prevent arbitrage that would substitute the more-circuitous supply of the good in question to the arbitrage-buyer via the arbitrage-seller for the direct supply of the arbitrage-buyer by the producer of the good in question, they will increase economic efficiency by reducing private and allocative delivery costs, preventing the deterioration of goods that are perishable, and speeding up delivery-time. I wrote "almost certainly" because, if the deterred arbitrage would have resulted in the supply of the arbitraged good to an arbitrage-buyer that would not otherwise have purchased the good in question directly from its producer, the deterrence of the arbitrage might decrease economic efficiency. However, for what it is worth, in my judgment, this possibility is not sufficiently empirically important to call into question the conclusion that this functional type of tie-ins and reciprocity agreements would increase economic efficiency if its exemplars would not cause their employers to use the fancy pricing-techniques that give their buyer-participants an incentive to engage in arbitrage. However, to the extent that these tie-ins and reciprocity agreements do cause their employers (1) to shift from non-discriminatory single pricing to inter-buyer price discrimination, perfect price discrimination, or the mixed pricing-technique in which the seller charges a combination of a lump-sum fee and a supra-TSM-unit-output-marginal-cost per-unit price (or its "meter pricing" analogue when the good in question is the individual use of a durable machine, franchise, or production process) or (2) to shift from the mixed pricing-technique just delineated (meter pricing) to perfect price discrimination (the outright sale of the durable machine, franchise, or right to use the production process), the analysis of the economic efficiency of these tie-ins and reciprocity agreements will have to take account of the economic inefficiency of the pricing-technique shifts just referenced. Your assessment of the relevance of this possibility may be as good as mine, but, for what it is worth, my judgment is that this possibility does not critically undermine the conclusion that this category of tie-ins and reciprocity agreements increases economic efficiency. (I also suspect that it will not be TBLE for enforcement authorities to investigate this possibility and its possible economic-efficiency relevance in individual cases or any subcategory of cases.) If the relevant seller's ability to use such tie-ins does not affect its decision to engage in inter-buyer price discrimination, such tie-ins will increase economic efficiency because the private-cost savings the tie-ins generate will if anything be lower than the allocative-cost savings they generate. However, to the extent that a seller's ability to use tie-ins for this purpose induces it to practice inter-buyer price discrimination when it otherwise would engage in non-discriminatory single pricing, one will have to take account of the economic inefficiency of that shift (even when the tie-in reduces its economic inefficiency) when analyzing the economic efficiency of this functional category of tie-ins. Once more, although your assessment of the empirical importance and economic-efficiency relevance of this possibility is probably as good as mine, I believe that this possibility does not critically affect the conclusion that this functional type of tie-in is economically efficient. I also doubt that it will be TBLE for enforcement authorities to consider the possibility that exemplars of this functional category of tie-ins will induce their employer to practice price discrimination when they would not otherwise do so when deciding whether to prohibit individual or larger subsets of tie-ins in this functional category.

A fourth functional category of non-pricing-technique tie-ins and reciprocity agreements function by concealing the existence, extent, or locus of their employer's inter-buyer price discrimination, predatory pricing, price-retaliation in the service of contrived-oligopolistic pricing, violations of maximum-price or minimum-price regulations, or contract or tax fraud. Tie-ins and reciprocity agreements that function by concealing inter-buyer price discrimination, predatory pricing, and retaliatory pricing in the service of contrivance are economically inefficient because they are allocative-transaction-costly to design and negotiate and because, to the extent that they increase the amount of inter-buyer price discrimination, predatory, and contrived-oligopolistic pricing their employer practices, they generate economic inefficacy on that account. The economic efficiency of tie-ins and reciprocity agreements that function by concealing price-regulation violations is somewhat less clear. On the one hand, such tie-ins and reciprocity will tend to increase economic inefficiency because their design and negotiation is allocative-transaction-costly. On the other hand, any tendency they have to increase the number of magnitude of the price-regulation violations their employer commits can be either economically efficient or economically inefficient: (1) violations of minimum-price regulations tend to increase economic by reducing poverty and material inequality, (2) tend to increase/decrease economic efficiency when the good in question was created by a QV investment when the violation is against/in the collective interest of the producers of the good in question by decreasing/increasing equilibrium QV investment in the ARDEPPS concerned, and (3) tend to increase/decrease economic efficiency when the good in question is a production process discovered by PPR when the violation is in/against the collective interest of the relevant production-process researchers by increasing/decreasing equilibrium PPR in the ARDEPPS concerned. Relatedly, violations of maximum-price regulations tend to decrease economic efficiency (1) by increasing poverty and material inequality, (2) tend to decrease economic efficiency when the good in question was created by a QV investment by increasing equilibrium QV investment in the ARDEPPS concerned, and (3) tend to increase economic efficiency when the good in question is a discovered production process by increasing equilibrium PPR in the ARDEPPS concerned (whose productive activity is the execution of PPR). Tie-ins and reciprocity agreements that function by concealing contract fraud cause economic inefficiency by increasing their employer's practice of contract fraud, which decreases economic efficiency by the allocative transaction costs the fraudster generates to perpetrate the fraud (the allocative transaction cost of drafting and negotiating the concealing tie-in or reciprocity agreement), by inducing their contract partners to devote allocatively-valuable resources to checking whether they have been cheated, and by inducing their contract partners to make related claims inside and outside legal fora whose making and processing are allocative-transaction-costly. Tie-ins and reciprocity agreements that function by concealing tax fraud reduce economic efficiency by increasing the amount of tax fraud in which their perpetrators engage (1) because the concealment-efforts are allocative-transaction-costly, (2) because the fraud induces the government to expend resources to detect it, (3) because the plea-bargaining and trial of tax-fraud claims are allocative-transaction-costly, (4) because the carrying out of various sentences imposed on those found guilty of tax fraud is both allocative-transaction-costly and allocative-costly in other ways, (5) because any loss of tax-revenue tax fraud generates and any fiscal costs the government incurs to detect, prosecute, and penalize tax fraud reduce economic inefficiency by causing the government to forego economically-efficient expenditures or to raise offsetting revenues in other ways that are allocative-costly, and (6) because successful tax fraud generates economic inefficiency by increasing poverty and material inequality.

A fifth functional category of non-pricing-technique tie-ins and reciprocity agreements enables its employers to render more cost-effective its "meter pricing" of a durable machine, franchise, or the right to use a discovered production process. I will assume initially that the use of this functional type of tie-in or reciprocity agreement will not cause an employer that would not otherwise have practiced meter pricing to do so. On this assumption, to the extent that the use of meter-pricing-effectuating tie-ins or reciprocity agreements is profitable for the producer of a "product" A because it is privately cheaper to implement such pricing through an appropriate tie-in or reciprocity agreement than to do so by attaching and reading a meter to a machine A, requiring the owner of a franchise A to pay the franchisor a percentage of its sales, or requiring a firm that uses a production process A to pay a fee for each unit of its product D it employs the production process to produce, the tie-in or reciprocity agreement in question will increase economic efficiency by the private-transaction-cost saving times the ratio of the associated allocative-cost savings to its private counterpart (which I assume will exceed the number one). On the assumption that the availability of such a tie-in or reciprocity agreement would not affect the relevant seller's decision about engaging in meter pricing, to the extent that the producer's use of a tie-in or reciprocity agreement to implement its meter pricing yields it profits by reducing the losses it sustains because its customer cheats by tampering with the meter, underreporting its franchise's sales, or underreporting its unit output of the D it produces with the seller's production process, the tie-in or reciprocity agreement will not affect economic efficiency on that account. If the availability of a meter-pricing tie-in or reciprocity agreement causes its employer to practice meter pricing when it would not otherwise have done so, the impact that such agreements will have on economic efficiency on that account will depend *inter alia* on the economic efficiency of the seller's shifting from the outright sale of its durable machine, franchise, or the right to use its production process for a lump-sum fee to meter pricing implemented without using tying or reciprocity agreements. Such a shift will tend to increase economic efficiency by reducing the allocative transaction costs the seller and buyer generate when trying to estimate the dollar value of the machine, franchise, or production process to the buyer and (in most cases) by reducing the sum of the risk costs that the buyer and seller face, but it will tend to decrease economic efficiency by requiring the seller to purchase, install, inspect, and read a meter or to scrutinize the buyer's books and by causing at least some buyers to generate allocative costs by tampering with the meter or keeping an inaccurate or misleading set of books. Although this point may seem airy-fairy, such a shift will also tend to decrease economic efficiency if members of society perceive it to be associated with additional cheating on contracts and suffer a "non-material" equivalent-dollar loss on that account. Because sellers' uses of tie-ins and reciprocity to implement their meter pricing will (presumably) increase the profits yielded by the associated QV or PPR investments they made, their profitable use of meter-pricing-implementing tie-ins and reciprocity will tend to decrease economic efficiency when the "product" involved is not a production process by increasing equilibrium QV investment in the relevant ARDEPPS and in the economy and will tend to increase economic efficiency when the "product" involved is a discovered production process by increasing equilibrium PPR in the relevant ARDEPPS and in the economy. To be honest, in part because I have little sense of the (purely-private) contribution that this shift makes to the seller's profits by enabling the seller to reduce the loss it sustains because of its own and the buyer's pessimism about the dollar-value of the seller's product to the buyer relative to the contribution that this shift makes to the seller's profits in other ways, I am unable to predict the impact that this functional category of tying and reciprocity agreements will have on economic efficiency as a result of their inducing the seller to shift from the pure lump-sum pricing of its machine, franchise, or right to use a production process to a pricing-technique in which meter pricing plays a role. In part for this reason and in part because I am doubtful about the percentage of this functional type of tying and reciprocity agreements that cause their employers to shift from pure lump-sum pricing to a pricing-technique that involves some meter pricing, I will proceed on the assumption that this functional category of tie-ins and reciprocity agreements increases economic efficiency. I will also assume in the next subsection that it will not be TBLE for antitrust-law-enforcement authorities to investigate whether particular tie-ins or reciprocity agreements in this functional category or one or more specifiable subsets of such agreements increase or decrease economic efficiency.

Sixth and finally, it is conceivable that some agreements that require firms Y1…n that buy one product A from its producer X to purchase their full requirements of a complement of A—say, product B—from X as well function perhaps *inter alia* by deterring prospective independent producers of B or a variant of B from entering into the A ARDEPPS. Section 13.2.1 states that, in my judgment, few if any tie-ins (and no reciprocity agreements) have this effect or *a fortiori* are critically motivated by their employer's belief that they will have this effect. Tie-ins that do have this effect will.

(1) tend to decrease economic efficiency because they are allocative-transaction-costly to draft, negotiate, and enforce,
(2) tend to increase economic efficiency when the tying good was created by a QV investment to the extent that the tie-ins reduce equilibrium QV investment in the ARDEPPS in which they are used,
(3) tend to decrease economic efficiency when the tying good is a production process to the extent that the tie-ins reduce equilibrium PPR in the ARDEPPS in which they are used,

(4) tend to decrease economic efficiency by concentrating the seller-side of the ARDEPPS in which they are used and hence increasing the total expenditures its sellers make on political parties/campaigns/candidates and government-decisionmaking-process participation,
(5) tend to decrease economic efficiency by increasing poverty and material inequality by reducing equilibrium investment in the ARDEPPSes in which they are used and concentrating the seller-sides of those ARDEPPSes, and
(6) may tend to increase economic efficiency by preserving the tying seller's incentive to identify buyers of their products and convince these buyers that it would be in their interest to purchase the sellers' products.

My admittedly-contrastable belief is that any tie-ins that perform this function will on this account tend to decrease economic efficiency all tolled even when the investments in the ARDEPPS of practice are QV investments.

13.2.2.2 The Ability of the Government of a Liberal-Moral-Rights-Based Society to Increase Economic Efficiency by Deterring Non-Pricing-Technique Tie-Ins and Reciprocity Agreements That Are Economically Inefficient and Allowing Those That Are Economically Efficient

If my conclusions about the economic efficiency of non-pricing-technique tying and reciprocity agreements' performing various functions are correct and if as I assert it would not be TBLE for antitrust-policy enforcement-authorities to attempt to determine whether in individual cases or particular subsets of cases tie-ins and reciprocity agreements that perform the various particular functions that non-pricing-technique tying and reciprocity agreements can perform will increase or decrease economic efficiency, the only obstacle to a government of a liberal-moral-rights-based society's increasing economic efficiency by deterring economically-inefficient non-pricing-technique tying and reciprocity agreements and allowing economically-efficient tying and reciprocity agreements of these kinds is the allocative cost of determining with various degrees of accuracy (1) whether and the extent to which individual package-pricing tie-ins increase their seller-employer's profits by enabling it (A) to control more-cost-effectively the quality of the complements B that the relevant buyer combines with the seller's product A, (B) to reduce the market-research cost, checkout-counter-personnel-training cost, and checkout-counter-sales-processing cost of practicing price discrimination, (C) to reduce the transaction cost of selling two products to one buyer by substituting one sale of two products for two sales of one product, and (D) to conceal its non-specific-anticompetitive-intent-motivated price discrimination, its predatory pricing, its retaliatory pricing in the service of contrivance, its price-regulation violations, or its contract or tax fraud and (2) whether and the extent to which individual reciprocity agreements increase a participant's profits by enabling (A) a buyer to control more-cost-effectively the quality of the ingredients or other inputs its supplier uses to produce the good it is supplying the buyer in question, (B) a seller to practice inter-buyer price discrimination more profitably by reducing the market-research cost, checkout-counter-personnel-training cost, and checkout-counter-sales-processing costs of such discrimination, (C) its participants to reduce the transaction cost of selling goods to each other by substituting for two transactions involving one product one transaction involving two products, and (D) a seller to conceal its non-specific-anticompetitive-intent-motivated inter-buyer price discrimination, its predatory pricing, its retaliatory pricing, its price-regulation violations, and its contract or tax fraud. In my judgment, this obstacle will not render it *ex ante* economically inefficient for antitrust-policy enforcement-authorities to attempt to prohibit economically-inefficient and allow economically-efficient non-pricing-technique tying and reciprocity agreements.

13.2.3 The Liberal-Moral-Rights-Violativeness of Non-Pricing-Technique Tie-Ins and Reciprocity Agreements and the Ability of the Government of a Liberal-Moral-Rights-Based Society to Secure Liberal-Moral-Rights-Related Interests by Responding Appropriately to Such Tie-Ins and Reciprocity Agreements

13.2.3.1 The Liberal-Moral-Rights-Violativeness of Non-Pricing-Technique Tie-Ins and Reciprocity Agreements

Because contrived-oligopolistic pricing, predatory behavior, and contract fraud are liberal-moral-rights-violative, tie-ins and reciprocity agreements that conceal, implement, or increase the profitability of any such conduct in any other way (say, by reducing the market-research, checkout-counter-personnel-training cost, and checkout-counter-sales-processing cost of charging discriminatorily-low prices that are predatory or retaliatory in the service of contrivance) are liberal-moral-rights-violative. Because I also subscribe to the admittedly-contestable position that violations of maximum-price regulations, minimum-price regulations, legal prohibitions of inter-buyer price discrimination, and tax laws are liberal-moral-rights-violative in liberal-moral-rights-based societies (that violations of laws that are constitutional in and were promulgated in a liberal-moral-rights-based society violate a liberal moral right of the non-violator citizens of and participants in such a society to have their society's laws obeyed), I believe that tie-ins and reciprocity agreements that lead to or increase the profitability of such violations are liberal-moral-rights-violative. Because I do not think that inter-buyer price discrimination that is not motivated by prejudice and is not prohibited by law is liberal-moral-rights-violative, I do not think that tying and reciprocity agreements that conceal such price discrimination to prevent legally-unwarranted suits against the discriminator or the loss of goodwill of buyers who discover that they have been charged discriminatorily-high prices are liberal-moral-rights-violative. (I am assuming perhaps contestably that sellers do not have a duty to disclose their practice of price discrimination to discriminated-against buyers or a duty not to take steps to conceal their practice of price discrimination from such buyers.) I do not think that any other non-pricing-technique functional type of tie-in or reciprocity agreement is liberal-moral-rights-violative: the fact that an exemplar of such an agreement that would not otherwise be liberal-moral-rights-violative imposes equivalent-dollar losses on one or more individuals that deprive them of the wherewithal that critically affects their ability to take their lives morally seriously does not render those agreements liberal-moral-rights-violative because, when acting in non-political capacities, the firms that or individuals who execute such agreements have no liberal moral duty to supply "strangers" with the resources and services that give the strangers a meaningful opportunity to take their lives morally seriously.

13.2.3.2 The Ability and Moral Duty of the Government of a Lbieral-Moral-Rights-Based Society to Secure Liberal-Moral-Rights-Related Interests by Preventing Tie-Ins and Reciprocity Agreements That Are Liberal-Moral-Rights-Violative and Allowing Tie-Ins and Reciprocity That Enable the Government to Finance Liberal-Moral-Rights-Securing Actions by Increasing Economic Efficiency and Thereby the Government's Ability to Raise Revenue and Finance Such Policies

Governments that are not prevented from doing so by limitations in their society's natural resources, human resources, and knowledge-base are morally obligated to deter liberal-moral-rights-violative tying and reciprocity agreements to the greatest extent they can without violating liberal investigative, proof, and sentencing/penalty constraints or foregoing expenditures that would secure on balance weightier liberal-moral-rights-related interests. I suspect that in societies that have antitrust policies the only relevant limitation on the government's ability and duty to prevent liberal-moral-rights-violative tying and reciprocity agreements relates to the possible difficulty of determining whether or the extent to which package-pricing tie-ins and certain reciprocity agreements are performing concealing and economic-efficiency-decreasing functions. I am disposed to think that antitrust-enforcement authorities will be able to resolve these issues and prove their conclusions in court with the morally-required degree of certainty.

One final point: If the society whose antitrust policy is being considered is unable to or chooses not to supply some of its moral-rights bearers with the material goods, services, education, and exposure to alternative conceptions of the moral good, religions, and life-styles that give them an appropriate opportunity to lead a life of moral integrity, its government may have a liberal moral duty to allow firms to employ non-pricing-technique tying and reciprocity agreements that increase economic efficiency—at least if the economic-efficiency increase will enable the government to finance and result in the government's financing expenditures that give the moral-rights bearers for whom it is responsible a meaningful opportunity to take their lives morally seriously or secure other liberal-moral-rights-related interests.

13.2.4 The Impact of Non-Pricing-Technique Tying and Reciprocity Agreements on the Instantiation of the Utilitarian and Various Non-Utilitarian-Egalitarian Conceptions of the Moral Good and the Ability of the Government of a Liberal-Moral-Rights-Based Society to Instantiate These Conceptions of the Moral Good by Deterring and Allowing Such Tying and Reciprocity Agreements

13.2.4.1 The Impact of Non-Pricing-Technique Tying and Reciprocity Agreements on the Instantiation of the Utilitarian and Other Egalitarian Conceptions of the Moral Good

As we have seen, the impact of any choice or natural event on total utility depends on its impact on economic efficiency and its impact on material equality while the impact of any choice or natural event on the instantiation of any non-utilitarian-egalitarian conception of the moral good depends exclusively on its impact on material equality. I will first analyze the impact of each functional type of non-pricing-technique tying and reciprocity agreement I have distinguished on total utility and on the various non-utilitarian-egalitarian conceptions of the moral good on the assumption that such agreements perform only one of the 6 functions or related sets of functions I have described. I will then analyze the moral-good effects of those tie-ins and reciprocity agreements that perform more than one of the 6 non-pricing-technique functions I have distinguished.

Section 13.2.2.1 establishes that tie-ins that increase the cost-effectiveness of their employer's efforts to control the quality of the complements B that its customers combine with its product A and reciprocity agreements that increase the cost-effectiveness of a buyer's efforts to control the quality of the ingredients or other inputs a supplier uses to produce the good it supplies the buyer in question always or virtually always increase economic efficiency. I will limit myself to pointing out what I take to be the most salient distributive impacts of such tying and reciprocity agreements. Such tie-ins will confer equivalent-dollar gains on the tying seller. To the extent that such tie-ins deter the tying seller's customers from using inferior complements when it is not in those buyers' parochial interest to do so, they will confer equivalent-dollar gains on those of the seller's customers the tie-ins prevent from mistakenly using inferior complements. Such tie-ins will also confer equivalent-dollar gains on those of the tying seller's potential customers who would have been deterred from buying the tying seller's product by the incorrect inference they drew about its quality as a result of other buyers' combining it with inferior complements. On the other hand, such tie-ins will impose equivalent-dollar losses both on those of the tying seller's customers who would have profited from using inferior complements, on the firms that would have supplied inferior complements to the customers of the tying seller that would have purchased such complements absent the tie-ins, and on the firms that would have taken sales away from the tying seller if the tying seller's customers' use of inferior complements had led other buyers to underestimate the quality of the tying seller's product(s). Since I see no reason to believe that the tying sellers' shareholders'/creditors'/managers/'employees' weighted-average income/wealth position would be different from its counterpart for the tying seller's rivals or that the weighted-average income/wealth position of the buyers that would benefit from the tie-ins would be different from its counterpart for the buyers on whom the tie-in would impose losses, I suspect that this functional type of tie-in will have no significant impact on poverty or material equality. I therefore expect that this type of tie-in will increase total utility, will have no impact on the instantiation of the various non-utilitarian-egalitarian conceptions of the moral good, and will tend to instantiate mixed conceptions of the moral good that value both total utility and one or more non-utilitarian-egalitarian *desiderata*. Section 13.2.2.1 also establishes that reciprocity agreements that increase the cost-effectiveness of a buyer-participant's efforts to control the quality of the ingredients or other inputs its supplier uses to produce the final good the supplier supplies the buyer always or virtually always increase economic efficiency. Such reciprocity agreements will confer equivalent-dollar gains on the buyers that employ them and, to the extent that they prevent the final-good producers they involve from using inferior ingredients or other inputs, will impose equivalent-dollar losses on the final-good suppliers and on the firms that would have supplied them with the inferior ingredients and others inputs they would have used absent the reciprocity agreement while conferring equivalent-dollar gains on the firms that supply the superior ingredients and inputs the reciprocity agreement cause the final-good-producer reciprocity-participant to use and on the customers of the buyers of the final good the reciprocity agreements involve (by preventing them from being disappointed by the quality of the final good the relevant final-good suppliers would have supplied absent the reciprocity agreement). Because I do not know the relative magnitudes of the equivalent-dollar gains and losses just referenced, my best guess is that this type of reciprocity agreement has no significant effect on poverty or material equality. In combination with my conclusion that such reciprocity agreements increase economic efficiency, this last "result" implies that such reciprocity agreements serve the instantiation of the utilitarian conception of the moral good and mixed conceptions of the moral good in which total utility is positively valued. It also implies that such reciprocity agreements will have no impact on the instantiation of non-utilitarian-egalitarian conceptions of the moral good, be they pure or mixed.

Section 13.2.2.1 also argues (or should I write: "claims") that tie-ins and reciprocity agreements that increase the cost-effectiveness of their employers' efforts to prevent their customers from engaging in arbitrage tend to increase economic efficiency. Such agreements confer an equivalent-dollar gain on their employers and, to the extent that they deter arbitrage, impose an equivalent-dollar loss on the original buyers of their employers' respective products (at least if one ignores the possibility that, if their employers could not employ tying and reciprocity agreements to deter arbitrage, they would change the pricing-technique they use to prevent arbitrage). On the assumption articulated in the preceding parenthetical, such tying and reciprocity agreements would also impose equivalent-dollar losses on the buyers that would have engaged in any arbitrage the relevant tying and reciprocity agreements deterred, though I must acknowledge that such agreements might be profitable even if they deterred less arbitrage then the arbitrage-preventing techniques their employer would otherwise have used (because the tying and reciprocity agreements in question were less private-transaction-costly to employ than these alternative arbitrage-preventing techniques). My inability to assess the probability that sellers that are prohibited from using tie-ins or reciprocity agreements to prevent arbitrage will respond to this prohibition by changing their pricing-technique or using any one of several other methods of preventing arbitrage inclines me to conclude that this functional type of tying and reciprocity agreements will not affect equality. The combination of this equality-conclusion and my conclusion that these agreements increase economic efficiency imply that they increase total utility; the equality conclusion implies that these agreements will have no tendency to serve or disserve the instantiation of non-utilitarian-egalitarian conceptions of the moral good; and the combination of the total-utility-impact conclusion and the "impact on the instantiation of any non-utilitarian-egalitarian conception of the moral good" conclusion implies that this functional type of tying and reciprocity agreements will serve the instantiation of mixed conceptions of the moral good in which total utility and one or more non-utilitarian conceptions of equality are positively valued.

Section 13.2.2.1 contends that tie-ins that increase the profitability of inter-buyer price discrimination by lowering the market-research, checkout-counter-personnel-training, and checkout-counter-sales-processing cost of practicing price discrimination will increase economic efficiency (at least on the admittedly-contestable assumption that such tie-ins do not cause a sufficient percentage of their employers to substitute inter-buyer price discrimination for non-discriminatory single pricing to render this functional category of tie-ins economically inefficient). Tie-ins that perform this function without increasing the incidence of inter-buyer price discrimination will yield equivalent-dollar gains to the firms that employ them and impose equivalent-dollar losses on market researchers and checkout-counter-employee trainers and probably will tend to increase inequality. Tie-ins that increase the incidence of inter-buyer price discrimination by performing this function will, in addition to generating the previously-referenced distributive impacts, tend to increase equality by conferring equivalent-dollar gains on those buyers who are charged discriminatorily-low prices and imposing equivalent-dollar losses on those potential and actual buyers who are charged discriminatorily-high prices (since the favored buyers will tend to be poorer than the disfavored buyers). I suspect that exemplars of this functional category of tie-ins that do not increase the incidence of inter-buyer price discrimination will increase total utility because their positive impact on economic efficiency will (so to speak) outweigh their negative impact on equality. I suspect that tie-ins in this category that substantially increase the incidence of inter-buyer price discrimination will increase total utility because their positive impact on economic efficiency will (so to speak) outweigh their negative impact on equality. I suspect that tie-ins in this category that substantially increase the incidence of inter-buyer price discrimination will decrease total utility because their negative impact on economic efficiency will (so to speak) outweigh any positive impact they may have on equality. I have already asserted that it will not be TBLE for antitrust-policy-enforcement authorities to investigate the impact that individual tie-ins or subsets of tie-ins in this functional category have on the incidence of price discrimination. The utilitarian case for such authorities' investigating this issue may be stronger. If utilitarianism disfavors the authorities' responding to exemplars of this functional category of tie-ins selectively so that the salient issue is whether all tie-ins in this category increase or decrease total utility, neither resolution would seem more convincing to me. However, I am disposed to conclude that, taken together, taken as a group, the exemplars of this functional category of tie-ins do disserve the instantiation of the various non-utilitarian-egalitarian conceptions of the moral good and therefore the instantiation of any mixed conception of the moral good that values both utility and one or more non-utilitarian-egalitarian conceptions of the moral good.

Section 13.2.2.1 reached reached 3 sets of conclusions that relate to the economic efficiency of any tie-ins or reciprocity agreements that function by concealing its employer's price discrimination that is not motivated by specific anticompetitive intent, retaliatory price discrimination in the service of contrived-oligopolistic pricing, predatory pricing, violation(s) of regulations of maximum and/or minimum prices, or tax or contract fraud:

The first set relates to the fact that concealing tie-ins will tend to increase/decrease economic efficiency to the extent that they decrease/increase poverty and material inequality. First, Sect. 13.2.2.1 argues that concealing tie-ins and reciprocity agreements that increase the incidence of (1) retaliatory pricing in the service of contrived-oligopolistic pricing and hence the incidence of contrived-oligopolistic pricing, (2) predatory pricing, (3) violations of maximum-price regulations, (4) tax fraud, and probably (5) contract fraud will tend to increase poverty and material inequality. Second, Sect. 13.2.3.1 argues that concealing tie-ins and reciprocity agreements that increase the incidence of price discrimination that is not related to contrived-oligopolistic or predatory pricing will have various impacts on poverty and material inequality—will increase material inequality by benefiting the discriminator but may decrease material inequality on balance by virtue of its conferring equivalent-dollar gains on favored buyers (who are poorer) and imposing equivalent-dollar losses on disfavored buyers (who are richer), and will tend to decrease poverty by conferring equivalent-dollar gains on favored buyers (who tend to be poorer). Section 12.2.2.1 also points out that concealing tie-ins and reciprocity agreements that increase the incidence of minimum-price-regulation violations will tend to decrease poverty and material inequality (even though they may impose losses on the violators, who are likely to be better-off than the average member of the society in question).

The second relevant point that Sect. 13.2.2.1 makes is that, to the extent that such tie-ins or reciprocity agreements are more-allocative-costly to design, draft, and implement than the set of two or more one-product agreements they replace, they will tend to decrease economic efficiency on that account (in my judgment by more than they increase the private transaction costs their participants incur).

The third set of relevant points that Sect. 13.2.2.1 makes relates to the impact that concealing tie-ins and reciprocity agreements will have on economic efficiency by altering equilibrium QV and equilibrium PPR in the ARDEPPS of practice and in the economy as a whole. The general point is that if the conduct concealed is profitable for the practitioners taken as a collective (see below) the concealing tie-ins and reciprocity agreements will, by increasing the practice's profitability and the profitability of the investments to which the practices relate decrease/increase economic efficiency if they increase/decrease equilibrium investment in the ARDEPPS of practice and the economy as a whole when the relevant investments are QV investments and will tend to increase/decrease economic efficiency if they increase/decrease equilibrium PPR in the ARDEPPS of practice and the economy as a whole. Section 13.2.2.1 also points out that most variants of the conduct being concealed will tend to increase equilibrium investment in the ARDEPPS of practice and the economy as a whole. The exceptions it references are predatory pricing, which may decrease equilibrium investment in the ARDEPPS of practice as a result of its reducing the intensity of its investment-competition, and minimum-price-regulation violations, which may be against the collective interest of all producers in the relevant ARDEPPS even when each individual seller finds it profitable to violate the minimum-price regulation.

Concealing tie-ins and reciprocity agreements that increase the incidence of (1) retaliatory pricing in the service of contrived-oligopolistic pricing and hence the incidence of contrived-oligopolistic pricing, (2) predatory pricing, (3) violations of maximum-price regulations, (4) tax fraud, and probably (5) contract fraud will tend to increase material inequality. Concealing tie-ins and reciprocity agreements that increase the incidence of price discrimination that is not related to contrived-oligopolistic or predatory pricing will have an uncertain impact on material inequality—will increase material inequality by benefiting the discriminator but may decrease material inequality on balance by virtue of its conferring equivalent-dollar gains on favored buyers (who are poorer) and imposing equivalent-dollar losses on disfavored buyers (who are richer), and will tend to decrease poverty by conferring equivalent-dollar gains on favored buyers (who tend to be poorer). Section 12.2.2.1 also points out that concealing tie-ins and reciprocity agreements that increase the incidence of minimum-price-regulation violations will tend to decrease poverty and material inequality (even though they may impose losses on the violators who are likely to be better-off than the average member of the society in question).

I suspect that with the almost-certainly-empirically-trivial exception of some concealing tying and reciprocity agreements that increase the incidence of violations of minimum-price regulations which violations are against the collective interest of QV investor violators, violations of minimum-price regulations and maximum-price regulations which violations are in the interest of their production-process-researcher violators, and predatory pricing by QV investors that decreases equilibrium QV investment in the ARDEPPS of practice and the economy, concealing tying and reciprocity agreements will disserve the instantiation of the utilitarian conception of the moral good. With what I assume is the empirically-unimportant exception of some concealing tying and reciprocity agreements that increase the incidence of minimum-price-regulation violations and some concealing tying and reciprocity agreements that increased the incidence of price discrimination that is not predatory or retaliatory in the service of contrived-oligopolistic pricing, concealing tying and reciprocity agreements will disserve the instantiation of all non-utilitarian-egalitarian conceptions of the moral good. The preceding two conclusions imply that the percentage of concealing tying and reciprocity agreements that serve the instantiation of mixed conceptions of the moral good in which total utility and one or more non-utilitarian-egalitarian *desiderata* are positively valued is even lower than the exceedingly-low percentage of such agreements that instantiate a pure utilitarian or non-utilitarian-egalitarian conception of the moral good.

Section 13.2.2.1 argues that tying and reciprocity agreements that function by increasing the cost-effectiveness and possibly on that account the incidence of the meter pricing of durable machines, franchises, or the use of production processes (1) will tend to increase economic efficiency to the extent that they are substituted for more-privately-transaction-costly methods of implementing meter pricing (using meters, contractual clauses that obligate franchisees to pay the franchisor a percentage of the franchisee's sales, or endproduct-royalty schemes)—indeed, in my judgment will decrease allocative transaction costs by more than they decrease private transaction costs—and (2) will also tend to increase economic efficiency when they induce a seller to substitute meter pricing for the outright sale of its durable machine, franchise, or the right to use its production process (since that substitution will tend to reduce the private and *a fortiori* the allocative transaction costs the seller generates to determine the dollar value of its "product" to various buyers and decrease the sum of the seller's and buyer's risk costs by shifting some of the risk that the buyer's quantity deemed will be different from what is expected from the buyer to the seller though it will increase private and allocative transaction costs to the extent that it is more private-transaction-costly and *a fortiori* more allocative-transaction-costly to draft, negotiate, and enforce the meter-pricing tying or reciprocity agreement than to draft and negotiate the outright sale). The preceding analysis ignores the fact that to the extent that meter-pricing tie-ins and reciprocity agreements increase the profitability of (QV investments)/PPR, they may tend to decrease/increase economic efficiency by increasing equilibrium (QV investment)/PPR in the ARDEPPS of practice and the economy as a whole.

To the extent that meter-pricing tying agreements increase the incidence of meter pricing, they will tend to increase material inequality because their use will lead to increases in the marginal cost to the machine/production-process buyer of using the machine/production process they involve and hence in the price of the good the machine/production-process buyer uses the machine or production process to produce. To the extent that meter-pricing reciprocity agreements increase the incidence of meter pricing, they will also tend to increase material inequality because their use will lead to (1) a downward shift in the marginal-revenue curve the machine/production-process buyer faces when selling the good it uses the machine or production process to produce),[19] hence a decrease in this party's profit-maximizing output of the good it produces (the output of this good the reciprocity agreement obligates it to sell to the "producer" of the relevant machine or production process for [say] $\$\alpha$ less per unit than it would otherwise charge for that output), hence a decrease in the output of the final good in question that the machine/production-process "producer" sells below the output that the final-good producer would have sold of the final good had it paid only a lump-sum fee for the machine or production process in question, hence an increase in the price of the final good in question.

The combination of the preceding conclusions that meter-pricing tying and reciprocity agreements will increase both economic efficiency and material inequality leaves one uncertain about their impact on total utility (though I am disposed to believe that across all exemplars they increase total utility). The conclusion that meter-pricing tying and reciprocity agreements tend to increase material inequality implies that they disserve the instantiation of all non-utilitarian-egalitarian conceptions of the moral good. And the preceding two findings imply that meter-pricing tying and reciprocity agreements can either serve or disserve the instantiation of conceptions of the moral good that place a positive value on total utility and one or more non-utilitarian-egalitarian *desiderata*, though they are less likely to serve the instantiation of such mixed conceptions of the moral good than they are to serve the instantiation of the utilitarian conception of the moral good.

The final functional category of non-pricing-technique tying agreements I distinguished have no reciprocity-agreement counterparts. This category contains tying agreements that are designed to prevent one or more potential entrants from entering the tying-product ARDEPPS by preventing them from reducing the (Π_D + R) barriers to entry they face in relation to entering the tying-product market by supplying the tying-product-producer's customers with complements of the tying product (by placing the tying seller's customers under a legal obligation to purchase their full requirements of those complements from the tying seller).

Section 13.2.2.1 argues (1) that few if any tie-ins are critically motivated by a desire to deter such entries, (2) that the tie-ins that critically raise entry-barriers probably increase economic efficiency on this account (A) because the investments that would be deterred in this way would almost always be QV investments and it is economically efficient to reduce equilibrium QV investment and (B) because it is probably economically efficient to entitle firms to keep their customer-lists secret (to increase their incentives to identify potential buyers to whom they could make profitable sales and to convince those buyers to purchase their products), but (3) that tie-ins in this category executed by sellers that would not have perceived them to be *ex ante* profitable but for the possibility that they could render an otherwise-effective potential competitor ineffective might be economically inefficient because they might prevent complement-sales from being made by more-economically-efficient complement-producers (if the tying-good seller would be deterred from buying the complements from a superior independent complement-producer out of concern that closing down its own complement-producing operation would make it vulnerable to the independent's resulting economic power).

Any tie-ins that perform this entry-deterring function will tend to increase inequality by imposing equivalent-dollar losses on the tying seller's customers both in the short run to the extent that those buyers could have shared in any transaction-surplus gain that would have resulted had the barred independent complement-producer been privately-better-placed (entry-effect-considerations aside) to supply the complement than the tying seller was and in the long run by rendering ineffective a barred complement-producer that would otherwise have been an effective potential competitor.

The preceding conclusions imply that if any tie-ins do function is this way (1) their impact on total utility will be uncertain, (2) they will disserve the instantiation of any non-utilitarian-egalitarian conception of the moral good, and (3) their impact on the instantiation of mixed conceptions of the moral good that place a positive value on both total utility and one or more non-utilitarian-egalitarian *desiderata* will be uncertain.

13.2.4.2 The Ability of a Liberal-Moral-Rights-Based Society to Serve the Instantiation of the Utilitarian, Non-Utilitarian-Egalitarian, and Any Mixed Conception of the Moral Good by Deterring and Allowing Non-Pricing-Technique Tying and Reciprocity Agreements

I have acknowledged (1) that the impact of some functional categories of non-pricing-technique tying and reciprocity agreements on the instantiation of the utilitarian conception of the moral good and on the instantiation of some mixed conceptions of the moral good in which total utility is positively valued is rendered uncertain by the fact that exemplars of the relevant functional categories of such agreements increase both utility and material inequality and (2) that the moral-goodness from various morally-defensible normative perspectives of some actual tying and reciprocity agreements is made more difficult to assess by their performing more than one of the categories of non-pricing-technique functions I have identified. However, I believe that in the vast majority of "cases," the government of a liberal-moral-rights-based society will be able to promote the instantiation of the various conceptions of the moral good that are morally defensible by prohibiting and allowing various non-pricing-technique categories of tying and reciprocity agreements—that the allocative and material-inequality cost of such a government's making such decisions will not prove to be prohibitive from the relevant normative perspectives.

13.3 Minimum-Price-Setting-Resale-Price-Maintenance (RPM) Clauses and Vertical-Customer-Allocation (VCA) Clauses That Are Surrogates for Vertical Integration

13.3.1 The Functions of Minimum-Price-Setting-RPM Clauses and VCA Clauses That Are Surrogates for Vertical Integration

Firms that are vertically integrated from production through distribution employ hierarchical controls to induce their distributive employees to make demand-increasing-expenditure decisions, shelf-space-allocation decisions, and retail-pricing decisions that are in the firm's interest as well as to incentivize such employees to communicate to higher-ups information about the possible uses of the firms' products, the best ways to employ the firm's products, and sales-techniques that are cost-effective that the firm can profit by communicating to other distributors, distributive employees, and/or buyers. When producers do not find it profitable to vertically integrate forward into distribution (because these hierarchical controls are costly to implement and/or imperfectly efficacious, because the relevant distributors find it profitable to sell not only the producer's product but other products as well and the producer in question would not be as good at selling these other products as independent distributors would be, because the producers can make more profitable uses of its retained earnings and underutilized managers and workers or of any capital and "staff" it can raise from the outside, and/or because it is expensive to raise/hire capital externally and costly and difficult to find good new managers and employees and integrate them into the firm, their most profitable course of action is to use independent distributors and to influence these independents' conduct by employing resale-price-maintenance clauses, vertical-customer-allocation clauses, demand-increasing-(expenditure/shelf-space-allocation) subsidies, and/or sales/franchise-renewal policies (as well as by employing the fancy pricing-techniques and "non-pricing" tying and reciprocity agreements. Sections 13.1 and 13.2 analyzed).

I will now be more specific about (1) the "organizationally"-unprofitable decisions that would be made by the independent distributors of a producer's product if the producer uses multiple independent distributors to sell its product, permits those distributors to compete against each other for the patronage of given buyers of the producer's product, and charges those distributors a per-unit price that exceeds the shadow price it would instruct its own employees to assume they were being charged for the firm's product when identifying the choices that would be most profitable for the "organization" (in this case, the vertically-integrated firm) for them to make—a shadow price equal to the marginal cost the firm would have to incur to produce and deliver to the relevant distributive employee the last unit of its product it would produce if it were producing the transaction-surplus-maximizing output of the good in question—and (2) the way in which minimum-price-setting-RPM clauses, VCA clauses, and demand-increasing-(expenditure/shelf-space-allocation) subsidies can enable a producer that is not vertically integrated forward into distribution can reduce the losses its non-integration imposes on it.

A producer's independent distributors can charge a retail price for the producer's product that is lower than the price that would maximize the organization's profits for at least 5 reasons: (1) it underestimates the price that would maximize its own profits; (2) it operates a franchise (say, a fast-food restaurant) that will find it profitable to supply only one price-quality combination, that supplies both locals (who prefer a lower price-quality combination) and interstate travelers (who prefer a higher price-quality combination) at least some or many of whom are not prospective repeat-customers, find it costly or difficult to assess in advance the price/quality combination a particular franchisee is offering and therefore value price-quality predictability, (3) it charges that price to outbid a rival independent distributor of the producer's product that could otherwise have obtained a higher price for the producer's product; and (4) it does not consider the fact that its charging the lower price will reduce the demand curve that other distributors of the producer's product face and on that account the profits "the organization" makes because some buyers that would patronize other distributors of the producer's product (A) believe that the material quality of the producer's product is positively correlated with its price and/or (B) value positively in itself a higher price being charged for the good in question—purchase goods in part to communicate to others their ability to pay high prices for products and services and in part to induce others to attribute to them non-wealth attributes possessed by other buyers of high-prices goods and services. A producer that uses independent distributors can reduce the losses it sustains on all 4 of these accounts by using minimum-price-setting-RPM clauses to prohibit its independent distributors from charging prices that are unprofitably low from the perspective of the organization (and for the producer, given that the operating profits its independent distributors realize affect the lump-sum fees it can induce them to pay). (A producer that uses independent distributors can reduce the losses it sustains on the third and, derivatively and partially, on the fourth of these accounts by using vertical territorial restraints [including non-overlapping exclusive dealerships] and other sorts of vertical-customer-allocation clauses to prevent intra-brand competition between or among its independent distributors.)

A producer's individual independent distributors may also find it individually profitable to make and may therefore make organizationally-unprofitable decisions about producer-product-related demand-increasing expenditures on media advertizing, in-store promotional displays, in-store sales-efforts, door-to-door sales-efforts, and warranteed maintenance-and-repair efforts[20] and on the quantity and quality of shelf-space to allocate to the producer's product(s). Each individual distributor will tend to make organizationally-unprofitable demand-increasing expenditures/(shelf-space allocations) to the extent that its expenditures/allocations take sales away from other independent distributors of the producer's product(s) and will tend not to make demand-increasing expenditures/(shelf-space allocations) that would be organizationally profitable when its expenditures/allocations yield sales to other distributors of the producer's product(s) and/or the per-unit price the producer charges the distributor for the producer's product exceeds the marginal cost the producer incurs to supply its product to the relevant distributor. A producer that is not vertically integrated forward into distribution may be able to reduce the losses it sustains because of its independent distributors' demand-increasing expenditure/(shelf-space-allocation) decisions by using VCA clauses that ideally will prevent any individual distributor's expenditure/allocation either from taking a sale away from another distributor of the producer's product or from generating a sale for another distributor of the producer's product. Such a non-integrated producer might also be able to reduce the losses it sustains on this account by using minimum-price-setting-RPM clauses since they will reduce the likelihood that any individual distributor's demand-increasing expenditure/(shelf-space allocation) will take a sale away from or generate a sale for another distributor of the producer's product by eliminating or at least reducing the possibility that a buyer who is persuaded or would have been persuaded by such an expenditure/allocation to purchase the producer's product will make or would otherwise have made its purchase from another distributor by eliminating or reducing the possibility that the buyer will have a price-reason for purchasing the producer's product from a distributor other than the one whose expenditure/allocation induced its purchase (for example, from a discount house). I should acknowledge that producers whose individual independent distributors seem likely to make "too low" demand-increasing expenditures or inadequate shelf-space allocations from the producer's perspective can also protect their interests by subsidizing their independent distributors' media advertizing and in-store promotions or paying for their independent distributors' warrantee services or shelf-space allocations. When such responses are rendered cost-ineffective by the possibility of distributor fraud, the producer may find it profitable to partially integrate forward itself—that is, to place its own local advertizing and set up its own local maintenance and repair services (though these moves are disfavored respectively by the producer's knowing less than its independent distributors about the kinds of advertizements that would appeal most to locals and the media outlets whose use would be most cost-effective and by the producer's inability to take as much advantage of economies of scale as could distributors that would in any event supply repair and maintenance services for all the products they sell).

A producer's individual independent distributors may also find it individually unprofitable to inform the producer of uses to which its products can be put, of the best way to employ its products, and of sales-pitches or promotional displays that are profitable when such communications would be organizationally profitable if the individual distributor is concerned that rival distributors of the producer's product will use such information in competition with it. Producers that are not vertically integrated forward into distribution may reduce the losses they sustain on this account by using VCA clauses or minimum-price-setting-RPM clauses to reduce or eliminate the possibility of such intra-brand competition respectively by prohibiting such competition directly and by preventing buyers from having a price-reason to patronize any distributor other than the distributor that is privately-best-placed to supply it. I should acknowledge that a producer that is not vertically integrated forward into distribution may also be able to mitigate this problem by paying its independent distributors for any such information they provide it.

13.3.2 The Economic Efficiency of Minimum-Price-Setting-RPM Clauses and VCA Clauses That Are Surrogates for Vertical Integration and the Ability of the Government of a Liberal-Moral-Rights-Based Society to Increase Economic Efficiency by Responding Appropriately to a Producer's Use of Such Vertical-Integration Surrogates

13.3.2.1 The Economic Efficiency of Minimum-Price-Setting RPM Clauses and VCA Clauses That Are Surrogates for Vertical Integration

I will start by reviewing and elaborating on the functions that such clauses can perform for the producers that include them in their contracts with their independent distributors: (1) preventing one or more such distributors from engaging in intra-brand price-competition that decreases the organization's profits directly by reducing the prices that buyers of the producer's product who or that would have been willing to purchase it at a higher price (2) preventing one or more distributors from charging lower prices for the producer's products that reduce the organization's profits regardless of whether they enable the distributor that charges them to make sales of the producer's product that would otherwise have been made by another distributor of the producer's product or take sales away from suppliers of another product because the lower price causes other actual and potential buyers of the producer's product who believe that the material quality of the producer's product increases with its price to undervalue the producer's product, (3) preventing one or more distributors of the producer's product from charging lower prices for the producer's products that reduce the organization's profits regardless of whether the distributor charges those prices to take sales away from another distributor of the producer's product or to engage in inter-brand price-competition because the lower prices reduce the actual value of the producer's product to buyers who positively value being seen to have paid a higher price for the good or who want to be perceived by others to have non-wealth attributes possessed by buyers of the high-priced variant of the type of product the producer produces, (4) preventing one or more distributors from reducing the organization's profits by offering a low price-quality combination that it finds most profitable to supply because its local customers prefer that combination in circumstances in which it is not possible or profitable for it to offer both that low price-quality combination and the higher price-quality combination that travelers prefer when the travelers cannot determine *ex ante* without incurring significant costs the price-quality combination that a particular member of "the producer's" distributive chain is offering and it is profitable for the producer-franchisor to assure its prospective customers that all its franchisees will be supplying the same higher price-quality combination, (5) preventing one or more distributors from making demand-increasing expenditures on media advertizing, in-store promotional displays, or in-person salesmanship or shelf-space allocations that are rendered organizationally unprofitable by the fact that some of the sales that the relevant expenditures would yield the distributor that made them would be taken from other distributors of the producer's product(s), (6) inducing one or more distributors to make organizationally-profitable demand-increasing expenditures on media advertizing, in-store promotional displays, or in-person salesmanship or on positive shelf-space allocations that increase the demand for the producer's product(s) by making potential buyers aware of the producer's product's or products' existence, (7) inducing one or more distributors to make organizationally-profitable demand-increasing expenditures that increase the demand for the producer's product(s) by increasing the quality of the producer's product(s) expansively defined (when the expenditure is on warrantee-covered repair and maintenance services), by improving the product's or products' image, and/or by supplying accurate positive information about the producer's product and/or accurate negative information about products that compete with the relevant producer's product(s), (8) inducing one or more distributors to make organizationally-profitable demand-increasing expenditures usually on media advertizing, in-store promotional displays, or in-person salesmanship that increase the demand for the producer's product(s) by providing potential buyers with inaccurate or misleading positive information about the producer's product's or products' material quality, image, and /or lifetime-ownership cost or with inaccurate or misleading negative information about one or more rival products' material quality, image(s), or lifetime-ownership costs, and (9) increasing the organization's profits by inducing one or more distributors to pass on to the producer information about its product's or products' possible uses, about the best way to employ its products, or about advertizing/promotional displays/sales-pitches that are cost-effective.

I will now analyze the economic efficiency of minimum-price-setting-RPM clauses and VCA clauses that function in one or more of the above ways. I will proceed initially on the usually-unrealistic assumption that a producer that would find it profitable to use such clauses for one or more of the purposes just listed would not do anything to achieve the relevant objective if it did not use the clauses to do so. I will then reanalyze the economic efficiency of minimum-price-setting-RPM clauses and VCA clauses on more-realistic assumptions about the choices that producers that would actually usually such clauses to achieve one or more of the above objectives for some reason would make instead to achieve the objective(s) in question if they did not use these clauses to do so despite their profitability.

The economic efficiency of the minimum-price-setting-RPM clauses and VCA clauses that a producer uses to achieve the objectives such clauses can enable the producer to secure when the producer would do nothing to achieve those objectives if it did not use these clauses to do so depends both on the allocative transaction cost of drafting, negotiating, and enforcing the clauses (which will be higher than their private-transaction-cost counterparts) and the distortion in the private benefits the producer can obtain by securing these objectives. The only point I will make about the relevant allocative transaction costs is that they include not only the allocative transaction cost associated with the private transaction cost the producer incurs but also the allocative transaction costs associated with the private transaction costs the distributor incurs (including the transaction costs the distributor incurs to conceal its violations of the relevant clauses and to defend itself in any related litigation) and the allocative transaction costs associated with the private transaction costs the government incurs to adjudicate any relevant disputes including the allocative transactions the government generates to finance its adjudicative efforts. (Although the following are not allocative *transaction* costs, any assessment of the economic efficiency of minimal-price-setting-RPM clauses and VCA clauses should also take into account the non-transaction-cost-related economic inefficiency generated by the government's financing of its adjudicative efforts.)

I will now analyze the economic efficiency of using minimum-price-setting-RPM clauses and VCA clauses to achieve the various objectives they can be used to secure, ignoring the allocative transaction costs the use of such clauses to secure each of these objectives will generate on the assumption that the producer in question would do nothing to achieve these objectives if it did not use such clauses to do so (would use no other surrogate for vertical integration to achieve the objective in question and would not vertically integrate froward into distribution to achieve the relevant objective). The first objective that minimum-price-setting-RPM clauses and VCA clauses can be used to secure is preventing the organizational losses that intra-brand price-competition will generate by enabling buyers to purchase the producer's product for a lower price than they would have been willing to pay for it (even if the intra-brand-price-competition does not reduce the organization's profits by reducing the demand for the producer's product indirectly by reducing relevant buyers' perception of the material quality of the producer's product, by reducing the value of the producer's good to buyers that place a positive value on the good's being priced higher, or by leading individual franchisees to supply a lower price-quality combination that is dispreferred by travelers who find it costly or impossible to determine *ex ante* the quality of the goods and services the individual franchisee is supplying [see below]). If one ignores the allocative transaction costs of drafting, negotiating, and enforcing the relevant clauses, minimum-price-setting-RPM clauses and VCA clauses whose use does not deter their employers from doing anything else to achieve this objective will have an uncertain net impact on economic efficiency—(1) will increase economic efficiency (A) by decreasing the number of bids that are made for the patronage of affected buyers and concomitantly the allocative transaction costs generated by the efforts of distributors to secure those buyers' patronage, (B) by decreasing the amount of intra-brand intra-ARDEPPS UO-to-UO misallocation that is generated (by decreasing the frequency with which sales are made by worse-than-privately-best-placed distributors that are presumptively also worse-than-allocatively-best-placed to make the sales in question), and (C) (by increasing the profits the producer realizes by selling the relevant product) by increasing equilibrium PPR in the ARDEPPS of practice when the "product" involved is a discovered production process and (2) will decrease economic efficiency (A) (by increasing the profits the producer realizes by selling the relevant product) by increasing the equilibrium QV investment in the ARDEPPS of practice in what I take to be the more typical case in which the relevant product was created by a QV investment, (B) by increasing poverty and material inequality in the typical case in which, on the weighted average, the shareholders/creditors/managers/employees of the relevant producer and its product-rivals are materially-better-off and less likely to be poor than the customers of the producer in question and its product-rivals by increasing the relevant sellers' profits and imposing equivalent-dollar losses on their customers, (B) by increasing the misallocation that the managers and employees of the producers in question generate by making economically-inefficient substitutions of lower-taxed or untaxed pleasant working-conditions and fringe-benefits for the goods they would have purchased had they accepted monetary compensation rather than the just-referenced types of "compensation" (if producers whose potential supernormal profit-rates are increased by their use of the clauses in question share those potential profits with their managers and employees), and (C) by generating conventional production-optimum misallocation (if [contrary to my own view] producers whose potential supernormal profit-rates are increased by their uses of the clauses in question squander some of those potential profits by operating sloppily).

The second set of objectives that minimum-price-setting-RPM clauses and VCA clauses can enable their employer to secure by deterring intra-brand price-competition is to prevent the producer from suffering losses because the lower prices that intra-brand price-competition leads its independent distributors to charge for its product reduce the demand for its product because some relevant buyers (1) mistakenly assume that the material quality of the producer's product is positively correlated with its price, (2) place a positive dollar value on increases in the price of the producer's product because they want to be perceived to be wealthy and believe that their purchase of high-priced goods induces this perception, (3) place a positive dollar value on increases in the price of the producer's product because they want to be perceived to possess various non-wealth attributes that are possessed by buyers of high-priced variants of the producer's product but not by buyers of low-priced variants of that product, and (4) because some relevant buyers (say, travelers) (A) prefer a higher price-quality combination of goods and services than some individual franchisees of the producer (franchisor) find it most profitable to supply (given the preferences of local potential patrons), (B) cannot assess *ex ante* the quality of the goods and services an individual franchisee is supplying either at all or without incurring significant costs, and therefore (C) place a positive dollar-value on franchisors' taking steps to assure that all their franchisees are providing goods and services of a predictable, "higher" quality-standard. In my judgment, allocative-transaction-cost considerations aside, minimum-price-setting-RPM clauses and VCA clauses that enable an employer that would otherwise do nothing to achieve these objectives to prevent decreases in the prices of their product that would lead buyers to underestimate its quality will increase economic efficiency on that account by preventing relevant buyers from making mistaken and misallocative product-purchasing decisions (from generating UO-to-UO misallocation), and minimum-price-setting-RPM clauses and VCA clauses that enable their employer to increase its organization's profits by assuring potential buyers that all its franchisees will be providing a stated minimum quality of goods and services increase economic efficiency on that account as well. However, although I recognize that many if not most economists will consider the following conclusions to be not only ungrounded but elitist and incorrect, I think that (allocative-transaction-cost considerations aside) minimum-price-setting-RPM clauses and VCA clauses that enable producers to increase their profits by inducing their distributors to charge higher prices for the producer's product that at least some buyers positively value because they want to be seen to be purchasing high-priced goods because they want observers to conclude that the buyers are wealthy or possess non-wealth attributes possessed by other buyers of high-priced variants of the producer's product will if anything decrease economic efficiency on this account because this kind of personal-image-consciousness disserves the interest of those who have this disposition and producer-decisions that enable buyers to satisfy such preferences disserve the interests not only of the buyers directly involved but also of the relevant society's population more generally by disposing them to be more image-conscious and "other-directed." I am not really "sorry about that" conclusion.

The third function that minimum-price-setting-RPM clauses and VCA clauses can perform is to deter individual distributors of the producer's product from making organizationally-unprofitable expenditures on media advertizing, in-store promotional displays, and in-person (including, door-to-door) salesmanship efforts and organizationally-unprofitable shelf-space allocations that are organizationally unprofitable despite the fact that they would by profitable for the individual distributors that made them because some of the sales they yield those individual distributors are taken from other distributors of the producer's product. In my judgment, the fact that minimum-price-setting-RPM clauses and VCA clauses that function perhaps *inter alia* by deterring such organizationally-unprofitable expenditures/allocations favors the conclusion that the clauses in question are economically efficient. This conclusion is favored by the organizational unprofitability of the deterred expenditures in question as well as by the fact that the allocative cost of the expenditures in question is likely to exceed their private cost.

The fourth function that minimum-price-setting-RPM clauses and VCA clauses can perform for their employer is to induce the producer's individual distributors to make additional organizationally-profitable demand-increasing expenditures and shelf-space allocations by eliminating or at least reducing the probability that those expenditures will increase the sales of one or more other distributors of the producer's product. The allocative efficiency of a producer's using such clauses for this purpose when it would otherwise do nothing to achieve this objective depends on the way in which the expenditures/allocations in question increase the demand for the producer's product. When the expenditures/allocations increase the demand for the producer's product by providing accurate information about the uses of the producer's product, the ease of using the producer's product, the performance of the producer's product, and/or the lifetime cost of purchasing, maintaining, and repairing the producer's product or accurate information about the counterpart facts that relate to products that compete with the producer's product, I would assume that (on this account) the clauses in question would tend to increase economic efficiency (although this conclusion is disfavored by the likely deflation in the private cost of the expenditures in question). However, when the induced demand-increasing expenditures increase the demand for the producer's product by conveying misleading or inaccurate information about the producer's product and/or about products that compete with the producer's product, I would assume that the clauses would on this account tend to be economically inefficient. I have not yet addressed the economic efficiency of minimum-price-setting-RPM clauses and VCA-clauses that function by inducing the producer's independent distributors to make additional demand-increasing expenditures that increase the demand for the producer's product by improving the product's image or denigrating the image of one or more products that compete against the producer's product. As some comments I made earlier imply, because I am skeptical of what I take to be the conventional view that expenditures that are profitable because they improve a products' image are economically efficient, I doubt the economic efficiency of RPM and VCA clauses that function by inducing distributors to make additional product-image-enhancing expenditures. It should therefore be no surprise that I agree with what I take to be the conventional view that expenditures that increase the demand for one product by denigrating the image of a rival product are economically inefficient and that RPM and VCA clauses that function by eliciting additional rival-product-image-denigrating expenditures tend to be economically inefficient on that account. (Indeed, I suspect that those would be the conventional views regardless of whether the denigrating expenditure elicited counteracting expenditures by the producer of the denigrated product.)

The fifth function that minimum-price-setting-RPM clauses and VCA clauses can perform is increasing the producer's independent distributors to provide it with information it would not otherwise possess about possible uses of its product, about the best way to make use of its product, and/or about cost-effective advertizing, promotional displays, and in-person sales-techniques by assuring the distributor that supplies such information that the information will not be used by other distributors of the producer's product to compete against the information-providing distributor will tend to increase economic efficiency on this account (at least if the privately-cost-effective advertizing, promotional displays, and sales-pitches do not convey inaccurate or misleading information).

The preceding analyses of the economic efficiency of minimum-price-setting-RPM clauses and VCA clauses that are surrogates for vertical integration proceed not only on the assumption that such clauses would be profitable for the producers that employed them if they were not illegal but also on the assumption that those producers would do nothing to achieve the objectives the clauses would enable them to secure if, for some reason, they did not use the clauses for these purposes. I will now analyze the economic efficiency of such clauses on the (more realistic) assumption that if producers did not use those clauses to secure the objectives the clauses could most profitably secure they would (1) use one or more other surrogates for vertical integration to achieve these objectives or (2) achieve these objectives by vertically integrating forward into distribution.

Producers can make many moves short of vertically integrating forward into distribution to achieve the objectives that minimum-price-setting-RPM clauses and VCA clauses can enable them to secure. Specifically, a producer that wants to prevent its independent distributors from engaging in intra-brand price-competition that reduces its "organization's" and hence its profits (1) directly by reducing the prices that ultimate consumers pay for the producer's product below the prices they would have been willing to pay for its product, (2) by increasing the total private transaction costs its independent distributors incur to secure the patronage of given buyers because it entails multiple independent distributors' of its product bidding for the patronage of given buyers, and (3) by resulting in sales of the producer's product being made by an independent distributor that is worse-than-privately-best-placed to supply a given buyer than is another independent distributor of its product (say, because the distributor that makes the sale had to incur higher costs to deliver the product to the buyer in question) can also prevent intra-brand price-competition that lowers its profits in these ways without vertically integrating forward into distribution by (1) lowering the lump-sum fee and raising the per-unit price it charges its distributors for its product so as to make it unprofitable for any distributor of the producer's product that is worse-placed to supply the producer's product to a buyer than is another distributor of the producer's product that is that buyer's privately-best-placed supplier to bid for the patronage of or actually supply the buyer in question and (2) combining that pricing-technique shift with other moves that are designed to mitigate some of the losses the pricing-technique shift would otherwise impose on the producer—for example, (A) moves that are designed to prevent the associated increase in the producer's product per-unit price to the distributor from deterring the distributor from making "organizationally"-profitable demand-increasing expenditures by reducing the profits the distributor will realize on any resulting sales below the sum of the profits the distributor and producer will realize on those sales (subsidies equal to the percentage of the cost of any such expenditure the distributor makes that equals the percentage that the producer's profits on any resulting sales constitutes of the sum of the profits that the producer and distributor make on the sales the expenditure yields, contractual clauses obligating the distributor to make all demand-increasing expenditures or shelf-space allocations that are "organizationally"-profitable, communications to distributors that the producer will cease supplying them if they do not make all "organizationally"-profitable demand-increasing expenditures/(shelf-space allocations), and/or decisions by the producer to place additional media-advertizements and in-store demand-increasing promotional displays itself).

A producer that would find it most profitable to use minimum-price-setting-RPM clauses and/or VCA clauses to prevent its independent distributors from charging prices below some specific level (regardless of whether the distributor wants to charge the lower price to engage in intra-brand or inter-brand competition) because the lower price reduces the demand for the producer's product because some buyers believe that the low price justifies a conclusion that the producer's product is materially less good than it actually is, because some buyers want the goods they buy to be priced high because they want observers to infer from their buying those goods that they are wealthy or possess other attributes possessed by other buyers who purchase high-priced variants of the producer's product, or because preventing distributors from charging low prices renders it unprofitable for the distributors to offer low price-quality combinations the relevant distributor would find profitable to supply whose supply would be against the interest of a producer that finds it profitable to assure potential patrons of its franchises that they will be supplied with the higher-quality goods and services they prefer to purchase that for some reason does not use such clauses to obtain these objectives may very will try to secure these goals by using the combination of pricing-techniques and other surrogates for vertical integration delineated and explained in the preceding paragraph.

Finally, a producer that would find it profitable to use minimum-price-setting-RPM clauses and/or VCA clauses to induce its independent distributors to make organizationally-profitable communications to it about uses of its product, the best way to make use of its product, and/or organizationally-profitable demand-increasing expenditures/(shelf-space allocation) because (ideally) such clauses would assure them that other distributors of the producer's good would not use this information in competition with them may if for some reason it does not use such clauses for this purpose try to secure this information by compensating distributors that provide it with such information, by doing relevant research itself, or (least promisingly) by communicating to its distributors its intention to discontinue supplying distributors that it discovers have obtained such information but not passed it on to the producer.

As indicated previously, when a producer that would find it most profitable to use (non-horizontal-price-fixing/non-horizontal-market-dividion)-effectuating minimum-price-setting-RPM clauses and VCA clauses to achieve various objectives by inducing its distributors to make various choices that are in "the organization's" interest would—if for some reason it did not use such clauses to achieve these objectives—try to achieve them by (1) increasing the per-unit prices it charges its independent distributors, (2) subsidizing the demand-increasing expenditures/(shelf-space allocations) its independent distributors make/provide, (3) including in its contracts with distributors clauses that obligate them to make specified (demand-increasing expenditures)/(shelf-space allocations) (where the specification covers not only the magnitudes but also the content/quality of the expenditures/[shelf-space allocations] in question), (4) adopting sales-policies of not renewing the franchises of independent distributors that compete against privately-better-placed distributors of the producer's product or fail to follow the producer's (demand-increasing expenditure)/(shelf-space allocation) "recommendations" (and perhaps cancel their franchises if they do not follow its recommendations), and/or (5) making additional demand-increasing expenditures itself (on local advertizing and warranteed repair-and-maintenance services), the economic efficiency of the minimum-price-setting-RPM clauses and VCA clauses in question equals the economic efficiency of their being substituted for these alternative producer-choices.

Before proceeding to outline the analytic protocol I will use to assess the economic efficiency of substitutions of minimum-price-setting-RPM clauses and VCA clauses for their just-referenced alternatives and the ability of the government of a liberal-moral-rights-based society to increase economic efficiency by responding appropriately to such substitutions, I must explain why the following analysis will focus on the economic efficiency of all members of a set of rivals' making such substitutions in the relevant set of circumstances rather than on the economic efficiency of an individual producer's making such substitutions in the relevant set of circumstances. In brief, the former analysand is appropriate because (1) when one member of a set of rival-producers would find it profitable to employ the referenced alternatives to RPM and VCA clauses to achieve those clauses' objectives if it did not use RPM and VCA clauses in question for these purposes despite the fact that the producer would find it most profitable to use such RPM and VCA clause to achieve the objectives in question, the other members of the relevant set of product-rivals would also find it profitable to employ those alternatives in the circumstances in question, (2) the economic-efficiency effect of all members of a set of product-rivals' using one of the just-referenced alternatives to RPM and VCA clauses (say, raising their per-unit prices to prevent their independent distributors from charging resale prices that are unprofitably low from "their organizations'" respective perspective) is different from the sum of the economic-efficiency effects of each member of the relevant set of product-rivals' making the alternative move in question (say, raising its per-unit price) if it was the only member of the relevant set of product-rivals to do so), and (3) the relevant policy-issue is the economic-efficiency impact of the government of a liberal-moral-rights-based society's responding in various ways to all members of a set of product-rivals' substituting minimum-price-setting-RPM clauses and VCA clauses for these alternatives (since allowing marginal competitors and potential entrants to make such substitutions because doing so will result respectively in their surviving and being effective potential entrants/investors while prohibiting well-established firms from making such substitutions because such prohibitions will help marginal competitors survive and tend to make them and potential entrants effective potential investors by worsening the well-established firm's array of competitive positions and concomitantly improving the latter firms' arrays of actual/prospective competitive positions [1] will be economically inefficient in that it will deflate the incentives of firms to become well-established and preclude them from using RPM and VCA clauses when they are well-established and the use of these clauses would increase their employer's organizational economic efficiency, [2] may be liberal-moral-rights-violative if the owners, creditors, and perhaps even the managers and employees of well-established firms have a liberal moral right for their firm to be allowed to compete on a "level-playing-field," and [3] might disserve the instantiation of the utilitarian and non-utilitarian-egalitarian conceptions of the moral good as well).

I will now analyze the economic efficiency of all members of a set of product-rivals' using minimum-price-setting-RPM clauses and VCA clauses to secure the non-horizontal-(price-fixing)/(market-division)-effectuating objectives such clauses can enable the producers to secure when they would, in essence, be substituting the RPM and VCA clauses in question for the just-referenced alternative choices. The analysis has five components. The first simply states the truism that the economic efficiency of any such substitution equals the profits it yields the producer that makes it *minus* any positive aggregate distortion in those profits or *plus* any negative distortion in those profits. The second component is simply the iteration of the analysis' assumption that the relevant substitutions would yield the respective producers that made them profits if they could make them without incurring any costs related to their (possible) legal prohibition. The third component explains (A) that the aggregate distortion in the profits a producer would realize by substituting minimum-price-setting-RPM clauses and VCA clauses that do not effectuate horizontal price-fixing or horizontal market-divisions for the alternative choices that I am now assuming it would make if it did not use such clauses reflect both any aggregate distortion in "the private benefits" the substitution would yield the producer because (I am assuming) the clauses achieve their objectives to a greater extent than the choices it would otherwise make to achieve them would secure them and any aggregate distortion in the "cost-related" profit-effects of the substitution—in the impact the substitution has on the private transaction costs the producer incurs (directly and/or because it must compensate its distributors for the related transaction costs they incur) and in the impact that the substitution has on the private proficiency of the organization for other reasons (e.g., because the producer will place less-cost-effective local advertizements than the distributor would or must incur higher costs than the distributor would to supply warranteed maintenance-and-repair services of given quality [on account of the fact that the distributor could take better advantage of relevant economies of scale in that it serviced not only the products of the relevant producer but also the products of other producers])—and (B) that (i) any positive distortion in a private benefit or private-cost advantage yielded by the substitution of a minimum-price-setting-RPM or VCA clause for an alternative set of actions other than total vertical integration forward into distribution will be associated with an equal positive distortion in (inflation of) the profits yielded by the substitution in question, (ii) any negative distortion in a private benefit or private-cost advantage yielded by the substitution of a minimum-price-setting-RPM clause or VCA clause for alternative actions other than total vertical integration forward into distribution will be associated with an equal negative distortion in (deflation of) the profits yielded by the substitution in question, (iii) any positive distortion in a private-benefit-related loss or a private-cost disadvantage yielded by the substitution of a minimum-price-setting-RPM clause and/or VCA clause for alternative actions other than total vertical integration forward into distribution will be associated with an equal negative distortion in (deflation of) the profits yielded by the substitution in question (since the statement that there is a positive distortion in a private loss or disadvantage indicates that the private loss [disadvantage] exceeds its allocative counterpart), and (iv) any negative distortion in a private-benefit-related loss or a private-cost disadvantage yielded by the positive distortion in (inflation of) the profits yielded by the substitution will be associated with an equal positive distortion in (inflation of) the profits yielded by the substitution in question (since the statement that there is a negative distortion in a private loss or disadvantage indicates that that private loss [disadvantage] is lower than its allocative counterpart). The fourth comments on (A) whether non-(horizontal-price-fixing)/(horizontal-market-division)-effectuating minimum-price-setting-RPM clauses and VCA clauses tend to secure more or less of the various producer-benefits they are designed to secure than the alternative choices other than total vertical integration forward into distribution for which these clauses would be substituted would secure and (B) whether such RPM and VCA clauses are more or less private-transaction-costly to use than are these alternatives and have other non-transaction-cost-related advantages and/or disadvantages relative to these alternatives that are not related to their securing the objectives they are used to secure. And the fifth combines the "theoretical" conclusions previously delineated and the assumption that the substitutions on which the analyses focuses are profitable for the producers that make them with (to be generous to myself) crude guesstimates of the magnitudes of the parameters whose salience the theory reveals to generate a conclusion about the economic efficiency of non-(horizontal-price-fixing)/(horizontal-market-division)-effectating minimum-price-setting-RPM and VCA clauses that are substituted for the alternative surrogates for vertical integration previously referenced that producers would use to achieve the objectives that the clauses in question can enable them to secure if for some reason they did not use the clauses to achieve these objectives and would not substitute vertical integration for these clauses if they did not use them.

Before proceeding, I want to state and explain two points that will play an important role in my analysis of the economic efficiency of a producer's substituting minimum-price-fixing-RPM clauses and VCA clauses for the other choices short of total vertical integration forward into distribution that it could make to achieve the objectives other than effectuating horizontal price-fixing and horizontal market-divisions it could use the relevant RPM and VCA clauses to secure. The first of these points is that the substitution of these other moves for the relevant RPM and VCA clauses will reduce the extent to which the objectives in question are secured. The second, somewhat-more-troubling point is that the TBLE guesstimates I can make about the extents to which these other choices would be substituted for the RPM and VCA clauses whose economic efficiency is currently at issue are extremely crude.

I will start by explaining why a producer that chooses not to use minimum-price-setting-RPM clauses and VCA clauses to secure the non-(horizontal-price-fiing/horizontal-market-division)-effectuating objectives they can achieve will not use any of the other techniques short of vertical integration it could use to secure those objectives to the extent that perfectly-implemented minimum-price-fixing-RPM clauses and VCA clauses would achieve them and why I suspect that if a producer chose not to use such RPM and VCA clauses despite the profitability of doing so it would not substitute for such clauses a combination of other surrogates for total integration forward into distribution that is as efficacious as the relevant RPM and VCA clauses would be at securing the objectives that the RPM and VCA clauses in question are designed to achieve.

In my judgment, (1) the fact that the unit-price increases that could be substituted for the relevant RPM and VCA clauses would decrease the organization's profits both by causing the distributors to charge resale-prices that are higher than the resale-prices that are in the organization's interest and by deterring the distributors from making organizationally-profitable (demand-increasing expenditures)/(shelf-space allocations) by reducing the profits the distributors realize on any sales yielded by such expenditures/allocations below the profits those sales yield the distributors and the producer combined even when one takes account of the higher resale-prices' tendencies to increase the organization's profits by leading some potential buyers to increase their estimates of the producer's product's material quality and to yield some potential buyers self-perceived dollar gains by enabling them to induce others to infer from their purchasing the good that they are wealthy or have other desirable attributes and (2) the fact that the producer will be able to eliminate only part of the loss that unit-price increases inflict on the organization in the second of the above two ways by subsidizing its distributors' (demand-increasing expenditures)/(shelf-space allocations), by replacing the demand-increasing expenditures its distributors do not make with expenditures of its own, and by communicating and implementing sales-policies of not renewing the distributorships of distributors who make less demand-increasing expenditures and shelf-space allocations than would be in the organization's interest warrant the conclusion that producers that do not use minimum-price-setting-RPM clauses and VCA clauses to achieve the non-(horizontal-price-fixing/horizontal-market-division)-effectuating objectives those clauses can achieve will substitute for them unit-price increases (and related subsidy policies, expenditures of its own, and sales-policies) that are far lower than the prices that would prevent intra-brand price-competition or the charging of prices that are organizationally-unprofitably-low for other reasons. I should add that producers that do not use minimum-price-setting-RPM clauses and VCA clauses to deter their distributors from charging resale-prices that are almost always lower than the resale-prices that would maximize the organization's profits will find it profitable to raise their per-unit prices to some extent. Similar conclusions are warranted about the extent to which a producer will make the other moves it might make to induce its distributors to behave in the way in which the relevant RPM and VCA clauses would cause them to behave. Thus, the extent to which a producer will find it profitable to use (demand-increasing-expenditure)/(shelf-space-allocation) subsidies to reduce the loss the organization sustains because the producer's supra-marginal-cost per-unit-prices makes (distributor-expenditures)/(shelf-space allocations) that are profitable for the organization unprofitable for the distributor is reduced by the possibility that the subsidies may induce the distributor to engage in fraud (to exaggerate their media-advertizing expenditures, shelf-space allocations, and/or warrantee-related maintenance-and-repair-services expenditures, to induce media to raise the prices they are charged for advertizements of the producer's product and lower the price they are charged for advertizements of other products, to perform unnecessary "repair-and-maintenance services" or make some repairs more expensively than was necessary). In the same vein, the extent to which the producer attempts to reduce the loss it sustains because its supra-marginal-cost per-unit pricing deters its distributors from making demand-increasing expenditures that would be in the organization's interest by placing advertizements itself or supplying warrantee-related repair-and-maintenance services itself will be reduced by the producer's being less adept than its distributors at devising and placing local advertizements (where some local advertizing would be more profitable than additional national advertizing) and less able to take advantage of economies of scale in supplying warrantee-related repair-and-maintenance services than are local distributors, which in addition to acting as distributors supply repair and maintain not only for the products of the producer in question but for the products of other producers. Once more, I am not maintaining that a producer that (1) for some reason does not use minimum-price-setting-RPM clauses and VCA clauses for various purposes other than effectuating horizontal price-fixing or a horizontal market-division despite the fact that it would be most profitable for it to use such clauses for these purposes and (2) does not find total vertical integration forward into distribution its second-most-profitable option will not substitute for the RPM and VCA clauses some expenditures on local advertizing and repair-and-maintenance services of its own.

I will now address (1) the distortion in the private benefits that a producer will secure by substituting non-(horizontal-pric-fixing/horizontal-market-division)-effectuating minimum-price-setting-RPM clauses and VCA clauses for the previously-referenced other surrogates for total vertical integration forward into distribution (because that substitution increases the extent to which these clauses' relevant objectives are secured), (2) the distortion in any benefits/costs the substitution confers/imposes on the producer because it increases/decreases the private transaction costs the producer incurs directly and/or indirectly because the producer must compensate its distributors for some of the private transaction costs their transactions with the producer impose on them, (3) the distortion in the private benefits the substitutions yield the producer that makes them that is associated with any impact the substitutions have on the "private" transaction costs the government of the society in question incurs to handle legal disputes between the producer and its distributors, (4) the distortion in the private benefits the substitutions yield the producer that makes them by preventing price-reductions that would cause some buyers to underestimate the material quality of the producer's product, and (5) the distortion in the private benefits the substitution confers on the producer because the additional demand-increasing expenditures the substitution induces its distributors to make are more privately-cost-effective than the expenditures the producer would make to replace the distributor-expenditures that would not be made if it did not employ minimum-price-setting-RPM clauses and VCA clauses, because the additional warranteed repair-and-maintenance services the substitutions induce the producer's distributors to supply are more cost-effective than the services of this kind the producer would supply if it did not make the substitutions in question, and because the substitutions would obviate the producer's adopting sales-policies whose implementation results in its replacing more-cost-effective established producers that do not follow its "recommendations" with less-cost-effective alternative distributors.

The distortion in the private benefits the relevant substitution yields the producer by increasing the extent to which its various non-(horizontal-price-fix/horizontal-market-division)-effecuation objectives are achieved varies with the objective in question. The distortion in the private benefits the clauses yield the producer by increasing the demand curve for its product by making potential purchasers aware of its existence, by providing potential purchasers with accurate information about its uses, the proper way to employ it, the quality of its performance, its durability and/or by providing them with accurate information about these features of its product-rivals products will be affected by all the other factors that determine the distortion in the profits yielded (to simplify) by the allocation of resources from the production of relevant units of the producer's rivals' product to the production of the units of the producer's product to which the above information relates—differences in the producer's relevant products (pre-tax P)/MC ratios and the weighted-average (pre-tax P)/MC ratios for the relevant products of the producer's rivals, differences in the (sales/excise) tax-rate applied to the producer's relevant product and the weighted-average (sales/excise) tax-rate applied to the relevant rival-products, differences in the external-marginal-cost to internal-marginal-cost ratio for the producer's product and its weighted-average ratio counterpart for the producer's product-rivals' relevant products, etc. However, I suspect that it will be TBLE to ignore such differences and assume that the private benefits that any producer's substitution of relevant RPM and VCA clauses for the alternative surrogates for vertical integration for which I am now assuming these clauses would be substituted will be undistorted.

By way of contrast, I believe that it would be TBLE to assume that there is a positive distortion in the private benefits that a producer's substitution of minimum-price-setting-RPM clauses and VCA clauses for these other surrogates for vertical integration yield the producer by increasing the demand curve for its product by causing its distributors to provide additional misleading or inaccurate information about the producer's products and/or about the products of its product-rivals. Indeed, I think that it is TBLE to assume that the relevant benefit-inflation exceeds the private benefits in question since the provision of such misleading and inaccurate information will tend to induce buyers to make economically-inefficient purchase-decisions. My analysis of the distortion in the private benefits that minimum-price-setting-RPM and VCA clauses that are substituted for other surrogates for total vertical integration forward into distribution yield the producers that use such clauses by increasing the amount of misleading and inaccurate information that is conveyed to prospective buyers about the products of the producer and its product-rivals will focus on the extent to which the relevant society has passed and fully implemented consumer-protection and business-tort policies that prohibit the dissemination of any such inaccurate or misleading product-information.

I also think that it is TBLE to assume that there is no distortion in the private benefits that the use of the RPM and VCA clauses on which I am now focusing under the conditions I am now assuming are satisfied generate for any producer that uses them by increasing the demand curve for its product by preventing reductions in the resale-price of its product that would cause some relevant buyers to underestimate the material quality of its product.

The distortion in the private benefits that the substitutions of relevant RPM and VCA clauses for other surrogates for total vertical integration forward into distribution generate for the producer by preventing reductions in the resale-price of the producer's product because some prospective buyers and some existing owners of the producer's product place a positive dollar-value on a higher price's being charged for it in that (1) they want to be seen to be paying or to have paid a high price for the product to induce observers to infer from the buyers' payment of that higher price that the buyers are wealthy and/or (2) they want the relevant product's price to be higher because increases in the product's price alters the attributes of the buyers of the product—more specifically, by changing the identities of the product's purchasers, causes the purchasers of the product to possess non-wealth attributes that some prospective purchasers of the product want observers to attribute to them—depends on whether the dollar-benefits that the buyers and owners of the producer's product believe they obtain when its price is increased are real as well as on whether external costs are generated by anything that encourages some members of a society to be personal-image-conscious and to try to improve their personal images by buying higher-priced goods. If, as I am disposed to believe, individuals who believe that they are obtaining personal-image-related benefits in this way are self-deceived (at best get nothing of value from increases in the prices of the goods they purchased) and individuals' attempts to improve their images by buying expensive goods generate external costs not just by worsening the relative quality of the personal images of others but by making others unhealthfully personal-image-conscious, the benefits that relevant RPM and VCA clauses yield producers on this account will be inflated (by more than the benefits themselves). If, on the other hand, you adopt the assumption (more generally made by economists) that (except in extreme cases such as preferences for addictive drugs) individual preferences should not be questioned, you will conclude that the benefits that relevant substitutions of relevant RPM and VCA clauses yield the producers that make them on this account may not be inflated all tolled—will tend to be inflated to the extent that any related improvement in the personal images of the relevant product's buyers and pre-existing owners are associated with deteriorations in the personal images of others (images are relative) and will tend to be deflated to the extent that the producer cannot internalize the benefits that increases in its product's resale-prices yield existing owners of its product by improving their personal images (a benefit that would be internalized to the producer to the extent that past buyers took account of the price that would be charged for the relevant product in the future when determining its value to them).

If the relevant society's consumer-protection and business-tort laws completely deterred misleading and inaccurate "factual advertizing," individual preferences for improving their image by purchasing high-priced goods when the high price is valued at least in part for its image-creating capacity should be treated like most other preferences, and the improvement of one individual's image did not in itself worsen the personal images of others, it might well be TBLE to assume that there is no distortion in the non-(horizontal-price-fixing/horizontal-market-division)-related benefits that producers secure by substituting minimum-price-fixing RPM clauses and VCA clauses for other surrogates for total vertical integration into distribution. To the extent that such substitutions (1) increase the amount of inaccurate or misleading information that is conveyed to prospective buyers about the products of the producer and/or its rivals and (2) to the extent that (A) such substitutions yield price-increases that consumers value for personal-image-creating reasons, (B) such preferences are misguided, and (C) the indulgence of such preferences yields external costs, the private benefits that such substitutions yield the producers that make them will be inflated (will exceed the associated allocative benefits).

I turn now to the distortion that might exist in the "cost-related" benefit/loss a producer might secure/suffer because the private transaction costs it must incur directly or indirectly (in that it must compensate its distributors for the private transaction costs their relationship with the producer imposes on them) to design, negotiate, and implement the minimum-price-setting-RPM clauses and VCA clauses whose economic efficiency is at issue exceed/(are lower than) the private-transaction-cost-related expenses it will have to incur to use the other surrogates for total vertical integration forward into distribution that I am now assuming the producer would use if for some reason it did not use the RPM and VCA clauses in question despite the profitability of using them. For reasons I have previously explained, I believe that, although every economy contains different Pareto imperfections, the Pareto imperfections that are present in any individual economy deflate private transaction costs and in so doing deflate any decrease-in-private-transaction-cost-generated gain and any increase-in-private-transaction-cost-generated loss the substitution on which I am now focusing would yield. Unfortunately, for a combination of three "reasons," the implications of this conclusion for even the sign of the private-transaction-cost-related component of the aggregate distortion in the profits yielded by this substitution are unclear: (1) the sign of the impact-on-private-transaction-cost-related aggregate-distortion component depends on whether the relevant substitution increases or decreases private transaction costs; (2) whether the relevant substitution increases or decreases private transaction costs depends in part on the set of other surrogates for vertical integration the producer would substitute for the relevant RPM and VCA clauses; and (3) I cannot be anything like precise about the various other surrogates for vertical integration that producers in general or any particular producer would substitute for RPM and VCA clauses in the circumstances in question and doubt that it would be TBLE for antitrust-policy implementers to investigate such issues. Thus, I do not know the extents to which relevant producers would substitute for their relevant RPM and VCA clauses (1) unit-price increases, (2) subsidies for media advertizing, in-store promotional displays, shelf-space allocations, and warranteed repair-and-maintenance services, (3) rewards for the supply of valuable information about product-uses, the best way to employ the producer's product, and cost-effective media advertizing, in-store displays, shelf-space allocations and/or sales-pitches, (4) decisions to place local advertizements or supply repair-and-maintenance services itself, and (5) sales-policies of not renewing the franchises of independent distributors that have not followed the producers "recommendations." Although I acknowledge the contestability of the following judgment and admit that the following list of private transaction costs is almost certainly incomplete, my own view is that (1) the sum of (A) the private transaction costs a producer will have to incur to devise, negotiate, and enforce a series of minimum-price-setting-RPM clauses and VCA clauses and (B) the private transaction costs its distributors will have to incur to place the media advertizements, arrange the in-store promotional displays, make and implements the shelf-space-allocation decisions, and provide the repair-and-maintenance services they would place/arrange/make/provide under the (RPM/VCA)-clause regime *will be lower than* (2) the sum of the private transaction costs (A) a producer will have to incur (i) to decide on the per-unit-price increase (if any) it makes, (ii) to determine how much to subsidize its distributors' media advertizing, in-store-promotional display, shelf-space-allocation, repair-and-maintenance-service expenditures, (iii) to determine whether its distributors' expense-claims are accurate or justified, (iv) to pay the relevant subsidies, (v) to handle claim-disputes with its distributors, (vi) to place local advertizements itself and/or supply repair-and-maintenance services itself, (vii) to communicate relevant sales-policies to its distributors, and (viii) to determine whether its distributors have followed its "recommendations" and to identify and negotiate distributorship-agreements with the new distributors it would choose to replace the disenfranchised distributors and (B) its distributors will have to incur (i) to place the probably-smaller amount of media-advertizements they will place if the producer does not use RPM and VCA clauses, (ii) to make the probably-smaller amount of in-store promotional-display expenditures they will make if the producer does not use RPM and VCA clauses, (iii) to make and implement the different shelf-space-allocation decisions they will make if the producer does not use RPM and VCA clauses, (iv) to supply the probably-smaller amount of repair-and-maintenance services it will supply if the producer does not use RPM and VCA clauses, and (v) to process the sales-policy communications the producer makes to them when it foregoes RPM and VCA clauses. (I am assuming that the producer will not have to compensate its distributors for the private transaction costs they incur to defraud it in various ways if the producer substitutes subsidies for RPM and VCA clauses.) If this conclusion is accurate, the associated component of the profits yielded by the substitution of relevant RPM and VCA clauses for other surrogates for total vertical integration will be deflated—that is, will be lower than the associated economic-efficiency gain.

I turn next to the distortion in the profits producers realize by substituting minimum-price-setting-RPM clauses and VCA clauses for other surrogates for total vertical integration forward into distribution that is generated by the substitution's affecting the private (and allocative) transaction costs the relevant society's government incurs/(itself generates) to process any related legal disputes between the producer and its distributors. Two initial points should be made. First, all such governmental "private" transaction costs are lower than their allocative counterparts not only because (1) in my judgment, the relevant economies' Pareto imperfections will deflate the private cost to the government of the resources its processing of these disputes "consumes" but also because (2) in my judgment, any government's financing of any such "private" transaction costs it incurs will also be allocative-costly (will involve its generating allocative transaction costs, levying misallocative additional taxes, charging misallocative higher prices for government-supplied goods and services, and/or canceling other expenditures that are collectively economically inefficient—a last claim whose contestability I acknowledge). Second, the first point implies that any tendency of the substitution of RPM and VCA clauses for other surrogates for total vertical integration forward into distribution to increase/decrease the amount of "private" transaction costs the government incurs by affecting the number and character of the legal disputes between the producer and its distributors will be associated with an inflation/deflation in the profits yielded by the substitution (because the producer's court-costs do not equal even the "private" transaction costs in question much less the sum of their allocative counterparts and the allocative costs of the government's financing them). The sign of this distortion in the profits the substitution on which I am now focusing will yield the producer that effectuates it therefore depends on whether the non-party-reimbursed court-costs the government will incur to process the suits the producer would bring against its distributors for allegedly violating the contractual obligations the producer's minimum-price-setting-RPM clauses and VA clauses would impose on them *exceed* their counterparts for the suits the producer would bring against its distributors for allegedly making fraudulent claims for partial reimbursement of expenses they stated they incurred (properly) to advertize the producer's product in local media or to provide maintenance-and-repair services to buyers of the producer's durable product. I cannot provide any useful speculations about the answer to this question and doubt that it would be TBLE for an antitrust-policy-implementation authority to investigate it. I will therefore assume that no distortion in the profits that would be yielded by a firm's substituting minimum-price-setting-RPM clauses and VCA clauses for other surrogates for total vertical integration forward into distribution will be associated with its possible effect on the unreimbursed "private" transaction costs the government incurs to handle disputes between the producer and its distributors.

The final component of the aggregate distortion in the profits that producers would obtain by making the substitution on which I am now focusing relates to the possibility that the substitution would confer gains on the producer by entailing (1) its substituting more effective local-media advertizing by its distributors for its own less-effective local-media advertizing, (2) its substituting the more-cost-effective repair-and-maintenance services its distributors would provide for the less-cost-effective repair-and-maintenance services it would provide, and (3) its obviating its replacing a distributor that was more-cost-effective (but did not follow the producer's "recommendations") with a distributor that was less-cost-effective (assuming the two distributors followed the producer's "recommendations" to the same extent). If I assume that the distributors' local-media advertizing was more-cost-effective than the producers would have been because the producer had a worse understanding than the local distributor of the accurate product-information that would be valuable to locals and/or of the local media that were best-placed to reach potential buyers of the producer's product, I would conclude that any related private gain the producer obtains by substituting relevant RPM and VCA clauses for other surrogates for relevant vertical integration would be undistorted. If I assume that the producer would be a less-cost-effective supplier of warranteed repair-and-maintenance services than its distributors would be (because the producer was less able to take advantage of relevant economies of scale), the profits the relevant RPM and VCA clauses would yield it on this account would be deflated (because costs and cost-savings are deflated). To the extent that the replacement-distributor with which the producer would contract if it discontinued its relationship with an established distributor that did not follow its recommendations would be less-cost-effective than the established distributor would have been because the replacement-distributor would incur higher costs than the established distributor would (in part because it was inherently less cost-effective and in part because it would have to learn things the established distributor had already learned), the gains the RPM and VCA clauses would enable the producer to secure by obviating its terminating its relationships with "non-obedient" distributors will be deflated. (If the gains the clauses enable the producer to secure by substituting distributor-advertizing and distributor-[repair-and-maintenance services] for its own efforts and by obviating its discontinuing its relationships with "disobedient" distributors are attributable to the fact that the new distributor would perform distributive functions less well than the established distributor did/would, I do not think there would be any general tendency for the associated producer-gains to be distorted).

A summary is in order. Here are the conclusions I have so far established or at least argued for:

(1) the economic efficiency of a producer's substitutions of non-(horizontal-price-fixing/horizontal-market-division)-effectuating minimum-price-setting-RPM clauses and VCA clauses for other surrogates for total vertical integration forward into distribution (henceforth of "the substitution[s]") equals the profits the substitutions of interest yield the producer in question *minus* any positive distortion in those profits or *plus* any negative distortion in those profits;

(2) the current analysis assumes that the substitutions of interest are profitable for the producer that makes them;

(3) it is TBLE to assume that there is no distortion in the private benefits that the substitutions of interest yield the producer by increasing the amount of accurate information the producer and its distributors provide prospective buyers about the uses, best way to employ, ease-of-use, performance-quality, durability, and lifetime cost of the producer's product and/or of products produced by the producer's product-rivals;

(4) to the extent that the substitutions yield the producer that makes them private benefits by increasing the amount of misleading or inaccurate information the producer and its distributors provide buyers about the possible uses of, best way to use, ease-of-use of, performance-quality, durability, and lifetime cost of the producer's product or the products of one or more of the producer's

product-rivals, those private benefits will be inflated (by the sum of the private benefits the provision of such information yields the producer and the economic inefficiency the provision of such information generates);

(5) given the conclusion articulated in Item (4) in this list, it will probably be TBLE for an antitrust-policy-enforcement authority to consider the extent to which any additional advertizements the substitution results in the producer's and its distributors' placing communicate such inaccurate or misleading information (*inter alia*, on the extent to which the relevant society's consumer-protection and business-tort laws deter the communication of such inaccurate or misleading information);

(6) if (A) one accepts as "real" the private benefits that buyers believe they secure when the image of a product they purchase or own is improved and the private benefits that buyers or owners of a product believe they obtain when the price of a product they buy or own increases because the increase in the product's price enables its buyers and owners to lead others to conclude that the buyers and owners are wealthy or possess other positively-valued non-wealth attributes that are possessed by the different and smaller set of individuals that would pay the higher price for the good but are possessed to a lesser extent by the different and larger set of individuals who would buy the product if it were priced lower, (B) one rejects the claim that product-image promotion and individuals' efforts to promote their images by purchasing high-priced goods that others will know they have purchased will encourage an other-directedness that is psychologically damaging to those who have it, and (C) one also rejects the claim that product-image promotion and such individual self-promotion would generate external costs even if it did not promote other-directedness that was harmful to the individuals who had such a disposition in that product-status and personal status are "competitive 'goods'" (because increases in the status of one product or of one individual are inevitably associated with decreases in the status of other goods or individuals with which/whom the first good or individual is "competitive"—that is, because status is relative), it would be TBLE to assume that the private benefits that the substitutions of interest yield the producers that made them on these image-related accounts are undistorted;

(7) if buyers/owners of products overvalue product-images and the personal images created by purchasing high-priced goods and/or if efforts to promote product-images and personal images in the way detailed in Item (6) harm the persuaders, those persuaded, and the society's members more generally, the private benefits that the substitutions of interest yield a producer that makes them by increasing the amount of product-image-enhancing expenditures that are made on its product and by catering to the desires of its customers to have its product priced high will be inflated;

(8) it will be TBLE to assume that the private benefits that the substitutions of interest yield the producer that makes them by preventing price-reductions that would lead some buyers to underestimate the material quality of the producer's product are undistorted;

(9) the substitutions of interest will tend to reduce the private transaction costs that the producer and its distributors incur as a result of their respective relationships;

(10) the benefits the substitutions of interest confer on the producer by virtue of its reducing the private transaction costs referenced in Item (9) in this list will be deflated;

(11) although any "private" benefits/costs the substitutions of interest confer/impose on the government by decreasing/increasing the uncompensated "private" transaction costs it incurs to deal with disputes arising out of the relationship between any relevant producer and its distributors would be deflated, if I am correct in believing that existing data justifies no conclusion about the impact of substitutions of interest on such uncompensated government transaction costs and that it would not be TBLE for antitrust-policy implementors to investigate this impact of such substitutions, it will be TBLE to assume that the aggregate distortion in the profits yielded by the substitutions of interest is not affected by any distortion related to the impact of the substitution of interest on uncompensated government transaction costs;

(12) to the extent that the substitutions of interest reduce the private cost to the organization of placing given media advertizements or supplying given warranteed repair-and-maintenance services by arranging matters so that the relevant tasks are preformed by distributors rather than by the producer, the profits the substitutions yield the producer on this account will be deflated;

(13) to the extent that the substitutions of interest reduce the private costs the repair-and-maintenance-service providers incur to provide given amounts of such services (perhaps under warrantees), the profits the substitutions yield the producer will be deflated;

(14) to the extent that the substitutions of interest result in the producer's warranteeing its product when it would otherwise not do so, the associated producer-profit will not be distorted on that account;

(15) to the extent that the substitutions in question cause more efficacious advertizements to be placed by distributors rather than less-efficacious advertizements to be placed by the producer, the distortion in the profits, the substitution yields the producer on this account will depend on the reason why the distributor ads are more efficacious—if the distributor's ads convey accurate information that is more valuable to local buyers than the information that the producer's ads would be or if the distributor's ads reach more local buyers than would the ads that the producer would select, it will probably be TBLE to assume that the associated profit-gain to the producer is undistorted, but if the distributors' ads are more efficacious because they convey inaccurate or misleading information more persuasively or to a larger audience, it will probably be TBLE to assume that the associated profit-gain to the producer is inflated; and

(16) the distortion in the profits the substitutions of interest yield the producer by increasing the efficacy of the organization's local ads therefore depends in part on how effective the relevant society's consumer-protection law and business-tort law are in deterring inaccurate and misleading advertizing.

I wish (1) that the conclusions expressed in the preceding 16 points were all established through a priori argument, (2) that any conclusion I express about the aggregate distortion in the profits yielded by or the economic efficiency of the substitutions of interest could be generated by a priori argument, or (3) that I could provide reliable, persuasive empirical evidence to back up my conclusions about the aggregate distortion in the profits yielded by and the economic efficiency of the substitutions of interest. Unfortunately, I must admit that none of these wishes is fulfilled. Nevertheless, it may be of interest for you to know that the conclusions I have just articulated lead me to believe (1) that the substitutions of current interest will clearly be economically efficient when they do not increase the amount of inaccurate or misleading information that the producer and its distributors convey to relevant buyers, do not yield the producer benefits by improving its product's image, by increasing the amount or efficaciousness of the product-image-enhancing ads the producer's organization places, and do not benefit the producer by enabling some buyers who believe that their personal image will be improved if they are seen to be purchasing goods whose prices are high to secure this "benefit" by purchasing the producer's product because the substitutions prevent reductions in its price, (2) that the empirical importance of the (inaccurate/misleading)-information possibility just referenced is substantially reduced by the consumer-protection law and business-tort law of most societies that have antitrust laws, (3) that it may sometimes by TBLE for an antitrust-policy-implementation authority to take account of the (inaccurate/misleading)-information possibility when analyzing the economic efficiency of a particular substitution of interest, and (4) that it will probably not be the TBLE to investigate the accuracy of my suspicions about the effects of product-image advertizing and individuals' efforts to impress others by being seen to purchase goods whose prices are high.

I turn now to the economic efficiency of a producer's substituting minimum-price-setting-RPM clauses and VCA clauses (that do not effectuate horizontal price-fixing or market-divisions) for total vertical integration forward into distribution (of a producer's using such clauses when it would otherwise totally vertically integrate forward into distribution). Once more, the economic efficiency of what I will denominate this substitution for vertical integration (VI) equals the profits it will yield the producer that makes it *plus* any deflation in those profits or *minus* any inflation in those profits—that is, *plus* any inflation or *minus* any inflation of the benefits this substitution for VI yields the producer that effectuates it and *plus* any inflation or *minus* any deflation of the private cost the substitution for VI imposes on it. I will analyze these distortions on 4 assumptions, each of which requires some discussion and justification.

First, I will assume that substitutions of the RPM and VCA clauses on which I am now focusing for VI will not affect equilibrium investment in either the relevant production-ARDEPPS or the relevant distribution-ARDEPPS. I make this assumption because (1) I believe that across all cases a rule allowing producers to substitute relevant RPM and VCA clauses for VI will not tend to change equilibrium investment in these ARDEPPSes by altering the height of any highest-supernormal-profit curve at the pre-choice equilibrium investment-quantity in the relevant ARDEPPSes or the magnitudes of any relevant barrier to expansion, barrier to entry, and/or investment-incentive/disincentive at or beyond the pre-choice equilibrium-investment quantities in question, (2) VI that is executed through merger or acquisition will not directly affect investment in the ARDEPPSes of consummation, and (3) although VI through internal growth will increase investment in the distribution ARDEPPS in the short run, it will not affect equilibrium investment in that ARDEPPS or produce even a medium-run effect on investment in that ARDEPPS if the ARDEPPS' equilibrium-investment quantity increases through time.

Second, I will assume that substitutions of the RPM and VCA clauses on which I am now focusing for VI into distribution will increase not only the skill with which various distributive functions are performed but the economic efficiency of their performance. These assumptions reflect my belief that individuals who want to be independent distributors tend to have preferences for being their own bosses that make it economically efficient to substitute them for integrated-firm employees.

Third, I will assume that substitutions of relevant RPM and VCA clauses for relevant VI will reduce the extent to which the relevant objectives of the RPM and VCA clauses in question are secured. I base this conclusion on an assumption that vertically-integrated firms are more able to control their own distributive employees' relevant decisions through hierarchical techniques (e.g., by making appropriate basic-salary, bonus, and promotion decisions) than non-vertically-integrated firms are able to control their independent distributors by enforcing relevant RPM and VCA clauses.

Fourth, I will assume that substitutions of relevant RPM and VCA clauses for VI forward into distribution will substantially reduce the "transaction costs" broadly understood (see below) that the producer incurs to influence the distributive decisions that its "organization" makes. The "private transaction cost" the producer will have to incur to use the relevant RPM and VCA clauses are the private transaction costs of devising, negotiating, and enforcing those clauses. What I am calling the "private transaction cost" of the relevant VI encompass (1) the conventional private transaction or other related costs of (A) consummating the relevant merger or acquisition and controlling the resulting company's distributive employees—the private cost of (i) identifying an appropriate merger or acquisition participant, (ii) negotiating the relevant deal, (iii) financing an acquisition either externally or from retained earnings (by foregoing other expenditures), (iv) integrating the distributive enterprise into the producer's organization, and (v) the transaction cost of devising and implementing the hierarchical controls the integrated firm will use to induce its distributive employees to make decisions in the organization's interest or (B) planning, executing, and taking advantage of the relevant internal growth—the private cost of (i) thinking through the internal growth, (ii) financing the internal growth either externally or from retained earnings (by foregoing other expenditures) (iii) any short-term or medium-term losses the producer must incur because its internal growth into distribution raises investment in the distribution ARDEPPS in the short run or medium run, and (iv) the transaction cost of devising and implementing the hierarchical controls the integrated firm will use to induce its distributive employees to make decisions in the organization's interest.

I will now analyze on the above assumptions the distortion in the profits that a producer will realize by substituting relevant RPM and VCA clauses for VI into distribution. I will make 7 points or clusters of related points and then state my conclusion.

First, I see no reason to believe that any benefits a producer obtains directly because its substitution of RPM and VCA clauses for VI allows it to satisfy the preferences of those individuals who would act as its independent distributors to be their own bosses would be distorted.

Second, I think it would be TBLE to assume that there is no distortion in the private loss a producer sustains because its substitution of relevant RPM and VCA clauses for VI decreases the extent to which prospective buyers are aware of its product, decreases the amount of accurate information prospective buyers have about its product and its competitors' products, increases the amount of money it loses directly because intra-brand competition allows actual buyers to purchase its product for lower prices than they would be willing to pay for it, and increases the amount of money it loses because intra-brand price-competition causes prospective buyers to underestimate the material quality of its product.

Third, I think it would be TBLE to assume that there is a positive distortion in the private losses a producer sustains because its substitution of the RPM and VCA clauses on which I am now focusing for VI decreases the amount of inaccurate or misleading information its "organization" conveys to prospective buyers, decreases the amount of product-image-enhancing expenditures its organization makes on the producer's products, and/or decreases the extent to which its prospective customers attempt to impress others by paying higher prices for its product.

Fourth, the private conventional-transaction-cost savings a producer will secure by substituting RPM and VCA clauses for VI will be deflated.

Fifth, any short-run or medium-run benefit a producer obtains because its substitution of RPM and VCA clauses for internal growth into distribution decreases investment in the distribution-ARDEPPS in question in the short run or medium run will be deflated.

Sixth, any benefits a producer's substitution of RPM and VCA clauses for VI forward into distribution yields it by enabling it to make other QV investments will tend to be inflated when its investment raises the equilibrium quantity of QV investment in the ARDEPPS in which it is made.

Seventh, any benefits a producer's substitution of RPM and VCA clauses for VI forward into distribution yields it by enabling it to execute additional PPR projects will tend to be deflated when its PPR investment increases equilibrium PPR in the ARDEPPS in question.

Finally, my contestable conclusion. Primarily because I think that the most-empirically-important point in the preceding list is the fourth—that the substitution of minimum-price-setting-RPM and VCA clauses for VI forward into distribution will substantially reduce conventional private transaction costs and that the reduction in such private transaction costs will be far lower than the reduction in allocative transaction costs with which it will be associated, I believe that the profits that would be yielded by a producer's decision to substitute relevant RPM and VCA clauses for VI into distribution will be substantially deflated and therefore that profitable decisions by producers to make such substitutions will be economically efficient.

The preceding analysis and the analysis that I will execute next ignores the possibility that the substitution of the RPM and VCA clauses of current interest for VI forward into distribution might increase horizontal price-fixing and horizontal market-divisions, both of which are economically inefficient—that is, ignores the fact that the private benefits that any such substitution yields the producer that makes it will be inflated on this account. I have ignored this possibility both because I think that minimum-price-setting-RPM clauses and VCA clauses rarely perform these functions and because, when they do, they will not be functioning as surrogates for vertical integration in so doing. However, I should acknowledge that my conclusion that substitutions of minimum-price-setting-RPM clauses and VCA clauses for VI forward into distribution are economically efficient would be disfavored if such clauses were more likely to effectuate competition-reducing horizontal price-fixing and horizontal market-divisions than the VI alternative was to increase the amount of predation in which the producer/(integrated firm) engaged.

I have now argued that it is TBLE to assume that economic efficiency will be increased (1) by profitable decisions by producers to use non-(horizontal-price-fixing/horizontal-market-division)-effectuating minimum-price-setting-RPM clauses and VCA clauses to achieve their objectives as opposed to (1) doing nothing to achieve those objectives and (2) attempting to achieve those objectives less profitably by (A) using other surrogates for VI or (B) vertically integrating forward into distribution. If these conclusions are correct, it will be TBLE to assume that the use of such clauses will increase economic efficiency, regardless of the behavior in which the producer that employs them would engage if it did not use them.

13.3.3 The Liberal-Moral-Rights-Violativeness of Minimum-Price-Setting-RPM Clauses and VCA Clauses and the Ability of the Antitrust-Policy-Implementation Authorities of a Liberal-Moral-Rights-Based Society to Secure Liberal Moral Rights by Responding Appropriately to the Use of Such Clauses

In my judgment, a producer's use of minimum-price-setting-RPM clauses and VCA clauses will violate the liberal moral rights of both its competitors and affected potential customers when the producer intends the clauses to induce its distributors to provide inaccurate or misleading information about the producer's product or the products of its product-rivals, regardless of whether the producer's *ex ante* perception that its use of such clauses would be at least normally profitable was critically affected by its belief that the clauses would or might have such an effect. In my judgment, a firm's use/(acceptance and enforcement of) a minimum-price-setting-RPM clause or VCA clause to (enable it and its product-rivals)/(its distributors and their competitors) to effectuate a horizontal price-fix or a horizontal market-division violates the liberal moral rights of the buyers that are directly negatively affected and of any possibly-non-cooperating sellers, who have a right not to be asked to participate in liberal-moral-rights-violative conduct, not to be threatened with retaliation, and not to be subjected to retaliation. Before proceeding, I should explain how minimum-price-setting-RPM clauses and VCA clauses could effectuate horizontal price-fixes or horizontal market-divisions and why I think that few if any such clauses perform these functions. The claim that some minimum-price-setting-RPM clauses effectuate a horizontal price-fix is actually, more specifically,a claim that distributors will sometimes induce their producer/suppliers to help the distributors effectuate a distributor horizontal price-fix by agreeing to bind their respective independent distributors not to charge prices below the prices the distributors have fixed--that is, to enforce the distributor price-fix by suing or discontinuing the supply of distributors that violate the distributors' horizontal price-fix. I think that few if any minimum-price-setting RPM clauses effectuate distributor horizontal price-fixes (1) because I believe that distributors will rarely if ever be better-placed to execute a horizontal price-fix than their producer/suppliers are and (2) because I doubt that even when the distributors are better-placed than their suppliers to execute a horizontal price-fix they will find it possible or profitable to induce their producer/suppliers to help them enforce the distributor horizontal price-fix. The claim that some VCA clauses effectuate a producer horizontal "market"-division is a claim that producers that are seeking to prevent themselves from competing against each other will sometimes find it profitable to secure this outcome by preventing their respective sets of distributors from competing against each other not just by limiting the set of buyers for whose patronage each individual distributor may compete but by assigning to each producer's distributors non-overlapping sets of buyers for whose patronage each producer's distributors may compete. If, for example, there are (1) 10 producers X1...10, (2) 100 distributors Y1...100 where X1's distributors are Y1...10, X2's distributors are Y11...20, etc., and (3) 10,000 buyers Z1...10,000, the VCA clauses would effectuate a horizontal market-division if X1 limited its distributors Y1...10 to competing for buyers 1-1000, X2 limited its distributors Y11...20 to competing for buyers 1001-2000, and so on and so forth. I doubt that any significant number of VCA clauses are included to effectuate horizontal market-divisions. However, I do acknowledge that a set of rival producers could conceivably include minimum-price-setting-RPM clauses in their contracts with their independent distributors to increase the efficacy of the producers' horizontal price-fix by reducing the incentives any producer has to reduce the price it charges its distributors by (in theory) precluding the distributors from making additional sales of the producer's product by passing on the producer's price-cut to final consumers. Because the efficacy of this arrangement depends on the price-fix cheater's enforcing its minimum-price-setting-RPM clause, I doubt that any significant number of minimum-price-setting-RPM clauses perform this function. With the two exceptions just referenced (the second of which [for reasons I have just explained] I do not think is empirically important), the use of minimum-price-setting-RPM clauses and VCA clauses is not liberal-moral-rights-violative. Indeed, I am tempted though hesitant to conclude that, unless the State can provide an adequate reason for preventing firms from doing so (see below), the shareholders and at-risk creditors (and possibly, derivatively, the managers and employees) of firms have a property-right-based liberal moral right to use such clauses to increase the extent to which buyers are aware of their firm's products, to increase the amount of accurate information their firm's organization conveys to prospective buyers about the firm's respective products and the products of the firm's rivals, to prevent intra-brand competition from costing them money directly by lowering the prices their firm's customers pay for its products, to prevent intra-brand price-competition that costs them money indirectly by yielding price-reductions that would lead some buyers to underestimate the material quality of their firm's products, and/or to avoid the various costs of vertically integrating forward. I am far from convinced that the government of a liberal-moral-rights-based society could offer adequate justification for restricting firms' uses of such clauses: (1) few if any such clauses effectuate horizontal price-fixing or horizontal market-divisions, and there may be less-restrictive means of deterring or dealing with this possibility, and (2) there clearly are less-restrictive means of dealing with the possibility that such clauses will increase the amount of inaccurate or misleading product-information their employers' organizations' convey. The best case for the moral appropriateness of a liberal-moral-rights-based society's government's restricting the use of such clauses is the argument that (1) such restrictions will reduce the amount of product-image-enhancing expenditures that are made and the extent to which individuals try to enhance their personal images by being seen to be purchasing high-priced goods and (2) such expenditures and behaviors disserve the interest of the society's members. However, were it not for the fact that product-promotion and self-promotion of this kind yields external costs, the use of the preceding argument might be illiberal (since it would otherwise have to be based on an assumption that individuals do not have a moral right to decide what is in their own interest). In any event, unless one believes that a liberal State has a moral obligation to protect the moral-rights bearers for whom they are responsible from product-image-enhancing advertizing and to prevent them from promoting their personal images by making publicly-observed purchases of expensive products, liberalism (1) would imply that the government of a liberal-moral-rights-based society has no duty to prevent producers from using minimum-price-setting-RPM clauses and VCA clauses that they did not believe *ex ante* would increase the amount of inaccurate or misleading information conveyed to prospective buyers or effectuate horizontal price-fixing or horizontal market-divisions and (2) might imply that such a government has a moral duty to allow producers to use such clauses when they would not do so to increase the amount of inaccurate or misleading information conveyed to potential buyers or to enable themselves or their immediate customers to practice horizontal price-fixing or effectuate a horizontal market-division.

13.3.4 The Impact of Minimum-Price-Setting-RPM Clauses and VCA Clauses on the Instantiation of the Utilitarian and Various Non-Utilitarian-Egalitarian Conceptions of the Moral Good and the Ability of a Government of a Liberal-Moral-Rights-Based Society to Secure the Moral Good by Responding Appropriately to Such Clauses

I will proceed on the assumption that the relevant society's consumer-protection and business-tort laws prevent the use of these clauses from increasing the amount of inaccurate and/or misleading product-information conveyed to consumers and that these clauses (or the subset of these clauses on which I am now focusing) do not effectuate horizontal price-fixing or horizontal market-divisions. Section 13.3.2 argued that on these assumptions the use of these clauses will increase economic efficiency. Even if I make the usually-correct assumption that, taken as groups, the shareholders/creditors/managers/employees of the relevant producers are better-off than the producers' customers, I suspect that, on the above two assumptions, the use of such clauses will decrease material inequality. This suspicion reflects (1) my assumption that these clauses will normally be substituted for various other surrogates for VI rather than for VI forward into distribution, (2) my belief that in the vast majority of situations the substitution of these clauses for the other surrogates for VI that would be employed in their stead will increase the demand-increasing expenditures the relevant organizations make to call attention to the producer's product, to provide accurate product-related information about the products of the producers and its product-rivals, and to supply warranteed repair-and-maintenance services, (3) my view that relevant buyers will gain more from the increases in the types of demand-increasing expenditures just listed than they will lose because the substitution of relevance reduces intra-brand price-competition, and

(4) my belief that a rule allowing all members of a set of rival producers to use such clauses will not increase the producers' profits because the competitive advantages each individual member of the set of product-rivals obtains by using the clauses cancel each other out. If these somewhat-informed guesstimates are accurate, the use of minimum-price-setting-RPM clauses and VCA clauses will instantiate both the utilitarian conception of the moral good (by increasing economic efficiency and decreasing material inequality) and all non-utilitarian-egalitarian conceptions of the moral good (by reducing material inequality) if the use of these clauses does not increase the amount of inaccurate or misleading information conveyed to consumers or effectuate horizontal price-fixing/market-divisions. Indeed, in my judgment, it will almost always be morally good from any of these egalitarian normative perspectives for antitrust-policy-implementation authorities to permit producers to use minimum-price-setting-RPM clauses and VCA clauses (at least if the relevant society's consumer-protection and business-tort laws can be relied on to prevent producers from conveying inaccurate or misleading product-information).

13.4 Maximum-Price-Setting-RPM Clauses

13.4.1 The Functions That Maximum-Price-Setting-RPM Clauses Can Perform

Even if I ignore the possibility that clauses that a producer includes in its contracts with its independent distributors that purport to be setting the maximum resale-price the distributors can charge for its product are actually establishing the minimum resale-price its distributors can charge as part of a scheme in which the producer and its rivals or the producer's distributors are engaging in horizontal price-fixing, maximum-price-setting-RPM clauses can perform one to 6 functions for any producer that includes them in its distributorship agreements:

(1) preventing one or more individual distributors from charging prices that are higher than the price that is most profitable from their own respective individual parochial perspectives for them to charge as well as being higher for straightforward reasons than the price that maximizes the organization's profits (I did not include in the list of functions that maximum-price-setting-RPM clauses can perform "preventing individual independent distributors from charging prices that are lower than the prices that would be in the individual distributor in question's interest to charge as well as being lower than the prices that would be in the organization's interest for it to charge" because, given the high probability that the producer will be charging its individual distributors per-unit prices that exceed the producer's marginal units, such distributor pricing-mistakes will rarely be against organizational interest);
(2) preventing a producer's or wholesaler's supra-TSM-marginal-cost per-unit pricing from inducing its retailers to charge per-unit prices that exceed the

per-unit price that maximizes the organization's interest directly by reducing the retailer's sales by making sales that would be directly profitable for the organization unprofitable for the retailer by raising the retailer's marginal costs above the organization's;

(3) preventing distributors from charging higher prices that the individual distributor finds profitable to charge but are against the organization's interest because the individual distributor does not consider the losses its higher price imposes on other distributors of the producer's product and on the producer by preventing deterred buyers from making repeat-purchases from other distributors of the producer's product, by preventing deterred buyers from making purchases of complements of the higher-priced goods from other distributors that would have yielded profits on those sales, by preventing deterred buyers who would have been impressed by the high quality of the product in question from purchasing unrelated products produced by the relevant producer, by deterring a sale to a buyer who would have recommended the producer's product to one or more other buyers who would on that account have purchased it and perhaps one or more of its complements from another distributor, or by preventing a sale to a buyer whose use of the producer's product would have caused one or more other potential buyers who would have observed its good performance for the deterred buyer in question to purchase it and perhaps one or more of its complements from another distributor;

(4) less importantly, preventing distributors from charging higher prices that are against the organization's interest because those prices reduce the dollar-value of the producer's product to potential customers who do not want to be perceived to be purchasing high-priced goods or to have non-wealth characteristics possessed by buyers that would purchase the good at the high price;

(5) preventing distributors from charging higher prices that are against the organization's interest because it is in the organization's interest to guarantee the maximum price that would be charged for its product in that such a guarantee will induce some buyers to consider purchasing its product when they would not otherwise have done so and will induce some buyers (say, travelers) who know that they would purchase its product at the allowed maximum price to buy it when they would otherwise have been deterred from doing so by the cost they would have to incur to ascertain the prices that particular distributors are charging for it; and

(6) preventing distributors from charging higher prices that are against the organization's interest because, by reducing the organization's unit sales of the product in question, it prevents the producer or another distributor from making profitable sales of a related product—for example, the higher price charged for a newspaper by a newspaper dealer may reduce the profits the newspaper can make by selling advertzing-space since the demand for its advertizing-space increases with its newspaper's circulation or the higher price charged for a one-quart pot might be unprofitable for the organization even if it was profitable for the individual dealer that charged it if some of the buyers that

would have bought the one-quart pot at a lower price would subsequently have bought from a different dealer other members of the same product-line (because people like to buy multiple members of a given product-line for aesthetic reasons and/or because the proper way to use different lines of [say] cookware vary from product-line to product-line and it is costly to learn how to use the members of any given line of pots and pans.)

13.4.2 The Economic Efficiency of Maximum-Price-Setting-RPM Clauses and the Ability of the Government of a Liberal-Moral-Rights-Based Society to Increase Economic Efficiency by Responding Appropriately to a Producer's Using Such Clauses

A producer can try to achieve the objectives that maximum-price-setting-RPM clauses can help it secure by combining such clauses with one or more other choices that are designed to help the producer achieve the objectives in question, by substituting a number of other choices for such clauses, or by vertically integrating forward into distribution, instructing its distributive employees to make the choices that maximize the organization's profits, and using hierarchical controls to induce its distributive employees to make those choices. The list of other choices a producer could make to achieve the objectives that maximum-price-setting-RPM clauses can help it secure includes (1) changing the pricing-technique the producer uses when supplying its distributors to one that involves its charging lower per-unit prices and higher lump-sum (franchise) fees, (2) paying each distributor a fee for each unit-sale it makes (say, a fee equal to the profit that each unit-sale the given distributor makes enables other members of the producer's organization to realize in the various ways previously described) and increasing the lump-sum fee it charges the distributor (to offset the payments in question), (3) implementing a sales-policy of not renewing the franchises of distributors that charge more than a specified maximum price for the producer's product, and/or (4) vertically integrating forward into distribution (as newspapers do to the extent that they sell subscriptions themselves and use their own employees to deliver newspapers to subscribers). When a producer that would not otherwise have vertically integrated forward into distribution simply adds maximum-price-setting-RPM clauses to the other surrogates for vertical integration it would have used anyway to secure the objectives the clauses help it achieve, the economic efficiency of the clauses is the economic efficiency of adding them to the other surrogates for vertical integration the producer would have used in any event. When a producer substitutes maximum-price-setting-RPM clauses for the other surrogates for vertical integrations it would otherwise have used to secure the objectives the clauses help it achieve, the economic efficiency of the clauses equals the impact on economic efficiency of their being substituted for these other substituted-out surrogates for vertical integration. When a producer that uses maximum-price-setting-RPM clauses substitutes them for vertical integration forward into distribution, the economic efficiency of the clauses equals the impact that this substitution would have on economic efficiency. In each of these cases, the economic efficiency of a producer's using maximum-price-setting-RPM clauses equals the profits the producer realizes by using them *minus* any net positive distortion in those profits or *plus* any net negative distortion in those profits.

The following analyses of the economic efficiency of maximum-price-setting-RPM clauses assume (1) that the clauses whose economic efficiency is at issue are not designed to effectuate and do not effectuate horizontal price-fixing and (2) that any producer's use of such clauses will increase its profits (regardless of whether the producer's use of such clauses [A] does not deter it from engaging in relevant vertical integration and alters no other choice it makes, [B] does not deter it from engaging in relevant vertical integration but does induce it to forego some or all of the other choices it would otherwise make to achieve the objectives the clauses can enable it to secure, or [C] induces it to forego total vertical integration forward into distribution in which it would otherwise have engaged). I will now execute four separate economic-efficiency analyses. The first will assume that the producer's use of the maximum-price-setting-RPM clauses whose economic efficiency is at issue will not deter it from vertically integrating forward into distribution and will not cause it to change its use of any other surrogate for vertical integration. The second will assume that the producer's use of the relevant clauses will not deter it from vertically integrating but will induce it to stop employing some of the other surrogates for vertical integration it would otherwise have employed. The third will assume that the producer's use of the relevant clauses will deter it from vertically integrating forward into distribution. And the fourth will assume that the analyst does not know and will not be able to increase economic efficiency by investigating what if any other choices a relevant-producer's use of such clauses will cause it to alter—that it will be TBLE for the analyst to proceed on its guesstimates of the frequency with which producers' use of maximum-price-setting-RPM clauses causes them to alter no other relevant choices, causes them to stop using other surrogates for vertical integration, or deters them from vertically integrating forward into distribution.

I focus first on the economic efficiency of maximum-price-setting-RPM clauses that are being added to another set of surrogates for vertical integration that the producer would be using in any event to achieve the objectives these RPM clauses could help it secure. My assumption that the uses of the maximum-price-setting-RPM clauses on which I am currently focusing are profitable implies that the private benefits the clauses yield the producer by deterring its independent distributors from charging higher prices for its product than is in its organization's interest *exceed* any increase in the private transaction costs the use of these clauses imposes on any producer that employs them in addiction to the other surrogates for vertical integration it would in any event employ because the private transaction costs the drafting, negotiation, and enforcement of these RPM clauses cause it to incur both directly and on account of its having to compensate its distributors for the private transaction costs they must incur to consider its offers exceed (as they may not) the private-transaction-cost savings the clauses' use enables the producer to obtain because its distributors violate the maximum-resale-price contractual obligations the clauses impose on them less often than they would refuse to follow the price- "recommendations" that are backed up by sales-policies of not renewing the franchises of distributors that do not follow the recommendations in question. I turn now to the distortions that are likely to exist in the benefits the clauses will confer on the producer if it adds them to the other surrogates for vertical integration it would in any event employ by increasing the extent to which the objectives the clauses are designed to achieve are secured. First, I suspect that, if anything, there will be a positive distortion in the private benefits that the RPM clauses on which I am now focusing yield the producer by preventing its individual distributors from charging prices that are unprofitably high from their respective individual perspectives. This suspicion reflects my belief that, in realistically-Pareto-imperfect economies, unless the deterred independent distributors would have charged prices that massively exceed the prices they would have found individually most profitable to charge, the deterred price-increases would not have caused intra-ARDEPPS UO-to-UO misallocation (a conclusion that holds *a fortiori* if the analysand is a rule allowing all members of a set of product-rivals to use maximum-rice-setting-RPM clauses). Admittedly, RPM clauses that deter distributors from charging individually-mistaken higher prices will tend to increase economic efficiency by causing additional resources to be allocated to UO production from a relevant combination of QV-creating and PPR-executing resource-uses and will tend to do so as well by reducing poverty (their impact on material inequality is less certain). However, my admittedly-contestable conclusion is that the increase in economic efficiency that maximum-price-setting-RPM clauses generate on these accounts by deterring individual distributors from charging prices that exceed the prices that maximize their individual profits will be lower than the private benefits that such clauses yield the producer by preventing such distributor-mistakes. For the same reason, I also suspect that it will be TBLE to assume that there is no distortion in the private benefits a producer's use of maximum-price-setting-RPM clauses enables it to secure by preventing its distributors from charging higher prices that are in the individual distributor's interest but are rendered unprofitable for the organization by the fact that the producer is charging its individual distributors per-unit prices for its product that exceed the producer's marginal costs. Contrastingly, I think it is TBLE to assume that there is no distortion in the private benefits that a producer's addition of maximum-price-setting-RPM clauses to the other surrogates for vertical integration it would use in any event to obtain the following objective enables it to secure by preventing its individual distributors from charging higher prices that deter the purchases of buyers who would otherwise not only have made a first purchase of the producer's product from the high-pricing distributor but would also have made repeat-purchases of the producer's product or purchases of other products the producer produced from other distributors because their use of the producer's product would provide them with valuable information about its possible uses, the ease of using it, the quality of its performance, its durability, and its lifetime repair-and-maintenance costs. This "case" seems to me to be different from its predecessor because the fact that the additional "first purchases" the RPM clauses in question yield provide the "first purchasers" accurate product-information favors the conclusion that on this account the RPM clauses will tend to increase economic efficiency by decreasing buyer-non-sovereignty-generated intra-ARDEPPS and perhaps even inter-ARDEPPS UO-to-UO misallocation. (Admittedly, however, this argument will be undercut to the extent that the alternative "first purchases" the RPM clauses in question deter would have yielded equally-valuable product-information to the relevant first purchasers about the alternative products the relevant buyers would have purchased had the RPM clauses not prevented the relevant distributors from raising the prices of the clause-perpetrator's products.) For the same reasons, I think it TBLE to assume that there is no distortion in the private benefits that a producer secures because its addition of maximum-price-setting-RPM clauses to the other surrogates for vertical integration it employs prevents its distributors from charging higher prices whose charging would decrease the organization's profits by deterring sales by other distributors of the producer's product(s) of (A) the product directly involved to other buyers to whom the initial deterred buyer would have recommended it or who would have observed its performance for the initial deterred buyer, (B) of other products produced by the producer in question to other buyers who would have been induced to purchase them by the initial deterred buyer's recommendation, their observation of the product's performance for the initial deterred buyer, or their own experience with consuming the product directly involved, (C) of complements of the product directly involved that the relevant producer produces, and (D) of other members of the product-line the producer produces to which the product directly involved belongs. In what may be the special case in which the first product is a newspaper or some other publication and the second product is advertizing-space in that publication, whether there is no distortion or a positive distortion in the private benefits that maximum-price-setting-RPM clauses yields the publisher because the increases in the sales of its publication that those clauses generate increase the dollar-value to advertizers of its advertizing-space depends on the relationship between the private value of the advertizements to the advertizer and the allocative value of the advertizements: if the advertizements convey accurate information about the advertizer's product and/or the product of the advertizer's product-rivals, it may be TBLE to assume that there is no distortion in the relevant private benefits to the publisher; if the advertizements convey influential but inaccurate or misleading information (or promote the advertizer's products' images in ways that are profitable for the advertizer but of no real value to the buyers that are influenced by them or impose external costs on owners of other products), the private benefits that the relevant RPM clause confers on the publishers by increasing the value of its advertizing-space to potential advertizers are likely to be inflated (there is likely to be a positive distortion in the private benefits the clauses yield the producer on this account). For reasons I explored when discussing the possible distortion in some of the benefits that minimum-price-setting-RPM clauses can yield producers that use them,

I do not know whether it is appropriate to assume that the benefits that a producer obtains from the effects that maximum-price-setting-RPM clauses have on the profits it realizes because the reduction in its products' resale-price increases its product's dollar-value to those buyers who do not want to be perceived to be paying the higher price for its good (who do not want their purchase of its product to cause others to conclude that the buyers in question are wealthy or have non-wealth attributes whose incidence in the product's other buyers is increased by increases in the product's price) are inflated or undistorted. I am inclined to conclude that there is no distortion in the benefits a producer's use of maximum-price-setting-RPM clauses yields it by enabling it to guarantee to potential buyers of its product that its resale-price will not exceed some maximum because such a guarantee has real economic value to prospective buyers who must decide whether to incur the cost of considering whether to buy the producer's product or whether to "visit" a distributor of the producer's product with the intent of purchasing its product if its price is below some maximum. I recognize the contestability of many of the preceding conclusions. However, for what it's worth, the preceding analyses dispose me to conclude that, if anything, it would be TBLE to assume that there is a positive distortion in the private benefits that a producer obtains by supplementing its uses of other surrogates for vertical integration with maximum-price-setting-RPM clauses.

Of course, a full analysis of the distortion in the profits a producer obtains by supplementing its use of other surrogates for vertical integration with such RPM clauses must also take account of any distortion in the impact that its use of such a supplement has on the private costs it incurs to run its business. For reasons Chap. 8 explains, I believe that any increase or decrease in the private transaction costs that a producer incurs that is generated by the producer's "supplementary" use of such RPM clauses will be lower than their allocative counterparts—that the distortion in this cost-impact of the supplementary use of such RPM clauses will deflate the profitability of their use if their use reduces the operating costs of the producer and will inflate the profitability of their use if their use increases the producer's operating costs. If—as I believe—producers that use maximum-price-setting-RPM clauses to supplement the other surrogates for vertical integration they would in any event employ to achieve the objectives the clauses help them secure would in any event use sales-policies to achieve those objectives—that is, would tell their distributors that they would not renew their franchises if the distributors charged more than a "recommended" maximum price for their products and/or would stop supplying distributors that did not follow those recommendations, my view would be that the use of such clauses as supplements to other surrogates for vertical integration would reduce the operating costs of the producers that employed them because (1) it would reduce the incidence of non-compliance and (2) the private cost of designing, negotiating, and enforcing the RPM clauses would not be particularly high. If this is correct, it would favor the conclusion that the profits the supplementary use of such clauses yields their employer are deflated. On the other hand, to the extent that distributors violate any such supplementary maximum-price-setting-RPM clause and the relevant producers collect damages from the distributors that do so, each dollar of such damages must be counted as a dollar inflation of the profits the supplementary use of such clauses yields their employer (in any analysis that, like this one, considers separately the allocative benefits that the prospect of having to pay such damages yields by deterring distributors from charging higher prices for the producer's product). I am inclined to think that the combination of the relevant RPM clauses and sales-policies will deter almost all of a producer's distributors from charging higher resale-prices than the producer's RPM clauses/sales-policies (permit them to)/(recommend that they) charge. However, to the extent that this claim is incorrect, its inaccuracy favors the conclusion that the profits that a producer obtains by supplementing its other surrogates for vertical integration with maximum-price-setting-RPM clauses are inflated.

The preceding analyses imply that the economic efficiency of a producer's supplementing the other surrogates for vertical integration it uses to secure the benefits that maximum-price-setting-RPM clauses will enable it to achieve with such RPM clauses depends on (1) the profits such conduct yields the producer that engages in it and (2) the magnitudes of a host of other factors that determine the distortion in those profits. In my judgment, across all cases and in the vast majority of individual cases, the decisions that producers make to add maximum-price-setting-RPM clauses to the other surrogates for vertical integration they employ to achieve the objectives the clauses will tend to help them secure increase economic efficiency. If this economic-efficiency conclusion is correct, it implies that it would be economically inefficient for any government to prohibit such supplementary uses of maximum-price-setting-RPM clauses. If, contrary to my view, the supplementary use of maximum-price-setting-RPM clauses decreases economic efficiency across all cases, it might still be economically inefficient for any government to prohibit and fully enforce the prohibition of such uses of such clauses, given the allocative cost of drafting and implementing such a prohibition and the allocative cost of financing such a prohibition's drafting and implementation. In my judgment, it would not be TBLE for the government of a liberal-moral-rights-based society (indeed, for the government of an exemplar of any moral category of society) to promulgate and implement a more-selective policy that prohibited individual exemplars of such clauses or subsets of such clause that analysis reveals are economically inefficient.

Recall: the preceding analyses assumed that the maximum-price-setting-RPM clauses whose economic efficiency is at issue were not minimum-price-setting-RPM clauses in disguise that were being used by the producer or producers that were using them to effectuate horizontal price-fixing or were being used by the producers or distributors that agreed to them (in combination with an apposite set of VCAs) to execute a horizontal market-division. When this assumption does not apply, the use of the faux maximum-price-setting-RPM clauses will be economically inefficient for the reasons that Sect. 9.1.1.1.2 explained contrived-oligopolistic pricing is economically inefficient. I suspect that very few RPM clauses that purport to be maximum-price-setting-RPM clauses are faux in the above sense. However, I am confident that it will virtually always be TBLE for the government of a liberal-moral-rights-based society to prohibit the use of such faux maximum-price-setting-RPM-clauses and to instruct its antitrust-policy implementers to devote some resources to determining whether particular RPM clauses that purport to be maximum-price-setting-RPM clauses are actually created to effectuate (horizontal price-fixing)/(horizontal market-divisions) and to convicting and punishing those that employ RPM clauses that fall into this category. These points apply equally to the next two subcases of maximum-price-setting-RPM clauses I will investigate, but I will not repeat them in those contexts.

I proceed now to cases in which the relevant producer would or did substitute the maximum-price-setting-RPM clauses whose economic efficiency is at issue for some or all of the other surrogates for vertical integration (reductions in its per-unit prices, unit-sales subsidies, relevant sales-policies) it would otherwise use to deter its distributors from charging per-unit resale-prices that are higher than those that would maximize the organization's profits. I acknowledge that a wide variety of subsubcases in this category of subcases could be distinguished according to the identity of the alternative surrogates for vertical integration the producer's use of the relevant RPM clauses causes the producer to abandon and/or by the extent to which the producer's use of maximum-price-setting -RPM clauses leads it to reduce its usage of the alternative surrogates for vertical integration it would use to achieve the objectives that its maximum-price-setting-RPM clauses enable it to secure if it did not use the RPM clauses in question. However, believe it or not, even I have my limits. The analyses that follow will assume that any producer that decides to substitute maximum-price-setting-RPM clauses for other surrogates for vertical integration will combine its decision to use such RPM clauses with decisions (1) to raise the per-unit prices it charges its distributors, (2) to eliminate its unit-sales subsidies to its distributors, and (3) to abandon its policy of not renewing the franchises of distributors that do not follow its per-unit resale-price "recommendations." The discussion that follows will assume that a producer that finds it profitable to make any such substitutions will not remove from their distribution-contracts clauses that prohibit their distributors from engaging in arbitrage. The analysis that follows will also assume that any such use of RPM clauses by a producer will decrease the extent to which its distributors' charging higher resale-prices than is in the organization's interest reduces the organization's profits (will increase the extent to which the various objectives of the relevant RPM clauses are secured), (2) will enable the producer to obtain profits by making claims against distributors that violate their maximum-resale-price contractual obligations (because the damages it collects exceed the private transaction costs it must incur to secure them), and (3) will reduce the profits the producer obtains by making claims against distributors that have violated their contractual obligation not to engage in arbitrage (by reducing the frequency with which its distributors engage in such arbitrage).The discussion that follows will assume as well that the substitution on which I am now focusing will yield any effectuating producer private benefits by making it profitable for the producer to increase the per-unit prices it charges its distributors and concomitantly (1) by reducing its distributors' incentives to engage in arbitrage (say, to cross-sell its product to discount-house distributors whose arbitrage-purchases enable them to resell the producer's products without paying the producer any franchise fee) and (2) (usually) by reducing the sum of the risk costs borne by the producer and its distributors by shifting from the distributors to the producer some of the "risk" associated with the possibility that final-consumers' demand for the producer's product may be lower or higher than is expected on the weighted average.

No surprise: the economic efficiency of a producer's substituting maximum-price-setting-RPM clauses for the other surrogates for vertical integration just referenced equals the profits the substitution yields the producer that effectuates the substitution *plus* any negative distortion in the private benefits the substitution yields its producer-effectuator *minus* any positive distortion in the private benefits the substitution yields its producer-effectuator *minus* any negative distortion in the private cost of the substitution to its producer-effectuator *plus* any positive distortion in those costs. Once more, I will not speculate about the mean or dispersion of the distribution of profits yielded by profitable substitutions of this kind. However, I will comment on the (distortions in the private benefits)/(distortions in the private costs) that such substitutions confer/impose on their producer-effectuators.

I will make 4 statements or sets of related statements about the distortion in the private benefits that the substitution whose economic efficiency is now at issue will yield any producer that effectuates it. First, the conclusions I reached about the distortions in the private benefits a producer would obtain because its addition of maximum-price-setting-RPM clauses to the other surrogates for vertical integration it would in any event have employed increase the extent to which it secures the objectives the clauses are designed to achieve apply fully to the distortions in the private benefits the substitution of minimum-price-setting-RPM clauses for other surrogates for vertical integration yield the producer-effectuator because this latter substitution increases the extent to which the objectives of these RPM clauses are secured.

Second, I suspect that it will be TBLE to assume that there is no distortion in the private benefits a producer obtains because the per-unit price-increases it finds profitable to conjoin with its use of maximum-price-setting-RPM clauses reduce its distributors' incentives to cross-sell the producer's product to other potential distributors of its product (most likely, to discount houses). I base this conclusion on two "facts": (1) to the extent that the combination of the RPM clauses in question and the associated increases in the per-unit prices the producer charges its distributors reduce such arbitrage, they will tend to increase economic efficiency on that account in that (A) the circuitous supply of the discount house via the franchised distributor is less-economically-efficient than the discount house's direct supply by the producer and (B) the operation of the discount house will probably be economically inefficient in that it will reduce the incentives of "full-service" distributors to make demand-increasing expenditures that are economically efficient (in that they provide allocatively-valuable information to prospective buyers who take their business to the discount house) and (2) to the extent that the combination of the RPM clauses in question and the associated increases in the per-unit prices the producer charges its distributors reduces the private transaction costs the producer incurs to prevent arbitrage (say, by enforcing contractual provisions that prohibit cross-selling), the private transaction costs the distributors incur to conceal their arbitrage and to defend themselves against the producer's arbitrage-related claims, and the compensated and uncompensated transaction costs the government incurs to process any antiarbitrage-clause litigation, the private-cost saving the clause and per-unit-price increase yield the producer by reducing the incidence of arbitrage will by deflated (by the sum of [1] the difference between the allocative value and the private value to the producer of its private-transaction-cost savings *plus* [2] the reduction in arbitrage-related distributor-generated allocative transaction costs [which will also be higher than the reduction in arbitrage-related distributor-incurred private transaction costs) *plus* [3] the difference between the reduction in arbitrage-related government-generated allocative transaction costs and the reduction in court costs the producer must bear).

Third, because private risk costs are allocative as well as private, there will be no distortion in the private benefits the substitution on which I am now focusing yields its producer-effectuator by reducing the sum of the risk costs it and its distributors directly bear because ultimate buyer demand for the producer's product could be stronger or weaker than is expected on the weighted average.

Fourth, I need to make two comments on the possible distortion in any benefits the substitution on which I am now focusing yields its effectuator by enabling the producer in question to collect (additional) damages from distributors that violate the contractual obligations under which they would respectively be operating if the producer respectively did or did not place them under a maximum-price-setting-RPM-clause obligation. The first comment is that it is unclear whether the substitution with whose economic efficiency I am now concerned would increase or decrease the damages its effectuator will obtain because it is unclear whether this substitution would increase or decrease the amount of contract-violations the producer's distributors commit (and/or their detectability). True, the substitution whose economic efficiency is now at issue creates the maximum-resale-price-related contractual obligation that the relevant distributors would not otherwise have, but it is also true that this substitution reduces the likelihood that the distributors in question will violate their contractual obligation not to engage in arbitrage (an obligation they would have under either of the contractual regimes in question). The second comment or set of comments relates to the calculation of the distortion in any net benefits a producer obtains by collecting damages from distributors that have violated relevant contract obligations. At least two points are relevant. First, because (1) the private transaction costs the producer incurs to collect such damages will be lower than the allocative value the resources it uses up in the course of so doing would have generated in their specified uses, (2) the producer's private benefits will not reflect the allocative transaction costs its efforts to collect such damages cause its distributors to generate, and (3) the private court costs the producer must pay if its efforts to collect damages extend to its instituting litigation or trying the relevant case will be lower than the allocative costs the government generates when participating in the relevant litigation and when financing its participation, any additional profits the substitution now under consideration would enable the producer to obtain by enforcing its legal rights will be inflated on this account and any loss of such benefits the substitution imposes on the producer will be associated with a negative distortion is the overall benefits the substitution yields its producer-effectuator. The second point is even trickier. Because I have independently considered the benefits that any such contract-enforcement efforts yield the producer by increasing the extent to which the objectives of the relevant RPM clauses are secured as well as the distortion in those benefits, at this juncture (to avoid a kind of double-counting), I should assume that—ignoring any distortion in the private cost the producer incurs to obtain damages from its distributors—the net private benefits the producer obtains by collecting such damages are 100% inflated.

I turn now to the effects of a producer's substituting maximum-price-fixing-RPM clauses for some of the other surrogates for vertical integration it would otherwise employ to secure the benefits the clauses would yield on the private operating costs the producer incurs to run its organization. To avoid double-counting, I will ignore at this juncture the impact that this substitution will have on the private costs the producer will incur to prevent arbitrage and to collect damages from distributors that have violated their contractual obligations not to charge a price that exceeds a contractually-specified maximum price and/or not to sell the producer's product to another firm that would resell it to final consumers.

At least 5 points are relevant. First, I think it will be less-private-transaction-costly for the producer to draft and negotiate the maximum-price-setting-RPM clauses than to figure out the per-unit-sale subsidy the substitution whose economic efficiency is at issue would eliminate (where the private transaction costs the subsidy causes to be generated include the private costs the producer must incur to pay its distributors and the private transaction costs the producer's distributors incur to consider the subsidy-plus-increase-in-franchise-fee proposal: the substitution will not reduce the private transaction costs the producer must incur by obviating its spending money to prevent its distributors from exaggerating their unit sales because those sales will be inferrable from the distributors' unit-purchases).

Second, the substitution now under consideration will not affect the private transaction cost the producer incurs to determine whether any particular distributor's price exceeds the maximum resale-price the producer "recommends"/(contractually permits) or whether any particular distributor has engaged in forbidden arbitrage.

Third, because the substitution of maximum-price-setting-RPM clauses for other surrogates for vertical integration increases the certainty-equivalent cost to a distributor of charging a higher-than- "recommended"/allowed resale-price (by creating a possibility that it will have to pay damages to the producer if it does so) and in so doing reduces the frequency with which the producer's distributors charge such prices and because the substitution now under consideration includes increases in the producer's per-unit prices to its distributors (which reduce their incentives to engage in forbidden arbitrage), the substitution may reduce the private transaction costs the producer incurs by reducing the amount of "violation"-detection expenditures it is profitable for the producer to make to enforce its contractual right), the substitution will on this account yield it private benefits ("negative costs").

Fourth, the private-transaction-cost savings referenced in Items (1) and (3) in this list will be lower than the associated allocative-transaction-cost savings.

Fifth, because I believe that the substitutions on which I am now focusing will yield substantial private-transaction-cost savings and that those savings will be substantially deflated, I am inclined to conclude that the distortions in the private-cost effects of substituting maximum-price-setting-RPM clauses for other surrogates for vertical integration will deflate the profits yielded by such substitutions.

I think that, all tolled, the net effect of (1) the distortions in what I have been calling "the private benefits a producer secures by substituting maximum-price-setting-RPM clauses for other surrogates for vertical integration" and (2) the distortions in what I have been calling "the operating-cost effects of such substitutions" is to deflate the profits such substitutions yield the producers that effectuate them. If this net-distortion conclusion is correct, such substitutions (which I am assuming are profitable) will be economically efficient. Indeed, even if there is a positive distortion in the profits such substitutions yield the producers that effectuate them, the substitutions will be economically efficient if those positive profit-distortions are smaller than the profits the substitutions yield. Given the allocative cost of government's promulgating and implementing prohibitions of such substitutions, I would be very surprised if the promulgation and implementation of any universal prohibition of such substitutions would not be economically inefficient. Moreover, I doubt that the government of a liberal-moral-rights-based society could increase economic efficiency by promulgating and implementing more selective prohibitions of such substitutions.

I turn finally to cases in which the producer that is including maximum-price-setting-RPM clauses in its contracts with its distributors is substituting such clauses for total vertical integration forward into distribution. I will analyze the economic efficiency of such substitutions on the assumption that they (1) reduce the extent to which the producer secures the objectives the clauses are designed to achieve but (2)(A) reduce the private transaction costs the producer incurs to operate its organization, (B) enables the producer to avoid the finance and opportunity costs it would have to incur to vertically integrate forward into distribution, and (C) enable the producer to make substitutions of independent distributors for employees when it would be more-cost-effective for it to use the independent distributors even if transaction-cost and finance considerations could be ignored (because the individuals who would act as independent distributors place a significant positive dollar-value on "being their own bosses" and because they are more skilled and assiduous than its own employees would be and the related differences in their proficiencies would not be associated with equal differences in their wages even if the independent distributors' desire to be their own bosses played no role).

For reasons I explained when analyzing other maximum-price-setting-RPM-clause cases, I suspect that—if anything—there will be a positive distortion in the loss the substitution now under consideration imposes on the producer because its RPM clauses secure their objectives to a lesser extent than they would be secured by vertical integration. For reasons I explained when analyzing the "cost-related" effects of substituting minimum-price-setting-RPM clauses for vertical integration, I also think that the private-transaction-cost savings the substitution of maximum-price-setting-RPM clauses for vertical integration will secure will be deflated and that it will be TBLE to assume that the preference-for-being-one's-own-boss-related, differential-skills-and-assiduity-related, and finance-related opportunity-cost savings such a substitution generates will not be distorted. Moreover, although any damage-award-related benefits a producer secures by substituting maximum-price-setting-RPM clauses for vertical integration would be inflated, I doubt that the substitution will yield much in the way of damage-awards—that is, I doubt that covered distributors will often violate the relevant RPM obligations. These "claims" imply that there will be a negative distortion in the profits a producer obtains by substituting maximum-price-setting-RPM clauses for vertical integration. If that conclusion is correct, profitable substitutions of maximum-price-setting-RPM clauses for vertical integration will be economically efficient.

I will close this discussion by repeating two points I made in relation to the other maximum-price-setting-RPM-clause cases I distinguish: (1) even if, taken as a group, all substitutions in this category would decrease economic efficiency, it might well not be economically efficient to prohibit them and enforce that prohibition, and (2) I suspect it will not be TBLE for the government of a liberal-moral-rights-based society to promulgate and implement a more selective set of prohibitions of those maximum-price-setting-RPM clauses that are being substituted for vertical integration that are economically efficient (even if some such substitutions exist).

So far, I have been tacitly assuming that it would be both possible and TBLE for antitrust-policy implementers to determine whether a producer that included maximum-price-setting-RPM clauses in its contracts with its distributors (1) was supplementing the other surrogates for vertical integration it was using with those clauses, (2) was substituting those RPM clauses for these other surrogates for vertical integration, or (3) was substituting such clauses for vertical integration. That assumption seems to me to be highly implausible. If as I suspect it will not be TBLE for antitrust-policy implementers to determine the subcategory into which an individual producer's use of such RPM clauses belongs or the subcategory to which any subclass of such RPM-clause uses belongs, what do the preceding analyses imply for the economic efficiency of such clauses' prohibition? In my judgment, these analyses imply that, taken as an indivisible class, the maximum-price-setting-RPM clauses that producers employ are likely to increase economic efficiency and that the probability that any effort to prohibit the use of such clauses would decrease economic efficiency is even higher than the probability that the clauses would increase economic efficiency.

I wish that the approach to economic-efficiency prediction I claim is TBLE would yield a priori arguments or partly-empirically-based arguments that would establish respectively irrefutable or totally-convincing conclusions about the economic efficiency of maximum-price-setting-RPM clauses and/or their prohibition. If any such economic-efficiency conclusion would clearly be correct, the fact that my approach generated that conclusion irrefutably or overwhelmingly-convincingly would certainly count in my approach's favor. But, in reality, the economic efficiency of such clauses and their prohibition depends on the magnitudes of many parameters whose size is contestable. In these circumstances, I would be more than satisfied to settle for an assessment that concludes that my approach identifies the parameters that are relevant, explains why these parameters are relevant and how they interact to affect the outcome of interest, and puts the analyst in a position to generate defensible conclusions from known data and plausible guesstimates of the magnitudes of the relevant parameters.

No doubt, my being a lawyer as well as an economist disposes me to offer conclusions when pure economists might tend to be more reticent. But it is important to emphasize that the value of the approach I am prescribing does not depend on the accuracy of the conclusions to which the combination of the theory I have developed and my guesstimates of the magnitudes of the parameters whose salience that theory has established have led me.

13.4.3 The Liberal-Moral-Rights-Violativeness of Maximum-Price-Setting-RPM Clauses and the Ability of the Government of a Liberal-Moral-Rights-Based Society to Secure Liberal Moral Rights by Responding Appropriately to a Producers' Using Such Clauses

I will ignore faux maximum-price-setting-RPM clauses that actually communicate the minimum prices that one or more contrived-oligopolistic pricers are agreeing to or seeking to charge (which clauses violate the liberal moral rights of the disadvantaged actual and potential customers of the contrivers and of any innocent rivals of the contrivers to which they make contrived-oligopolistic communications or against which they threaten or practice any related retaliation). All non-faux (actual) maximum-price-setting-RPM clauses are not liberal-moral-rights-violative. In fact, it is arguable that the owners, in some circumstances the at-risk creditors, and conceivably the managers and employees of a producer have a (property-right-related) liberal-moral-rights-related interest in the producer's being allowed to increase its profits by using maximum-price-setting-RPM classes. Correlatively, the government of a liberal-moral-rights-based society has no moral duty to proscribe the use of such clauses and may not be able to prohibit their use without violating one or more of the above sets of individuals' liberal moral rights.

13.4.4 The Impact of a Producer's Using Maximum-Price-Setting-RPM Clauses on Total Utility and the Instantiation of Various Non-Utilitarian-Egalitarian Conceptions of the Moral Good and the Ability of the Government of a Liberal-Moral-Rights-Based Society to Instantiate Any Such Conception of the Moral Good by Responding Appropriately to a Producer's Use of Maximum-Price-Setting-RPM Clauses

Section 13.2 argued that it is TBLE to assume that maximum-price-setting-RPM clauses increase economic efficiency. Such clauses will also tend to reduce material inequality. (Remember: for the purpose of moral-good analyses as opposed to for the purpose of liberal-moral-rights-violation analyses, the relevant analysand is a rule allowing all members of a set of product-rivals to engage in the conduct at issue, and there is no reason to believe that such a rule will increase the profits of the firms to which it applies.) The preceding two conclusions imply that (with rare exceptions) the use of maximum-price-setting-RPM clauses will increase total utility and that (with rare exceptions) government prohibitions of the use of such clauses will reduce total utility. The second sentence of this paragraph implies that (with rare exceptions) the use of maximum-price-setting-RPM clauses will instantiate all non-utilitarian-egalitarian conceptions of the moral good and that (with rare exceptions) government prohibitions of the use of such clauses will disserve the instantiation of all non-utilitarian-egalitarian conceptions of the moral good.

13.5 Single-Brand Exclusive Dealerships

Single-brand exclusive dealerships are dealerships in which the dealer is prohibited from selling products that are competitive with the producer's product(s).

13.5.1 The Functions of Single-Brand Exclusive Dealerships

Single-brand exclusive dealerships can perform at least four functions for the producer that establishes them (though only the first two I list will relate to such dealerships' being surrogates for vertical integration): (1) preventing the dealer from selling products that are competitive with the dealership-establishing producer's products when the dealer's selling such rival-products will reduce the sum of the distributor's and the dealership-establishing producer's profits—a problem that will arise when the dealership-establishing producer's per-unit price to the dealer exceeds the producer's marginal costs and/or when the dealer's sale of a product that is competitive with the dealership-establishing producer's products will deprive other distributors of the dealership-establishing purchaser's products of sales (for most of the reasons in which we saw in Sect. 13.4.1 that a distributor's charging a high price for a producer's product can, by reducing the distributor's unit-sales of the producer's product, reduce the sales of the producer's product that other distributors make), (2) preserving the incentives of a producer to give its distributors organizationally-profitable advice about their premises' architectural and interior design, the protocols they should use to hire, reward, and promote their employees, and the information their salespersons should provide potential customers and the other sales-techniques these salespersons should use by precluding the distributors from using this advice to sell products of the advice-giving producer's product-rivals, (3) enabling a producer to induce the exit of an established rival, to deter an established rival from expanding its total investment in the relevant ARDEPPS, and/or to deter the entry into that ARDEPPS of a potential competitor) in what I take to be the rare case in which (A) the producer that is arranging single-brand exclusive dealerships reduces the number of unrestricted dealers below the number that must distribute a relevant rival's product for the rival in question to find it profitable to continue to operate or to invest unless the rival can profitably enter the distribution business itself, can profitably execute a distribution joint venture, or can rely on or profitably induce an independent distributor's entry, (B) the target cannot render survival or investment profitable by making one or more such moves, (C) the target-investment that is removed or deterred would not be immediately replaced by an equally-competitive investment by someone else, and (D) the gains the prospective single-brand-exclusive-dealership-establishing producer will obtain by driving out or deterring a rival investment in this way exceed the cost of arranging the single-brand exclusive dealerships in question—a function whose perpetrator-expected performance would render the single-brand exclusive dealerships predatory if but only if the perpetrator's *ex ante* conclusion that the creation of the dealership(s) in question would be at least normally profitable was critically positively affected by its perception that the operation of such dealerships would or might increase the perpetrator's profits in this way; and (4) enabling a set of product-rivals to secure a horizontal market-division by combining the single-brand restrictions in their distributorship-agreements with appropriate VCA clauses (which restrict the participants' respective distributors to dealing for the patronage of non-overlapping sets of customers).

13.5.2 The Economic Efficiency of Single-Brand Exclusive Dealerships and the Economic Efficiency of the Government of a Liberal-Moral-Rights-Based Society's Responding to Single-Brand Exclusive Dealerships in Various Ways

I believe that it will be TBLE to assume that the VCA clauses whose combination with single-brand exclusive dealerships will effect a horizontal market-division (VCA clauses in which [ideally from the relevant producers' perspective] the members of the relevant set of product-rivals restrict their respective distributors to dealing for the patronage of non-overlapping sets of prospective buyers) will always be economically inefficient. Relatedly, I believe that it will be TBLE for the government of a liberal-moral-rights-based-society to effectively prohibit the use of such VCA clauses and, by extension, the use of single-brand exclusive dealerships to effectuate horizontal market-divisions. I also believe that any predation that single-brand exclusive dealerships effectuate will be economically inefficient (that even if the predation prevents ARDEPPS-equilibrium-QV-investment-increasing QV investments that would be economically inefficient, it would be more economically efficient to reduce the relevant ARDEPPS' equilibrium QV-investment quantity in other ways) and that it will be TBLE for the government of a liberal-moral-rights-based -society effectively to prohibit predatory single-brand exclusive dealerships (that is, to effectively prohibit any producer's entering into single-brand exclusive dealerships when the producer's *ex ante* perception that doing so would be at least normally profitable was critically affected by its belief that this conduct would cause a rival to exit or deter an actual or potential competitor from investing in the perpetrator's ARDEPPS). However, the last sentence leaves unresolved issues of (1) the economic efficiency of single-brand exclusive dealerships arranged by producers that believe *ex ante* that they will cause one or more exits or deter one or more rival investments when that belief did not cause the producer to perceive as being at least normally profitable single-brand exclusive dealerships it would not otherwise have perceived to be at least normally profitable and (2) the TBLE of a liberal-moral-rights-based society's prohibiting such single-brand exclusive dealerships: even if such dealerships' tendency to reduce the investment against which the perpetrating producer will have to compete makes them less economically efficient than they would otherwise have been, their performance of other economically-efficient functions may render them economically efficient all tolled when their perpetrator's perception of their *ex ante* profitability was not critically positively affected by the prospect of their reducing its rivals' investment in the ARDEPPS in question. More importantly, to the extent that a producer's use of single-brand exclusive dealerships yields it profits by making it profitable for it to provide its distributors organizationally profitably with various kinds of information, I suspect that the single-brand exclusive dealerships will tend to increase economic efficiency on that account (though I acknowledge that this conclusion is disfavored by the possibility that the allocative cost of providing such information may exceed the private cost of doing so as well as by the possibility that some of the sales-techniques advice that is given may be to provide inaccurate or misleading information about the products of the producer and/or its product-rivals). I acknowledge as well that the claim that single-brand exclusive dealerships will tend to increase economic efficiency by increasing the accuracy of the information that buyers have about the perpetrator's product by increasing its sales and thereby the information that its use provides its purchasers, those to whom its purchasers provide information, and observers of the purchasers' use of the product is undercut by the fact that the rival-product sales that the single-brand exclusive dealership deters would have provided the same types of information in the same ways about the relevant rival-products.

Obviously, the preceding observations also have implications for the economic efficiency of single-brand exclusive dealerships that do not effectuate horizontal market-divisions or predation. It will come as no surprise that the economic efficiency of such single-brand exclusive dealerships depends on (1) the profits they yield the producer that arranges them, (2) the distortion in the benefits they yield the perpetrator, and (3) the distortion in the private cost to the perpetrator of effectuating them. I have nothing useful to say about the profits single-brand exclusive dealerships yield the producers that would employ them. I turn now to the distortion in the private benefits such exclusive dealerships yield the producers that establish them. As I stated previously, such single-brand exclusive dealerships may increase their perpetrator's profits (1) by enabling the perpetrator (A) to avoid losing profitable sales to rivals and/or (B) to avoid making otherwise-unprofitable changes in its pricing-technique (to avoid reducing its per-unit prices and increasing its lump-sum fees) (2) by making it profitable for the perpetrator to provide its distributors with information that is organizationally-profitable for them to receive from the perpetrator, and (3) by enabling the perpetrator to profit from the rival-investment-deterring effects of even those single-brand exclusive dealerships that are not predatory. I suspect that (1) the private benefits referenced in Item (1)(A) in the immediately-preceding list are 100 percent inflated (have no allocative-efficiency-gain counterpart), (2) the private benefits referenced in Item (1)(B) in the immediately-preceding list are inflated but by less than 100 percent because the deterred change in pricing-technique would have decreased economic efficiency by increasing the distributors' incentive to engage in arbitrage and would probably have increased the sum of the risk costs borne by the producer and its distributors, (3) it will be TBLE to assume that the private benefits referenced in Item (2) in the immediately-preceding list are undistorted at least if the relevant society's consumer-protection and business-tort law deters the provision of inaccurate or misleading product-information. All tolled, the preceding conclusions imply that the private benefits that single-brand exclusive dealerships yield the producers that employ them will be significantly but far from totally inflated.

I turn next to the distortion in the private cost a producer must incur to make its independent distributors single-brand. I will first address the distortions in (1) the private benefit and (2) the private costs that single-brand exclusive dealerships will respectively confer on and impose on any producer that created them on the assumption that it will conjoin its creation of them with increases in the per-unit prices it charges its distributors, decreases in the per-unit-sales subsidies it pays its distributors, and removals of its sales-policy of cutting off distributors that sell rival-products that are competitive with the products of the producer that the producer authorizes them to sell. Although my analyses of the benefits that a producer can obtain by placing its distributors under a single-brand obligation and of the impacts that a producer's decisions to do so will have on other choices it makes reveal the determinants of the profits that a producer will be able to obtain by placing its distributors under a single-brand obligation, I will not comment on the amount of profits that profitable decisions by a producer to create such obligations will yield it (because I have nothing useful to say on this quantitative issue).

However, I hope I can offer some informative observations about the distortions in the various private benefits that a producer can obtain by imposing and enforcing single-brand obligations on its distributors and about the distortions in the private cost to the producer of creating and enforcing such obligations. I will address initially the case in which the producer substitutes its decision to create and enforce single-brand exclusive dealerships (as opposed to non-single-brand exclusive dealerships) for decisions to raise the per-unit prices it charges its distributors for its products and decisions to subsidize the unit-sales of its distributors (while continuing to announce and/or implement a sales-policy of cutting off distributors that sell products that compete with the products of the perpetrator that the distributors sell). In my judgment, a producer's substitution of single-brand obligations for the just-referenced other surrogates for vertical integration will increase the extent to which its distributors are deterred from selling rival-products and in so doing increase or tend to increase all 4 of the benefits Sect. 13.5.1 indicated single-brand obligations could yield producers. I will begin by analyzing the distortion in the private benefits the single-brand contract-obligation yields the producer by increasing its distributors' sales of its products by deterring its distributors from selling rival-products by more than they would be deterred from doing so by the per-unit-price decreases and distributor-unit-sales subsidies for which the producer would substitute the contract-obligations in question. To do so, I will have to analyze the economic-efficiency concomitants of any such increase in the producer's sales (ignoring any allocative-transaction-cost consequences, which will be analyzed separately subsequently). I think it would be TBLE to assume that any increase in the unit sales a producer obtains by placing its distributors under single-brand obligations will have no impact on intra-ARDEPPS or inter-ARDEPPS UO-to-UO misallocation and that this no-economic-efficiency-impact conclusion holds *a fortiori* when the analysand is the choices of the members of a set of product-rivals to create such single-brand obligations. Moreover, because the relevant analysand is the impact of all members of a set of product-rivals' placing their distributors under single-brand obligations and there is no reason to believe that their doing so would increase either the height of their ARDEPPS' $H\Pi_E$ curve or the intensity of their ARDEPPS' investment competition if the creation of the single-brand obligations would not induce the withdrawal of an existing investment or deter the execution of a new investment (a possibility that will be addressed below), with that qualification, the creation of single-brand obligations that perform only the function on which I am now focusing will not affect economic efficiency by altering equilibrium investment in the producer's ARDEPPS. By way of contrast, any tendency that a producer's creation of single-brand contract-obligations has to cause it to increase the per-unit prices it charges its distributors (because the single-brand obligation reduces its concern that its charging its distributors high per-unit prices will induce them to sell units of a rival's product) will tend (1) to increase economic efficiency by decreasing the distributors' incentives to engage in arbitrage by selling the producer's product to unauthorized (discount-house) distributors (arbitrage whose practice is economically inefficient to the extent that it replaces the direct supply of the arbitrage-buyers by the producer or results in the discount houses' generating misallocation by taking a free ride on the sales-efforts of authorized distributors), (2) to increase economic efficiency by decreasing the sum of the producer's and distributors' risk costs by shifting from the distributors to the producer the risk of demand for the producer's product's being different from what is expected on the weighted average, and (3) to decrease economic efficiency by increasing poverty and material inequality (to the extent that the consumers of the producer's product are absolutely poor or less-materially-well-off than the average member of the society in question). Finally, because I am considering separately the possible allocative benefits that are generated when a producer collects damages from distributors that have violated their single-brand obligations and because the private cost a producer incurs to collect such damages are deflated (in that on balance the producer pays less than the allocative cost of the resources it uses to collect such damages, does not pay any of the allocative costs its claims cause the relevant distributors to generate, and pays court fees that are lower than the allocative costs the government's handling of the relevant disputes generates), "the net benefits" a producer's decisions to place its distributors under single-brand obligations enable it to secure by collecting damages from distributors that have violated these obligations should also in the context of this analysis be deemed to be highly inflated. All tolled, the preceding benefits-distortion analyses seem to me to warrant the conclusion that the private benefits a producer obtains by substituting single-brand-obligations-creating contractual clauses for decreases in their product's per-unit prices, payments of unit-sales subsidies to its distributors, and sales-policies of cutting off distributors that sell rival-products are inflated, though the magnitude of the inflation will clearly be reduced if as I suspect few dealers violate their single-brand obligations (if producers obtain little in the way of damage-awards on these clauses' account).

I turn next (1) to the effects of such a substitution on the producer's costs and (2) to the distortion in those cost-effects. I see no reason to believe that the private cost to a producer of drafting and negotiating single-brand-obligation-creating clauses will be different from the private cost it will have to incur to devise and negotiate the unit-sales-subsidy clauses for which the single-brand clauses would in part be substituted. It will also clearly not be more privately costly for a producer to determine whether a particular distributor has sold a product that is rivalrous with the producer's product when it is investigating this issue to implement the combination of its sales-policy and its single-brand exclusive-dealership agreement than when it is doing so simply to implement the sales-policy. In fact, I suspect that the producer's adding its single-brand arrangement to its sales-policy will reduce the private transaction costs it incurs to detect violations of its contract rights and refusals to follow its "recommendations" to distributors by increasing the cost to any distributor of its rival-product sales being detected, hence reducing the likelihood that any relevant distributor will make such unauthorized sales, and hence reducing the costs that the producer will find most profitable to incur to detect such "illicit" distributor sales. However, I should admit that the preceding point is not likely to be empirically significant: distributor ("illicit") sales of products that are competitive with a relevant producer's product(s) will almost always be public and detectable by the "prohibiting" producer at virtually no cost. A producer's placing its distributors under a single-brand obligation will also reduce the producer's operating costs by obviating its having to calculate the subsidies it will pay its distributors for each unit of its product they sell and its actually paying those subsides (by causing it to eliminate those subsidies). (I do not think that the elimination of the subsidies will reduce the producer's costs by obviating its checking to see whether its distributors are exaggerating their unit-sales since the producer will be able to infer its distributors' unit-sales from their unit-purchases.) Because a producer's decision to place its distributors under a single-brand obligation will make it profitable for the producer to raise its per-unit prices to its distributors and in so doing to reduce the amount of arbitrage in which they engage (their opportunities to engage in profitable arbitrage), the producer's creation of such obligations will tend to reduce the private transaction costs it incurs to detect its distributors' cross-selling to distributors the producer has not authorized to sell its product(s). Admittedly, a producer's placing its distributors under a single-brand obligation will cause it to incur additional costs by giving it the opportunity to collect damages from distributors that violate this obligation. However, because I expect that the contractual prohibition, the related sales-policy, and the visibility of the prohibited or "discouraged" rival-product sales will deter virtually all such illicit sales, I do not think that a producer's decision to place its distributor under a single-brand obligation will result in its incurring significant costs to enforce this obligation.

All tolled, my best guess is that substitutions of single-brand-obligation-creating clauses for unit-price decreases and unit-sales subsidies will reduce the private transaction costs that the producers incur and that the private-cost savings in question will if anything tend to be deflated.

Everything considered, I suspect that it will be TBLE to assume (1) that the profits a producer that finds it profitable to substitute decisions to place its distributors under single-brand obligations for decisions to charge lower per-unit prices and pay unit-sale subsidies to its distributors realizes by making this choice are undistorted—that any inflation of the relevant benefits are "pretty-much-perfectly" (sorry about that) offset by the deflation in the cost-savings the substitution yields the producer that effectuates it—and (2) that those substitutions of this kind that yield the producers that effectuate them profits are economically efficient. I also suspect that it will not be TBLE for the government of a liberal-moral-rights-based society to respond to exemplars of this category of substitutions selectively—that is, to prohibit those examples that are economically inefficient and instruct its antitrust-policy implementers to investigate whether particular exemplars or particular subclasses of exemplars of this category of substitutions are economically inefficient and to prohibit those it concludes are economically inefficient.

I turn now to the impact that a producer's decision to substitute for vertical integration forward into distribution decisions to place its independent distributors under single-brand obligations, to increase the per-unit prices it charges its distributors, and to continue its sales-policy of disenfranchising distributors that sell rival-products. I will assume that this substitution reduces the extent to which the producer in question prevents rival-products from being sold, replaces the producer's prospective better-designed distributive facilities with worse-designed facilities owned by the producer's independent distributors, and replaces the better-advised distributive employees the producer would have hired with less-well-advised distributive employees of its independent distributors. I will also assume that this substitution reduces what I will call "the operating costs" the producer that effectuates it incurs—that (1)(A) the private cost to the producer of devising, negotiating, and enforcing the single-brand clauses and of determining the unit-price increases it wants to effectuate *is lower than* (B) the sum of (i) the private transaction cost of effectuating a vertical merger, acquisition, or joint venture or vertical internal growth, (ii) the private transaction cost of devising and implementing the hierarchical controls it would use to influence its own distributive employees' decisionmaking, (iii) (if I count these separately) the cost of financing the vertical integration including the opportunity cost of doing so, and (iv) the loss the vertical integration would have imposed on the producer because independent distributors value being their own bosses and would in any event be better "buys" than the individuals who would work as the producer's employees.

I turn finally in this subsection to the distortions in the negative private benefits and the private costs the substitution on which I am now focusing "confers"/imposes on the producer that effectuates the substitution in question. I suspect that the "negative private benefits" the substitution generates by increasing the amount of rival-products sold are associated with economic-efficiency gains (to the extent that the per-unit-price increases that are substituted for vertical integration reduce distributor-arbitrage and the sum of the producer's and distributors' risk costs) so that the percentage-inflation of the negative benefits is over 100 percent. I suspect that it will be TBLE to assume that there is no distortion in the negative private benefits the substitution generates by reducing the amount of advice the producer gives its distributors below the information the producer would bring to bear on tits decisions if it were fully integrated forward into distribution. I suspect that the private costs the substitution of the clauses for vertical integration will impose on the producer by putting it in a position in which it will pursue claims against clause-violating distributors are substantially deflated (though I suspect that such private costs will be low—that the combination of the clauses, the sales-policy, and the visibility of the sale of the relevant rival products will deter almost all violations of single-brand clauses). I suspect that the private-cost saving the substitution of single-brand clauses, unit-price increases, and sales-policies for vertical integration will enable the producer to obtain will be both substantial and significantly deflated.

All tolled but particularly for the last reason, I suspect (1) that across all cases the profits producers obtain by substituting single-brand clauses, per-unit-price increases, and sales-policies for vertical integration forward into distribution are substantially deflated, (2) that taken as a group all such substitutions that are profitable are economically efficient, (3) that universal prohibitions of such substitutions would be economically inefficient even if (contrary to my view) taken as a group such substitutions reduced economic efficiency, and (4) that it would not be TBLE for a government to try to prohibit such substitutions selectively.

So far, I have implicitly assumed that it will be possible and TBLE to determine whether particular producers' uses of single-brand clauses are being substituted for (1) vertical integration or (2) some other set of surrogates for vertical integration. I actually do not think that is so. In my judgment, each of the 4 conclusions I articulated in the immediately-preceding paragraph that applied to decisions to substitute single-brand clauses and per-unit-price increases and sales-policies for vertical integration apply when it is not known whether the alternative to the single-brand-clause-including combination is vertical integration.

Because I doubt that few if any producer-uses of single-brand clauses will or might drive a rival out or deter a rival from making an investment in the ARDEPPS of practice because I think the services of the constrained distributors would rarely critically affect the profitability of any producer-rival's decision to stay in business or invest in the relevant ARDEPPS even if the rival could do nothing to mitigate any associated loss and because I believe that any affected rival will unusually be able to mitigate any such losses that would otherwise be generated by vertically integrating forward into distribution on its own, executing a distribution joint venture, or inducing one or more independent firms to enter and distribute its products ([by supplying the firm(s) in question with information, capital, and/or an assured source of patronage or supply]), I have not yet addressed single-brand exclusive dealerships that function by driving producer-rivals out or deterring investments by potential investors in the producer's ARDEPPS (be they established firms in that ARDEPPS or potential entrants into that ARDEPPS). If as will usually be the case the investments at issue are QV investments and the clauses will reduce equilibrium QV investment in the ARDEPPS in which they are being used, their having this impact increases their economic efficiency and strengthens the preceding conclusion. (Admittedly, if the relevant ARDEPPS investments are investments in PPR, any tendency of one or more single-brand exclusive-dealership clauses to reduce the ARDEPPS' equilibrium-investment quantity will count against its or their economic efficiency.) I admit, however, that if the relevant producer's *ex ante* perception that its use of the clause was at least normally profitable was critically positively affected by its perception that these clauses would or might have one or more such effects (if the producer's use of the clauses was predatory) the fact that the clause was inherently unprofitable and would generate other effects that would decrease its economic efficiency would strongly favor the conclusion that the clause was economically inefficient.

13.5.3 The Liberal-Moral-Rights-Violativeness of Single-Brand Exclusive Dealerships and the Ability of the Government of a Liberal-Moral-Rights-Based Society to Secure Liberal Moral Rights by Responding Appropriately to the Creation of Such Dealerships

A producer's creation of single-brand exclusive dealerships will violate liberal moral rights if it was predatory (in which case the liberal moral rights that are violated are those of the driven-out or excluded competitors of the single-brand-exclusive-dealership-creating producer and those of the negatively-affected actual and prospective customers of the perpetrator and its driven-out/excluded competitors). One or more members of a set of rivals' creation of single-brand exclusive dealerships will violate liberal moral rights if the perpetrator(s) in question was (were) trying to secure a horizontal market-division by combining the creation of a number of such dealerships with VCA clauses that limited the respective dealers to trying to sell one-product-variant to non-overlapping sets of buyers (in which case the parties whose liberal moral rights are violated are the adversely-affected buyers and any seller that was being threatened with retaliation or subjected to retaliation for not participating in the scheme). It may be that the shareholders, at-risk creditors, and possibly the managers and employees of any firm that wants to create single-brand exclusive dealerships for licit reasons have a liberal moral right in the firm's being allowed to do so. The preceding conclusions imply that—within the operative liberal-moral-rights constraints—the government of any liberal-moral-rights-based society has a liberal moral duty to prevent morally-illicit uses of single-brand exclusive dealerships and to provide the victims of such illicit dealerships with an appropriate opportunity to obtain legal redress. It may also be that the government of a liberal-moral-rights-based society has a moral duty to allow firms to make licit uses of single-brand exclusive dealerships.

13.5.4 The Impact of Single-Brand Exclusive Dealerships on the Instantiation of the Utilitarian and Various Non-Utilitarian-Egalitarian Conceptions of the Moral Good and the Ability of the Government of a Liberal-Moral-Rights-Based Society to Instantiate These Conceptions of the Moral Good by Responding Appropriately to Uses of Single-Brand Exclusive Dealerships

Illicit uses of single-brand exclusive dealerships will (1) decrease economic efficiency, (2) increase poverty and material inequality, (3) reduce total utility, and (4) disserve the instantiation of all non-utilitarian-egalitarian conceptions of the moral good, regardless of the behaviors for which they will be substituted. I suspect that the government of a liberal-moral-rights-based society will be able to secure the instantiation of both the utilitarian and the various non-utilitarian-egalitarian conceptions of the moral good by devoting an appropriate amount of resources to deterring illicit uses of single-brand exclusive dealerships, though I doubt that any significant number of single-brand exclusive dealerships are illicit.

In my judgment, regardless of the behaviors for which they are substituted, licit uses of single-brand exclusive dealerships (1) will tend to increase economic efficiency (especially if they are substituted for vertical integration), (2) will have an uncertain impact on poverty and material inequality (because they will tend to be conjoined with increases in the per-unit prices the producer charges its independent distributors), and (3) will probably tend to increase total utility (especially when they are substituted for vertical integration). I (1) think that the prohibition of licit uses of single-brand exclusive dealerships will decrease total utility, (2) doubt that the government of a liberal-moral-rights-based society will be able to secure the instantiation of non-utilitarian-egalitarian conceptions of the moral good by prohibiting licit uses of single-brand exclusive dealerships, and (3) am concerned that even if the prohibition of licit uses of such dealerships would serve the instantiation of some egalitarian conceptions of the moral good, it would be moral-rights-violative.

13.6 Long-Term Full-Requirements Contracts and Long-Term Total-Output-Supply Contracts

13.6.1 The Functions of Long-Term Full-Requirements Contracts and Long-Term Total-Output-Supply Contracts

Long-term full-requirements contracts and long-term total-output-supply contracts perform many legitimate functions: can increase their participants' profits (1) by reducing their contracting costs by substituting one long-term contract for more than one short-term contract, (2) by making it individually-profitable for the participants to make jointly-profitable adjustments in their operations (for example, better to coordinate their truck-selections and loading/unloading-dock selections), (3) by lowering the sum of the risk costs they bear by providing them with assured sources of supply and/or patronage and making the prices that they will (have to pay)/(be paid) more predictable, (4) when the long-term provision is included in a full-requirements tie-in that functions by increasing the private-cost-effectiveness of the tying seller's efforts to prevent the buyer from making a jointly-unprofitable choice to combine the seller's product with an inferior complement, by increasing the private-cost-effectiveness of the seller's efforts to control the quality of the complement(s) the buyer combines with the seller's product, (5) when the long-term provision is included in a full-requirements tying agreement or a total-output-supply reciprocity agreement that is designed to increase the private-cost-effectiveness of the seller's efforts to practice meter pricing on a durable machine, the right to use a production process, or the right to operate a distributive outlet for whose distinguishing characteristics, brand, and promotion the "seller" is responsible, by increasing the private-cost-effectiveness of the seller's meter pricing, sometimes by rendering the use of tie-ins and/or reciprocity agreements for these purposes profitable, and sometimes by rendering the meter pricing profitable, and (6) when the long-term provision is included in a full-requirements tying agreement or a total-output-supply reciprocity agreement that is designed to increase the private-cost-effectiveness of the efforts of a producer of an input against which substitution is possible to prevent the buyer from making jointly-unprofitable substitutions against the seller's input, by increasing the private-cost-effectiveness of those efforts, sometimes by rendering profitable the use of tie-ins or reciprocity agreements to achieve this objective, indeed sometimes by rendering profitable any effort to achieve this objective. Admittedly, long-term full-requirement contracts and long-term total-output-supply contracts may also be used by a seller predatorily to drive an extant rival out or to deter an extant or potential competitor from making a new investment in the ARDEPPS of practice by locking up enough sales or inputs to reduce the sales that the target can make or the inputs the target can buy to a level that would preclude the target from realizing a normal rate-of-return on its extant or prospective investment(s) in the ARDEPPS of practice, However, I suspect that few if any long-term full-requirements contracts or total-output-supply contracts are predatory, in part because their targets will sometimes if not often be able to reduce the effectiveness of such contracts as predation-devices by vertically integrating forward into distribution or backward into the input-production business, by entering into joint ventures that will supply the relevant distributive service or input, and/or by helping independent firms to enter into the relevant distributive or input-manufacturing business, especially when the equilibrium-QV-investment quantity in the relevant distributive or input-manufacturing business is increasing through time.

13.6.2 The Economic Efficiency of Long-Term Full-Requirements Contracts and Long-Term Total-Output-Supply Contracts and the Ability of the Government of a Liberal-Moral-Rights-Based Society to Increase Economic Efficiency by Responding Appropriately to Them

Like the economic efficiency of the other surrogates for vertical integration this chapter addresses, the economic efficiency of the long-term contract-provisions on which this section focuses depends in part on the conduct their employer would substitute for them if for some reason the possible employer chose not to use them despite the (assumed) profitability of using them. I will assume (it seems to me, plausibly) that when the long-term provisions under consideration function by reducing their participants' mechanical contracting costs, inducing the participants to make mutually-profitable adjustments in their operations, and reducing the sum of the participants' risk costs, their employers would either be substituting the provisions for vertical integration or including them in their contracts without altering any other decisions they make. I will assume that, when the long-term full-requirements or total-output supply provisions at issue are components of tying or reciprocity agreements that function by increasing the private-cost-effectiveness of the seller's efforts to prevent its buyers from using inferior complements, the decisions to include the long-term provision will be substituted for a decision either (1) to stop trying to control the buyer's complement-choice in any way, (2) to try to control the buyer's complement-choice by including in the contract a clause obligating the buyer to use complements with stated attributes and to enforce that obligation, or (3) to vertically integrate forward into distribution. I will assume that, when the long-term full-requirements or total-output-supply provisions at issue are components of tying or reciprocity agreements that function by enabling the seller to practice meter pricing, the decision to include the long-term provision at issue will be substituted for a decision either (1) to sell for a lump-sum fee the relevant machine, the right to use the relevant production process, or the right to operate the relevant franchise or (2) to use an endproduct-royalty scheme or share-in-total-distributive-revenue scheme or (3) to vertically integrate forward. Finally, I will assume that, when the long-term full-requirements or total-output-supply provisions at issue are components of tying or reciprocity agreements that are designed to enable a seller to prevent its customer from making jointly-unprofitable substitutions against the seller's substitutable input, the provision's long length will be relevant to the overall arrangement's profitability only to the extent that it reduces the mechanical contracting costs and risk costs the participants incur and promotes their coordination in ways other than by deterring the buyer's jointly-unprofitable substitutions against the seller's input, and the decision to make the arrangement long-term will be substituted for either (1) a decision to do nothing to prevent the input-substitutions in question, (2) a decision by the input-producer to make an otherwise-unprofitable reduction in its per-unit price and increase in its lump-sum fee, (3) a decision to use endproduct royalties, or (4) a decision by the input producer to vertically integrate forward into final-good production.

In my judgment, taken as a class, each functional category of non-predatory long-term full-requirements contracts and long-term total-output-supply contracts is economically efficient, and it would not be TBLE for any antitrust-policy-enforcement authority to try to identify and prohibit the exceptions to this generalization. I will focus first on long-term provisions that are not part of complement-controlling meter-pricing-effectuating or input-substitution-preventing tie-ins and/or reciprocity agreements. If such long-term provisions are not substituted for vertical integration, I believe that such provisions will be economically efficient. I reach this conclusion because (1) on this analysis' assumptions, they are profitable, (2) the reduction in private mechanical contracting costs they yield will tend to be lower than the allocative gains they generate on that account, (3) the private coordination-benefits they yield the participants will tend to be lower than the associated economic-efficiency gains they generate to the extent that the coordination benefits are reductions in private operation-costs, and

(4) the private risk-cost gains they generate equal their allocative counterparts—that is, because by assumption the long-term provisions are profitable and analysis suggests that the distortions in their profits are negative.

When the long-term provisions are not components of tie-ins or reciprocity agreements that increase the private-cost-effectiveness of a participant's efforts to control the quality of the complements its customers combine with its product, to effectuate meter pricing, or to prevent jointly-unprofitable substitutions against an input it produces but are being substituted for vertical integration, it is more complicated to determine their economic efficiency and their economic efficiency is more questionable. There are at least 3 sets of related sources of difficulty and doubt.

The first set relates to the distortion in the conventional-transaction-cost effects of the substitution of the long-term provisions for vertical integration. Although I am confident that any private-transaction-cost-related benefits or costs the substitution of long-term clauses for vertical integration will generate will be deflated, it is not clear whether this substitution will yield the participants private-transaction-cost-related benefits or costs—will reduce or increase the private transaction costs the participants incur. Will (1) the private transaction cost of devising, negotiating, and enforcing the long-term provisions be higher or lower than (2)(A) the private transaction cost of identifying a suitable (M or A) co-participant, negotiating the (M or A), and using hierarchical control to influence the resulting firm's employers or (B) the private transaction cost of identifying an appropriate joint-venture participant and of running the joint venture in the parents' joint interest or (C) the private transaction cost of planning and executing the vertical internal growth and using hierarchical controls to influence the new operation's employees?

The second set of sources of difficulty and doubts relates to the financing of the vertical integration. If the vertical integration is financed externally, what will be the mechanical transaction cost of securing the external finance? Will the vertical integrator have to reckon with its efforts' to obtain external financing imposing costs on it because, to secure the external financing, it will have to reveal information about its operations or plans to possible external financers that may to its detriment sell or pass on the information to the vertical integrator's rivals? Will the vertically-integrating firm have to compensate its external financer to cover risk costs the financer bears because it is less-well-informed about the vertical-integration project than the integrator is? Will the external financer be able to obtain supernormal profits on its loan or investment? Regardless of whether the vertical integrator finances the integration externally or with retained earnings, will it have to forego other investments that would have yielded it supernormal profits if their execution would not require it to forego the at-least-normally-profitable vertical integration? What is the distortion in these various finance-related costs?

The third set of sources of difficulty and doubt relates to the various ways in which vertical integration can yield the integrator benefits and the distortions in the private benefits that vertical integration would yield the integrator in each of these ways. As Sect. 14.1 states, vertical integration can yield the integrator benefits in a large number of ways—in all the ways that horizontal (M&A)s can yield their participants profits other than by freeing them from each other's active competition and in a series of additional ways as well—not only, by enabling the resulting firm to use hierarchical controls rather than contract clauses, independent-contractor subsidies, sales-policies, etc. to secure certain objectives but also by creating a resulting firm that can take advantage of continuous-flow economies and conceal more-private-cost-effectively price-regulation violations, tax fraud, and contract fraud. Since the vertical integration that a firm's use of long-term contractual provisions might induce it to reject could yield it benefits in many ways that are unrelated to the functions that the provisions perform, a full analysis of the economic efficiency of long-term provisions that are substituted for vertical integration would have to take account of all the other functions that the foregone vertical integration would have performed and any distortion that would exist in the private benefits the vertical integration would have yielded the integrator by performing those functions.

Where does all this leave me? The analysis assumes that the substitution of the long-term provisions for the vertical integration that would be profitable but for the long-term provisions yields its participants profits. I am confident that the substitution of the long-term full-requirements or total-output-supply contracts that are not components of tying or reciprocity agreements for vertical integration will substantially reduce the non-financial and financial private transaction costs the parties incur and that this private benefit will be significantly deflated. I am confident that the substitution will reduce the extent to which the upstream and downstream actors coordinate their behavior and that the portion of the lost benefits that reflect increases in operation costs will be significantly deflated. I suspect that the substitution will not have much effect on the parties' risk costs and that any impact on their risk costs will not be distorted. Clearly, some but not all of the substitutions will impose losses on the parties by forfeiting the static cost-efficiencies the vertical integration would have yielded, especially when it would have yielded continuous-flow economies, and I am confident that any such losses will be deflated. I am certain that some but not all of the substitutions will impose losses on the parties by forfeiting the dynamic efficiencies that the forewent vertical integration would have generated, that the losses will be substantially inflated when the dynamic efficiencies the vertical integration would have generated would have caused the resulting firm to make a QV investment that would increase the relevant ARDEPPS' equilibrium-QV-investment quantity (though the likelihood of any such effect is enormously reduced by the fact that the relevant analysand is the impact of the choices of all members of a set of product-rivals to make the substitution in question), will be substantially deflated when the dynamic efficiencies the vertical integration would have generated would have caused the resulting firm to execute a PPR project that would have increased the relevant ARDEPPS' equilibrium-PPR quantity (but see the preceding parenthetical), but may not be distorted when the dynamic efficiencies would have caused the resulting firm to make a QV investment or execute a PPR project that deters a rival from making an equally-large QV investment or executing an equally-large PPR project that was less-profitable and presumably was less-economically-efficient. I doubt that it will be TBLE for an antitrust-policy-implementation authority to attempt to determine which of the preceding scenarios would result (much less to investigate whether the dynamic efficiencies all relevant firms' relevant substitutions would have generated would have reduced equilibrium investment in the relevant ARDEPPS by creating a situation in which two or more vertically-integrated firms would have confronted each other with critical natural-oligopolistic investment-disincentives when one would otherwise have made an investment). I suspect (or at least hope) that it will be TBLE to assume that the forgone vertical integrations would not have created resulting firms that engage in more contrived-oligopolistic conduct, more predatory conduct, and more tax and contract fraud or committed more price-regulation violations. I am disposed to support the contestable conclusion that all tolled the preceding points favor the conclusion that the negative distortion in the private benefits the relevant substitutions generate by reducing private transaction costs (by a larger amount) is bigger than any negative distortion in the (smaller-amount of) private losses the relevant substitutions generate by sacrificing the efficiencies the forgone vertical integration would have generated. But, of course, the accuracy of that conclusion depends not only on the relative magnitudes of the private benefits and private costs the substitutions in question would generate but also on the proportions of the private costs that are attributable to sacrificed static marginal-cost efficacies, static fixed-cost efficiencies, dynamic cost-efficiencies, static and dynamic product-improvements as well as on whether the dynamic efficiencies would increase, leave unchanged, or even decrease equilibrium investment in the relevant ARDEPPS. In any event, if I am right, the combination of the fact that the relevant substitutions are profitable and my "surmise" that their profitability would be deflated (that the deflation in the private benefits such substitutions yield will exceed the deflation in the private costs they generate) would justify the conclusion that across all instances such substitutions will be economically efficient. Although it might be TBLE for an antitrust-policy-implementation authority to do more-refined analyses that aim to identify subclasses of substitutions of this kind that would be economically inefficient with the view of prohibiting those that are, I doubt that it will be TBLE to make any such attempt. If it is any consolation, I am no more pleased than you are.

I turn next to long-term provisions in full-requirements tying or reciprocity agreements that function by deterring buyers from combining the seller's durable product with inferior complements when it is against the seller's and buyer's joint interest for the buyers to do so. Section 13.2.2.1 argued that—(implicitly) regardless of their duration—the profitable substitution of full-requirement tie-ins that perform this function for (1) decisions to do nothing to prevent buyers from making such "organizationally-unprofitable" decisions to use inferior complements or (2) decisions to prevent such complement-choices by placing buyers under a contractual obligation to use complements that possess specified appropriate attributes and enforcing that obligation are economically efficient—that it is TBLE to assume that the private benefits of deterring such inferior-complement uses are undistorted, that the substitution of the tie-ins for the inclusion and enforcement of clauses specifying the attributes that the complements that buyers use must possess will reduce transaction costs, that the associated transaction-cost savings will be deflated, and that any deflation in the private cost of drafting, negotiating, and enforcing the tie-in (relative to the zero cost of doing nothing) will almost always be lower than the profits yielded by choices to use full-requirements tie-ins to prevent buyers from using inferior complements. If this argument and its conclusion is correct, the decision to make the duration of the full-requirements provision match the durability of a durable tying product will also be economically efficient. For similar reasons, I also believe that it will be economically efficient for a producer to make a profitable substitution of a complement-quality-controlling long-term full-requirements contract for vertical integration when the tying product is durable.

Section 13.2.2.1 made an analogous argument for the economic efficiency—(again implicitly) regardless of their duration—of input-full-requirements provisions in reciprocity agreements through which a firm in its capacity as a buyer attempts to control the quality of the ingredients/machines a supplier (incorporates into)/(uses to produce) the product the former firm is purchasing from the latter. An analogous argument to the argument made in the preceding paragraph seems to me to justify the conclusion that when for good reasons the overall arrangement is long-term the inclusion of the long-term input-full-requirements provision in the reciprocity agreement will increase economic efficiency if it is substituted for a decision to do nothing to control the quality of the inputs the supplier uses, clauses that specify the attributes of the inputs the supplier must use, or vertical integration of the final-good buyer into its production.

Long-term provisions in tie-ins and reciprocity agreements that are designed to increase the private-cost-effectiveness of the seller's meter pricing could be substituted for (1) decisions to forego meter pricing (to sell outright for a lump-sum fee the durable machine, the right to use the production process, or the right to operate the differentiated, branded franchise), (2) decisions to use endproduct royalties or share-in-franchise-sales provisions, or (3) decisions to vertically integrate. Because for reasons that Sect. 13.2.2.1 explains, the economic efficiency of substituting meter pricing for outright sales of durable "products" is contestable, I am not sure whether long-term provisions in meter-pricing tie-ins or reciprocity agreements that critically affect their use are economically efficient. However, for analogous reasons to those that led me to conclude that profitable substitutions of complement-quality-controlling long-term full-requirements tie-ins for either required-complement-quality-attribute-specifying clauses or vertical integration are economically efficient, I think that profitable substitutions of long-term meter-pricing-effectuating full-requirements tie-ins or total-output-supply reciprocity agreements for endprodcut-royalty/share-of-total-franchise-sales clauses or vertical integration are economically efficient. Moreover, because I suspect that only a small percentage of meter-pricing-effectuating long-term full-requirements tie-ins or total-output-supply reciprocity agreements are substituted for decisions not to engage in meter pricing and doubt that it will be TBLE for antitrust-policy-enforcement authorities to try to identify those exemplars of such long-term provisions that are in essence substituted for the outright sale of the durable machine/production process/branded distribution franchise to which they relate, I suspect that the policy-salient conclusions are that long-term provisions in meter-pricing-effectuating tie-ins and reciprocity agreements are economically efficient and that it would be economically inefficient for government to prohibit and prevent such provisions either totally or selectively.

The final set of economic-efficiency-related issues relates to long-term full-requirements or total-output-supply contracts that are predatory. 5 points seem to me to be most salient. First, few if any long-term full-requirements or total-output-supply contracts are predatory. Second, those predatory exemplars of such contracts that seek to drive out existing investments are economically inefficient. Third, those predatory exemplars of such contracts that seek to prevent new PPR investments from being made in the ARDEPPS of practice are clearly economically inefficient. Fourth, the economic efficiency of those predatory exemplars of such contracts that deter a target from making a QV investment in the ARDEPPS of practice may depend on whether they reduce equilibrium QV investment in the ARDEPPS of practice: if they do, their economic efficiency may be contestable; if they do not—that is, if they result in the predator's making a QV investment that deters a rival from making an equally-large QV investment (particularly in what I take to be the usual case in which the predator's investment was inherently-less-profitable than the target's would have been), they will be economically inefficient. Fifth, although I do not think this case is practically important (because I believe few if any long-term contractual provisions are predatory), I am disposed to think that it will be third-best-economically-inefficient for an antitrust-policy-enforcement authority to try to increase economic efficiency by prohibiting and deterring individual or subclasses of long-term full-requirements or total-output-supply contractual provisions.

13.6.3 The Liberal-Moral-Rights-Violativeness of Long-Term Provisions in Full-Requirements Contracts or Total-Output-Supply Contracts and the Ability of the Government of a Liberal-Moral-Rights-Based Society to Secure Liberal Moral Rights by Responding Appropriately to Such Long-Term Provisions

Because, for reasons that Sect. 13.6.1 explained, I suspect that few if any long-term provisions in full-requirements or total-output-supply contracts are predatory, because only predatory exemplars of such provisions are liberal-moral-rights-violative, and because relevant parties may have a property-rights-related liberal-moral right that "their" firm be allowed to profit by using long-term full-requirements or total-output-supply contracts to secure objectives that such provisions can enable them to achieve, I suspect that, with rare and possibly no exception, the government of a liberal-moral-rights-based society will have no moral duty to prohibit the conclusion of long-term provisions in such contracts and may sometimes have a moral duty to allow firms to include such provisions in such contracts.

13.6.4 The Impact of the Inclusion of Long-Term Provisions in Full-Requirements and Total-Output-Supply Contracts on Total Utility and the Instantiation of Various Non-Utilitarian-Egalitarian Conceptions of the Moral Good and the Ability of the Government of a Liberal-Moral-Rights-Based Society to Instantiate Various Egalitarian Conceptions of the Moral Good by Responding Appropriately to the Inclusion of Such Provisions in Such Contracts

I will restrict myself to making 7 points. First, all or virtually all full-requirements and total-output-supply contracts that are not predatory are economically efficient. Second, virtually all long-term full-requirements contracts and total-output-supply contracts that are predatory are economically inefficient. Third, virtually no long-term full-requirements contract or total-output-supply contract is predatory. Fourth, a rule allowing all members of a set of product-rivals to enter into non-predatory full-requirements contracts and/or total-output-supply contracts is unlikely to increase poverty or material inequality—is unlikely to impose an equivalent-dollar loss on final consumers of the products covered by the rule in question because (1) most exemplars of such individual contracts will benefit the ultimate buyers they affect taken as a class by lowering their suppliers' marginal costs and/or preventing the buyers from making mistakes—indeed, the only individual contracts in this category that may impose an equivalent-dollar loss on ultimate consumers are non-predatory meter-pricing-facilitating long-term contracts that cause producers to substitute meter pricing for the outright sale for a lump-sum fee of their machines, the right to use the production processes they are selling, or the right to operate trademarked franchises they designed and promoted and few such contracts have such an effect, (2) the rule is unlikely to lessen the competition faced by the producers that use such contracts, and relatedly, (3) the rule is not likely to benefit the shareholders/creditors/managers/employees of the sellers that enter into such contracts. Fifth, virtually all non-predatory long-term full-requirements and total-output-supply contracts will increase total utility. Sixth, non-predatory long-term full-requirements and total-output-supply contracts will not tend to disserve the instantiation of non-utilitarian or mixed utilitarian/non-utilitarian conceptions of the moral good, and the government of any liberal-moral-rights-based society is unlikely to be able to instantiate any of the just-referenced conceptions of the moral good by attempting to identify those exemplars of such conduct that disserve such conceptions of the moral good and selectively deterring and prohibiting them. Seventh, given the rarity of predatory long-term full-requirements and total-output-supply contracts and the difficulty and allocative cost of identifying exemplars of such contracts that are predatory, it is unlikely that the government of a liberal-moral-rights-based society will be able to serve the instantiation of any morally-defensible egalitarian conception of the moral good by attempting to identify, prohibit, and deter those exemplars of such contracts that are predatory.

Notes

1. The claim the footnoted sentence in the text makes will not be correct if the seller is not a perfect competitor and faces a horizontal demand curve that (1) is kinked at some output, (2) is higher than the seller's marginal-cost curve at the output at which it is kinked, and (3) is associated with a marginal-revenue curve that drops below the seller's marginal-cost curve at the output at which the demand curve for the seller's product is kinked.
2. In these terms, the per-unit price that is more profitable than any alternative per-unit price is the per-unit price that strikes the most profitable trade-off between destroying transaction surplus and allowing buyer surplus to escape.
3. A seller can prevent arbitrage in three privately-costly ways: (1) by including clauses in written contracts of sale prohibiting the buyer from cross-selling and enforcing those prohibition legally, (2) by communicating its intention to stop supplying buyers that engage in arbitrage, investigating whether buyers have engaged in cross-selling, and cutting off buyers it has determined have engaged in arbitrage, and (3) in some rare cases, by altering the product it provides each buyer in a way that critically reduces its attractiveness to other buyers without critically reducing its attractiveness to the buyer in question.
4. Admittedly, when the seller is smaller than the buyer (for example, when the seller is an orange grower and the buyer is a large national chain of grocery stores), the seller may be more risk-averse than the buyer, and the shift from single pricing to at least the third variant of perfect price discrimination I distinguish may raise the seller's certainty-equivalent profits by reducing the sum of its and the buyer's risk costs.
5. Of course, when the buyer overestimates its weighted-average-expected-quantity-demand for the seller's product at the seller's transaction-surplus-maximizing price, this variant of perfect price discrimination will on this account tend to yield the seller higher profits than single pricing would.
6. Admittedly, the seller may be able to reduce these demand-increasing-expenditure-related losses by subsidizing the buyer's demand-increasing expenditures, increasing its own local or national media advertizing expenditures, and/or contractually obligating the buyer to engage in specified quantities and qualities of in-store promotions and to allocate to its products specified quantities and qualities of shelf-space, but all these seller-responses are costly.
7. This description ignores the fact that in most situations sellers that use these types of tie-ins will find it profitable to reduce the lump-sum fee they charge the buyer and increase the amount of buyer surplus they remove by charging the buyer supra-marginal-cost per-unit prices. The text will also ignore the fact that, when the buyer has bargaining power, it may be able to obtain part of the joint gain this type of tie-in generates for the seller and buyer "combined" by bargaining for a reduction in the lump-sum fee it must pay.
8. For a diagrammatic demonstration of these claims, see Markovits (2014b) at pp. 267–272.
9. For a diagrammatic illustration of the text's argument, see *id*. at 287–300.

10. For a diagrammatic illustration of the text's argument, see *id*. at 300–305.
11. For an analysis of this possibility, see Markovits (2014b) at pp. 314–320 and p. 303.
12. This list ignores possible promotional-pricing and learning-by-doing benefits price discrimination may yield its practitioner in part because conventional price discrimination will yield such benefits primarily by increasing its practitioner's unit output and sales and conventional price discrimination can either increase or decrease its practitioner's unit sales.
13. As the following text reveals, I am drawing a non-critical distinction between tie-ins and reciprocity agreements that deserve to be called "pricing-techniques" and tie-ins and reciprocity agreements that increase the cost-effectiveness of a pricing-technique.
14. Such tie-ins can increase the cost-effectiveness of X's efforts to control the quality of the complements that its customers Y combine with its product at the same time that it increases the cost-effectiveness of X's meter pricing.
15. See, e.g., Carlton and Waldman (2002), Choi and Stefandis (2001), Whinston (1990), Farrell and Saloner (1986), and Ordover et al., (1985).
16. For detailed analyses of systems rivalry, see Markovits (2014a) at pp. 694–721.
17. See *inter alia* the titles of the articles referenced in note 15 and cited fully in the References entry in this chapter.
18. The preceding discussion implicitly assumes that reciprocity agreements cannot be used to increase the profitability of inter-buyer price discrimination by reducing the market-research, personnel-training, and checkout-counter sale-processing cost of practicing such discrimination. For a brief discussion of the conditions under which reciprocity agreements could perform this function and the reasons why those conditions are unlikely to be fulfilled, see Markovits, (2014b) at p. 417.
19. If, as I have been assuming, meter-pricing reciprocity agreements place the buyer of the machine or production process they involve under a legal obligation to supply its total output of the good it uses the machine or production process to produce for a price $\$\alpha$ below the price the final-good producer would otherwise charge for each unit of the final good it produced of its product, the final-good producer's marginal-revenue curve for its product under the reciprocity agreement would be parallel to but $\$\alpha$ lower than the marginal-revenue curve it would face on its product if it purchased the machine/production process for a lump-sum fee.
20. A producer will find it profitable to warrantee the performance of its product when its customers are more risk-averse than it is and when the risk that the products that its individual customers purchase will perform worse-than-expected is greater than the risk that all units of all the products the producer produces will perform worse-than-expected.

References

Carlton, D. W., & Waldman, M. (2002). The strategic use of tying to preserve and create market power in evolving industries. *Rand Journal of Economics, 33*, 194–220.

Choi, J. P., & Stefanadis, C. (2001). Tying, investment, and the dynamic leverage theory. *Rand Journal of Economics, 32*, 52–71.

Farrell, J., & Saloner, G. (1986). Installed base and compatibility: Innovation, product preannouncements, and predation. *American Economic Review, 76*, 940–955.

Markovits, R. (2014a). *Economics and the interpretation and application of U.S. and E.U. antitrust law* Vol. I *Basic concepts and economics-based analyses of oligopolistic and predatory conduct.* Springer.

Markovits, R. (2014b). *Economics and the interpretation and application of U.S. and E.U. antitrust law* Vol. II *Economics-based legal analyses of mergers, vertical practices, and joint ventures.* Springer.

Ordover, J., Sykes, A. O., & Willig, R. D. (1985). Nonprice anticompetitive behavior by dominant firms toward producers of complementary products. In F. M. Fisher, (Ed.) *Antitrust and regulation: Essays in memory of John J. McGowen* (pp. 115–130). MIT Press.

Whinston, M. D. (1990). Tying, foreclosure, and exclusion. *American Economic Review, 80*, 837–859.

References

Vertical Mergers and Acquisitions 14

Mergers and acquisitions are vertical when their participants are in a supplier-supplied relationship to each other. For example, a producer of aluminum can engage in a vertical (M or A) with a producer of aluminum pots and pans or a producer of aluminum pots and pans can engage in a vertical (M or A) with a distributor of pots and pans (and other kitchenware).

This chapter has the same structure as Chaps. 12 and 11, which focus respectively on conglomerate and horizontal (M&A)s. Section 14.1 discusses the various ways in which vertical (M&A)s can yield their participants profits and the determinants of the amount of profits a vertical (M or A) yields its participants in each of these ways. Section 14.2 analyzes the economic efficiency of vertical (M&A)s and the ability of the government of a liberal-moral-rights-based society to increase economic efficiency by responding appropriately to vertical (M&A)s. Section 14.3 analyzes the conditions under which a vertical (M or A) will be liberal-moral-rights-violative and the ability of a liberal-moral-rights-constrained government to secure liberal moral rights by responding appropriately to vertical (M&A)s. And Section 14.4 analyzes the impact of vertical (M&A)s on the instantiation of the utilitarian and other egalitarian conceptions of the moral good and the ability of a liberal-moral-rights-constrained government to secure the instantiation of any egalitarian conception of the moral good by responding appropriately to vertical (M&A)s.

In one important respect, this chapter's analyses of vertical (M&A)s resemble their Chap. 12 conglomerate-merger-focused counterparts more than their Chap. 11 horizontal-(M&A) counterparts. To save space and avoid repetition, this chapter focuses on the differences between the relevant vertical-(M&A) analyses and their horizontal-(M&A) counterparts.

R. S. Markovits, *Welfare Economics and Antitrust Policy—Vol. II*,
https://doi.org/10.1007/978-3-030-96482-5_14

14.1 The Differences Between the Ways in Which Vertical (M&A)s and Horizontal (M&A)s Can Yield Their Participants Profits

Vertical (M&A)s can yield their participants profits in most of the ways in which horizontal (M&A)s can do so—for example, (1) by generating the same sorts of static and dynamic efficiencies that horizontal (M&A)s can generate, (2) by enabling one participant to take advantage of a tax-loss that the other participant could not use, (3) by enabling one participant to liquidate his or her assets and escape the burdens of management, (4) by creating a resulting firm that is better-placed to engage in contrived-oligopolistic[1] and predatory pricing[2] (especially when the resulting firm faces one or more rivals that individually operate in at least one market of each participant but in any event by creating a resulting firm that is better-placed to take advantage of organizational economies of scale in building and maintaining a reputation for engaging in strategic conduct), (5) by creating a resulting firm that, because of its enhanced prominence, is better able to successfully initiate (A) a series of price-announcements whose sequential timing increases the seller's HNOP arrays and/or (B) a series of premature price-announcements and related behaviors that enable the relevant sellers to obtain OMs naturally, (6) by reducing the investment competition and derivatively the price competition one participant faces by "eliminating as an independent entity" one participant that was an effective potential competitor of the other, etc. However, there are several differences in the ways in which vertical and horizontal (M&A)s can yield their participants profits. In the one direction, unlike horizontal (M&A)s, vertical (M&A)s cannot yield their participants profits by freeing them from each other's extant price competition (though it can have a related effect by preventing one participant from entering the other's ARDEPPS when the participants are respectively an established firm and an effective potential entrant into the established firm's ARDEPPS). In the other direction, vertical (M&A)s can yield their participants profits in at least 5 ways in which horizontal (M&A)s cannot:

(1) as Chap. 13 suggested, by creating a resulting company that realizes more profits than its non-vertically-integrated components would realize because the integrated firm does not have to worry about the fact that its charging a downstream final-product manufacturing/distribution division a marginal-cost price for (a non-final-product input)/(a final good) will result in the downstream division's books showing that it realized profits whereas the non-integrated firm would have to take steps (e.g., charge franchise fees) to internalize any buyer surplus its sales to an independent downstream firm generated;
(2) as Chap. 13 suggested, in some cases, by creating a resulting firm that can use hierarchical controls to induce its downstream division's employees to make decisions that are in the overall organization's interest that are more privately-cost-effective than the contractual clauses, downstream-firm

subsidies, upstream-firm downstream actions, and sales-policies that a non-integrated upstream firm would have to use to induce downstream independent firms to act in their and its joint interest,

(3) in some situations—for example, when the upstream company produces molten metal and the downstream company produces final goods or more-finished inputs with that metal, by creating a vertically-integrated firm that can take advantage of continuous-flow economies,

(4) when the maximum price that can be charged by an upstream business is regulated but the maximum price that can be charged by the downstream business is not regulated, when different tax rates are applied to the profits yielded by the members of a related pair of upstream and downstream businesses, or when different commission-rates or royalty-rates apply to the revenues generated by the members of a related pair of upstream and downstream businesses, by creating a resulting firm that can better conceal its rate-regulation violations, tax frauds, or contract frauds than the relevant participant could, and

(5) when to secure a mutually-profitable decision from an input-supplier (including a financier) or a distributor a producer would have to reveal information to that party about its operations or plans that the information-recipient could sell to a rival of the information supplier, by creating a resulting firm that can secure the supply of the input that the independent supplier could supply without running the risk that an independent supplier would sell relevant information to a rival of the "buyer"—a benefit that will be reduced if the country in question has applicable effective Codes of Ethics or contract-law doctrines (such as the *culpa in contrahendo* civil-law doctrine or conceivably but probably not the common-law promissory-estoppel doctrine) that deter the illicit sale or even communication of such information.

Before closing this section, I want to comment on the importance of the first item in the preceding list as well as on the likelihood that vertical (M&A)s will yield their participants profits by creating a resulting company that can profit by predatorily refusing to distribute one or more rivals' products through its downstream distributive division (which, pre-[M or A], was independently owned) or by predatorily refusing to supply a target with an input produced by an input-production division (which, pre-[M or A], was independently owned). In my experience, many U.S. economists who think that vertical (M&A)s should be permitted exaggerate the extent to which such (M&A)s will yield reductions in final-product prices (which is connected to the extent to which they will yield their participants profits by creating a resulting firm that does not have to be concerned with any tendency that its charging a marginal-cost per-unit price for the upstream product would have had prior to the [M or A] to yield the relevant downstream buyer profits [that does not have to worry about the upstream division's charging the downstream division a shadow price for the upstream division's product equal to the upstream division's marginal cost's resulting in a conventionally-kept set of downstream-division books' showing that the downstream division had generated substantial profits]). These economists make this error (which has less bearing on the actual desirability of the [M &A]s in question than they perceive it to have) because they are implicitly assuming that a non-vertically-integrated upstream company would engage in single pricing when selling its product to the non-vertically-integrated downstream company. To the extent that that is not the case, the per-unit price the non-vertically-integrated upstream company would charge the non-vertically-integrated downstream company will be lower (will be closer to if not equal to the upstream company's marginal cost) and the vertical (M&A)s will have less of a tendency to reduce the per-unit prices final consumers must pay for the goods the integrated firms produce.

In the other direction, I think that those U.S. economists and economics-conversant law professors who believe that it would be desirable to prohibit many if not most vertical (M&A)s (and who also believe that many if not most such [M&A]s violate the Clayton and Sherman Acts) vastly exaggerate the frequency with which such (M&A)s will create resulting companies that find it possible and profitable to drive extant rival investments out or to deter new investments by extant and potential competitors by refusing to make otherwise-profitable sales of distributive services or inputs that the vertically-integrated concern "produces." As I indicated several times in Chap. 13 as well as in Chapter 10, such refusals to deal are unlikely to be successful (such predation is therefore unlikely to be practiced) both because—to be successful—the refuser or refusers would have to lock up enough of the supply of the relevant "goods" or services to prevent their target's being able to satisfy its needs with unlocked-up goods or services and because any target whose investment's or investments' profitability would otherwise be endangered by such predatory refusals to deal will frequently be able to defend itself by engaging in vertical integration through internal growth, an (M or A), or a joint venture or by inducing an independent distributor or input-supplier to enter.

14.2 The Economic Efficiency of (Profitable) Vertical (M&A)s and the Ability of the Liberal-Moral-Rights-Constrained Government of a Liberal-Moral-Rights-Based Society to Increase Economic Efficiency by Responding Appropriately to Vertical (M&A)s

I believe that the vast majority of profitable vertical (M&A)s are economically efficient and that the most-allocatively-efficient way for a liberal-moral-rights-constrained government to respond to any vertical (M&A) is to allow it unless the State or a private plaintiff can establish that, more probably than not, its participants' *ex ante* perception that it was at least normally profitable was critically positively affected by the perpetrator's *ex ante* belief that the (M or A) would or might contribute to its participants' profits by creating a resulting firm that profited more from contrived-oligopolistic pricing, causing itself and its across-the-board-pricing rivals to announce their prices in a sequence that increases their HNOP array, engaging in natural-oligopolistic pricing, from predation, price-regulation violations, and tax and/or contract fraud than the participants would have done as separate entities. I believe that it will sometimes be TBLE for the government of a liberal-moral-rights-based society (1) to investigate whether the participants in a vertical (M or A) have profited in one or more of the just-listed ways and whether the participants' *ex ante* expectation that the (M or A) in question would be at least normally profitable was critically positively affected by their belief that it would enable them to profit in one or more of these ways and (2) to prohibit those vertical (M&A)s whose expected or actual at-least-normal profitability was positively and critically affected by its having had one or more of these effects. I acknowledge that this set of conclusions does not reflect the "facts" that (1) vertical (M&A)s that increase the COMs and/or NOMs of a participant that is in the business of doing production-process research may increase economic efficiency on that account and (2) vertical (M&A)s that decrease the investment-competition faced by a participant whose investments are QV investments (say, because one participant was an effective potential competitor of the other) may increase economic efficiency on that account. However, I doubt that these two possibilities will critically affect the economic efficiency of a profitable vertical (M or A) to whose economic efficiency one is or both are relevant sufficiently often for it to be TBLE for an antitrust-policy-implementation authority to consider them. If I am wrong, it will be TBLE to alter the policy to instruct the enforcement-authority to take these possibilities into account (at least when there are sufficient grounds to believe that they are sufficiently likely to be critical).

I will now list the facts or considerations that are relevant to the economic efficiency of vertical (M&A)s and explain why I think it will be TBLE for a government to assume they are economically efficient. At least the following 20 assumptions, relationships, or factual claims are relevant:

(1) by assumption, the vertical (M&A)s on whose economic efficiency I am now focusing are profitable;
(2) a profitable vertical (M&A) will be economically efficient unless the profits it yields are inflated and the inflation in the profits it yields equals or exceeds the profits it yields;
(3) vertical (M&A)s can generate static-marginal-cost efficiencies, static-fixed-cost efficiencies, and dynamic efficiencies: (A) admittedly, vertical (M&A)s are less likely to generate standard production and distribution economies-of-scale-related efficiencies (except to the extent that the vertically-integrated firm's unit output is higher than the non-vertically-integrated firm's unit output would have been), but (B) like horizontal (M&A)S, vertical (M&A)s can generate operating efficiencies by creating a resulting firm that can take advantage of more general organizational economies of scale, (C) unlike horizontal (M&A)s, vertical (M&A)s can generate operating efficiencies by creating a resulting firm that can use hierarchical controls when the non-vertically-integrated upstream participant would have had to rely on contract clauses, independent-distributor subsidies, or sales-policies, and (D) unlike horizontal (M&A)s, vertical (M&A)s can generate static and dynamic

marginal-cost efficiencies by creating a resulting firm that can take advantage of continuous-flow economies;

(4) the profits a vertical (M or A) (or any other choice) yields a perpetrator by lowering its costs will tend to be deflated;

(5) vertical (M&A)s will also tend to increase their participants' profits by increasing and improving the shelf-space allocations to the resulting company's products, the media advertizing of its products, the in-store promotional displays of its products, the salesmanship-efforts devoted to its products, and the product-warrantees the resulting-company supplies relative to the counterparts that would have been allocated/provided if the (M or A) had not been executed;

(6) if one assumes that the government of the relevant society has prevented companies from providing inaccurate or misleading information about its own products or the products of its rivals, it will probably be TBLE to assume that the benefits that vertical (M or A)s yield their participants by increasing the allocations, expenditures, and efforts referenced in Item (5) in this list are undistorted;

(7) vertical (M&A)s will tend to decrease their participants' profits to the extent that the owners of the independent distributorships for which the vertically-integrated firm substitutes its own distributive divisions place a positive dollar value on "being their own bosses" and to the extent that for other reasons the owners of the independent distributorships would be better "hires" for the independent upstream participants in the vertical (M or A) than the individuals that would be hired in their stead by the vertically-integrated firm would be;

(8) the loss the participants in the vertical (M or A) would sustain because of the independent distributors' valuing being their own losses will not be distorted, but any loss they sustain because the employees they hire to replace the independent-distributorship owners obtain more surplus from their employment-contracts than the independent distributors would have secured from their franchise-agreements—a difference whose existence I recognize is questionable—will be 100 per cent inflated;

(9) vertical (M&A)s can also yield their participants profits by improving the quality of their participants' products and/or the quality of their participants' products' performance (vertical [M&A]s can increase the quality of a final-product-producer participant's product by increasing the quality of the inputs used to produce the final product and can increase the quality of the performance of a participant's product without changing the quality of the product by increasing the product-producer's ability to prevent its product's users from combining it with inferior complements);

(10) I suspect that it will be TBLE to assume that any profits a vertical (M or A) yields its participants by improving the quality of the final product the integrated firm produces or the quality of that product's performance are not distorted;

(11) vertical (M&A)s whose upstream participant would not otherwise have used contractual clauses, downstream-participant subsidies, and/or sales-policies to induce the downstream participant to make choices that are jointly profitable for the upstream and downstream participant will clearly increase the amount of private transaction costs the participants incur because it will be private-transaction-costly for the (M or A) participants to identify each other, negotiate their transaction, obtain external financing for any related acquisition (if the acquirer needs to finance the acquisition externally), and use the hierarchical controls it will employ to induce its downstream employees to make choices that maximize the integrated company's profits;

(12) although the following "claim" is a claim against interest (i.e., disfavors my ultimate economic-efficiency conclusions) and is contestable, I also suspect that profitable vertical (M&A)s executed by an upstream participant that would otherwise have used contractual clauses, distributor-subsidies, and sales-policies to induce the downstream participants to act in their and its joint interest will tend to increase the private transaction costs the participants incur;

(13) any "cost" or loss a vertical (M or A) imposes on its participants by increasing the private transaction costs they incur will be deflated;

(14) I suspect that it will be TBLE to assume that there is no distortion in any loss that a participant in an externally-financed vertical acquisition incurs because, to obtain the financing, it had to reveal information about its operations and plans to one or more possible external financers that would sell it or pass it on (in exchange for goodwill or specific transactions) to a competitor of the information-provider;

(15) I assume that there is no distortion in the private costs a vertical acquirer that externally finances its acquisition incurs because the external financer is less-well-informed about the acquirer's prospects than the acquirer is (because the financer's normal rate-of-return on its loan to the acquirer is increased by the financer's relative lack of knowledge);

(16) if I assume that there is no distortion in the private opportunity cost to an external financer of financing a vertical integrator's acquisition, any costs a vertical integrator incurs because it finances its acquisition externally and its external financer obtains supernormal profits on the transaction will be 100 per cent inflated;

(17) I assume there is no distortion in the benefits a vertical (M or A) yields its participants by reducing the sum of the risk costs they bear;

(18) I assume that it will be TBLE to assume that any profits that a vertical (M or A) yields its participants by creating a resulting firm that profits more by increasing its and its rivals across-the-board-HNOP arrays by altering the sequence in which they announce and commit themselves to prices, by increasing its and its rivals NOMs by increasing their OCAs, or by orchestrating a series of premature price-announcements and related acts that lock themselves into their announced prices, by engaging in contrived-oligopolistic conduct, and engaging in predatory behavior are more than 100

per cent inflated (though I admit that it might be TBLE for an antitrust-policy-implementation authority to consider the possibility that contrived-oligopolistic investment-restrictions and predatory conduct that decreases equilibrium investment in any ARDEPPS of practice whose investments are QV investments may increase economic efficiency on this account);

(19) I assume that it will be TBLE to assume that there is no distortion in any loss any vertical (M or A) imposes on its participants by increasing the contrived-oligopolistic retaliation or predation to which they are subjected by creating a resulting firm whose defenses are more-widely-spread than the individual participants' defenses would have been (by enabling any rival of the resulting firm to retaliate against it or target it for predation by "attacking" either or both participants' operations); and

(20) if the vertical integrator's decision to participate in a vertical merger or, more likely, a vertical acquisition causes it not to make an alternative investment, the distortion in the associated opportunity cost to it of participating in the vertical (M or A) whose economic efficiency is at issue (yes, I am assuming that such opportunity costs are taken into consideration when calculating the profits yielded by the vertical [M or A] under consideration) equals the distortion in the profits that would have been yielded by the foregone investment.

Like you, I would be more pleased if this list of observations yielded a clear conclusion about the economic efficiency of all profitable vertical (M&A)s. I admit that it does not—that the economic efficacy of any given profitable vertical (M or A) depends *inter alia* on (1) the profits it yields its participants, (2) the ratio of the non-transaction-cost private-cost efficiencies it generates to the amount by which it raises the private transaction costs the participants incur, (3) any difference that, contrary to my suspicions, exist in the percentage-deflation in the non-transaction-cost private-cost-efficiency-generated benefits the (M or A) confers on its participants and the percentage-deflation in the private-transaction-cost-increase-generated losses the (M or A) imposes on its participants, (4) the relative extents to which the (M or A) increases the amount of accurate information and the amount of inaccurate or misleading information conveyed to relevant buyers, (5) the extent to which a vertical (M or A) consummated by an across-the-board pricer increases the HNOP array in an ARDEPPS by creating a resulting firm that is better able to influence the order in which the ARDEPPS' sellers announce and lock themselves into their prices and the amount of contrived-oligopolistic, natural-oligopolistic, and predatory conduct in which the participants (and their rivals) engage, and (6) the extent to which the vertical (M or A) increases the amount of maximum-price-regulation violations and tax and contract fraud in which its participants engage.

The conclusions I articulated at the beginning of this section reflect assumptions that (1) most vertical (M&A)s that are consummated (that are profitable) yield their participants substantial profits, (2) the substantial profitability of most profitable vertical (M&A)s primarily reflects the fact that the non-transaction-cost efficiency-generated benefits they confer on their participants exceed the increase-in-conventional-transaction-cost-generated private costs they impose on their participants, (3) it is TBLE to assume that the percentage-deflations in the private benefits and costs just referenced are the same, (4) the relevant societies' consumer-protection and tort law have deterred the dissemination of almost all inaccurate or misleading product-information, (5) the antitrust-policy regime of which the vertical-(M&A) policy is a component has substantially reduced (though admittedly not eliminated) contrived-oligopolistic, natural-oligopolistic, and predatory conduct and has prevented across-the-board pricers from increasing their and their rivals HNOPs by influencing the order in which they and their rivals announce their prices—partly for this reason, vertical (M&A)s are unlikely to increase the incidence of such conduct, (6) the relevant society's price-regulation policies, tax-law-enforcement policies, and contract law have deterred almost all price-regulation violations and tax and contract frauds—partly for this reason, vertical (M&A)s are unlikely to increase the incidence of such conduct, and (7) although it may be TBLE to investigate the accuracy of the above assumptions as they relate to particular individual or subclasses of vertical (M&A)s, it will usually not be TBLE to do so, given the allocative cost of executing and publicly financing the relevant research and any suit against the proposed or consummated vertical (M or A) or (M or A)s in question. I acknowledge that assumptions (4)–(6) in this list are optimistic.

Obviously, if I am wrong, it will be TBLE more often than I believe for antitrust-policy-implementation authorities to investigate the facts that affect the economic efficiency of a vertical (M or A) and, at least sometimes, to bring suits against parties that have proposed or consummated such an (M or A).

14.3 The Liberal-Moral-Rights-Violativeness of Vertical (M&A)s and the Ability of the Government of a Liberal-Moral-Rights-Based Society to Secure Liberal Moral Rights by Responding Appropriately to Vertical (M&A)s

No surprises. A vertical (M or A) will be liberal-moral-rights-violative if and only if (1) one or both is its participants' *ex ante* perception that the (M or A) would be at least normally profitable was critically, positively affected by its/their perception that it would or might yield it/them profits by increasing the profits it/they realized post-(M or A) by engaging in conduct that is liberal-moral-rights-violative (contrived-oligopolistic conduct, [possibly] natural-oligopolistic pricing, predatory conduct, [possibly] arranging for it/them and its/their rivals to announce their prices in a sequence that will increase their HNOP array if they implement those price-announcements, price-regulation violations, tax and/or contract fraud) and/or (2) one or both participants believed that the (M or A) would provide them with an opportunity to earn more profits in one or more liberal-moral-rights-violative ways and intended *ex ante* to take advantage of that opportunity. I think that few vertical (M or A)s are liberal-moral-rights-violative. The government of a liberal-moral-rights-based society is morally obligated to prohibit and deter liberal-moral-rights-violative vertical (M&A)s to the extent that it can do so without disserving the instantiation of the liberal conception of justice all tolled. It is possible that liberalism imposes a moral duty on such a government not to prohibit profitable vertical (M&A)s that are not liberal-moral-rights-violative, but although liberalism may value the institution of private property not only for economic-efficiency-related utilitarian reasons but also because the legal protection of property interests may provide property-owners with some protection against the government or private actors' violating their autonomy interests, I hesitate to endorse any such conclusion (which would certainly not imply the liberal impermissibility of redistributive tax policies designed to give moral-rights bearers resources and experiences that significantly increase their opportunity to lead a life of moral integrity or that would effectuate a morally-defensible conception of the moral good).

14.4 The Impact of Profitable Vertical (M&A)s on the Instantiation of the Utilitarian and Other Pure or Mixed Egalitarian Conceptions of the Moral Good and the Ability of a Liberal-Moral-Rights-Constrained Government to Instantiate These Conceptions of the Moral Good by Responding Appropriately to Profitable Vertical (M&A)s

In a liberal-moral-rights-based society, the impact of individual or subsets of vertical (M&A)s on the moral good is of policy-interest only if the (M or A)s in question are not liberal-moral-rights-violative because the government of any such society is morally obligated to prohibit all liberal-moral-rights-violative vertical (M&A)s regardless of whether they promote a morally-defensible conception of the moral good. The relevant analysands are therefore (1) the impact on the referenced egalitarian conceptions of the moral good of the profitable, non-liberal-moral-rights-violative vertical (M&A)s that would be executed by those members of a set of product-rivals that would choose to engage in them if it were lawful for them to do so and (2) the ability of a liberal-moral-rights-constrained government to instantiate those conceptions of the moral good by promulgating and enforcing policies that relate to the legality of the profitable, non-liberal-moral-rights-violative vertical (M&A)s that some or all of the members of sets of product-rivals would consummate if it were lawful or them to do so.

5 points are salient. First, for reasons that Sect. 14.2 articulated, I believe that the non-liberal-moral-rights-violative vertical (M&A)s that would be consummated if such vertical (M&A)s were permitted would increase economic

efficiency. Second, although I have not even attempted to execute the extremely-complicated analysis one would have to execute to determine whether such a permissive vertical-(M&A) policy would increase or decrease material inequality, I am disposed to think that the profitable, non-liberal-moral-rights-violative vertical (M&A)s that any set of product-rivals will execute if the law permitted them to do so will usually decrease material inequality and poverty by benefiting relevant consumers by creating firms with lower marginal costs that produce better products and convey more useful product-information to prospective buyers without reducing price or investment competition and therefore without having much of an effect on the participant firms' shareholders/creditors/managers/employees (since the relevant set of vertical [M&A]s will increase the organizational proficiency of each member of any relevant set of rivals that consummates such an [M or A] and will therefore not tend to increase the profits the relevant firms realize). Third, the combination of the first two points implies that a policy of allowing all non-liberal-moral-rights-violative vertical (M&A)s would increase total utility if the antitrust-policy-implementation authorities could determine sufficiently accurately at sufficiently low allocative cost whether particular individual or subclasses of vertical (M or A)s were liberal-moral-rights-violative. Fourth, at least in combination with an assumption that taken as classes the customers of any set of product-rivals that might want to consummate non-liberal-moral-rights-violative vertical (M or A)s are poorer than the average member of the society in question, the distributive-impact conclusions made in Point (2) imply that a policy of allowing all non-liberal-moral-rights-violative vertical (M&A)s would serve the instantiation of all non-purely-utilitarian egalitarian conceptions of the moral good. Fifth, I think that from the perspectives of both the utilitarian and the other egalitarian conceptions of the moral good it will be third-best-morally-desirable for the government of a liberal-moral-rights-based society that has already devoted the amount of resources its commitment to liberalism requires it to devote to determining whether a vertical (M or A) or subset of vertical (M or A)s is/are liberal-moral-rights-violative to permit all such (M&A)s it has concluded are not liberal-moral-rights-violative.

Notes

1. For a fuller account, see Markovits (2016) at 478–480.
2. For a fuller account, see *id.* at 479–480.

Reference

Markovits, R. (2014). *Economics and the interpretation and application of U.S. and E.U. antitrust law* Vol. II *Economics-based legal analyses of mergers, vertical practices, and joint ventures.* Springer.

Joint Ventures (and Functionally-Analogous Collaborative Arrangements) 15

A joint venture is a business entity created by two or more other business entities (its "parents") to engage in one or more business activities. For simplicity, this chapter will assume that the joint venture is created by two parents. Joint ventures can be horizontal, conglomerate, or vertical, depending on the relationship between the business activity in which the joint venture engages and the business activity in which its parents engage. Thus, a joint venture created by two parents that manufacture automobiles to produce a particular type of car (say, a subcompact) that will compete with the parents' other cars is horizontal. A joint venture created by two parents that manufacture cars to produce kitchen appliances is conglomerate. And a joint venture created by two parents that manufacture cars to produce fabrics and paints they will use to upholster and paint their automobiles is vertical.

Two or more business entities can also participate in a collaborative arrangement that does not involve the creation of another legal entity (a joint venture) that performs one or more functions that a joint venture could perform. For example, rather than creating a vertical production-process-research and/or product-research joint venture, two or more firms may enter into a patent-pool agreement in which they agree to give each other free access to their respective patents (sometimes while limiting the ability of their mutual or respective rivals to gain access to the pool) or two or more newspapers (which may not be significantly competitive with each other because they are published in different locations and contain a lot of local news [in addition to national and foreign news]) may agree to allow each other to publish the stories they, respectively, produce (perhaps while limiting the ability of other newspapers [especially those that are significantly competitive with an initial participant] to join the arrangement at all or to join it on terms that do not place the others at a disadvantage or at an unjustifiable disadvantage).

This chapter focuses on joint ventures. Its analyses apply *mutatis mutandis* to functionally-analogous collaborative arrangements that do not involve the

R. S. Markovits, *Welfare Economics and Antitrust Policy—Vol. II*,
https://doi.org/10.1007/978-3-030-96482-5_15

creation of a separate business entity (a joint venture). This chapter has four sections. Section 15.1 explains the functions of joint ventures. Section 15.2 analyzes the economic efficiency of joint ventures and the ability of a liberal-moral-rights-constrained government to increase economic efficiency by responding appropriately to joint ventures. Section 15.3 examines the liberal-moral-rights-violativeness of joint ventures and any restrictive provisions a joint-venture agreement contains and the ability of government to secure liberal moral rights by responding appropriately to joint ventures and such restrictive provisions. And Sect. 15.4 analyzes the impact of joint ventures and any restrictive provisions a joint-venture agreement contains on total utility, the instantiation of various pure non-utilitarian-egalitarian conceptions of the moral good, and various mixed egalitarian conceptions of the moral good and the ability of a liberal-moral-rights-constrained government to serve the instantiation of these various egalitarian conceptions of the moral good by responding appropriately to joint ventures.

All of the preceding analyses will be made more complicated by three related facts. First, many if not most joint-venture agreements contain clauses that prohibit the joint venture from entering the parents' ARDEPPSes, that prohibit the parents from entering the joint venture's ARDEPPSes, and/or that prohibit the parents from entering each other's ARDEPPSes. Second, these restrictions (1) can increase the economic efficiency of the joint venture's operations by causing the parents to provide the joint venture with information and personnel that will increase the economic efficiency of the joint venture's operations by assuring each parent that the information and personnel it provides the joint venture will not be used by the joint venture or the other parent to compete more effectively against the (information/personnel)-providing parent, (2) can reduce competition (indeed, can be motivated by specific anticompetitive intent) by resulting in one joint-venture investment's being substituted for two parental investments (an outcome that can be generated by each parent's partial ownership of the joint venture even if the joint-venture agreement does not prohibit the parents from entering the joint venture's ARDEPPSes), and/or by deterring one or both parents from entering the other's ARDEPPSes when their failure to make the investments in question does not lead anyone else to invest or to make an investment that is as economically efficient and as competitive with the other parent's investment as the deterred investment would have been—outcomes that are clearly relevant to the joint venture's economic efficiency, liberal moral permissibility, and impact on the instantiation of any egalitarian conception of the moral good, or (3) can both increase the economic-efficiency proficiency of the joint venture's operation and lessen competition. Third, there is no easy or allocatively-cheap way to determine whether or the extent to which the restrictive clauses that a particular joint-venture agreement contains increase the economic-efficiency proficiency of the joint venture's operations and/or decrease competition. Both for the above reasons and because—as Sect. 15.1 explains—it is complicated and difficult to determine the economic-efficiency impact of any cost-reductions or profitable product-alterations a joint venture generates, it will be allocative costly to generate predictions of these effects that are sufficiently accurate for their use to be economically efficient, liberal-moral-rights-securing, and moral-good-promotive.

15.1 The Functions of Joint Ventures

Joint ventures can increase their parents' profits in 12 or 13 ways that are not essentially linked to their reducing competition (that are in the preceding sense "licit") and in six or seven ways that are essentially linked to their reducing competition (that are in the preceding sense "illicit"). I will now list separately the 12 or 13 licit functions and the 6 or 7 illicit functions that joint ventures can perform.

However, before proceeding, I want to explain why (1) the profits that a joint venture yields the parents because it reduces the fixed costs the parents (acting through the joint venture) have to incur to create a given investment, reduces the variable and/or marginal costs the parents (acting through the joint venture) have to incur to use a given investment, enables the parents via the joint venture to create and produce for the same cost a product or distributive outlet that enough relevant buyers sufficiently prefer to the product or distributive either parent could have created on its own to make the joint venture profitable, enables the parents via the joint venture to create and produce at a higher average total cost a product that enough relevant buyers prefer sufficiently to the product or distributive outlet either parent could have created on its own to render it profitable for the parents to incur the additional costs, or enables the parents to create/produce via the joint venture a lower average-total-cost product that enough relevant buyers disprefer by sufficiently little relative to the product or distributive outlet either parent could have created on its own to render it profitable for the joint venture to "substitute" the creation and production of the less-preferred product (distributive outlet) for the more-preferred product (distributive outlet) a parent would have found (most profitable)/(least unprofitable) to create and produce depend (2) on whether the joint venture is horizontal, on whether the joint-venture investment deters a parent from making an investment in the joint venture's ARDEPPS, on whether the joint-venture investment deters a non-parent from making an investment in the joint venture's ARDEPPS, and on whether the joint venture reduces equilibrium investment in the ARDEPPS in which it might operate as well as on a number of other facts that relate to the possibilities just referenced.

I will reveal these connections by considering 7 possible scenarios. First, if the joint venture is not horizontal, the joint venture's investment deters a parent from creating the same product or service the joint venture's investment creates, and the private costs the joint venture must incur to create and produce the same product or service a parent would have created and produced had the joint venture not been established, the profits the joint venture will yield the parents on this account will equal the amount by which the joint venture's fixed costs are lower than the parents' fixed costs would have been *plus* the amount by which the variable costs the joint venture would have had to incur to produce the output of the relevant created product or service that the parent would have produced are lower than the variable costs the relevant parent would have had to incur to produce that output *plus*, if the marginal-cost curve the joint venture faces is lower than the marginal-cost curve the parent would have faced over the relevant range of output, the profits the joint venture realizes by producing units of the product or service in question that the parent would not have found profitable to produce.

Second, if the joint venture is not horizontal, the joint venture's investment deters a parent from making an investment in the joint venture's ARDEPPS, and the joint venture's investment is more profitable than the deterred parent's investment would have been because the joint venture will create a different product or service than the deterred parent would have created—a different product or service whose creation and production yield the joint venture more profits than the creation and production of the alternative product or service the parent would have created would have yielded the parent, the profits the joint venture will yield the parents on this account will equal the difference between the profits the joint venture's investment yield the joint venture and the profits the parent's deterred investment would have yielded the parent.

Third, if the joint venture is horizontal, the joint venture's investment deters a parent from creating the same product or service that a parent would have created, but the joint venture charges a lower price for that good or service than the parent would have charged for it because the joint venture's relevant marginal costs are lower, the profits the joint venture will yield, the parents will equal the profits I indicated it would yield the parents in the first scenario *minus* any loss the parents sustain on their other investments because the joint venture's price is lower than the price the deterred parent would have charged for the product in question.

Fourth, if the joint venture is horizontal, the joint venture's investment deters a parent from creating a product or service that is different from the product or services that the joint venture creates, the profits the joint venture will yield the parents will equal the profits I indicated it would yield the parents in the second scenario I addressed *minus* (*plus*) any amount by which the substitution of the joint venture's product/service for the product/service that would have been created by the parent's deterred investment increased (decreased) the "investment"-generated reduction in the profits yielded by the parents' other investments in the ARDEPPS in question.

Fifth, if the joint venture is horizontal, the joint venture's investment does not deter any active or potential mutual competitor of the parents from making an investment in the joint venture's ARDEPPS, and the fact that the joint venture must incur lower costs to create and produce a new product or service than either parent would have had to incur to do so or can create a more-profitable, different product or service than either parent could have created renders it profitable for the joint venture to make an investment when it would not have been profitable for either parent to do so, the profits that the joint venture's investment will yield the parents will equal the profits I indicated it would yield the parents in the first or second scenario *minus* the amount by which the joint venture's investment would lower the profits yielded by the other investments the parents owned in the joint venture's ARDEPPS.

Sixth, if the joint venture is horizontal and the fact that the joint venture can create and produce a new product or service more cheaply than either parent could do or can create a more profitable, different product or service than either parent could produce renders it profitable for the joint venture to make an investment that deters a mutual rival of the parents from investing when neither parent would have made such an investment, the profits the joint venture's investment will yield the parents equal the profits I indicated it would yield them in the first and second scenarios *plus* (*minus*) any amount by which the substitution of the joint venture's investment for the parents' rival's deterred investment would reduce (increase) the additional-investment-generated reduction in the profit-yields of the parents' other investments in the joint venture's ARDEPPS.

Seventh, and almost certainly least importantly empirically, if the joint venture is horizontal and the joint venture substitutes for a situation in which a mutual rival of the parents would make an investment in the joint venture's and the parents' ARDEPPS a situation in which neither the relevant rival nor the joint venture would make an investment in that ARDEPPS by creating a situation in which the joint venture and the relevant parent rival confronted each other with critical natural-oligopolistic investment-disincentives when neither parent would cause the mutual rival to face such disincentives (because the parents faced barriers to investment expansion that critically exceed any such barriers facing the joint venture), the joint venture's creating an entity that faced lower barriers to investment than its parents faced would benefit its parents not by resulting in the joint venture's making an investment but by preventing the parents from suffering the losses they would have sustained from the mutual-rival investment that would be deterred by the creation of a joint venture that faced critically-lower barriers to investment than its parents faced.

Joint ventures (and functionally-analogous collaborative arrangements) can increase their participants' profits in 12 or 13 licit ways. Specifically, a joint-venture agreement can increase its participants' profits

(1) by reducing the distributive costs that the parents have to incur to supply each other with inputs of some type that the parents continue to produce (*e.g.*, with news stories or the right to use product or production-process patents) by creating an entity that can take better advantage of economies of scale or that employs personnel that are relevantly complementary for non-scale reasons,
(2) by reducing the production costs that the parents have to incur to supply themselves with an input they all use or some final product they all resell by enabling the parents to produce that input or product more cheaply by creating an entity that combines assets that are complementary for scale and/or non-scale reasons,
(3) by reducing the costs the parents have to incur to purchase inputs from others (when the parents are producers) or final products from others (when the parents are resellers) by creating an entity that can take advantage of economies of scale or scope in purchasing that relate to (A) the per-unit

mechanical transaction cost of the transactions in question and (B) the benefits that assured sales give suppliers (i) by obviating their incurring costs to identify potential buyers, to advertize their products, and to direct more individualized sales-efforts at buyers and (ii) by reducing the risk costs that the suppliers incur because they do not know how many units of their product they will sell (when the related gains increase more than proportionately with the amount of sales that are assured),

(4) by increasing the proficiency of their doing market research by creating an entity that combines relevant assets that are complementary for scale and/or non-scale reasons,

(5) by increasing the cost-effectiveness of the parents' efforts to establish credible quality-standards for the goods they produce and/or distribute by creating an entity that can take advantage of the fact that an industry-wide organization's pronouncements are more credible than are an individual company's and that combines resources that are complementary for scale and non-scale reasons (the scale possibility is salient because each parent competes with and therefore is interested in the quality-rating of only a subset of the products produced by all parents and there are economies of scale in applying the quality-standards),

(6) by increasing the proficiency with which the parents can control the quality of the goods the parents produce and/or distribute, can establish a brand-name for those products, and can advertize that brand and/or the type of product the parents produce/distribute,

(7) by increasing the proficiency with which the parents can assess the credit-worthiness of potential customers, bill actual buyers, and/or collect and process payments from actual buyers by creating an entity that combines relevant assets that are complementary for scale or non-scale reasons,

(8) by increasing the proficiency with which the parents can execute a given innovative product-research or production-process-research project by creating an entity that combines relevant assets that are complementary for scale or non-scale reasons,

(9) by increasing the proficiency with which the parents can make a non-innovative QV investment or plant-modernization investment again by creating an entity that combines assets that are complementary for scale and/or non-scale reasons,

(10) by enabling the parents to execute a more profitable set of product-research or production-process-research projects without increasing the proficiency with which any individual project is executed by permitting the parents to substitute a more-privately-profitable because less-jointly-unprofitably-duplicative set of research-projects for a less-privately-profitable because more-jointly-unprofitably-duplicative set of research-projects (even if the two sets of projects are equally costly),

(11) by enabling the parents to create one profitable innovative or non-innovative QV investment or to execute one profitable PPR project when they would not have done so when acting separately because—as independent agents—they would have confronted each other with critical natural-oligopolistic investment-disincentives,

(12) by increasing the parents' profits by creating an entity that would in any event find that the investment it could make that would yield it and the parents the most supernormal profits if the "organization" has no monopolistic investment-incentive to make it would also yield the organization profits because (A) that investment would be less competitive with the other investments of the joint venture and the parents than the rival investment it would deter would have been—that is, would reduce the OCAs of these other investments by a smaller total amount than those OCAs would otherwise have been reduced by the deterred rival investments—and/or (B) the joint venture would take full account of the impact that the decisions it made to advertize, sell, and price the product its investment created on the profits yielded by its other investments and the investments the parents owned whereas the deterred investor would have taken no account of these impacts of its decisions (at least if it ignored the possibility that its decisions might elicit retaliatory or predatory responses), and perhaps

(13) by enabling the parents to purchase more cheaply from others inputs or final products by creating a joint-purchasing organization that has more buying power than the sum of any buying power the parents had when acting separately ("perhaps" because in essence this function involves buyer price-fixing and buyer price-fixing may be liberal-moral-rights-violative [may in the sense in which I am currently using this modifier be "illicit"]).

Joint ventures can also perform at least 6 and perhaps 7 illicit functions. I should say at the outset that joint ventures will perform some of these functions only when the parents abuse the opportunity for communication that their participation in the joint venture affords them, will perform some of these functions because the joint-venture agreement contains one or more provisions that impose restraints on the parents and/or the joint venture, and can perform some of these functions even when (1) the parents do not abuse the opportunity for communication their participation in the joint venture affords them and (2) the joint-venture agreement does not impose any relevant restraints on the parents and/or the joint venture.

The first illicit function that joint ventures can perform is increasing the profits the parents earn by practicing contrived-oligopolistic pricing both by making it profitable for them to practice additional contrived-oligopolistic pricing and by increasing the profits they realize by charging contrived-oligopolistic prices they would have charged absent the joint venture. Joint-sales-agency joint ventures that prohibit the parents from making sales on their own perform this function most obviously: indeed, it would probably be more accurate to say that they obviate the parents' price-fixing in the same way that horizontal mergers obviate the merger partners' fixing prices or horizontal acquisitions obviate the acquiring and acquired firms' fixing prices. However, various sorts of joint ventures that do not in essence fix prices directly (that do not obviate the parents' engaging in price-fixing) can facilitate the parents' price-fixing. Thus, when the parents would find it inherently profitable to undercut or undermine each other's contrived oligopolistic prices, joint ventures can perform this illicit function by facilitating the parents' agreeing not to undercut each other's contrived oligopolistic prices and/or by enabling one or both parents to communicate their intention to retaliate against the other should the other not acquiesce in its contrivance. When the parents have one or more common rivals that could undercut or undermine the parents' contrived-oligopolistic pricing, these other sorts of joint ventures can also facilitate the parents' contrived-oligopolistic pricing by enabling them (1) to communicate to each other information about their own sales-records and about those rivals' sales-records that increase the ability of the parents in individualized-pricing contexts to determine whether undercutting from an inferior competitive position has taken place, to identify the undercutter, to identify opportunities to reciprocate to a cooperator or to increase the benefits a parent can bestow on a cooperator through reciprocation when the parents are uniquely-equal-privately-second placed or respectively uniquely-privately-second placed and uniquely-privately-third placed to supply one or more buyers the cooperator was privately-best-placed to supply, and to identify the customers of their undercutter to which it would be most-cost-effective to offer retaliatory price-cuts or at which it would be most-cost-effective to direct retaliatory advertizing campaigns, (2) to put at each other's disposal any excess reciprocatory power each has in relation to a common rival that has cooperated with the other's contrivance, and (3) to retaliate cooperatively against each other's undercutters (in individualized-pricing contexts) or underminers (in across-the-board-pricing contexts), (4) when the joint venture is operating in a parent's ARDEPPS or in an ARDEPPS in which one or more of a parent's rivals are operating, to use the joint venture's sales-records to help the parent identify whether undercutting from a position of inferiority is taking place, to reciprocate to a cooperator, and/or to retaliate against an undercutter/underminer.

The second illicit function that joint ventures can perform is increasing the profits the parents can realize by confronting their rivals with retaliation barriers to entry or expansion, usually by increasing the effectiveness of their threats of retaliation but conceivably as well by enabling them to reward rival potential QV investors that choose not to invest. Joint ventures can yield the parents such benefits *inter alia* (1) by increasing the profits they can realize by confronting each other with retaliation barriers by facilitating their communication of relevant intentions to each other, (2) by enabling them to provide each other with information about another rival's competitive-position array that will enable each parent to retaliate more-cost-effectively or better to perceive its opportunities for reciprocation, (3) by increasing the amount of benefits the parents can provide cooperators by not beating their contrived-oligopolistic offers (in situations in which the parents are uniquely-equal-privately-second placed or respectively uniquely-privately-second placed and uniquely-privately-third placed to supply one or more customers that the cooperator is privately-best-placed to supply), (4) by putting at each other's disposal any excess reciprocatory power either has in relation to a cooperator, (5) by facilitating their joint retaliation against an investor, and (6) by enabling them to use the joint venture to reciprocate to a non-investor and/or retaliate against an investor.

The third illicit function that joint ventures can perform is enabling the parents to profit more by engaging in other sorts of predation by enabling them better to coordinate their predatory pricing, predatory advertizing, predatory investments, or predatory refusals to deal. For example, vertical joint ventures in which the parents agree to supply each other with inputs (say, news stories or other types of intellectual property [to allow each other to use patent-protected information]) or distributive services may contractually organize predatory refusals to deal by prohibiting the parents/participants from supplying the inputs or distributive services in question to any non-participant (e.g., to each other's rivals) unless all participants, some burdensome percentage of participants, or the participant(s) that are rivals of the non-participant accept terms of participation that place the non-participants at a critical disadvantage. Of course, such contractual provisions will be predatory and illicit only if one or more of their perpetrators' *ex ante* perception that the provisions were profitable was critically affected by the perpetrators' belief that the provisions would or might reduce the absolute attractiveness of the offers against which they would have to compete.

The fourth illicit function that joint ventures can perform is enabling the parents to substitute one investment (a smaller number of investments) made by the joint venture for the larger number of investments the parents would have made absent the joint venture when no remaining rival would replace the deterred parent investment(s) immediately, at all, or with equally-competitive investments. Sometimes, the joint venture will secure this result by including in its by-laws a provision precluding the parents from investing on their own in the joint venture's ARDEPPS. The parents might believe that they will be able to escape liability for including such a provision in the joint venture's by-laws by arguing that (1) no parent could have entered the joint venture's ARDEPPS on its own had it not learned things from the other parent(s) in the course of their participation in the joint venture and (2) the parents would not have found the joint venture profitable had they not been assured that the information they would supply it would not be used by any fellow parent to compete against the joint venture—*i.e.*, by arguing that the by-law provision in question was "ancillary" to the formation of a joint venture (ideally that it increased competition [say] by making an investment that raised total investment in the relevant area of product-space to a level to which it would not otherwise have been raised). I should say that in many situations, the parents may not need to include such a by-law provision in their joint-venture agreement to achieve this result: the mere fact that each parent (say, in a two-parent joint venture) owns 50% of the joint venture and therefore would suffer 50% of the loss that its entry into the joint venture's ARDEPPS would impose on the joint venture may suffice to deter each parent from entering the joint venture's ARDEPPS.

The fifth illicit function a joint venture can perform is to enable the parents to profit by making a predatory joint-venture investment—that is, a joint-venture investment that would not have been profitable for the joint venture and the parents all together had these firms not had a critical monopolistic investment-incentive to make the investment in question (in other words, to make an investment that would not have been profitable for the joint venture and the parents all together were it not for the fact that its operation would reduce the profits yielded by the joint venture's and the parents' other investments by less than those profits would otherwise have been reduced by the rival investment the joint-venture investment deterred [because the joint-venture investment was less competitive with its and its parents other investments than the deterred investment would have been, because the joint venture will use its investment in the way that maximizes its and the parents' profits whereas the deterred rival would not have been influenced by the impact that its deterred-investment-use decisions would have on the profits yielded by the investments of the joint venture and its parents, and/or because the joint-venture investment would elicit non-retaliatory responses from other rivals of the joint venture and the parents that lowered their profits by a smaller amount than they would have been lowered by the rival non-retaliatory responses the deterred investment would have elicited]). More specifically, the joint venture will perform this function when, by creating an entity that could make an investment that was less unprofitable than any investment a parent could make in the joint venture's ARDEPPS if the relevant profit-calculations ignored any monopolistic investment-incentives the joint venture and relevant parent(s) would have to make the investments in question, the joint-venture agreement created a situation in which the monopolistic investment-incentive the joint venture had was critical, whereas the monopolistic investment-incentive either parent would have had was not critical.

The sixth illicit function that joint ventures can perform is enabling the parents to agree not to enter each other's ARDEPPSes when each was an effective potential competitor of the other. To perform this function, the joint venture would have to include in its by-laws a provision prohibiting the parents from entering each other's ARDEPPS. Once more, even if these by-laws were motivated by specific anticompetitive intent, the parents might be able to persuade triers-of-fact that they were not—in particular, might be able to persuade triers-of-fact that the parents could not have entered each other's ARDEPPSes had they not participated in the joint venture, that the joint venture would enable them to profit by entering each other's ARDEPPSes because they would learn things necessary for doing so in the course of collaborating in the running of the joint venture, perhaps that none of them would have found the joint venture profitable had it not been able to prevent the other parent(s) from using against it information it conveyed to the other parent(s) in the course of participating in the joint venture, and perhaps that the joint venture increased competition in the ARDEPPSes in which it operated because it added one or more investments to the ARDEPPSes in which it operated that would not otherwise have been made or introduced investments into those ARDEPPSes that were more effective competitively than the investments of others the joint venture's investments deterred.

The seventh illicit function that joint ventures can perform is actually only possibly illicit. As I indicated previously, joint ventures that create a purchasing agent that has more buying power than the sum of the buying power that each parent would have acting separately on its own and prohibits the parents from competing against each other as buyers may be illicit on that account.

15.2 The Economic Efficiency of Joint Ventures and the Ability of a Liberal-Moral-Rights-Constrained Government to Increase Economic Efficiency by Responding Appropriately to Joint Ventures

I will start by making 15 general economic-efficiency-related sets of points, each of which focuses on a particular way in which a joint-venture agreement can increase or affect the parents' profits. The first set of points relates to the profits that a joint-venture agreement can confer on the parents by reducing the private cost the joint venture/parent organization incurs to perform tasks the parents would have performed in any event (to create and use a QV investment a parent would have created anyway), to execute a PPR project the parent would have executed anyway and use the discovery generated by that PPR project, to control the quality of exemplars of one or more products the joint venture/parent organization or the parents would have produced in any case, to develop/promote/apply quality-standards the parents would have developed/promoted/applied anyway, to ascertain the credit-worthiness of prospective customers, to purchase (i.e., to reduce the transaction cost as opposed to the purchase-price cost of) given amounts of one or more inputs or final products, or to determine that it would be more profitable to create and use one QV investment rather than another or to execute one PPR project rather than another. The relevant points are that the private-cost savings in question are deflated and that the contribution that the joint-venture agreement makes to the "parents' profits" (i.e., to the sum of the joint venture's profits and the profits the parents would be calculated to realize if the latter profits were calculated without considering the profits they realize because they share in the joint venture's profits) on this account are therefore equal to the private-cost savings *plus* the deflation in these private-cost savings.

The second set of points relates to the profits the joint-venture agreement yields the parents by creating a joint venture that recognizes and acts on its realization that it will be profitable for it to produce a more-privately-costly-to-create-and-produce product variant (on which some relevant buyers place a higher-dollar value) rather than a less-privately-costly-to-create-and-produce product variant (on which relevant buyers place a lower dollar value) or vice versa. The first point that is relevant to this possibility is that any associated private-cost increase or decrease will be deflated. The second point that relates to this possibility is that the profits that a joint-venture agreement yields the parents by creating a joint venture that creates and produces a more-expensive/less-expensive rather than a less-expensive/more-expensive product are inflated/deflated—that the associated economic-efficiency effect will equal the profits (*minus* the deflation) in the relevant private-cost increase (*plus* the deflation in the relevant private-cost decrease).

The third set of points relates to the effects that a joint-venture agreement has on the parents by altering relevant buyers' perceptions of the dollar value of the parents and the joint venture's products (by causing the organization to substitute a [privately-cheaper/lower-dollar value] product variant for a [privately-more-expensive/higher-dollar value] product variant or vice versa, to provide better quality-control, to provide a better warrantee, to provide more information about its/their products, and to provide the same information about the relevant products more effectively). I suspect that it will be TBLE to assume that any change-in-buyer-dollar-valuation-of-product-related effects on the parents are not distorted. Fourth, for the same (admittedly-unstated) reason, I think it will be TBLE to assume that any benefits a joint-venture agreement yields the parents by improving the accuracy of their assessments of prospective buyers' credit-worthiness are not distorted.

Fifth, any profits a joint-venture agreement yields the parents by increasing the profits they and the joint venture realize by engaging in natural-oligopolistic pricing, contrived-oligopolistic pricing, and predation of all sorts will be inflated by more than 100%. Thus, the fact that a joint-venture agreement yields the parents profits in one or more of these ways will render the agreement less economically efficient than it otherwise would have been.

The sixth set of points relates to the profits a joint-venture agreement yields its parents because the joint venture makes an investment that deters a parent rival from creating a product (A) that would have been more competitive with (privately-better placed to compete against) the parents' investments and the joint venture's other investments than the joint venture's investment was and (B) that would in any event have been advertized and priced more aggressively vis-à-vis the parent's products and the joint venture's other products than the joint venture's product would be. I suspect that it will be TBLE to assume that the inflation in the parents' gains attributable to "(A) above" will be 100% since there is no reason to believe that the joint venture's product's product-space location will be either more or less economically efficient than the product-space location of the rival product whose creation the joint venture's investment would deter and that the inflation in the parents' gains attributable to "(B) above" will be over 100% since the reduction in competition generated by the substitution of the joint ventures' conduct for the deterred rival's conduct will cause economic inefficiency. All tolled, the fact that a joint-venture agreement yields the parents profits in this way will cause it to be less allocatively efficient than it otherwise would have been—will reduce its economic efficiency by the contribution it makes to the parents' profits in this way *minus* the inflation in those profits (which, all tolled, will exceed 100% of those profits).

The seventh set of points relates to the profits that a joint venture that restricts the parents from entering each other's ARDEPPSes yields the parents by substituting for a parental investment that would reduce the sum of the parents' profits by a larger number of dollars a rival investment that would reduce the sum of the parents' profits by a smaller number of dollars, presumably because the rival investment would sufficiently be less competitive with the parents' investments than the deterred parental investment would have been with the non-investing parent's investment(s) for this difference to more than compensate for the fact that the deterred parental investment would have yielded the parent that would have made it some (supernormal) profits. I want to make three points about this possibility. First, I think it is less empirically important than the other items in this list. Second, I think that across all instances the profits that joint ventures yield the parents in this way will, if anything, be more than 100% inflated because across all instances the only reason to believe that the rival investments that will be made will be more or less economically efficient than the parental investments that are deterred is that (presumably) the relevant rival investments will be less profitable than the deterred parental investments. Third, a point that is really not separate from its predecessor: in these instances, the restrictive provisions will tend to decrease economic efficiency at the same time that they yield the parents profits.

The eighth set of points relates to any joint venture that increases equilibrium QV investment in the ARDEPPS in which the joint venture operates. A joint venture can produce this effect by creating an entity that faces lower barriers to investment than either parent faced (by generating dynamic efficiencies). In some such cases, the fact that the joint venture faces lower barriers to investment than either parent faced will result in its making an ARDEPPS-equilibrium-QV-investment-increasing QV investment because the investment barriers it faces are critically lower than the investment barriers the parents or any other potential investor faced. In some such cases, the fact that the joint venture faces lower barriers to investment than either parent faced will result in another firm's in the joint venture's ARDEPPS making an equilibrium-QV-investment-increasing QV investment in the joint venture's ARDEPPS by converting a situation in which that other firm faced critical monopolistic QV-investment disincentives into one in which it faced lower, non-critical monopolistic QV-investment disincentives, no monopolistic QV-investment disincentives, or monopolistic QV-investment incentives (by creating a joint venture that would invest if the other firm did not when, absent the joint venture, no firm would invest if the relevant other firm would not). In the case in which the joint venture leads the joint venture to make an ARDEPPS-equilibrium-QV-investment-quantity-increasing QV investment, the joint venture's generation of such dynamic efficiencies will increase the profits it yields the joint venture and its parents taken together. In the case in which the joint venture-generated reduction in QV-investment barriers causes a non-parent rival of the joint venture to make an ARDEPPS-equilibrium-QV-investment-quantity-increasing QV investment, the joint venture's generation of dynamic efficiencies will decrease the profits it yields the joint venture and its parents taken together. If as I suspect it is realistic to assume that the government of the society in which the joint venture is created has not eliminated the positive distortion in the profits yielded by QV investments, any additional QV investments a joint venture causes to be made in the joint venture's ARDEPPS by generating dynamic efficiencies will affect economic efficiency positively/negatively by the positive/negative difference between the profits the additional QV investment yielded the investor that made it and the positive distortion in those profits. (I suspect that, across all cases, the additional QV investments a joint venture's dynamic efficiencies cause to be made will decrease economic efficiency.) In the case in which the dynamic efficiencies a joint venture generates causes the joint venture to make an ARDEPPS-equilibrium-QV-investment-increasing QV investment, the profits the dynamic efficiencies yield the joint venture and its parents by causing the joint venture to make that investment will clearly be inflated. In the case in which the dynamic efficiencies a joint venture would generate cause a rival of the joint venture to make an ARDEPPS-equilibrium-QV-investment-increasing QV investment, the loss the joint venture would impose on the joint venture and its parents by generating prospective (unrealized) dynamic efficiencies could either be higher than, equal to, or lower than the associated economic-efficiency loss—could be inflated, undistorted, or deflated—depending on whether the associated joint venture/parental loss was higher than, equal to, or lower than the associated economic-efficiency loss.

The ninth set of points I want to make relates to the profits that the dynamic efficiencies a joint venture confer on the joint venture and its parents taken together by reducing equilibrium QV investment in the joint venture's ARDEPPS by substituting for a situation in which a joint venture/parental rival would have made an ARDEPPS-equilibrium-QV-investment-increasing QV investment *inter alia* because it did not have any natural-oligopolistic QV-investment disincentives to make that investment a situation in which neither it nor the joint venture would make such an investment because they confronted each other with natural-oligopolistic QV-investment disincentives. In this case, the fact that the joint venture had the potential to generate dynamic efficiencies would yield the joint venture (and the parents if the joint venture was horizontal) profits by deterring the execution and use of a rival QV investment and would increase/decrease the joint venture's contribution to economic efficiency by the positive/negative difference between the profits the deterred QV investment would have yielded the deterred investor natural-oligopolistic QV-investment disincentives aside and the amount by which those profits would have been inflated had the investor faced no natural-oligopolistic QV-investment disincentives. Because I believe that in virtually all cases the equilibrium-QV-investment-increasing QV investment that the joint venture's prospective dynamic efficiencies would deter would have decreased economic efficiency (given that the profits QV investments yield are inflated now and will probably be inflated in the future as well), I think that the profits that such prospective dynamic efficiencies would yield the joint venture and its parents in these cases could be inflated, undistorted, or deflated, depending on whether those profits exceeded, equaled, or were lower than the positive distortion in the profits the deterred QV investment would have yielded.

The tenth set of points I will make at this juncture relates to the possibility that a joint venture may reduce equilibrium QV investment in the joint venture's ARDEPPS by substituting for the larger amount of QV investment the parents would have made as separate entities not involved in the joint venture the smaller amount of QV investment the joint venture (and perhaps the parents) would make in the joint venture's ARDEPPS in circumstances in which no other firm makes investments that "replace" the just-referenced deterred investments. Joint-venture agreements can generate this outcome both by binding the parents contractually not to enter the joint venture's ARDEPPS and by relying on the individual parents' partial ownerships of the joint venture to make it unprofitable for any parent to invest in the joint venture's ARDEPPS. Given the fact that the profits yielded by QV investments are inflated, it is probably TBLE to assume that any such effect of a joint venture will increase its economic efficiency.

The eleventh set of points that are relevant here relates to the profits the joint-venture agreement will yield the parents by reducing equilibrium QV investment in their ARDEPPSes by prohibiting them from investing in each other's ARDEPPSes and the joint venture from investing in a parent's ARDEPPS when the deterred QV investment will not be replaced by a rival investment. The points made at the end of the preceding paragraph apply fully in the current context.

With one important set of related differences, the twelfth through fifteenth sets of points I could make at this juncture parallel, respectively, the eighth through eleventh sets of points I just made. The twelfth through fifteenth sets of points are different from their preceding counterparts because they focus on the possible effects that a joint venture can have on the joint venture's and its parents' profits, on economic efficiency, and on the distortion in the profits the joint-venture agreement yields the joint venture and its parents by increasing or decreasing equilibrium PPR (rather than equilibrium QV investment) in the joint venture's ARDEPPS or the parents' ARDEPPSes. The relevant economic-efficiency-focused analyses are different when the investments in question are investments in PPR rather than QV investments because the profits yielded by investments in PPR are deflated rather than inflated so that decreases/increases in an ARDEPPS' equilibrium-PPR quantity will be associated with decreases/increases in economic efficiency, a difference that is relevant both for the economic efficiency of joint ventures that alter relevant equilibrium-PPR-investment quantities and to the distortion in the profits that the relevant joint ventures yield. To save space and avoid testing readers' patience, I will write no more about these issues.

It is important to emphasize that all the preceding points apply not only to any joint-venture agreement including the restrictive provisions it contains but also to the restrictive provisions analyzed in isolation—provisions that prohibit a joint venture's parents from investing in a joint venture's ARDEPPS(es) and from investing in each other's ARDEPP(es) and provisions that prohibit the joint venture from investing in its parents' ARDEPPS(es) or from making certain investments in its own ARDEPPS (when the joint venture is horizontal). By inducing each parent to provide a greater quantity and quality of valuable information and personnel to the joint venture (by preventing the other parent or the joint venture from using the personnel and/or information in question to compete against the parent that provided it), such restrictive provisions can increase economic efficiency by (1) reducing the costs the joint venture incurs to perform given tasks, (2) enabling the joint venture to create investments that are intrinsically more profitable for reasons unconnected with the cost the joint venture must incur to perform given tasks, (3) enabling the joint venture to obtain more benefits from (A) advertizing and salesmanship, (B) product-quality control, (C) input-quality control, (D) potential-buyer creditworthiness assessment, and (E) as a result of items (1) (A)-(C) in this list, increasing price and investment competition. However, by prohibiting the parents and the joint venture from competing against each other, such restrictive provisions can also decrease economic efficiency by decreasing price and investment competition both directly and by making it profitable for the parents to engage in more oligopolistic and predatory conduct.

The preceding analyses imply that some joint-venture agreements including the restrictive provisions they contain and some joint-venture-agreement restrictive provisions viewed in isolation will increase economic efficiency and some will decrease economic efficiency. The preceding analyses also imply that it will be extremely complicated and allocative costly to determine with the liberalism-required degree of accuracy whether a given (joint-venture agreement)/(set of restrictive clauses in a joint-venture agreement) or some identifiable subset of such agreements or sets of joint-venture-agreement restrictive provisions will increase or decrease economic efficiency. For example, it will be far from easy to determine whether or the extent to which a joint venture must incur lower costs to perform particular tasks than a parent would have had to incur to do so, the percentage deflation in any joint-venture-generated private-cost savings, whether and the extent to which the joint venture will secure more quality-control (of inputs, final goods, and customers) than a parent would have done, whether and the extent to which the joint venture will create more-economically-efficient QV investments or execute more-economically-efficient PPR projects than the parents would have done, whether any joint-venture-generated reduction in barriers to investment will lead to an increase/decrease/(no change in) the equilibrium-investment quantity of the joint venture's or a parent's ARDEPPS, whether a parent that a joint-venture agreement prohibits from investing in another parent's ARDFEPPS was an effective potential investor in that ARDEPPS and, if another firm would invest in the ARDEPPS in which the prohibited parent would otherwise have invested, how much less-economically-efficient than the deterred parent's investment this alternative investor's investment would have been, the extent to which the joint-venture agreement with or without its restrictive provisions will increase the parents' and their rivals' practice of natural-oligopolistic pricing, cause the parents and their mutual rivals to confront each other with natural-oligopolistic investment-disincentives, increase the parents' practice of contrived-oligopolistic and/or predatory pricing, and the extent to which any joint-venture-generated increase in such oligopolistic or predatory conduct will decrease economic efficiency, etc.

I do not think that the preceding conclusions imply that the government of a liberal-moral-rights-based society will be unable to increase economic efficiency by responding somewhat selectively to particular joint ventures or identifiable subclasses of joint ventures. In some cases, such a government will be given sufficient information by eyewitnesses or individuals who have access to relevant company studies or e-mails to enable it to determine that a particular joint venture will be economically inefficient or economically efficient. And in some cases, the antitrust-policy-implementation authorities will be able to secure through its own initiative sufficient eyewitness testimony, company reports, and company e-mails without violating any liberal moral right to put it in a position to determine that a particular joint venture (would be)/was economically efficient or economically inefficient even if the government had not required firms that want to create a joint venture (or, possibly, to continue their ownership of a joint venture) to obtain the approval of an antitrust-policy-implementation authority or reviewing court *inter alia* by supplying the relevant government-decision-makers with information on the determinants of the proposed or operating joint venture's economic efficiency. And it will clearly be TBLE for such a government to pass and implement legislation that conditions the right of firms to create a joint venture or to continue to operate a joint venture on their convincing a relevant antitrust-policy-implementation authority that the proposed joint venture or their continued operation of a joint venture would not decrease economic efficiency (in the latter case, taking account of the economic efficiency of providing firms with incentives to create joint ventures that increase economic efficiency over their lifetimes). I recognize that I have not specified any of the details of this joint-venture-review process—*inter alia*, the characteristics that a proposed joint venture or a consummated joint venture or its parents must have for the joint venture to be covered by this proposal, the speed with which the authority would be legally obligated to make its decision, the obligation of the authority to explain a negative or positive decision (which would in part be affected by the economic efficiency of allowing the parents or the joint venture to keep some relevant information secret as well as their liberal moral right to do so), the nature of any judicial review of negative or positive implementation-authority joint-venture decisions, the conditions if any under which any such authority would be authorized to review the legality of a consummated joint venture, etc. But the point I am making is that the government of a liberal-moral-rights-based society will be able to put its antitrust-policy-implementation authority in a position to increase economic efficiency by responding selectively to proposed (or consummated) joint ventures by establishing for joint ventures the kind of review protocol that the U.S.' Hart-Scott-Rodino Act[1] and the E.U.'s Council Regulation 139/2004 on the Control of Concentrations Between Undertakings[2] establish for horizontal mergers.[3]

Perhaps I would be wise to stop here. But, by now, you will not be surprised by my proceeding to comment on the economic efficiency of six functional categories of joint ventures and on the TBLE of the government's responding to exemplars of each of these categories of joint ventures in particular ways. I should acknowledge at the outset that this plan is somewhat undercut by the fact that some individual joint ventures belong in more than one of the functional categories I distinguish—for example, both jointly sell and regulate the quality of the parents' products.

The first functional category of joint ventures or functionally-analogous collaborations are arrangements to sell multiple producers' products.[4] Such joint ventures or functionally-analogous contracts increase economic efficiency by arranging matters so that the actor that makes the relevant sales can take advantage of private economies of scale in selling that presumptively are associated with allocative economies of scale in selling. Unfortunately, at least if the producers in question grant the joint venture or "sales agent" the exclusive right to sell their products, the increase in economic efficiency the (joint venture)/collaboration generates by lowering allocative transaction costs will be more or less offset by the decrease in economic efficiency the arrangement generates by reducing or eliminating the price competition the participating producers would otherwise wage against each other and derivatively increasing both QV investment in the producer's ARDEPPS (when the good involved is not a discovered production process) and poverty/material inequality (by raising the price of the good in question). Indeed, I am disposed to think that arrangements (joint ventures or other sorts of contracts) in which the original seller reserves the right to sell its product on its own are not much different in the latter regard from arrangements in which they do not. I am also disposed to conclude that joint-sales joint ventures created by sellers that substantially reduce each other's OCAs decrease economic efficiency all tolled while joint-sales joint ventures created by sellers that do not substantially reduce each other's OCAs increase economic efficiency, particularly when the parents are small firms that are competing against large rivals that can take advantage of economies of scale in selling. This conclusion needs to be qualified in one important way: decisions by the original parents of a sales-agency joint venture or the original "employers" of a truly-independent marketer to exclude others from participating in the arrangement or to allow others to participate only on disadvantageous terms seem to me to be economically inefficient except insofar as the advantaging of the original participants increases economic efficiency by incentivizing the founders to create the arrangements: in fact, some such decisions may be not only economically inefficient but liberal-moral-rights-violative—that is, predatory. I wish that I could be more precise. Perhaps, I should have confined myself to stating that it will be TBLE for antitrust-policy-implementation authorities to devote a significant amount of resources to analyzing the economic efficiency of joint-sales-agency joint ventures and of any features of related joint-venture agreements that disadvantage non-founders.

Joint ventures and analogous collaborations that function primarily by enabling producers to take advantage of standard-transaction-cost economies of scale in identifying, negotiating, and physically supplying buyers also sometimes function by increasing the private-cost-effectiveness of the parents'/seller participants' efforts to do other things related to their selling their products (to regulate the rules of the game when the product is an athletics contest, to promulgate and apply quality-standards, to promote the products being sold, to monitor uses of non-material products (copyrighted music, etc.). In fact, joint ventures and other sorts of collaborations could be created exclusively to perform these latter functions. The second category of such arrangements I will consider perform these latter functions. As I indicated earlier, any profits the joint venture or other collaboration yields its participants by lowering the private costs they must incur to achieve these objectives to any given extent will be deflated, and in my judgment, it will be TBLE to assume that any profits such arrangements yield their participants by improving their products in these ways will be undistorted. With two important exceptions, I think it will be TBLE to assume that joint ventures or other sorts of collaborations that function exclusively in these ways will increase economic efficiency. The first relates to any action the founders take to bar non-founders from joining the arrangement or to price the admission of non-founders to the arrangement in a way that places the non-founders at a disadvantage that, from the perspective of economic efficiency is not warranted by the need to incentivize firms to create the joint venture or analogous arrangement. The second exception relates to the possibility that the joint venture or other collaboration may establish quality-standards that disadvantage some members or, more likely, some non-members when there is no quality-difference justification for doing so and/or may misapply defensible quality-standards to the disadvantage of such parties—that is, to the possibility that quality-standards may be used to wage unfair competition or to practice predation. I think it will be TBLE for an antitrust-policy-implementation authority to investigate these possibilities, to penalize actors that have engaged in such unfair competition or predation, to give victims of such conduct a reasonable opportunity to obtain legal redress, and to prohibit joint ventures or other arrangements whose *ex ante* participant-perceived profitability was critically affected by the participants' belief that the arrangement's quality-standards would themselves be unfair or predatory or would be applied unfairly or predatorily.

The third functional category of joint ventures or related collaborations I will discuss are joint-buying arrangements. Joint-buying joint ventures can be created to reduce the mechanical transaction cost of identifying advantageous potential suppliers, negotiating purchases, and securing deliveries and can also function by enabling the participants to increase their profits by picking better suppliers, developing and promoting private labels for the products bought, and by promoting the private brands and/or the participants more generally. Such purchasing joint ventures are often formed by small distributors to improve their competitive positions vis-à-vis large chains.[5] I think such joint-buying arrangements are economically efficient, though, once more, it will almost certainly be TBLE for an antitrust-policy-implementation authority to check to see whether the arrangement allows a participant to place a competitor under a disadvantage by vetoing its joining the arrangement or allows the parents to establish terms for joining the arrangement that place rivals under a disadvantage that cannot be rationalized in economic-efficiency terms by the value of giving founders an incentive to create an economically-efficient arrangement. From the perspective of economic efficiency, I do not think it problematic that some joint-buying joint ventures also function by enabling the parents to avoid competing against each other as buyers, though this possibility may be problematic from a liberal perspective.

The fourth category of joint ventures or analogous collaborations contains arrangements whose participants agree to supply each other with inputs at no cost or for less than they would otherwise charge for these *desiderata*. The "inputs" that are involved in the most prominent U.S. cases that deal with such arrangements are "news stories"[6] and intellectual property.[7] The economic efficiency of such joint ventures is complicated to analyze. They will clearly increase economic efficiency by reducing the allocative transaction costs the participants must generate to complete any given amount of related transactions between themselves and (I suspect) by increasing the extent to which the "traded goods" are used. However, the effect they will have on economic efficiency by reducing the amount of resources devoted to researching and writing news stories or doing product researcher and production-process research by reducing the private advantage the newspaper/researcher obtains by (discovering and writing) the story (making the discovery) would be complicated to analyze even if it were clear that these arrangements do reduce the amount of investigative reporting, product research, and production-process research that is done. Because I think that the private profits yielded by investigative reporting are deflated, that the profits yielded by product research are inflated, and that the profits yielded by production-process research are deflated, I think that the impact that any such pool has on economic efficiency by reducing such resource-uses varies with what is pooled—is negative when the pooled object is investigative reporting or production-process discoveries and is positive when the pooled object is product related. I am also concerned in this context with the possibility that such pools may reduce or distort competition by barring non-participants that are rivals of participants or by admitting them on disadvantageous terms that cannot be given an economic-efficiency justification. I suspect that it may be TBLE to strike down all such disadvantageous terms but to allow pools that do not contain such terms.

The fifth functional category of joint ventures contains joint ventures that are formed to create a company that can make a more profitable QV investment or investment in PPR than either parent could or to make a profitable investment of either kind when neither parent could profit by making such an investment.[8] As we have seen, the economic efficiency of any such joint venture depends *inter alia* on (1) the amount by which the profits the joint venture's investment would yield the parents exceed the profits that the parental investment for which it would be substituted would have yielded the relevant parent, (2) the relative extent to which the joint-venture investment would be more profitable than any investment it deters because it would be privately cheaper to create and use or because the product or production process it would discover would be superior, (3) the percentage deflation in any associated private-cost savings, (4) whether the investment the joint venture would create would be a QV investment or an investment in PPR, and (5) whether the joint venture would increase its ARDEPPS' equilibrium-investment quantity, and (6) if it would increase its ARDEPPS' equilibrium-investment quantity, the size of the inflation/deflation in the profits yielded by the added (QV investment)/(investment in PPR). I suspect that it will be TBLE for an antitrust-policy-enforcement authority to consider all of these issues (aided by evidence the joint venture's parents are legally obligated to supply) when deciding whether a particular joint venture in this category would increase or decrease economic efficiency.

The sixth and final functional category of joint ventures contains joint ventures that are designed admittedly *inter alia* to help their parents fix their prices[9] or increase the prices they obtain by making it more difficult for buyers to obtain price-information.[10] Any joint venture's performance of this function is economically inefficient for the reasons that Chapter 9 explained contrived-oligopolistic pricing is economically inefficient. It will clearly be TBLE for antitrust-policy-implementation authorities to investigate whether a joint venture is performing this function, to declare illegal its performance of this function, and in those cases in which the joint venture would be economically inefficient even if it did not perform this function to declare the relevant joint venture illegal.[11]

15.3 The Liberal-Moral-Rights-Violativeness of Joint Ventures, Functionally-Analogous Collaborations, and Any Restrictive Provisions Joint-Venture Agreements Contain and the Ability of a Government to Secure Liberal Moral Rights by Responding Appropriately to Such Arrangements and Provisions

Joint ventures, functionally-analogous collaborations, and any restrictive provisions joint-venture agreements contain will be liberal-moral-rights-violative (1) if one or more participants' *ex ante* perception that they would be profitable was critically affected by a belief that they would or might decrease the absolute attractiveness of the best offers against which they would have to compete in one or more ways that would render the relevant efforts economically inefficient in an otherwise-Pareto-perfect economy and/or (2) if one or more participants believed that they would put them in a position to profit from engaging in independently-liberal-moral-rights-violative acts (contrived-oligopolistic pricing, possibly natural-oligopolistic pricing, or predatory conduct) and intended *ex ante* to take advantage of any such opportunity the arrangement in question created. The government of a liberal-moral-rights-based society is morally obligated to deter liberal-moral-rights-violative arrangements and provisions of these kinds and to provide their victims (the actual and potential customers of the perpetrators and the targets of any associated predation or contrived-oligopolistic-pricing-related retaliation) with an appropriate opportunity to obtain legal redress to the extent that it can do so in ways that do not decrease the extent to which liberal-moral-rights-related interests are secured overall. I am optimistic that the government of a liberal-moral-rights-based society will be able to secure liberal-moral-rights-related interests by responding appropriately to proposed and consummated joint ventures, analogous collaborations, and restrictive provisions in joint-venture agreements (1) by requiring firms that want to participant in such arrangements and/or use such provisions to secure the permission of an antitrust-policy-implementation authority or reviewing court by providing information that relates *inter alia* to the impact that their proposed conduct will have on liberal moral rights, (2) by instructing the relevant public authority to take advantage of testimony volunteered by eyewitnesses and participants, and (3) (A) by soliciting such testimony, (B) by searching for and considering relevant studies done by the participants, e-mails sent by the participants, and minutes of participant meetings, and (C) by doing other sorts of investigations on its own into the parameters that affect the legitimate profitability of the arrangements and provisions in question and the potential profitability of any liberal-moral-rights violations.

A final point that is contestable. It may be that the members of and participants in a liberal-moral-rights-based society have a liberal moral property right to use their property in any profitable way that is not liberal-moral-rights-violative. If that is the case, that property-right-related liberal-moral interest would have to be taken into consideration when determining the number that an antitrust-policy-implementing authority or reviewing court must assign to the probability that a joint venture, related collaborative arrangement, or restrictive provision in a joint-venture agreement was liberal-moral-rights-violative to prohibit it.

15.4 The Impact of Joint Ventures, Functionally-Analogous Collaborative Arrangements, and Any Restrictive Provisions in Joint-Venture Agreements on the Instantiation of Various Egalitarian Conceptions of the Moral Good and the Ability of the Government of a Liberal-Moral-Rights-Based Society to Instantiate Various Egalitarian Conceptions of the Moral Good by Responding Appropriately to Such Arrangements and Provisions

I will start by analyzing the impact of these arrangements and provisions on total utility (i.e., on the instantiation of this variant of the utilitarian conception on the moral good). As already indicated, this impact depends on whether (1) (the equivalent-dollar gains the arrangements and provisions at issue confer on their beneficiaries) *times* (the average marginal utility generated by the equivalent-dollars gained) is higher or lower than (2) (the equivalent-dollar losses the arrangements and provisions at issue impose on their "victims") *times* (the average marginal utility that would have been generated by the equivalent-dollars lost) where (1) the difference between the first terms in these two expressions is the economic efficiency of the arrangement/provision and (2) the desirability of the distributive impact of the arrangement/provision in question from this utilitarian perspective depends on whether the second term in the first of the above two expressions is higher/lower than the second term in the second of the above two expressions.

Section 15.2 showed that some exemplars of joint ventures, functionally-analogous collaborative arrangements, and restrictive provisions in joint-venture agreements increase economic efficiency and some decrease economic efficiency. Section 15.2 also revealed why it is complicated to determine whether particular exemplars of such arrangements/provisions are economically efficient or inefficient but that a liberal-moral-rights-based society will often be able to make this determination third-best allocative efficiently.

It will also be difficult to determine whether the distributive impact of particular (joint ventures)/(functionally-analogous collaborations)/(restrictive provisions in joint-venture agreements) will be desirable or undesirable from a utilitarian perspective. I suspect that it will prove to be TBLE, liberally-appropriate, and desirable from the perspective of the utilitarian or any other egalitarian conception of the moral good to assume that (1) taken as classes, the income/wealth positions of and hence the marginal utility of money to the shareholders/creditors/managers/employees of the joint-venture/collaboration participants are no different from the income/wealth positions of and hence the marginal utility of money to their counterparts for the participants' rivals and (2) that (except in the rare instances in which there is good reason to suspect that this is not true), taken as classes, the customers of the perpetrators and their rivals are less-well-off than the shareholders/creditors/managers/employees of the perpetrators and their rivals (that the marginal utility of money is higher for these buyers than for the relevant shareholders/creditors/managers/employees). I also suspect (3) that it will be third-best desirable to ignore the general-equilibrium distributive effects of these phenomena when analyzing their desirability from a utilitarian (or any other egalitarian perspective).

However, even on these simplifying assumptions, the required distributive analysis will be complicated. I will assume *ad arguendo* that the conduct has no net equivalent-dollar impact on parties other than the perpetrators' and their product-rivals' shareholders/creditors/managers/employees and the perpetrators' and their product-rivals' possible and actual customers. If the conduct at issue would increase economic efficiency (on my current assumptions, would yield the perpetrators profits that exceed [the equivalent-dollar losses it would impose on the perpetrators' product-rivals] *plus* [any net equivalent-dollar losses it would impose on the possible and actual customers of the perpetrators and their product-rivals] or *minus* [any equivalent-dollar gains it would confer on these buyers]), whether the conduct would increase or decrease total utility will depend not only on the magnitudes of the equivalent-dollar gains and losses it would generate but also on whether it would confer equivalent-dollar losses on the relevant buyers and, if it would, on the ratio of the (average) marginal utility of money over the relevant ranges to the relevant buyers to the (average) marginal utility of money over the relevant ranges to the relevant shareholders/creditors/managers/employees (which depends both on the differences in their pre-conduct income/wealth positions and on the relationship between those income/wealth positions and the marginal utility of money to the individuals who occupy them). If the conduct at issue would decrease economic efficiency (on my current assumptions, would yield the perpetrators profits that would be lower than the equivalent-dollar losses it would impose on their product-rivals *plus* any equivalent-dollar losses it would impose on the relevant buyers or *minus* any equivalent-dollar gains it would confer on the relevant buyers), whether the conduct increases or decreases total utility will depend on whether it would confer an equivalent-dollar gain on or impose an equivalent-dollar loss on relevant buyers and, if it would confer an equivalent-dollar gain on these buyers, on their income/wealth positions relative to those of the relevant firms' shareholders/creditors/managers/employees and on the difference any such income/wealth-position difference makes to the (average) marginal utility of money to the two groups over the relevant ranges. All of these distributive-impact enquiries will be difficult. Thus, it will be hard to determine whether the equivalent-dollar gains the conduct confers on relevant buyers by increasing equilibrium-investment in the ARDEPPS of practice and by reducing prices by lowering marginal costs exceed or are exceeded by the equivalent-dollar losses the conduct imposes on the relevant buyers by decreasing equilibrium-investment in the ARDEPPS of practice (an alternative possible outcome) and by increasing the extent to which the ARDEPPS' sellers practice natural and/or contrived oligopolistic pricing. It will also be hard to ascertain the distributions of the income/wealth positions of (1) the relevant buyers and (2) the relevant shareholders/creditors/managers/employees as well as the relationship between differences in such income/wealth distributions and the differences in the (average) marginal utility of money to members of the two groups over the relevant ranges. Moreover, although the perpetrators may have some information about the income/wealth positions of both their shareholders/creditors/managers/employees and their possible and actual customers, I do not think that the antitrust-policy implementers will be able to rely exclusively on them to provide such information. I suspect that it will be desirable for the antitrust-policy-implementation authority to obtain more information on these parameters than the perpetrators possess or could "reasonably" be required to discover and disclose.

Nevertheless, I do think that the government of a liberal-moral-rights-based society will be able to increase total utility by responding appropriately to joint ventures, functionally-analogous collaborations of other sorts, and restrictive provisions in joint-venture agreements that are not liberal-moral-rights-violative. This conclusion is made more plausible by the fact that (this analysis' assumption that) the relevant government has already collected a great deal of the information that bears on the impact of such conduct on total utility in the process of assessing whether the conduct in question is liberal-moral-rights-violative.

I turn next to (1) the impact that joint ventures, functionally-analogous collaborative arrangements, and restrictive provisions in joint-venture agreements can have on the instantiation of the various pure non-utilitarian-egalitarian conceptions of the moral good and (2) the ability of the government of a liberal-moral-rights-based society to instantiate these equal-resource, equal-utility, and equal-opportunity conceptions of the moral good by responding appropriately to such conduct. The impact of the conduct at issue on the instantiation of these pure non-utilitarian-egalitarian conceptions of the moral good depends entirely on their impact on material inequality. As I previously indicated, such conduct will confer equivalent-dollar gains on its perpetrators (i.e., on their shareholders, creditors, managers, employees), will usually impose equivalent-dollar losses on their perpetrator's product-rivals (though they may confer equivalent-dollar gains on such parties if they reduce equilibrium investment in the ARDEPPS of practice by creating a situation in which the joint venture and a mutual rival of the parents that would otherwise have invested confront each other with critical natural-oligopolistic investment-disincentives), and can confer equivalent-dollar gains, impose equivalent-dollar losses, or have no net effect on the possible and actual customers of the perpetrators and their product-rivals. The conduct at issue will almost always increase material inequality and therefore disserve the instantiation of all non-utilitarian-egalitarian conceptions of the moral good if it imposes an equivalent-dollar loss on the possible and actual customers of the perpetrators and their product-rivals. It may also increase material inequality if it confers equivalent-dollar gains on these buyers depending *inter alia* on the size of those gains relative to the equivalent-dollar gains the conduct confers on its perpetrators, the size of the buyer-gains relative to the magnitude of the losses the conduct imposes on its perpetrators' product-rivals, the pre-conduct differences in the income/wealth positions of the relevant buyers, the shareholders/creditors/managers/employees of the perpetrators, and the shareholders/creditors/managers/employees of the perpetrators' product-rivals, and the metric for material inequality that the relevant pure non-utilitarian-egalitarian conception of the moral good deems morally appropriate. I recognize the difficulty of doing the required analyses, but I believe that a government of a liberal-moral-rights-based society that has already analyzed whether an exemplar of the conduct in question is liberal-moral-rights-violative through a process that obligates actors that want to engage in such conduct to provide the authorities with relevant information will be able to respond to conduct in these categories that is not deemed to be liberal-moral-rights-violative in a way that instantiates any of the pure non-utilitarian-egalitarian conceptions of the moral good.

I turn finally to mixed egalitarian conceptions of the moral good that value two or more of the pure conceptions of the moral good already considered. The preceding analyses lead me to conclude that (1) individual exemplars of joint ventures, functionally-analogous collaborations, and restrictive provisions in joint-venture agreements can either serve or disserve any of these mixed egalitarian conceptions of the moral good, (2) it will be complicated to determine whether any exemplar of or subclass of such conduct serves or disserves any of these mixed conceptions of the moral good, but (3) a government of a liberal-moral-rights-based society that has fulfilled its duty to prevent liberal-moral-rights-violative exemplars of such conduct and to provide the victims of such moral-rights-violative conduct with an appropriate opportunity to obtain legal redress will be able to secure the instantiation of any mixed egalitarian conception of the moral good by responding appropriately to exemplars of such conduct that it has concluded are not liberal-moral-rights-violative.

Notes

1. Public Law 94-435 (1976).
2. OJ L24/1 (May 1, 2004).
3. The third-best economic efficiency of the government of a liberal-moral-rights-based society's investigating the economic efficiency of individual joint ventures or individual restrictive provisions in joint-venture agreements or subclasses of joint ventures or joint-venture agreement restrictive provisions will (in one sense) be enhanced by the facts that (1) any such government will presumably have fulfilled its moral obligation to respond to joint ventures and restrictive provisions in joint-venture agreements in the way that maximizes the extent to which

liberal-moral-rights-related interests are secured, (2) in the course of fulfilling this obligation, any such government will have collected the information that bears on whether particular joint ventures or the restrictive provisions in particular joint-venture agreements are liberal-moral-rights-violative, and (3) much of this information is also relevant to the joint venture's or provision's economic efficiency.

4. In the U.S., the 3 most renowned cases that deal with joint-selling joint venture or joint-venture-type arrangements are (1) *Appalachian Coals, Inc. v. United States*, 288 U.S. 344 (1933), in which the "good" sold was lumps of coal (of various quality and size), (2) *National Collegiate Athletic Association v. Board of Regents of the University of Oklahoma*, 468 U.S. 85 (1984), in which the "good" sold was the right to broadcast collegiate athletic events, and (3) *Broadcast Music, Inc. v. Columbia Broadcasting System*, 441 U.S. 1 (1979), in which the "good" sold was the right to use copyrighted music, a case that is usually treated as a tie-in case because it involved copyright-holders' authorizing a firm to sell the right to play their music, which the firm did by issuing blanket licenses (allowing subscribers to play or use on specified terms every piece of music covered by the license). *Broadcast Music* did not involve the creation by parents of a separate entity but the independent creation of a firm that subsequently sold its services to the music copyright-holders. Strictly speaking, it therefore involves an "analogous collaborative arrangement" rather than a joint venture.
5. For an example of such a joint venture (in which a group of small independent grocers and local small grocery chains created a joint venture to perform these functions), see *United States v. Topco Associates*, 405 U.S. 596 (1972).
6. See *Associated Press v. United States*, 326 U.S. 1 (1945).
7. The relevant cases are patent-pool cases.
8. For U.S. cases that involve this functional category of joint ventures, see, *e.g.*, *General Motors Corp.*, 103 F.T.C. 374 (1984), a joint venture created by General Motors and Toyota to produce in an idle GM-plant a subcompact car based on a Toyota product sold only in Japan, *United States v. Sealy*, 388 U.S. 350 (1967), a joint venture formed by manufacturers of mattresses and other bedding products to manufacture and sell Sealy-brand mattresses and other bedding products that permitted the parents to manufacture and sell other brands of mattresses and bedding products under separate labels, and *United States v. Penn-Olin Chemical Co.*, 378 U.S. 158 (1964) a joint venture (Penn-Olin) proposed by a manufacturer of sodium chlorate in the U.S. Northwest (Pennsalt) and a purchaser and distributor of sodium chlorate that had patented certain uses of the product (Olin) to produce and distribute sodium chlorate in the U.S. Southeast.
9. For U.S. cases that focus on joint ventures deemed to be performing this function, see *FTC v. Superior Court Trial Lawyers Association*, 493 U.S. 413 (1989), *Arizona v. Maricopa County Medical Society*, 437 U.,S. 332 (1982), and *Goldfarb v. Virginia Bar*, 421 U.S. 773 (1975).
10. Far a U.S. case that falls into this functional category, see *National Society of Professional Engineers v. United States*, 435 U.S. 679 (1978).

11. It might be informative for me to comment on the relationship between the position I have just taken in the text and the U.S. courts' position that restrictive provisions in joint-venture agreements are lawful (under the Sherman Act) if and only if they are "ancillary" to a lawful joint venture. This task is complicated by the U.S. courts' taking inconsistent positions on the conditions that must be satisfied for a restrictive provision in a joint-venture agreement to qualify as "ancillary" and therefore be lawful. Some statements by U.S. courts imply that a restrictive provision in a joint-venture agreement is "ancillary" if and only if (1) the parents have a legitimate interest in preventing each other or the joint venture from engaging in the conduct the provision prohibits and (2) the restraint is necessary to preserve the profitability of an otherwise-lawful joint venture. Other statements by U.S. courts imply that only the first of the above two conditions must be satisfied for a restrictive provision to be "ancillary." The text is arguing that neither the fact that a restrictive provision enables a parent to increase the profitability of the joint venture by contributing information or personnel to a joint venture (without running any risk that those assets will be used in competition against it) nor the fact that the restrictive provision did not critically increase the profitability of a joint venture whose *ex ante* parent-perceived profitability was critically affected by a belief that it might reduce the absolute attractiveness of the best offers against which it would have to compete guarantees either the economic efficiency of the restrictive provision or the economic efficiency of the joint venture with or without the restrictive provision.

References

Appalachian Coals, Inc. v. United States, 288 U.S. 344 (1933).
Associated Press v. United States, 326 U.S. 1 (1945).
Arizona v. Maricopa County Medical Society, 437 U.S. 332 (1982).
Broadcast Music, Inc. v. Columbia Broadcasting System, 441 U.S. 1 (1979).
European Union Council Regulation 139/2004 on the Control of Concentrations Between Undertakings, OJ L24/1 (May 1, 2004).
FTC v. Superior Court Trial Lawyers Association, 493 U.S. 413 (1989).
General Motors Corp., 103 F.T.C. 374 (1984).
Goldfarb v. Virginia Bar, 421 U.S. 773 (1975).
Hart-Scott-Rodino Act, Public Law 94-435 (1976).
National Collegiate Athletic Association v. Board of Regents of the University of Oklahoma, 468 U.S. 85 (1984).
National Society of Professional Engineers v. United States, 435 U.S. 679 (1978).
United States v. Penn-Olin Chemical Co., 378 U.S. 158 (1964).
United States v. Sealy, 388 U.S. 350 (1967).
United States v. Topco Associates, 405 U.S. 596 (1972).

References

16 Internal Growth

Firms can grow internally by expanding their capacity, making quality-or-variety-increasing investments, executing production-process research, or (I suppose) by investing in new production facilities that incorporate known technology. For many years, economic analyses of a variety of issues (such as the impact of effective potential competition) proceeded on an implicit assumption that existing firms owned a given set of QV investments or investments in PPR and that, although owners of existing firms could decide to retire or not renew an extant investment or to grow through merger or acquisition or by creating a joint venture, they could not or would not choose to grow internally by (in my terms) by creating new QV investments or executing new PPR projects (e.g., again in my terms, by responding to effective potential competition by making a limit investment). Obviously, the economists who were making this assumption knew that firms could and did engage in internal growth. They just chose not to investigate this phenomenon and not to consider its implications for issues they did address.

In fact, firms can engage in horizontal, conglomerate, and/or vertical internal growth, and their decisions to do so can affect economic efficiency, violate or perhaps exercise liberal moral rights, and serve or disserve the instantiation of the various egalitarian conceptions of the moral good this study has considered. Relatedly, it is worth considering whether the government of any liberal-moral-rights-based society will be able to increase economic efficiency, secure liberal moral rights, and/or promote the instantiation of various egalitarian conceptions of the moral good by responding appropriately to firms' proposals or decisions to engage in internal growth.

This chapter's analyses of internal growth are presented in four sections. Section 16.1 analyzes the functions of internal growth (the ways in which internal growth can increase the growing firm's profits or yield its shareholders gains). Section 16.2 analyzes the possible impacts of internal growth on economic efficiency and the ability of a liberal-moral-rights-constrained government to increase economic efficiency by responding appropriately to internal growth. Section 16.3

R. S. Markovits, *Welfare Economics and Antitrust Policy—Vol. II*,
https://doi.org/10.1007/978-3-030-96482-5_16

analyzes the circumstances in which a firm's decision to grow internally will be liberal-moral-rights-violative and the ability of a government to increase the extent to which liberal moral rights are secured by responding appropriately to internal growth. And Sect. 16.4 analyzes the possible impacts of internal growth on the instantiation of the utilitarian, equal-utility, equal-resource, equal-opportunity, and various mixed-egalitarian conceptions of the moral good and the ability of a liberal-moral-rights-constrained government to instantiate egalitarian conceptions of the moral good by responding appropriately to firms' decisions to grow internally.

This chapter treatments of these issues are much shorter than their treatments in Chaps. 11, 12, 14, and 15. This chapter's treatments of these issues is abbreviated because it relies on those chapters' analyses of the issues in question as they relate to horizontal, conglomerate, and vertical (M&A)s and joint ventures and focuses primarily on any differences between the conclusions of the relevant internal-growth analyses and the conclusions of the counterpart analyses in the earlier chapters.

16.1 The Functions of Internal Growth

As just indicated, this section focuses on the differences between the ways in which internal growth on the one hand and (M&A)s and joint ventures on the other can contribute to a firm's profits. I will start by examining three ways in which it might be correct to say internal growth is either more able or more directly able to yield its perpetrator profits or its perpetrator's shareholders gains than (M&A)s or joint ventures can.

The first way assumes that the tax laws of the society in question do not classify as taxable income the unrealized capital gains individuals covered by the tax law secure when the price of stocks they own rises but do classify as taxable income any dividends such individuals receive on shares they own. These tax rules (which I believe are operative in all societies that have antitrust policies) tend to make it advantageous for shareholders for their companies to retain earnings rather than declare dividends even when those companies can earn a lower rate-of-return on their retained earnings than the shareholders could earn on the net-of-tax dividends they receive from those companies. Concomitantly, these tax rules cause internal growth financed by retained earnings to yield shareholders benefits if the company could not earn a higher rate-of-return on its retained earnings in some other way (say, by buying bonds or shares of other companies) even when the shareholders would realize a higher rate-of-return on the investments they would make with the after-tax proceeds of the dividends they would be paid if the company decided not to retain the relevant earnings than the company could realize by investing itself the earnings in question.[1] Admittedly, acquisitions and joint ventures can also yield shareholders tax advantages in this way, but mergers can do so only to the extent that the resulting firm must devote additional resources to its consolidation (to making it operate more proficiently).

The second possibility I want to discuss is a way in which internal growth can yield its perpetrator more profits than equally-large (M&A)s and joint ventures can. This possibility relates to three facts or sets of facts about a company's managers: first, unlike almost all other firm-assets, the (private) productivity of a manager tends to appreciate rather than depreciate as the manager grows older because managerial productivity increases with experience; second, part of the experience that increases a manager's productivity is firm-specific in the sense that it relates to knowledge a manager obtains through time about (A) the firm's underutilized capabilities and weaknesses, (B) the identity of the individual(s) in the firm that must be convinced of the profitability of a decision for the firm to make it, and (C) the most effective arguments to make or the most effective way to persuade those influential firm-members; and third, because for the reasons just stated a manager is likely to be more productive for a firm for which he or she has worked for a considerable period of time than for a new employer and the compensation that an experienced manager will be able to secure from a new employer is likely to be lower than his or her product for the firm for which he or she has worked for a significant period of time, firms will be likely to be able to profit by retaining the services of their experienced managers and by taking advantage of their increasing capabilities by promoting them to higher positions. To do so, firms will have to grow, and, I suspect, for this purpose, internal growth will be superior both to growth by engaging in (M&A)s or growth by creating joint ventures. In this respect, a given dollar-investment in internal growth will be superior to the same dollar-investment in (M&A)s because more managerial resources are required to manage a given dollar-amount of internal growth than to consolidate the operations of a firm that would result from an acquisition of the same size. In this respect, I also think that a given dollar-investment in internal growth will be superior to the same dollar-investment in a joint venture because existing managers' knowledge of the firm will be more relevant to their managing its internal growth than to their managing a joint venture that their firm partly owns many of whose managers will come from the other parent or from other sources.

The third way in which internal growth may be "more able" than (M&A)s or joint ventures to contribute to its perpetrators' profits relates to critical monopolistic investment-incentives. Internal growth will at least sometimes contribute to its perpetrator's profits because the perpetrator has a monopolistic investment-incentive to make the internal-growth investment. This will occur both when the firm's *ex ante* perception that the growth would be at least normally profitable was critically affected by its belief that it did or might have a monopolistic investment-incentive to make the investment in question (in which case I call the investment a "limit investment") and when the monopolistic investment-incentive did not critically affect the firm's *ex ante* perception that the investment would be at least normally profitable. Admittedly, as previously indicated, both (M&A)s and joint ventures can create situations in which a participant that would not otherwise have a monopolistic investment-incentive to make a particular investment did have such an incentive, but this effect (which internal growth can also produce) is (so to speak) indirect.

I will now list six of the ways in which (M&A)s and/or joint ventures can increase their participants' profits that have no internal-growth counterpart:

(1) unlike (M&A)s, internal growth cannot yield its perpetrator profits by enabling it to take advantage of tax losses another actor (participant) could not use;
(2) unlike (M&A)s, internal growth cannot enable its perpetrators respectively to liquidate his or her assets and retire from management and share in the gains one of its participants realized by liquidating his or her assets and retiring from management;
(3) unlike horizontal (M&A)s, internal growth cannot yield its perpetrator profits by directly freeing the perpetrator from another firm's price and investment competition (though internal growth can reduce the price-competition its perpetrator faces by deterring a rival from investing);
(4) unlike joint ventures, internal growth does not enable its perpetrator to engage in communications with another firm that enable it (them) to secure more COMs and NOMs and to coordinate their predatory moves;
(5) unlike joint ventures that contain restrictive provisions, internal growth cannot directly enable its perpetrator (perpetrators) to secure a rival's contractual agreement not to invest in its ARDEPPS; and
(6) unlike joint ventures, internal growth cannot benefit each perpetrator by giving the other participant a share in an enterprise whose possession will deter that firm from investing in the ARDEPPS in which the internal growth/joint-venture investment is located.

Of course, internal growth can also yield its perpetrator profits in many of the ways in which (M&A)s and/or joint ventures can yield their perpetrators profits—for example, (1) because the internally-made investment yields profits even if one ignores its effect on the profits yielded by the "grower's" other investments, (2) because the investment increases the grower's profits on its other projects by filling out its product-line or enhancing its reputation for producing high-quality products, (3) because, by increasing its prominence, the internal growth enhances the grower's ability to initiate a series of price-announcements that increase the announcers' HNOP arrays or enable them to obtain NOMs, (4) because the investment increases the profits the grower can realize by engaging in strategic behavior (A) by enabling it to take advantage of organizational economies of scale in building and maintaining a reputation for engaging in such conduct, (B) by increasing its sales and hence its ability to infer non-cooperation with its contrived-oligopolistic pricing from sales-evidence, (C) by enhancing its ability to reciprocate to cooperators or to retaliate against non-cooperators by pricing the newly-created product to achieve these objectives, and (D) by enhancing its ability to engage in predation by enabling it to predatorily advertize and price the new product.

16.2 The Impact of Internal Growth on Economic Efficiency and the Ability of a Liberal-Moral-Rights-Constrained Government to Increase Economic Efficiency by Responding Appropriately to Internal Growth

The economic efficiency of any investment a firm creates when it grows internally equals the profits it yields the firm that makes it *plus* any deflation in those profits or *minus* any inflation in those profits. The fact that an investment was (1) a "real" investment made by a growing firm to create a new product, execute a new PPR project, or enable it to use a known alternative production process as opposed to being (2) a monetary investment made by one extant firm to acquire another extant firm or (3) a real investment made by the parents of a joint venture via the joint venture (if I distinguish such investments from other sorts of internal growth) or (4) a real investment made by a new business entity can affect the distortion in the profits it yields the investing firm or the benefits it yields that firm's shareholders only if these various categories of investment yield profits (shareholder benefits) in different ways where the distortion in the profits/benefits in question vary with the way in which they were generated.

These anodyne claims imply (1) that the analysis of the distortion in the profits yielded by real investments made by growing existing firms will differ from the analysis of the distortion in the profits yielded by the other "sorts of investments" referenced above only to the extent that these various categories of investments yield profits (shareholder benefits) in different ways where the distortion in any relevant amount of profits (shareholder benefits) an investment yields in any particular way varies with "the way" in question and (2) that the economic efficiency of real investments made by growing extant firms taken either as a group or individually will differ from the economic efficiency of investments made by firms that result from (M or A)s, investments in acquisitions, joint-venture investments, or investments made by start-ups only to the extent that the proportions of the profits (shareholder benefits) generated by these five categories of investment that derive from different sources vary among the categories of investment in question.

To illustrate these points, I will point out 4 of the differences in the distortions in the profits yielded respectively by horizontal-internal-growth investments and horizontal-acquisition investments:

(1) unlike the profits yielded by some horizontal-acquisitions investments, the profits yielded by horizontal-internal-growth investments will not be inflated by the inflation in the profits that the relevant horizontal-acquisition investments yields by creating a resulting firm that can take advantage of a tax loss of one participant that that participant could not use;
(2) unlike the profits yielded by horizontal-acquisition investments, the profits yielded by horizontal-internal-growth investments will not be inflated by their eliminating the price-competition the participants waged against each other;
(3) to the extent that a horizontal-acquisition investment increases the profits its participants realize by practicing natural and contrived oligopolistic pricing by

more than a horizontal-internal-growth investment of the same size increases the profits the growing firm realizes by engaging in oligopolistic pricing, the profits yielded by the horizontal acquisition will be inflated more by its increasing its participants' oligopolistic pricing than the profits yielded by the horizontal internal growth will be inflated by its increasing the amount of profits the growing firm realizes by practicing oligopolistic pricing; and

(4) to the extent that, over the long run, a horizontal-acquisition investment of given size decreases equilibrium investment in the ARDEPPS of consummation by more than a horizontal-internal-growth investment decreases equilibrium investment in that ARDEPPS, the impact of this difference on the aggregate distortion in the profits yielded by the two investments will depend on (A) whether investments in the ARDEPPS of consummation are QV investments or investments in PPR, and (B) the absolute magnitudes of the positive distortions in the profits that would have been yielded by the deterred QV investments and the the negative distortions in the profits that would have been yielded by the deterred investments in PPR.

However, although I hope that the four sets of points just made are of interest, they are relevant in the current context only to the extent that they shed light on the probable economic efficiency of internal-growth investments and on the ability of a liberal-moral-rights-constrained government to increase economic efficiency by responding appropriately to internal growth. If it would be third-best allocatively inefficient for the antitrust-policy implementers of a liberal-moral-rights-based society to attempt to assess the economic efficiency of individual internal-growth investments or various subsets of such investments, it would be economically efficient for the government of such a society to allow all internal-growth investments unless it concluded that as a group they would decrease economic efficiency by more than the allocative cost of prohibiting them. I doubt that an economic-efficiency case could be made for prohibiting all internal growth under the information-conditions specified. Admittedly, some internal-growth investments will decrease economic efficiency by increasing the incidence of oligopolistic and predatory conduct, and some will reduce economic efficiency by deterring other firms from making investments whose substitution for the relevant internal-growth investments would be economically efficient (because of the incentives tax law gives shareholders to support the companies' they own retaining earnings and [this I have not yet said] because the managers of established companies have a parochial incentive to make their companies grow that is not much controlled by boards of directors and that is insufficiently countered by the threat of hostile takeovers). However, I suspect that, taken together, internal-growth investments are rendered economically efficient by their enabling established firms to make more-profitable and more-economically-efficient use of their existing managers' increasing, firm-specific productivity.

For me, the more salient issue is the third-best allocative efficiency of a liberal-moral-rights-constrained government's prohibiting some internal growth and allowing some internal growth. I am disposed to conclude that selective prohibitions would be TBLE if the government required at least some prospective internal growers to obtain the permission of an antitrust authority or reviewing count after having supplied a great deal of information about their investment plan and relevant surrounding conditions that bear on their proposed internal-growth investment's economic efficiency—that is, if the government adopted a review protocol similar to the protocol that the Hart–Scott–Rodino Act[2] and the E.U. Council Regulation 139/2004 on the Control of Concentrations Between Undertakings[3] promulgated for (M&A)s. I also think that—even if no such protocol is promulgated—it will sometimes (perhaps even frequently) be TBLE for a liberal-moral-rights-constrained antitrust-policy-implementation authority to base prohibitions of particular internal-growth investments on information volunteered by eyewitnesses, information solicited or elicited from eyewitnesses by offering them rewards, and company-reports, meeting-minutes, and e-mails the authority discovered on its own.

16.3 The Liberal-Moral-Rights-Violativeness of Internal Growth and the Ability of the Government of a Liberal-Moral-Rights-Based Society to Secure Liberal Moral Rights by Responding Appropriately to Internal Growth

Same old story. An internal-growth investment will be liberal-rights-violative (1) if the growing firm's *ex ante* perception that the growth would be profitable (or beneficial to shareholders) was critically positively affected by its perception that the investment in question would reduce the absolute attractiveness of the best offers against which the firm would have to compete in one or more ways that would render the investment profitable though economically inefficient in an otherwise-Pareto-perfect company (by the firm's perception that it had a critical monopolistic investment-incentive to make the relevant investment or that the investment would critically increase the profits the firm would realize by engaging in oligopolistic or predatory conduct) or (2) if *ex ante* the firm believed that the investment would or might increase the profits it could realize by engaging in strategic behavior and intended to take advantage of any such opportunity the investment created. Some internal-growth investments are liberal-moral-rights-violative, and some are not. I am certain that the percentage that are not is far too high for it to be morally permissible for the government of a liberal-moral-rights-based society to ban them all, even if some subset of the shareholders/creditors/managers/employees of a company did not have a property-type liberal moral right that it be allowed to make profitable internal-growth decisions that are not liberal-moral-rights-violative but certainly if some such individuals have such a liberal moral right. But I suspect that the more salient point is that it will be feasible and just for the government of a liberal-moral-rights-based society to respond to internal-growth investments selectively: to use (1) information provided under legal orders by firms that want to engage in internal growth, (2) testimony provided by witnesses, and (3) e-mail/meeting-minute/company-study information it unearths to assess the liberal-moral-rights-violativeness of particular proposed internal-growth investments and to then prohibit those exemplars of internal growth that it concludes are sufficiently likely to be liberal-moral-rights-violative (or perhaps are sufficiently likely to disserve a relevant conception of the moral good—see below).

16.4 The Impact of Internal-Growth Investments on the Instantiation of Various Egalitarian Conceptions of the Moral Good and the Ability of the Government of a Liberal-Moral-Rights-Based Society to Secure the Instantiation of These Conceptions of the Moral Good by Responding Appropriately to Internal-Growth Investments

I will be brief, at least for me. Some internal-growth investments will increase total utility (by increasing economic efficiency and either benefiting the growing firm's actual and possible buyers or generating a distributive impact that is insufficiently undesirable from a utilitarian perspective to outweigh the pro-utility effects of the increase in economic efficiency they generate), and some internal-growth investments will decrease total utility by reducing economic efficiency and/or inflicting losses on directly-affected buyers (I am simplifying). Some internal-growth investments will serve the instantiation of pure non-utilitarian-egalitarian conceptions of the moral good by decreasing material inequality, and some will disserve the instantiation of these pure non-utilitarian-egalitarian conceptions of the moral good by increasing material inequality. Some internal-growth investments will serve and some will disserve each of the possible mixed egalitarian conceptions of the moral good. I have no opinion worth consideration about the percentages of internal-growth investments that serve and disserve these various conceptions of the moral good. The fact that the percentages in question are "unclear" to say the least is not really problematic because it will almost certainly be morally good from the perspective of any of these egalitarian conceptions of the moral good for the government of a liberal-moral-rights-based society to determine more selectively whether particular internal-growth investments serve or disserve the instantiation of a relevant conception of the moral good by requiring those who want to make such investments to supply the authorities with moral-good-relevant information, to supplement such information with volunteered and induced eyewitness testimony and with information gleaned from company e-mails, meeting-minutes, and studies and to use this information to instantiate the moral good by controlling the decisions of firms to make investments that are not liberal-moral-rights-violative.

I want to close this chapter with a Coda that focuses on the possibility that it might be economically efficient, liberal-moral-rights-securing, and/or moral-good-promoting for a government to break up firms whose dissolution would increase economic efficiency, secure liberal moral rights, and/or promote some defensible conception of the moral good even though these firms had never violated any antitrust policy. I chose not to write a separate chapter on this issue in part for nominalist reasons: such policies seem to me to be regulated-industry policies, not antitrust or competition policies. I am not going to reverse this decision at this juncture. I will confine myself to making one, admittedly-obvious point about such company-dissolution policies. Even if a decision to partially or totally dissolve a company whose great size cannot be attributed to its illegal behavior would otherwise increase economic efficiency or secure the moral good in a relevant defensible sense, such a decision might not do so because it might deter firms from making economically-efficient and moral-good-promoting choices that will cause them to grow out of a concern that those decisions might subsequently lead to the government's dissolving them or might induce firms that fear that the government might dissolve them to split themselves up to avoid the government intervention when their self-dissolution decreases economic efficiency and disserves the moral good. I should add that it might also be liberal-moral-rights-violative to break up a company that has not grown through illegal conduct without compensating the shareholders, creditors, and possibly the managers and employees who would be harmed by the dissolution. I hasten to add that I am far from convinced that this last concern is warranted.

Notes

1. I should add that the ability of internal growth to benefit shareholders will be further enhanced if the tax laws of the society in question enable beneficiaries of the shareholders' estates to use a stepped-up basis when calculating any capital gains they obtain by selling shares they have inherited from the original-shareholders/testator—that is, to calculate their capital gains to equal the difference between the price they received for the shares and the price the shares had on the date of the testator's death as opposed to the price the testator paid for the shares.
2. Public Law 94–435 (1976).
3. OJ 24/1 (May 1, 20,004).

References

European Union Council Regulation 139/2004 on the Control of Concentrations Between Undertakings, OJ L24/2 (May 1, 2004).
Hart-Scott-Rodino Act, Public Law 94–435 (1976).

Part III

The Economic Efficiency, Liberal Justness, and Non-Liberal-Egalitarian Moral Desirability of U.S. Antitrust Law and E.U. Competition Law, Correctly Interpreted and Applied as a Matter of Law

Introduction to Part III

On the admittedly-contested but to my mind uncontestable premise that the major U.S. antitrust statutes—the Sherman Act,[1] the Clayton Act,[2], and the Federal Trade Commission Act[3]—and the sources of E.U. competition law—what is now the 2009 Treaty of Lisbon[4] and the European Community's Merger Control Regulation (EMCR)[5]—promulgate judicially-cognizable and (in principle) outcome-determinative tests of illegality and contain provisions whose conduct and business-entity coverages are judicially cognizable, Part III analyzes the economic efficiency, liberal justness, and moral desirability from the perspectives of the utilitarian and other egalitarian conceptions of the moral good (justice-considerations aside) of U.S. antitrust law as written and E.U. competition law as written. Part III does not consider what I take to be the mistakes that U.S. and E.U. courts have made when interpreting and applying respectively U.S. antitrust law and E.U. competition law. Nor does it consider the mistakes that I believe (1) U.S. antitrust-law-enforcement authorities (the Antitrust Division of the U.S. Department of Justice [DOJ] and the Federal Trade Commission [FTC]) have made when interpreting and applying U.S. antitrust law (e.g., those made in the DOJ/FTC horizontal-merger guidelines[6]) or the mistakes that I believe E.U.-competition-law-enforcement authorities (the European Commission [EC]) has made when interpreting and applying E.U. competition law (e.g., those made in the EC merger-guidelines,[7] in various Director General [DG] Discussion Papers[8] and EC Guidance publications,[9] and in the various Block Exemption Regulations [BERs] the EC has promulgated under authority granted by the Council of Ministers to control various vertical practices[10]). Finally, Part III does not consider (1) the proposed (M&A) notification-provisions and proposed-(M&A) administrative-review protocols of U.S. antitrust law and E.U. competition law, (2) the civil-and-criminal damages/civil-fine/criminal-fine/non-incarcerative-penalty/incarcerative-penalty provisions of U.S. antitrust law and E.U. competition law (though it does consider the fact that one U.S. antitrust law [the Sherman-Act] entitles legally-entitled victims to obtain treble damages whereas E.U. competition law provides no opportunity for victims of its violation to obtain legal redress), (3) the (antitrust-law/competition law) enforcement-budget decisions made by the U.S. and E.U. governments, (4) the enforcement-priorities of U.S. and E.U. (antitrust/competition)-law-enforcement authorities, and (5) the criteria used to select relevant judges and enforcement-authority personnel, the remuneration paid such personnel, the criteria used to decide whether to retain and promote them, the restrictions imposed on the emoluments they may receive from non-government sources during their government-service and the jobs they may take and emoluments they may receive after leaving government-service.

Part III contains two chapters. Chapter 17 describes and compares U.S. antitrust law as written and E.U. competition law as written. Chapter 17 has three sections. Section 17.1 describes the test(s) of illegality promulgated by and the conduct-coverage and business-entity coverage of the major U.S. antitrust laws (the Sherman Act, the Clayton Act, and the Federal Trade Commission Act). Section 17.2 describes the tests of illegality promulgated by and the conduct and business-entity coverages of Article 101 of the 2009 Treaty of Lisbon, of Article 102 of the 2009 Treaty of Lisbon, and of the EMCR. Section 17.3 compares the tests of illegality promulgated by and conduct and business-entity coverages of U.S. antitrust law as written and E.U. competition law as written.

Chapter 18 analyzes and compares the economic efficiency, liberal justness, and egalitarian moral desirability (liberal-justice considerations aside) of U.S. antitrust law and E.U. competition law as written, taking account of their respective tests of illegality and conduct and business-entity coverages but ignoring those features of the two legal regimes that Chap. 17 does not address. Chapter 18 contains 8 sections, each of which focuses on the two systems' treatments of a category of conduct covered by Chaps. 9–16. Chapter 18 addresses those categories of conduct in the order in which they are analyzed in those chapters.

Notes

1. Sherman Act, 26 Stat. 209 (1890) (codified as amended at 15 U.S.C. Section 1–11).
2. Clayton Act, 38 Stat. 730 (1914) (codified as amended at 15 U.S.C. Sections 12–27).
3. Federal Trade Commission Act, 38 Stat. 717 (1914) (codified as amended at 15 U.S.C. Sections 41–45).
4. Treaty of Lisbon Amending the Treaty on European Union and the Treaty Establishing the European Community (hereinafter 2009 Treaty of Lisbon), 2007 OJ C306 p.1 (December 13, 2007). The 2009 Treaty of Lisbon is the currently-operative variant of the Treaty Establishing the European Economic Community (also known as the Treaty of Rome), 298 U.N.T.S. 11 (March 25, 1957). The Articles of the 2009 Treaty of Lisbon that are most relevant for European Union (E.U.) competition law are now numbered Articles 101 and 102.
5. Council Regulation 139/2004 on the Control of Concentrations Between Undertakings, OJ L 24/1 (May 1, 2004).
6. Department of Justice and Federal Trade Commission 2010 Horizontal Merger Guidelines (August 19, 2010).

7. EC Guidelines on the Assessment of Horizontal Mergers, OJ C31/5 (2004). OJ L241 (May 1, 2004).
8. See, *e.g.*, DG Competition Discussion Paper on the Application of Article 82 of the Treaty (which is now Article 102 of the 2009 Treaty of Lisbon) to Exclusionary Abuses (Dec. 2005).
9. See, *e.g.*, EC Guidelines on the Commission's Enforcement Priorities in Applying Article 82 of the E.C. Treaty to Abusive Exclusionary Conduct by Dominant Undertakings, C 45/02 (2009). In this study, "EC" stands for "European Commission," and "E.C." stands for "European Community" just as "U.S." stands for "United States" and "E.U." stands for "European Union."
10. See, *e.g.*, Commission Regulation (EC) 2790/1999 of 22 December 1999 on the Application of Art. 81(3) of the Treaty (which is now Article 101(3) of the 2009 Treaty of Lisbon) to Categories of Vertical Agreements and Concerted Practices, OJ L336 (1999).

References

Clayton Act, 26 Stat. 209. (1890). (codified as amended at 15 U.S.C. Section 1–11).
Commission Regulation on the Application of Art. 81(3) to Categories of Vertical Agreements and Concerted Practices. (1999).
Council Regulation 139/2004 on the Control of Concentrations Between Undertakings, OJ L24/2. (May 1, 2004).
DG Discussion Paper on the Application of Article 82 of the Treaty to Exclusionary Abuses (2005).
EC Guidelines on the Assessment of Horizontal Mergers, C 31/5 OJ. (2004).
EC Guidelines on the Commission's Enforcement Priorities in Applying Article 82 of the EC Treaty to Abusive Exclusionary Conduct by Dominant Undertakings. (2009).
Federal Trade Commission Act, 38 Stat. 717. (1914). (codified as amended at 15 U.S.C. Sections 41–45).
Sherman Act, 26 Stat. 209. (1890). (codified as amended at 15 U.S.C. Sections 1–11).
Treaty Establishing the European Community (Treaty of Rome), 298 U.N.T.S. 11. (May 25, 1957).
Treaty of Lisbon Amending the Treaty on European Union and the Treaty Establishing the European Community, 2007 OJ C306 p.1. (December 13, 2007).

17 U.S. Antitrust Law and E.U. Competition Law, Correctly Interpreted and Applied as Matters of Law: The Tests of Illegality They Respectively Promulgate and the Business Entities and Conduct to Which Those Tests Respectively Apply

This chapter contains three sections. Section 17.1 delineates the tests of illegality promulgated by U.S. antitrust law and the business entities and conduct to which U.S. antitrust law applies those tests. Section 17.2 provides parallel descriptions of E.U. competition law. Section 17.3 compares U.S. antitrust law's and E.U. competition law's respective treatments of exemplars of each of the eight categories of conduct analyzed respectively in Chaps. 9–16.

Here is a partial list of this chapter's conclusions: (1) both legal regimes promulgate specific-anticompetitive-intent, lessening-competition, and distorting-competition tests of illegality; (2) E.U. competition law also promulgates an "exploitative abuse of a dominant position" test of illegality; (3) in some important respects, the business-entity and conduct coverages of the two legal regimes differ—for example, E.U. competition law covers natural-oligopolistic conduct, which U.S. law does not cover, and U.S. law prohibits contrived-oligopolistic conduct that does not involve an agreement and single-firm predatory conduct by any firm whereas E.U. law prohibits such conduct only when the perpetrator occupies a dominant position; (4) the (antitrust/competition)-law-creating provisions of both regimes contain some text that cannot be operationalized at all or without making policy-judgments—thus, the U.S. Clayton Act refers to "any line of commerce" and "any line of commerce in any section of the country," Article 102 refers to "a dominant position," the U.S. Clayton Act contains the expression "*substantially* to lessen competition" (emphasis added), and the EMCR contains the expression "*significantly* impeded *effective* competition" (emphases added), and (5) clause (e) of Article 101(1) and clause (d) of Article 102 manifest the E.U. treaty's drafters' and ratifiers' failure to understand the non-illegal functions of the various types of contractual provisions producers use to control their independent distributions.

This chapter's accounts of and comparisons of the tests of illegality promulgated by U.S. antitrust law and E.U. competition law and the categories of business conduct and business entities to which these two legal regimes apply the various tests of illegality they promulgate is designed to prepare the way for Chap. 18's

R. S. Markovits, *Welfare Economics and Antitrust Policy—Vol. II*,
https://doi.org/10.1007/978-3-030-96482-5_17

comparison of the two legal regimes' economic efficiency, liberal justness, and egalitarian moral attractiveness.

17.1 The Business Entities Covered by, the Tests of Illegality Respectively Promulgated by, and the Conduct Respectively Covered by the Sherman Act, the Clayton Act, and the Federal Trade Commission Act—The 3 Major Sources of U.S. Federal Antitrust Law

Because all 3 of these U.S. antitrust statutes cover all business firms (regardless of their size or economic power), all trade associations, and all actors of other sorts, the rest of Sect. 17.1 will not allude to the entity-coverage issue.

17.1.1 The Test of Illegality Promulgated by and the Conduct-Coverage of the Sherman Act

Section 1 of the Sherman Act prohibits "contracts, agreements, or conspiracies in restraint of trade," and Section 2 of the Sherman Act prohibits "monopoliz[ing] conduct" or attempts to monopolize. In my judgment, the Sherman Act promulgates a specific-anticompetitive-intent test of illegality. According to this test, covered conduct is illegal if one or more of its participants' *ex ante* perception that it was at least normally profitable was critically affected by a belief that it would or might increase the participant's profits by reducing the absolute attractiveness of the best offers against which it would have to compete in one or more ways that would render the conduct profitable even if it would be economically inefficient in an otherwise-Pareto-perfect economy—paradigmatically, by reducing or eliminating the price and/or investment competition the participants wage against each other and/or by reducing or eliminating the price and/or investment competition a non-perpetrator will wage against one or more perpetrators (perhaps by driving the non-perpetrator rival out of business or deterring a potential competitor from entering) when the relevant conduct's doing do would critically inflate the participant's *ex ante* perception of the conduct's *ex ante* profitability in an oPp economy. *Inter alia*, this conclusion implies that, in the sense in which this concept is used in the Sherman Act, a firm does not "monopolize" simply by charging a price that exceeds its marginal cost or by realizing a supernormal rate-of-return. This conclusion is favored by 4 facts: (1) the fact that, increasingly as the nineteenth century progressed, U.S. courts understood "monopolizing conduct" to refer to what I call conduct motivated by specific anticompetitive intent, (2) the fact that the Sherman Act was passed in response to and to prevent what was perceived to be conduct that manifested in essence its perpetrators' specific anticompetitive intent (predatory conduct and mergers and acquisitions that were critically motivated by their participants' desire to free each other from the competition they would otherwise have waged as independent entities), (3) the admittedly-contestable "fact" that, by and large, the comments that the legislators who passed the Sherman Act made about their objectives that did not focus on the business conduct that led to its passage were most consistent with my conclusion that the statute promulgates a specific-anticompetitive-intent test of illegality, and (4) the fact that U.S. industrial policy as a whole (which includes its intellectual-property [IP] law) is based on the premise that competition on the merits that puts its perpetrators in a position to charge supra-competitive prices and/or realize supernormal rates-of-return is morally legitimate and promotes the public interest [admittedly inchoately] by increasing economic efficiency).

In my judgment, with 4 exceptions, the Sherman Act covers all categories of antitrust-policy-coverable business-conduct. The first exception is unsuccessful attempts to enter into contracts that manifest at least one perpetrator's specific anticompetitive intent. My conclusion that, correctly interpreted as a matter of U.S. law, the Sherman Act would not be read to cover unsuccessful attempts to enter into and execute contracts motivated by specific anticompetitive intent is based on the following facts: (1) the Sherman Act is a federal (central-government) statute; (2) the U.S. federal government has not passed a "general attempt-statute" (that is, a statute that prohibits all unsuccessful attempts to do something whose successful commission is prohibited); (3) the U.S. federal courts have consistently refused to read an attempt-provision into any statute that does not contain one; (4) the argument for this legal practice (which focuses on the moral right of individuals to receive "fair notice" of their legal duties) is particularly strong when the statute in question is a criminal statute; (5) the Sherman Act is (in part) a criminal statute; (6) Section 1 of the Sherman Act, which prohibits "contracts, agreements, or conspiracies in restraint of trade" does not include an attempt-provision; (7) although Section 2 of the Sherman Act does prohibit "attempts to monopolize," the U.S. courts' refusal to read attempt-provisions into a section of a criminal statute that does not prohibit unsuccessful attempts to do something whose successful completion it prohibits favors the conclusion that it would be incorrect as a matter of U.S. law to hold that in the Sherman Act context the concept of "attempts to monopolize" covers unsuccessful attempts to enter into contracts, agreements, or conspiracies motivated by specific anticompetitive intent in addition to unsuccessful attempts to engage in single-firm behavior motivated by specific anticompetitive intent.

The second type of antitrust-policy-coverable business-conduct that the Sherman Act does not cover is natural-oligopolistic behavior. Natural-oligopolistic conduct is not covered by the Sherman Act because natural-oligopolistic conduct does not involve the communication or fulfillment of any promise or threat that is motivated by specific anticompetitive interest—does not involve the making of any contract in restraint of trade or the making or execution of any threat to respond to non-cooperation by making inherently-unprofitable moves to inflict losses on the non-cooperators.

The third type of antitrust-policy-coverable conduct that I think it correct as a matter of U.S. law to conclude that the Sherman Act does not cover is devoting resources to political parties/campaigns/candidates and/or participation in government-decision-making processes without behaving "unfairly" (say, without lying, intentionally making misleading statements, or hiring one or more perceived neutral experts or observers to make public statements that favor the actor's policy-preferences without revealing that the hiree was being paid to do so). Although the text of the Sherman Act does not ground this last exception, it is favored (1) by individuals' possession of a liberal-moral-rights-related interest in engaging in political speech, participating in politics in other ways, and participating in government-decision-making processes, (2) by the related possibility that any law that restricts an individual's ability to engage in such conduct would be unconstitutional on that account, and (3) by the practice of U.S. courts' that are confronted with statutes whose texts' conventional reading would result in some of their applications being unconstitutional adopting a so-called saving construction of the statute that renders it constitutional.

The fourth type of antitrust-policy-coverable business conduct that I think it would be correct as a matter of U.S. law to interpret the Sherman Act not to cover (or, perhaps better-expressed, not to prohibit) is contracts between buyers not to compete against each other in their roles as buyers—joint-purchasing agreements or the creation of joint-purchasing joint ventures. I acknowledge that no textual argument can be made for this conclusion—that, linguistically, joint-purchasing agreements and joint ventures are "contracts in restraint of trade." My admittedly-contestable argument for the conclusion that the Sherman Act does not cover or at least does not prohibit such contracts is that (1) the legislators that passed the Sherman Act did so in part to benefit ultimate consumers, (2) in the United States, it is correct as a matter of law for courts to interpret or apply a statute to effectuate the goals it was designed to achieve when the court concludes that a legislative text has been mis-drafted in a way that disserves the legislators' goals, and (3) because the buyers that agree to enter into a joint-purchasing agreement or that create a purchasing joint venture face sellers that have monopoly and/or oligopoly power (that such buyers do not become monopsonists in the traditional sense of being buyers that face an upward-sloping supply curve), their participation in the joint-purchasing agreement or joint venture reduces not only the average cost to them of purchasing the "input" they are buying (as distributors or final-good producers) but also the marginal cost to them of buying the marginal unit of the input(s) involved, hence the marginal cost to them of reselling the "input" in question when they are distributors and the "input" is a final good or the marginal cost to them of producing the final good they use the relevant input they are purchasing together, hence the price(s) they charge final consumers for the relevant good(s) they distribute or produce. I acknowledge that this legal interpretation would be hard to justify if joint-purchasing arrangements or purchasing joint ventures violated the liberal moral rights of the joint purchasers' affected suppliers.

17.1.2 The Conduct-Coverage of and Test of Illegality Promulgated by the Clayton Act

Unlike the Sherman Act, whose two relevant sections cover a wide range of business-conduct, each of the three relevant sections of the Clayton Act covers a narrow range of business-conduct. I will now discuss the conduct-coverage of each of these three sections of the Clayton Act.

Section 2 covers "price discrimination" defined idiosyncratically to reference the charging of different prices to different buyers at (about) the same time for "commodities" of like grade and quality. Two points need to be made about the conduct-coverage of Section 2. First, Section 2 does not cover a seller's charging the same price for a commodity of given quality at a given time when the cost to the seller of supplying the different buyers in question differs—for example, because the commodity in question is a good that is delivered to the buyer and the cost of delivery differs from buyer to buyer because of differences in their locations and/or their delivery docks: that is why I indicated that the Clayton Act defines "price discrimination" idiosyncratically (differently from the way in which it is defined in economics). I should add that, although the Clayton Act does allow what it calls "price discrimination" if the difference in prices is cost-justified, the Clayton Act places on defendants the burden of proof on the cost-justification issue, and U.S. courts have been unjustifiably reluctant to be persuaded by cost-justification evidence. (The Clayton Act also allows sellers that have engaged in "price discrimination" in its sense of that expression to exonerate themselves by establishing that they charged the lower price to match what would otherwise be a lawful superior offer of a rival.) Second, the Clayton Act's reference to "commodity" has been read (linguistically plausibly) to imply that the Act does not cover "price discrimination" on services or insurance.

Section 3 of the Clayton Act covers decisions by "any person…to lease or make a sale of goods…or fix a price charged therefore, or discount from, or rebate upon, such price, on the condition, agreement or understanding that the lessor or purchaser thereof shall not use or deal in the goods…of a competitor or competitors of the lessee or seller"—that is, covers single-brand exclusive dealerships and full-requirements clauses in tie-ins and long-term sales-agreements). Two points should also be made about Section 3. First, Section 3's use of the word "goods" has been read (again, plausibly literally) to imply that it does not cover otherwise-covered arrangements that involve services or insurance. Second, Section 3 does not cover an actor's entering into a reciprocity agreement that conditions its obligation to purchase a trading-partner's good on the trading partner's agreeing not to use or deal in the goods of a competitor of the relevant "actor" or agreeing to sell to the actor first referenced its total output of a good the trading partner produces with the first actor's substitutable input, durable machine, or discovered production process.[1]

The post-1950 variant of Section 7 covers (M&A)s of all sorts—decisions "to acquire…the whole or any part of the stock or other share capital assets of another entity." One point needs to be made about Section 7. It does not cover joint ventures or functionally-related collaborations of other sorts.[2]

I turn now to the test of illegality the Clayton Act promulgates. With one empirically-unimportant exception,[3] the Clayton Act's various provisions prohibit the category or categories of conduct they respectively cover if and only if their "effect…may be substantially to lessen competition" "in any line of commerce" or "in any line of commerce in any section of the country." Of course, the phrase "lessens competition" does not have self-declaring meaning. In my judgment, in the Clayton Act context, conduct should be deemed to have "lessened competition" (or be predicted to "lessen competitions") if and only if it imposed (is predicted to impose) a net equivalent-dollar loss on the potential and actual customers of the perpetrator(s) and on the potential and actual customers of the product-rivals of the perpetrator(s) "combined" by worsening the absolute attractiveness of the best offer they respectively receive from any inferior supplier. In my view (with some elaboration), this operationalization is correct as a matter of U.S. law because it captures the intent of the legislators who voted for the Clayton Act and makes good policy-sense (at least on the relevant legislators' first-best assumptions). Certainly, my operationalization is superior to those proposed or used by the various Industrial Organization economists and economics-conversant U.S.-antitrust-law legal scholars who have addressed this issue—operationalizations that deem conduct to have "lessened competition" if it (1) reduces the unit output(s) of the perpetrator(s), (2) increases their prices, (3) increases their (P−MC) differences, (4) increases their ([P−MC]/P) ratios, or (puzzlingly) (5) increases their profits. These alternative operationalizations must be rejected because they (1) are ill-specified in that they do not take account of the facts (A) that sellers may charge lump-sum fees as well as per-unit prices, (B) that sellers may charge different buyers different per-unit prices or different buyers different (average-lump-sum-fee *plus* per-unit-price) prices, (C) that covered transactions may directly involve the pricing and unit-outputs of more than one product, and (D) that covered transactions may affect the attributes of the product(s) or (product/service)-packages supplied by the perpetrator(s), (2) yield different conclusions in a given case (e.g., an exemplar of a covered category of conduct can simultaneously reduce price and increase [P−MC]), and (3) make no functional or normative sense (e.g., do not distinguish between conduct that raises its perpetrators' prices by enabling them to improve their products and conduct that increases its perpetrators' prices by enabling them to eliminate the price competition they would otherwise have waged against each other).[4]

I acknowledge that the Clayton Act text I have just quoted contains language that may favor the conclusion that the Clayton Act's test of illegality differs from my rendition of the lessening-competition test of legality. The first statutory text that raises this possibility is "may be," which in isolation could mean that the Act prohibits the conduct it covers whenever there is the remotest chance that the conduct would lessen competition. I reject this inference because no legislative history supports it, because it would create a test of illegality that was in this respect unique or virtually unique, and because the test of illegality it would imply the Clayton Act promulgates would be undesirable (think of an [M or A] that may lessen competition to a given extent but is far more likely to increase competition to that extent).

The second statutory text that may justify the conclusion that the Clayton Act's test of illegality differs from my reading of the lessening-competition test is the word "substantially." I might be willing to adjust my interpretation to make it compatible with the word "substantially" if the concept of "substantiality" were defined more clearly—say, to refer to a specific quantity of net equivalent-dollar losses the relevant buyers must sustain or a minimum percentage that those losses must constitute of the sales the conduct affected or the profits the conduct yielded its perpetrator(s): indeed, such an adjustment might make policy-sense, given the allocative cost that antitrust suits generate, though this policy-conclusion is disfavored by the fact that the inclusion of an operationalized "substantiality-of-loss" requirement would make it necessary for another issue to be investigated and litigated whose investigation and litigation would itself be allocative-transaction-costly and misallocative to finance.

The third Clayton-Act text that bears on the Clayton Act's test of illegality is the Clayton Act's reference to a "line of commerce" or a "section of the country." These phrases refer respectively to what economists conventionally denominate "product markets" and "geographic markets"—concepts whose operational definitions I believe are inherently arbitrary not just at their peripheries but comprehensively. Since any conclusion that this language must be interpreted literally (as opposed, for example, to interpreting it to reinforce the requirement that—to be illegal—the conduct in question must lessen competition substantially) would endanger the constitutionality of the statute by making it "void for vagueness" and reduce the statute's desirability by leading to the conclusion that conduct that increased competition overall (or did not decrease competition, all things considered) would be illegal if it lessened competition in one product or geographic "market,"[5] I think that it would be correct as a matter of U.S. law to interpret this language to provide a regrettably-redundant reinforcement of the Clayton Act's "substantiality" requirement.

Five additional "interpretive" issues that relate to the Clayton Act's (primary) test of illegality must be addressed. First, what is the Clayton Act's baseline for competitive-impact calculation? Is it the situation that would prevail if the perpetrator(s) did nothing relevant, or is it the situation that would prevail if the perpetrators made the choice that would yield the largest net equivalent-dollar gain to Clayton-Act-relevant buyers and still be at least as profitable for the perpetrator(s) as doing nothing? This issue has never been explicitly addressed by any U.S. court or antitrust-law-enforcement authority, though, with two exceptions,[6] these institutions have always implicitly assumed that the legally-correct baseline is the perpetrator-does-nothing-relevant baseline. In my judgment, the baseline for competitive-impact measurement that is correct as a matter of U.S. law is the "perpetrator does nothing relevant" baseline. This conclusion is consistent with liberalism's disfavoring placing positive obligations on moral-rights-bearers and, with the two exceptions previously noted, with the general (implicit) position of U.S. courts and antitrust-law-enforcement authorities.

The second additional Clayton-Act-"interpretive" issue that relates to the Act's (primary) test of illegality that needs to be discussed is whether a kind of "organizational-allocative-efficiency" defense should be read into the Clayton Act. Such a defense would render lawful (for example) (M&A)s that would impose a net equivalent-dollar loss on the customers of the participants and the customers of the participants' rivals "combined" by reducing the absolute attractiveness of the best offer they respectively receive from any inferior supplier when the proposed (M or A) would not do so if it would not drive out a rival of the resulting firm or deter a rival investment by generating static or dynamic allocative efficiencies that would improve the resulting firm's array of competitive positions and concomitantly critically worsen the existing rival's array of competitive positions or critically worsen a potential rival-investor's array of prospective competitive positions. Although the Clayton Act's text provides no basis for such a defense, I would argue for it on the ground that it is consistent with the assumption of U.S. industrial policy (antitrust policy, IP policy, regulated-industries policy) that firms should be allowed to profit from choices they make that increase their allocative proficiency.

Like the second additional "interpretive" issue just discussed, the third additional issue that relates to the Clayton Act's test of illegality that needs to be addressed may not best be characterized as "interpretive." The question is: When assessing the impact of a proposed or consummated (M or A), should a court or antitrust-law-enforcement authority take account of the predicted effect that the (M or A) will have on the amount of contrived-oligopolistic and predatory conduct in which the resulting firm will engage relative to the amount of such conduct in which the participants would have engaged as well as on the predicted impact the (M or A) will have on the amount of contrived-oligopolistic and predatory conduct in which the resulting firm's rivals will engage? One could argue that, since contrived-oligopolistic and predatory conduct are illegal, the appropriate response to an (M or A)'s possible tendency to increase the incidence of such conduct is to prosecute any such resulting conduct if it is perpetrated. However, one could also argue (indeed, I would argue) that, since it is extremely difficult to detect and prove contrived-oligopolistic and predatory conduct, it is correct as a matter of U.S. law for a court or antitrust-law-enforcement authority to take account of a proposed/consummated (M or A)'s predicted/detected impact on such conduct when calculating its impact on competition. I should add that, because natural-oligopolistic conduct is not prohibited by U.S. antitrust law (in particular, by the Sherman Act), courts and antitrust-law-enforcement authorities clearly should take account of any predicted/detected impact that a proposed/consummated (M or A) will/did have on the incidence of natural-oligopolistic conduct when predicting/assessing the competitive impact of an (M or A).

The fourth additional Clayton-Act "interpretive" issue that relates to the Clayton Act's test of illegality that needs to be addressed concerns the "unit of conduct" whose competitive impact is legally salient when the category of conduct whose Clayton-Act legality is at issue is vertical conduct and the conduct is not liberal-moral-rights-violative—is not price discrimination that involves the charging of a discriminatorily-low price that is predatory or retaliatory in the service of contrived-oligopolistic pricing, does not involve exemplars of Section 3-covered conduct that are predatory, and does not involve vertical (M or A)s that would not have been perceived by a participant to be *ex ante* at least normally profitable but for the participant's belief that it would or might create a resulting firm that would or might realize more profits by engaging in oligopolistic and/or predatory conduct than the participants would have realized by doing so or that was created by a participant that believed that the (M or A) would or might increase the profits it could realize by engaging in such conduct and intended the resulting firm to take advantage of any such opportunity the (M or A) created. The question is whether in such cases the Clayton Act's competitive-impact-oriented test of illegality focuses on is the competitive impact of an individual producer's engaging in the conduct in question or the competitive impact of a rule allowing all members of a set of product-rivals to engage in the relevant category of vertical conduct. I have no doubt that in such cases it is correct as a matter of U.S. law to interpret the Clayton Act's test of illegality to focus on the impact of the rule rather than of the conduct of an individual seller. The opposite conclusion is incorrect as a matter of U.S. law because it is inconsistent with the premise of U.S. law that firms should be allowed "to compete on the merits"—to operate "on a level playing-field." Thus, the conclusion that it is incorrect as a matter of U.S. law to focus on the competitive impact of an individual seller's including such provisions in its distributorship contracts that restrict the choices the distributors may make is correct because that approach would sometimes lead to the conclusions that (1) a well-established firm's engaging in such vertical conduct when it would increase its organizational allocative efficiency would be deemed illegal because, by improving its array of competitive positions, such conduct would lessen competition by causing one or more of the firm's rivals to exit or by deterring one or more of the firm's actual or potential rivals from investing (by worsening respectively their actual and prospective arrays of competitive positions) while (2) a marginal competitor's or potential entrant's engaging in such vertical contracts would be deemed lawful because their doing so would increase competition by enabling the marginal competitor to survive and/or expand its ARDEPPS-investment and making it profitable for the potential entrant to enter by improving their respective actual and prospective arrays of competitive positions.

To repeat: any 'interpretation" of the Clayton Act that produces such results is incorrect as a matter of U.S. law because the "handicapping" it entails is inconsistent with the "competition on the merits"/"level-playing-field" paradigm not only of U.S. antitrust law but of U.S. industrial policy more generally. (I acknowledge that this argument is somewhat undercut by the possibility of the well-established firm's making out an organizational-allocative-efficiency defense for its conduct: I wrote "somewhat" because of the difficulty of proving the economic efficiency of the restrictions in question and persuading courts and antitrust-enforcement authorities to overcome their reluctance to accept such organizational-economic-efficiency defenses). I hasten to add that the preceding argument has no bearing on the appropriate unit for legal analysis when the test of illegality that is being applied to vertical conduct is the specific-anticompetitive-intent test of illegality: when the question is whether vertical conduct violates this Sherman Act test of illegality, the critical legal issue is the motivation of an individual firm (or of two or more cooperators in joint predation), not the motivation of non-participating members of the set of rivals to which the perpetrator(s) belong.

The fifth and final interpretive issue that relates to the Clayton Act's (primary) test of illegality is connected to the final sentence of the preceding paragraph. When conduct covered by the Clayton Act violates the Sherman Act's specific-anticompetitive-intent test of illegality, should the Clayton Act's lessening-competition test of illegality be applied to the conduct of an individual perpetrator or perpetrator-pair as opposed to the impact of a rule allowing all members of a set of product-rivals to engage in the conduct in question? I have no doubt that in such cases the analysand that is correct as a matter of Clayton Act law is still a rule allowing all members of a set of product-rivals to engage in the conduct at issue. I should add that, in cases in which the individual perpetrators are motivated by specific anticompetitive intent, the rule in question will presumably lessen competition in the Clayton-Act sense.

17.1.3 The Test of Illegality and Conduct-Coverage of the Federal Trade Commission Act

The Federal Trade Commission Act (Section 5) prohibits any "unfair method of competition"—in my terms, promulgates a "distorting competition" test of illegality that prohibits conduct that yields its perpetrator(s) a private-competitive-position advantage that is not allocative-efficiency-warranted.

17.2 The Business Entities Respectively Covered by, the Tests of Illegality Respectively Promulgated by, and the Conduct Respectively Covered by What Is Now Article 101 of the 2009 Treaty of Lisbon, What Is Now Article 102 of the 2009 Treaty of Lisbon, and the EMCR

17.2.1 Article 101 of What Is Now the 2009 Treaty of Lisbon

I find it useful to distinguish three components of what is now Article 101 of the 2009 Treaty of Lisbon. The first contains the initial part of the text of Article 101(1), the part that precedes the words (in English) "and in particular those which…." This component (1) specifies that Article 101 covers "undertakings" ("firms" in U.S. parlance) regardless of whether they occupy a "dominant position" (whatever that is, see Sects. 7.2 and 17.2.2) and "associations of undertakings" ("trade associations" in the U.S. parlance), specifies that Article 101 covers "all agreements between undertakings, decisions by association of undertakings or concerted practices," and (read in isolation) declares illegal those exemplars of all such covered behavior by all such covered actors that "have as their object or effect the prevention, restriction or distortion of competition within the common market." In my judgment, it is correct as a matter of E.U. law to interpret (1) "all agreements between undertakings" to cover not only formed agreements but unsuccessful attempts to form agreements,[7] (2) "concerted practices" (so-called concertations) to cover natural-oligopolistic conduct, (3) conduct whose "object" is "the prevention…[or] restriction…of competition" to reference conduct that is motivated by specific anticompetitive intent, (4) conduct whose "effect" is "the prevention…[or] restriction of competition" to reference conduct that "lessens competition" in the sense in which I argue this concept should be understood when used in the Clayton Act, and (5) conduct whose "object or "effect" is the "distortion of competition" to reference conduct that is critically motivated by a desire to or has the effect of "distorting competition" in the sense in which I have defined this expression when discussing the Federal Trade Commission Act. Read in isolation, this component of Article 101(1) prohibits all agreements between business-firms or attempts to form such agreements that are motivated by specific anticompetitive intent, that lessen competition, or that distort competition, including (contrary to what in my admittedly-limited experience is the academic, judicial, and E.U.-competition-law-enforcement-official consensus) all mergers and acquisitions, joint ventures, and functionally-analogous collaborative agreement's, (2) all trade-association decisions that are motivated by specific anticompetitive intent, lessen competition, or distort competition, and (3) all firm natural-oligopolistic decisions that lessen or distort competition. However, read in isolation or for that matter read in combination with the rest of Article 101(1) and Article 101(3), this component of Article 101 does not cover single-firm contrived-oligopolistic conduct whose initiator relies exclusively on threats of retaliations to secure compliance or single-firm predation—an omission that Article 102 remedies for any perpetrator that occupied a dominant position prior to engaging in the conduct at issue but does not remedy for perpetrators that did not occupy a dominant position prior to engaging in that conduct.

The second component of Article 101(1) contains a list of categories of between-firm agreements, decisions by trade associations, or concerted practices that Article 101(1) covers—namely, inter-firm agreements, trade-association decisions, and concerted practices that

(a) directly or indirectly fix purchase or selling prices or any other trading conditions;
(b) limit or control production, markets, technical developments, or investment;
(c) share markets or sources of supply;
(d) apply dissimilar conditions to equivalent transactions with other trading parties, thereby placing them at a competitive disadvantage;
(e) make the conclusion of contracts subject to acceptance by the other parties of supplementary obligations which, by their nature or according to commercial usage have no connection with the subject of such contracts.

I want to make 5 points about this component of Article 101. The first relates to the following issue: Is it correct as a matter of E.U. law to read the list of categories of conduct provided by clauses (a) to (e) to be comprehensive (to articulate all the categories of conduct that Article 101(1) covers)? I am American, and although I have lived in England for more than 20 years all tolled, my ear for British English is not so good as my ear for American English. As I indicated previously, the English version of Article 101(1)—there is no official E.U. language—precedes clauses (a) through (e) with the words "in particular," which to my American ear implies that the list that follows is intended to be comprehensive: had the list been preceded with the adverb "particularly," the use of that word (which is synonymous with "especially" in this context) would not have implied that the list that follows is comprehensive. Instead of "in particular," the Italian and Spanish versions of Article 101(1) contain words that also imply that the list that follows is intended to be comprehensive—specifically and respectively, *in particulare* and *en particular*, both of which I believe would be translated as "in particular" in English. By way of contrast, instead of "in particular," the French and German versions of Article 101(1) contain words whose English translation would be "particularly" or "especially"—respectively, *notamment* ("most notably" or "especially") and *insebesondere* ("especially"). I think there are two arguments for concluding in the face of this linguistic uncertainty that clauses (a) through (e) should not be interpreted to provide a comprehensive list of categories of conduct that may violate Article 101. First, as I will indicate below, the largely-overlapping list of categories of illegal ("abusive") behavior that Article 102 contains is preceded (in English) with the words "*may, in particular*" (emphasis added), which suggests that that list is not intended to be comprehensive, and there is no reason to believe that Article 102's list should be different in this regard from Article 101's list. Second, there is no good policy-argument for limiting Article 101's conduct-coverage to the categories of conduct listed in clauses (a)–(e). For these reasons, I conclude that it is not correct as a matter of E.U. law to interpret the list specified by the second component of Article 101 to be comprehensive. I should add that my conclusion that Article 101 does cover mergers, acquisitions, joint ventures, and functionally-analogous contractual relationships between separate firms does not depend on my conclusion that the component-two list should not be read to be comprehensive: exemplars of such conduct that manifest specific anticompetitive intent and/or lessen or distort competition fall into the categories of conduct specified by clauses (b) and (c) in Article 101(1). I simply do not understand why E.U.-competition academic commentators and appliers subscribe to the opposite position. The fact that European legal academics believe that Article 101 does not cover mergers, acquisitions, joint ventures, and functionally-analogous collaborations is made even more puzzling by the disposition of European academic lawyers to believe that the answer that is correct as a matter of law to a legal-rights question (say, under the German civil code—the BGB) is often not the answer that judges have given to that question.

The second point relates to clauses (a) and (c). The fact that clause (a) references agreements between firms that directly or indirectly "fix *purchase*…prices or any other trading conditions" (emphasis added) and the fact that clause (c) references agreements between firms or decisions by trade associations (that is, the members of trade associations) to "share…sources of supply" through their trade association favor the conclusion that, correctly read as a matter of E.U. law, Article 101 prohibits joint-purchasing agreements (which "fix" purchasing prices "directly") or purchasing joint ventures or mergers or acquisitions that affect ("fix" is not quite the right word) purchasing prices and other trading conditions "indirectly." Since I believe that such conduct benefits final consumers by lowering the marginal cost of inputs to the perpetrators, hence their marginal costs, hence the prices they charge their customers, the preceding legal conclusion seems inconsistent with E.U. competition law's goals of benefiting the buyers "directly" affected by covered conduct (which is manifest both in Article 101(3)—see below—and in the "exploitative abuse of a dominant position" test of illegality some claim it is legally correct to interpret Article 102 to promulgate—see below). It may be possible to counter the argument that clause (a) implies the illegality of covered conduct that "fixes" purchase prices and other purchasing terms of trade by demonstrating that this element of clause (a) reflects its drafters' and ratifiers' mistaken belief that joint purchasing imposes equivalent-dollar losses on ultimate consumers (a mistaken conclusion to which many U.S. economists and economically-literate U.S. antitrust-law scholars also subscribe) and that interpreters or appliers of clause (a) should not be bound by text that manifests an economics mistake when that text's literal interpretation would disserve its drafters' and ratifiers' goals.

The third point relates to clause (b) of Article 101(1). I believe that clause (b) should not be read to prohibit agreements between undertakings, trade-association decisions, or (least-empirically-importantly) concertations that "control" technical developments or investments to make them not only less duplicative but more-economically-efficient: although, if the relevant words are interpreted literally, such conduct could be said to "prevent," "restrict," or "lessen" competition, prohibiting it would not secure any of the goals of E.U. competition law, and although, as I will indicate below, Article 101(3) may come to the rescue, Article 101(3) does not legally obligate Article 101 appliers to make desirable decisions in these cases and may in some instances legally obligate them not to do so.

The fourth point relates to clause (d), which is concerned with the possibility that a firm may lessen or distort competition by discriminating against certain customers, "thereby placing them at a competitive disadvantage." As I indicated when discussing a similar provision of the Clayton Act—Section 2(f) of that Act, this possibility is almost certainly far less empirically important than the drafters and ratifiers of Article 101 seem to believe: sellers are unlikely to find it profitable to engage in discrimination that disadvantages one or more disfavored customers in their competition with other customers of the seller because such discrimination will tend to disserve the seller's interest by increasing the bargaining power of the favored customers by driving the disfavored buyers out.

The fifth and final point relates to another aspect of clause (a) and to clause (e). Clause (a) does not explicitly distinguish between horizontal and vertical price-fixes and clause (e) implies that the "supplementary obligations" that some contracts (most importantly, contracts between producers and their independent distributors) "impose" on one of the parties to them (namely, on the independent distributors) "by their nature or according to commercial usage…have no connection with the subject of such contracts." In fact, as Chap. 13 reveals, vertical price-fixes perform different functions for their perpetrators than do horizontal price-fixes and have different effects on competition, economic efficiency, liberal moral rights, and the instantiation of various egalitarian conceptions of the moral good than do horizontal price-fixes, and the supplementary obligations that some contracts impose on one of the parties to them (most often, obligations imposed by producers on their independent distributors to charge resale prices that do not exceed a stated maximum or do not fall below a stated minimum, to expend a stated amount of money on advertizing the producer's products, to give the producer's products stated amounts and quality of shelf-space, to provide buyers with warrantee services, to limit their sales-efforts to buyers in stated geographic areas or to buyers defined not by their geographic locations, not to sell competitive products of the producer's rivals) are connected by their nature and commercial usage to the "subject of the contract"—almost always perform legitimate functions, are frequently economically efficient, rarely violate liberal moral rights, and usually do not disserve the instantiation of utilitarian or non-utilitarian-egalitarian conceptions of the moral good. The interpretive issue is: Are interpreters of Article 101(1) bound by the failure of its promulgators to understand the differences between vertical and horizontal price-fixes or the functions and effects of "supplementary obligations" imposed on some parties to contracts: do interpreters have to base their legal analyses on these promulgators' mistakes? My answer to this question is: No. That is why I believe that most of the BERs (block-exemption regulations) promulgated by the EC are wrong as a matter of E.U. law.

The third component of Article 101 is Article 101(3). Article 101(3) provides that the provisions of Article 101(1) "may...be declared inapplicable" (I disapprove of and am baffled by the strong discretion that "may...be" appears to give Article 101 appliers) if the following conditions are fulfilled—namely, if the undertakings-agreement, trade-association decision, or concerted practice at issue

(1) "contributes to improving the production and distribution of goods or to promulgating technical or economic progress while allowing consumers a fair share of resulting benefit,"
(2) is the least restrictive means of achieving those objectives ("imposes [only] those restrictions which are...indispensable to...those objectives"), and
(3) does not "afford...[the relevant] undertakings the possibility of eliminating competition in respect to a substantial part of the products in question."

I will restrict myself to making 3 points.[8] First, because profitable product R&D and even profitable PPR can be economically inefficient, it is not always economically efficient to make technical progress. Second, even if Article 101(3) did not give appliers of Article 101 strong discretion when deciding whether to allow otherwise-Article 101-violative conduct on Article 101(3) grounds, it would not create the equivalent of the organizational-economic-inefficiency defense I claim it is correct as a matter of U.S. law to read into the Clayton Act (1) because it counts in favor of conduct its yielding technical progress, (2) because it allows interpreters to permit conduct that would otherwise violate Article 101 only if the conduct allows consumers a fair share of the resulting benefit,[9] and (3) because it forbids interpreters from allowing otherwise-Article 101-violative conduct that satisfies conditions (1) and (2) if the conduct creates "the possibility" (whatever that means) of "eliminating competition" (whatever that means) in respect to "a substantial part" (whatever that means) of the products in question. Third, a point I have made previously: condition (1) manifests the fact that one goal of the drafters and ratifiers of E.U. competition law is to benefit final consumers.

17.2.2 Article 102 of What Is Now the 2009 Treaty of Lisbon

I start by quoting Article 102 in full:

Any abuse by one or more undertakings of a dominant position within the internal market or a substantial part of it shall be prohibited as incompatible with the internal market in so far as it may affect trade between Member States.

Such abuse may, in particular, consist in:

a. directly or indirectly imposing unfair purchase or selling prices or other unfair trading conditions;
b. limiting production, markets, or technical development to the prejudice of consumers;
c. applying dissimilar conditions to equivalent transactions with other trading parties, thereby placing them at a competitive disadvantage;
d. making the conclusion of contracts subject to acceptance by other parties of supplementary obligations which, by their nature or according to commercial usage, have no connection with the subject of such contracts.

I will start by making 8 points about the first paragraph of Article 102. First, that paragraph indicates that Article 102 covers the conduct only of firms that occupied a dominant position prior to engaging in the conduct at issue, not of firms that did not occupy a dominant position or to trade associations. Second, as Section 7.2 demonstrates, the concept of "a dominant position" is complicated and may not be definable non-arbitrarily—more positively, can be defined non-arbitrarily only if one can appropriately link a particular operationalization of the concept of a dominant position to a justified conclusion about the maximand of the ratifiers of the relevant E.U. treaty. Third, although Article 102 has been interpreted to apply not only to individual undertakings that occupied a dominant position before engaging in the conduct under review but also to sets of rivals that jointly occupied a collectively-dominant position at that time, the fact that it is even more difficult to justify an operational definition of "a set of rivals' collectively-dominant position" than it is to justify an operationalization of "an individual undertaking's dominant position" counsels against this expansion of Article 102's business-entity coverage. Fourth, Article 101's concept of "abuse of a dominant position" has been interpreted to cover both exclusionary abuses of a dominant position and exploitative abuses of a dominant position. Fifth, the concept of "conduct that constitutes an exclusionary abuse of a dominant position" coincides with the concept of "conduct by a firm that occupied a dominant position that manifests that firm's specific anticompetitive intent." This conclusion implies that, although E.U. competition law does not prohibit any individual firm that does not occupy a dominant position from engaging in contrived-oligopolistic behavior solely by threatening to retaliate against non-cooperators or from engaging in predatory behavior on its own, E.U. competition law does prohibit any firm that did occupy a dominant firm from engaging in such contrived-oligopolistic conduct and/or single-firm predatory conduct of any type. Given that paragraph two of Article 102 states that "abuse *may*...consist in" (emphasis added) exemplars of the categories of conduct it references, this conclusion also implies that Article 102 prohibits any dominant firm from consummating (M or A)s and/or participating in joint ventures or other sorts of functionally-analogous collaborative arrangements when the relevant conduct is motivated by specific anticompetitive intent. (I should point out that U.S.-antitrust-law analyses use the expression "exclusionary conduct" to refer to conduct that in my terminology manifests its perpetrator's specific anticompetitive intent.) Sixth, given E.U. competition law's concern with benefiting the actual and potential customers of covered business entities as manifest by both condition (1) of Article 101(3) and clause (b) of Article 102, it is probably correct as a matter of E.U. law to interpret Article 102 to prohibit exploitative abuses of a dominant position as well as exclusionary abuses of a dominant position. Seventh, contrary to what appears to be the consensus of E.U.-competition-law scholars and officials that the concept of "an exploitative abuse of a dominant position" is not judicially cognizable, I believe that this concept can be given a judicially-cognizable operational definition: according to this definition, a firm would be deemed to have exploitatively abused its position if the seller surplus it realized by selling the products produced in some (arbitrarily-) defined portion of product-space exceeded some percentage of the sum of the seller surplus and buyer surplus its sales in that area of product-space generated. Eighth, a dominant firm's engaging in competition on the merits can never constitute an exploitative abuse of a dominant position, and dominant-firm conduct that puts the dominant firm in a position in which it could exploitatively abuse its dominant position by making pricing-decisions that result in its realizing an exploitatively-high percentage of the transaction surplus its sales in a relevant ARDEPPS generates will not violate Article 102 on that account.

I turn now to the list of categories of abusive conduct contained in paragraph two of Article 102. I will make 5 points. First, the fact that this list is preceded by the words "*may*, in particular, consist in" (emphasis added) implies that the list is not comprehensive and that not all exemplars of all items in the list are abusive. Second, clause (a)'s statement that a dominant firm's "imposing unfair purchase...prices or other unfair...[purchase] conditions" constitutes an abuse of its dominant position has no counterpart in U.S. antitrust law. Third, U.S. antitrust law has no counterpart to clause (b)'s prohibition of a dominant firm's "limiting production, markets [whatever that means] or technical development to the prejudice of consumers." Fourth, I suspect that clause (c)'s inclusion reflects the Treaty's drafters' and ratifiers' overestimating the frequency with which a dominant firm (indeed, any firm) will find it profitable to place a customer at a competitive disadvantage by discriminating against it. Fifth, like its clause-(e) Article 101 counterpart, clause (d) of Article 102 manifests the Treaty's drafters' and ratifiers' failure to understand the functions, economic efficiency, and morally-salient effects of clauses in contracts that place "supplementary obligations" on one of the parties to the contract: since such contractual clauses do "by their nature" and "according to commercial usage" have a legitimate "connection with...such contracts," I do not think that appliers of Article 102 are bound by its drafters' and ratifiers' perception that such contractual clauses are abusive.

17.2.3 The European Merger Control Regulation (EMCR)

> Article 2(3) of the 1994 EMCR states:
> A concentration [the English word for "merger or acquisition"] which would significantly impede effective competition, in the common market or in a substantial part of it, in particular as a result of the creation or strengthening of a dominant position, shall be declared incompatible with the common market.

Supposedly by way of clarification ("in the interest of legal certainty"), EC Recital 25 on the meaning of the 1994 EMCR states:

> The notion of "significant impediment to effective competition" in Article 2(2) and (3) [of the EMCR] should be interpreted as extending, beyond the concept of dominance, only to the anticompetitive effects of the concentration resulting from the non-coordinated behavior of undertakings which would not have a dominant position in the market concerned.

I will take the EC at this word and ignore its inconsistent Recital 26: "A significant impediment to effective competition generally results from the creation or strengthening of a dominant position." (Now you see it: now you don't.)

I will make five points about the EMCR. First, as my comments on Articles 101 and 102 of the 2009 Treaty of Lisbon imply, the EMCR seems to me to be essentially otiose since (M&A)s are covered by both Article 101 (which covers agreements between undertakings and promulgates both a specific-anticompetitive-intent and a lessening-competition test of illegality) and Article 102 (which covers all conduct in which a dominant firm may engage and promulgates both a specific-anticompetitive-intent [exclusionary abuse of a dominant position] and an exploitative abuse-of-a-dominant-position test of illegality). Second, I believe that it is correct as a matter of E.U. law to interpret the EMCR to use a defendants-do-nothing-relevant baseline when calculating the competitive impact of a concentration: I reach this conclusion because (with the two exceptions I discussed) this baseline has always been used by U.S. Clayton Act appliers and Europeans have generally tended to follow American practice on antirust/competition)-law-interpretation matters (though I acknowledge that a contrary conclusion would be favored by both [1] by the fact that E.U. competition law is more concerned with effects on buyers than is U.S. antitrust law if the use of a "most-pro-competitive [M or A] the defendants could have consummated that they would have found more profitable than consummating no [M or A] baseline" would actually benefit relevant buyers and [2] by the "fact" that the E.U. is less committed to instantiating a liberal conception of justice than is the United States ("fact" enquoted because I admit the contestability of this claim).[10] Third, I believe that, correctly interpreted as a matter of E.U. law, the *prima facie* test of illegality that the EMCR promulgates is the lessening-competition test of illegality I claim the U.S. Clayton Act promulgates: this conclusion is consistent with the EC's post-2004 application-practice. Fourth, I am disposed to conclude that it would be incorrect as a matter of E.U. law to read into the EMCR (or, for that matter, into Articles 101 or 102) the kind of organizational-economic-efficiency defense I believe it is correct as a matter of U.S. law to read the Clayton Act to recognize. This conclusion primarily derives from my perception that E.U. competition law is more concerned with effects on "Clayton-Act-relevant buyers" and less concerned with economic efficiency than is U.S. antitrust law. It is also consistent with the EC's treatment of (M or A)-generated efficiencies: such efficiencies will render an otherwise-illegal (M or A) lawful only if, because of the efficiencies, "consumers will not be worse off as a result of the merger."[11] Fifth, the EMCR does not cover joint ventures or other forms of functionally-analogous collaborations.

I have put off to the end two questions about E.U. competition law whose U.S.-antitrust-law counterparts I addressed. The responses I will give to these questions reflect not only the research I have been able to do on my own but also the research of a colleague who is far more adept than I am at securing information about E.U. law from websites, case-law data-bases, and academic articles and treatises that address E.U. law in general and E.U. competition-law in particular.

The first question is whether E.U. competition law covers unsuccessful attempts to do things whose successful completion it prohibits—for example, any unsuccessful attempt of firms to enter into and execute an agreement whose object or effect is to prevent, restrict, or distort competition (agreements whose successful formation and execution would violate what is now Article 101(1) of the 2009 Treaty of Lisbon), any unsuccessful attempt by a dominant firm to exclusionarily or exploitatively abuse its dominant position (attempts whose successful execution violate what is now Article 102 of the 2009 Treaty of Lisbon), or unsuccessful attempts to consummate a merger or acquisition (concentration) that would significantly lessen competition (in violation of Article 101 and the EMCR)—unsuccessful either because the (M or A)-negotiation failed or because the (M or A) did not or would not significantly lessen competition even though its proponents could be shown to have believed it would. My colleague and I have found no discussion of "attempt" in E.U. law. If it is true that the relevant primary and secondary sources do not address the concept of "attempt," I do not think one can attribute this omission to the fact that the E.U. has not promulgated criminal law: the fact that E.U. law does not contain criminal-law provisions might imply that E.U. courts would be more willing to read attempt-provisions into sources of law that do not contain them than they would be if the relevant provisions were criminal-law provisions since the fact that relevant laws are not criminal laws somewhat weakens the liberal fair-notice-related argument against reading attempt-provisions into "laws" that do not contain them, but it does not explain much less justify the failure of officials and academic commentators to note that E.U. law in general or E.U. competition law in particular does not explicitly cover unsuccessful attempts or to address the response that would be correct as a matter of E.U. law or morality for E.U.-law interpreters/appliers to make to this omission (which might include announcing that prospectively the relevant law would be read to cover unsuccessful attempts, though past unsuccessful attempts would be deemed not to be covered).

The second E.U.-competition-law issue I have not yet addressed is: When deciding whether specific-anticompetitive-intent-motivated efforts by two or more firms to enter into an agreement to make expenditures, decisions by an association of undertakings to make expenditures, or decisions by a dominant firm to make expenditures that are designed to benefit the perpetrators, members of the trade association, or dominant firms by inducing the government to make decisions that will reduce the absolute attractiveness of the best offers against which the above parties will have to compete in one or more ways that would render the perpetrator-conduct in question profitable though it would be economically inefficient in an otherwise-Pareto-perfect economy, will the EC and E.U. courts be influenced by the possible legal/moral interest of the actor(s) to participate in government electoral or decision-making processes, at least if they do so in a manner that is "fair"—for example, that does not involve their lying or paying experts or others to take positions that favor the perpetrator's or perpetrators' interest without revealing that they are paying the experts or concerned citizens to do so? Once more, neither I nor my helpful colleague has been able to discover any primary or secondary source that bears on this issue.

What if any conclusion should I reach about the answers to the two questions just referenced that are correct as a matter of E.U. law? If it were true that (1) the E.U. is committed to instantiating a liberal conception of justice, (2) in legal regimes that are committed to instantiating a liberal conception of justice, arguments that focus on the concrete extensions of the liberal conceptions of justice are the dominant mode of legal argument, and (3) U.S. federal courts have correctly discerned the concrete implications of liberalism for (A) the correctness as a matter of U.S. law of reading attempt-provisions into federal legislation that does not contain them (given that there is no general attempt-provision in federal U.S. law) and (B) the correctness as a matter of U.S. law of interpreting any statute that prohibits one of more firms from engaging in covered conduct that manifests its or their specific anticompetitive intent not to cover one or more firms' seeking to influence the government to make one or more decisions that would benefit the perpetrator(s) by reducing the absolute attractiveness of the best offers against which it or they will have to compete so long as the firm or firms "play fair" when engaging in the relevant government electoral or decision-making process, I would probably be justified in concluding that the responses that the U.S courts have given to the referenced questions would be correct as a matter of E.U. law as well. However, although I do think that both the second—see Markovits (1998), pp. 53–78—and the third of the above three premises are correct, my doubts about whether the E.U. is committed to instantiating a liberal conception of justice[12] prevent me from venturing any conclusion about the answers to the two questions on which I am now focusing that are correct as a matter of E.U. law. My reluctance is strengthened by what I take to be the failure of E.U. officials and academic E.U.-competition-law experts to note much less address these issues (which, it seems to me, if anything, disfavors the conclusion that E.U. law is designed to instantiate a liberal conception of justice). I will therefore proceed on the assumption that the answer to the referenced E.U.-law questions are unclear.

17.3 The Relationship Between the Business-Entity Coverages of, the Conduct-Coverage of, and the Tests of Illegality Promulgated Respectively by U.S. Antitrust Law, Correctly Interpreted and Applied, and E.U. Competition Law, Correctly Interpreted and Applied

I begin by making three related preliminary points about the relationship between written U.S. antitrust law and written E.U. competition law that are general in that they apply regardless of the business conduct whose antitrust-law/competition-law legality is at issue: (1) unlike written E.U. competition law, written U.S. antitrust law does not distinguish between dominant and non-dominant firms when it comes either to the categories of conduct it covers or the tests of illegality it applies to categories of conduct it covers; (2) to the extent that a perpetrator's dominance is relevant to whether an exemplar of covered conduct in which it has engaged has violated a test of illegality that applies to its engaging in that category of conduct, both written U.S. antitrust law and written E.U. competition law would deem relevant the dominance of a perpetrator; and (3) if one ignores the fact that a firm cannot exploitatively abuse a dominant position unless it occupies a dominant position (N.B., a firm can exploitatively abuse a non-dominant position), a firm's occupying a dominant position has virtually no bearing on the probability that any exemplar of any category of covered conduct in which a business can engage violates any test of illegality that written U.S. antitrust law or written E.U. competition law promulgates—in particular, on whether business conduct is motivated by specific anticompetitive intent, lessens competition, distorts competition, or exploitatively abuses the business' position.

17.3.1 Contrived-Oligopolistic and Natural-Oligopolistic Conduct

17.3.1.1 Contrived-Oligopolistic Conduct

Both written U.S. antitrust law (the Sherman Act and sometimes [when the conduct results in "discriminatory prices" being charged] Section 2 of the Clayton Act) and written E.U. competition law (Articles 101 and 102) prohibit any firm that occupies a dominant position from forming and carrying out a contrived-oligopolistic agreement with a rival that manifests its perpetrators' specific anticompetitive intent. Both written U.S. antitrust law (the Sherman Act and sometimes the Clayton Act) and written E.U. competition law (Article 101) prohibit any firm that does not occupy a dominant position from forming and carrying out a contrived-oligopolistic agreement with a rival that manifests its perpetrators' specific anticompetitive intent. U.S. antitrust law (the Sherman Act) prohibits any firm, regardless of its dominance, from engaging in specific-anticompetitive-intent-motivated contrived-oligopolistic conduct without offering to enter into or actually entering into any agreement with a rival (exclusively by threatening to retaliate against or threatening to retaliate against and actually retaliating against non-cooperating rivals) whereas written E.U. competition law prohibits such conduct if and only if its perpetrators occupied a dominant position prior to engaging in it. This last claim about written E.U.-competition law assumes that the fact that contrived-oligopolistic pricing that involves exclusively the making and possibly or actually the carrying out of threats of retaliation affects the price charged in an agreement between undertakings does not bring it within Article 101's coverage because that sales-contract does not prevent or restrict competition (though its content reflects the fact that competition has been prevented or restricted): Article 101 would not cover contrived-oligopolistic pricing on the ground that it affected the price-term in a contract in any event if the relevant buyer was an individual rather than an undertaking because Article 101 covers only those contracts that are contracts between undertakings. U.S. antitrust law does not prohibit any unsuccessful attempt by any firm (regardless of its dominance) to practice contrivance exclusively by forming and carrying out a specific-anticompetitive-intent-motivated contrived-oligopolistic agreement. It is not clear whether E.U.

competition-law Articles 101 and 102 prohibit respectively any firm or any firm that occupies a dominant position from attempting unsuccessfully to form and carry out a contrived-oligopolistic agreement that manifests its perpetrators' specific anticompetitive intent, though I believe that written U.S. antitrust law does not prohibit such unsuccessful attempts. It is not clear whether E.U. competition law (Article 102) prohibits any firm that occupies a dominant position from unsuccessfully attempting to exclusionarily and/or exploitatively abuse its position by engaging in specific-anticompetitive-intent-motivated contrived-oligopolistic conduct exclusively by threatening to retaliate against or threatening to retaliate against and actually retaliating against non-cooperators whereas U.S. antitrust law (Section 2 of the Sherman Act) prohibits any attempt by any firm regardless of its dominance to engage in specific-anticompetitive-intent-motivated contrivance by threatening to retaliate against or threatening to retaliate against and actually retaliating against non-cooperators regardless of whether the attempt is successful.

There is therefore at least one and possibly up to three differences between written U.S. antitrust law's and written E.U. competition law's treatments of (specific-anticompetitive-intent-motivated) contrived-oligopolistic conduct:

(1) U.S. antitrust law (the Sherman act) does prohibit and E.U. competition law (Article 101) does not prohibit firms that do not occupy a dominant position from engaging in such contrivance exclusively by threatening to retaliate against or threatening to retaliate against and actually retaliating against non-cooperators;
(2) written U.S. antitrust law (Section 2 of the Sherman Act) does prohibit unsuccessful attempts to engage in the variant of contrived-oligopolistic conduct that involves no agreements but involves threats or threats and acts of retaliation against non-cooperators whereas it is unclear whether the component of E.U. competition law (Article 102) that prohibits such contrived-oligopolistic conduct when it is practiced by a firm that occupied a dominant position covers unsuccessful attempts to profit by engaging in such conduct; and
(3) written U.S. antitrust law (Section 1 of the Sherman Act) does not prohibit any unsuccessful attempt by any firm, regardless of its dominance, to engage in contrived-oligopolistic conduct exclusively by forming or forming and carrying out a specific-anticompetitive-intent-motivated contrived-oligopolistic agreement whereas it is unclear whether written E.U. competition law prohibits such unsuccessful attempts.

17.3.1.2 Natural-Oligopolistic Conduct

U.S. antitrust law does not prohibit natural-oligopolistic conduct (since such conduct does not involve the making of any agreement or the communication or communication and carrying out of any threat of retaliation against one or more potential/actual non-cooperators). Article 101 of E.U. competition law does prohibit natural-oligopolistic conduct that lessens or distorts competition because it covers "concerted practices" (concertations), and Article 102 of E.U. competition law does prohibit dominant-firm-committed natural-oligopolistic pricing that results in that firm's exploitatively abusing its dominant position. The Article 101 point made in the first half of the last sentence may have to be qualified when the natural-oligopolistic "conduct" in question is decisions not to do something—for example, not to invest, not to disclose to buyers negative information about the non-discloser's product's performance or lifetime cost to buyers, or not to disclose to government such information or information about the external costs generated by a product's production and/or consumption. The argument that written Article 101 does not prohibit negative decisions that result from natural-oligopolistic interactions is:

(1) the E.U. is committed to instantiating a liberal conception of justice;
(2) although this disposition is not always decisive, liberalism is disposed not to impose moral duties on moral-rights bearers to provide benefits to others because liberalism places a lexically-highest value on creatures' that have the neurological prerequisites for taking their lives morally seriously having a meaningful opportunity to do so and seizing that opportunity and imposing positive duties on moral-rights bearers to benefit others militates against their taking their lives morally seriously by undermining their perception that they are the authors of their own lives; and
(3) with the possible exception of situations in which (A) the issue is the legal duty to disclose (as opposed to the legal duty to invest) and (B) the relevant buyers are in long-term or repeated commercial relationships with the non-disclosers, the relevant buyers are relatives or other non-commercial intimates of the non-disclosers, or the non-disclosures are life-of-moral-integrity-imperiling, for the reason articulated in Item (2) of this list, the conclusion that all tolled liberalism would be opposed to interpreting Article 101 or Article 102 to impose a positive duty to benefit others on businesses would seem to be warranted.

I reject the claim that it is correct as a matter of E.U. law to interpret Articles 101 and 102 not to impose positive duties on firms (1) because I doubt that the E.U. (as opposed to several of its Member Nations) is committed to instantiating a liberal conception of justice, (2) because I suspect that imposing a positive duty to benefit others on a firm undermines its "connectees'" perception that they are the authors of their own lives less than a similar order directed at them individually would do, and (3) because at least in the non-disclosure case many of the directly-affected buyers will be in a long-term or in repeated short-term relationships with the non-discloser.

17.3.2 Predatory Conduct

Both written U.S. antitrust law (Section 1 of the Sherman Act) and written E.U. competition law (Article 101) prohibit agreements by two or more firms (regardless of their individual dominance) or decisions by any trade association to engage in predation. Written U.S. antitrust law (Section 2 of the Sherman Act and in some instances [namely, when the predatory conduct involves Clayton Act price discrimination on a commodity or a seller/lessor's restricting a buyer/lessee's dealing in a commodity produced the seller/lessor] Sections 2 and 3 of the Clayton Act [since, if the predatory act succeeds, it will lessen competition]) prohibit an individual firm's predatory conduct (regardless of the firm's dominance). Written E.U. competition law prohibits individual-firm predation if and only if the perpetrator occupied a dominant position prior to engaging in the conduct alleged to be predatory. Thus, Article 102's prohibition of any exclusionary abuse of a dominant position covers dominant-firm predation (although Article 102's prohibition of a dominant firm's exploitatively abusing its position does not cover predation, it does prohibit a predator that was dominant before the predation or became dominant through the predation from taking advantage of the competitive positions the predation yielded it by setting prices that result it in its realizing an exploitatively-high percentage of the transaction surplus its sales in a relevant portion of product-space generate). Article 101 (which applies to undertakings that are not dominant as well as to undertakings that are dominant) covers predation only if it involves one or more agreements between competitors to coordinate their predation against a mutual rival or agreements between undertakings (say, between a predator and another firm that is a potential customer of the target not to patronize or supply goods or services to the target). Written U.S. antitrust law (Section 2 of the Sherman Act) does prohibit unsuccessful as well as successful attempts to practice predation by any firm (regardless of its dominance) or any trade association, but it is unclear whether written E.U. competition law (Article 102) covers unsuccessful predatory efforts by a dominant firm.

17.3.3 Horizontal Mergers and Acquisitions

Both written U.S. antitrust law and written E.U. competition law (correctly interpreted and applied as matters of the two jurisdictions' law) prohibit horizontal (M or A)s if they will lessen competition (see respectively [1] Section 7 of the Clayton Act and [2] Article 101 and the EMCR) or if they are motivated by specific anticompetitive intent (see Section 1 of the Sherman Act and Article 101). In my view, in both jurisdictions, it is correct as a matter of law to conclude that the baseline for measuring the competitive impact of a horizontal (M or A) is the participants-do-nothing-relevant baseline. However, although I believe that it is correct as a matter of U.S. law to read the Clayton Act to permit horizontal-(M or A) participants to exonerate themselves by establishing an organizational-allocative-efficient defense, the first clause of Article 101(3) of what is now the 2009 Treaty of Lisbon and the "exploitative abuse of a dominant position" branch of Article 102's test of illegality warrant the conclusion that it would be incorrect as a matter of E.U. law to allow defendants in any horizontal-(M or A) case—or indeed, in any case brought correctly under Article 101(1)—to exonerate themselves in this way.

17.3.4 Conglomerate Mergers and Acquisitions

The horizontal-(M and A)-related conclusions of Sect. 17.2.2 apply fully to conglomerate (M&A)s.

17.3.5 Surrogates for Vertical Integration

I will proceed on the assumption that, under both U.S. antitrust law and E.U. competition law correctly interpreted as matters of law, the relevant analysand when the question is whether something related to a surrogate for vertical integration should be deemed to have lessened competition is not (1) an individual firm's use of the surrogate for vertical integration but (2) a rule allowing all members of a relevant set of product-rivals to use the surrogate for vertical integration in question. (I will make the same assumption when the behavior in question is vertical [M or A]s, vertical joint ventures, or vertical internal growth.) I am confident that this analysand-conclusion is correct as a matter of U.S. antitrust law since U.S. antitrust law approves of firms' competing on the merits and seeks to allow firms to compete on a level playing-field and since U.S. industrial policy in general rewards firms' economically-efficient conduct. However, I admit that this legal conclusion is more contestable in relation to E.U. competition law. Although various E.U. officials have often made statements approving competition on the merits, some components of E.U. competition law suggest that such competition is illegal if it imposes an equivalent-dollar loss on what I call Clayton-Act-relevant buyers. I have in mind the clause of Article 101(3) that proclaims that conduct that would otherwise violate Article 101(1) cannot be granted an exemption even if it increases its perpetrator's organizational economic efficiency if it does not "allow…consumers a fair share of the resulting benefit" and the "exploitative abuse of a dominant position" reading of Article 102, which prohibits a dominant firm from taking advantage of conduct that increases its organizational economic efficiency (that is, of the associated improvement in its competitive-position array) by charging prices that result in its realizing an exploitatively-high percentage of the transaction surplus it generated in the ARDEPPS of practice. I also have in mind clause (e) of Article 101(1) and clause (d) of Article 102 and a variety of BER decisions the EC has made that declare illegal or limit the use of vertical practices that are economically efficient (though as I previously indicated these texts and decisions could also be attributed to their promulgators' failure to understand the functions and economic efficiency of the practices in question). In any event, I will proceed on the assumption that as written E.U. competition law does not permit defendants whose conduct (be it vertical or not vertical) would otherwise be deemed illegal under a lessening-competition test of illegality to exonerate themselves by establishing an organizational-allocative-efficient defense.

I will also proceed on the assumption that, under U.S. antitrust law correctly interpreted as a matter of law, firms whose uses of surrogates for vertical integration would otherwise be deemed illegal because a rule allowing a relevant set of product-rivals to which the firms belonged would "lessen competition" in the relevant sense of that expression will be allowed to exonerate themselves by establishing that the rule would not have had this effect had the practice in question not increased the organizational allocative efficiency of some of the relevant sellers more than of others and on that account led to the exit of sellers whose organizational economic efficiency the practice increased by a "less-than-average" amount or raised the ($\Pi_D + R$) barriers to investment faced by potential entrants or established sellers whose organizational allocative efficiency the practice increased by a "less-than-average" amount.

17.3.5.1 Pricing-Techniques

I continue to define the concept "pricing-techniques" to cover perfect price discrimination in all its variants, the charging of a combination of a lump-sum fee and a supra-transaction-surplus-maximizing per-unit price, conventional "single pricing"—charging all buyers the same per-unit price and no lump-sum fee, tie-ins and reciprocity agreements that effectuate and/or conceal inter-buyer price discrimination or reduce the amount of transaction surplus a seller must directly destroy to remove a given amount of buyer surplus through supra-marginal-cost per-unit pricing, and inter-buyer price discrimination in all its variants.

I will start with 5 preliminary points: (1) all these pricing-techniques could be employed predatorily and all could be used by firms that were engaged in contrived-oligopolistic pricing; (2) a low percentage of the exemplars of any of these techniques is predatory or is associated with contrived-oligopolistic pricing; (3) the percentage of the exemplars of any pricing-technique that involves inter-buyer price discrimination that is associated with predatory or contrived-oligopolistic pricing is significantly higher than the percentage of the exemplars of that pricing-technique that does not involve inter-buyer price discrimination (these claims reflect respectively the fact that predatory pricing usually involves the charging of discriminatorily-low prices to the target's customers and the fact that contrived-oligopolistic pricing often involves the charging of discriminatorily-low retaliatory prices to the customers of non-cooperators and discriminatorily-high prices to the customers of cooperators); (4) although de facto choices to substitute for single-pricing "fancier" pricing-techniques that increase the seller's unit -sales may "lessen competition" or "prevent or restrict competition" in the sense in which those expressions should be understood when interpreting respectively the Clayton Act and what is now Article 101 of the 2009 Treaty of Lisbon by causing one or more perpetrator-rivals to exit or deterring one or more actual or potential competitors of the perpetrator from making an investment in the relevant ARDEPPS by lowering the demand curve they face on an extant product or would face on a new product they could introduce, when such choices are not motivated by specific anticompetitive intent, they will rarely have such an effect; and (5) even in what I take to be the extremely-rare instances in which an individual firm's non-specific-anticompetitive-intent-motivated use of a fancier pricing-technique does impose a net dollar-loss on relevant buyers by reducing the absolute attractiveness of the best offers they respectively receive from any supplier other than their privately-best-placed supplier, the individual firm's conduct should not be deemed to violate a law that covered it and its pricing-technique choice because (A) the relevant "unit" for the legally-salient competitive-impact analysis is not the impact of an individual firm's using the technique but the impact of a rule allowing all members of a set of rivals to use the technique in question and (B) such a rule would be far less likely than an individual seller's conduct to impose dollar-losses on relevant buyers in this way.

I will now make 4 comparative observations about written U.S. antitrust law's and written E.U. competition law's respective treatments of a firm's pricing-technique choice:

(1) both written U.S. antitrust law (the Sherman Act) and written E.U. competition law prohibit all specific-anticompetitive-intent-motivated pricing-technique choices by dominant-firms;
(2) written E.U. competition law (Article 102) (probably) prohibits but written U.S. antitrust law does not prohibit any dominant firm's making any non-exclusionary pricing-technique choice that results in its securing an exploitatively-high percentage of the transaction surplus its sales in a relevant portion of product-space generate;
(3) written U.S. antitrust law (the Sherman Act) also prohibits specific-anticompetitive-intent-motivated pricing-technique choices made by non-dominant firms regardless of whether those choices involve the making of any agreement with or sale to a final consumer as opposed to another firm (undertaking) whereas written E.U. competition law (Article 101) prohibits specific-anticompetitive-intent-motivated pricing-technique choices by undertakings that are not dominant only if the choices are embedded in an agreement with another undertaking; and
(4) written U.S. antitrust law (respectively Sections 2 and 3 of the Clayton Act) prohibits firms (regardless of their dominance) from lessening competition by charging discriminatory prices on "commodities" (that is goods, not services or insurance) to any category of buyer (to final consumers as well as to other firms) or by using full-requirement tie-ins or single-brand exclusive dealerships to prevent any category of buyer from purchasing or leasing the right to use a "good" (a commodity not a service or insurance) of a rival when a rule allowing the seller in question and all its rivals to engage in such behavior would lessen competition and the sellers could not establish an organizational-allocative-efficiency defense for their conduct whereas written E.U. competition law (Article 101) prohibits any undertaking from lessening ("preventing" or "restricting") competition by using any pricing-technique (not just price discrimination, tie-ins, and single-brand exclusive dealerships)—which it will always do in the course of forming an agreement—when a rule allowing the seller in question and all its product-rivals to engage in such conduct would lessen competition if and only if the relevant buyer is another undertaking (not when the relevant buyer is a final consumer), regardless of whether what is sold or leased is a commodity or service or insurance (written E.U. law does not recognize the organizational-collective-efficiency defense

that I think it correct as a matter of U.S. law to interpret the Clayton Act to recognize).

I want to close by emphasizing that the empirical importance of the just-referenced differences between the treatment of pricing-technique choices by written U.S. antitrust law and written E.U. competition law is substantially diminished by the facts that such choices are rarely motivated by specific anticompetitive intent and a rule allowing all members of a set of product-rivals to use any such pricing-techniques will rarely lessen competition.

17.3.5.2 Tie-Ins and Reciprocity Agreements That Do Not Function Either by Increasing the Profitability of Price Discrimination in Other Ways Than by Concealing It or by Reducing the Amount of Transaction Surplus a Seller Must Directly Destroy to Eliminate a Given Amount of Buyer Surplus by Charging Supra-Marginal-Cost Per-Unit Prices, Resale-Price-Maintenance Clauses, Vertical Territorial Restraints and Oher Restrictions on the Set of Buyers to Which an Independent Distributor May Make Sales, Clauses That Control the Expenditures That an Independent Distributor Must Make on Media Advertizing, In-Store Promotions, and Door-to-Door Sales-Efforts, Clauses That Control the Shelf-Space That an Independent Distributor Must Give a Producer's Products, Clauses That Require Independent Distributors to Supply Warrantee Services, Producer Subsidies of Independent-Distributor Advertizing and/or In-Store-Promotional Display Expenditures and Shelf-Space Allocations, Sales Policies That Are Designed to Influence Such Independent-Distributor Decisions, Single-Brand Exclusive Dealerships, and Long-Term Full-Requirements Contracts or Total-Output-Supply Contracts

Subsections 13.1.2, 13.1.3, 13.1.4, and 13.1.5 explain the various ways in which the practices referenced in this subsection's heading can increase a firm's profits without reducing the absolute attractiveness of the best offers against which it must compete. Subsection 13.1 also explains that some tie-ins and reciprocity agreements increase their employer's profits by concealing the existence, location, and/or magnitude of the employer's price discrimination or predatory pricing, price-regulation violations, or tax or contract fraud, that some minimum-price-setting and some allegedly maximum-price-setting RPM agreements may effectuate contrived-oligopolistic pricing by the sellers or buyers they involve, that some vertical territorial restraints may play a role in sellers' dividing up "markets," and that some single-brand exclusive dealerships and long-term full-requirements contracts may be predatory. Section 13.1 explains as well why at most only a tiny percentage of RPM clauses, customer-allocation restraints, single-brand exclusive dealerships, long-term full-requirements contracts, and long-term total-output-supply contracts are predatory or contribute to contrived-oligopolistic pricing. Moreover, although tie-ins and reciprocity agreements formed by (antitrust/competition)-law-covered actors that conceal predatory pricing and those rare exemplars of non-predatory inter-buyer price discrimination that are illegal because a rule allowing all members of a set of rivals to practice it lessens competition violate the applicable antitrust/competition law, tie-ins and reciprocity agreements that conceal and effectuate price-regulation violations, tax fraud, or contract fraud do not violate antitrust or competition law, though the price-regulation violations, tax fraud, and contract fraud they conceal and effectuate are illegal.

I will now make 8 comparative observations about written U.S. antitrust law's and written E.U. competition law's respective treatments of these surrogates for vertical integration:

(1) the rare exemplars of these surrogates for vertical integration that are motivated by specific anticompetitive intent that are engaged in by a dominant firm are prohibited by both written U.S. antitrust law (the Sherman Act) and written E.U. competition law (Article 102);
(2) the fact that clause (e) of Article 101(1) of what is now the 2009 Treaty of Lisbon and clause (d) of what is now Article 102 of that Treaty reveal that their drafters and ratifiers suspected that these categories of conduct manifest their perpetrators' specific anticompetitive intent does not make it correct as a matter of E.U. law to conclude that this is the case, a legal conclusion that is rendered salient by the non-mandatory character of Article 101(3)'s "exemption"-authorization and by Article 101(3)'s requirement that, to be eligible for an exemption, conduct must 'allow…consumers a fair share of the…benefit [it yields]";
(3) the tiny percentage of sales-policies in this category that are used by firms that do not occupy a dominant position that are motivated by specific anticompetitive intent are prohibited by written U.S. antitrust law (the Sherman Act) but are prohibited by written E.U. competition law—Article 101—only if they are successful in securing distributor-compliance and the sales-policies and the distributor-compliance they elicit can be said to constitute a concertation (since sales-policies do not involve agreements between undertakings);
(4) although like written U.S. antitrust law written E.U. competition law (Article 102) does not prohibit any dominant firm from engaging in these categories of conduct whenever its doing so puts it in a position to price its product(s) in a way that would result in its exploitatively abusing its dominant position, unlike written U.S. antitrust law written E.U. competition law does prohibit any dominant firm whose use of any of these categories of conduct has put it in a position to realize an exploitatively-high percentage of the transaction surplus its sales in a relevant portion of product-space generate from pricing its products in a way that results in its exploitatively abusing its dominant position;

(5) written U.S. antitrust law (the Sherman Act) does prohibit the (rare) exemplars of tie-ins and reciprocity agreements that manifest a participant's specific anti-competitive intent even when the relevant agreement is formed by a firm that is not dominant and involves a buyer that is a final consumer whereas written E.U. competition law (Article 101) does not cover tie-ins and reciprocity agreements formed by a firm that is not dominant when the trading-partner is a final consumer (is not another undertaking);
(6) under both written U.S. antitrust law (the Clayton Act) and written E.U. competition law (Article 101), when the illegality of something related to a covered surrogate for vertical integration turns on whether that "something" lessens competition, it is correct as a matter of law to conclude that the salient "something" is not (A) an individual firm's use of the surrogate for vertical integration but (B) a rule allowing all members of a set of product-rivals to use the covered vertical-integration surrogate in question;
(7) under both written U.S. antitrust law and written E.U. competition law, the impact on relevant buyers of a firm's use of a surrogate for vertical integration or of a rule allowing all members of a set of rivals to use some surrogate for vertical integration should be analyzed by comparing the outcome that was or would be generated by the surrogate's use with the outcome that would have resulted if the firm was or firms were prohibited firm using the surrogate—an extremely-complicated analysis that must take into consideration the behavior(s) the firm(s) in question would substitute for the forbidden surrogate for vertical integration (*inter alia*, whether the "defendant" would respond to the prohibition by making no other changes in its behavior, by advertizing or supplying warrantee services itself rather than by relying on its independent distributors to perform these tasks, by changing the prices it charged it independent distributors, or by vertically integrating forward into distribution);
(8) although I think it is correct as a matter of U.S. law to read the Clayton Act to allow firms whose use of a covered surrogate for vertical integration (non-cost-justified "price discrimination" in the Clayton-Act sense practiced on commodities, full-requirements tie-ins, minimum-price-setting and maximum-price-setting resale-price-setting agreements, vertical-customer-allocation clauses, and single-brand exclusive dealerships) to exonerate themselves when a rule allowing all members of a set of relevant rivals to engage in the relevant conduct would otherwise be deemed to be illegal because the conduct such a rule would elicit would lessen competition—an outcome I suspect rarely if ever occurs—by establishing that the rule would not have generated this effect had the surrogate not increased relevant firms' organizational allocative efficiency by different amounts, Article 101(3)'s "allowing consumers a fair share of the resulting benefit" requirement and (admittedly less-directly-relevantly) the "exploitative abuse of a dominant position" branch of Article 102's test of illegality disfavor reading Article 101 to promulgate an organizational-allocative-efficiency defense: although the EC and E.U. courts often state that E.U. competition law permits firms to compete on the merits,

the just-cited treaty provisions and numerous EC and E.U./E.C.-court decisions or pronouncements belie this declaration.

I should not conclude this subsection without acknowledging that the empirical importance of many of the differences between written U.S. antitrust law and written E.U. competition law just referenced is largely if not entirely eliminated by the fact that almost no exemplars of these surrogates for vertical integration are motivated by specific anticompetitive intent and that rules allowing all members of a set of product-rivals to employ any of these surrogates for vertical integration (indeed, even an individual firm's use of such a surrogate for vertical integration) will rarely if ever lessen competition.

17.3.6 Vertical Mergers and Acquisitions

Vertical (M&A)s can increase their participants' profits in a variety of ways other than by reducing the absolute attractiveness of the best offers against which their participants will have to compete—for example, by enabling their participants to take advantage of organizational allocative economies of scale, to combine personnel that are complementary for non-scale reasons, to take advantage of continuous-flow economies, to evade price-regulations, and to profit by substituting hierarchical controls of the resulting firm's employees and managers for the contractual controls, distributor-expenditure-subsidy policies, and sales-policies one participant would have had to use to control the other, independent-distributor participant. Vertical (M&A)s that eliminate as an independent entity one participant that was an effective potential competitor of the other participant or that create a resulting firm that will profit by engaging in predatory refusals to deal can also be motivated by specific anticompetitive intent and/or lessen competition (though I suspect that the conditions that would have to be fulfilled for the vertically-integrated firm to be able to profit by predatorily refusing to deal will rarely be satisfied). Although many economists overestimate the tendency of vertical (M&A)s—indeed, of vertical integration regardless of whether it is achieved by an (M or A) or through internal growth—to benefit consumers by creating a vertically-integrated firm that charges lower prices than would be charged by independent distributors (because the economists implicitly assume that the integrating producers would have charged the integrating distributors only per-unit prices rather than a combination of a lump-sum [franchise] fee and a lower per-unit price had they remained separate) and overestimate the tendency of vertical integration to place non-vertically-integrated distributors at a competitive disadvantage that does not reflect their being less allocatively efficient than their vertically-integrated rivals (for the same reason), vertical integration will tend to distort competition between vertically-integrated firms and the non-vertically-integrated competitors of their downstream divisions because, profitably-run vertically-integrated firms will charge their downstream divisions (shadow) prices equal to their upstream divisions' marginal costs while charging independent buyers supra-marginal-cost per-unit prices and, although such independents may be able to eliminate this disadvantage by vertically integrating themselves, the net result may be a decrease in investment-competition (if, put crudely, the barriers to investment facing investors that will have to operate at two levels are higher than those that would face potential investors that would have to enter at only one level).

I will now make 4 comparative observations or sets of related observations about written U.S. antitrust law's and written E.U. competition law's respective treatments of vertical (M&A)s:

(1) what I take to be the rare exemplars of vertical (M&A)s that are motivated by specific anticompetitive intent are prohibited both by U.S. antitrust law (the Sherman Act) and E.U. competition law (by Article 101 regardless of whether a participant occupied a dominant position prior to consummating the M or A, by Article 102 when a participant was a dominant firm prior to executing the [M or A], and by the EMCR if as will usually be the case a rule allowing all members of a set of rivals to execute vertical [M or A]s that are motivated by specific anticompetitive intent will lessen competition regardless of whether a perpetrator occupied a dominant position prior to consummating the [M or A]);

(2) both written U.S. antitrust law (the Clayton Act) and written E.U. competition law (Article 101 and the EMCR) declare *prima facie* illegal "vertical (M or A)s" if and only if a rule allowing all members of a set of product-rivals to execute vertical (M&A)s would lessen competition;

(3) although I believe that it is correct as a matter of U.S. law to interpret the U.S. antitrust statute (the Clayton Act) that applies a lessening-competition test of illegality to vertical (M&A)s to enable participants to exonerate themselves by demonstrating that a rule allowing all members of a set of rivals to which they belong to execute vertical (M&A)s would not have lessened competition had the vertical (M&A)s the relevant firms were in a position to execute not increased their respective organizational allocative efficiency to different extents, the fact that Article 101(3) and the "exploitative abuse of a dominant position" branch of Article 102 manifest the European treaty's drafters' and ratifiers' concern with benefiting relevant buyers favors the conclusion that it would not be correct as a matter of E.U. competition law to read Article 101(1) and the EMCR to allow vertical-(M or A)-case defendants to exonerate themselves by establishing such an organizational-allocative-efficiency defense; and

(4) although neither written U.S. antitrust law nor written E.U. competition law prohibits any dominant firm from executing a vertical (M or A) that creates a resulting firm that is in a position to realize an exploitatively-high percentage of the transaction surplus its sales in the relevant area of product-space generate, written E.U. competition law (Article 102) does prohibit any firm that occupied a dominant position after consummating a vertical (M or A) from exploitatively abusing its dominant position (from taking advantage of

any opportunity the vertical [M or A] gave it to realize an exploitatively-high percentage of the transaction surplus its sales in the relevant ARDEPPS generate).

17.3.7 Joint Ventures and Functionally-Analogous Collaborative Arrangements of Other Sorts (Such as Patent Pools)

To save space, I will not reference "functionally-analogous collaborative arrangements of other sorts" in the rest of this section. I begin with 3 preliminary points or sets of related preliminary points. First, if one subdivides joint ventures by the relationship between the joint venture and its parents, joint ventures can be horizontal, conglomerate, or vertical. Second, it is useful to distinguish between (1) the components of a joint-venture agreement that deal with the financing of the joint venture, the personnel and information the parents will supply the joint venture, the personnel and information the joint venture will supply the parents, and the ownership-shares of the respective parents and (2) the components of the joint-venture agreement that restrict the products the joint venture may produce and the potential buyers to which the joint venture may sell those products (for example, the permissibility of the joint venture's competing with one or more parents) and the rights of the parents to make investments or sales in the joint venture's ARDEPPSes or in each other's ARDEPPSes. Third, it is important to recognize (1) that some of the restrictive clauses just referenced are and some are not motivated by specific anticompetitive intent and that some do and some do not lessen competition, (2) that some joint-venture agreements that do not contain such restrictive clauses are and some are not motivated by specific anticompetitive intent and that some such joint ventures do and some do not lessen competition (because, for example, the very fact that each parent is a partial owner of the joint venture will deter each parent from entering the joint venture's ARDEPPS when—absent the joint venture—more than one parent would have invested in or made sales in the joint venture's ARDEPPS), and (3) that all combinations of these possibilities will obtain in some instances.

I will now make 7 comparative observations or sets of related comparative observations about written U.S. antitrust law's and written E.U. competition law's treatment of joint ventures:

(1) both written U.S. antitrust law (the Sherman Act) and written E.U. competition law (Articles 101 and 102) do prohibit joint ventures that manifest one or more seller-participants' specific anticompetitive intent (in the case of Article 102, only if the relevant participant occupied a dominant position prior to participating in the joint venture);
(2) *inter alia*, Item (1) in this list implies that both U.S. antitrust law (the Sherman Act) and Article 101 prohibit (A) the formation of a trade association if

its formation is motivated by specific anticompetitive intent (e.g., if the participants' *ex ante* perception that it would be profitable for them to create a trade association was critically affected by their belief that the trade association would promulgate and communicate predatory, competition-distorting "quality" or "safety" standards whose promulgation and communication would violate those sources of law even if it did not critically affect the *ex ante* perpetrator-perceived profitability of the trade association), (B) the formation of a patent pool by participants' whose *ex ante* perception that it would be at least normally profitable was critically positively affected by their belief that they would benefit by the pool's excluding or unfairly disadvantaging actual or potential rivals of the founders (whose formation was motivated by specific anticompetitive intent), or (C) the formation of a new-product production-and-distribution joint venture if one or both of its parents' *ex ante* perception that it would be at least normally profitable was critically positively affected by its or their belief that its formation would deter both parents from investing in the joint venture's ARDEPPS and/or the parents from investing in each other's ARDEPPS;

(3) written U.S. antitrust law's and written E.U competition law's treatments of purchasing joint ventures and joint-purchasing collaborations of other sorts are each contestable: (A) although in my judgment, read non-functionally, Section 1 of the Sherman Act would be interpreted to cover and prohibit such arrangements as "contracts in restraint of trade or commerce" when their founders' *ex ante* perception that they would be at least normally profitable was critically positively affected by their belief that the arrangements would benefit them by freeing them from each other's competition as buyers, the facts that (i) the Sherman Act was passed at least in part to protect the interest of final consumers, (ii) joint-purchasing arrangements almost always relate to purchases their participants are making from sellers that are not perfect competitors (that have some economic power) with which the joint purchasers engage in individualized bargaining, (iii) in such individualized-bargaining situations, joint purchasing reduces not only the average cost but the marginal cost to the producers of the good purchased by the joint purchasers, (iv) on this account, even when it does not yield any purchasing-related allocative efficiencies, joint purchasing will reduce the prices that the joint purchasers charge final consumers for the goods they produce with the input they jointly purchased (when the joint purchasers are manufacturers that use the jointly-purchased good to produce a final product) or for the goods they or their retailer-customers resell to final consumers (when the joint purchasers are wholesalers or retailers and the jointly-purchased good is a final product), and (v) the fact that U.S. courts tend to "interpret" statutes whose non-functional reading would disserve the goals of their promulgators in the way that would serve the promulgators' goals favors the conclusion that, correctly read as matter of U.S. law, Section 1 of the Sherman Act would not be read to prohibit purchasing joint ventures or other sorts of joint-purchasing arrangements, even when they were motivated

by specific anticompetitive intent and (B) (i), article 101(1) covers purchasing joint ventures formed by undertakings and other sorts of joint-purchasing agreements into which two or more undertakings enter and (ii) read in isolation, Article 101(1) would prohibit a purchasing joint venture or any other sort of joint-purchasing agreement if the conduct did not yield any allocative purchasing-economies or was not expected *ex ante* by the participants to yield sufficient allocative purchasing-economies to be rendered *ex ante* at least normally profitable on their account alone because in such cases the conduct in question would have as its object the prevention or restriction of competition (would be motivated by specific anticompetitive intent), but (iii) Article 101(3) provides that the provision of Article (101)(1) that by itself would yield the conclusion that a purchasing joint venture or other sort of joint-purchasing agreement was illegal for one of the above reasons "may...be deemed inapplicable" so that the purchasing joint venture or other sort of joint-purchasing agreement in question may be deemed lawful if it "contributes to improving the...distribution of goods" (by generating allocative purchasing-economies), "allow[s] consumers a fair share of resulting benefit," "imposes [only] those restrictions which are...indispensible to...those objectives," and "does not afford...[the defendant] undertakings the possibility of eliminating competition in respect to a substantial part of the product in question": I assume that this last condition applies to the competition the defendants face as sellers, not as buyers, and that Article 101(3) does not authorize Article 101(1)'s appliers to deem Article 101(1) inapplicable if the conduct in question "allow[s] consumers a fair share of the resulting benefit" but does not improve the distribution of goods—a conclusion that is legally salient because I believe that when the purchasing joint venture or the joint buyers face sellers with economic power (when the situation is a bilateral-monopoly situation) the purchasing joint venture or other sort of joint-purchasing arrangement may well benefit ultimate consumers even if it does not generate any allocative purchasing-efficiencies (does not "improve the distribution of goods");

(4) although neither the EMCR nor the Clayton Act (Sect. 7) covers joint ventures, written E.U. competition law (Article 101) prohibits joint ventures that lessen competition even if they are not motivated by specific anticompetitive intent whereas written U.S. antitrust law does not prohibit such joint ventures;

(5) it is correct as a matter of both written U.S. antitrust law and written E.U. competition law to calculate the competitive impact of a joint venture by using a participant-does-nothing-relevant baseline;

(6) Article 101(3) makes it clear that participants in non-purchasing joint ventures that lessen competition in the relevant sense cannot exonerate themselves by establishing an organizational-allocative-efficiency defense since such joint ventures will not have given relevant buyers a fair share of the resulting benefit; and

(7) written E.U. competition law (Article 102) but not written U.S. antitrust law prohibits a dominant firm whose joint venture has created or increased its ability to exploitatively abuse its dominant position from taking advantage of that ability.

17.3.8 Internal Growth

Decisions to engage in internal growth can be motivated by specific anticompetitive intent (are predatory when the firm had a critical monopolistic investment-incentive to make the investment in question) and can "lessen competition" in the relevant sense even if they are not motivated by specific anticompetitive intent (will lessen competition if they inflict a net equivalent-dollar loss on relevant buyers by deterring rival investments whose "substitution" for the investment in question would have yielded the relevant buyers a net equivalent-dollar gain by improving the absolute attractiveness of the best offers they respectively received from an inferior supplier).

I will make 3 comparative observations or sets of related comparative observation about written U.S antitrust law's and written E.U. competition law's respective treatments of internal growth. My accounts of the relevant positions of written E.U. competition law will be based on the admittedly-contestable assumption that an undertaking's decisions to obtain financing for its internal growth from another undertaking or to hire one or more independent undertakings rather than relying solely on its own employees to execute an investment that it will own exclusively does not legally justify the conclusion that its internal growth is covered by Article 101—does not warrant the Article 101 conclusion that it involves an "agreement between undertakings":

(1) written U.S. antitrust law (the Sherman Act) prohibits internal growth that is motivated by specific anticompetitive intent, regardless of whether the perpetrator occupied a dominant position prior to engaging in the growth in question, while written E.U. competition law (Article 102) prohibits internal growth motivated by specific anticompetitive intent when the perpetrator occupied a dominant position prior to growing but does not prohibit non-dominant firms from engaging in specific-anticompetitive-intent-motivated internal growth since Article 101, which covers the conduct of all undertakings regardless of their dominance, does not cover internal growth (on my legal assumption that internal growth should never as a matter of E.U. law be deemed to involve an agreement between undertakings).
(2) neither U.S. antitrust law nor E.U. competition law prohibits internal growth that lessens competition because the provisions of these two jurisdictions' antitrust/competition law that promulgate a lessening-competition test of illegality (the U.S. Clayton Act and the E.U. Article 101 and the EMCR) do not cover internal growth; and
(3) although Article 102 of E.U. competition law should not be interpreted to prohibit any dominant firm from engaging in internal growth that gives it the ability to exploitatively abuse its dominant position or increases its ability to do so, Article 102 does prohibit a dominant firm from pricing its products post-internal-growth so as to yield it seller surplus that constitutes an exploitatively-high percentage of the transaction surplus its relevant sales yield.

Notes

1. I should note that the Clayton Act prohibits contrived-oligopolistic pricing and natural-oligopolistic pricing when (1) they result in the relevant seller's or sellers' charging prices that are "discriminatory" in the idiosyncratic Clayton-Act sense of that adjective and (2) that "price discrimination" lessens competition.
2. For a U.S. Supreme Court opinion that mistakenly assumes that the Clayton Act does cover joint ventures, see United States v. Penn-Olin Chemical Co., 378 U.S. 158 (1964).
3. The exception is the "injury to competitor" test of illegality promulgated by Section 2(f) of the Clayton Act, which is part of the 1936 Robinson-Patman Act revision of the original Clayton Act. Section 2(f) of the Clayton Act makes it illegal for a buyer "knowingly to induce or receive a discrimination in price" in the Clayton Act sense of that concept (a lower price than the seller was charging other buyers, regardless of whether the price-difference was cost-justified) when its doing so lessens competition or *injures one or more of its rivals* (emphasis added). I consider the exception articulated in the italicized position of the preceding sentence to be empirically unimportant because a seller will rarely if ever grant a price-concession to one or more buyers when its doing so will injure one or more of the favored buyer's rivals since those rivals are also potential customers of the seller and the seller will have a stake in preventing any buyer it might supply from obtaining monopsony (purchasing) power and, given that fact, I suspect buyers will rarely solicit discriminatory price-concessions from their suppliers when those concessions would lessen competition by disadvantaging a rival of the buyer. Still, it is worth noting that Section 2(f) of the Clayton Act prohibits individual buyers from soliciting discriminatory price-concessions under certain circumstance—that is, covers buyer-behavior whereas the rest of Section 2 focuses on seller-behavior. See Robinson-Patman Act, 15 U.S.C. Section 13 (1936).
4. For elaborations, see Markovits (2014a) at pp. 94–95.
5. For a U.S. case that promulgates precisely this holding, see United States v. Philadelphia National Bank, 365 U.S. 320 (1961).
6. The first exception relates to the so-called "failing-company defense" in (M or A) cases, which permits a company that faces "the grave possibility of business failure" to consummate an (M or A) that would otherwise be deemed illegal because it would otherwise lessen competition to consummate that (M or A) if—given the high probability that the company would otherwise fail—the (M or A) would not lessen competition relative to the state of the world that would prevail if the (M or A) was not consummated. The exception is that in these cases the courts and antitrust-enforcement agencies have stated that in order to prevail the failing company must establish that it has made a reasonable effort to identify an (M or A) whose consummation would increase competition more than the proposed (M or A) would do (usually an [M or A] with a non-competitor when the actual or proposed [M or A] was with a competitor) and failed to identify such an alternative partner. See International Shoe Co. v. Federal

Trade Commission, 280 U.S. 291 (1930), Citizen Pub. Co. v. United States, 394 U.S. 131 (1969), Department of Justice and Federal Trade Commission 1992 Horizontal Merger Guidelines, Section 5.1, 4 Trade Reg. Rep. (CCH) Section 13, 104, 57 Fed. Reg. 41, 532, and Department of Justice and Federal Trade Commission 2010 Horizontal Merger Guidelines, Section 11 (August 19, 2010). I should note that the decision to require failing companies to make reasonable efforts to identify more-pro-competitive (M or A)s that are more profitable than consummating no (M or A) may lessen competition by deterring failing companies from consummating any (M or A) because the cost of search is prohibitively high. The second exception is that, in some cases in which a firm that is established in one geographic "market" is proposing to merge with or acquire a non-small firm that produces the first firm's product or a variant of the first firm's product in a different geographic market, some lower courts and the FTC have held that to prevail the firm proposing the geographic-diversification conglomerate merger or acquisition must demonstrate not only that the proposed (M or A) would not lessen competition relative to the situation that would prevail if the firm did nothing to enter its (M or A)-partner's market but also that (1) the firm would not have entered its (M or A)-partner's market on its own if prohibited from consummating such an (M or A) and (2) it had devoted a reasonable amount of resources to identifying a small firm in the relevant market with which it could consummate an (M or A) that would be more profitable than doing nothing and had failed to do so. I should note that this toe-hold-merger doctrine may also lessen competition both because it may deter firms from engaging in geographic-diversification (M or A)s that would increase competition (by increasing the search-costs they must incur to be allowed to consummate such [M or A]s and by reducing the certainty-equivalent profitability of the [M or A] they are allowed to consummate [search-costs aside]) and because there is little reason to believe that geographic-diversification (M or A)s with small firms tend to be more-pro-competitive than the more-profitable geographic-diversification (M or A)s for which they would be substituted, For a thorough economic and legal analysis of the toe-hold-merger doctrine, see Markovits, R. 2014(b) at pp. 201–218. See also SKF Indus., 1979 Trade Reg. Rep. ¶21, 595; Bendix Corp., 77 F.T.C. 731 (1976); and Budd Co., 86 F.T.C. 518 (1975).

7. As the text below indicates, neither I nor a colleague who is more knowledgeable than I have been able to find any legislative or treaty provision, any case-law, or any scholarly commentary that addresses or informs the analysis of this issue.
8. For a more complete analysis of Article 1011(3), see Markovits 2014(a), pp. 123–127.
9. It is unclear whether the referent of "resulting benefit" is (1) the total benefit the conduct yielded the perpetrator(s) and its/their customers (and perhaps the customers of its/their rivals) or (2) the total benefit yielded these parties by the improvement in production and distribution and the promotion of technical and economic progress the conduct yielded.
10. It does seem to me that the post-World-War-II German constitution (which was in force in 1956) commits Germany to instantiating a liberal conception of

justice (a liberal conception of "human dignity") and that France (the home of the Enlightenment) is also committed to instantiating a liberal conception of justice (though I doubt that some of the officially-accepted extensions of the principle of *laicité* can be reconciled with liberalism). However, I do not know enough about the moral commitments of the other founding members of the European Community and a *fortiori* of the non-original members that ratified later versions of the 1956 Treaty of Rome or about the "legislative history" of the Treaty of Rome and its successors to be able to justify any conclusions about the E.U.'s moral commitments.

11. See EC Guidelines on the Assessment of Horizontal Mergers at Section VII, OJ C31/5 (2004). The U.S. DOJ and FTC take the same position as the EC on the legal relevance of (M or A)-generated efficiencies. See, *e.g.*, Department of Justice and Federal Trade Commission Horizontal Merger Guidelines Section 10 (August 19, 2010).
12. See note 10 *supra*.

References

Bendix Corp., 77 F.T.C. 731 (1975).
Budd Co., 86 F.T.C. 518 (1975).
Citizen Pub. Co. v. United States, 394 U.S. 131 (1969).
Clayton Act, 38 Stat. 730 (1914) (codified as amended at 15 U.S.C. Sections 12–27).
Council Regulation 139/2004 on the Control of Concentrations Between Undertakings (also known as the European Merger Control Regulation [EMCR]), OJ L24/1 (2004, May 1).
Department of Justice and Federal Trade Commission 1992 Horizontal Merger Guidelines, 4 Trade Reg. Rep. (CCH) Sect. 13, 104, 57 Fed. Reg. 41, 532 (1992).
Department of Justice and Federal Trade Commission 2010 Horizontal Merger Guidelines (2010, August 19).
EC Guidelines on the Assessment of Horizontal Mergers, OJ C31/5 (2004).
Federal Trade Commission Act, 38 Stat. 717 (1914) (codified as amended at 15 U.S.C. Sections 41–45).
International Shoe Co. v. Federal Trade Commissions, 280 U.S. 291 (1930).
Markovits, R. (2014a). *Economics and the interpretation and application of U.S. and E.U. antitrust law* Vol. I *Basic concepts and economics-based analyses of oligopolistic and predatory conduct.* Heidelberg, New York, Dordrecht, London: Springer.
Markovits, R. (2014b). *Economics and the interpretation and application of U.S. and E.U. antitrust law* Vol. II *Basic Concepts and economics-based analyses of oligopolistic and predatory conduct*. Heidelberg, New Work, Dordrecht, London: Springer.
Robinson-Patman Act, 15 U.S.C. Section 13 (1936).
Sherman Act, 26 Stat. 209 (1890) (codified as amended at 15 U.S.C. Sections 1–11).
SKF Indus., 1979 Trade Reg. Rep. ¶21, 595.
Treaty of Lisbon Amending the Treaty on European Union and the Treaty Establishing the European Community, 2007 OJ C306 p. 1 (December 13, 2007).
United States v. Penn-Olin Chemical Co., 378 U.S. 158 (1964).
United States v. Philadelphia National Bank, 365 U.S. 320 (1961).

18 The Differences in the Potentials of U.S. Antitrust Law and E.U. Competition Law as Written to Increase Economic Efficiency, Secure Liberal Moral Rights, and Instantiate Various Utilitarian and Other Egalitarian Conceptions of the Moral Good

Chapter 17 delineated the differences in the tests of illegality promulgated by and the differences in the conduct-coverages and actor-coverages of U.S. antitrust law and E.U. competition law when both are correctly interpreted as matters of law. This chapter analyzes the implications of these differences for the respective potentials of these two bodies of law to increase economic efficiency, secure liberal moral rights, and achieve the moral good in the utilitarian and other egalitarian conceptions of that concept.

This chapter contains 8 sections, each of which focuses on the two bodies' of law treatment of one category of (antitrust/competition)-policy-coverable conduct. This chapter addresses these categories of conduct in the same order in which they are treated in Part II—that is, in Chaps. 9–16. Each section of this chapter has 4 subsections. The first delineates any differences in the treatment of the category of conduct on which it focuses by U.S. and E.U. antitrust/competition law, correctly interpreted and applied as matters of law. The second, third, and fourth respectively indicate the significance of any such differences for the potentials of the two bodies of written law to increase economic efficiency, secure liberal moral rights, and instantiate various egalitarian conceptions of the moral good.

R. S. Markovits, *Welfare Economics and Antitrust Policy—Vol. II*,
https://doi.org/10.1007/978-3-030-96482-5_18

18.1 Oligopolistic Conduct: The Differences Between Written U.S. Antitrust Law's and Written E.U. Competition Law's Respective Potentials to Increase Economic Efficiency, Secure Liberal Moral Rights, and Instantiate Any Egalitarian Conception of the Moral Good That Are Attributable to Their Disparate Treatments of Oligopolistic Conduct

18.1.1 Natural Oligopolistic Pricing and Contrived-Oligopolistic Pricing

There are 5 differences between written U.S. antitrust law's and written E.U. competition law's treatments of contrived-oligopolistic and natural-oligopolistic pricing. First, written U.S. antitrust law (the Sherman Act) prohibits the practice of contrived-oligopolistic pricing by non-dominant firms when it involves exclusively the making or making and carrying out of threats of retaliation (not exclusively the making of an agreement with a competitor) whereas the written E.U. competition law does not prohibit non-dominant firms' practicing contrived-oligopolistic pricing in this way. Second, written U.S. antitrust law (the Sherman Act) prohibits a non-dominant firm's practicing contrived-oligopolistic pricing when the buyer involved is an individual rather than a firm (an undertaking) whereas the component of E.U. competition law that covers some contrived-oligopolistic pricing of non-dominant firms (Article 101) does not cover the charging of contrived-oligopolistic prices to individuals even when its other requirements for coverage are satisfied (because the contrived-oligopolistic pricing involved an agreement between practicing sellers). Third, U.S. antitrust law gives buyers that or who can prove that they have been charged contrived-oligopolistic prices and sellers that have been subjected to retaliation in the service of contrivance a right to obtain legal redress in the form of (treble) damages whereas E.U. competition law as written does not entitle such buyers and contriver-rivals (indeed, any victim of oligopolistic pricing) an opportunity to obtain legal redress. Fourth, what is now Article 101 of the 2009 Treaty of Lisbon prohibits the practice of natural-oligopolistic pricing as a concertation when the buyer involved is an undertaking, regardless of whether the relevant seller is dominant, and what is now Article 102 of the 2009 Treaty of Lisbon prohibits any dominant firm from charging any type of buyer natural-oligopolistic prices that result in its exploitatively abusing its dominant position whereas written U.S. antitrust law (most relevantly, the Sherman Act) does not prohibit natural-oligopolistic pricing at all (given that its practice involves neither the formation of an agreement in restraint of trade nor the making or carrying out of any threat of retaliation). (I am ignoring the possibility that Section 2 of the Clayton Act will prohibit natural-oligopolistic pricing if [1] the practice results in "price discrimination" in the Clayton Act sense, [2] the good involved is a commodity (is not a service or insurance), and [3] the resulting "price discrimination" or, in my view, a rule allowing all members of a set of product-rivals to practice the relevant "price discrimination" will lessen competition because I do not think that an individual seller's practice of such price discrimination or *a fortiori* a rule allowing all members of a set of product-rivals to practice price discrimination will lessen competition in any significant number of cases.) Fifth, if it is correct as a matter of U.S. law to conclude that the Sherman Act "as written" does not cover unsuccessful attempts to enter into agreements with rivals to practice contrived-oligopolistic pricing or unsuccessful attempts to enter into agreements with buyers that contain contrived-oligopolistic prices and if it is correct as a matter of E.U. law to interpret E.C. law to contain a general attempt-provision, which would be incorporated into E.U. competition law "as written," the "written" E.U. competition law would prohibit otherwise-covered attempts to practice contrived-oligopolistic or natural-oligopolistic pricing that were unsuccessful whereas U.S. antitrust law would not cover unsuccessful attempts to enter into contrived-oligopolistic-pricing agreements even when they impose an equivalent-dollar loss on the buyers in question (e.g., because the deal the contriver's customer made with a non-cooperating rival of the contriver was worse than the deal it would have made with the contriver had the contriver not tried to obtain a contrived-oligopolistic price). I should add that this possible unsuccessful-attempt-coverage difference is relevant not only when the attempt that is unsuccessful is an attempt to enter into a contrived-oligopolistic-pricing agreement but also when the attempt is an attempt to obtain an OM naturally (which a rival defeats by beating the natural-oligopolistic-pricer's offer and persuading the buyer not to solicit or accept its privately-best-placed supplier's rebid in order to deter that supplier and its other privately-best-placed suppliers from charging it NOMs): In this case, the privately-best-placed supplier's attempt to secure an NOM will inflict a loss on the relevant buyer because the offer of the worse-than-privately-best-placed supplier it accepts will be worse than its perfectly-best-placed supplier's HNOP-containing offer.

What do these differences imply for the relative potentials of written U.S. antitrust law and written E.U. competition law to increase economic efficiency, secure liberal moral rights, and instantiate various egalitarian conceptions of the moral good? To facilitate the analysis of these issues, I will review my conclusions about the economic efficiency, liberal-moral-rights-violativeness and impact on egalitarian conceptions of the moral good of contrived-oligopolistic and natural-oligopolistic pricing.

In my judgment, although natural-oligopolistic pricing is less economically inefficient than contrived-oligopolistic pricing (in that its practice is less allocative-transaction-costly and does not involve offensive and defensive retaliation, which are both allocative-transaction-costly and prone to generate intra-ARDEPPS UO-to-UO misallocation) and both variants of oligopolistic pricing could conceivably increase economic efficiency all tolled as a result of their increasing equilibrium PPR in the ARDEPPS of practice when the "good" involved is the right to use a production process, it will be TBLE to assume that all exemplars of contrived-oligopolistic and natural-oligopolistic pricing decrease economic efficiency. I also believe that contrived-oligopolistic pricing is always liberal-moral-rights-violative, and—although this conclusion is contestable—that natural-oligopolistic pricing is liberal-moral-rights-violative as well. If oligopolistic pricing always decreases economic efficiency, natural-oligopolistic and contrived-oligopolistic pricing will virtually always decrease total utility because, in addition to decreasing economic efficiency, they will increase material inequality in the overwhelming majority of cases (the only exceptions are cases in which the relevant buyers are substantially better-off than the oligopolistic pricers' shareholder/creditors/managers/employees). Natural- and contrived-oligopolistic pricing will also virtually always disserve the instantiation of all other pure or mixed egalitarian conceptions of the moral good because, as just stated, they will almost always increase material inequality. This subsection assumes that—to the extent that they are effective and can be effectuated without incurring allocative costs or generating distributive consequences that defeat these conclusions—prohibitions of natural-oligopolistic and contrived-oligopolistic pricing will increase economic efficiency, secure liberal moral rights, and instantiate any pure or mixed egalitarian conception of the moral good.

The preceding economic-efficiency, liberal-moral-rights, and egalitarian-moral-good conclusions have the following implications for the impacts of the differences between written U.S. antitrust law's and written E.U. competition law's respective treatments of oligopolistic pricing for their relative potentials to increase economic efficiency, secure liberal moral rights, and instantiate various egalitarian conceptions of the moral good:

(1) the facts that written E.U. competition law does not cover non-dominant firms' practicing contrived-oligopolistic pricing without attempting to or actually entering into a collaborative agreement with one or more rivals or practicing contrived-oligopolistic pricing in their relations with persons (not undertakings) whereas written U.S. competition law does cover and prohibit this variant of contrived-oligopolistic pricing and contrived-oligopolistic pricing that involves buyers who are persons reduces the potentials of written E.U. competition law to increase economic efficiency, secure liberal moral rights, and instantiate the various egalitarian conceptions of the moral good below the potentials of written U.S. antitrust law to achieve these objectives;
(2) the fact that written U.S. antitrust law (the Sherman Act) gives victims of contrived-oligopolistic pricing an opportunity to obtain legal redress whereas E.U. competition law does not given victims of even the contrived-oligopolistic pricing it prohibits an opportunity to obtain legal redress raises the potential of written U.S. antitrust law to increase economic efficiency, secure liberal moral rights (both because the victims of contrived-oligopolistic pricing have a liberal moral right to secure compensation from its perpetrator[s] and because legally entitling them to obtain such redress will deter contrived-oligopolistic pricing, which is liberal-moral-rights-violative) and instantiate the various egalitarian conceptions of the moral good;
(3) the fact that written E.U. competition law (Article 101) prohibits natural-oligopolistic pricing when the buyer is an undertaking whereas written U.S. competition law does not prohibit natural-oligopolistic pricing (remote

Section 2 Clayton Act possibilities aside) makes E.U. competition law more economically efficient, more liberal-moral-rights-securing (if natural-oligopolistic pricing is liberal-moral-rights-violative), and more instantiative of egalitarian conceptions of the moral good than is written U.S. antitrust law; and

(4) if E.U. law does contain a general attempt-provision whereas federal U.S. law does not, this difference will increase the potential of "written" E.U. competition law above the potential of "written" U.S. antitrust law to secure the 3 objectives at issue.

18.1.2 Natural-Oligopolistic Investment-Restrictions and Contrived-Oligopolistic Investment-Restrictions

I will start by making 3 points about the relationships between (1) the differences between written U.S. antitrust law's and written E.U. competition law's respective treatments of natural-oligopolistic and contrived-oligopolistic investment restrictions and (2) the differences between these two bodies' of written law respective treatments of natural-oligopolistic and contrived-oligopolistic pricing. The first two of these 3 points relate to the relative practical significance of two differences in these two bodies of written law as these differences relate to contrived-oligopolistic and natural-oligopolistic pricing on the one hand and contrived-oligopolistic and natural-oligopolistic investment-restrictions on the other. First, the fact that Article 101 of the 2009 Treaty of Lisbon covers agreements only when they are agreements between undertakings whereas the Sherman Act covers agreements between undertakings and individuals as well as agreements between undertakings has no practical significance when the conduct at issue is natural and contrived investment-restrictions, whereas it is consequential when the conduct at issue is natural-oligopolistic and contrived-oligopolistic pricing. Second, the possibility that Article 101 may cover unsuccessful attempts to engage in conduct whose successful perpetration is illegal whereas the Sherman Act does not is less relevant when the conduct at issue is natural-oligopolistic investment-restrictions than when it is natural-oligopolistic pricing (though it is equally relevant when the conduct at issue is contrived-oligopolistic conduct of the two sorts) because (in my judgment) decisions by firms not to invest because they confront each other with *O*s never are unsuccessful whereas efforts by a seller to obtain an NOM can sometimes be unsuccessful. Third, because *O*-generated decisions not to invest do not involve any positive act whereas decisions to practice natural-oligopolistic pricing always involve the positive act of charging a price that includes an NOM (even if they do not involve positive acts such as making "premature" price-announcements that put firms in a position to obtain OMs naturally), it may be that Article 101 should not as a matter of law be read to cover *O*-generated decisions not to invest even though it does cover and prohibit as concertations all decisions that lead to natural-oligopolistic prices being obtained. Such a reading would be correct as a matter of law if (1) the E.U. were committed to instantiating a liberal conception of justice and (2) the liberal reasons for not imposing positive moral duties on moral-rights bearers warranted the conclusion that the liberal conception of justice does not impose a moral obligation on firms to invest when the investment in question was rendered subnormally profitable by the prospect of its inducing a rival investment to be made (when no additional investment would otherwise have been made in the ARDEPPS in question). In part because (1) I doubt that the E.U. as opposed to a number of its individual Member Nations (such as Germany) is committed to instantiating a liberal conception of justice and in part because (2)(A) written E.U. competition law manifests its drafters' and ratifiers' desire to prevent business choices that impose equivalent-euro losses on the buyers they directly affect and to assure that businesses share the euro-gains their conduct generates with their customers and (B) the investment-restrictions that result from critical natural-oligopolistic investment-disincentives impose equivalent-euro losses on the customers of the potential investors and the customers of their product-rivals, I will assume that Article 101 does cover and prohibit as a concertation decisions by two or more undertakings not to invest because of the critical natural-oligopolistic investment-disincentives with which they confronted each other. (I should add that if one or more of the potential investors in question were dominant or would be rendered dominant by its and its rival's or rivals' *O*-induced decisions not to invest and the negative investment-decisions in question would give one or more of the relevant dominant firms the opportunity to exploitatively abuse its dominant position or increase the extent to which it could exploitatively abuse its dominant position, Article 102 would prohibit the firm's taking advantage of that opportunity.)

To determine the impacts that the differences between written U.S. antitrust law's and written E.U. competition law's respective treatments of natural-oligopolistic and contrived-oligopolistic investment-restrictions have on their relative abilities to increase economic efficiency, secure liberal moral rights, and instantiate egalitarian conceptions of the moral good, one must first analyze the effects of contrived-oligopolistic and natural-oligopolistic investment-restrictions on the 3 *desiderata* just referenced.

I will start by analyzing the relevant effects of *O*-induced decisions not to make an investment and then analyze the relevant effects of investment-reduction-focused contrivance. Decisions not to invest that are critically motivated by the natural-oligopolistic investment-disincentives the potential investors faced will usually decrease economic efficiency by increasing poverty and material inequality (by imposing equivalent-dollar losses on the customers of the deterred investors and on the customers of their product-rivals in the relevant ARDEPPS while conferring equivalent-dollar gains on the deterred investors and their product-rivals), can increase/decrease economic efficiency by increasing/decreasing the expenditures the sellers in the ARDEPPS in question make on political parties/campaigns/candidates and government-decision-making-process participation (depending on whether they increase or decrease the concentration of the seller-side of the relevant ARDEPPS), will increase economic efficiency by decreasing

ARDEPPS equilibrium investment if the relevant ARDEPPS' investments are QV investments, will decrease economic efficiency by decreasing the relevant ARDEPPS' equilibrium investment if the relevant ARDEPPS' investments are investments in PPR, and will decrease economic efficiency to the extent that a firm's ability to make one or more choices that will result in its and a rival's facing critical natural-oligopolistic investment-disincentives induces firms to make decisions they would not otherwise have found profitable to achieve this objective. I do not know whether the negative investment-decisions induced by *O* disincentives will increase or decrease economic efficiency all tolled when the investment(s) not made would have been QV investments, but I am certain that such negative investment-decisions will decrease economic efficiency when the investments not made would have been investments in PPR.

I turn now to the effect of *O*-induced incentives not to invest on liberal moral rights. Although this conclusion is contestable, the liberal reasons for not requiring individuals to make positive decisions (that benefit others) dispose me to conclude that *O*-generated decisions not to invest are not liberal-moral-rights-violative, though decisions to make otherwise-unprofitable choices to create a situation in which *O* disincentives are present and critical are liberal-moral-rights-violative.

I turn finally to the impact of *O*-induced decisions not to invest on the instantiation of the various egalitarian conceptions of the moral good. Although the fact that virtually all decisions not to invest for *O*-related reasons will increase poverty and material inequality implies that virtually all such decisions not to invest will disserve the instantiation of non-utilitarian-egalitarian conceptions of the moral good, the likelihood that many such decisions that are made in ARDEPPSes whose investments are QV investments will increase economic efficiency implies that some percentage of such decisions that are made in ARDEPPSes whose investments are QV investments will increase total utility (though the percentage of such decisions in such ARDEPPSes that increase total utility will be lower than the percentage that will increase efficiency).

I turn now to the relevant effects of contrivance that aims to restrict investment. Efforts to contrive investment-restrictions will be more economically inefficient (in some instances, will be less economically efficient) than *O*-generated decisions not to invest both because the communications contrivance always involves are allocative-transaction-costly and because any offensive and defensive retaliation such contrivance elicits will not only be allocative-transaction-costly but will generate intra-ARDEPPS UO-to-UO misallocation when the retaliator makes the sale. The preceding sentence's point implies that the practice of investment-restricting contrivance is even more economically inefficient than natural-oligopolistic investment-restrictions when the relevant ARDEPPS' investments are investments in PPR and leads me to conclude (admittedly contestably) that investment-restricting contrivance will usually decrease economic efficiency (indeed, that it will be TBLE to assume that it always will decrease economic efficiency) when the relevant ARDEPPS' investments are QV investments.

I turn now to the liberal-moral-rights-violativeness of efforts to contrive investment-restrictions. The only efforts to contrive investment-restrictions that might not be liberal-moral-rights-violative would be those made by firms that believed *ex ante* after doing appropriate research into this issue that their conduct was economically efficient because it would reduce equilibrium QV investment in their ARDEPPS, and I suspect that few if any firms will be able to exonerate their contrivance of investment-restrictions in this way even if one assumes that such an argument would be exonerative.

I turn next to the impact of investment-restricting contrivance on the instantiation of egalitarian conceptions of the moral good. Virtually all efforts to contrive investment-restrictions will disserve the instantiation of all non-utilitarian-egalitarian conceptions of the moral good because virtually all such efforts will increase poverty and material inequality, and the percentage of such efforts that increase total utility will be lower than the percentage of *O*-generated decisions not to invest that do so because the contrivance in question is less likely to be economically efficient and is less economically efficient when it is economically efficient than the *O*-generated decisions not to invest.

I should now be able to analyze the impacts that the differences between written U.S. antitrust law's treatment of natural and contrived investment-restrictions and written E.U. competition law's treatment of such conduct have on their relative potentials to increase economic efficiency, secure liberal moral rights, and instantiate the various egalitarian conceptions of the moral good. I will make 3 points or sets of related points.

First, the fact that written E.U. competition law does not prohibit non-dominant firms from contriving investment-restrictions exclusively by threatening to retaliate against investments whereas written U.S. antitrust law does prohibit such contrivance (1)(A) clearly raises the potential of U.S. antitrust law above the potential of E.U. competition law to increase economic efficiency by increasing the potential of U.S. antitrust law above the potential of E.U. competition law to deter the contrivance of PPR-investment restrictions and (B) has an uncertain impact on the relative potentials of U.S. antitrust law and E.U. competition law to increase economic efficiency by increasing the potential of U.S. antitrust law above the potential of E.U. competition law to deter the contrivance of QV-investment restrictions (although the deterred QV investments would have been economically inefficient, doubts are raised by the allocative-transaction-costliness of the communications the deterred contrivance would have entailed and by the fact that the deterred contrivance would tend to have led to offensive and defensive retaliation that would have been allocative-transaction-costly, would sometimes have involved the placement of economically-inefficient advertizements, and would have tended to generate intra-ARDEPPS UO-to-UO misallocation if the retaliator would have made the sale), (2) raises the potential of U.S. antitrust law to secure liberal moral rights above the potential of written E.U. competition law to do so (since contrived-oligopolistic investment-restricting conduct is liberal-moral-rights-violative in all or the overwhelming majority of cases), and (3)(A) raises the potential of U.S. antitrust law to instantiate non-utilitarian-egalitarian conceptions of the moral good above the potential of E.U. competition law to do so (since contrived-oligopolistic investment-restrictions almost always increase material inequality) and (B) raises the potential of U.S. antitrust law to increase total utility above the potential of E.U. competition to do so (clearly serves the instantiation of the utilitarian conception of the moral good when the deterred investments are investments in PPR and is more likely to increase total utility than to increase economic efficiency when the deterred investments are QV investments, given the undesirability from a utilitarian perspective of the distributive impact of contrived-oligopolistic investment-restrictions).

Second, for deterrence-related reasons, the fact that written U.S. antitrust law entitles buyers that would purchase the products that would have been created by the deterred investments, buyers of other products produced in the ARDEPPS of practice, and producers that were deterred from investing by threats of retaliation or were subjected to retaliation when they did not cooperate with the contriver to obtain legal redress whereas written E.U. competition law gives such parties no such opportunity affects the 3 relevant relative potentials of U.S. antitrust law and E.U. competition law in the same ways that they are affected by written U.S. antitrust law's covering and written E.U. competition law's not covering contrivance by never-dominant firms that is practiced solely by making or making and carrying out threats of retaliation: In addition, this right-to-legal-redress-related difference makes U.S. law more liberal-moral-rights-securing than E.U. competition law directly because victims of liberal-moral-rights-violating acts have a liberal moral right to obtain redress from their perpetrator(s) (if the fact that U.S. law entitles the relevant victims to *treble* damages does not justify the opposite conclusion).

Third, the "fact" that written E.U. competition law (Article 101) prohibits all firms from not investing for *O*-related reasons whereas U.S. antitrust law does not cover natural-oligopolistic conduct of any kind ("fact" enquoted because of the possibility that it might not be correct as a matter of E.U. law to interpret Article 101 to cover negative decisions) and the fact that Article 102 prohibits dominant firms from exploitatively abusing any position in which its and its rivals' *O*-related decisions not to invest put it whereas U.S. antitrust law does not prohibit any firm from exploitatively abusing any competitive position (1)(A) raises the potential of written E.U. competition law to increase economic efficiency above the counterpart potential of written U.S. antitrust law when the investments not made are investments in PPR and (B) has an uncertain effect on the above potentials when the investments not made are QV investments (because *O*-related investment-restrictions do not result from allocative-transaction-costly communications and do not involve retaliation, which is misallocative for more than one reason), (2) raises the potential of written E.U. competition law to secure liberal moral rights above its counterpart for written U.S. antitrust law (for deterrence reasons) if one assumes (contestably) that decisions not to invest for *O*-related reasons are liberal-moral-rights-violative, and (3)(A) raises the potential of written E.U. competition law to serve the instantiation of non-utilitarian-egalitarian conceptions of the moral good above the potential of written U.S. antitrust law to do so because *O*-induced decisions not to invest increase material inequality and (B)(i) raises the potential of written E.U. competition law to increase total utility above the potential of written

U.S. antitrust law to do so when the deterred investments are investments in PPR but (ii) has an uncertain effect on the relative potentials of written E.U. competition law and written U.S. antitrust law to increase total utility when the deterred investments are QV investments (given that investment-restrictions that result from natural-oligopolistic interactions are not secured by allocative-transaction-costly communications and do not involve misallocative retaliation).

18.1.3 Contrived-Oligopolistic Conduct That Is Designed to Enable Its Participants to Make a Different Set of Investments That Are Collectively More Economically Efficient as Well as More Profitable Because They Are Less-Economic-Inefficiently-Duplicative

Such conduct does not violate written U.S. antitrust law. Such conduct also does not violate written E.U. competition law. Of course, if one or more of such conduct's participants are dominant post-conduct and the conduct gives them an opportunity to exploitatively abuse their dominant position, Article 102 prohibits their taking advantage of that opportunity (a prohibition that has no counterpart in written U.S. antitrust law).

How does this difference between written E.U. competition law's and written U.S. antitrust law's treatments of the pricing-conduct to which this kind of contrivance might lead its participants to engage affect their relative potentials to increase economic efficiency, secure liberal moral rights, and instantiate the various egalitarian conceptions of the moral good? I will focus first on the economic-efficiency-related issue. I will assume that—if one ignores the impact that this sort of contrivance has on equilibrium investment in the ARDEPPSes of practice—this type of contrivance will increase economic efficiency, that the increase in the economic efficiency of the set of investments made exceeds the allocative transaction cost of the contrivance and any other sort of misallocation generated by any retaliation it entails. On this assumption, to the extent that Article 102's prohibition of any dominant firm's exploitatively abusing its dominant position deters some exemplars of this kind of contrivance (those exemplars whose *ex ante* profitability would be critically reduced if its perpetrators were prohibited from exploitatively abusing any dominant positions it led them to occupy), Article 102's prohibition of exploitative abuses of a dominant position (1) would decrease economic efficiency if the investment-location contrivance that prohibition deterred would not have affected equilibrium investment in the ARDEPPS of practice, (2) would decrease economic inefficiency even more when the investment-location contrivance that prohibition deterred would have increased equilibrium investment in the ARDEPPS of practice and that ARDEPPS' investments were investments in PPR, and (3) would have an uncertain effect on economic efficiency when the investment-identity contrivance that prohibition deterred would have increased equilibrium investment in the ARDEPPS of practice and that ARDEPPS' investments were QV investments. In my contestable judgment, all tolled, to the extent that Article 102's prohibition of exploitative abuses of any dominant position deters the kind of contrivance on which this subsection is focusing, it will tend to make written E.U. competition law less economically efficient than written U.S. antitrust law. My disposition to reach this conclusion is strengthened by the fact that in two ways the fact that E.U. competition promulgates and U.S. antitrust law does not promulgate an "exploitative abuse of a dominant position" test of illegality renders the written E.U. competition law on this type of contrivance more economically efficient than its U.S.-antitrust-law counterpart by causing the E.U. law to be more prone to reduce poverty than is the U.S. law: (1) on this account, the written E.U. law will deter some relevant contrivers from taking as much advantage as they otherwise would of the increases in their competitive advantages the relevant contrivance yields them, and (2) on this account, the E.U. law will deter some exemplars of this type of contrivance that would have imposed equivalent-dollar losses on relevant buyers by substituting less-duplicative investments (whose owners would have had higher competitive advantages) for more-duplicative investments whose owners would have had lower competitive advantages.

The fact that written E.U. competition law prohibits dominant firms from exploitatively abusing their dominant positions, whereas written U.S. antitrust law does not will render written E.U. competition law liberal-moral-rights-violative when written U.S. antitrust law is not if liberalism implies that the shareholders, possibly the at-risk creditors, and conceivably the managers and employees of a firm have a moral right that the firm be allowed to engage in economically-efficient conduct and to profit from such conduct by setting prices that maximize their gains from it. However, I doubt that such firm-"connectees" have such a liberal moral right. The combination of (1) my belief that the contrivance of economically-efficient investment-location changes will increase economic efficiency, (2) my concern that such contrivance may impose equivalent-dollar losses on what I call Clayton-Act-relevant buyers by substituting investments that are less competitive with each other for investments that are more competitive with each other, (3) my suspicion that Article 102's prohibition of dominant firms' exploitatively abusing their dominant positions may decrease poverty and material inequality both by causing firms that do engage in the kind of contrivance now at issue to charge lower prices than they otherwise would and by deterring firms from substituting less-duplicative for more-duplicative investments, and (4) the high likelihood that any reduction in such contrivers' prices that is generated by Article 102's "exploitative abuse of a dominant position" prohibition would increase total utility if the prohibition did not affect any other seller-decision lead me to conclude that as it applies to this type of contriver written E.U. competition law's promulgation of this "exploitative abuse of a dominant position" test of illegality has an uncertain impact on the instantiation of the utilitarian conception of the moral good but probably serves the instantiation of all other egalitarian conceptions of the moral good and would on this account be more likely than U.S. antitrust law as written to increase total utility and instantiate any of the various non-pure-utilitarian-egalitarian conceptions of the moral good.

18.1.4 Contrived-Oligopolistic Purchasing

I think that contrived-oligopolistic purchasing will almost always increase economic efficiency by enabling its participants to take advantage of conventional-transaction-cost-related economies of scale and to make better use of purchasing expertise and by reducing poverty and material inequality by lowering the marginal cost the purchasers have to incur to purchase whatever they are purchasing and hence the prices they charge ultimate consumers. I also think that contrived-oligopolistic purchasing will increase total utility by increasing economic efficiency and redistributing income in a way that utilitarianism favors. Moreover, because I think that contrived-oligopolistic purchasing will reduce material inequality by benefiting ultimate consumers, I think that such contrivance will serve the instantiation of all non-pure-utilitarian-egalitarian conceptions of the moral good. However, I acknowledge that contrived-oligopolistic purchasing may violate the liberal moral rights of the sellers with which the contrivers deal, though I think that such a conclusion is disfavored both by the economic efficiency of such contrivance and by the fact that the equivalent-dollar gains it confers on its perpetrators exceed the equivalent-dollar losses it imposes on its seller-victims, given that the price-reductions it generates increase the amount of transaction surplus generated by the (larger unit-quantity) of purchases it results in the contriving buyers making from the relevant sellers.

Read literally, U.S. antitrust law (Section 1 of the Sherman Act) prohibits contrived-oligopolistic purchasing that is effectuated through agreement, but Section 2's proscription of monopolizing conduct would not be read to cover monopsonizing conduct. My own, admittedly-contestable view is that the Sherman Act should not be read literally when the issue is the legality of contrived-oligopolistic purchasing. In my view, the combination of (1) the fact that the Sherman Act was partly motivated by a desire to protect ultimate consumers, (2) the high likelihood that joint purchasing will benefit ultimate consumers, and (3) the fact that U.S. courts tend not to be bound by the literal meaning of legislative text when that meaning favors conclusions that disserve the goal the relevant legislature promulgated the legislation to achieve warrants the conclusion that, correctly interpreted as a matter of U.S. law, the Sherman Act does not prohibit contrived-oligopolistic purchasing. However, I fully acknowledge the contestability of this legal conclusion.

Read literally, the text of Article 101(1) of the 2009 Treaty of Lisbon that prohibits "all agreements between undertakings…[and] decisions by associations of undertakings…which have as their object or effect the prevention…[or] restriction of competition…" would prohibit contrived-oligopolistic purchasing executed through the formation of an agreement (though not contrived-oligopolistic purchasing secured exclusively by an individual undertaking's threat of retaliation or threat and practice of retaliation against non-cooperative fellow-buyers). To be honest, I do not know whether E.U. courts ignore statutory or treaty text that disserves its promulgators' objectives. But, to the extent that they do and relevant participants and observers consider their doing so to be correct as a matter of E.U.

law, the combination of (1) those facts, (2) the fact that both clause (1) of what is now Article 101(3) of the 2009 Treaty of Lisbon and the exploitative-abuse branch of Article 102's "abuse of a dominant position" test of illegality manifest the treaty's promulgators' desire to benefit ultimate consumers, and (3) the fact that it is far from clear that the E.U. is committed to a liberal conception of justice favor the conclusion that E.U. competition law (Article 101) does not prohibit contrived-oligopolistic purchasing.

Obviously, if neither U.S. antitrust law as written nor E.U. competition law as written prohibit contrived-oligopolistic purchasing, no difference in these two bodies of law potential to increase economic efficiency, secure liberal moral rights, or instantiate any egalitarian conception of moral good will be attributable to differences in their treatment of such conduct. If E.U. competition law as written permits contrived-oligopolistic purchasing but U.S. antitrust law as written prohibits it, the E.U. law will on this account be more economically efficient and more promotive of egalitarian conceptions of the moral good than is the "written" U.S. law but may be less protective of liberal moral rights on this account than is the "written" U.S. law (though I doubt it).

18.2 Predatory Conduct: The Differences (If Any) Between Written U.S. Antitrust Law's and Written E.U. Competition Law's Respective Potentials to Increase Economic Efficiency, Secure Liberal Moral Rights, and Serve the Instantiation of any Egalitarian Conception of the Moral Good That Can Be Attributed to Their Disparate Treatments of Predatory Conduct

I will assume (admittedly without much basis) that, like U.S. antitrust law, E.U. competition law does not prohibit predatory participation in government electoral processes or government-decisionmaking processes unless the conduct in question violates norms of "fair play." I know that both written U.S. antitrust law (the Sherman Act) and written E.U. competition law (Article 102) cover and prohibit all positive predatory acts by dominant firms. However, there are 3 important differences between written U.S. antitrust law's and written E.U. competition law's treatment of predatory acts.

First, as written, E.U. competition law (Article 101) does not cover positive predatory acts (other than participation in government electoral or decisionmaking processes) committed by non-dominant firms if the conduct in question does not involve the formation of a contract between rival undertakings (does not involve joint predation). In other words, as written, E.U. competition law does not cover or prohibit predation by an individual non-dominant firm that is executed without forming an agreement with another firm to engage in joint predation—that is, does not cover an individual firm's predation carried out solely by threatening to make or threatening to make and actually making predatory moves. (This last claim assumes, perhaps contestably, that [1] the fact that predatory pricing that results in a sale to a buyer that is offered the predatorily-low price involves an agreement between the predator and the buyer does not bring the predatory act within the coverage of Article 101 even when the buyer is an undertaking because the buyer does not have predatory intent, [2] the fact that a predatory advertizement has been placed through a contract between the predator and an undertaking that publishes printed matter or operates a radio station, TV station, or website does not bring the predatory act within the coverage of Article 101 because the "publishing" firm does not have predatory intent, and [3] the fact that a predatory flyer, poster, or promotional display that was printed/created by a firm other than the predator involved an agreement between the predator and the other undertaking does not bring the predation within the purview of Article 101 because the second firm did not have predatory intent).

Second, unlike written U.S. antitrust law (the Sherman Act), written E.U. competition law does not provide the rival and buyer victims of the predation it prohibits with any opportunity much less with an appropriate opportunity to obtain legal redress.

Third, unlike written U.S. antitrust law, written E.U. competition law (Article 102) does provide customers of dominant firms that have for some reason gotten away with predation and customers of pre-conduct non-dominant firms that are rendered dominant by the predation with some protection against the losses the predation could impose on them by increasing or creating the dominance of the perpetrator by prohibiting the perpetrator from exploitatively abusing the dominant position the predation enhanced or created.

Each of the following subsubsections of Sect. 18.2 will focus on a particular type of predatory conduct. Each will focus initially on the economic efficiency, liberal-moral-rights-violativeness, and impact on the instantiation of the various egalitarian conceptions of the moral good of exemplars of the type of predation it addresses and then examine in the light of its determination of these impacts the effects that the differences between written U.S. antitrust law's and written E.U. competition law's treatments of the relevant variant of predation will have on these two bodies' of law potentials to increase economic efficiency, secure liberal moral rights, and instantiate egalitarian conceptions of the moral good.

18.2.1 Predatory Pricing

Predatory pricing decreases economic efficiency by generating additional allocative transaction costs—to the extent that (1) it entails the predator's generating such costs to identify the customers of its target to which it is going to offer predatory prices and to make predatory offers to target-customers to whom it would not otherwise have made bids, (2) it leads the target to make allocative-transaction-costly rebids to its customers, (3) it leads targets to generate allocative transaction costs to engage in defensive retaliation against the predator, and (4) it leads the predator to engage in allocative-transaction-costly offensive retaliation against the defensive retaliation of its target. Predatory pricing also decreases economic efficiency by causing intra-ARDEPPS UO-to-UO misallocation to the extent that the initial predatory prices, the target's defensively-retaliatory prices, and the predator's offensively-retaliatory prices result in a worse-than-privately-best-placed seller's making sales (since it is TBLE to assume that the sellers that are worse-than-privately-best-placed are also worse-than-allocatively-best-placed). Predatory pricing also decreases economic efficiency by increasing poverty and material inequality: Though predatory pricing reduces poverty and material inequality in the short run by benefiting the buyers who receive the predatorily-low prices, the counter-offers from their privately-best-placed suppliers, and any retaliatory pricing, it increases poverty and material inequality in the long run by increasing the prices the relevant buyers pay in the long run. Predatory pricing decreases economic efficiency by increasing the expenditures that the sellers in the ARDEPPS of practice make on political parties/campaigns/candidates and on government-decisionmaking-process participation by increasing the concentration of the seller-side of the ARDEPPS of practice. Predatory pricing will decrease economic efficiency in the short run if it drives out the target's investment (as opposed to causing the target to sell its investment to the predator at a distressed price) because the continued use of an investment that would have yielded operating profits absent the predation will usually be economically efficient. In what I take to be the unusual case in which the "good" on which predatory pricing is practiced is a patented production process, predatory pricing may also tend to decrease economic efficiency by reducing equilibrium investment in the ARDEPPS of practice by decreasing the intensity of investment-competition in that ARDEPPS (though I acknowledge that any tendency the predatory pricing has to decrease price-competition at various relevant ARDEPPS-investment quantities will tend to have the opposite effect on equilibrium investment in the ARDEPPS of practice). Admittedly, predatory pricing will tend to increase economic efficiency to the extent that the investments in the ARDEPPPS of practice are QV investments and its practice reduces equilibrium investment in that ARDEPPS. However, I am confident that, even when predatory pricing increases economic efficiency by reducing equilibrium QV investment in the ARDEPPS of practice, it will decrease economic efficiency all tolled.

Predatory pricing is also always liberal-moral-rights-violative. It violates the liberal moral rights of the target, of the customers of the predator, and of the customers of the predator's rivals on whom it imposes an equivalent-dollar loss.

Predatory pricing also always or virtually always disserves the instantiation of the utilitarian conception of the moral good because it decreases economic efficiency and increases material inequality. In addition, predatory pricing always or almost always disserves the instantiation of all non-purely-utilitarian-egalitarian conceptions of the moral good because it increases material inequality.

The fact that written U.S. antitrust law does cover and prohibit while written E.U. competition law does not cover or prohibit predatory pricing by any non-dominant firm that is not practiced jointly through an agreement with a cooperating-rival predator raises written U.S. antitrust law's potential to increase economic efficiency, secure liberal moral rights, and instantiate each egalitarian conception of the moral good above the counterpart potentials of written E.U. competition law. The fact that written U.S. antitrust law (the Sherman Act) gives the seller-victims and buyer-victims of predatory pricing an opportunity to obtain legal redress whereas written E.U. competition law does not also raises the relevant potentials of written U.S. antitrust law above their written-E.U.-competition-law counterparts not only by increasing the deterrent powers of written U.S. antitrust law above that of written E.U competition law but also by securing the liberal moral right of victims of practiced predatory pricing to obtain redress from its perpetrators. The fact that written E.U. competition law prohibits predatory pricers that are dominant post-conduct from exploitatively abusing their created or enhanced dominant position increases the relevant potentials of written E.U. competition law above their counterparts for written U.S. antitrust law to the extent that such firms might get away with their predatory pricing.

18.2.2 Predatory Investing

An investment is predatory if two conditions are fulfilled: (1) the investor believed *ex ante* that it would deter a rival investment and (2) *ex ante*, the investor would not have perceived the investment to be at least normally profitable had the investor not believed that the investment would or might reduce the profit-yields of the investor's other investments relative to the *status quo ante* by less than the profit-yields of those other investments would have been reduced relative to the *status quo ante* by the investment the investment in question would deter (because the investor's investment's product-space location would make it less competitive with the investor's other projects than the differently-placed deterred investment would be, because [unlike the investor that would have made the investment that the investment in question would deter] the investor whose investment's predatory character is at issue would take full account of the consequences that its pricing and other decisions that relate to its use of the investment at issue would have on the profits yielded by the investor's other investments, and because the investor's investment would induce its other existing rivals to react in non-retaliatory ways that reduce the investor's profits by less than they would be reduced by those rivals' non-retaliatory reactions to the deterred investment). In other words, this second condition is that the investor believed *ex ante* that it had a critical monopolistic investment-incentive (*M*) to make the investment in question.

I will begin this subsection by comparing written U.S. antitrust law's and written E.U. competition law's respective treatments of predatory investments. The two bodies' of law treatments of predatory investments differ in the same 3 ways that their treatments of predatory pricing differ.

First, although both written U.S. antitrust law (the Sherman Act) and written E.U. competition law (Article 102) prohibit dominant firms from making predatory investments, written U.S. antitrust law (the Sherman Act) does prohibit but written E.U. competition law (most relevantly, Article 101) does not prohibit non-dominant firms from making predatory investments. In particular, at least if I assume that any contract a predatory investor makes with another firm to supply it with inputs it uses to execute its predatory investment does not bring the conduct under the coverage of Article 101 by warranting the conclusion that the conduct involves an agreement between undertakings, Article 101 does not cover a firm's making a predatory investment because such conduct does not involve the making of an agreement between undertakings, trade-association behavior, or a concertation.

Second, written U.S. antitrust law but not written E.U. competition law gives the rival-victims and the buyer-victims of predatory investments an opportunity to obtain legal redress.

Third, written E.U. competition law (Article 102) but not written U.S. antitrust law prohibits firms that are dominant post-conduct from exploitatively abusing the dominant position that the predatory investment created or enhanced.

I turn now to the impact of predatory investments on economic efficiency, liberal moral rights, and the instantiation of the various egalitarian conceptions of the moral good. I focus first on the impact of predatory investments on economic efficiency.

I begin this analysis by considering the "direct" economic efficiency of the predatory investment. The economic efficiency of any predatory investment depends on (1) the profits it yields the investor that makes it, which equal the monopolistic investment-incentive the predatory investor had to make it *minus* the loss the investment would have imposed on the investor if the investor had no monopolistic investment-incentive to make it, (2) the distortion in the private benefits it yields the investor, and (3) the distortion in the private cost to the investor of making the investment. The fact that the predatory investor had an *M* incentive to make the investment implies that on that account the private benefits the investment did/would yield the investor are inflated by more than the dollar monopolistic investment-incentives it had to make the investment, given that the fact that (1) the investment in question is less competitive with the investor's other investments than the investment it deters would have been has no implications for its economic efficiency and the facts that (2) the investment in question will be used in a way that reduces the investor's other projects' profits by less than the use of the deterred investment would have reduced them and (3) will elicit less in the way of competitive responses from the investor's other rivals than the deterred investment would have elicited implies that on these accounts the predatory investment will reduce economic efficiency. The distortion in the private cost to the investor of making the predatory investment equals the distortion in the private benefits the deterred investment would have yielded the deterred investor. If the deterred investor is a potential competitor or an established firm that had no monopolistic incentive (or disincentive) to make the deterred investment, it will probably be TBLE to assume that the distortion in the private benefits the deterred investment would have yielded the deterred investor equal the distortion in the private benefits that all distorting factors other than the monopolistic investment-incentives in question would/did generate in the private benefits yielded by the predatory investment. The preceding results imply that two conclusions are TBLE. First, if the investment the predatory investment would deter would have been made by a potential competitor or an established rival that had no monopolistic investment-incentive to make the deterred investment, the predatory investment would/did decrease economic efficiency by the loss it would have imposed on the predator if the predator had no monopolistic investment-incentive to make it *plus* the economic inefficiency the investment would cause because of the facts that result in the investor's having monopolistic investment-incentives to make it. Second, if the investment the predatory investment would/did deter would have been made by an investor that had a monopolistic investment-incentive to make it (regardless of whether the deterred investment would have been predatory), the economic efficiency of the predatory investment will equal (1)(A) the difference between the dollar-loss the deterred investment would have imposed on the deterred investor if it had no monopolistic investment-incentive to make it (if it would have imposed such a loss on the deterred investor on this assumption) and the dollar-loss the predatory investment whose economic efficiency is at issue would have imposed on the predatory investor if it had no monopolistic investment-incentive to make it and/or (B) the negative of (1) the sum of the dollar-gain the deterred investment would have yielded the deterred investor if it had no monopolistic investment-incentive to make it and the dollar-loss the predatory investment whose economic efficiency is at issue would have imposed on the predatory investor if it had no monopolistic investment-incentive to make it *minus* (2) the difference between the economic inefficiency the predatory investment at issue would cause by virtue of the facts that gave the predator a monopolistic investment-incentive to make it and the economic inefficiency the deterred investment would have generated by virtue of the facts that gave the deterred investor a monopolistic investment-incentive to make it. In my judgment, this second conclusion implies that the vast majority of predatory investments that deter an established rival from investing in the relevant ARDEPPS that are made by firms that have a higher share of the relevant ARDEPPS' investments than the deterred established rival possesses will be economically inefficient because the monopolistic investment-incentive a firm has to make an investment in an ARDEPPS increases with its share of that ARDEPPS' investment. Although I acknowledge that it may be TBLE to investigate whether particular predatory investments increased or decreased economic efficiency (or that it might be TBLE to do so if economically-efficient predatory investments were not liberal-moral-rights-violative and the government of the relevant society were not duty-bound to prohibit them on that account), I suspect that, everything considered it, will be TBLE to assume that all predatory investments decrease economic efficiency.

Predatory investments that decrease economic efficiency violate the liberal moral rights of the firms whose investments they deter and the liberal moral rights of the buyers they disadvantage. I am uncertain whether a predatory investment that (1) is economically efficient and (2) was made by an investor that did appropriate research into this issue and concluded its predatory investment would be economically efficient is liberal-moral-rights-violative. If one concludes that under such conditions the predatory investment would not be liberal-moral-rights-violative, I think it would be liberal-moral-acceptable for the government to require the investor to provide the evidence establishing the fulfillment of the relevant conditions.

Because predatory investments will tend to reduce price competition, I think they will increase material inequality. On that account, they will disserve the instantiation of all non-utilitarian-egalitarian conceptions of the moral good. If as I believe it will be third-best desirable to assume that all predatory investments decrease economic efficiency and increase material inequality, it will be third-best desirable to conclude that all predatory investment decrease total utility.

Written U.S. antitrust law's treatment of predatory investments differs from written E.U. competition law's treatment of predatory investments in 3 ways:

(1) written U.S. antitrust law (the Sherman Act) prohibits non-dominant firms' making predatory investments whereas written E.U. competition law (most relevantly, Article 101) does not,
(2) written U.S. antitrust law gives the victims of the predatory investments it prohibits an opportunity to obtain legal redress (indeed, to collect treble damages) whereas written E.U. competition law does not give the victims of the predatory investments it prohibits (namely, predatory investments made by already-dominant firms) no opportunity to obtain legal redress, and
(3) written E.U. competition law prohibits firms whose positions have been rendered dominant by the predatory investment(s) they made or whose dominance has been increased by the predatory investment(s) they made from exploitatively abusing their dominant positions (the latter point is salient because some time may pass before a dominant firm's predatory investment is detected and found unlawful and because some dominant-firms' predatory investments may not be declared illegal) whereas written U.S. antitrust law does not prohibit the exploitative abuse of any set of competitive positions (regardless of the dominance of the firm that occupies them).

These differences in the written-U.S.-antitrust-law and written-E.U.-competition-law treatments of predatory investments affect these bodies' of law relative potentials to increase economic efficiency, secure liberal moral rights, and instantiate various egalitarian concepts of the moral good in the following ways:

(1) the facts that U.S. antitrust law prohibits predatory investments by non-dominant firms whereas written E.U. competition law does not and that U.S. antitrust law gives rival-victims and buyer-victims of illegal predatory investments an appropriate opportunity to obtain legal redress implies that on their account the potentials of written U.S. antitrust law to secure these 3 *desiderata* are greater than are their written-E.U.-competition-law counterparts, and
(2) the fact that written E.U. competition law but not written U.S. antitrust law prohibits firms that get away with predatory investments from exploitatively abusing their created or enhanced dominant position raises the potentials of written E.U. competition law to secure these 3 *desiderata* above their written-U.S.-antitrust-law counterparts.

18.2.3 Predatory Advertizing That Is Not Unfairly Competitive

This subsection focuses on predatory advertizing that is not "unfairly competitive"—that is, that does not drive a rival out or deter an investment by doing something that improves the predator's array of competitive positions and concomitantly worsens its target's array of actual or prospective competitive positions by conveying misleading or false information about the performance-attributes or lifetime-cost-to-buyers of the predator's product(s) and/or one or more target-product(s). Advertizing is correctly said to be predatory if the advertizer's *ex ante* perception that it would be at least normally profitable was critically affected by its belief that the advertizing would or might drive a rival out, deter an established rival or potential competitor from making an investment in the ARDEPPS of practice, or induce an established rival or potential competitor to change the location of an extant or future investment. I will first address the differences between written U.S. antitrust law's treatment of predatory advertizing and written E.U. competition law's treatment of predatory advertizing, then analyze the impacts of predatory-advertizing on economic efficiency, liberal moral rights, and the instantiation of the various egalitarian conceptions of the moral good, and finally consider the impacts of the relevant legal differences on the two bodies' of written law potentials to secure the above 3 *desiderata.*

There are 3 differences between written U.S. law's and written E.U. law's treatments of predatory advertizing that is not unfairly competitive. First, although written U.S. antitrust law (the Sherman Act) covers and prohibits predatory advertizing regardless of whether the advertizer occupied a dominant position (and regardless of whether it was inaccurate or misleading), if (as I assume) the fact that an exemplar of such advertizing involves a contract with a broadcaster, printer, or promotional-display producer that has no predatory intent does not bring the predatory advertizing in question within the coverage of Article 101, written E.U. competition law does not cover and therefore does not prohibit predatory advertizing (regardless of whether it was unfairly competitive) when the predator did not occupy a dominant position before placing the predatory advertizement(s). Second, unlike written E.U. competition law, written U.S. antitrust law gives the victims of predatory advertizing an opportunity to obtain legal redress when it does prohibit the predatory advertizing. Third, unlike written U.S. antitrust law, written E.U. competition law prohibits any dominant firm from exploitatively abusing any dominant position that predatory advertizing creates or enhances. This difference is salient to the extent that dominant firms sometimes get away with predatory advertizing or could exploit any dominant position that predatory advertizing created or enhanced prior to their being found to have engaged in predatory advertizing.

I will make 6 points about the impact on economic efficiency of predatory advertizing that is not unfairly competitive. First, I think it will be TBLE to assume that the fact that such advertizing would be less-than-normally-profitable if it did not alter any rival's investment-decision implies that it would be economically inefficient if it did not alter my rival's investment-decision. Second, if such advertizing causes its target to sell its investment to the predator at a distressed price, it will decrease economic efficiency by causing allocative transaction costs to be generated by the sale, by increasing poverty and material inequality, and by increasing the expenditures the sellers in the ARDEPPS of practice make on political parties/campaigns/candidates and participation in government-decisionmaking processes by increasing the concentration of the seller-side of the ARDEPPS of practice. Third, it will be TBLE to assume that predatory advertizing that causes the target's investment to be withdrawn when its operation would otherwise have yielded at least a normal rate-of-return but does not affect the relevant ADREPPS' equilibrium investment-quantity will tend to cause economic inefficiency on that account. Fourth, if the investments in the ARDEPPS of practice are QV investments, the predatory advertizing will increase/decrease economic efficiency if it decreases/increases equilibrium investment in the ARDEPPS of practice: It could do either, depending on the relative extents to which it reduced price competition at relevant QV-investment quantities in the relevant ARDEPPS and reduced QV-investment competition in that ARDEPPS. Fifth, in the less-common cases in which the investments in the ARDEPPS of practice are investments in PPR, predatory advertizing will decrease/increase economic efficiency if it decreases/increases equilibrium investment in that ARDEPPS. Sixth, in my judgment, predatory advertizing that is not unfairly competitive will almost always decrease economic efficiency. Moreover, I doubt that it will be TBLE for analysts to consider the possibility that such advertizing might increase economic efficiency in either individual instances or in any definable subset of cases.

I will now address the liberal-moral-rights-violativeness of predatory advertizing. Predatory advertizing always violates the liberal moral rights of its target(s). If, as I suspect, *ex ante* the relevant predatory advertizers will rarely if ever have reached the conclusion that the advertizing would increase economic efficiency after doing appropriate research, I will be able to avoid considering the possibility that predatory advertizing that is not unfairly competitive may not be liberal-moral-rights-violative if after due consideration the predator concluded *ex ante* that its advertizing would be economically efficient.

I suspect that predatory advertizing that is not unfairly competitive will almost always increase material inequality by inflicting equivalent-dollar losses on the buyers in the ARDEPPS of practice—that any dollar-gains the accurate, non-misleading information such advertizing conveys to buyers enables them to secure by improving their relevant knowledge-base will be lower than the dollar-losses it will impose on them by reducing price competition (and possibly investment-competition). If correct, this last (admittedly-contestable) conclusion implies that predatory advertizing that is not unfairly competitive will disserve the instantiation of any pure or mixed non-utilitarian-egalitarian conception of the moral good. Moreover, in combination with my conclusion that such advertizing will decrease economic efficiency, this last distributive conclusion implies that it will also disserve the instantiation of the utilitarian conception of the moral good.

If the preceding practice-impact conclusions are correct, (1) the fact that written U.S. antitrust law prohibits non-dominant-firm predatory advertizing that is not unfairly competitive whereas written E.U. competition law does not and the fact that written U.S. antitrust law gives predator-rival and relevant-buyer victims of illegal predation an opportunity to obtain legal redress whereas written E.U. competition law does not imply that on these accounts written U.S. antitrust law is more economically efficient, more liberal-moral-rights-securing, and more instantiative of egalitarian conceptions of the moral good than is written E.U. competition law and (2) the fact that written E.U. competition law but not written U.S. antitrust law prohibits dominant firms from exploitatively abusing their dominant positions raises the potential of written E.U. competition law above the potential of written U.S. antitrust law to secure these 3 *desiderata*.

18.2.4 Predatory Unfair Competition

Business conduct is "unfairly competitive" if it improves its perpetrator's array of competitive positions without increasing its perpetrator's relative allocative efficiency—in the words of Article 101 of the 2009 Treaty of Lisbon, if it "distorts competition" and, in the words of Section 5 of the U.S. Federal Trade Commission Act, if it is an "unfair method of competition." Unfair methods of competition can either be predatory or non-predatory. They are predatory if their perpetrator's *ex ante* perception that the conduct in question would be at least normally profitable was critically affected by its belief that the conduct would or might reduce the absolute attractiveness of the best offers against which it would have to compete by driving a rival out, deterring a rival investment, or inducing a rival or potential rival to change the location of an existing or planned investment: Unfair competition can be profitable and practiced even if it is not predatory—even if its *ex ante* normal profitability is secured by the prospect of its improving its perpetrator's array of competitive positions without altering any rival's investment-related decision. Although the heading of this subsection references predatory unfair competition, all its conclusions apply to non-predatory unfair competition.

As Sect. 10.4 indicated, unfair competition can take many forms. *Inter alia*, the following kinds of conduct constitute unfair competition—(1) placing advertizements that contain inaccurate or misleading information about the products of the advertizer or of one or more of its rivals, (2) promulgating unjustified quality-standards that disadvantage one or more rivals or misapplying quality-standards to the disadvantages of one or more rivals, (3) deterring potential suppliers or customers of a rival from dealing with the rival by communicating false or misleading information about the rival's credit-worthiness, legal position, or likely survival, (4) obstructing a rival's place of business, (5) bribing potential suppliers or customers of a rival to forego what would otherwise be profitable transactions with the perpetrator's rival, (6) inducing suppliers of a rival to supply it with inferior services or goods, (7) making otherwise-unprofitable purchases of workers, managers, raw materials, IP rights, other inputs and refusing inherently-profitable sales of them to the target, (8) making unjustifiable legal claims against the rival or attempting to secure legislation or administrative regulations that would unfairly disadvantage one or more rivals.

I will now discuss (1) any differences in written U.S. antitrust law's and written E.U. competition law's treatments of unfair competition, (2) the impacts of unfair competition on economic efficiency, liberal moral rights, and the instantiation of egalitarian conceptions of the moral good, and (3) the impact of any differences in the two bodies' of written law treatments of unfair competition on their relative potentials to secure the above 3 *desiderata*. I focus initially on the relevant law-differences.

I will assume that neither written U.S. law nor written E.U. law firms prohibit firms from engaging in unfair competition by inducing government to make legislative, administrative, and/or judicial decisions that unfairly disadvantage their rivals so long as the firms' participation in government electoral and decisionmaking processes does not violate norms of fair play. I believe that that is the law in the U.S., but I admit that I have not been able to ascertain the E.U. law on this matter. Even on this assumption, there are 3 differences between the treatment of unfair competition by written U.S. antitrust law and written E.U. competition law.

First, written U.S. antitrust law prohibits an individual firm's engaging in unfair competition on its own regardless of whether its perpetrator is dominant in the ARDEPPS of practice whereas written E.U. competition law prohibits unfair competition practiced by an individual firm on its own only if its perpetrator is dominant in the ARDEPPS of practice. Thus, Section 5 of the Federal Trade Commission Act prohibits non-dominant-individual-firm unfair competition as an "unfair method of competition," and the Sherman Act prohibits such unfair competition when its perpetrator's *ex ante* perception that it was at least normally profitable was critically affected by the perpetrator's belief that it would or might increase the perpetrator's profits by reducing the absolute attractiveness of the best offers against which it would have to compete in a way that would render the conduct profitable though economically inefficient in an oPp economy, whereas Article 101 of the 2009 Treaty of Lisbon prohibits unfair competition only if it involves an agreement between undertakings, trade-association conduct, or a concertation. Second, when the unfair competition violates the Sherman Act, written U.S. law provides rival-victims and buyer-victims an opportunity to obtain legal redress whereas E.U. competition law does not provide such victims with such an opportunity even when it does prohibit the unfair competition (because its practice involves an agreement between undertakings, trade-association conduct, or a concertation or its practitioner occupied a dominant position before engaging in the unfair competition). Third, in those cases in which the practitioner of unfair competition occupies a dominant position after engaging in the unfair competition, written E.U. competition law prohibits the unfair-competition practitioner from exploitatively abusing the dominant position the unfair competition created or enhanced whereas written U.S. antitrust law does not prohibit dominant firms from exploitatively abusing their dominant positions.

I will now address the impact of unfair competition on economic efficiency. Regardless of whether acts that are unfairly competitive are predatory, they will reduce economic efficiency in the short run because (1) they are allocative-transaction-costly, (2) they will tend to cause their target(s) to make allocative-transaction-costly responses and will cause the government to generate allocative transaction costs, (3) they will deter economically-efficient transactions, and (4) some types of such conduct (e.g., obstructing a rival's place of business or calling into question a target's credit-worthiness or likely longevity) will cause the target-rival's potential customers or trading-partners to generate allocative transaction costs (to surmount the obstruction or to check out the negative allegation) even if they do not deter them from making what would otherwise be economically-efficient purchases. If the conduct induces one or more unfairly-disadvantaged rivals to sell out to the perpetrator, it will reduce economic efficiency by the allocative transaction costs the business-sales generate. If the conduct induces one or more rivals simply to stop using their investment when it would otherwise have been profitable for it or them to use the investment(s) in question, it will decrease economic efficiency on that account. Because such conduct will tend to increase prices and the associated loss to the relevant buyers will almost certainly not be eliminated by any related increase in the ARDEPPPS' equilibrium investment, unfair competition will also decrease economic efficiency by increasing poverty and material inequality. Because such conduct will tend to increase the concentration of the seller-side of the ARDEPPS of practice, it will tend to decrease economic efficiency by increasing the expenditures the ARDEPPS' sellers make on political parties/campaigns/candidates and government-decisionmaking-process participation. Admittedly, predatory unfair competition may increase economic efficiency by decreasing equilibrium QV investment in an ARDEPPS of practice whose investments are QV investments or (less likely) by increasing equilibrium investment in an ARDEPPS of practice whose investments are investments in PPR, but it seems to me that such conduct is too likely to decrease economic efficiency by increasing equilibrium QV investment in the ARDEPPS of practice or decreasing equilibrium PPR in the ARDEPPS of practice for these possible equilibrium-investment effects to significantly reduce the probability that unfair competition will decrease economic efficiency. Moreover, I doubt that it will be TBLE to consider that possibility in individual unfair-competition cases or in any identifiable subset of such cases.

I turn now to the impact of unfair competition on liberal moral rights. Predatory or not, unfair competition violates the liberal moral rights of the shareholders, at-risk creditors, and possibly the managers and employees of the firms it disadvantages and of the buyers it directly disadvantages.

I turn finally to the impact of unfair competition on the instantiation of the various egalitarian conceptions of the moral good. Unfair competition imposes equivalent-dollar losses not only on the firms that are unfairly disadvantaged but also on the buyers in the ARDEPPS of practice. If as I suspect it is third-best morally good to assume that these buyers are materially less-well-off than the average member of the society in question, unfair competition will on this account disserve the instantiation of all non-purely-utilitarian egalitarian conceptions of the moral good. And the combination of the preceding distributive-impact conclusion and the earlier conclusion that such conduct is economically inefficient implies that unfair competition will also disserve the instantiation of the utilitarian conception of the moral good.

If as I believe unfair competition decreases economic efficiency, violates liberal moral rights, and disserves the instantiation of all egalitarian conceptions of the moral good, (1) the fact that written U.S. antitrust law prohibits unfair competition practiced individually (non-oligopolistically) by non-dominant firms whereas written E.U. competition law does not and the fact that the Sherman Act gives victims of unfair competition that violates it an opportunity to obtain legal redress whereas written E.U. competition law does not provide such an opportunity to victims of its violation imply that on these accounts the potentials of written U.S. antitrust law to increase economic efficiency, secure liberal moral rights, and instantiate egalitarian conceptions of the moral good are greater than their written-E.U.-competition-law counterparts, but (2) the fact that written E.U. competition law (Article 102) prohibits dominant firms from exploitatively abusing their dominant position whereas written U.S. antitrust law does not prohibit any firm from exploitatively abusing its position implies that on that account written E.U. competition law has more potential than written U.S. antitrust law to secure the 3 *desiderata* on which I am focusing by virtue of their respective treatments not of unfair competition directly but of a possible consequence of its practice.

18.2.5 Predatory Refusals to Deal

Even if I ignore refusals to deal that are connected to systems rivalry (which Sect. 18.2.6 considers), at least 9 varieties of refusals to deal are worth distinguishing. In particular, (1) an individual firm can refuse to deal with a potential supplier or a customer, (2) two or more firms can agree to refuse to deal with a potential customer, (3) an individual seller/buyer may enter into (a long-term full-requirements contract with its customer)/(a long-term total-output-supply contract with its supplier), (4) the parents of a joint venture or the founders of a patent pool can agree not to supply the good they have agreed to supply each other (usually for free) to non-members, to supply non-members with that good only on disadvantageous terms, or to allow any parent or participant to veto the supply of the good to one of its rivals, (5) an individual firm can condition its employing someone, patronizing another firm, or supplying another firm with goods to distribute on that other individual's or other firm's agreeing not to deal with one or more other parties, (6) two or more individuals that are forming a partnership may agree that they will not compete for the patronage of any of the partnership's actual or potential customers either in their individual capacities or as an employees of another firm during the operation of the partnership or for some time after the partnership is dissolved, (7) two or more firms that are forming a joint venture or some other functionally-analogous collaborative arrangement may prohibit the joint venture from dealing with the parents' customers and/or each parent from dealing with the other parent's or parents' customers, (8) a seller of a professional practice or a business may agree not to compete against the buyer of that practice or business ever or for a specified period of time, and (9) a producer may decide to prohibit its individual independent distributors from competing for the patronage of specified individual or classes of buyers.

I will now consider in this order (1) the differences between written U.S. antitrust law's and written E.U. competition law's treatments of refusals to deal, (2) the impacts of refusals to deal on economic efficiency and liberal moral rights (which I will analyze together because [if I ignore the possibility that some refusals to deal may be motivated by prejudices] refusals to deal will be liberal-moral-rights-violative only if they are predatory or unfairly competitive and, in my judgment, it is TBLE to assume that the effects of refusals to deal that render them non-predatory or not unfairly competitive render them economically efficient), (3) the impact of refusals to deal on the instantiation of the various egalitarian conceptions of the moral good, and (4) the impacts that the differences between written U.S. law's and written E.U. law's treatments of refusals to deal have on their relative potentials to increase economic efficiency, secure liberal moral rights, and instantiate egalitarian conceptions of the moral good.

Written U.S. antitrust law's and written E.U. competition law's respective treatments of refusals to deal differ in the same 3 ways that their treatments of the other kinds of conduct considered in this section differ: (1) Written U.S. antitrust law prohibits any non-dominant firm from engaging in a refusal to deal that is predatory or is an unfair method of competition (see the Sherman Act and the Federal Trade Commission Act) whereas written E.U. competition law does not (because Article 101 does not cover such refusals, given that they do not result from any agreement between undertakings, trade-association decisions, or concertations and Article 102 does not cover them because the perpetrator does not occupy a dominant position); (2) written U.S. antitrust law gives any victim of a refusal to deal the Sherman Act prohibits the opportunity to obtain legal redress whereas written E.U. competition law does not give any victim of a refusal to deal it prohibits an opportunity to obtain legal redress; and (3) when the perpetrator of the refusal to deal occupied a dominant position before refusing to deal or the refusal to deal caused its perpetrator to occupy a dominant position, E.U. competition law prohibits the perpetrator from taking advantage of the refusal to deal by exploitatively abusing its dominant position whereas U.S. law does not prohibit any firm (dominant or not) from exploitatively abusing its dominant position.

I will now analyze the economic efficiency and moral-rights-violativeness of the various exemplars of each of the categories of refusals to deal I distinguished. As indicated previously, I am combining these analyses because (with what I hope are rare exceptions) business refusals to deal are liberal-moral-rights-violative only if they are predatory or unfairly competitive and it is TBLE to assume that the effects that render refusals to deal non-predatory or fairly competitive render them economically efficient.

In my judgment, the overwhelming majority of exemplars of each category of refusals to deal I distinguished are neither predatory nor unfairly competitive and are, by virtue of the facts that render them non-predatory and fairly competitive, economically efficient. I will now attempt to justify these claims for each of the 9 categories of refusals to deal I distinguished.

First, in my judgment, most individual-firm individual refusals to deal are neither predatory nor unfairly competitive—reflect nothing more than the inherent unprofitability of the refused deals. The refused deals may be inherently unprofitable because the price offered does not cover the incremental cost of supply or because the amount by which the price offered exceeds the conventional incremental cost of supply is lower than the loss the supply would impose on the supplier by damaging its product's reputation because the relevant buyer would combine it with one or more inferior complements. It is almost certainly TBLE to assume that refusals of inherently-unprofitable deals increase economic efficiency.

Second, I suspect that the overwhelming majority of decisions of sellers/buyers to enter into long-term (full-requirements)/(total-output-supply) contracts that in effect require their contract partner not to deal with others are not predatory or unfairly competitive because they are rendered profitable by their reducing the mechanical transaction costs the parties must incur, by their reducing the risk costs the parties incur, by their encouraging the parties to adjust their operations (say, their delivery-truck and loading-dock/unloading-dock choices) in their mutual interest, and if the long-term-clause-containing agreements are tying agreements by their enabling the seller to profit by using the tying agreement to perform legitimate functions. The facts that make these contracts legitimately profitable also make the refusals to deal they "command" economically efficient.

Third, although I acknowledge that some provisions in vertical joint-venture or patent-pool agreements that restrict access to the good produced or distributed by the joint venture to its parents or the intellectual property distributed by the patent pools to its members are predatory or unfairly competitive as are provisions allowing non-parents/non-members to purchase the "goods" involved only on unfavorable terms and provisions allowing parents/members to veto the supply of the goods involved to their rivals, some related refusals to deal may be rendered non-predatory or fairly competitive by the economic-efficiency gains that are generated by providing potential "founders" with incentives to create the joint venture or patent pool (which is itself economically efficient). Obviously, joint-venture or patent-pool refusals to deal or discrimination against "non-founders" that are not predatory or not unfairly competitive for this reason will increase economic efficiency.

Fourth, an employer's decision to prohibit its employees or independent suppliers from dealing with any rival may be rendered non-predatory and fairly competitive by its increasing the profits the employer can realize (1) by revealing information about its business or business-plans to its employees or independent distributors that would increase the contribution they could make to its profits when the information-recipients could otherwise sell the information to a rival of the information-provider and/or (2) by its training its employees in a way it would find profitable if it could retain their services but not if they could profit from the training by selling their labor to a competitor or competing against it themselves on their own. Once more, it seems TBLE to assume that refusals to deal that are executed for these reasons increase economic efficiency.

Fifth, I suspect that most decisions by founders of a partnership and most decisions by parents of a joint venture to prohibit each partner from competing against the other or each parent from competing against the other or the joint venture and to prohibit the joint venture from competing against the parents are rendered non-predatory and fairly competitive by their increasing the profits the partnership/(joint venture) will generate by encouraging each founder/parent to communicate to the (other partner)/(the joint venture) information that will increase the partnership's/(joint venture's) profit-yield but could also be used by the partner or joint venture that received the information to compete against its communicators. Once more, it seems TBLE to assume that refusals to deal that are executed for this reason increase economic efficiency.

Sixth, I suspect that most decisions by a seller of a professional practice or other sort of business to agree not to compete against the buyer are rendered non-predatory and fairly competitive by the fact that part of what is being sold is the seller's goodwill and client/patient/customer-list and the value of that list and goodwill would be substantially diminished if the seller could re-enter and supply goods and services to his or her former clients/patients/customers. It seems to me that refusals to deal that are generated for these reasons increase economic efficiency both (1) by causing economically-efficient transfers of ownership to be executed and (2) by removing what would otherwise be a negative distortion in the profits individuals can realize by identifying potential customers and building up goodwill.

Seventh, decisions by producers to include vertical-customer-allocation clauses in their agreements with their independent distributors will not be predatory if they are rendered non-predatory and fairly competitive by their enabling the producer to deter intra-brand price competition and to induce its distributors to make advertizing, promotional-display, shelf-space-allocation, salesmanship, warrantee-service-provision decisions and organizationally-profitable decisions to pass on valuable information to the producer. Although the relevant analysis is complicated by the need to take account of the decisions the producer would substitute for the vertical-customer-allocation clauses if it were prohibited from using them, for reasons that Sect. 13.3 explains, I think that the refusals to deal that VCA clauses generate increase economic efficiency all tolled.

Of course, some exemplars of many categories of refusal-to-deal-related conduct are predatory or unfairly competitive. Although I believe that this is rarely if ever the case, some decisions by vertically-integrated firms to refuse to supply or buy from rivals may be predatory or unfairly competitive. I also acknowledge that some agreements by two or more vertically-integrated firms not to deal with a non-vertically-integrated rival that is an actual or potential competitor may be predatory or unfairly competitive. It is possible that some decisions of individual firms to enter into long-term full-requirements contracts with buyers or long-term total-output-supply contracts with one or more sellers are predatory or unfairly competitive, but I very much doubt that even a trivial number of such contracts are. I think that many decisions of patent pools to exclude or disadvantage non-founders are predatory or unfairly competitive. I admit as well that some decisions by firms to prohibit their employees or independent contractors from working for or selling information to the prohibitor's rivals may be predatory or may constitute unfair competition though I suspect that the percentage of such decisions that can be correctly characterized in one or the other of these ways is small. I recognize that the same conclusions apply to decisions by buyers of professional practices or businesses to prohibit the seller from competing with them and to decisions by individuals forming a partnership to prohibit themselves from competing against each other. I would not be surprised if a significant percentage of provisions in joint-venture agreements prohibiting the parents from competing against each other or the joint venture and prohibiting the joint venture from competing against the parents were predatory, but I am pessimistic about the TBLE of identifying those restrictive provisions in joint-venture agreements that are predatory (in part because I suspect that taken together all such restrictive provisions increase economic efficiency). I think it is TBLE to assume that all refusals to deal that are predatory or unfairly competitive reduce economic efficiency because the refused deals would have been economically efficient and because predatory refusals to deal will tend to decrease economic efficiency by increasing the expenditures made on political parties/campaigns/candidates and government-decisionmaking-process participation by increasing the concentration of the seller-side of the ARDEPPSes of practice, by increasing poverty and material inequality, and (possibly) by increasing the supernormal profits the predators could realize if they operated proficiently and did not increase the compensation made to their managers and employees and relatedly increasing the misallocative X-inefficiency they generated and the misallocation the predator's managers and employees generated by substituting untaxed or lower-taxed fringe benefits for the goods and services they would have purchased with the monetary compensation they forewent to obtain the fringe benefits. I think it is TBLE to assume that all refusals to deal that are not predatory or unfairly competitive increase economic efficiency.

I turn next to the impact of refusals to deal on the instantiation of the utilitarian and non-utilitarian-egalitarian conceptions of the moral good. In my judgment, refusals to deal that are predatory or unfairly competitive will tend to increase poverty and material inequality (by imposing equivalent-dollar losses on the perpetrator's customers and the customers of its rivals and by conferring equivalent-dollar gains on the perpetrator's connectees). In my judgment, refusals to deal that are neither predatory nor unfairly competitive will if anything decrease poverty by benefiting Clayton-Act-relevant buyers and will have no predictable impact on material inequality. The combination of these admittedly-contestable claims and my conclusions that (1) refusals to deal that are neither predatory nor unfairly competitive will increase economic efficiency and (2) refusals to deal that are predatory or unfairly competitive will decrease economic efficiency imply that refusals to deal that are neither predatory nor unfairly competitive will increase total utility while refusals to deal that are predatory and/or unfairly competitive will decrease total utility. The distributive-impact conclusions previously articulated imply that across all instances refusals to deal that are neither predatory nor unfairly competitive will tend neither to serve nor to disserve the instantiation of non-utilitarian-egalitarian conceptions of the moral good.

The preceding refusal-to-deal-impact conclusions imply that (1) the facts that written U.S. antitrust law does prohibit predatory or unfairly-competitive refusals to deal executed or induced by an individual actor that was not an undertaking or a dominant undertaking whereas written E.U. competition law does not and that the written Sherman Act provides victims of the refusals to deal it prohibits with an appropriate opportunity to obtain legal redress whereas written E.U. competition law does not provide victims of the refusals to deal it prohibits with any such opportunity support the conclusions that on these accounts the potentials of written U.S. antitrust law to increase economic efficiency, secure liberal moral rights, and instantiate the various egalitarian conceptions of the moral good exceed their written-E.U.-competition-law counterparts and (2) the fact that written E.U. competition law (Article 102) prohibits dominant firms from exploitatively abusing their competitive positions whereas written U.S. antitrust law does not implies that the difference between written E.U. competition law's and written U.S. antitrust law's treatments of the exploitative conduct to which successful predatory or unfairly-competitive might lead its perpetrator to engage raises the potentials of written E.U. competition law to increase economic efficiency, secure liberal moral rights, and instantiate egalitarian conceptions of the moral good above their written-U.S.-antitrust-law counterparts.

18.2.6 Allegedly-Predatory Systems Rivalry

The expression "systems rivalry" refers to conduct in which a producer of one product (say, a camera or a computer mainframe) makes decisions to prevent potential suppliers of complements of its product (film and developing services or peripherals and repair-and-maintenance services) from being able to supply them. Those decisions include decisions not to reveal to such potential complement-suppliers attributes of the basic product the potential complement-producer would have to be aware of to produce a desirable complement, decisions to contractually obligate buyers of the basic product to purchase their full requirements of the complement(s) from either the basic-product producer or an independent firm that the basic-product producer designates, decisions not to provide would-be repair-and-maintenance-service providers with the information they require to provide such services satisfactorily, decisions not to sell to independent service organizations (ISOs) replacement-parts the basic-product producer manufacturers itself, and decisions to contractually prohibit independent replacement-part producers to which the basic-product producer provided important information and from which the basic-product producer buys replacement-parts for use by its own repairment-and-maintenance divisions or that the basic-product producer authorizes to supply repair-and-maintenance services to some specified basic-product purchasers from supplying replacement-parts to other ISOs.

The conclusion that systems rivalry is predatory is based on the claim that the basic-product producer would not find the practice *ex ante* profitable but for its believing that the practice would or might deter the firms that want to provide the complements from entering the basic-product ARDEPPS by denying them (1) the financial wherewithal they would obtain by producing and selling the complements, (2) the knowledge they would gain about the basic product and its production by producing the complementary goods or supplying the repair-and-maintenance services, (3) the knowledge of the basic-product-buyers' identities, particular economic needs, and salesmanship-relevant predilections, and (4) the opportunity to make a good impression on these buyers. I doubt that systems rivalry is predatory or unfairly competitive because I think its perpetrators' *ex ante* perceptions that it is profitable almost always reflect their beliefs that it will yield them profits (1) by enabling them to control more private-cost-effectively the quality of the complements their customers combine with their basic products, (2) by enabling them to practice meter pricing on their basic goods more-private-cost-effectively, (3) by increasing the profits they can realize by making expenditures to identify buyers for their products and persuading those buyers of their products' value, and (4) by enabling them to prevent the profits they can realize by making use of the investment that created the basic product from being deflated by entries by complement-producers. I recognize the contestability of this fourth ground for concluding that systems rivalry is legitimate—that it is undercut both by what I assume to be the reality that the complement-producer's creation of its own basic product would not have violated any IP right of the firm practicing systems rivalry and (perhaps) by the possibility that the Pareto imperfections the relevant economy contains (taking account of its IP law) may otherwise have inflated the profits the systems-rivalry perpetrator expected *ex ante* that its investment in the basic product would yield.

Because I doubt that any exemplar of systems rivalry is predatory or unfairly competitive, I do not think that the possible differences between written U.S. antitrust law's and written E.U. competition law's respective treatments of systems rivalry have any practical consequences. However, given that my assessment of systems rivalry is undoubtedly contested even if I do not think it is contestable, it behooves me to consider the difference between the two bodies' of law treatments of those exemplars of systems rivalry that (contrary to my view) are deemed predatory or unfairly competitive. Once more, there are 3 such differences: The first relates to differences in written U.S. antitrust law's and written E.U. competition law's coverages of systems rivalry. First, because the interpretation of U.S. statutes that is correct as a matter of law is influenced by liberalism's implication that unless one or more special conditions are fulfilled that are not fulfilled in systems-rivalry situations moral-rights bearers have no moral duty to benefit others, it may be correct as a matter of U.S. law to interpret the Sherman Act and Federal Trade Commission Act not to cover a firm's decision to practice systems rivalry by not communicating to potential complement-producers information about its product or the proper way to maintain and repair its product or by not supplying to ISOs replacement-parts or maintenance-and-repair implements regardless of whether the systems-rivalry practitioner is dominant whereas written E.U. competition law (Article 101) clearly will not cover such types of systems rivalry when the perpetrator is not dominant (because such types of systems rivalry do not involve an agreement between undertakings, a trade-association decision, or a concertation) but will cover such types of systems rivalry when the perpetrator is dominant (if I am correct in concluding that liberalism plays no generic role in the interpretation of E.U. sources of law). Second, written U.S. antitrust law (the Sherman Act) does give victims of systems rivalry that violates the Sherman Act an opportunity to secure legal redress whereas written E.U. competition law does not provide victims of any system rivalry it deems illegal with an opportunity to obtain legal redress. Third, in cases in which the perpetrator of systems rivalry occupies a dominant position after practicing systems rivalry, written E.U. competition law (Article 102) prohibits the systems-rivalry perpetrator from taking advantage of the improvement in its array of competitive positions the systems rivalry generated by exploitatively abusing its dominant position whereas written U.S. antitrust law contains no such prohibition. To repeat: I do not think that these differences are consequential because I do not think that systems rivalry ever violates any U.S. antitrust law or E.U. competition law test of illegality, but if you disagree with this latter claim you will disagree with my assessment of the consequences of the 3 written-law differences just specified.

I turn now to the impact of systems rivalry on economic efficiency. At least 7 effects are relevant. First, systems rivalry will increase economic efficiency by increasing the extent to which its perpetrator controls the quality of the complements its basic-product buyers combine with its basic product and by reducing the allocative cost the perpetrator generates when controlling its customers' complement-choices. Second, systems rivalry will increase economic efficiency if it decreases the allocative cost its practitioner generates to practice "a given amount" of meter pricing. Third, the impact that systems rivalry has on economic efficiency by increasing the extent to which its perpetrator practices meter pricing is uncertain. Fourth, if as I suspect, systems rivalry tends to increase the concentration of the seller-sides of its ARDEPPSes of practice by encouraging potential perpetrators to invest and deterring entry, it will on that account decrease economic efficiency by increasing the expenditures the ARDEPPSes' sellers make on political parties/campaigns/candidates and on government-decisionmaking-process participation. Fifth, I do not know how systems rivalry will impact economic efficiency by affecting equilibrium investment in the ARDEPPSes of practice because I do not know whether it will increase or decrease those ARDEPPS' equilibrium-investment quantities: It will increase those quantities by making the investments in relation to which it is practiced more profitable, but it will decrease those quantities by raising the barriers to entry (preventing reductions in the barriers to entry) faced by some potential entrants. Sixth, to the extent that systems rivalry increases the potential supernormal profits of its practitioners, it *may tend* to decrease economic efficiency by causing them to generate misallocative X-inefficiency and by causing its practitioners' managers and employees to generate misallocation by substituting lower-taxed fringe benefits for the goods and services they would have purchased with the wages they forewent to obtain those fringe benefits. Seventh, I do not want to speculate about whether systems rivalry will increase/decrease economic efficiency by decreasing/increasing poverty and material inequality because, for reasons I will discuss below, I am too uncertain about whether systems rivalry will increase or decrease poverty and material inequality. I am disposed to conclude that, all tolled, systems rivalry increases economic efficiency, but I recognize the contestability of this conclusion.

I turn next to the liberal-moral-rights-violativeness of systems rivalry. Two sets of points are salient. First, systems rivalry will be liberal-moral-rights-violative only if it is predatory or unfairly competitive, and the arguments I made for system rivalry's being neither predatory nor unfairly competitive imply that systems rivalry is not liberal-moral-rights-violative. Second and relatedly, it is possible that prohibitions of systems rivalry would be liberal-moral-rights-violative—that firm-connectees have a liberal moral right that the firm be allowed to protect the profits its investment could generate by keeping secret various matters that relate to its "discovery" and by pricing its product in the way that is most profitable so long as its pricing is not predatory or oligopolistic (though I would not endorse this second contention).

I will now address the impact of systems rivalry on total utility and on the instantiation of non-utilitarian-egalitarian conceptions of the moral good, which depends entirely on whether its practice increases or decreases material inequality. Here is a list of some of the most important distributive impacts of systems rivalry. Systems rivalry (1) confers equivalent-dollar gains on its practitioner's "connectees"—that is, shareholders, at-risk creditors, and probably managers and employees, (2) imposes equivalent-dollar losses on the deterred aspiring-complement-producers' "connectees," (3) confers equivalent-dollar gains on buyers who would otherwise mistakenly use inferior complements, (4) imposes equivalent-dollar losses on buyers who would profit from using inferior complements, (5) confers equivalent-dollar gains on buyers who use the basic product less often than its average buyer does if the practice causes meter pricing to replace non-discriminatory untied sales, (6) imposes equivalent-dollar losses on buyers who use the basic product more often than its average buyer does if the practice causes meter pricing to replace non-discriminatory untied sales, and (7) can either (A) confer equivalent-dollar gains on buyers of the basic product and equivalent-dollar losses on the connectees of the producers in the basic-product-production ARDEPPS if the practice increases that ARDEPPS' equilibrium-investment quantity or (B) have the opposite effect on those parties if the practice decreases equilibrium investment in that ARDEPPS. I will resist the temptation to speculate about the relative income/wealth positions of the just-referenced affected groups. I have no usefully-informed view of the net effect of system rivalry on material inequality. I will therefore assume that systems rivalry has no tendency either to serve or to disserve the instantiation of any non-utilitarian-egalitarian conception of the moral good.

The final systems-rivalry impact I will consider is the practice's impact on total utility. I recognize the contestability of the following claim, but, in my view, the combination of my inability to judge system rivalry's impact on material inequality, my view that the practice tends to increase economic efficiency, and my suspicion that efforts to determine whether individual exemplars or particular classes of exemplars of systems rivalry will increase or decrease total utility will decrease total utility warrants the conclusion that it is third-best desirable from the perspective of utilitarianism to assume that the practice increases total utility.

If as I believe no exemplar of systems rivalry violates any test of illegality promulgated by written U.S. antitrust law or written E.U. competition law, the only difference in these two bodies' of law treatments of systems rivalry or the conduct to which it could lead is the fact that written Article 102 prohibits any firm that is dominant post-conduct from exploitatively abusing any improvement in its competitive position the systems rivalry generated whereas written U.S. antitrust law contains no such prohibition. To the extent that this written-E.U.-competition-law prohibition deters some systems rivalry (because individual exemplars of systems rivalry that would otherwise be *ex ante* profitable though they could yield losses *ex post* would be rendered *ex ante* unprofitable by the prohibition), this provision might reduce the potential of written E.U. competition law to increase economic efficiency and total utility below their written-U.S.-antitrust-law counterparts. If, contrary to my view, some exemplars of systems rivalry are predatory and/or unfairly competitive (do violate the tests of illegality promulgated by the Sherman Act, the Federal Trade Commission Act, Article 101, and Article 102), the potentials of written U.S. antitrust law to increase economic efficiency, secure liberal moral rights, and increase total utility would be reduced below their written-E.U. competition-law counterparts if (because of liberalism's disinclination to impose duties on moral-rights bearers to benefit others) "written" U.S. antitrust law does not cover failures to communicate relevant product-information or product-maintenance-and-repair information and refusals to supply maintenance-and-repair implements to ISOs. If, contrary to my view, some exemplars of systems rivalry are predatory and/or unfairly competitive, the fact that written U.S. antitrust law does not prohibit while written E.U. competition law (Article 102) does prohibit dominant firms from exploitatively abusing dominant positions regardless of whether those positions have been created or enhanced by prohibited systems rivalry reduces the potentials of written U.S. antitrust law to increase economic efficiency, secure liberal moral rights, and increase total utility below their written-E.U.-competition-law counterparts. If, contrary to my view, some exemplars of systems rivalry do violate the Sherman Act, the fact that the Sherman Act does afford the victims of any systems rivalry that is illegal an opportunity to obtain legal redress whereas written E.U. competition does not provide such an opportunity to victims of prohibited systems rivalry implies that on this account the potentials of written U.S. antitrust law to increase total utility, secure liberal moral rights, and increase total utility are higher than their written-E.U.-competition-law counterparts.

18.3 Horizontal Mergers and Acquisitions

As Sect. 17.3.3 explains, the treatments of horizontal (M&A)s, respectively, by written U.S. antitrust law and written E.U. competition law differ in 3 respects. First, written U.S. antitrust law (the Sherman Act) provides victims of horizontal (M&A)s that were motivated by specific anticompetitive intent with an opportunity to obtain legal redress while written E.U. competition law provides no victim of any horizontal (M or A) it prohibits with an opportunity to obtain legal redress. Second, unlike written U.S. antitrust law, which does not promulgate any exploitative-abuse test of illegality, written E.U. competition law (Article 102) prohibits any firm that results from a horizontal (M or A) that is dominant from exploitatively abusing its dominant position—a provision that admittedly relates not to the illegality of the horizontal (M or A) itself but to the illegality of the way in which some resulting firms take advantage of the competitive positions the (M or A) gives them. Third, though it may not be appropriate to ascribe this possible difference between U.S. antitrust law's and E.U. competition law's respective treatments of horizontal (M&A)s to written features of the two bodies of law, it may be correct as a matter of U.S. law to interpret the Clayton Act, which promulgates a lessening-competition test of illegality that applies *inter alia* to any horizontal (M or A) that "lessens competition," to allow participants in horizontal (M or A)s that "lessen competition" to exonerate themselves by demonstrating that their (M or A) would not have imposed a net equivalent-dollar loss on the customers of the participants and the customers of their product-rivals "combined" as a result of its reducing the absolute attractiveness of the best offers these buyers respectively received from any worse-than-privately-best-placed supplier had the (M or A) not driven a rival out or deterred a new investment by creating a resulting firm whose operations were more economically efficient (as well as more privately efficient) than the participants' would have been and thereby critically worsened one or more existing firms' arrays of actual competitive positions or one or more deterred potential investors' arrays of prospective competitive positions whereas it would not be correct as a matter of E.U. law to interpret Article 101 (which promulgates a lessening-competition test of illegality and covers horizontal [M&A]s) or the European Merger Control Regulation (which also promulgates a lessening-competition test of illegality and covers horizontal [M&A]s) to permit horizontal-(M or A) participants to establish such an organizational-allocative-efficiency defense. As Sect. 17.3.3 points out, (1) the case for reading such a defense into the Clayton Act is that not only U.S. antitrust law in general but U.S. industrial policy in general (including its IP law) permits and encourages firms to do things that are economically efficient, and (2) the case for not reading such a defense into Article 101 or the EMCR is that, despite many officials' and commentators' claims to the contrary, E.U. competition law is not disposed to allow firms to compete on the merits when its doing so harms relevant consumers. This written-E.U.-competition-law position is most manifest by the fact that Article 101(3) authorizes decisionmakers to declare Article 101 and its prohibitions inapplicable to covered conduct Article 101 would otherwise prohibit despite the fact that the conduct "contributes to improving the production or distribution of goods or to promoting technical or economic progress" only if the conduct (its perpetrators) "allow...consumers a fair share of the resulting benefit." The relevant disposition of written E.U. competition law is also manifest in Article 102's prohibiting dominant firms from exploitatively abusing their dominant position even if they achieved their position by engaging in economically-efficient conduct.

My assessments of the effects of these differences between the written U.S. antitrust law's and the written E.U. competition law's treatments of horizontal (M&A)s and the pricing-conduct to which they may lead is based on the following 4 crude conclusions or should I say assertions:

(1) horizontal (M&A)s that manifest one or more participants' specific anticompetitive intent (A) reduce economic efficiency, (B) are liberal-moral-rights-violative, (C) reduce total utility because they reduce economic efficiency and redistribute income to their participants' connectees" (who tend to be richer) from the customers of their participants and the customers of their participants' rivals (who tend to be poorer), and (D) disserve the instantiation of non-utilitarian-egalitarian conceptions of the moral good,
(2) horizontal (M&A)s that do not manifest any participant's specific anticompetitive intent but do lessen competition and are consummated by firms that could not establish an organizational-allocative-efficiency defense for them if such a defense were available will tend to decrease economic efficiency, decrease total utility, and disserve the instantiation of non-utilitarian-egalitarian conceptions of the moral good but are not liberal-moral-rights-violative,
(3) horizontal (M&A)s that do not manifest any participant's specific anticompetitive intent but do lessen competition and are consummated by participants that could make out an organizational-allocative-efficiency defense if such a defense were available (A) probably tend to increase economic efficiency, (B) have an uncertain impact on total utility, (C) disserve the instantiation of non-utilitarian-egalitarian conceptions of the moral good, and (D) are not liberal-moral-rights-violative, and
(4) prohibitions of dominant firms' exploitatively abusing their dominant positions (A) have an uncertain impact on economic efficiency, (B) also have an uncertain effect on total utility (given that they may deter economically-efficient conduct that benefits consumers), though their "direct" impact will be to increase total utility by redistributing income from dominant-firm-connectees to "Clayton-Act-relevant buyers," (C) also have an uncertain effect on the instantiation of non-utilitarian-egalitarian conceptions of the moral good, and (D) neither secure nor violate liberal moral rights.

I will now address the impacts that the 3 differences between the written U.S. antitrust law's and the written E.U. competition law's treatments of horizontal (M&A)s or the conduct to which they may lead their participants to engage on these two bodies' of law relative potentials to increase economic efficiency, secure liberal moral rights, and instantiate various egalitarian conceptions of the moral good.

The fact that written U.S. antitrust law (the Sherman Act) gives victims of specific-anticompetitive-intent-motivated horizontal (M&A)s an opportunity to obtain legal redress whereas written E.U. competition law gives no victims of horizontal (M&A)s such an opportunity implies that on this account the potentials of written U.S. antitrust law to increase economic efficiency, secure liberal moral rights, and instantiate the utilitarian and other egalitarian conceptions of the moral good are higher than their written-E.U.-competition-law counterparts. The fact that written E.U. competition law prohibits firms that occupy a dominant position from exploitatively abusing that position whereas written U.S. antitrust law does not has an uncertain impact on their relative potentials to increase economic efficiency, to increase total utility, and to serve the instantiation of non-utilitarian-egalitarian conceptions of the moral good (since the E.U. prohibition applies to firms that occupy a dominant position regardless of whether their doing so reflects their engaging in exclusionarily-abusive conduct, luck, or their having made economically-efficient choices) but probably does increase the potential of written E.U. competition law above the potential of U.S. antitrust law to secure liberal moral rights at least to the extent that liberal-moral-rights-violating horizontal (M&A)s will not in practice be found to violate the respective jurisdictions' laws (if it is not liberal-moral-rights-violative to prohibit firms that have secured their dominant positions by competing on the merits from exploitatively abusing that position). In my judgment, the "fact" that (enquoted because I recognize the contestability of the following claim) "written" U.S. antitrust law's lessening-competition test of illegality is qualified by an organizational-allocative-efficiency defense whereas written E.U. competition law's lessening-competition test of illegality is not qualified in this way implies that on this account the potential of written U.S. antitrust law to increase economic efficiency exceeds the potential of written E.U. competition law to do so, probably tends to favor the conclusion that on this account the potential of written U.S. antitrust law to increase total utility exceeds the potential of written E.U. competition law to do so, has no bearing on the relative potentials of the two bodies' of written law to secure liberal moral rights (if as I assume the connectees of a firm have no liberal moral right that it be allowed to engage in the horizontal [M&A]s that the organizational-allocative-efficiency defense would render lawful), and probably raises the potential of written E.U. competition law to instantiate non-utilitarian-egalitarian conceptions of the moral good above its written-U.S.-antitrust-law counterpart.

18.4 Conglomerate Mergers and Acquisitions

Written U.S. antitrust law's and written E.U. competition law's respective treatments of conglomerate (M&A)s differ in the same 3 ways as do their respective treatments of horizontal (M&A)s. As Chap. 12 explains, conglomerate (M&A)s may differ from horizontal (M&A)s in some ways that affect the impacts of these written-law differences on the two bodies' of law potentials to increase economic efficiency, secure liberal rights, and instantiate various egalitarian conceptions of the moral good. For example, (1) unlike horizontal (M&A)s, conglomerate (M&A)s do not directly eliminate the price-competition their participants wage against each other (though they may eliminate such price-competition indirectly by deterring the entry of an effective-potential-competitor participant), and (2) conglomerate (M&A)s may increase their participants' contrived and natural oligopolistic pricing less than horizontal (M&A)s do. However, the above differences and others that Chap. 13 delineates affect only the magnitudes not the sign of the law-differences' impacts on the potentials of the two bodies of written law to increase economic efficiency, secure liberal moral rights, and instantiate various egalitarian conceptions of the moral good. I will therefore restrict myself to stating that all the analyses and conclusions that Sect. 18.3 reached about the relevant potentials of the U.S. and E.U.'s written law on horizontal (M&A)s apply *mutatis mutandis* to those bodies' of law treatments of conglomerate (M&A)s.

18.5 Surrogates for Vertical Integration

I will start by reviewing the 6 most important points or related sets of points that Sect. 17.3.5 makes about the relationship between the written U.S. law and the written E.U. law on surrogates for vertical integration:

(1) correctly interpreted as matters of law, the provisions of both legal regimes that promulgate lessening-competition tests of illegality make the analysand in lessening-competition cases not an individual firm's using the surrogate for vertical integration but a rule permitting all members of a set of product-rivals to use the relevant surrogate for vertical integration (the analysand in specific-anticompetitive-intent cases [monopolization, object-of-restricting-competition, exclusionary-abuse-of-a-dominant-position cases] is the motivation of the individual actor),

(2) although it is correct as a matter of U.S. law to read the statute (the Clayton Act) that promulgates a lessening-competition test of illegality and covers some surrogates for vertical integration to permit defendants to exonerate themselves by establishing an organizational-economic-efficiency defense, it is probably not correct as a matter of E.U. law to read the treaty provision (Article 101) that promulgates a lessening-competition test of illegality and covers some surrogates for vertical integration to permit defendants to

exonerate themselves by establishing an organizational-economic-efficiency defense,

(3) (A) the U.S. Sherman Act, which promulgates a specific-anticompetitive-intent test of illegality, covers all actors regardless of their dominance and all successful uses of all varieties of surrogates for vertical integration, regardless of whether the buyers involved are firms or individuals but does not cover unsuccessful attempts to form contracts whose formation would constitute a use of a surrogate for vertical integration; (B) the U.S. Clayton Act, which promulgates a lessening-competition test of illegality and an "injury to rival" test of illegality when the conduct whose illegality is at issue is a decision by a buyer "knowingly to induce or receive a discrimination in price," covers any decision of any actor regardless of its dominance to practice "price discrimination" in the Clayton-Act sense on a commodity (but not on a service or insurance) on sales to either other firms or to individuals and any decision by any actor to contractually obligate any lessor or buyer of a "good" (but not of a service or insurance) it supplies on the lessee's or buyer's agreement not to "use or deal in the goods…of a competitor or competitors of the lessor or seller" regardless of whether the lessee or buyer is a firm or an individual; (C) Article 101 of the 2009 Treaty of Lisbon covers firms (undertakings) regardless of their dominance, promulgates specific-anticompetitive-intent, lessening-competition, and distorting-competition tests of illegality, applies only to those surrogates for vertical integration that involve an agreement between undertakings, applies to sales-agreements between undertakings that involve the sale of services and insurance policies as well as sales-agreements between undertakings that involve the sale of commodities, and (I will assume) covers any unsuccessful attempt to form an agreement between undertakings; and (D) Article 102 of the current E.U. treaty covers only undertakings that occupied a dominant position prior to engaging in the conduct at issue, covers all surrogates for vertical integration, and prohibits them if they manifest the perpetrator's specific anticompetitive intent (constitute an exclusionary abuse of its dominant position): Article 102 also prohibits any firm that occupies a dominant position (including a dominant position that was created or enhanced by its use of a surrogate for vertical integration) from exploitatively abusing that dominant position, regardless of whether the "good" in question is a commodity or a service or insurance and regardless of whether the buyer(s) in question is (are) other firm(s) or one or more individuals,

(4) it is not correct as a matter of E.U. law to read clause (a) of Article 101, which references agreements between undertakings that "directly or indirectly fix…selling prices" to imply that Article 101 prohibits vertical price-fixing,

(5) it is not correct as a matter of E.U. law to read clause (b) of Article 101 or clause (c) of Article 102, which refer to agreements between undertakings that "apply dissimilar conditions to equivalent transactions with other trading parties, thereby placing them at a competitive disadvantage," to imply that Article 101 or Article 102 prohibit all instances of a seller's engaging in price discrimination when selling its product to buyers that are rivals,

(6) it is not correct as a matter of E.U. law to read clause (e) of Article 101's or clause (d) of Article 102's references to clauses in agreements between undertakings that "make the conclusion of contracts subject to acceptance by other parties of supplementary obligations which, by their nature or according to commercial usage, have no connection with the subject of such contracts" to imply that Article 101 or Article 102 prohibits minimum-price-setting or maximum-price-setting RPM clauses, vertical-customer-allocation (VCA) clauses, clauses requiring distributors to engage in stipulated quantities and qualities of media advertizing, to provide stipulated quantities and qualities of in-store promotional displays or shelf-space, to provide waranteed repair-and-maintenance services, and/or not to sell products that compete with the products of the supplier-participant in the contract, and

(7) the provisions of U.S. antitrust law that covers "price discrimination" and applies a lessening-competition test of illegality to it (Section 2 of the Clayton Act) defines "price discrimination" to refer to the charging of different prices to different buyers for in essence a given good at in essence the same time—that is, does not count as price discrimination charging the same price to different buyers at (about) the same time despite the fact that the cost to the seller of supplying that good to the different buyers was different, and although this provision permits defendants in price-discrimination cases to exonerate themselves by establishing a cost-justification for any inter-buyer price-differences, it places the burden of proof on the cost-justification issue on the defendant whereas the provision of E.U. competition law that covers price discrimination and applies *inter alia* a lessening-competition test of illegality to it clearly should be read to define price discrimination in the way that economists define it and may or may not place the burden of establishing cost-justifications on defendants.

18.5.1 Pricing-Techniques

I will focus first on predatory uses of any pricing-technique. There are 4 differences in the treatment of the predatory use of a pricing-technique by U.S. antitrust law as written and E.U. competition law as written. First, U.S. antitrust law as written covers and prohibits any non-dominant firm's predatory use of a pricing-technique in sales-contracts with individuals (with buyers that are not undertakings) whereas E.U. competition law as written does not cover or prohibit any predatory use of a pricing-technique by a non-dominant seller in a sales-contract with an individual. Second, I am assuming admittedly contestably that E.U. competition law as written or at least as correctly interpreted as a matter of E.U. law covers unsuccessful attempts to incorporate one or more predatory exemplars of any type of pricing-technique into contracts of sale between undertakings whereas U.S. competition law as written or at least as correctly interpreted as a matter of U.S. law does not cover such unsuccessful attempts. Third, E.U. competition law as written (Article

102) but not U.S. antitrust law as written (the Sherman Act) prohibits any firm that is dominant after using a pricing-technique predatorily from exploitatively abusing its dominant position. Fourth, U.S. antitrust law as written (the Sherman Act) but not E.U. competition law as written (Articles 101 and 102) do not give the rival-victims and buyer-victims of predatory pricing an opportunity to obtain legal redress. The first and fourth differences just referenced raise the potentials of U.S. antitrust law as written to increase economic efficiency, secure liberal moral rights, and instantiate the utilitarian and non-utilitarian-egalitarian concepts of the moral good above the potentials of E.U. competition law to do so. The second difference renders E.U. competition law as written more potential economically efficient, liberal-moral-rights-securing, and egalitarian-moral-good-promoting than is U.S. antitrust law as written. The third difference raises the potentials of written E.U. competition law to increase economic efficiency and instantiate all egalitarian conceptions of the moral good above their written-U.S.-antitrust-law counterparts both directly and by tending to make written E.U. competition law more effective at deterring predatory pricing and raises the potential of written E.U. competition law to secure liberal moral rights above its written-U.S.-antitrust-law counterpart by increasing the extent to which E.U. law deters predatory pricing.

I focus next on non-predatory uses of pricing-techniques—uses whose execution by all members of a set of product-rivals may lessen competition or uses by a dominant firm that may result in the user's exploitatively abusing its dominant position. There are 5 sets of differences in the treatment of such pricing-technique uses by written U.S. antitrust law and written E.U. competition law. First, the provision of U.S. antitrust law that promulgates a lessening-competition test of illegality and that applies to "price discrimination" (Section 2 of the Clayton Act) (1) does not cover "price discrimination" in the economics sense that is practiced by charging different buyers the same price for essentially the same good essentially contemporaneously when the seller must incur different incremental or marginal costs to supply the buyers in question, (2) does not apply to the sale of services or insurance as opposed to goods but does apply to the use of the pricing-technique it calls price discrimination both when the relevant buyers are firms and when the buyers are individuals whereas the provision of E.U. competition law that will sometimes apply to price discrimination (Article 101) applies to "price discrimination" even when it does not involve charging different buyers different prices, applies to price discrimination practiced on the sale of services and insurance policies as well as on the sale of commodities, but does not apply when the buyers involved are individuals as opposed to undertakings. Second, the provision of U.S. antitrust law that promulgates a lessening-competition test of illegality (the Clayton Act) does not apply to the use of perfect price discrimination, the charging of a combination of a lump-sum fee and a supra-TSM-marginal-cost per-unit price, and the (pricing-technique) use of reciprocity agreements to prevent substitutions against inputs when the relevant pricing-technique implementations do not involve inter-buyer price discrimination whereas the provision of E.U. competition law that promulgates a lessening-competition test of illegality and covers pricing-technique uses covers the use of all pricing-techniques when the seller and buyer are firms.

Third, unlike written U.S. antitrust law, written E.U. competition law contains a provision (Article 102) that makes a dominant firm's use of any pricing-technique illegal if it results in the dominant firm's exploitatively abusing its dominant position. Because I think that non-predatory price discrimination in the economics sense decreases economic efficiency, does not violate any liberal moral right, probably tends to instantiate all non-utilitarian-egalitarian conceptions of the moral good (because it tends to reduce material inequality by conferring equivalent-dollar gains on poorer buyers [who tend to be charged the discriminatorily-low prices] and imposing equivalent-dollar losses on better-off buyers [who tend to be charged discriminatorily-high prices]), and has an uncertain impact on total utility, I think that the fact that as written U.S. antitrust law does not cover non-predatory price discrimination in the economics sense that does not involve the charging of different buyers different prices or non-predatory price discrimination in the Clayton Act's sense on services and insurance policies whereas E.U. competition law as written does cover such pricing makes E.U. competition law as written potentially more economically efficient and potentially less-instantiative of the non-utilitarian conceptions of the moral good than is U.S. antitrust law as written. Because I believe that a rule allowing all members of a set of product-rivals to use the pricing-techniques whose use Article 101 covers but the Clayton Act does not cover will never or virtually never lessen competition, I think this difference between E.U. competition law as written and U.S. antitrust law as written does not affect their respective potentials to increase economic efficiency, secure liberal moral rights, or instantiate any egalitarian conception of the moral good. In my judgment, the fact that E.U. competition law as written prohibits dominant firms from exploitatively abusing their dominant positions *inter alia* by making choices that are not predatory or do not lessen competition whereas U.S. antitrust law as written promulgates no such prohibition implies that on this account E.U. competition law as written has more potential to increase economic efficiency as written (because the use of all the fancy pricing-techniques whose use can cause their user to obtain an exploitatively-higher percentage of the transaction surplus its sales in a relevant ARDEPPS yield [except for the use of tie-ins and reciprocity agreements to prevent substitutions against inputs and probably the use of tie-ins to prevent purchases of more complements to basic products than is economically efficient] will decrease economic efficiency) and to serve the instantiation of all egalitarian conceptions of the moral good as well (because the fancy pricing-techniques both decrease economic efficiency and increase material inequality [by transferring surplus from the dominant firm's customers to the dominant firm]).

18.5.2 Non-Pricing-Technique Tying and Reciprocity Agreements

There are 3 differences between written U.S. antitrust law's and written E.U. competition law's treatments of such tying and reciprocity agreements. First, although both U.S. antitrust law as written (the Sherman Act) and E.U. competition law as written (Article 101 and Article 102 when the perpetrator is a dominant firm) cover and prohibit predatory tying and reciprocity agreements, written E.U. competition law's lessening-competition test of illegality applies to all functional types of tying and reciprocity agreement whereas written U.S. antitrust law's lessening-competition test of illegality applies only to tie-ins and reciprocity agreements that effectuate inter-buyer price discrimination (Section 2 of the Clayton Act) and full-requirements tie-ins (Section 3 of the Clayton Act), which can perform a variety of functions. Second, unlike U.S. antitrust law as written, E.U. competition law as written prohibits any functional type of tie-in or reciprocity agreement that is not predatory that results in a dominant-firm practitioner's exploitatively abusing its dominant position. Third, written U.S. antitrust law (the Sherman Act) but not written E.U. competition law provides victims of predatory non-pricing tying and reciprocity agreements with an opportunity to obtain legal redress.

I think the first and third of these differences are not consequential because few if any tying or reciprocity agreements are predatory: The only possible (arguable) exceptions are agreements of these kinds that function by concealing the existence, extent, or location of predatory pricing. I think that the second difference is not consequential because rarely if ever will a rule allowing all members of a set of product-rivals to use any functional type of tying or reciprocity agreement lessen competition. (Admittedly, if a rule allowing all rivals to use such agreements does sometimes lessen competition, the second difference will be more salient given that it would be incorrect as a matter of E.U. law to read an organizational-economic-efficiency defense into the component of Article 101 that covers such conduct and promulgates a lessening-competition test of illegality but correct as a matter of U.S. law to read such a defense into the components of the Clayton Act that cover such conduct and promulgate a lessening-competition test of illegality).

18.5.3 Minimum-Price-Setting-RPM, Maximum-Price-Setting-RPM, and Vertical-Customer-Allocation (VCA) Clauses in Distributorship Agreements

In the few if any instances in which such clauses effectuate horizontal price-fixing or horizontal market-divisions, their use would be prohibited both by written U.S. antitrust law (the Sherman Act) and by written E.U. competition law (Article 101 and Article 102 when the user was a dominant firm). The fact that written U.S. antitrust law entitles victims of such conduct to obtain legal redress whereas written E.U. competition law does not clearly makes the written U.S. antitrust law's treatment of such exemplars of these clauses more liberal-moral-rights-securing than is the written E.U. competition law's treatment of them and may tend to make the written U.S. antitrust law more economically efficient and better at instantiating the utilitarian and other egalitarian conceptions of the moral good than is written E.U. competition law, though a complete analysis of these bodies' of law efficacy on these fronts would have to take account of differences in the penalties they prescribe and other differences that affect their respective abilities to deter horizontal price-fixing and horizontal market-divisions. The fact that E.U. competition law prohibits such exemplars of these clauses not only on the ground that they are motivated by specific anticompetitive intent but also on the ground that they lessen competition and (in some cases) enable one or more dominant firms to exploitatively abuse their dominant positions is not consequential.

The overwhelming majority (indeed, I suspect, perhaps all) of these clauses are not designed to and do not effectuate horizontal price-fixing or horizontal market-divisions. The only exemplars of such clauses that may manifest specific anticompetitive intent are exemplars used by a producer that would not have perceived its inclusion of such a clause to be *ex ante* at least normally profitable had it not believed that the clause would lead the distributor to make inaccurate or misleading statements about the product(s) of the producer and/or the product(s) of its product-rivals (in which case the clauses would also distort competition [violate Article 101 on that account] and constitute an unfair method of competition [violate the Federal Trade Commission Act on that account]), and I doubt that any significant number of such clauses induce such communications (certainly in societies that have effective consumer-protection and business-tort laws). In any event, both written U.S. antitrust law (the Sherman Act and the Federal Trade Commission Act) and written E.U. competition law (Article 101 and Article 102) would prohibit any exemplars of clauses that are motivated by specific anticompetitive intent. Once again, written U.S. antitrust law's treatment of these exemplars of such clauses differs from written E.U. competition law's treatment of them only in that written U.S. law affords their victims the opportunity to obtain legal redress, while written E.U. competition law does not. I have already indicated the relevant consequences of this difference.

There are two other differences between written U.S. antitrust law and written E.U. competition law as they apply to RPM and VCA clauses. These differences relate to uses of such clauses by sets of rivals that lessen competition even though the clauses do not effectuate horizontal price-fixing or horizontal market-divisions and are not designed to induce competition-distorting conduct. First, written E.U. competition law (Article 101) prohibits and written U.S. antitrust law does not prohibit such uses of such clauses that "collectively" lessen competition presumably because their use is more beneficial to some members of the set of rivals than to others and on that account their general use induces the exit of one or more firms whose respective arrays of competitive positions were critically worsened by the general use of the practice or deters an investment in the ARDEPPS in question by an established seller in it or a potential entrant whose prospective competitive-position array(s) was (were) critically worsened by the general use of the practice or the prospect of the clauses' being generally used (at least "written" E.U. competition law would prohibit such uses of such clauses if as I believe it would be incorrect as a matter of E.U. law to read an organizational-economic-efficiency defense into the lessening-competition test of Article 101). I should add that I doubt the empirical importance of this difference because I doubt that a rule allowing all members of a set of product-rivals to use RPM and VCA clauses will often or ever decrease competition by leading to exits or deterring investments.

Second, written E.U. competition law's treatment of RPM and VCA clauses that do not effectuate horizontal price-fixing or horizontal market-divisions and do not distort competition differs from written U.S. antitrust law's treatment of such clauses in that if the supplier of such clauses is dominant post-conduct Article 102 will prohibit its exploitatively abusing any improvement in its array of competitive positions its use of such clauses generates. I think that if, as I believe, it is correct as a matter of written E.U. law to conclude that Article 101 does not permit a perpetrator to establish an organizational-economic-efficiency defense in a lessening-competition case the fact that Article 101 applies *inter alia* a lessening-competition test of illegality to the use of RPM and VCA clauses whereas U.S. antitrust law does not would make written E.U. competition law less economically efficient and less promotive of total utility than written U.S. antitrust law is, at least if (as I suspect) such clauses' lessening-competition in the few cases in which their general use does so would not decrease economic efficiency sufficiently by increasing equilibrium QV investment in the ARDEPPS of practice (as it may well not do) for this economic-efficiency loss to exceed the economic-efficiency gains the clauses would generate on other accounts. (I am assuming that the relevant producers do not have a liberal moral right to use such clauses when they do so without specific anticompetitive intent and with no intention to distort competition and that the use of such clauses by all members of a set of product-rivals will not increase material inequality by imposing an equivalent-dollar loss on the relevant ARDEPPS' buyers, especially given the behaviors the relevant producers would substitute for the clauses if they were prohibited from using them).

If as I suspect RPM clauses and VCA clauses increase economic efficiency (more precisely, if such clauses' substitution for the conduct their employers would substitute for them if their use was prohibited would increase economic efficiency), the fact that Article 102 prohibits exploitative abuses of a dominant position, whereas U.S. antitrust law promulgates no such prohibition would warrant the conclusions that on this account this difference in the two bodies' of law treatments of RPM and VCA clauses would tend to raise the potential of written U.S. antitrust law to increase economic efficiency and total utility above the counterpart potentials of written E.U. competition law.

18.5.4 Contractual Clauses Obligating Distributors to Place Specific Quantities and/or Qualities of Media Advertizing, to Provide Specified Quantities and/or Qualities of Promotional Displays, to Supply Specified Quantities and Qualities of Salesmanship, to Provide Specified Quantities and Qualities of Shelf-Space, to Provide Specified Repair-and-Maintenance Services (Perhaps Related to Warrantees), and to Use Specified Architectural Layouts and Contractual Clauses in Which a Producer Agrees to Subsidize/(Pay for) Distributor (Expenditures of These Kinds)/(Shelf-Space Allocations)

The analyses of and conclusions about (1) the differences in the treatments of such clauses by written U.S. antitrust law and written E.U. competition law and (2) the impacts that any such differences have on the two bodies' of written law relative potentials to increase economic efficiency, secure liberal moral rights, and instantiate various egalitarian conceptions of the moral good are the same as their counterparts when the business conduct whose treatment is at issue is the use of RPM and VCA clauses.

18.5.5 Sales-Policies: A Producer's Communicating to Its Distributors Its Intention Not to Renew Their Distributorships If They Do Not Follow Its "Recommendations" and a Producer's Not Renewing the Distributorships of Distributors That Do Not Follow Its "Recommendations"

I will start by indicating the 4 differences or sets of differences in written U.S. law's and written E.U. law's respective treatments of such sales-policies. The first difference (set of differences) relates to the characteristics of the sellers whose sales-policies are covered by the two bodies of law and the "nature" of the sales-policies that those bodies of law, respectively, cover. With one possible exception that makes me uncomfortable, written U.S. antitrust law (the Sherman Act and the Federal Trade Commission Act) covers the sales-policy of any firm regardless of its dominance, regardless of whether it entails the linguistic communication of recommendations and/or related threats of discontinuance and regardless of whether it succeeds in securing any compliance by any distributor: The possible exception is that the U.S.' commitment to a liberal conception of justice might warrant the conclusion that sales-policies that are effectuated solely by discontinuing the supply of distributors that do not behave in certain ways may not be covered by the Sherman Act or Federal Trade Commission Act because prohibiting a producer from discontinuing a distributor would impose a positive legal duty on the producer to benefit the distributor (a conclusion that strikes me as too foolish to be warranted by liberalism). By way of contrast, written E.U. competition law covers sales-policies only if they are used by a dominant firm (in which case they are covered by Article 102) or if they succeed in inducing at least one of the distributors at which they are directed to follow the producer's "recommendations" (in which case the combination of the sales-policy and the distributor's acquiescence might be deemed to constitute a concerted practice covered by Article 101: Sales-policies cannot be found to be covered by Article 101 by virtue of their involving an agreement between undertakings because they do not involve an agreement between undertakings. The second difference relates to the tests of illegality that apply to sales-policies. Written U.S. antitrust law prohibits any sales-policy it covers if it is motivated by specific anticompetitive intent (the Sherman Act) or distorts competition (the Federal Trade Commission Act) whereas written E.U. competition law prohibits any sales-policy it covers if it is motivated by specific anticompetitive intent (Article 101 and Article 102), distorts competition (Article 101), or lessens competition—in my view, if a rule allowing all members of a set of product-rivals to use the relevant sales-policy did or would lessen competition—(Article 101). The third difference is that written U.S. antitrust law (the Sherman Act) entitles victims of sales-policies that are motivated by specific anticompetitive intent to obtain legal redress whereas no applicable E.U. treaty provision that prohibits some sales-policies entitles their victims to obtain legal redress. The fourth difference is that written E.U. competition law (Article 102) but not written U.S. antitrust law prohibits any perpetrator of a sales-policy that occupies a dominant position post-conduct from exploitatively abusing that position.

My assessment of the implications of these differences in the written-U.S.-antitrust-law and the written-E.U.-competition-law treatments of sales-policies is largely determined by my views that (1) unless the distributor is "recommending" that the distributor convey to potential buyers misleading or inaccurate information about the producer's product(s) and/or about the product(s) of one or more product-rivals of the producer or the sales-policy is designed to implement a predatory single-brand restriction, "sales-policies" are economically efficient (certainly relative to the behaviors that the producer would substitute for them if prohibited from using them), do not violate any liberal moral right, and do not disserve the instantiation of any utilitarian or non-utilitarian-egalitarian conception of the moral good, (2) at least in societies that have effective consumer-protection and business-tort laws, few if any sales-policies are designed to induce distributors to provide buyers with misleading or inaccurate information, (3) few if any sales-policies implement predatory single-brand restrictions (because few if any single-brand restrictions are predatory), (4) a rule allowing all members of a set of product-rivals to use sales-policies will rarely if ever (I will assume never) lessen competition, and (5) a rule allowing a dominant firm (and *a fortiori* a rule allowing a dominant firm and its rivals) to use sales-policies will rarely if ever critically affect the dominant firm's ability to exploitatively abuse its dominant position.

On these assumptions, the fact that E.U. competition law as written does not cover sales-policies adopted by non-dominant firms that do not secure distributor-compliance whereas written U.S. antitrust law does cover all sales-policies of non-dominant firms that involve linguistic communication and almost certainly covers all sales-policies of such firms that do not involve linguistic communication is not consequential. Similarly, on these assumptions, the fact that—if Article 101 does cover sales-policies that secure distributor-compliance—unlike U.S. antitrust law as written, E.U. competition law as written applies a lessening-competition test of illegality to those sales-policies (as well as specific-anticompetitive-intent and distorting-competition tests of illegality) is not consequential, even if (as I believe [with regret] it is correct as a matter of E.U. law to conclude that the organizational-economic-efficiency defense I have proposed should not be read into Article 101's lessening-competition test of illegality). Again, on these assumptions, the fact that, unlike U.S. law as written, E.U. competition law as written prohibits any dominant firm from exploitatively abusing its position will rarely if ever be consequential. Finally, on these assumptions, the fact that written U.S. antitrust law (the Sherman Act) entitles victims of sales-policies that are motivated by specific anticompetitive intent to obtain legal redress while E.U. competition law does not entitle the victim of any sales-policy that violates any of the tests of illegality it applies to them to obtain legal redress is inconsequential.

18.5.6 Clauses in Distributorship Agreements That Impose Single-Brand Restrictions on the Distributor

Written U.S. antitrust law covers all such clauses and applies specific-anticompetitive-intent (the Sherman Act), lessening-competition (Section 3 of the Clayton Act), and distorting-competition (Section 5 of the Federal Trade Commission Act) tests of illegality to them, though it is probably correct as a matter of law to read an organizational-economic-efficiency defense into the U.S. but not into the E.U. lessening-competition test of illegality. Written E.U. competition law covers all such clauses and applies not only the above 3 tests of illegality to them but also an "exploitative abuse of a dominant position" test to the pricing-decisions of any perpetrator that occupies a dominant position after establishing one or more single-brand exclusive dealerships. The component of U.S. antitrust law that promulgates a specific-anticompetitive-intent test of illegality (the Sherman Act) entitles victims of conduct that violates this test of illegality to obtain legal redress whereas E.U. competition law provides no victim of such clauses with an opportunity to obtain legal redress.

In my judgment, (1) few if any single-brand exclusive dealerships are motivated by specific anticompetitive intent (are liberal-moral-rights-violative), (2) virtually all single-brand clauses in distributorship agreements increase economic efficiency, (3) rules allowing all members of a set of product-rivals to create single-brand exclusive dealerships will rarely if ever lessen competition, (4) such rules will not tend to increase material inequality, (5) an individual firm's creating single-brand exclusive dealerships and perhaps more relevantly (given the possible existence of a liberal moral rights of firm-connectees to have their firm allowed to compete on a level playing-field) the members of a set of product-rivals' creating single-brand exclusive dealerships will rarely increase material inequality or disserve the instantiation of any egalitarian conception of the moral good, and (6) a rule allowing a dominant firm and all of its rivals to create single-brand exclusive dealerships will rarely if ever affect whether any dominant firm occupies a dominant position or the array of competitive advantages any firm enjoys (which the firm could abusively exploit).

If the preceding claims are correct, the fact that the U.S. law that promulgates a specific-anticompetitive-intent test of illegality entitles victims of conduct it prohibits to obtain legal redress while no component of E.U. competition law creates such a right to legal redress does not make the associated difference in the two bodies' of law treatments of single-brand exclusive dealerships consequential. And if the preceding claims are correct, the fact that E.U. law but not U.S. law prohibits any dominant firm's exploitatively abusing its dominant position would have no single-brand-exclusive-dealership-related impact on their relative potentials to secure desired objectives.

18.6 Vertical Mergers and Acquisitions

There are 3 differences between written U.S. antitrust law and written E.U. competition law as they apply to vertical (M&A)s: (1) in many of what I take to be the rare cases in which a rule allowing all members of a set of product-rivals to execute vertical (M&A)s lessens competition, it will be important that the U.S. lessening-competition test of illegality but not the E.U. lessening-competition test of illegality entitles the participants to exonerate themselves by establishing an organizational-economic-inefficiency defense; (2) E.U. competition law but not U.S. antitrust law prohibits any dominant firm whose ability to exploitatively abuse its dominant position was critically affected by its and its product-rivals' being permitted to participate in vertical (M&A)s from taking advantage of that opportunity; and (3) written U.S. antitrust law but not written E.U. competition law entitles victims of vertical (M&A)s that are motivated by specific anticompetitive intent and victims of any predatory refusals to deal that a firm that results from a vertical (M or A) perpetrates to obtain legal redress.

The impact of the first, organizational-economic-efficiency-defense-related difference on the vertical-(M&A)-related relative potentials of written U.S. antitrust law and written E.U. competition law will be substantially reduced if, as I believe, rules allowing all members of a set of product-rivals to participate (separately) in vertical (M&A)s rarely (if ever) lessen competition. However, if as I believe the rare sets of product-rival vertical (M&A)s that collectively reduce competition increase economic efficiency, the "fact" that E.U. competition law does not combine its lessening-competition test of illegality with an organizational-economic-efficiency defense whereas U.S. antitrust law does will make E.U. competition law's treatment of vertical (M&A)s less economically efficient than U.S. antitrust law's treatment of them. Moreover, if as is possible some connectees of any firm that engages in a non-predatory, economically-efficient vertical (M or

A) have a liberal moral right that it be permitted to do so (at least if its and its product-rivals being permitted to participate in such [M or A]s does not disserve any relevant conception of the moral good—see below), the fact that written U.S. law but not written E.U. law combines its lessening-competition test of illegality with an organizational-economic-efficiency defense will make written E.U. competition law less-liberal-moral-rights-securing than written U.S. antitrust law. Since I do not know whether, all tolled, a set of product-rivals' vertical (M&A)s that will lessen competition or has lessened competition that are executed by firms that could establish organizational-economic-efficiency defenses for these (M&A)s will increase or decrease material inequality (the reduction in competition will increase material inequality but many of the other effects of vertical [M&A]s will decrease material inequality by yielding buyers equivalent-dollar gains that exceed the equivalent-dollar gains the series of vertical [M&A]s in question yield the participants' connectees), I take no position on whether such vertical (M&A)s serve or disserve the instantiation of the utilitarian and various non-utilitarian-egalitarian conceptions of the moral good and concomitantly on whether E.U. competition law's failure to combine its lessening-competition test of illegality with an organizational-allocative-efficient defense whereas U.S. antitrust law does recognize such an organizational-economic-efficiency defense in the relevant cases makes E.U. competition law's treatment of vertical (M&A)s less promotive of the moral good than is U.S. antitrust law's treatment of vertical (M&A)s.

The impact of the second, "exploitative abuse of a dominant position"-test-of-illegality-related difference between written U.S. antitrust law's and written E.U. competition law's treatments of vertical (M&A)s on these two bodies' of law relative potentials to increase economic efficiency, secure liberal moral rights, and instantiate various egalitarian conceptions of the moral good is substantially diminished by what I take to be the fact that few if any of the series of vertical (M&A)s that were or would by consummated by the members of a set of product-rivals will put any dominant-firm members of such a set of rivals in a position to exploitatively abuse its dominant position. However, to the extent that this E.U. test of illegality that has no U.S. counterpart deters one or more firms that would be dominant after consummating one or more economically-efficient vertical (M&A)s from doing so by critically reducing the *ex ante* profitability of such (M&A)s by prohibiting a perpetrator from taking full advantage of the improvement in its competitive-position arrays the vertical (M&A)(s) would generate, the fact that written E.U. competition law promulgates such a test of illegality when written U.S. antitrust law does not will tend to make written E.U. law less economically efficient than written U.S. law, will make written E.U. competition law less-liberal-moral-rights-securing than written U.S. antitrust law if (and this is a big if) some connectees of firms have a liberal moral right that the firm be able to consummate and take advantage of non-predatory, economically-efficient vertical (M&A)s, and (for reasons I articulated in the preceding paragraph) will have an uncertain impact on the relative potentials of written E.U. competition law and written U.S. antitrust law to instantiate any egalitarian conception of the moral good.

In my judgment, very few if any individual perpetrators' vertical (M or A)s manifest specific anticompetitive intent either in the sense that the perpetrator's *ex ante* perception that the vertical (M&A)s in question would be at least normally profitable was positively critically affected by its perception that the resulting firm would engage in predatory refusals to deal or in the sense that the perpetrator believed *ex ante* that the (M or A)s would create a resulting firm that could profit more than the perpetrator could by refusing to deal predatorily and intended *ex ante* the resulting firm to take advantage of this opportunity. To the extent that an individual actor's vertical (M or A) or (M or A)s is/was or are/were motivated by specific anticompetitive intent, the fact that written U.S. antitrust law (the Sherman Act) entitles victims of such predatory vertical (M&A)s an opportunity to obtain legal redress whereas written E.U. competition law does not makes the written U.S. antitrust law's treatment of vertical (M&A)s more liberal-moral-rights-securing than is the written E.U. competition law on vertical (M&A)s, and to the extent that written U.S. antitrust law's providing victims of Sherman Act violations including victims of Sherman-Act-violating vertical (M&A)s an opportunity to obtain legal redress, whereas written E.U. competition law does not is associated with written U.S. antitrust law's providing greater disincentives to firms to consummate such vertical (M&A)s and to engage in such predatory refusals to deal, U.S. antitrust law's treatment of such vertical (M&A)s and related predatory refusals to deal will be more liberal-moral-rights-securing than is written E.U. competition law's treatment of such vertical (M&A)s and refusals to deal and will be more economically efficient and more egalitarian-conception-of-the-moral-good-instantiating than E.U. competition law's treatment of such conduct as well if (as I believe) vertical (M&A)s and refusals to deal that manifest their participants' specific anticompetitive intent reduce economic efficiency, decrease total utility, and disserve egalitarianism by increasing material inequality (though I acknowledge that it may be better on all three of these accounts to permit vertical [M&A]s whose perpetrator *ex ante* perceived profitability was not critically, positively affected by its participants' belief that the resulting firm would make additional profits by engaging in predatory refusals to deal while penalizing the perpetrators for planning to engage or actually engaging in predatory refusals to deal and entitling victims of any such planned or executed predatory refusals to deal to obtain legal redress).

18.7 Joint Ventures, Functionally-Related Collaborative Arrangements, and Any Restrictive Clauses the Contract That Creates Them Contain

I do not know whether the fact that written U.S. antitrust law does not prohibit joint ventures, collaborative arrangements of other sorts, or restrictive provisions in agreements that create joint ventures or arrange other sorts of collaborations that lessen competition but are not motivated by specific anticompetitive intent whereas E.U. competition law does prohibit them even if their participants could establish an organizational-allocative-efficiency defense for them if they were authorized to do so causes the potentials of written U.S. antitrust law to increase economic efficiency and to increase total utility to be higher or lower than the counterpart potentials of written E.U. competition law. I am inclined to believe that joint ventures, other sorts of functionally-analogous collaborations, and related restrictive provisions that do not manifest a participant's specific anticompetitive intent but do lessen competition will increase economic efficiency and total utility if the perpetrator could establish an organizational-allocative-efficient defense for it if they were legally entitled to do so but will decrease economic efficiency and total utility if they could not establish such a defense. But even if these suspicions are correct, I would not be able to predict whether this difference between written U.S. and written E.U. law causes the potentials of the written E.U. law to increase economic efficiency and total utility to be greater or lower than the potentials of written U.S. law to do so because I do not know the proportions of the joint ventures/other sorts of collaborations/related restrictive provisions that do not manifest specific anticompetitive intent but do lessen competition by creating a joint venture or other sort of collaboration that is more organizationally-economically-efficient than its participants would have been on their own or than any other investor whose investment was deterred by the relevant joint venture or other sort of collaboration would have been.

I do think that the fact that written U.S. antitrust law (the Sherman Act) entitles the victims of the (joint ventures)/collaborations/(restrictive provisions) it prohibits because they are motivated by specific anticompetitive intent to obtain legal redress whereas written E.U. competition law does not entitle the victims of those arrangements of these kinds that are so motivated to obtain legal redress increases the potentials of written U.S. antitrust law to increase economic efficiency, secure liberal moral rights, and instantiate egalitarian conceptions of the moral good above their written-E.U.-competition-law counterparts.

I also do not know whether the fact that written E.U. competition law (Article 102) prohibits firms that are dominant from exploitatively abusing their dominant positions whereas written U.S. antitrust law does not affects the relative potentials of written E.U. competition law and written U.S. antitrust law to increase economic efficiency and instantiate egalitarian conceptions of the moral good because (1) this written-E.U.-law prohibition applies regardless of whether the firm's dominant position was generated by exemplars of the categories of conduct now at issue that were motivated by specific anticompetitive intent, by exemplars that lessened competition for reasons unrelated to its creating an entity whose organizational allocative efficiency was higher than that of the entity it "replaced," by exemplars that lessened competition because it increased its perpetrators' organizational economic efficiency or created an entity that was more organizationally-allocatively-efficient than the entity it replaced would have been, or by exemplars that increased organizational allocative efficiency and did not lessen competition and (2) I do not know the percentages of the categories of conduct at issue that fall into these categories. On the other hand, I do think that this difference does increase the potential of written E.U. competition law to secure liberal moral rights above the counterpart potential of written U.S. antitrust law, though this difference causes written E.U. competition law to deter more conduct that is not liberal-moral-rights-violative as well as more conduct that is liberal-moral-rights-violative.

18.8 Internal Growth

There are 3 differences between the treatment of internal growth by written U.S. antitrust law and written E.U. competition law. First, written U.S. antitrust law (the Sherman Act) prohibits any decision by any firm regardless of its dominance to grow internally when the firm had a critical monopolistic investment-incentive to make the growth-generating investment and/or when the internal growth was perpetrated by a firm that believed *ex ante* that the growth would increase its ability to profit by engaging in specific-anti competitive-intent-motivated conduct and intended *ex ante* to take advantage of this opportunity whereas E.U. competition law prohibits such internal growth only if the firm that engages in it was dominant before engaging in the conduct in question. (This conclusion derives from my Sect. 17.3.8 conclusion that Article 101 does not cover internal growth even when the growing firm hires other firms to help it execute the internal growth.) Second, written E.U. competition law prohibits any firm that was dominant before engaging in internal growth or that was made dominant by its internal growth from taking advantage of any improvement in its array of competitive positions its internal growth yielded in any way that would justify the conclusion that it had exploitatively abused its dominant position (regardless of whether the internal growth itself was illegal) whereas U.S. antitrust law does not prohibit the exploitative abuse of any competitive position (be it dominant or not). Third, written U.S. antitrust law (again the Sherman Act) gives any rivals or potential/actual customers of any firm that has engaged in illegal internal growth that has imposed equivalent-dollar losses on them the legal right to obtain redress for the losses the illegal internal growth imposed on them whereas written E.U. competition law creates no such right to obtain legal redress.

The first of these 3 differences is consequential because (in my judgment) a significant amount of non-dominant-firm internal growth is motivated by specific anticompetitive intent (would not have been perceived by the growing firm *ex ante* to be at least normally profitable had the firm not had a monopolistic investment-incentive to make the associated investment and/or had the firm not believed that the growth would increase the amount of profits it would realize by engaging in contrived-oligopolistic or predatory conduct). Because I believe that almost all of the internal growth that written U.S. antitrust law prohibits but written E.U. competition law does not prohibit is economically inefficient (the only possible exceptions are [1] internal growth that involves the making of an investment in PPR that is larger than the investment it deters and on that account increases the relevant ARDEPPS' equilibrium PPR-quantity and [2] internal growth that was motivated by critical monopolistic investment-incentives that increases economic efficiency because it deters an investment that was even less economically efficient than the no-investment alternative because the latter investment would have been motivated by even larger monopolistic investment-incentives—a second possibility whose empirical importance is diminished by the fact that in this type of situation U.S. law would prohibit both the investment that was made and the investment it deterred), I think that this first difference in the two bodies' of law respective treatments of internal growth favors the conclusion that the potential of written U.S. antitrust law to increase economic efficiency is greater than the potential of written E.U. competition law to do so. Because the internal growth that written U.S. antitrust law prohibits and written E.U. competition law does not prohibit is liberal-moral-rights-violative, this first difference also favors the conclusion that written U.S. antitrust law has more of a potential than does written E.U. competition law to secure liberal moral rights. Because the internal growth that written U.S. antitrust law prohibits and written E.U. competition law does not prohibit decreases economic efficiency and probably tends to increase material inequality (by reducing the strength of the investor's rivals' pro-competitive [non-retaliatory] reactions and by leading to additional oligopolistic and predatory conduct—that is, by imposing equivalent-dollar losses on the customers of the internal grower and those of its rivals), this first difference also tends to favor the conclusion that written U.S. antitrust law has more of a potential to instantiate utilitarian and non-utilitarian-egalitarian conceptions of the moral good than does written E.U. competition law.

The second, "exploitative abuse of a dominant position"-test-of-illegality-related difference referenced in first paragraph of this section is operative both when the internal growth is illegal and when it is not. If I ignore the allocative transaction cost of implementing the "exploitative abuse of a dominant position" branch of Article 102's test of illegality, its existence will increase the potential of written E.U. competition law above the potential of U.S. antitrust law to increase economic efficiency, secure liberal moral rights, and instantiate any egalitarian conception of the moral good to the extent that it increases written E.U. law's deterrent effect on internal growth by dominant firms that is exclusionarily abusive but will not secure liberal moral rights and may or may not make written E.U. competition law more economically efficient and more instantiative of any egalitarian conception of the moral good to the extent that it increases E.U. competition law's deterrent effect on internal growth by dominant firms that would be economically efficient but could generate either losses or profits (if the perpetrator could abuse its dominant position).

The third difference between written U.S. antitrust law's and written E.U. competition law's respective treatments of internal growth—the fact that written U.S. law does and written E.U. competition law does not give victims of illegal acts an opportunity to obtain legal redress—also supports the conclusions that written U.S. antitrust law has more potential to increase economic efficiency, to secure liberal moral rights, and to instantiate egalitarian conceptions of the moral good than does written E.U. competition law (1) because, by increasing the total legal sanctions that will be imposed on violators and by making it more likely that victims will provide the government with relevant evidence, the creation of a right of victims to obtain legal redress will secure these objectives by increasing the law's power to deter internal growth that is economically inefficient, liberal-moral-rights-violative, and inimical to the instantiation of egalitarian conceptions of the moral good and (2) because parties whose liberal moral rights have been violated have a liberal moral right to be compensated by the rights-violators.

Conclusion

This study of antitrust policy is unusually complicated. Its complexity reflects *inter alia* (1) the study's recognition of (A) the fact that the moral desirability of an antitrust policy depends on its securing liberal moral rights and/or its instantiating a morally-defensible egalitarian conception of the moral good and (B) the fact that, although a policy's impact on some of these objectives depends in part on its impact on economic efficiency and consumer welfare, a policy's increasing economic efficiency and benefiting consumers does not guarantee that it will secure either of these moral *desiderata*, (2) the study's taking into account the ways in which antitrust-policy-coverable conduct affects quality-or-variety-increasing or production-process-research investment as well as prices, (3) the study's recognition that the impacts that antitrust-policy-coverable conduct has on the incidence of various types of oligopolistic conduct and predatory conduct and on the equilibrium quantity of quality-or-variety-increasing investment or production-process research in various portions of product-space depend on many factors that conventional analyses ignore, (4) the study's delineation of the various "legitimate" and "illegitimate" functions that can be performed by different categories of antitrust-policy-coverable business conduct and the factors that determine whether and the extent to which individual exemplars of each such category of conduct perform each such function, (5) the study's recognition that antitrust-policy-coverable conduct can affect the magnitudes of many categories of economic inefficiency that conventional analyses ignore, (6) the study's analyzing the economic efficiency of antitrust-policy-coverable conduct and government responses to such conduct in a way that takes appropriate account of The General Theory of Second Best, the fact that relevant research uses up allocatively-valuable resources, and the fact that the public financing of research is allocative-costly, (6) the study's analyzing the abstract definition and concrete extensions of the liberal conception of justice, (7) the study's analyzing the abstract definitions of the utilitarian, equal-utility, equal-resource, other-equal-opportunity, and mixed egalitarian conceptions of the

R. S. Markovits, *Welfare Economics and Antitrust Policy—Vol. II*,
https://doi.org/10.1007/978-3-030-96482-5

moral good, and (8) the study's careful delineation of the tests of illegality promulgated by U.S. antitrust law and E.U. competition law and of various other tests of illegality that could be applied to antitrust-policy-coverable conduct.

I know that it took those of you who have read this study in its entirety a great deal of time and effort to do so. I hope you found the "expenditure" cost-effective.

I also hope that readers of this study will build on it—will correct its errors of commission and omission and use its analytic protocols to analyze various other policy-issues. The general policy-analysis protocol this study develops and uses is equally applicable to the analysis of environmental policy, land-use policy, consumer-protection policy, tax policy, (tort/contract/property) policy, distributive policy, regulated-industries policy, international-trade policy, macro-economic policy, growth policy, developmental-economics policy, etc. as to antitrust policy. I would appreciate any feedback you choose to provide.

The manufacturer's authorised representative in the EU is Springer Nature Customer Service Centre GmbH, Europaplatz 3, 69115 Heidelberg, Germany. If you have any concerns regarding our products, please contact ProductSafety@springernature.com

Printed and bound by CPI Group (UK) Ltd, Croydon, CR0 4YY
30/09/2026
02225460-0019